MCSA/MCSE

Managing and Maintaining a Windows® Server™ 2003 Environment

Exam 70-290

Lee Scales
John Michell

Training Guide

MCSA/MCSE 70-290 Training Guide: Managing and Maintaining a Windows® Server™ 2003 Environment

International Standard Book Number: 0-7897-2935-0

Library of Congress Catalog Card Number: 2003101058

Printed in the United States of America

First Printing: November 2003

06 05 04 03 4 3 2 1

Trademarks

All terms mentioned in this book that are known to be trademarks or service marks have been appropriately capitalized. Que Publishing cannot attest to the accuracy of this information. Use of a term in this book should not be regarded as affecting the validity of any trademark or service mark.

Microsoft is a registered trademark of Microsoft Corporation.

Windows is a registered trademark of Microsoft Corporation.

Warning and Disclaimer

Every effort has been made to make this book as complete and as accurate as possible, but no warranty or fitness is implied. The information provided is on an "as is" basis. The authors and the publisher shall have neither liability nor responsibility to any person or entity with respect to any loss or damages arising from the information contained in this book or from the use of the CD or programs accompanying it.

Bulk Sales

Que Publishing offers excellent discounts on this book when ordered in quantity for bulk purchases or special sales. For more information, please contact

U.S. Corporate and Government Sales

1-800-382-3419

corpsales@pearsontechgroup.com

For sales outside the U.S., please contact

International Sales

1-317-428-3341

international@pearsontechgroup.com

PUBLISHER
Paul Boger

EXECUTIVE EDITOR
Jeff Riley

DEVELOPMENT EDITOR
Steve Rowe

MANAGING EDITOR
Charlotte Clapp

PROJECT EDITOR
Tonya Simpson

COPY EDITOR
Bart Reed

INDEXER
Mandie Frank

PROOFREADER
Katie Robinson

TECHNICAL EDITORS
Ed Tetz
Jeff Dunkelberger

TEAM COORDINATOR
Pamalee Nelson

MULTIMEDIA DEVELOPER
Dan Scherf

INTERIOR DESIGNER
Anne Jones

COVER DESIGNER
Charis Anne Santillie

PAGE LAYOUT
Susan Geiselman

Que Certification • 800 East 96th Street • Indianapolis, Indiana 46240

A Note from Series Editor Ed Tittel

Congratulations on your purchase of *MCSA/MCSE 70-290 Training Guide: Managing and Maintaining a Windows Server 2003 Environment,* the finest exam preparation book in the marketplace!

As Series Editor of the highly regarded Training Guide series, I can assure you that you won't be disappointed. You've taken your first step toward passing the *MCSA/MCSE 70-290* exam, and we value this opportunity to help you on your way!

As a "Favorite Study Guide Author" finalist in a 2002 poll of CertCities readers, I know the importance of delivering good books. You'll be impressed with Que Certification's stringent review process, which ensures the books are high-quality, relevant, and technically accurate. Rest assured that at least a dozen industry experts—including the panel of certification experts at CramSession—have reviewed this material, helping us deliver an excellent solution to your exam preparation needs.

We've also added a preview edition of PrepLogic's powerful, full-featured test engine, which is trusted by certification students throughout the world.

As a 20-year-plus veteran of the computing industry and the original creator and editor of the Exam Cram series, I've brought my IT experience to bear on these books. During my tenure at Novell from 1989 to 1994, I worked with and around its excellent education and certification department. At Novell, I witnessed the growth and development of the first really big, successful IT certification program—one that was to shape the industry forever afterward. This experience helped push my writing and teaching activities heavily in the certification direction. Since then, I've worked on more than 70 certification related books, and I write about certification topics for numerous Web sites and for *Certification* magazine.

In 1997 when Exam Cram was introduced, it quickly became the best-selling computer book series since "*...For Dummies*," and the best-selling certification book series ever. By maintaining an intense focus on the subject matter, tracking errata and updates quickly, and following the certification market closely, Exam Cram was able to establish the dominant position in cert prep books.

You will not be disappointed in your decision to purchase this book. If you are, please contact me at `etittel@jump.net`. All suggestions, ideas, input, or constructive criticism are welcome!

Ed Tittel

The test is in 2 weeks – are you ready?

You need a quick and efficient way to make sure you have what it takes to pass.

Where do you go?

Exam Cram2!

Why?

Que Certification Exam Cram2 titles have exactly what you need to pass your exam:

- Key terms and concepts highlighted at the start of each chapter
- Notes, Exam Tips, and Alerts advise what to watch out for
- End-of-chapter sample Exam Questions with detailed discussions of all answers
- Complete text-based practice test with answer key at the end of each book
- The tear-out Cram Sheet condenses the most important items and information into a two-page reminder
- A CD that includes PrepLogic Practice Tests for complete evaluation of your knowledge
- Our authors are recognized experts in the field. In most cases, they are current or former instructors, trainers, or consultants—they know exactly what you need to know!

MCSA/MCSE Managing and Maintaining a Windows Server 2003 Environment Exam Cram2
(Exam 70-290)
Dan Balter
0-7897-2946-6
$29.99 US/$45.99 CAN/£21.99 Net UK

Contents at a Glance

Table of Contents

About the Author

Lee Scales holds the MCSE+I (NT4) as well as the MCSE (W2K/W2K3) certifications and has been working in the computer industry for more than 20 years, including employment and consulting engagements with several Fortune 100 companies. He is currently employed as a senior consultant with a Microsoft Gold Partner, where his duties include working with companies that are migrating to the Windows Server 2003 platform with Active Directory.

In addition to his consulting duties, he has been developing courseware for the Windows platform for several years and has been a contributing/co-author to titles in the original *Exam Cram*, *Exam Cram 2*, and *Windows Power Toolkit* series. When time allows, he also performs contributing reviewer duties for *Microsoft Certified Professional Magazine.*

When not buried neck deep in a networking project, Lee enjoys camping, hunting, and fishing, especially in places where you can't plug in a laptop, and the cell phone doesn't work.

Lee lives in Overland Park, Kansas with his son Davin. You can reach Lee at `leescales@hotmail.com`.

About the Contributing Author

John Michell is a Microsoft Certified Trainer and MCSE. He was among the first MCSEs on the planet to certify on Windows 2000. He worked extensively on Windows 2000 in production settings and has been working with Windows Server 2003 since its beta versions. Before making the switch to Microsoft network operating systems, John was a Certified Novell Trainer and Master CNE. And before *that*, John worked with IBM mainframes. John is the owner of Startext Computing Services Ltd., a consulting firm based in Calgary, Alberta, Canada.

Dedication

To the true highlights of my life, Davin and Alayanna.

Acknowledgments

Lee Scales: Many people have worked hard to make this book possible. It is my great pleasure to acknowledge the efforts of these people.

First, special thanks to Ed Tittel, for giving me my first writing job and always finding writing projects for me. A very special thanks goes to my long-time editor and project manager, Dawn Rader, a fellow Scorpio, for all her hard work in keeping this project focused, especially in light of all the special trials and tribulations that were associated with it.

Thanks to my technical editors, Ed Tetz and Jeff Dunkelberger, for sharing their technical expertise and reviewing the contents of this book for correctness. Their constructive comments and suggestions also ensured that I did not miss anything that is of importance to the exam.

I would also thank Steve Rowe, Tonya Simpson, Bart Reed, Mandie Frank, and Katie Robinson, who were working behind the scenes to take the final manuscript and put it between covers and on the shelf.

A special thanks goes out to the KC Social Group members who acknowledged my absences from various social activities and were always available to commiserate with me on this project that became somewhat affectionately known as "The BLB."

And last, but definitely not least, a very, very special thanks to my son Davin, who was very understanding on those days when Daddy couldn't come out and play. Hey buddy, this book is done and we're going fishing!

John Michell: I'd like to thank Dawn Rader at LANWrights, Inc. for choosing to work with me and for bearing with me as I went through the trauma of moving (which I'm never going to do again!). I'd also like to thank my wife, Duff, and my daughter, Christine, for putting up with me as I worked on the book while I could have been packing or unpacking. And I'd like to acknowledge the support and encouragement I have received from my friends at Prairie Sky Cohousing Cooperative.

We Want to Hear from You!

As the reader of this book, *you* are our most important critic and commentator. We value your opinion and want to know what we're doing right, what we could do better, what areas you'd like to see us publish in, and any other words of wisdom you're willing to pass our way.

As an executive editor for Que Publishing, I welcome your comments. You can email or write me directly to let me know what you did or didn't like about this book—as well as what we can do to make our books better.

Please note that I cannot help you with technical problems related to the topic of this book. We do have a User Services group, however, where I will forward specific technical questions related to the book.

When you write, please be sure to include this book's title and author as well as your name, email address, and phone number. I will carefully review your comments and share them with the author and editors who worked on the book.

Email: `feedback@quepublishing.com`

Mail: Jeff Riley
Executive Editor
Que Publishing
800 East 96th Street
Indianapolis, IN 46240 USA

For more information about this book or another Que Certification title, visit our Web site at `www.examcram2.com`. Type the ISBN (excluding hyphens) or the title of a book in the Search field to find the page you're looking for.

How to Use This Book

Que Certification has made an effort in its Training Guide series to make the information as accessible as possible for the purposes of learning the certification material. Here, you have an opportunity to view the many instructional features that have been incorporated into the books to achieve that goal.

Chapter Opener

Each chapter begins with a set of features designed to allow you to maximize study time for that material.

List of Objectives: Each chapter begins with a list of the objectives as stated by Microsoft.

Objective Explanations: Immediately following each objective is an explanation of it, providing context that defines it more meaningfully in relation to the exam. Because Microsoft can sometimes be vague in its objectives list, the objective explanations are designed to clarify any vagueness by relying on the authors' test-taking experience.

Objectives

This chapter covers the following Microsoft-specified objectives for the "Managing and Maintaining Physical and Logical Devices" section of the Managing and Maintaining a Microsoft Windows Server 2003 Environment exam:

Manage basic disks and dynamic disks.

- When working in a Windows Server 2003 environment, you need to have a thorough understanding of the different types of disks available. In addition, it is important to understand how they are used and how to manage them.

Optimize server disk performance.

- **Implement a RAID solution.**
- **Defragment volumes and partitions.**

- The purpose of this objective is to teach you how to create, manage, and troubleshoot problems with the various RAID solutions available in Windows Server 2003. In addition, you should be familiar with maintaining volumes and partitions using the Disk Defragmenter utility.

CHAPTER 1

Managing Server Storage Devices

OUTLINE

Chapter Outline: Learning always gets a boost when you can see both the forest and the trees. To give you a visual image of how the topics in a chapter fit together, you will find a chapter outline at the beginning of each chapter. You will also be able to use this for easy reference when looking for a particular topic.

OUTLINE

STUDY STRATEGIES

- The sections in this chapter outline features that are basic to using and managing Windows Server 2003. The proper use of and recovery from problems with storage have always been major points on Microsoft exams. Expect the Windows Server 2003 exams to continue that tradition. Make sure you have a complete understanding of the capabilities of basic and dynamic disks, especially as far as how they are similar and how they are different.
- Most of the disk-related questions will probably concern the use of dynamic disks. Although basic disks can be used in Windows Server 2003, the advanced storage functionality is supported only on dynamic disks. Make sure you understand the various capabilities of dynamic disks, how they are configured, and how to recover from failures.

Study Strategies: Each topic presents its own learning challenge. To support you through this, Que Certification has included strategies for how to best approach studying in order to retain the material in the chapter, particularly as it is addressed on the exam.

INSTRUCTIONAL FEATURES WITHIN THE CHAPTER

These books include a large amount and different kinds of information. The many different elements are designed to help you identify information by its purpose and importance to the exam and also to provide you with varied ways to learn the material. You will be able to determine how much attention to devote to certain elements, depending on what your goals are. By becoming familiar with the different presentations of information, you will know what information will be important to you as a test-taker and which information will be important to you as a practitioner.

EXAM TIP

Know Your Partitions Be familiar with the two types of partitions, logical drives, and which drives are bootable.

Exam Tip: Exam Tips appear in the margins to provide specific exam-related advice. Such tips may address what material is covered (or not covered) on the exam, how it is covered, mnemonic devices, or particular quirks of that exam.

Note: Notes appear in the margins and contain various kinds of useful information, such as tips on the technology or administrative practices, historical background on terms and technologies, or side commentary on industry issues.

Chapter 1 MANAGING SERVER STORAGE DEVICES 33

Although multiple primary partitions can contain boot records, only one primary partition can be marked *active*. When a primary partition is marked as active, the system BIOS looks for the boot files needed to start the system in that partition.

The other type of partition is the *extended partition*, which allows you to create a theoretically unlimited number of logical drives inside that partition. Using older operating systems limits the number of drive letters that are available; however, in the later versions of Windows NT/2000/2003/XP, these logical drives can be mounted without a drive letter. The downside is that logical drives created inside an extended partition are not bootable.

You can have up to four primary partitions, or three primary partitions and an extended partition, on a single physical hard disk. The basic disk was the only type supported in versions of Windows prior to Windows 2000.

Before a physical hard disk can be used with an operating system, it must be *initialized*. The initialization process is used to write the master boot record (MBR) to the first sector of the hard drive. The MBR contains a small amount of startup code and a partition table that lists the configuration of the partitions. The hard drive can be initialized during a clean installation of Windows 2003 or by using the command-line utility FDISK.

When a Windows Server 2003 server is started, its Basic Input/Output System (BIOS) reads the MBR on the physical hard drive that is used to start the server. The MBR contains a pointer to the location of the active partition on the hard drive and the code needed to begin the startup process. The active partition is also referred to as the *system partition*. On an Intel-based system, the system partition contains the BOOT.INI, NTDETECT.COM, and NTLDR files. These files tell the server how to start the operating system.

The BOOT.INI file, shown in Figure 1.1, contains the physical path to the location of the folder that contains the operating system files. The BOOT.INI file can contain paths to multiple operating systems. At boot time, you are presented with a menu that allows you to choose which operating system to start. In the example shown, there is an additional option to boot to the Recovery Console.

NOTE

Watch the Terminology Beginning with Windows XP, Microsoft has started to refer to primary partitions and the logical drives that are contained in extended partitions as *basic volumes*. Do not confuse this with **simple volumes**, which are discussed later in the chapter. In addition, remember that a basic disk is a physical entity and that a basic volume is a logical one.

NTBOOTDD.SYS Another file that might be included is NTBOOTDD.SYS. This file is needed only if you are using a SCSI controller that has its BIOS disabled.

WARNING

Multiboot Limitations Dynamic disks can only be utilized by one operating system. If you plan on multibooting your computer with operating systems other than Windows 2000 or Windows 2003, do not convert your basic disks to dynamic disks.

Warning: In using sophisticated information technology, there is always potential for mistakes or even catastrophes that can occur through improper application of the technology. Warnings appear in the margins to alert you to such potential problems.

STEP BY STEP

1.4 Adding a New Disk

1. From the Start menu, select All Programs, Administrative Tools, Computer Management.
2. In the left pane of the Computer Management MMC, left-click the Storage entry and then select the Disk Management entry. This starts the Disk Management snap-in, which starts the wizard, as shown in Figure 1.14.

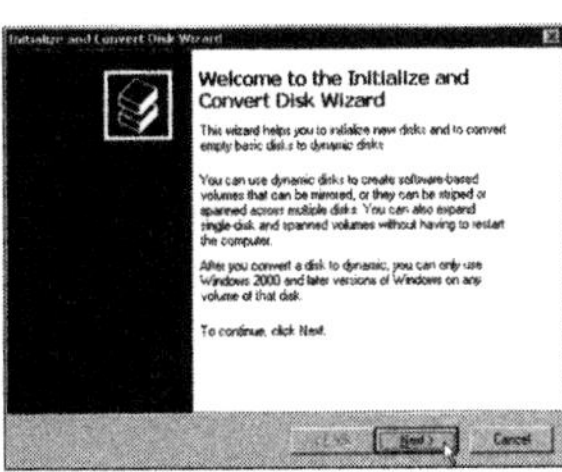

FIGURE 1.14
The opening window of the Initialize and Convert Disk Wizard, listing its purpose and guidelines for completing the installation of the new disk.

Step by Step: Step by Steps are hands-on tutorial instructions that walk you through a particular task or function relevant to the exam objectives.

Figure: To improve readability, the figures have been placed in the margins wherever possible so they do not interrupt the main flow of text.

Chapter 1 MANAGING SERVER STORAGE DEVICES

7. Power down the computer, replace the hard disk, and restart the computer.
8. Use your boot disk to start your Windows Server 2003 computer.
9. Remove and re-create the mirror as discussed in the previous procedure.

IN THE FIELD

PREBUILD THE RECOVERY FLOPPY

When you initially configure your boot/system drives in a mirrored configuration, that's when you should build your recovery boot floppy. You should configure the boot floppy and then use it for a few test boots to make sure you have the paths configured correctly in the BOOT.INI file. Then make two or more copies of it and put them away in a safe place.

When the server has crashed and the phones are ringing off the hook is not the proper time to learn how to build and test a recovery floppy.

Recovering a Failed RAID-5 Drive

Recovering from a disk failure in a RAID-5 array is a fairly simple process thanks to the fault tolerance provided by the array. Remember that RAID-5 arrays can only provide fault tolerance for one failed disk, so be sure to replace the failed disk as soon as possible. While the disk is failed and not replaced, you can still use the RAID-5 array; however, I/O performance will be severely degraded because the missing data must be re-created from the parity information. Again, you should replace a failed disk in a RAID-5 array as soon as you can by performing the procedure outlined in Step by Step 1.22.

In the Field Sidebar: These more extensive discussions cover material that perhaps is not as directly relevant to the exam, but which is useful as reference material or in everyday practice.
In the Field may also provide useful background or contextual information necessary for understanding the larger topic under consideration.

CASE STUDIES

Case Studies are presented throughout the book to provide you with another, more conceptual opportunity to apply the knowledge you are developing. They also reflect the "real-world" experiences of the authors in ways that prepare you not only for the exam but for actual network administration as well. In each Case Study, you will find similar elements: a description of a Scenario, the Essence of the Case, and an extended Analysis section.

CASE STUDY: DL CRAIG

ESSENCE OF THE CASE

Here are the essential elements in this case:

- Provide a fault-tolerant database configuration.
- Provide the best performance of the database.
- Archive old data using the least amount of space.

SCENARIO

DL Craig is a wholesaler for beverages based in the Midwest. DL Craig has decided to implement a third-party order-entry and sales-analysis program that uses several separate Microsoft SQL Server databases. Because the company has been wildly successful over the past year, its old order-entry system has become slow and overburdened.

DL Craig now wants to scale the hardware supporting the SQL Server databases for the best performance of the application. In addition, the solution must be fault tolerant. Due to the popularity and the competitive nature of the beverage business, DL Craig cannot afford to have its order-entry system suffer any downtime during normal business hours.

In addition to the requirements for the new order-entry system, due to a legal settlement, DL Craig needs to maintain all its correspondence for a period of 10 years. This correspondence consists of a large number of online documents. Although daily access to the documents is not required, they still need to be reasonably accessible.

continues

Essence of the Case: A bulleted list of the key problems or issues that need to be addressed in the Scenario.

Scenario: A few paragraphs describing a situation that professional practitioners in the field might face. A Scenario will deal with an issue relating to the objectives covered in the chapter, and it includes the kinds of details that make a difference.

CASE STUDY: DL CRAIG

continued

However, due to the enormous number of documents to be archived, DL Craig wants them to be stored as efficiently as possible.

ANALYSIS

The features in Windows Server 2003 will enable DL Craig to satisfy its fault tolerance, performance, and archival requirements. The first step is to install new Windows Server 2003 servers using a mirrored system boot partition. This will ensure that the servers will keep operating in case of a single system/boot volume failure.

The next step is to add several SCSI drives to the server in a RAID-5 configuration. This configuration will require at least three volumes, but better performance will be achieved by adding more drives to the volume set. Although a RAID-5 configuration provides excellent read performance, write performance is hindered because parity information has to be calculated and written with the data. However, this is a slight tradeoff considering the fault tolerance provided by this type of configuration.

The final requirement can be accomplished by building another Windows Server 2003 server to store the archived data. Because DL Craig did not request that the archival server provide any specific fault tolerance or performance features, any disk configuration should suffice. However, for the most efficient storage of the archived information, the data-storage volumes should be formatted with NTFS as compressed volumes. This will ensure that as documents are added to the volumes, they will automatically be compressed.

Here's an overview of the requirements and solutions in this case study:

Requirement	*Solution Provided By*
Provide a fault-tolerant data-base configuration.	Configuring Windows Server 2003 with a RAID-1 system/boot volume and a RAID-5 database volume
Provide the best performance of the database.	Configuring a RAID-5 volume
Archive old data using the least amount of space.	Configuring the data archival volumes to enable NTFS compression

Analysis: This is a lengthy description of the best way to handle the problems listed in the Essence of the Case. In this section, you might find a table summarizing the solutions, a worded example, or both.

EXTENSIVE REVIEW AND SELF-TEST OPTIONS

At the end of each chapter, along with some summary elements, you will find a section called "Apply Your Knowledge" that gives you several different methods with which to test your understanding of the material and review what you have learned.

CHAPTER SUMMARY

This chapter has covered a lot of ground; here are the main points:

- **Working with partitions and volumes**—This includes knowing the types of partitions available on a basic disk (primary, extended, and logical) and the types of volumes available on a dynamic disk (simple, spanned, mirrored, striped, and striped with parity). Know when and how to use them.
- **Optimizing server disk performance**—This includes knowing which of the partitions/volumes provide the best performance and how to configure and maintain them.
- **Implementing a RAID solution**—This includes knowing how to configure, troubleshoot, and repair the various RAID configurations available in Windows Server 2003.
- **Defragmenting volumes and partitions**—This is part of maintaining and optimizing server disk performance.

KEY TERMS

- Boot disk
- Boot partition
- System partition
- Basic disk
- Dynamic disk
- Mirror volume
- RAID-0
- RAID-1
- RAID-5
- BOOT.INI

Chapter Summary: Before the Apply Your Knowledge section, you will find a chapter summary that wraps up the chapter and reviews what you should have learned.

Key Terms: A list of key terms appears at the end of each chapter. These are terms that you should be sure you know and are comfortable defining and understanding when you go in to take the exam.

112 Part I EXAM PREPARATION

APPLY YOUR KNOWLEDGE

Exercises

1.1 Creating and Testing a Boot Disk

This exercise demonstrates how to create a boot disk. This boot disk can be used to start the server when your system files are corrupted, or when you need to boot to recover a failed mirrored set. This exercise requires a blank floppy disk.

Estimated Time: 20 minutes.

1. Format the floppy disk, either from the command line or from Windows Explorer or My Computer.
2. Using either Windows Explorer or My Computer, confirm that your view settings allow you to see hidden and system files.
3. From the system partition, copy `BOOT.INI`, `NTDETECT.COM`, `NTLDR`, and `NTBOOTDD.SYS` (if present) to your floppy disk. Remove the floppy disk.
4. Delete `NTDETECT.COM` on the system partition.
5. Reboot your server. The reboot should fail.
6. Insert your floppy disk and reboot the server. The reboot should be successful. Copy `NTDETECT.COM` from the floppy to your system partition.

1.2 Repairing a Mirrored Volume

This exercise demonstrates how to repair a mirrored volume. This exercise assumes that you are repairing the mirrored volume in a server that uses hot-plug drives. For a procedure for use in a server that does not have hot-plug drives, see Step by Step 1.20, "Repairing a Mirrored Volume."

Estimated Time: 30 minutes.

Review Questions

1. What is a Windows Server 2003 boot disk and how is it different from a DOS boot disk?
2. What are the two types of disks available in Windows Server 2003 and how are they different?
3. What tools can you use in Windows Server 2003 to configure disks?
4. Explain the differences between a basic disk and a dynamic disk in Windows Server 2003.
5. What are the two methods for compressing files, folders, and volumes?
6. Briefly explain the method used to upgrade a Windows NT 4.0 or Windows 2000 server that contains basic disks in a RAID-5 configuration to Windows Server 2003.

Review Questions: These open-ended, short-answer questions allow you to quickly assess your comprehension of what you just read in the chapter. Instead of asking you to choose from a list of options, these questions require you to state the correct answers in your own words. Although you will not experience these kinds of questions on the exam, these questions will indeed test your level of comprehension of key concepts.

Exercises: These activities provide an opportunity for you to master specific hands-on tasks. Our goal is to increase your proficiency with the product or technology. You must be able to conduct these tasks in order to pass the exam.

Exam Questions: These questions reflect the kinds of multiple-choice questions that appear on the Microsoft exams. Use them to become familiar with the exam question formats and to help you determine what you know and what you need to review or study more.

APPLY YOUR KNOWLEDGE

Exam Questions

1. You have been asked whether an older computer will operate properly with Windows Server 2003. What feature of the computer must be present for device resource settings to be assigned automatically by Windows Server 2003?

   A. APM

   B. SFC

   C. ACPI

   D. PnP

2. After installing a new driver for a printer, you find that it is not functioning properly, and you decide to return to the previous driver. What procedure(s) will give you the desired results?

   A. Uninstall the printer and then start again with the most recent functioning driver you can find.

   B. Use Device Manager to invoke Driver Roll Back.

   C. Run Driver Roll Back from Administrative Tools.

   D. On the Advanced tab of the printer's Properties dialog box, choose New Driver and use Have Disk to select the source of the previous driver.

3. A colleague has sent you a new driver for your server's RAID controller, which he says makes the drives it controls run more efficiently. You want to ensure that the driver is from a reputable source. How do you do that?

Answers to Exam Questions

1. **C.** ACPI must be present on the computer for Windows Server 2003 to be able to take over the configuration of devices. APM (Advanced Power Management) is a predecessor to ACPI that does not perform automatic configuration as completely as ACPI. SFC (System File Checker) is a tool for scheduling a run of the system files to identify any that are unsigned. PnP (Plug and Play) is a specification that states how devices should identify themselves and respond to configuration commands.

Answers and Explanations: For each of the Review and Exam questions, you will find thorough explanations located at the end of the section.

Suggested Readings and Resources: The very last element in every chapter is a list of additional resources you can use if you want to go above and beyond certification-level material or if you need to spend more time on a particular subject that you are having trouble understanding.

Suggested Readings and Resources

1. Microsoft Official Curriculum Course 2275: Maintaining a Microsoft Windows Server 2003 Environment
   - Module 5: Managing Disks
   - Module 6: Managing Data Storage
2. Microsoft Official Curriculum Course 2270: Updating Support Skills from Microsoft Windows NT 4.0 to the Windows Server 2003 Family
   - Module 12: Managing File Resources
   - Module 15: Performing Disk Management
   - Module 16: Implementing Disaster Protection
3. Microsoft Official Curriculum Course 2274: Managing a Microsoft Windows Server 2003 Environment
   - Module 5: Managing Access to Resources
4. Non-Microsoft Resources
   - Boswell, William. *Inside Windows Server 2003*. New Riders, 2003. ISBN: 0735711585.
   - Matthews, Marty. *Windows Server 2003: A Beginners Guide*. McGraw-Hill, 2003. ISBN: 0072193093.
   - Minasi, Mark, et al. *Mark Minasi's Windows XP and Server 2003 Resource Kit*. Sybex, 2003. ISBN: 0782140807.
   - Minasi, Mark, et al. *Mastering Windows Server 2003 Server*. Sybex, 2003. ISBN: 0782141307.
   - Shapiro, Jeffrey, et al. *Windows Server 2003 Bible*. John Wiley and Sons, 2003. ISBN: 0764549375.

Introduction

This book, *70-290 Training Guide: Managing and Maintaining a Windows Server 2003 Environment*, is for technicians, system administrators, and other technical professionals who are pursuing the goal of becoming a Microsoft Certified System Administrator (MCSA) or Microsoft Certified System Engineer (MCSE). This book covers the Managing and Maintaining a Windows Server 2003 Environment exam (70-290), which is a core exam for both of those certifications. The exam is designed to measure your skill in managing and maintaining servers in a Windows Server 2003 environment.

This book is designed to cover all the objectives Microsoft created for this exam. It doesn't offer end-to-end coverage of Windows 2003; rather, it helps you develop the specific core competencies that Microsoft says administrators that support Windows Server 2003 will need to master. You can pass the exam by learning the material in this book, without taking a class. Of course, depending on your own personal study habits and learning style, you might benefit from studying this book *and* taking a class.

Even if you are not planning to take the exam, you may find this book useful. The wide range of topics covered by the Microsoft exam objectives will certainly help you to accomplish the server-management tasks at your job. Experienced MCSA/MCSEs looking for a reference on the new features of Windows Server 2003 in particular should appreciate the coverage of topics here.

How This Book Helps You

This book gives you a self-guided tour of all the areas of the product that are covered by the Managing and Maintaining a Windows Server 2003 Environment exam. The goal is to teach you the specific skills that you need to achieve your MCSA or MCSE certification. You will also find helpful hints, tips, examples, exercises, and references to additional study materials. Specifically, this book is set up to help you in the ways detailed in the following subsections.

Organization

This book is organized around the individual objectives from Microsoft's preparation guide for the Managing and Maintaining a Windows Server 2003 Environment exam. Every objective is covered in this book. These objectives are not covered in exactly the same order you will find them on the official preparation guide (which you can download from `www.microsoft.com/traincert/exams/70-290.asp`) but are reorganized for more logical teaching. We have also tried to make the information more accessible in several ways:

- This introduction includes the full list of exam topics and objectives.
- After the introduction you will encounter the "Study and Exam Prep Tips" section. Read this section early on to help you develop study strategies. It also provides you with valuable exam-day tips and information.
- Each chapter starts with a list of objectives that are covered in that chapter.

- Each chapter also begins with an outline that provides an overview of the material for that chapter as well as the page numbers where specific topics can be found.
- We have also repeated each objective in the text where it is covered in detail.
- The tear card in the front of the book provides you with a handy cross-reference between test objectives and page numbers in the book.

Instructional Features

This book has been designed to provide you with multiple ways to learn and reinforce the exam material. Here are some of the instructional features you'll find inside:

- **Objective explanations**—As mentioned previously, each chapter begins with a list of the objectives covered in the chapter. In addition, immediately following each objective is a more detailed explanation that puts the objective in the context of the product.
- **Study strategies**—Each chapter also offers a selected list of study strategies—exercises to try or additional material to read that will help you in learning and retaining the material you'll find in the chapter.
- **Exam tips**—Exam tips appear in the margin to provide specific exam-related advice. Such tips might address what material is likely to be covered (or not covered) on the exam, how to remember it, or particular exam quirks.
- **Guided practice exercises**—These exercises offer you additional opportunities to practice the material within a chapter and to learn additional facets of the topic at hand.
- **Key terms**—A list of key terms appears at the end of each chapter. You'll find definitions for these terms in the glossary.
- **Notes**—These appear in the margin and contain various kinds of useful information, such as tips on technology, historical background, side commentary, or notes on where to go for more detailed coverage of a particular topic.
- **Warnings**—When using sophisticated computing technology, there is always the possibility of mistakes or even catastrophes. Warnings appear in the margin to alert you of such potential problems, whether they are in following along with the text or in implementing Windows Server 2003 in a production environment.
- **Step by Steps**—These are hands-on, tutorial instructions that lead you through a particular task or function relevant to the exam objectives.
- **Exercises**—Found at the end of each chapter in the "Apply Your Knowledge" section, the exercises may include additional tutorial material and more chances to practice the skills you learned in the chapter.

Extensive Practice Test Options

The book provides numerous opportunities for you to assess your knowledge and practice for the exam. The practice options include the following:

- **Review questions**—These open-ended questions appear in the "Apply Your Knowledge" section at the end of each chapter. They allow you to quickly assess your comprehension of what you just read in the chapter. The answers are provided later in the section.

- **Exam questions**—These questions also appear in the "Apply Your Knowledge" section. They reflect the kinds of multiple-choice questions that appear on the Microsoft exams. Use them to practice for the exam and to help you determine what you know and what you may need to review or study further. Answers and explanations are provided later in the section.
- **Practice exam**—The "Final Review" section includes a complete practice exam. The "Final Review" section and the Practice Exam are discussed in more detail later in this chapter.
- **PrepLogic practice tests**—The PrepLogic software included on the CD-ROM provides further practice questions.

> NOTE
> **PrepLogic Software** For a complete description of the Que Top Score test engine, please see Appendix E, "Using the PrepLogic Practice Exams, Preview Edition Software."

Final Review

This part of the book provides you with three valuable tools for preparing for the exam:

- **Fast Facts**—This condensed version of the information contained in the book will prove extremely useful for last-minute review.
- **Study and Exam Preparation Tips**—This section provides some general guidelines for preparing for a Microsoft certification exam. Included is an overview of the question types and general strategies for studying.
- **Practice Exam**—A full practice test for the exam is included. Questions are written in the style and format used on the actual exams. Use it to assess your readiness for the real thing.

This book includes several valuable appendixes as well, including a list of key online resources (Appendix A), a list of suggested readings and resources that contains useful information on Windows Server 2003 (Appendix B), a glossary (Appendix C), and a description of what is on the CD-ROM (Appendix D). Finally, Appendix E covers the use of the PrepLogic software.

These and all the other book features mentioned previously will provide you with thorough preparation for the exam.

For more information about the exam or the certification process, you should contact Microsoft directly:

- By email: `MCPHelp@microsoft.com`.
- By regular mail, telephone, or fax, contact the Microsoft Regional Education Service Center (RESC) nearest you. You can find lists of Regional Education Service Centers at `www.microsoft.com/traincert/support/northamerica.asp` (for North America) or `www.microsoft.com/traincert/support/worldsites.asp` (worldwide).
- On the Internet: `www.microsoft.com/traincert/`.

WHAT EXAM 70-290 COVERS

The Managing and Maintaining a Windows Server 2003 Environment exam covers five major topic areas:

- Managing and maintaining physical and logical devices
- Managing users, computers, and groups
- Managing and maintaining access to resources
- Managing and maintaining a server environment
- Managing and implementing disaster recovery

The exam objectives are listed by topic area in the following sections.

Managing and Maintaining Physical and Logical Devices

Manage basic disks and dynamic disks.

Monitor server hardware. Tools might include Device Manager, the Hardware Troubleshooting Wizard, and appropriate Control Panel items.

Optimize server disk performance.

- Implement a RAID solution.
- Defragment volumes and partitions.

Install and configure server hardware devices.

- Configure driver signing options.
- Configure resource settings for a device.
- Configure device properties and settings.

Managing Users, Computers, and Groups

Manage local, roaming, and mandatory user profiles.

Create and manage computer accounts in an Active Directory environment.

Create and manage groups.

- Identify and modify the scope of a group.
- Find domain groups in which a user is a member.
- Manage group membership.
- Create and modify groups by using the Active Directory Users and Computers Microsoft Management Console (MMC) snap-in.
- Create and modify groups by using automation.

Create and manage user accounts.

- Create and modify user accounts by using the Active Directory Users and Computers Microsoft Management Console (MMC) snap-in.
- Create and modify groups by using automation.
- Import user accounts.

Troubleshoot computer accounts.

- Diagnose and resolve issues related to computer accounts by using the Active Directory Users and Computers Microsoft Management Console (MMC) snap-in.
- Reset computer accounts.

Troubleshoot user accounts.

- Diagnose and resolve account lockouts.
- Diagnose and resolve issues related to user account properties.

Troubleshoot user authentication issues.

Managing and Maintaining Access to Resources

Configure access to shared folders.

- Manage shared folder permissions.

Troubleshoot Terminal Services.

- Diagnose and resolve issues related to Terminal Services security.
- Diagnose and resolve issues related to client access to Terminal Services.

Configure file system permissions.

- Verify effective permissions when granting permissions.
- Change ownership of files and folders.

Troubleshoot access to files and shared folders.

Managing and Maintaining a Server Environment

Monitor and analyze events. Tools might include Event Viewer and System Monitor.

Manage software update infrastructure.

Manage software site licensing.

Manage servers remotely.

- Manage a server by using Remote Assistance.
- Manage a server by using Terminal Services remote administration mode.
- Manage a server by using available support tools.

Troubleshoot print queues.

Monitor system performance.

Monitor file and print servers. Tools might include Task Manager, Event Viewer, and System Monitor.

- Monitor disk quotas.
- Monitor print queues.
- Monitor server hardware for bottlenecks.

Monitor and optimize a server environment for application performance.

- Monitor memory performance objects.
- Monitor network performance objects.
- Monitor process performance objects.
- Monitor disk performance objects.

Manage a Web server.

- Manage Internet Information Services (IIS).
- Manage security for IIS.

Managing and Implementing Disaster Recovery

Perform system recovery for a server.

- Implement Automated System Recovery (ASR).
- Restore data from shadow copy volumes.
- Back up files and system state data to media.
- Configure security for backup operations.

Manage backup procedures.

- Verify the successful completion of backup jobs.
- Manage backup storage media.

Recover from server hardware failure.

Restore backup data.

Schedule backup jobs.

What You Should Know Before Reading This Book

The Microsoft Managing and Maintaining a Windows Server 2003 Environment exam assumes that you are familiar with Active Directory and networking in general, even though there are no objectives that pertain directly to this knowledge. We show you tasks that are directly related to the exam objectives, but this book does not include a tutorial in working with the finer points of Active Directory and networking. If you are just getting started with Microsoft Windows and networking, you should check out some of the references in Appendix B for the information you will need to get you started. For beginners, we particularly recommend these references:

- *Mastering Windows Server 2003*, by Mark Minasi (Sybex, 2003). This is an excellent starting point for information on Windows Server 2003 and common tasks.
- *Windows XP Power Pack*, by Stu Sjouwerman, et al. (Que, 2003).
- *Microsoft Windows Server 2003 Delta Guide*, by Don Jones and Mark Rouse (Sams, 2003). This is a great book to have if you are already familiar with Windows 2000.

Hardware and Software You'll Need

The volumes in the *Microsoft Windows 2003 Training Guide* series are intended to be self-paced study guides. As such, the concepts presented are intended to be reinforced by the reader through hands-on experience.

To obtain the best results from your studies, you should have as much exposure to Windows Server 2003 as possible. The best way to do this is to combine your studies with as much lab time as possible. In this section, we will make some suggestions on setting up a test lab to provide you with a solid practice environment.

Microsoft Windows Server 2003 is available in the following versions:

- **Standard Edition**—Microsoft Windows Server 2003, Standard Edition is the entry-level product in the product line. This edition is designed for the small-to-medium-sized environments and departmental servers.
- **Enterprise Edition**—Windows Server 2003, Enterprise Edition is designed for medium-to-large environments. It includes features for enterprise environments, such as clustering and support for up to 8 processors and 32GB of memory.
- **Datacenter Edition**—Windows Server 2003, Datacenter Edition is designed for high-availability and large environments. It includes support for up to 32 processors and 64GB of memory. This version is only available preinstalled on high-end hardware.
- **Web Edition**—Microsoft Windows Server 2003, Web Edition is positioned and priced as a lower-cost Web platform. As such, it doesn't support features such as Terminal Services in Application mode, nor can it be used as a domain controller.

You should be able to complete all the exercises in this book with any of the first three editions of Windows Server 2003. (If you can afford to use a datacenter server as your lab machine, invite me over.) Your computer should meet the minimum criteria required for a Windows Server 2003 installation:

- Pentium or better CPU running at 133MHz or faster
- Minimum of 128MB RAM
- 2GB of disk space for a full installation
- CD-ROM or DVD drive
- Video card running at 800×600 with at least 256 colors
- Microsoft or compatible mouse

Of course, those are *minimum* requirements. I recommend the following, more realistic, requirements:

- Pentium III or better CPU running at 550MHz or faster
- At least 256 MB of RAM, and as much more as you can afford
- 5GB of disk space for a full installation
- CD-ROM or DVD drive
- Video card running at 1280×1024 or higher with at least 65,000 colors
- NIC
- Suitable switch or hub
- Microsoft or compatible mouse

In addition to a machine running Windows Server 2003, you might want one or more client workstations to test accessing shares over the network, Terminal Services, and other functions. For best results, Windows 2000 or Windows XP clients are recommended because they are required to support features such as Group Policy and the Software Update Service—items that will probably appear on the exam.

Two products that have proven invaluable to us in the writing field are VMWare (`www.vmware.com`) and Connectix Virtual PC (`www.connectix.com`). These products allow you to create and run multiple virtual client sessions on your PC.

Microsoft, of course, is highly motivated to spread the word about Windows Server 2003 to as many people as possible. So you can download trial versions of Windows Server 2003, along with other Microsoft products here:

`http://www.microsoft.com/windowsserver2003/evaluation/trial/default.mspx`

You may find it easier to obtain access to the necessary computer hardware and software in a corporate environment. It can be difficult, however, to allocate enough time within a busy workday to complete a self-study program. Most of your study time will probably need to occur outside of normal working hours, away from the everyday interruptions and pressures of your job.

ADVICE ON TAKING THE EXAM

You'll find more extensive tips in the "Final Review" section titled "Study and Exam Prep Tips," but keep this advice in mind as you study:

- **Read all the material**—Microsoft has been known to include material not expressly specified in the objectives for an exam. This book includes additional information not reflected in the objectives in an effort to give you the best possible preparation for the examination—and for the real-world experiences to come.
- **Do the Step by Steps and complete the exercises in each chapter**—They will help you gain experience with Windows Server 2003. All Microsoft exams are task and experience based and require you to have experience using the Microsoft products, not just reading about them.
- **Use the questions to assess your knowledge**—Don't just read the chapter content; use the questions to find out what you know and what you don't. Study some more, review, and then assess your knowledge again.

- **Review the exam objectives**—Develop your own questions and examples for each topic listed. If you can develop and answer several questions for each topic, you should not find it difficult to pass the exam.

Remember, the primary objective is not to pass the exam—it is to understand the material. After you understand the material, passing the exam should be simple. To really work with Windows Server 2003, you need a solid foundation in practical skills. This book, and the Microsoft Certified Professional program, are designed to ensure you have that solid foundation.

Good luck!

EXAM TIP

No Substitute for Experience The single best study tip anyone can give you is to actually work with the product you're learning! Even if you could become a "paper MCSA or MCSE" simply by reading books, you wouldn't get the real-world skills you need to be a success.

Object Matrix

Unit/Objective/Subobjective	*Chapter/Heading for Coverage*
Managing and Maintaining Physical and Logical Devices	
Manage basic disks and dynamic disks.	**Chapter 1** Managing Basic Disks and Dynamic Disks, p. 32 Using the Disk Management Console to Manage Disks, p. 40
Monitor server hardware. Tools might include Device Manager, theHardware Troubleshooting Wizard, and appropriate Control Panel items.	**Chapter 2** Monitoring Server Hardware, p. 140 Troubleshooting Server Hardware, p. 146 Diagnosing and Resolving Server Hardware Issues, p. 148
Optimize server disk performance.	**Chapter 1** Optimizing Server Disk Performance, p. 97
Implement a RAID solution.	
Defragment volumes and partitions.	Working with Dynamic Disks, p. 64
Install and configure server hardware devices.	**Chapter 2** Installing and Configuring Hardware Devices, p. 126
Configure driver signing options.	
Configure resource settings for a device.	Monitoring Server Hardware, p. 140
Configure device properties and settings.	
Managing Users, Computers, and Groups	
Manage local, roaming, and mandatory user profiles.	**Chapter 3** Managing Local, Roaming, and Mandatory User Profiles, p. 202
Create and manage computer accounts in an Active Directory environment.	**Chapter 3** Creating and Managing Computer Accounts in an Active Directory Environment, p. 224
Create and manage groups.	**Chapter 3** Creating and Managing Groups, p. 206
Identify and modify the scope of a group.	
Find domain groups in which a user is a member.	
Manage group membership.	
Create and modify groups by using the Active Directory Users and Computers Microsoft Management Console (MMC) snap-in.	
Create and modify groups by using automation.	

continues

continued

Unit/Objective/Subobjective	*Chapter/Heading for Coverage*
	Managing Users, Computers, and Groups
Create and manage user accounts.	**Chapter 3** Creating and Managing User Accounts, p. 167
Create and modify user accounts by using the Active Directory Users and Computers MMC snap-in.	
Create and modify user accounts by using automation.	
Import user accounts.	
Troubleshoot computer accounts.	**Chapter 3** Troubleshooting Computer Accounts, p. 227
Diagnose and resolve issues related to computer accounts by using the Active Directory Users and Computers MMC snap-in.	
Reset computer accounts.	
Troubleshoot user accounts.	**Chapter 3** Troubleshooting User Accounts, p. 196
Diagnose and resolve account lockouts.	
Diagnose and resolve issues related to user account properties.	
Troubleshoot user authentication issues.	**Chapter 3** Troubleshooting User Accounts, p. 196
	Managing and Maintaining Access to Resources
Configure access to shared folders.	**Chapter 4** Configuring and Managing Shared Folders, p. 260
Manage shared folder permissions.	
Troubleshoot Terminal Services.	**Chapter 4** Using Windows Server 2003 Terminal Services, p. 272
Diagnose and resolve issues related to Terminal Services security.	
Diagnose and resolve issues related to client access to Terminal Services.	Troubleshooting Terminal Services, p. 307
Configure file system permissions.	**Chapter 4** Configuring File System Permissions, p.242
Verify effective permissions when granting permissions.	
Change ownership of files and folders.	Verifying Effective Permissions when Granting Permissions, p. 256
	Changing Ownership of Files and Folders, p. 254
Troubleshoot access to files and shared folders.	**Chapter 4** Troubleshooting Access to Files and Shared Folders, p. 270

Unit/Objective/Subobjective	*Chapter/Heading for Coverage*
Managing and Maintaining a Server Environment	
Monitor and analyze events. Tools might include Event Viewer and System Monitor.	**Chapter 6** Using the Event Logs, p. 420
	Monitoring and Optimizing a Server Environment for Application Performance, p. 461
Manage a software update infrastructure.	**Chapter 5** Managing a Software Update Infrastructure, p. 384
Manage software site licensing.	**Chapter 4** Terminal Services in Application Server Mode, p. 277
Manage servers remotely.	**Chapter 5** Managing Servers Remotely, p. 329
Manage a server by using Remote Assistance.	
Manage a server by using Terminal Services Remote Administration mode.	Remote Assistance, p. 340
Manage a server by using available support tools.	Terminal Services in Remote Desktop for Administration Mode, p. 336
Troubleshoot print queues.	**Chapter 6** Managing and Monitoring Print Queues, p. 487
Monitor system performance.	**Chapter 6** Monitoring and Optimizing a Server Environment for Application Performance, p. 461
	Optimizing System Resources, p. 472
Monitor file and print servers. Tools might include Task Manager, Event Viewer, and System Monitor.	**Chapter 6** Monitoring File and Print Servers, p. 480
Monitor disk quotas.	Implementing and Monitoring Disk Quotas, p. 480
Monitor print queues.	Managing and Monitoring Print Queues, p. 487
Monitor server hardware for bottlenecks.	Monitoring System Resources, p. 461
Monitor and optimize a server environment for application performance.	**Chapter 6** Monitoring and Optimizing a Server Environment for Application Performance, p. 461
Monitor memory performance objects.	
Monitor network performance objects.	Optimizing System Resources, 472
Monitor process performance objects.	
Monitor disk performance objects.	

continues

continued

Unit/Objective/Subobjective	*Chapter/Heading for Coverage*
	Managing and Maintaining a Server Environment
Manage a Web server.	**Chapter 5**
	Managing Internet Information Services (IIS) 6.0, p. 347
Manage Internet Information Services (IIS).	
Manage security for IIS.	Managing Security for IIS, p. 377
	Managing and Implementing Disaster Recovery
Perform system recovery for a server.	**Chapter 7**
	Planning for Disaster Recovery, p. 579
Implement Automated System Recovery (ASR).	
Restore data from shadow copy volumes.	Implementing Automated System Recovery (ASR), p. 575
Back up files and system state data to media.	Restoring Data from Shadow Copy Volumes, p. 552
Configure security for backup operations.	System State Backups, p. 530
	Using Windows Backup, p. 516
	Configuring Security for Backup Operations, p. 540
Manage backup procedures.	**Chapter 7**
	Using Windows Backup, p. 516
Verify the successful completion of backup jobs.	
Manage backup storage media.	Managing and Rotating Backup Storage Media, p. 581
Recover from server hardware failure.	**Chapter 7**
	Using Other Recovery Tools, p. 551
	Planning for Disaster Recovery, p. 579
Schedule backup jobs.	**Chapter 7**
	Scheduling Backup Jobs, p. 533

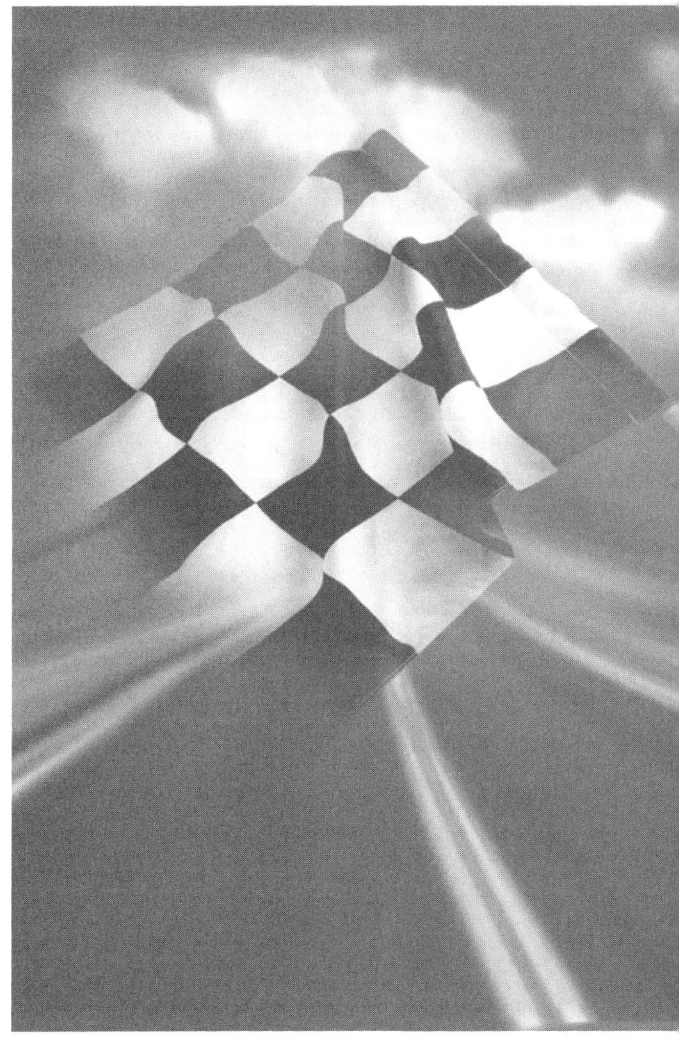

Study and Exam Prep Tips

This element of the book provides you with some general guidelines for preparing for any certification exam, including Exam 70-290, "Managing and Maintaining a Microsoft Windows Server 2003 Environment." It is organized into four sections. The first section addresses learning styles and how they affect preparation for the exam. The second section covers exam-preparation activities and general study tips. This is followed by an extended look at the Microsoft certification exams, including a number of specific tips that apply to the various Microsoft exam formats and question types. Finally, changes in Microsoft's testing policies and how they might affect you are discussed.

LEARNING STYLES

To best understand the nature of preparation for the test, it is important to understand learning as a process. You are probably aware of how you best learn new material. You might find that outlining works best for you, or, as a visual learner, you might need to see things. Or you might need models or examples, or maybe you just like exploring the interface. Whatever your learning style, test preparation takes place over time. Obviously, you shouldn't start studying for a certification exam the night before you take it; it is very important to understand that learning is a developmental process. Understanding learning as a process helps you focus on what you know and what you have yet to learn.

Thinking about how you learn should help you recognize that learning takes place when you are able to match new information to old. You have some previous experience with computers and networking. Now you are preparing for this certification exam.

Using this book, software, and supplementary materials will not just add incrementally to what you know; as you study, the organization of your knowledge actually restructures as you integrate new information into your existing knowledge base. This leads you to a more comprehensive understanding of the tasks and concepts outlined in the objectives and of computing in general. Again, this happens as a result of a repetitive process rather than a singular event. If you keep this model of learning in mind as you prepare for the exam, you will make better decisions concerning what to study and how much more studying you need to do.

STUDY TIPS

There are many ways to approach studying, just as there are many different types of material to study. However, the tips that follow should work well for the type of material covered on Microsoft certification exams.

Study Strategies

Although individuals vary in the ways they learn information, some basic principles of learning apply to everyone. You should adopt some study strategies that take advantage of these principles. One of these principles is that learning can be broken into various depths. Recognition (of terms, for example) exemplifies a rather surface level of learning in which you rely on a prompt of some sort to elicit recall. Comprehension or understanding (of the concepts behind the terms, for example) represents a deeper level of learning than recognition. The ability to analyze a concept and apply your understanding of it in a new way represents further depth of learning.

Your learning strategy should enable you to know the material at a level or two deeper than mere recognition. This will help you perform well on the exams. You will know the material so thoroughly that you can go beyond the recognition-level types of questions commonly used in fact-based multiple-choice testing. You will be able to apply your knowledge to solve new problems.

Macro and Micro Study Strategies

One strategy that can lead to deep learning includes preparing an outline that covers all the objectives and subobjectives for the particular exam you are working on. You should delve a bit further into the material and include a level or two of detail beyond the stated objectives and subobjectives for the exam. Then you should expand the outline by coming up with a statement of definition or a summary for each point in the outline.

An outline provides two approaches to studying. First, you can study the outline by focusing on the organization of the material. You can work your way through the points and subpoints of your outline, with the goal of learning how they relate to one another. For example, you should be sure you understand how each of the main objective areas for Exam 70-290 is similar to and different from another. Then, you should do the same thing with the subobjectives; you should be sure you know which subobjectives pertain to each objective area and how they relate to one another.

Next, you can work through the outline, focusing on learning the details. You should memorize and understand terms and their definitions, facts, rules and tactics, advantages and disadvantages, and so on. In this pass through the outline, you should attempt to learn detail rather than the big picture (the organizational information that you worked on in the first pass through the outline).

Research has shown that attempting to assimilate both types of information at the same time interferes with the overall learning process. If you separate your studying into these two approaches, you will perform better on the exam.

Active Study Strategies

The process of writing down and defining objectives, subobjectives, terms, facts, and definitions promotes a more active learning strategy than merely reading the material does. In human information-processing terms, writing forces you to engage in more active encoding of the information. Simply reading over the information leads to more passive processing.

You need to determine whether you can apply the information you have learned by attempting to create examples and scenarios on your own. You should think about how or where you could apply the concepts you are learning. Again, you should write down this information to process the facts and concepts in an active fashion.

The hands-on nature of the exercises at the end of each chapter provides further active learning opportunities that will reinforce concepts as well.

Common-Sense Strategies

You should follow common-sense practices when studying: You should study when you are alert, reduce or eliminate distractions, and take breaks when you become fatigued.

Pretesting Yourself

Pretesting allows you to assess how well you are learning. One of the most important aspects of learning is what has been called *meta-learning.* Meta-learning has to do with realizing when you know something well or when you need to study some more. In other words, you recognize how well or how poorly you have learned the material you are studying.

For most people, this can be difficult to assess. Review questions, practice questions, and practice tests are useful in that they reveal objectively what you have learned and what you have not learned. You should use this information to guide review and further studying. Developmental learning takes place as you cycle through studying, assessing how well you have learned, reviewing, and assessing again until you feel you are ready to take the exam.

You might have noticed the practice exam included in this book. You should use it as part of the learning process. The PrepLogic Practice Exams, Preview Edition test-simulation software included on this book's CD-ROM also provides you with an excellent opportunity to assess your knowledge.

You should set a goal for your pretesting. A reasonable goal would be to score consistently in the 90% range.

See Appendix E, "Using the PrepLogic Practice Exams, Preview Edition Software," for further explanation of the test-simulation software.

Exam Prep Tips

After you have mastered the subject matter, the final preparatory step is to understand how the exam will be presented. Make no mistake: A Microsoft Certified Professional (MCP) exam challenges both your knowledge and your test-taking skills. The following sections describe the basics of exam design and the exam formats, as well as provide hints targeted to each of the exam formats.

MCP Exam Design

Every MCP exam is released in one of three basic formats. What's being called *exam format* here is really little more than a combination of the overall exam structure and the presentation method for exam questions.

Understanding the exam formats is key to good preparation because the exam format determines the number of questions presented, the difficulty of those questions, and the amount of time allowed to complete the exam.

All the exam formats use many of the same types of questions. These types or styles of questions include several types of traditional multiple-choice questions, multiple-rating (or scenario-based) questions, and simulation-based questions. Some exams include other types of questions that ask you to drag and drop objects onscreen, reorder a list, or categorize things. Still other exams ask you to answer various types of questions in response to case studies you have read. It's important that you understand the types of questions you will be asked and the actions required to properly answer them.

The following sections address the exam formats and the question types. Understanding the formats and question types will help you feel much more comfortable when you take the exam.

Exam Formats

As mentioned previously, there are three basic formats for the MCP exams: the traditional fixed-form exam, the adaptive exam, and the case study exam. As its name implies, the fixed-form exam presents a fixed set of questions during the exam session. The adaptive exam, on the other hand, uses only a subset of questions drawn from a larger pool during any given exam session. It may present each test taker with a different number of questions, depending on how the person answers the initial questions. The case study exam includes case studies organized into testlets that serve as the basis for answering the questions. Most MCP exams these days utilize the fixed-form approach, with the case study approach running second. Microsoft seems to have backed off of the adaptive format, but it still lists that form as a possibility on its Training & Certification Web site.

Fixed-Form Exams

A fixed-form computerized exam is based on a fixed set of exam questions. The individual questions are presented in random order during a test session. If you take the same exam more than once, you won't necessarily see exactly the same questions. This is because two or three final forms are typically assembled for every fixed-form exam Microsoft releases. These are usually labeled Forms A, B, and C.

The final forms of a fixed-form exam are identical in terms of content coverage, number of questions, and allotted time, but the questions for each are different. However, some of the same questions are shared among different final forms. When questions are shared among multiple final forms of an exam, the percentage of sharing is generally small. Many final forms share no questions, but some older exams may have a 10%–15% duplication of exam questions on the final exam forms.

Fixed-form exams also have fixed time limits in which you must complete them.

The score you achieve on a fixed-form exam, which is always calculated for MCP exams on a scale of 0 to 1,000, is based on the number of questions you answer correctly. The passing score is the same for all final forms of a given fixed-form exam. Although Microsoft no longer reports the actual score to you, preferring to just tell you whether you passed, it is still calculated in this fashion.

The typical design of a fixed-form exam is as follows:

- The exam contains 50–60 questions.
- You are allowed 75–90 minutes of testing time.
- Question review is allowed, including the opportunity to change your answers.

Adaptive Exams

An adaptive exam has the same appearance as a fixed-form exam, but its questions differ in quantity and process of selection. Although the statistics of adaptive testing are fairly complex, the process is concerned with determining your level of skill or ability with the exam subject matter. This ability assessment begins with the presentation of questions of varying levels of difficulty and ascertaining at what difficulty level you can reliably answer them. Finally, the ability assessment determines whether your ability level is above or below the level required to pass that exam.

Examinees at different levels of ability see quite different sets of questions. Examinees who demonstrate little expertise with the subject matter continue to be presented with relatively easy questions. Examinees who demonstrate a high level of expertise are presented progressively more difficult questions. Individuals of both levels of expertise may answer the same number of questions correctly, but because the higher-expertise examinee can correctly answer more difficult questions, he or she receives a higher score and is more likely to pass the exam.

The typical design of an adaptive exam is as follows:

- The exam contains 15–25 questions.
- Testing time is shorter than that for a fixed-form exam.
- Question review is not allowed, so you have no opportunity to change your answers.

The Adaptive-Exam Process

Your first adaptive exam will be unlike any other testing experience you have had. In fact, many examinees have difficulty accepting the adaptive testing process because they feel that they are not provided the opportunity to adequately demonstrate their full expertise.

You can take consolation in the fact that adaptive exams are painstakingly put together after months of data gathering and analysis and that adaptive exams are just as valid as fixed-form exams. The rigor introduced through the adaptive testing methodology means that there is nothing arbitrary about the exam items you'll see. It is also a more efficient means of testing, requiring less time to conduct and complete than traditional fixed-form exams.

As you can see in Figure 1, a number of statistical measures drive the adaptive examination process. The measure that is most immediately relevant to you is the ability estimate. Accompanying this test statistic are the standard error of measurement, the item characteristic curve, and the test information curve.

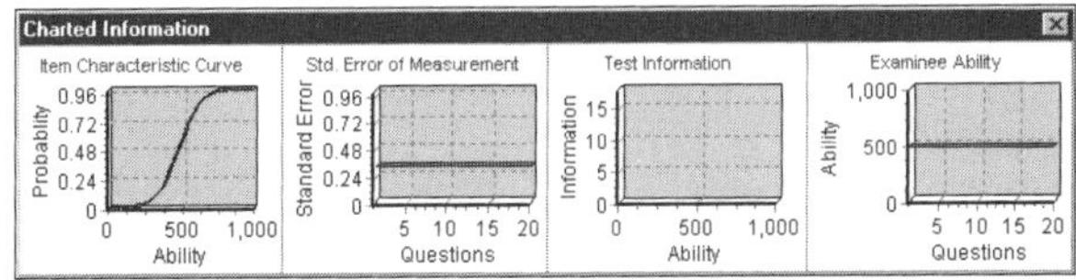

FIGURE 1
Microsoft's adaptive testing demonstration program.

The standard error, which is the key factor in determining when an adaptive exam terminates, reflects the degree of error in the exam ability estimate. The item characteristic curve reflects the probability of a correct response relative to examinee ability. Finally, the test information statistic provides a measure of the information contained in the set of questions the examinee has answered, again relative to the ability level of the individual examinee.

When you begin an adaptive exam, the standard error has already been assigned a target value below which it must drop for the exam to conclude. This target value reflects a particular level of statistical confidence in the process. The examinee ability is initially set to the mean possible exam score (typically 500 for MCP exams).

As the adaptive exam progresses, questions of varying difficulty are presented. Based on your pattern of responses to these questions, the ability estimate is recalculated. At the same time, the standard error estimate is refined from its first estimated value of 1 toward the target value. When the standard error reaches its target value, the exam is terminated. Thus, the more consistently you answer questions of the same degree of difficulty, the more quickly the standard error estimate drops, and the fewer questions you end up seeing during the exam session. This situation is depicted in Figure 2.

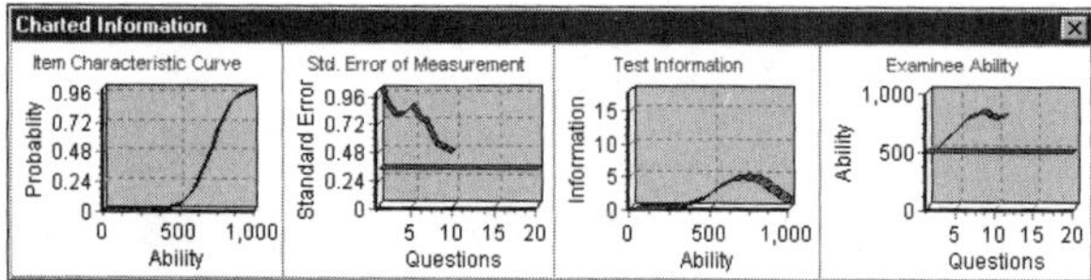

FIGURE 2
The changing statistics in an adaptive exam.

As you might suspect, one good piece of advice for taking an adaptive exam is to treat every exam question as if it were the most important. The adaptive scoring algorithm attempts to discover a pattern of responses that reflects some level of proficiency with the subject matter. Incorrect responses almost guarantee that additional questions must be answered (unless, of course, you get every question wrong). This is because the scoring algorithm must adjust to information that is not consistent with the emerging pattern.

Currently Microsoft is not utilizing adaptive exams much, but that could change. They are certainly still discussed on the Training & Certification Web site as a possibility (`www.microsoft.com/traincert/mcpexams/faq/security.asp`).

Case Study Exams

The case study–based format for Microsoft exams first appeared with the advent of the 70-100 exam (the original "Solution Architectures" exam) and then appeared in the MCSE sequence in the Design exams. The questions in the case study format are not the independent entities that they are in the fixed and adaptive formats. Instead, questions are tied to a case study, a long scenario-like description of an information technology situation. As the test taker, your job is to extract from the case study the information that needs to be integrated with your understanding of Microsoft technology. The idea is that a case study will provide you with a situation that is even more like a real-life problem than the other formats provide.

The case studies are presented as testlets. A *testlet* is a section within the exam in which you read the case study and then answer 10 to 20 questions that apply to the case study. When you finish that section, you move on to another testlet, with another case study and its associated questions. Typically, three to five of these testlets compose the overall exam. You are given more time to complete such an exam than to complete the other types because it takes time to read through the cases and analyze them. You might have as much as three hours to complete a case study exam—and you might need all of it. The case studies are always available through a linking button while you are in a testlet. However, when you leave a testlet, you cannot come back to it.

Figure 3 provides an illustration of part of such a case study.

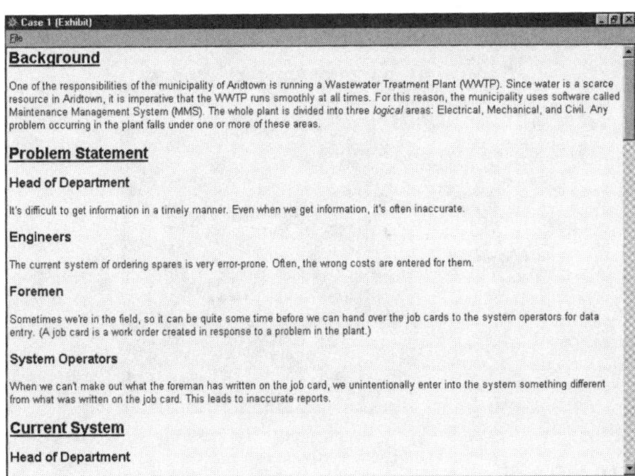

FIGURE 3
An example of a case study.

Question Types

A variety of question types can appear on MCP exams. We have attempted to cover all the types that are available at the time of this writing. Most of the question types discussed in the following sections can appear in each of the three exam formats.

A typical MCP exam question is based on the idea of measuring skills or the ability to complete tasks. Therefore, most of the questions are written so as to present you with a situation that includes a role (such as a system administrator or technician), a technology environment (for example, 100 computers running Windows XP Professional on a Windows Server 2003 network), and a problem to be solved (for example, the user can connect to services on the LAN but not on the intranet). The answers indicate actions you might take to solve the problem or create setups or environments that would function correctly from the start. You should keep this in mind as you read the questions on the exam. You might encounter some questions that just call for you to regurgitate facts, but these will be relatively few and far between.

The following sections look at the different question types.

Multiple-Choice Questions

Despite the variety of question types that now appear in various MCP exams, the multiple-choice question is still the basic building block of the exams. The multiple-choice question comes in three varieties:

- **Regular multiple-choice question**—Also referred to as an *alphabetic question*, a regular multiple-choice question asks you to choose one answer as correct.
- **Multiple-answer, multiple-choice question**—Also referred to as a *multi-alphabetic question*, this version of a multiple-choice question requires you to choose two or more answers as correct. Typically, you are told precisely the number of correct answers to choose.
- **Enhanced multiple-choice question**—This is simply a regular or multiple-answer question that includes a graphic or table to which you must refer to answer the question correctly.

Examples of multiple-choice questions appear at the end of each chapter in this book.

Simulation Questions

Simulation-based questions reproduce the look and feel of key Microsoft product features for the purpose of testing. The simulation software used in MCP exams has been designed to look and act, as much as possible, just like the actual product. Consequently, answering simulation questions in an MCP exam entails completing one or more tasks just as if you were using the product itself.

A typical Microsoft simulation question consists of a brief scenario or problem statement, along with one or more tasks that you must complete to solve the problem.

It sounds obvious, but your first step when you encounter a simulation question is to carefully read the question (see Figure 4). You should not go straight to the simulation application! You must assess the problem that's presented and identify the conditions that make up the problem scenario. You should note the tasks that must be performed or outcomes that must be achieved to answer the question, and then you should review any instructions you're given on how to proceed.

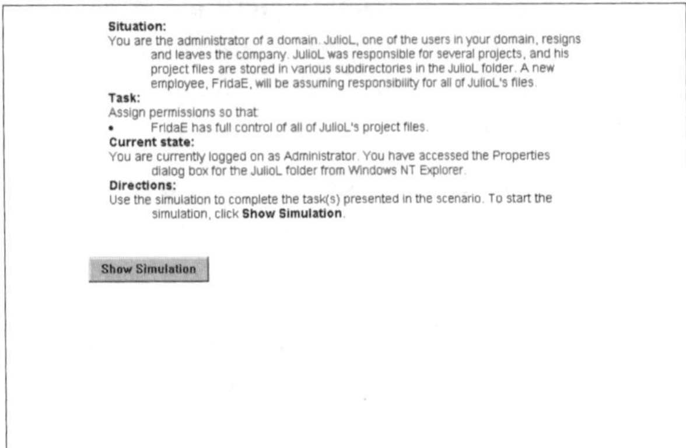

FIGURE 4
A typical MCP exam simulation with directions.

The next step is to launch the simulator by using the button provided. After you click the Show Simulation button, you see a feature of the product, as shown in the dialog box in Figure 5. The simulation application will partially obscure the question text on many test-center machines. You should feel free to reposition the simulator and to move between the question text screen and the simulator by using hotkeys or point-and-click navigation—or even by clicking the simulator's launch button again.

It is important for you to understand that your answer to the simulation question will not be recorded until you move on to the next exam question. This gives you the added capability of closing and reopening the simulation application (by using the launch button) on the same question without losing any partial answer you may have made.

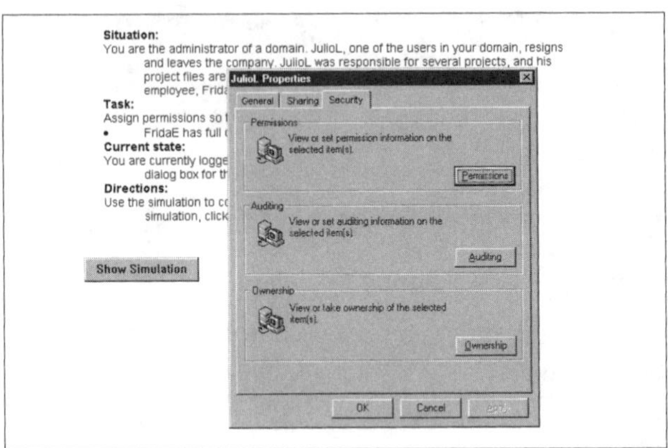

FIGURE 5
Launching the simulation application.

The third step is to use the simulator as you would the actual product to solve the problem or perform the defined tasks. Again, the simulation software is designed to function—within reason—just as the product does. But you shouldn't expect the simulator to reproduce product behavior perfectly. Most importantly, you should not allow yourself to become flustered if the simulator does not look or act exactly like the product.

Figure 6 shows the solution to the sample simulation problem.

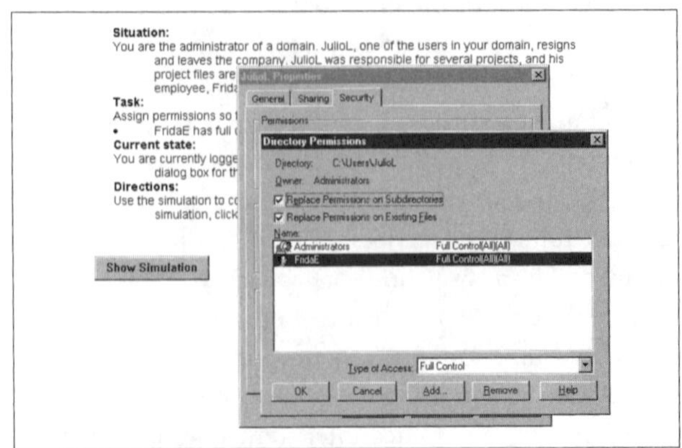

FIGURE 6
The solution to the simulation example.

Two final points will help you tackle simulation questions. First, you should respond only to what is being asked in the question; you should not solve problems that you are not asked to solve. Second, you should accept what is being asked of you. You might not entirely agree with conditions in the problem statement, the quality of the desired solution, or the sufficiency of defined tasks to adequately solve the problem. However, you should remember that you are being tested on your ability to solve the problem as it is presented.

The solution to the simulation problem shown in Figure 6 perfectly illustrates both of those points. As you'll recall from the question scenario (refer to Figure 4), you were asked to assign appropriate permissions to a new user, FridaE. You were not instructed to make any other changes in permissions. Therefore, if you were to modify or remove the administrator's permissions, this item would be scored wrong on an MCP exam.

Hot-Area Questions

Hot-area questions call for you to click a graphic or diagram to complete some task. You are asked a question that is similar to any other, but rather than click an option button or check box next to an answer, you click the relevant item in a screenshot or on a part of a diagram. An example of such an item is shown in Figure 7.

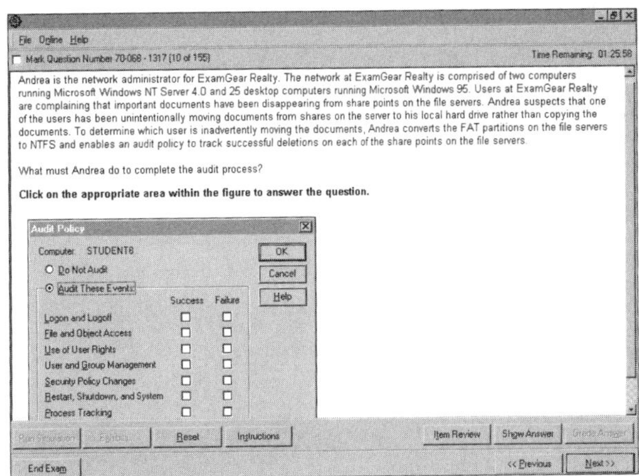

FIGURE 7
A typical hot-area question.

Drag-and-Drop Questions

Microsoft has utilized two different types of drag-and-drop questions in exams: select-and-place questions and drop-and-connect questions. Both are covered in the following sections.

Select-and-Place Questions

Select-and-place questions typically require you to drag and drop labels on images in a diagram so as to correctly label or identify some portion of a network. Figure 8 shows you the actual question portion of a select-and-place item.

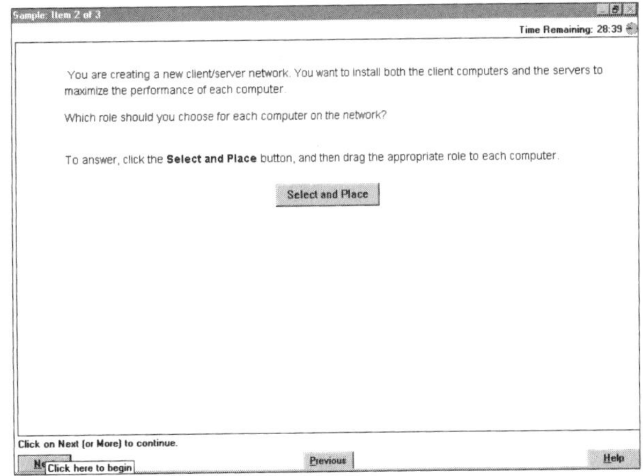

FIGURE 8
A select-and-place question.

Figure 9 shows the window you would see after you clicked Select and Place. It contains the actual diagram in which you would select and drag the various server roles and match them up with the appropriate computers.

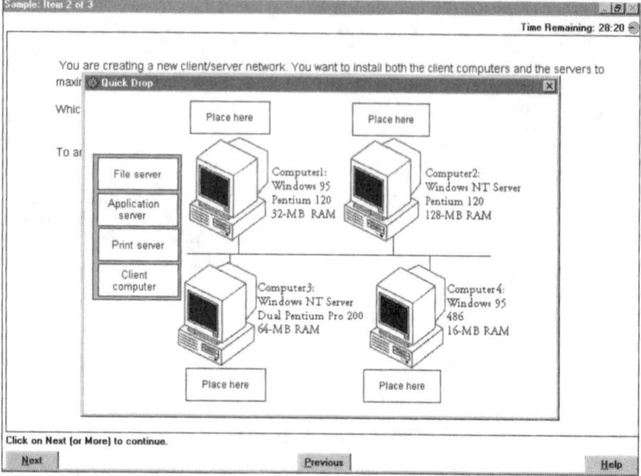

FIGURE 9
The window containing the select-and-place diagram.

Drop-and-Connect Questions

Drop-and-connect questions provide a different spin on drag-and-drop questions. This type of question provides you with the opportunity to create boxes that you can label, as well as connectors of various types with which to link them. In essence, you create a model or diagram in order to answer a drop-and-connect question. You might have to create a network diagram or a data model for a database system. Figure 10 illustrates the idea of a drop-and-connect question.

Microsoft seems to be getting away from this type of question, perhaps because of the complexity involved. You might see the same sort of concepts tested with a more traditional question utilizing multiple exhibits, each of which shows a diagram; in this type of question, you must choose which exhibit correctly portrays the solution to the problem posed in the question.

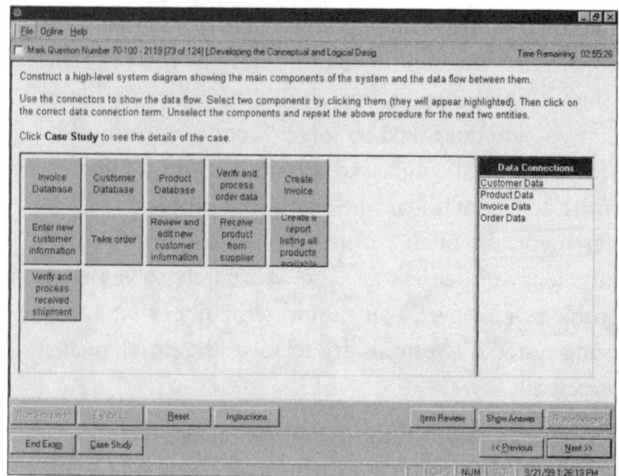

FIGURE 10
A drop-and-connect question.

Ordered-List Questions

Ordered-list questions require you to consider a list of items and place them in the proper order. You select items and then use a button or drag and drop to add them to a new list in the correct order. You can use another button to remove the items in the new order in case you change your mind and want to reorder things. Figure 11 shows an ordered-list question.

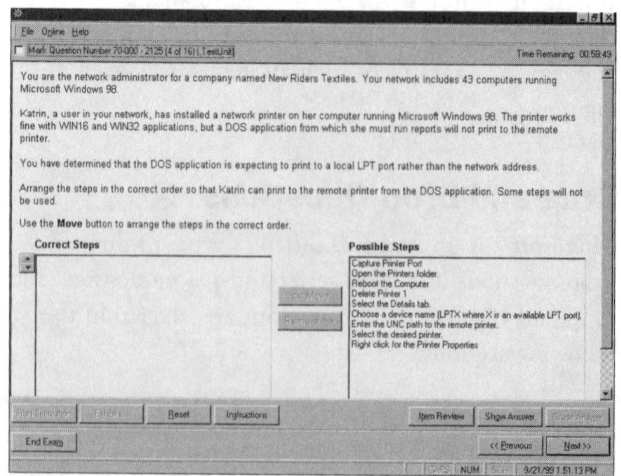

FIGURE 11
An ordered-list question.

Tree Questions

Tree questions require you to think hierarchically and categorically. You are asked to place items from a list into categories that are displayed as nodes in a tree structure. Such questions might ask you to identify parent-child relationships in processes or the structure of keys in a database. You might also be required to show order within the categories, much as you would in an ordered-list question. Figure 12 shows an example of a tree question.

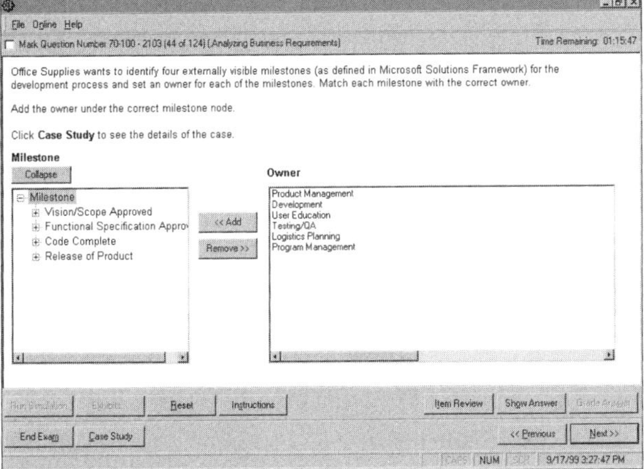

FIGURE 12
A tree question.

Putting It All Together

As you can see, Microsoft is making an effort to utilize question types that go beyond asking you to simply memorize facts. These question types force you to know how to accomplish tasks and understand concepts and relationships. You should study so that you can answer these types of questions rather than those that simply ask you to recall facts.

Given all the different pieces of information presented so far, the following sections present a set of tips that will help you successfully tackle the exam.

More Exam-Preparation Tips

Generic exam-preparation advice is always useful. Tips include the following:

- Become familiar with the product. Hands-on experience is one of the keys to success on any MCP exam. Review the exercises and the Step by Steps in the book.
- Review the current exam-preparation guide on the Microsoft Training & Certification Web site. The documentation Microsoft makes available on the Web identifies the skills every exam is intended to test.
- Memorize foundational technical detail, but remember that MCP exams are generally heavier on problem solving and application of knowledge than on questions that require only rote memorization.
- Take any of the available practice tests. We recommend the one included in this book and the ones you can create by using the PrepLogic software on this book's CD-ROM. As a supplement to the material bound with this book, try the free practice tests available on the Microsoft MCP Web site.
- Look on the Microsoft Training & Certification Web site for samples and demonstration items. (As of this writing, check `www.microsoft.com/traincert/mcpexams/faq/innovations.asp`, but you might have to look around for the samples because the URL may have changed.) These tend to be particularly valuable for one significant reason: They help you become familiar with new testing technologies before you encounter them on MCP exams.

Tips for During the Exam Session

The following generic exam-taking advice that you've heard for years applies when you're taking an MCP exam:

- Take a deep breath and try to relax when you first sit down for your exam session. It is very important that you control the pressure you might (naturally) feel when taking exams.
- You will be provided scratch paper. Take a moment to write down any factual information and technical detail that you have committed to short-term memory.
- Carefully read all information and instruction screens. These displays have been put together to give you information relevant to the exam you are taking.
- Accept the nondisclosure agreement and preliminary survey as part of the examination process. Complete them accurately and quickly move on.
- Read the exam questions carefully. Reread each question to identify all relevant detail.
- In fixed-form exams, tackle the questions in the order in which they are presented. Skipping around won't build your confidence; the clock is always counting down.
- Don't rush, but also don't linger on difficult questions. The questions vary in degree of difficulty. Don't let yourself be flustered by a particularly difficult or wordy question.

Besides considering the basic preparation and test-taking advice presented so far, you also need to consider the challenges presented by the different exam designs, as described in the following sections.

Tips for Fixed-Form Exams

Because a fixed-form exam is composed of a fixed, finite set of questions, you should add these tips to your strategy for taking a fixed-form exam:

- Note the time allotted and the number of questions on the exam you are taking. Make a rough calculation of how many minutes you can spend on each question, and use this figure to pace yourself through the exam.
- Take advantage of the fact that you can return to and review skipped or previously answered questions. Record the questions you can't answer confidently on the scratch paper provided, noting the relative difficulty of each question. When you reach the end of the exam, return to the more difficult questions.
- If you have session time remaining after you complete all the questions (and if you aren't too fatigued!), review your answers. Pay particular attention to questions that seem to have a lot of detail or that require graphics.
- As for changing your answers, the general rule of thumb here is *don't*! If you read the question carefully and completely and you felt like you knew the right answer, you probably did. Don't second-guess yourself. If, as you check your answers, one clearly stands out as incorrect, however, of course you should change it. But if you are at all unsure, go with your first impression.

Tips for Adaptive Exams

If you are planning to take an adaptive exam, keep these additional tips in mind:

- Read and answer every question with great care. When you're reading a question, identify every relevant detail, requirement, or task you must perform and double-check your answer to be sure you have addressed every one of them.

- If you cannot answer a question, use the process of elimination to reduce the set of potential answers and then take your best guess. Stupid mistakes invariably mean that additional questions will be presented.
- You cannot review questions and change answers. When you leave a question, whether you've answered it or not, you cannot return to it. Do not skip any question, either; if you do, it's counted as incorrect.

Tips for Case Study Exams

The case study exam format calls for unique study and exam-taking strategies:

- Remember that you have more time than in a typical exam. Take your time and read the case study thoroughly.
- Use the scrap paper or whatever medium is provided to you to take notes, diagram processes, and actively seek out the important information.
- Work through each testlet as if each were an independent exam. Remember that you cannot go back after you have left a testlet.
- Refer to the case study as often as you need to, but do not use that as a substitute for reading it carefully initially and for taking notes.

Final Considerations

Finally, a number of changes in the MCP program affect how frequently you can repeat an exam and what you will see when you do:

- Microsoft has an exam retake policy. The rule is "two and two, then one and two." That is, you can attempt any exam twice with no restrictions on the time between attempts. But after the second attempt, you must wait two weeks before you can attempt that exam again. After that, you are required to wait two weeks between subsequent attempts. Plan to pass the exam in two attempts or plan to increase your time horizon for receiving the MCP credential.
- New questions are always being seeded into the MCP exams. After performance data is gathered on new questions, the examiners replace older questions on all exam forms. This means that the questions appearing on exams change regularly.
- Any of the current MCP exams may be republished in adaptive form. The exception to this may be the case study exams because the adaptive approach does not work with that format.

These changes mean that the brute-force strategies for passing MCP exams have lost their viability. So if you don't pass an exam on the first or second attempt, it is likely that the exam's form could change significantly by the next time you take it. It could be updated from fixed-form to adaptive, or, even more likely, it could have a different set of questions or question types.

Microsoft's intention is not to make the exams more difficult by introducing unwanted change, but to create and maintain valid measures of the technical skills and knowledge associated with the different MCP credentials. Preparing for an MCP exam has always involved not only studying the subject matter but also planning for the testing experience itself. With the continuing changes, this is now truer than ever.

PART I

EXAM PREPARATION

OBJECTIVES

This chapter covers the following Microsoft-specified objectives for the "Managing and Maintaining Physical and Logical Devices" section of the Managing and Maintaining a Microsoft Windows Server 2003 Environment exam:

Manage basic disks and dynamic disks.

- When working in a Windows Server 2003 environment, you need to have a thorough understanding of the different types of disks available. In addition, it is important to understand how they are used and how to manage them.

Optimize server disk performance.

- **Implement a RAID solution.**
- **Defragment volumes and partitions.**

- The purpose of this objective is to teach you how to create, manage, and troubleshoot problems with the various RAID solutions available in Windows Server 2003. In addition, you should be familiar with maintaining volumes and partitions using the Disk Defragmenter utility.

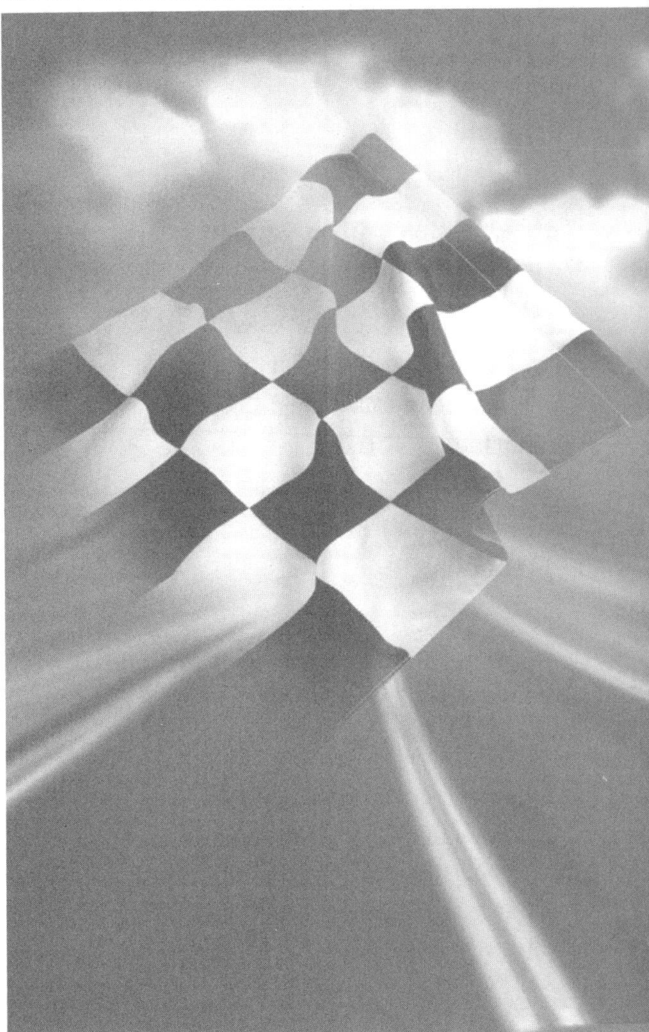

CHAPTER 1

Managing Server Storage Devices

OUTLINE

OUTLINE

STUDY STRATEGIES

- The sections in this chapter outline features that are basic to using and managing Windows Server 2003. The proper use of and recovery from problems with storage have always been major points on Microsoft exams. Expect the Windows Server 2003 exams to continue that tradition. Make sure you have a complete understanding of the capabilities of basic and dynamic disks, especially as far as how they are similar and how they are different.
- Most of the disk-related questions will probably concern the use of dynamic disks. Although basic disks can be used in Windows Server 2003, the advanced storage functionality is supported only on dynamic disks. Make sure you understand the various capabilities of dynamic disks, how they are configured, and how to recover from failures.

Introduction

One of the primary roles of Windows Server 2003 is that of a data repository, or file server. Many administrative tasks are involved in creating, configuring, and managing a file server. This can range from deciding what types of volumes or partitions to use, to recovering from a physical disk failure. This chapter covers the tasks required to maintain data on Windows Server 2003. This type of information is crucial for a job as a system administrator, and it is also very important for the exam.

Managing Basic Disks and Dynamic Disks

Windows Server 2003 supports two types of physical disk configurations: *basic* and *dynamic*. A single physical disk must be one type or the other; however, you can intermingle the physical disk types in a multiple disk server.

Introduction to Basic Disks

When a new disk is installed in Windows Server 2003, it is installed as a basic disk. The basic disk type has been used in all versions of Microsoft Windows dating back to 1.0, OS/2, and in MS-DOS. This configuration allows a basic disk created in Windows Server 2003 to be recognized by these earlier operating systems.

A basic disk splits a physical disk into units called *partitions.* Partitions allow you to subdivide your physical disk into separate units of storage. There are two types of partitions: *primary* and *extended.*

A primary partition can be used to store a boot record so that you can boot your server from that partition. A hard disk can be configured with one to four primary partitions. You can use these partitions to boot multiple operating systems, or to just contain data.

Although multiple primary partitions can contain boot records, only one primary partition can be marked *active*. When a primary partition is marked as active, the system BIOS looks for the boot files needed to start the system in that partition.

The other type of partition is the *extended partition*, which allows you to create a theoretically unlimited number of logical drives inside that partition. Using older operating systems limits the number of drive letters that are available; however, in the later versions of Windows NT/2000/2003/XP, these logical drives can be mounted without a drive letter. The downside is that logical drives created inside an extended partition are not bootable.

You can have up to four primary partitions, or three primary partitions and an extended partition, on a single physical hard disk. The basic disk was the only type supported in versions of Windows prior to Windows 2000.

Before a physical hard disk can be used with an operating system, it must be *initialized*. The initialization process is used to write the master boot record (MBR) to the first sector of the hard drive. The MBR contains a small amount of startup code and a partition table that lists the configuration of the partitions. The hard drive can be initialized during a clean installation of Windows 2003 or by using the command-line utility `FDISK`.

When a Windows Server 2003 server is started, its Basic Input/Output System (BIOS) reads the MBR on the physical hard drive that is used to start the server. The MBR contains a pointer to the location of the active partition on the hard drive and the code needed to begin the startup process. The active partition is also referred to as the *system partition*. On an Intel-based system, the system partition contains the `BOOT.INI`, `NTDETECT.COM`, and `NTLDR` files. These files tell the server how to start the operating system.

The `BOOT.INI` file, shown in Figure 1.1, contains the physical path to the location of the folder that contains the operating system files. The `BOOT.INI` file can contain paths to multiple operating systems. At boot time, you are presented with a menu that allows you to choose which operating system to start. In the example shown, there is an additional option to boot to the Recovery Console.

NOTE

Watch the Terminology Beginning with Windows XP, Microsoft has started to refer to primary partitions and the logical drives that are contained in extended partitions as *basic volumes*. Do not confuse this with *simple volumes*, which are discussed later in the chapter. In addition, remember that a basic disk is a physical entity and that a basic volume is a logical one.

`NTBOOTDD.SYS` Another file that might be included is `NTBOOTDD.SYS`. This file is needed only if you are using a SCSI controller that has its BIOS disabled.

EXAM TIP

Know Your Partitions Be familiar with the two types of partitions, logical drives, and which drives are bootable.

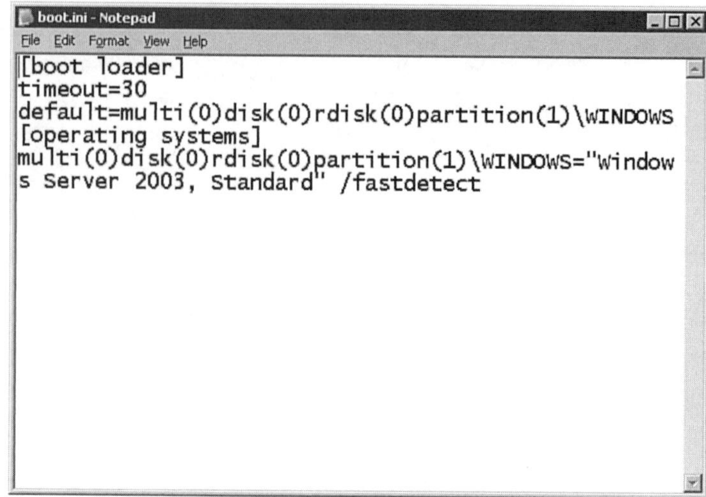

boot.ini - Notepad
File Edit Format View Help
[boot loader]
timeout=30
default=multi(0)disk(0)rdisk(0)partition(1)\WINDOWS
[operating systems]
multi(0)disk(0)rdisk(0)partition(1)\WINDOWS="Windows Server 2003, Standard" /fastdetect

FIGURE 1.1
A typical `BOOT.INI` file, showing the location of the system partition.

> **NOTE**
>
> **More on the Recovery Console** The Recovery Console is covered in Chapter 7, "Managing and Implementing Disaster Recovery."

> **EXAM TIP**
>
> There might be scenarios on the exam where you must understand the logical relationship between boot partitions and system partitions.

The partition that contains the operating system files is referred to as the *boot partition.* Of course, you don't have to have separate boot and system partitions. You can use a single partition to contain both the boot and the operating system files; for example, the common configuration for most servers is for both partitions to be located on the C: drive.

Although the system partition must be located on a physical partition, the boot partition can be contained on a logical drive in the extended partition. It is important to remember that although physical and extended partitions are physical entities, active, system, and boot partitions are logical entities.

Using the `DISKPART` Utility

A new feature in Windows Server 2003 is the ability to extend partitions on basic disks. This allows you to extend either primary or logical partitions into unallocated, adjacent, contiguous space. In Windows 2000, only dynamic volumes could be extended.

Extending partitions on a basic disk is performed using the `DISKPART` utility. `DISKPART` is a command-line utility that can be used to perform a variety of disk-management tasks. Because it is a command-line utility, it can be included in scripts or run from a remote session.

Although the Disk Management snap-in is what you use to perform the majority of disk-related tasks, `DISKPART` can perform more operations than the Disk Management snap-in. For example, extending a basic volume can be performed only through the `DISKPART` utility.

However, whereas the Disk Management snap-in prevents you from performing operations that might result in data loss, `DISKPART` has no safeguards and allows you to perform just about any operation on your disk with little or no warning. Here is a partial list of the operations that can be performed using the `DISKPART` utility:

- Set a partition to active.
- Add, create, and delete disks, partitions, and volumes, both basic and fault tolerant.
- Add or break mirrored volumes (RAID-1).
- Repair mirrored sets (RAID-1) or fault-tolerant volumes (RAID-5).
- Import foreign disks.
- List the size, configuration, and status of the physical and logical disks in the server.

In Windows Server 2003, a basic volume can be extended into the next contiguous, unallocated space on that disk. The limitations are that you cannot extend the system or boot partitions you used to start the current session, and the partition must be formatted with NTFS.

To extend a basic volume on a basic disk using the `DISKPART` utility, follow Step by Step 1.1.

> **NOTE**
>
> **Required Permissions** To perform disk-management tasks on a Windows Server 2003 server, you must be a member of either the Administrators or Backup Operators local group on the server. Alternatively, if the server is a member of a domain, you should be a member of the Domain Admins group.

STEP BY STEP

1.1 Using `DISKPART` to Extend a Basic Volume

1. From the Start menu, select Run. From the command line, enter `DISKPART` and press the Enter key.

continues

continued

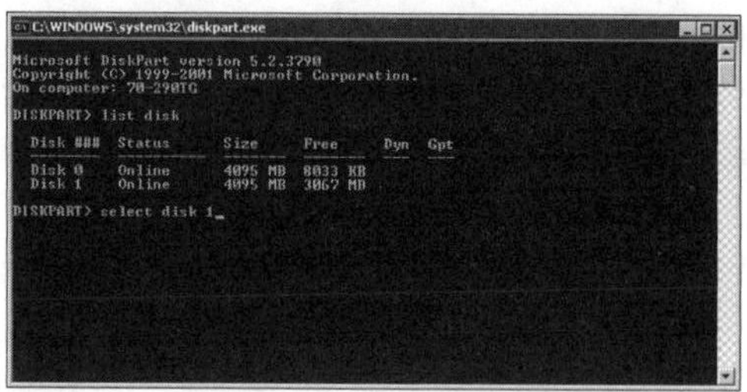

FIGURE 1.2
Output from the `DISKPART` utility, showing the results of the `list disk` command.

2. A command window opens with `DISKPART` in command mode. You need to select the disk and partition on which you want to perform operations. You can accomplish this by entering the `list disk` command to obtain a list of physical disks in your server, as shown in Figure 1.2. Note that an asterisk appears next to the disk, if any, that has the current focus.

3. After you determine the number of the disk you want to perform the operation on, you can set the focus to that disk by entering `select disk` *x*, where *x* is the number of the disk.

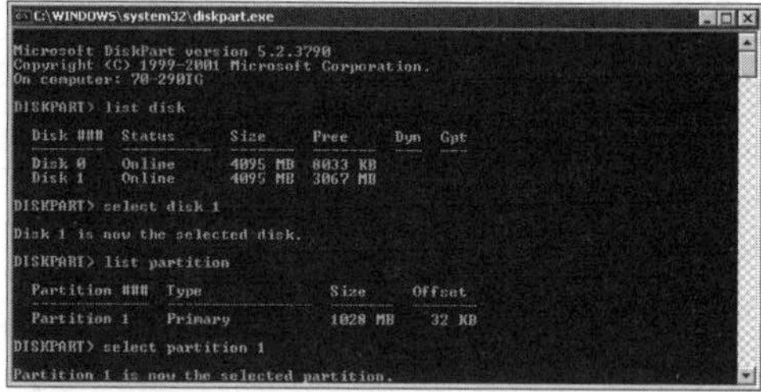

FIGURE 1.3
Output from the `DISKPART` utility, showing the results of the `list partition` command.

4. After you have set the focus to the desired disk, you can list the partitions or volumes on the disk by entering the `list partition` or the `list volume` command, as shown in Figure 1.3.

5. After you determine the number of the partition or volume you want to perform the operation on, set the focus to it by entering either `select partition` *x* or `select volume` *x*, as appropriate, where *x* is the number of the partition or volume.

6. After the desired disk and partition/volume are selected, use the `extend` command to extend the selected partition into the contiguous unallocated space. At the command prompt, enter `extend size=`*x*, where *x* is the amount in megabytes (MB) that you want to extend the partition or volume, as shown in Figure 1.4. If no size is specified, all the contiguous allocated space is added to the existing partition or volume.

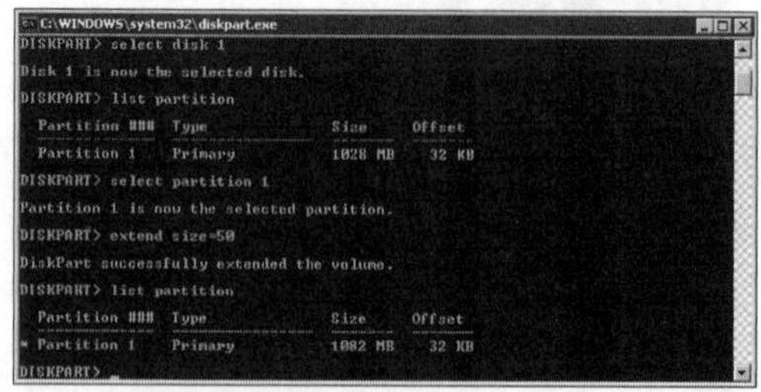

FIGURE 1.4
Output from the `DISKPART` utility, showing the results of the `extend` command. The asterisk is displayed next to the partition or volume that has the focus.

7. You can verify the results by entering the `list partition` or `list volume` command and then checking the new size.

> **NOTE**
>
> **Use the Proper Identification** On basic disks, you can specify the volume or partition by using the number, drive letter, or mount point. On dynamic disks, you can use only the volume number.

> **EXAM TIP**
>
> **Know the Uses for `DISKPART`** Be familiar with the things that `DISKPART` can do that can't be accomplished via the Disk Management MMC.

Introduction to Dynamic Disks

Dynamic disks were first introduced in Windows 2000 and are the preferred disk type for Windows Server 2003. Unlike a basic disk, a dynamic disk is divided into *volumes* instead of partitions. Although a clean installation of Windows Server 2003 creates a basic disk by default, any additional disks can be added as basic or dynamic disks. In addition, after the initial installation, the basic disk can be converted to a dynamic disk.

Unlike basic disks, which use the original MS-DOS–style master boot record (MBR) partition tables to store primary and logical disk-partitioning information, dynamic disks use a private region of the disk to maintain a *Logical Disk Manager (LDM)* database. The LDM contains volume types, offsets, memberships, and drive letters of each volume on that physical disk. The information in the LDM database is also replicated to all the other dynamic disks so that each dynamic disk knows the configuration of every other dynamic disk. This feature makes dynamic disks more reliable and recoverable than basic disks. This extra reliability and recoverability is necessary so that a disk move or failure does not cause the disk configuration to be lost. The LDM database is stored in a 1MB reserved area at the end of every dynamic disk.

In addition, configuration changes can be made to dynamic disks without rebooting the server. Dynamic volumes can be created, deleted, and expanded, all without a reboot.

The following are the five types of volumes available using dynamic storage disks:

- **Simple volumes**—Simple volumes are similar to a partition on a basic disk.

- **Spanned volumes**—Spanned volumes can take various amounts of disk space, from 2 to 32 physical disks, and use that space to create a single large volume. Spanned volumes provide no fault tolerance. In fact, they can be more prone to failure than other types of volume because if any disk fails, the entire set is lost. The advantage of spanned volumes is that you can quickly add more storage space.

- **Striped volumes**—Striped volumes can be created from 2 to 32 physical disks. Striped volumes write data to these disks in 64KB sequential stripes. The first stripe is written to the first disk, the second stripe is written to the second disk, and so forth. Striped volumes, also known as *RAID-0,* provide no fault tolerance. The advantage provided by striped volumes lies in the overall disk I/O performance increase of the computer because the total disk I/O is split among all the disks in the volume.

- **Mirrored volumes**—Mirrored volumes, also known as *RAID-1 volumes,* provide fault-tolerant data storage using two physical disks. Data is written simultaneously to each physical disk so that they contain identical information. If one of the drives in a mirrored volume fails, the system continues to run using the other volume. The total volume capacity will be equal to that provided by one of the physical disks.

- **RAID-5 volumes**—RAID-5 volumes are similar to striped volumes in that they use multiple disks—in this case, from 3 to 32 physical disks of the same size. The total volume capacity is equal to that provided by the number of physical disks minus one. Data is written sequentially across each physical disk and contains both data and parity information. For example, if you create a volume using four 1GB disks, your usable storage would be 3GB, because 1GB is devoted to storing the parity information. The parity information from the set is used to rebuild the set should one disk fail, thus providing fault tolerance. RAID-5 volumes in Windows Server 2003 cannot sustain the loss of more than one disk in the set while still providing fault tolerance.

After Windows Server 2003 is installed, you can convert a basic disk to a dynamic disk using the Disk Management snap-in or the `DISKPART` command-line utility. Using the Disk Management utility to covert disks is covered later in this chapter.

Limitations of Dynamic Disks

After reading about the wonderful features of dynamic disks, you're probably thinking that you should always use dynamic disks instead of basic disks. However, dynamic disks have some limitations, and there are situations in which they can't be used at all. Here are some of the limitations of dynamic disks:

- You cannot use dynamic disks if you want to dual boot a computer with an older operating system such as Windows 9*x* or Windows NT 4.0. Unfortunately, these older operating systems cannot access a dynamic disk, either as a boot device or for file storage. Only Windows 2000, 2003, and XP machines recognize dynamic disks. However, a dynamic disk can be accessed over the network by older operating systems.
- You can't set up multiple boot partitions on a dynamic disk.
- If you convert a basic disk that was configured to multiboot two or more operating systems to a dynamic disk, that disk is no longer bootable from any of the operating systems on it.
- Dynamic disks are not supported in laptops or removable disks, such as Zip disks or disks connected via a Universal Serial Bus (USB) or FireWire (IEEE 1394) interface. In addition, dynamic disks are not supported on disks used in cluster array configurations.
- Windows Server 2003 cannot be installed on a dynamic volume that was created from unallocated space on a dynamic disk.
- You can install Windows Server 2003 only on a basic disk, or on a dynamic volume that was converted from a basic boot volume/partition.

- After a basic disk is converted to a dynamic disk, it can't be converted back to a basic disk. The only way to revert to a basic disk is to back up the data, reinitialize the disk, repartition it, and restore the data.
- When installing Windows Server 2003 on a dynamic disk, you can't change the volume or partition sizes during the setup procedure.

EXAM TIP

Accessing Disks over the Network When accessing a disk over the network, the client PC doesn't know or care whether it's accessing a basic or dynamic disk, using FAT or NTFS. This could easily be part of an exam question.

Most of the dynamic disk limitations in the Windows 2000/2003/XP family are due to the requirement of these operating systems that the boot partition have an entry in the partition table. After a basic disk is converted to a dynamic disk, you cannot change the partition table to mark a volume as an active volume.

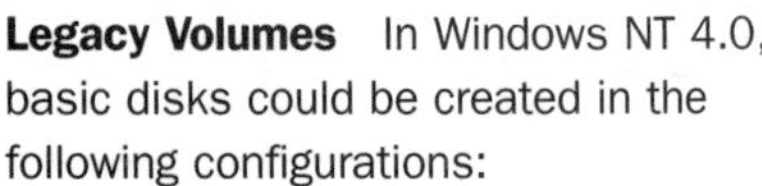

NOTE

Legacy Volumes In Windows NT 4.0, basic disks could be created in the following configurations:

- Spanned volume sets
- Mirrored volumes (RAID-1)
- Striped volumes (RAID-0)
- Striped volumes with parity (RAID-5)

Windows Server 2003 does not support the creation or use of any of these configurations on a basic disk. If any of these volumes are present in a server that is upgraded to Windows Server 2003, or are added after Windows 2003 is installed, they will no longer be accessible. These volumes must be mounted in either Windows NT 4.0 or Windows 2000 Server to recover the data. For more information, see the Microsoft Knowledge Base Article Q328520, "Disk Management Displays Previous FTDisk Volumes As 'Unknown' with No Drive Letter."

Using the Disk Management Console to Manage Disks

Regardless of what type of disk you are using in Windows Server 2003, the majority of management tasks are performed using the Disk Management snap-in. The Disk Management snap-in is an extremely useful GUI tool for performing the required management tasks on your computer's hard drives and volumes. Disk Management can be accessed in several ways, the easiest of which is via the Computer Management console, as outlined in Step by Step 1.2.

STEP BY STEP

1.2 Starting the Disk Management Snap-In

1. From the Start menu, select All Programs, Administrative Tools, Computer Management.
2. In the left pane of the Computer Management MMC, left-click the Storage entry and then select the Disk Management entry. This starts the Disk Management snap-in, as shown in Figure 1.5.

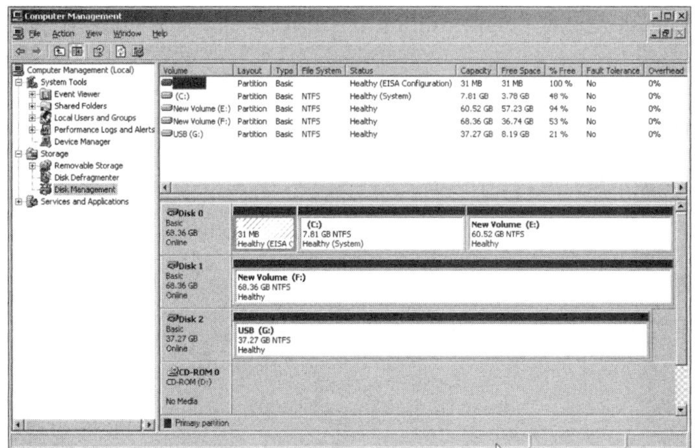

FIGURE 1.5

The Disk Management snap-in, shown here as part of the Computer Management MMC.

3. By default, Disk Management opens with the volume list displayed in the top-right pane and the graphical view displayed in the bottom-right pane. To change the view, for example, to display the disk list in the bottom-right pane, from the menu bar, select View, Bottom, Disk List (see Figure 1.6).

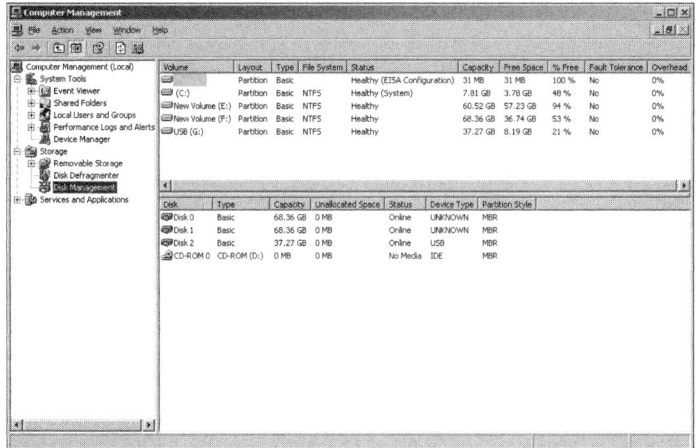

FIGURE 1.6

The Disk Management snap-in, showing the disk list in the bottom-right pane. The disk list displays the physical characteristics of the disks.

The Disk Management utility provides the following information:

- The type of disk, such as basic or dynamic
- The health status of each disk
- The partitions and/or volumes installed
- The health status of each partition or volume
- The file systems in use, such as FAT32 and NTFS
- The total size and free space for each disk, partition, or volume

MONITORING AND CONFIGURING DISKS AND VOLUMES

The bulk of your hard disk– and volume-management tasks are performed with the Disk Management utility. It can be used to perform the following tasks:

- Determine disk and volume information, such as size, file system, and other pertinent information.
- Determine disk health status.
- Convert basic storage to dynamic storage.
- Create new partitions and volumes.
- Format partitions and volumes.
- Delete partitions and volumes.
- Extend the size of dynamic volumes.
- Assign and change drive letters or paths to hard drives and removable storage drives.
- Add new physical disks.

Although you most commonly access the Disk Management utility from the Computer Management console, you can access Disk Management in any one of the following three ways, depending on your preferences:

- On the command line, enter `diskmgmt.msc`.
- On the command line, enter `MMC`. In the empty console, add the Disk Management snap-in. This can be useful for creating powerful, customized MMC consoles for a variety of management tasks.
- From within the Computer Management console, click Disk Management.

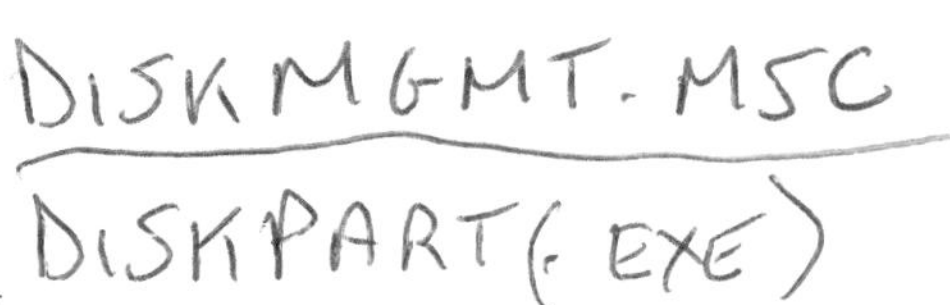

Viewing Disk Properties

You can quickly determine the properties of each physical disk in your computer by right-clicking the disk in question (see Figure 1.7) in the bottom area of the Disk Management window and selecting Properties from the shortcut menu.

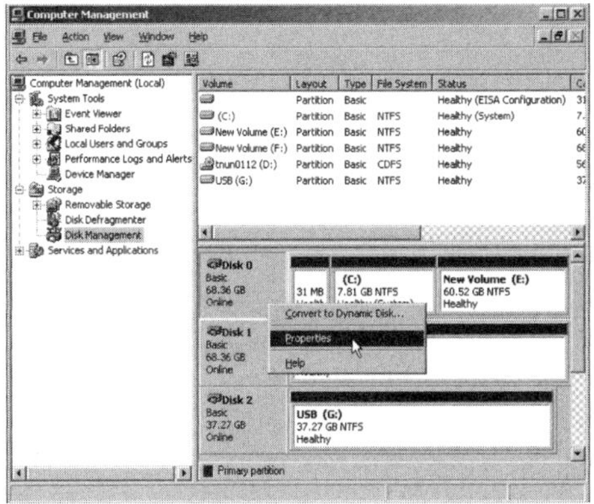

FIGURE 1.7
Getting disk properties from within the Disk Management snap-in.

As shown in Figure 1.8, the Disk Device Properties dialog box shows you the following information about your disks:

- The disk number, such as 0 or 1
- The type of disk (either basic or dynamic)
- The status and health of the disk
- The total capacity of the disk
- The unallocated space remaining on the disk
- The device type (either IDE or SCSI)
- The vendor of the hard disk, such as Maxtor or Fujitsu
- The adapter channel, such as primary IDE or secondary IDE
- The volumes or partitions that are located on the physical disk, such as C and D

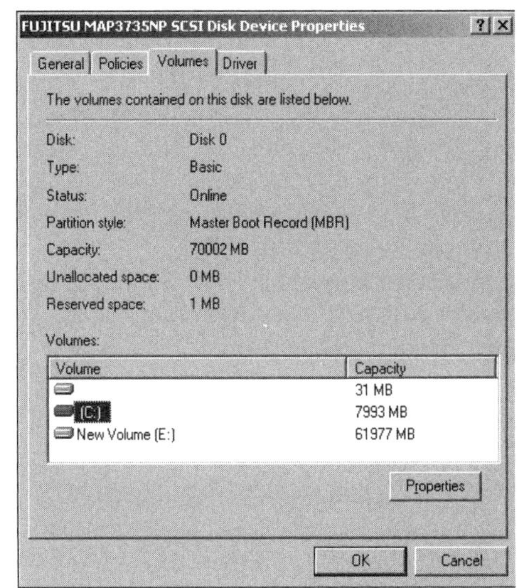

FIGURE 1.8
The Disk Device Properties dialog box, showing the Volumes tab. Most of the physical data about the disk configuration can be obtained here.

Viewing Volume Health Status

The health status of each volume is provided in the volume properties pane under the volume size in Disk Management (see Figure 1.9). The following are some of the more common items displayed in this area:

- **Online**—The disk is operating normally with no known problems.
- **Healthy**—The volume is operating normally.
- **Healthy (At Risk)**—The volume is operating but is experiencing I/O errors.
- **Online (Errors)**—Used only for dynamic disks, this status indicates that I/O errors have been detected.
- **Offline or Missing**—Used only for dynamic disks, this status indicates that the disk is not accessible.
- **Failed Redundancy**—One of the fault-tolerant volumes has failed.
- **Foreign**—Used only for dynamic disks, this status indicates that a dynamic disk was removed from a Windows 2000/2003/XP computer and placed into this Windows 2003 computer, but has not yet been imported.
- **Unreadable**—The disk is not accessible.
- **Unrecognized**—The disk is not recognized (for example, a disk that was used in a Linux or Unix system).
- **No Media**—Used only for removable-media drives such as CD-ROM and Zip drives. The status changes to Online when readable media is inserted into the drive.

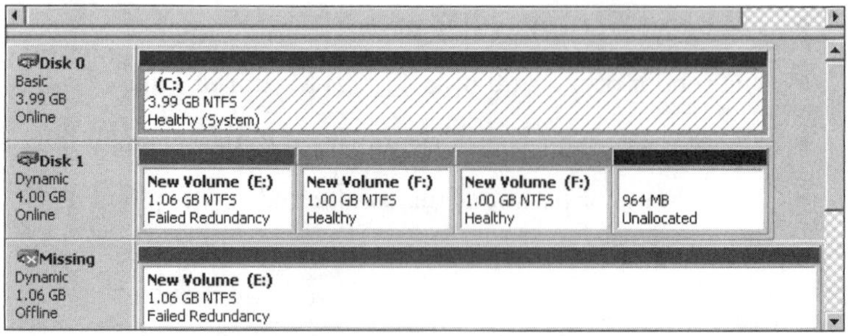

FIGURE 1.9
The Disk Management snap-in, focusing on the volume status. For redundant drives, this is your only indication of a failure.

Correcting problems with drives is discussed further in the "Recovering from Disk Failures" section later in this chapter.

Viewing and Configuring Volume Properties

To gather information about a specific volume, right-click the desired volume in the lower pane of the Disk Management window (refer to Figure 1.9) and select Properties from the shortcut menu. As shown in Figure 1.10, the volume's Properties dialog box shows you the following information about your volumes (from the General tab):

- ▶ The volume label
- ▶ The type of volume—either local disk (basic storage) or simple, spanned, or striped (dynamic storage)
- ▶ The file system in use (either as FAT32 or NTFS)
- ▶ The amount of space in use on the volume
- ▶ The amount of free space on the volume
- ▶ The total capacity of the volume
- ▶ Whether or not the volume has been configured for volume-level NTFS file and folder compression
- ▶ Whether or not the volume has been configured for indexing by the Indexing Service

If you click the Disk Cleanup button, the Disk Cleanup utility starts, which is discussed later in this chapter. From the Hardware tab (see Figure 1.11) of the volume's Properties dialog box, you can quickly get a summary of all installed storage devices in your computer. To open a troubleshooting wizard for a particular device, select it and click the Troubleshoot button. To view a device's properties, select the device and click the Properties button. The device's Properties dialog box opens. Device properties are discussed in Chapter 2, "Managing and Troubleshooting Hardware Devices."

The Sharing tab of the volume's Properties dialog box allows you to configure sharing of a volume for use by network clients across the network. Working with shared folders is discussed in Chapter 4, "Managing and Maintaining Access to Resources." The Security tab allows you to configure the NTFS permissions for the root of the volume; NTFS permissions are also discussed in Chapter 4.

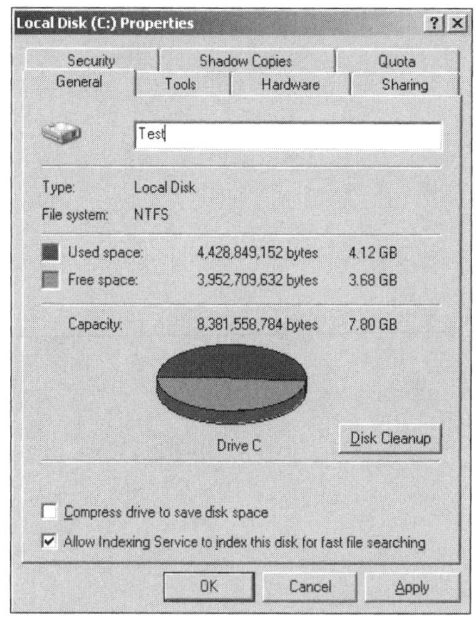

FIGURE 1.10
The General tab of Disk Properties displays the logical configuration of the individual volume.

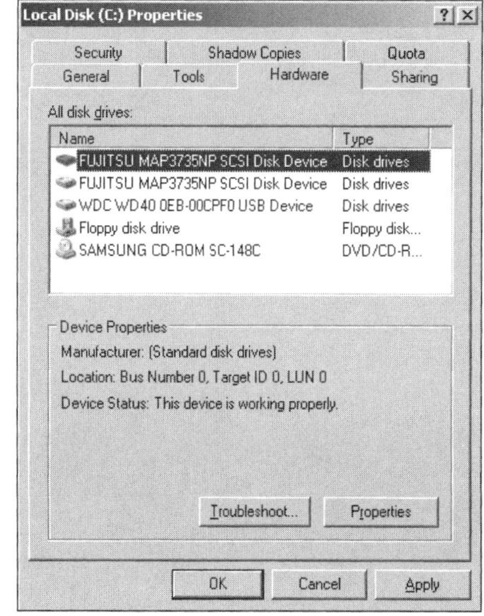

FIGURE 1.11
The Hardware tab of Disk Properties displays information about all the physical drives in the server.

The Quota tab allows you to configure and enforce disk usage quotas for your users. Working with disk quotas is discussed in the "Managing Disk Quotas" section of Chapter 4.

The last tab in the volume's Properties dialog box is the Web Sharing tab. If you have IIS installed on your computer, you will see this tab. Working with IIS and Web Sharing is discussed in Chapter 5, "Managing and Troubleshooting Servers."

Managing Disks on a Remote Computer

Because Disk Management is an MMC snap-in to the Computer Management MMC, it inherits the capabilities of all the Computer Management MMC's snap-ins to manage remote computers. This allows you to perform disk-management operations on any remote Windows 2000/2003/XP computer to which you have the required administrative authority.

To perform disk-management tasks on a remote computer, you must be a member of either the Administrators or Backup Operators local group on the remote computer. If the remote computer is a member of a domain, you should be a member of the Domain Admins group.

Step by Step 1.3 walks you through connecting to a remote computer to perform disk-management tasks.

STEP BY STEP

1.3 Connecting to a Remote Computer to Perform Disk-management Tasks

1. From the Start menu, select All Programs, Administrative Tools, Computer Management.
2. In the left pane of the Computer Management MMC, right-click the Computer Management (Local) entry.

Then select Connect to Another Computer from the pop-up menu. This opens the Select Computer dialog box, as shown in Figure 1.12.

3. From the Select Computer dialog box, you can either browse for or enter the name of the remote computer to manage. Enter the name of the computer and then click the OK button.

4. The Computer Management MMC opens with the focus assigned to the remote computer, as shown in Figure 1.13, with a remote computer named "PRO" as the management focus.

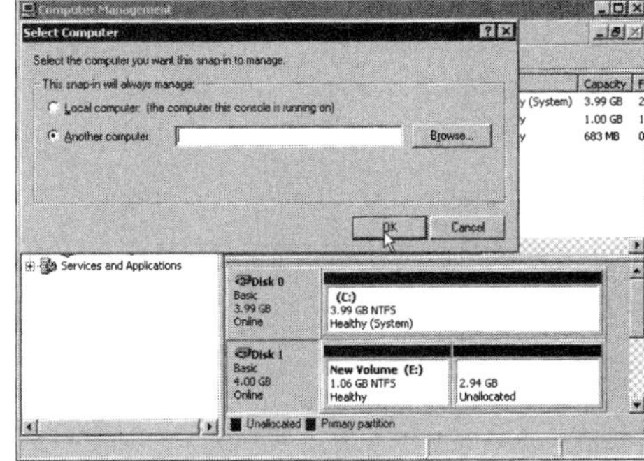

FIGURE 1.12▲
The Computer Management MMC, showing the Select Computer dialog box. Select Computer allows you to either browse for or enter the name of a remote computer to manage.

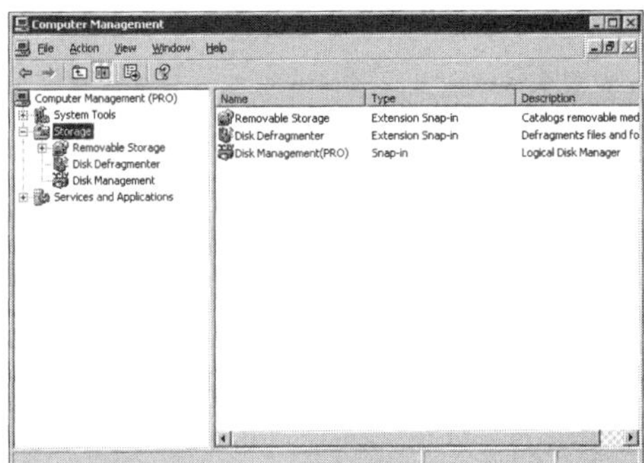

FIGURE 1.13◄
The Computer Management MMC, connected to a remote computer.

If the user has the proper permissions, any computer in the Windows 2000/2003/XP family can manage other family members. For example, a Windows 2000 Professional computer can be used to manage a Windows Server 2003 computer or a Windows XP Professional computer. Only the features that are supported on the remote computer are available in the MMC. For example, if you are using a Windows Server 2003 computer to manage a Windows XP Professional computer, the selection for RAID-5 will not be available because it is not supported on the remote computer, which in this case is Windows XP Professional.

Adding a New Disk

When you add a new disk to a Windows Server 2003 server, it must be initialized and a disk signature and MBR written to it before it can be used. When you open the Disk Management snap-in for the first time after the new disk has been installed, the Initialize and Convert Disk Wizard displays a list of any new disks detected by the operating system, and it prompts you as to whether you want to install the new disk as a basic disk or as a dynamic disk.

Step by Step 1.4 walks you through adding a new disk to your server using the Initialize and Covert Disk Wizard.

STEP BY STEP

1.4 Adding a New Disk

1. From the Start menu, select All Programs, Administrative Tools, Computer Management.
2. In the left pane of the Computer Management MMC, left-click the Storage entry and then select the Disk Management entry. This starts the Disk Management snap-in, which starts the wizard, as shown in Figure 1.14.

FIGURE 1.14
The opening window of the Initialize and Convert Disk Wizard, listing its purpose and guidelines for completing the installation of the new disk.

3. Click Next to continue. The next screen, as shown in Figure 1.15, displays a list of disks that require initialization before they can be used. Select the desired disks and then click Next to continue.

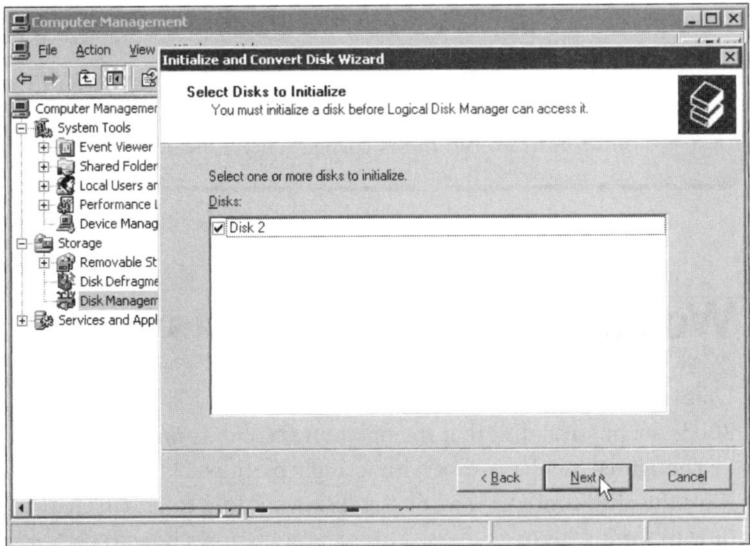

FIGURE 1.15
The Disk Manager snap-in, running the *Initialize and Convert Disk Wizard*, showing the disk list. The list displays the physical disks that have not yet been initialized.

4. The next screen, as shown in Figure 1.16, allows you to select which of the new disks, if any, you want to convert to dynamic disks. If you don't make a selection here, the new disks are configured as basic disks. Click Next to continue.

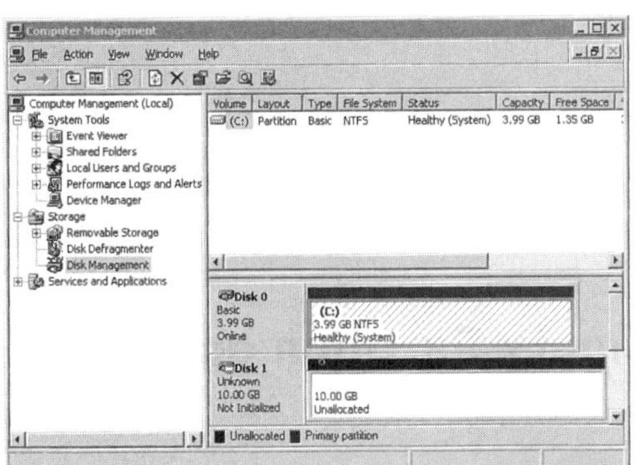

FIGURE 1.16
The Disk Manager snap-in, running the *Initialize and Convert Disk Wizard*, showing the disk list. The list displays the physical disks and allows you to specify whether they will be configured as dynamic disks.

continues

> **NOTE**
> **A Rescan May Be Necessary** If for some reason the Initialize and Convert Disk Wizard doesn't start automatically, the server might not have recognized the presence of the new disk. This sometimes happens with hot-plug disks. You can force the server to recognize the new disk by starting the Disk Management snap-in and then selecting Action, Rescan Disks from the system menu.

continued

5. On the next screen, confirm that the selected settings are correct. If you need to make any changes, click the Back button. If everything is correct, click Finish.

WORKING WITH BASIC DISKS

Unless you convert it after the initial installation of Windows Server 2003, the physical disk that the operating system is installed on will be configured as a basic disk with a single partition. If you choose to leave this disk configured as a basic disk, you need to understand how to work with basic disks. This section discusses how to perform the following tasks:

- Create primary partitions on a basic disk.
- Create extended partitions on a basic disk.
- Create logical drives in an extended partition on a basic disk.
- Delete partitions on a basic disk.
- Format a partition.
- Change the drive letter of a partition.
- Set a partition to active.

Creating a Primary Partition on a Basic Disk

As discussed earlier in this chapter, when Windows Server 2003 is initially installed on a new machine, it is installed on a basic disk in a primary partition. Usually, after the initial install of the operating system, unallocated free space is still available on the disk. This space can be used to create additional drives.

On a basic disk, you can have either four primary partitions or three primary partitions and an extended partition. Step by Step 1.5 walks you through creating a primary partition on a basic disk.

STEP BY STEP

1.5 Creating a Primary Partition

1. From the Start menu, select All Programs, Administrative Tools, Computer Management.
2. In the left pane of the Computer Management MMC, left-click the Storage entry and then select the Disk Management entry. This starts the Disk Management snap-in.
3. In the lower-right pane of the Computer Management MMC, right-click the unallocated space on the drive that you want to add a primary partition to (see Figure 1.17).
4. From the pop-up menu, select New Partition. This starts the New Partition Wizard. Click Next to continue.
5. The next screen, shown in Figure 1.18, prompts you to select the type of partition to create. Select the Primary Partition radio button and then click Next to continue.

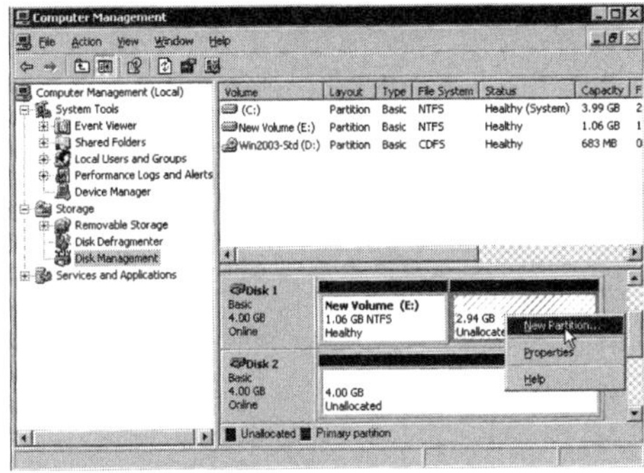

FIGURE 1.17▲
The Disk Manager snap-in, showing how to start the New Partition Wizard.

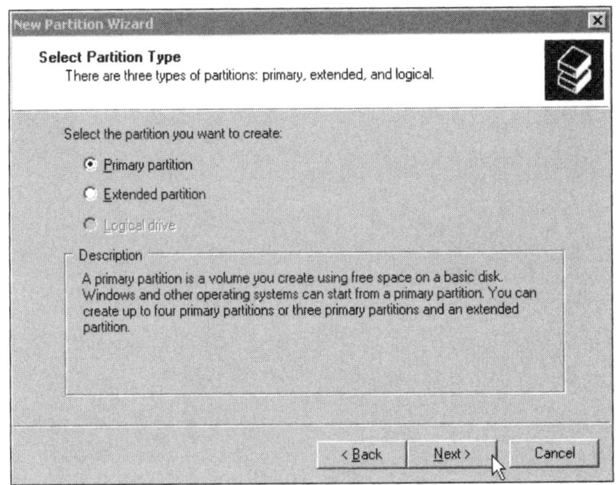

FIGURE 1.18◀
The New Partition Wizard, showing how to select the partition type. Notice that the logical drive selection is available only when an extended partition is selected.

6. The next screen, shown in Figure 1.19, prompts you to select the size of the new partition. The size can be anything from 8MB up to the size of the available free space. Enter the desired size and then click Next to continue.

continues

continued

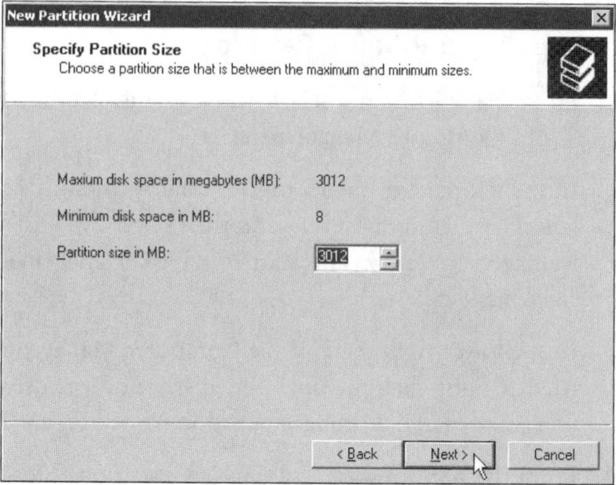

FIGURE 1.19
The partition size can be configured to be from 8MB up to the maximum amount of free space.

7. The next screen allows you to select the drive letter or NTFS folder to assign the new partition to. You also have the option to not assign it, opting instead to come back and do it later. Most of the time you will assign a drive letter, as shown in Figure 1.20. Click Next to continue.

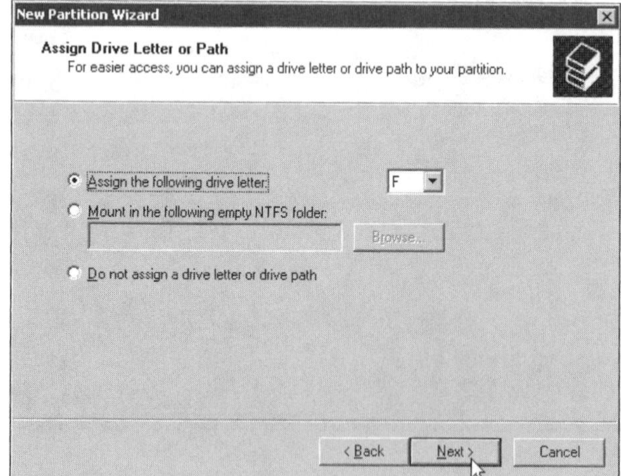

FIGURE 1.20
Assigning a drive letter to the new partition.

8. The Format Partition screen of the New Partition Wizard allows you to specify whether you want to format the partition, and what file system and cluster size to use.

There is also a selection to configure the new partition for file and folder compression. Normally, most partitions in Windows Server 2003 are formatted as NTFS with the default cluster size and no compression, as shown in Figure 1.21. The different file system formats along with file and folder compression are covered later in this chapter. Click Next to continue.

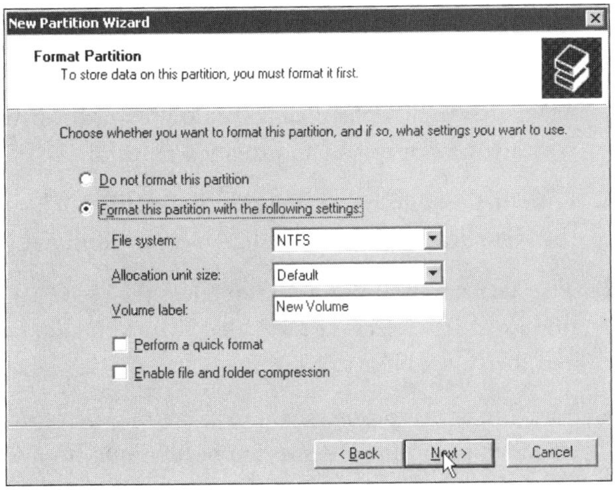

FIGURE 1.21
The Format Partition screen allows you to select from NTFS, FAT, and FAT32 formats.

9. Look over the settings on the Completing the New Partition Wizard screen. Confirm that the selected settings are correct. If you need to make any changes, click the Back button. If everything is correct, click Finish.

Creating an Extended Partition on a Basic Disk

If you need to create more than four partitions on a basic disk, you must create an extended partition so that you can create logical drives inside it. Step by Step 1.6 walks you through creating an extended partition on a basic disk.

STEP BY STEP

1.6 Creating an Extended Partition

1. From the Start menu, select All Programs, Administrative Tools, Computer Management.
2. Left-click the Storage entry and then select the Disk Management entry. This starts the Disk Management snap-in.
3. In the lower-right pane of the Computer Management MMC, right-click the unallocated space on the drive to which you want to add an extended partition.
4. From the pop-up menu, select New Partition. This starts the New Partition Wizard. Click Next to continue.
5. The next screen prompts you to select the type of partition to create. Select the Extended Partition radio button and then click Next to continue.
6. The next screen prompts you to select the size of the new extended partition. The size can be anything from 8MB up to the size of the available free space. Typically, the extended partition is the last partition created on the disk, so you will accept the default, which is the maximum. Click Next to continue.
7. Look over the settings on the Completing the New Partition Wizard screen. Confirm that the selected settings are correct. If you need to make any changes, click the Back button. If everything is correct, click Finish.

Creating a Logical Drive on a Basic Disk

By itself, an extended partition isn't worth much. However, within an extended partition, you can create a theoretically unlimited number of logical drives.

Step by Step 1.7 outlines how to create a logical drive:

STEP BY STEP

1.7 Creating a Logical Drive

1. From the Disk Management snap-in, as shown in Figure 1.22, right-click the extended partition entry on the drive to which you want to add a logical drive partition.

2. From the pop-up menu, select New Logical Drive. This starts the New Partition Wizard. Click Next to continue.

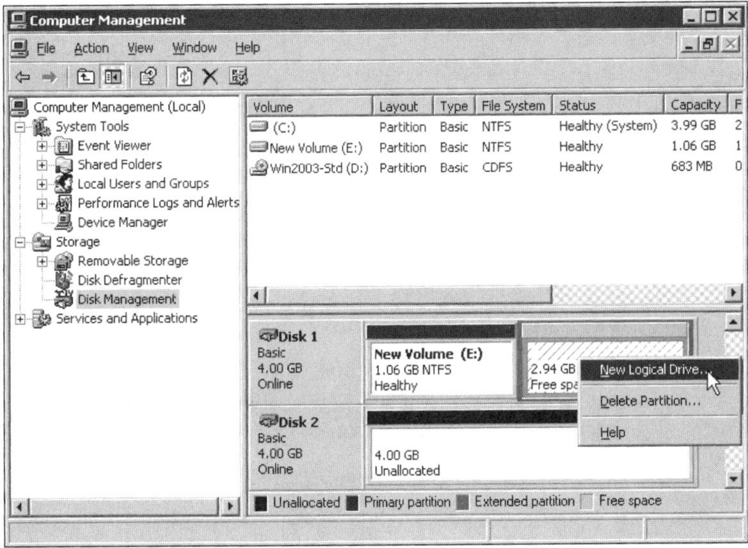

FIGURE 1.22
The Disk Manager snap-in, showing how to start the New Partition Wizard to create a logical drive.

3. The next screen, shown in Figure 1.23, prompts you to select the type of partition to create. Select the Logical Drive radio button and then click Next to continue.

continues

continued

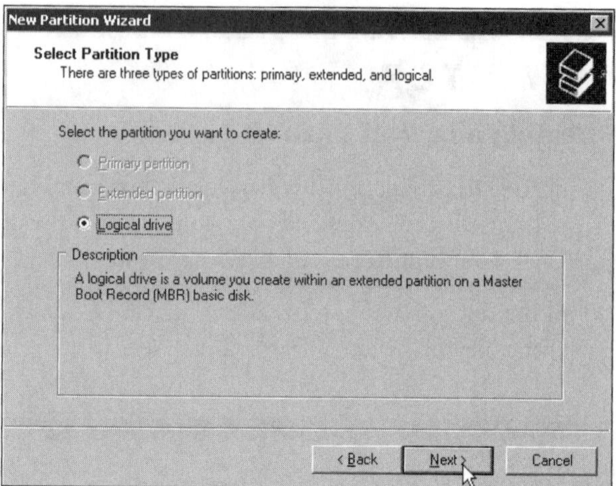

FIGURE 1.23
The New Partition Wizard, showing how to select the partition type. Notice that the Logical Drive selection is available only when an extended partition is selected.

4. The next screen prompts you to select the size of the new partition. The size can be anything from 8MB up to the size of the available free space. Enter the desired size and then click Next to continue.

5. The next screen allows you to select the drive letter or NTFS folder to assign the new partition to. You also have the option to not assign it, opting instead to come back and do it later. Most of the time you will assign a drive letter. Click Next to continue.

6. The Format Partition screen of the New Partition Wizard allows you to specify whether you want to format the partition, and what file system and cluster size to use. There is also a selection to configure the new partition for file and folder compression. Normally, most partitions in Windows Server 2003 are formatted as NTFS with the default cluster size and no compression. The different file system formats along with file and folder compression are covered later in this chapter. Click Next to continue.

7. Look over the settings on the Completing the New Partition Wizard screen. Confirm that the selected settings are correct. If you need to make any changes, click the Back button. If everything is correct, click Finish.

Deleting a Partition

Deleting a partition or logical drive is far easier than creating one. However, it is important to remember that when a partition or logical drive is deleted, the data that was on that drive or partition is gone. It cannot be recovered by any utility that is included with Windows Server 2003. Before deleting a partition or logical drive, always make sure you have a current backup!

> NOTE
>
> **Delete in the Proper Order** You cannot delete an extended partition until all the logical drives inside it have been deleted.

Step by Step 1.8 show you how to delete a partition or logical drive.

STEP BY STEP

1.8 Deleting a Partition or Logical Drive

1. From the Disk Management snap-in, right-click the partition or logical drive that you want to delete and select Delete Partition or Delete Logical Drive from the shortcut menu.
2. Acknowledge the warning dialog box notifying you that all data will be lost by clicking Yes.

Windows Server 2003 is self-preserving in that it does not allow you to delete the system or boot partitions from within the Disk Management GUI.

File Systems and Formatting a Partition

Before you can store data on a drive, it has to be formatted with a file system. Two main file systems are recognized by Windows Server 2003: File Allocation Table (FAT16 and FAT32) and the NT File System (NTFS). Although other file systems are in use in Windows Server 2003, such as the Universal Disk Format (UDF) and the CD-ROM File System (CDFS), they are read-only file systems and do not truly support detailed access controls. For this reason, this section—and the Microsoft exam—focuses on the capabilities and features of the FAT and NT file systems.

The File Allocation Table (FAT) File System

The FAT file system is recognized by Windows Server 2003 in order to provide legacy support for earlier Windows operating systems. Because FAT was originally designed to support disks that were much smaller than the devices in use today, it is not very efficient at handling large disks or files. Windows Server 2003 is able to read partitions formatted in two versions of FAT—the 16-bit version (FAT16) supported by early versions of MS-DOS and the 32-bit version (FAT32) first introduced with Windows 95 OEM Service Release 2 (OSR2). The first version of the FAT file system, FAT12, used in the earliest versions of MS-DOS, is not supported in Windows Server 2003.

Because FAT predates Windows NT and Windows 2000/2003/XP, it does not include support for extensive security or enhanced partition features such as compression. From a practical perspective, the biggest difference between FAT16 and FAT32 is the maximum supported partition size. This is achieved by doubling the size of the File Allocation Table from 16 bits to 32 bits. For FAT16 partitions, the maximum size is 4GB, even though most operating systems limit FAT16 to 2GB partitions. In theory, FAT32 partitions support a maximum size of 2,047GB. However, there is a 32GB limitation on creating FAT32 partitions in Windows 2003.

The NT File System (NTFS)

Introduced with the first versions of Windows NT, the NT File System (NTFS) is designed to provide a high-performance, secure file system for Windows NT Servers. Windows Server 2003 includes the same version of NTFS included with Windows 2000.

Here are some of the benefits of NTFS over FAT:

- **Recoverability**—To ensure data is consistently written to the volume, NTFS uses transaction logging and advanced recovery techniques. In the event of a failure, NTFS uses checkpoint and data-logging information to automatically maintain the consistency of the data on the volume.
- **Compression**—NTFS supports selective file, folder, and volume compression, which is not available on FAT volumes.

- **Encrypting File System (EFS)**—EFS is similar to NTFS compression in that it allows the user to selectively encrypt files and folders as desired. After a file is encrypted, all file operations continue transparently for the user who performed the encryption. However, unauthorized users cannot access the files. EFS is covered in detail in Chapter 4.
- **Disk quotas**—NTFS volumes include the use of disk quotas to limit the amount of drive space a user can consume.
- **Mount points**—NTFS allows you to attach volumes or partitions to a folder on an existing drive. This allows you to increase the size of the existing drive, and it doesn't use any additional drive letters.

The selectivity of the NTFS compression settings allows administrators the ability to pick and choose whether specific file system objects are compressed. Although data compression reduces the drive space required on the volume, it puts a greater burden on the system's resources. A small amount of processing overhead is involved in compressing and uncompressing files during system operation. Providing the option to selectively compress entire volumes, folders, or individual files ensures that the drive space is used as efficiently as possible, while still maintaining timely file services.

In an effort to provide the fastest file services available, NTFS uses smaller clusters and has been designed to require fewer disk reads to find a file on the volume. NTFS also supports significantly larger volumes than FAT—up to 16TB (terabytes) on a single volume.

Perhaps more importantly, individual files, folders, and volumes can be secured at the user and group level. This is significantly more secure than FAT, which is limited to three very basic permission settings (and then only when the volume is accessed via shared folders): Read, Change, and Full Control. Securing folders and, when possible, files is discussed in greater detail in Chapter 4.

Because NTFS offers such improvements over FAT, Microsoft (and just about anyone else you talk to) recommends that all Windows Server 2003 volumes be formatted with NTFS. However, there are some situations where this is not possible. For example, most multiple-boot configurations require a FAT file system on the boot partition. If you need to maintain a FAT volume on the server, it is important that you understand the security implications of the configuration.

Formatting the Partition or Logical Drive

After you decide which file system to use, you have to format your drives. During the initial install of Windows Server 2003, the install procedure formatted the install drive for you. In addition, when manually creating a partition or logical drive, the wizard prompts you for the file type and then formats the drive for you.

If you need to manually format a partition or logical drive, follow the procedure provided in Step by Step 1.9.

STEP BY STEP

1.9 Formatting a Partition or Logical Drive

1. From the Disk Management snap-in, right-click the partition or logical drive that you want to format. Then select Format from the shortcut menu.

2. From the Format dialog box, as shown in Figure 1.24, enter the volume name, the file system desired, and the allocation unit size. You can adjust the cluster size to tune performance for a specific disk size. However, NTFS compression is not supported for cluster sizes larger than 4,096 bytes. It's usually best to accept the default cluster size unless you have a specific reason not to. You can also select to perform a Quick Format, which removes the files but does not scan for bad sectors. This option should be used only on a disk that has been previously formatted and has no bad sectors. There is also an option to enable file and folder compression on the drive. This causes every file and folder either copied or created on this drive to be compressed. Select the desired options and then click OK to continue.

3. Acknowledge the warning dialog box notifying you that all data will be lost by clicking Yes.

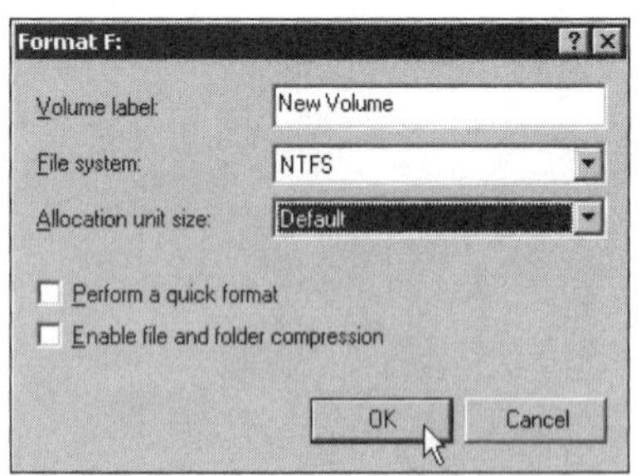

FIGURE 1.24
Drive formatting options.

Remember, Windows Server 2003 is self-preserving in that it does not allow you to format the system or boot partitions from within the Disk Management GUI.

Changing the Drive Letter of a Partition

In Windows Server 2003, only the system and boot partitions are required to maintain specific drive letters. Any other drives can be assigned whatever letters you desire. The only caveat is that if you have installed a program on a drive or if a program is looking for its data in a specific location, you might not be able to access it after you change the drive letter. This happens because many programs store their location in the Registry. When you change a drive letter, the program entries in the Registry aren't updated with the changes.

If you wish to rearrange drive letters, it should be done immediately after the initial install of Windows Server 2003 and before you install any programs.

Use the procedure outlined in Step by Step 1.10 to change drive letter assignments.

STEP BY STEP

1.10 Changing a Drive Letter

1. From the Disk Management snap-in, right-click the drive that you want to reconfigure and select Change Drive Letter and Paths from the shortcut menu.

2. From the Change Drive Letter and Paths For dialog box, click the Change button.

3. From the Change Drive Letter or Path dialog box shown in Figure 1.25, click the drop-down list and choose a new drive letter. Click OK to continue.

continues

continued

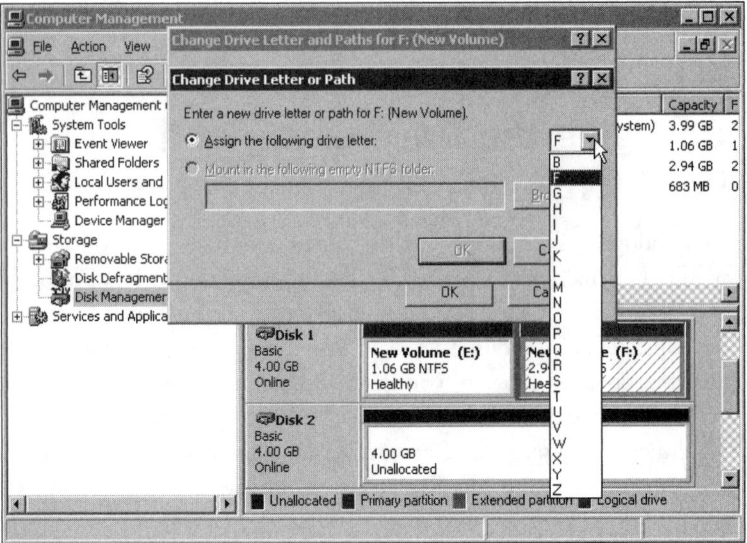

FIGURE 1.25
Click the drop-down list to see what drives are available.

4. When the warning prompt appears, click Yes to confirm the change.

Using Mount Points

A feature of NTFS is the capability of mounting a partition or volume as a folder on an existing drive. This is especially useful on data drives. For example, say that your user data drive is rapidly running out of free space. You could always go out and buy a larger drive and then move all the files over to the new drive. However, by using a mount point, you can mount the new drive as a folder on the existing drive, thereby adding additional space to the existing drive. This saves you from having to move the user files. The end users won't see any difference because they still access everything via the same drive letter or share. Additionally, you can create a volume from free space on an existing drive and then mount that volume as a folder.

Marking a Partition As Active

When an Intel-based computer starts, it looks for the active partition to start the system. This can be either a primary partition on a basic disk or a simple volume on a dynamic disk. However, the simple volume must have previously been created and marked as the active partition before the disk was converted from basic to dynamic. Although the active partition can be changed on a basic disk, it cannot be changed on a dynamic disk. Follow the procedure outlined in Step by Step 1.11 to mark a primary partition as Active.

STEP BY STEP

1.11 Marking a Primary Partition As Active

1. From the Disk Management snap-in, right-click the partition that you want to mark as Active.
2. Select Mark Partition As Active from the shortcut menu.
3. When the warning prompt appears, click Yes to confirm the change. The results are shown in Figure 1.26.

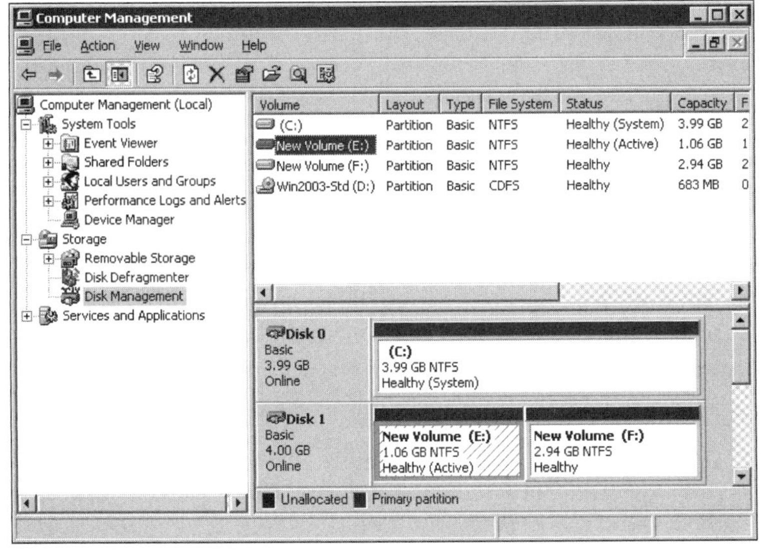

FIGURE 1.26
Disk Management snap-in, showing the results of marking disk 1, partition 1 as Active.

WORKING WITH DYNAMIC DISKS

Although the initial installation of Windows Server 2003 configures a new hard disk as a basic disk, you are not required to leave it that way. Unless you have to maintain a dual-boot configuration and have older operating systems accessing partitions on that disk, you can convert the disk to a dynamic disk and take advantage of the extended capabilities available.

As discussed earlier, dynamic disks offer more features and flexibility than basic disks. For example, fault-tolerant disk configurations are supported only on dynamic disks.

In this section you will learn how to perform the following tasks:

- Convert a basic disk to a dynamic disk.
- Create simple volumes on a dynamic disk.
- Extend a dynamic volume.
- Create a spanned volume.
- Create a mirrored volume.
- Create a striped volume.
- Create a RAID-5 (stripe with parity) volume.

Converting a Basic Disk to a Dynamic Disk

Should you want to take advantage of the capabilities offered by dynamic disks in Windows Server 2003, you must convert your basic disk to a dynamic disk. The conversion is performed on an entire physical disk, not just one particular partition.

Basic disks can be converted to dynamic disks at any time without data loss, provided that you meet all the following requirements. However, you cannot revert a dynamic disk back to a basic disk without complete data loss on the disk.

In addition to the limitations discussed earlier in the chapter, make sure your disks meet the following conditions before attempting to convert them to dynamic disks:

- A master boot record (MBR) disk must have at least 1MB of free space available at the end of the disk for the dynamic disk database to be created.
- Dynamic storage cannot be used on removable media such as Zip disks.
- Hard drives on portable computers cannot be converted to dynamic storage.
- The sector size on the hard disk must be no larger than 512 bytes in order for the conversion to take place. Use the following command on an NTFS volume, where *x:* is the volume in question, to determine the sector size:

```
fsutilfsinfo ntfsinfo x:
```

Step by Step 1.12 guides you through the process to convert a basic disk to a dynamic disk.

> **WARNING**
>
> **Multiboot Limitations** Dynamic disks can only be utilized by one operating system. If you plan on multibooting your computer with operating systems other than Windows 2000 or Windows 2003, do not convert your basic disks to dynamic disks.

STEP BY STEP

1.12 Upgrading a Basic Disk to a Dynamic Disk

1. From the Disk Management snap-in, right-click the disk indicator that you want to convert on the left side of the bottom-right pane and select Convert to Dynamic Disk from the shortcut menu (see Figure 1.27).

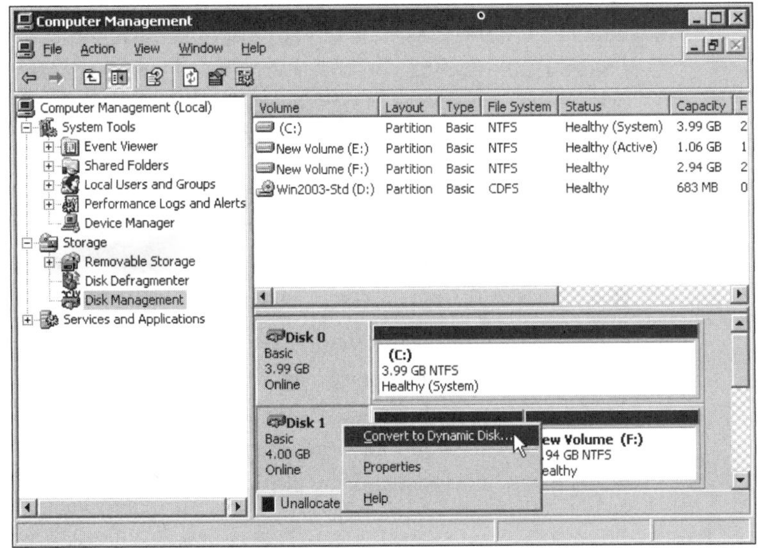

FIGURE 1.27
Disk Management snap-in, showing the Convert to Dynamic Disk selection.

continues

continued

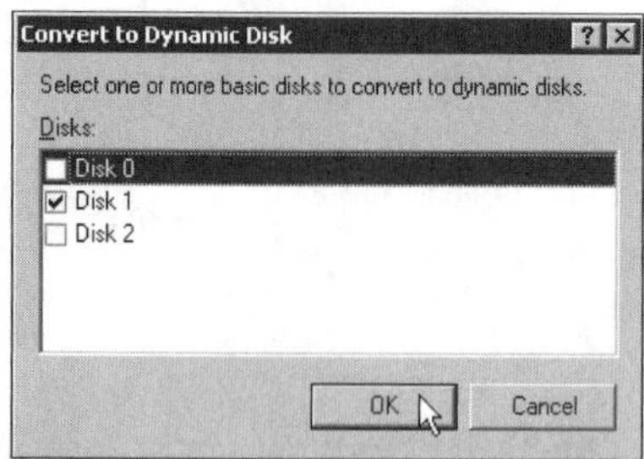

FIGURE 1.28▲
The Convert to Dynamic Disk dialog box allows you to select multiple disks to be converted.

2. When the Convert to Dynamic Disk dialog box appears (see Figure 1.28), verify that the disk you wish to convert is selected and then click OK.
3. The Disks to Convert dialog box (see Figure 1.29) lists the disks you have selected. Click Convert to continue.

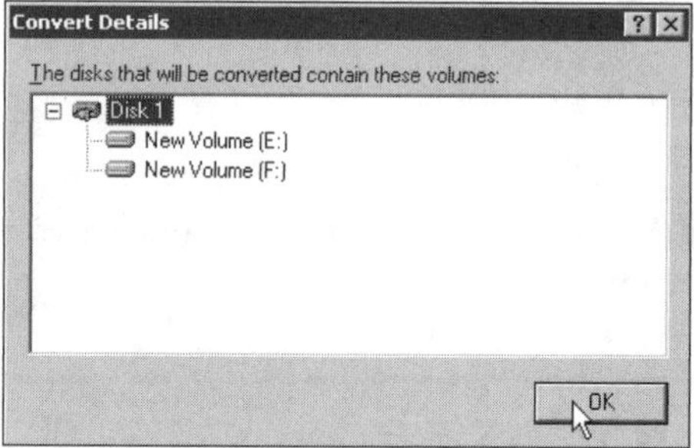

FIGURE 1.29▶
The Disks to Convert dialog box allows you view the volumes on the disk to be converted by clicking the Details button.

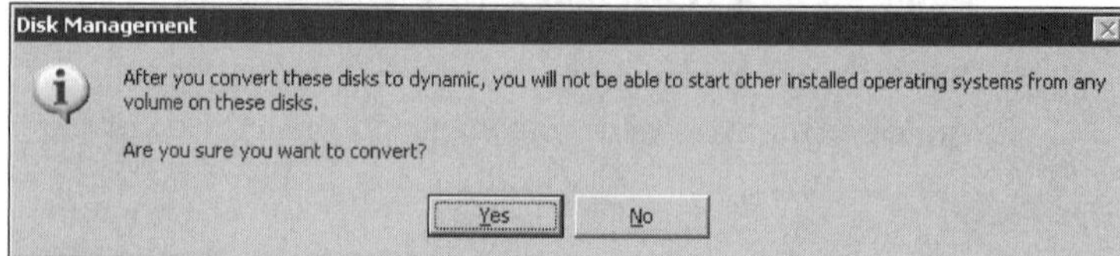

FIGURE 1.30▶
Because dynamic disks are unique to the Windows 2000/2003/XP family, they will not be readable or bootable from other operating systems.

4. The Disk Management dialog box appears, as shown in Figure 1.30, warning you that you will not be able to start other operating systems from this disk. Click Yes to continue.
5. A warning prompt appears, notifying you that any file systems existing on the disk will be dismounted as part of the convert process. Click Yes to proceed—this is your last chance to abort the process.
6. Click Yes to confirm the change. If you are converting the disk that contains the boot or system partition or a volume that is currently in use, you may be required to reboot. After the conversion is completed, the disk will be relabeled as Dynamic, and the partitions are labeled as Simple Volumes, as shown in Figure 1.31.

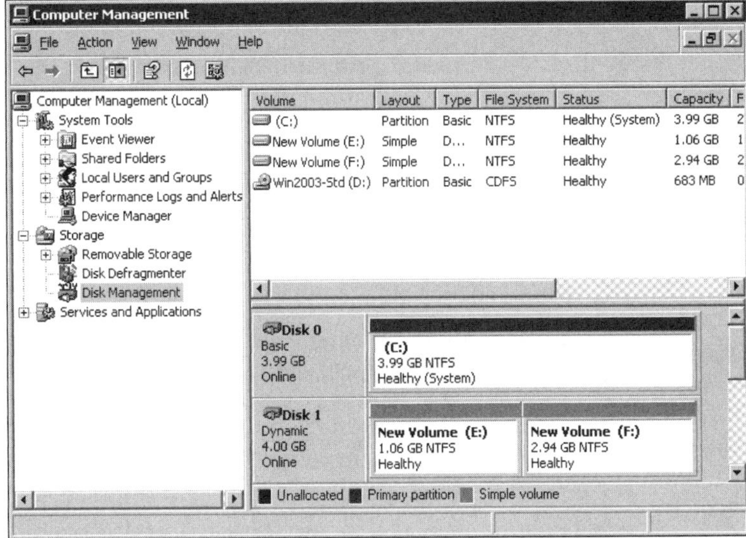

FIGURE 1.31

After the conversion is completed, the disk status bar changes color, and the disk is labeled as Dynamic with Simple Volumes.

Creating Simple Volumes on a Dynamic Disk

Should you happen to have any unallocated (free) space on one of your disks, you can create a new volume in that space. Creating a new dynamic volume follows the same basic process as does creating new basic disk partitions, with the exception that you can choose from one of the available volume types as previously mentioned in the "Introduction to Dynamic Disks" section. You are also given the opportunity to select the total size of the volume to be created in the case of a spanned volume. To create a new partition out of free space on a dynamic disk, refer to Step by Step 1.13.

STEP BY STEP

1.13 Creating a Simple Volume

1. From the Start menu, select All Programs, Administrative Tools, Computer Management.

continues

continued

2. In the left pane of the Computer Management MMC, left-click the Storage entry and then select the Disk Management entry. This starts the Disk Management snap-in.
3. In the lower-right pane of the Computer Management MMC, right-click the unallocated space on the drive that you want to add a simple volume to.
4. From the pop-up menu, select New Volume. This starts the New Volume Wizard. Click Next to continue.
5. The next screen, as shown in Figure 1.32, prompts you to select the type of volume to create. Select the Simple Volume radio button and then click Next to continue. It is important to note that in a server with a single dynamic disk, Simple Volume is the only selection available. All the other choices require the presence of two or more dynamic disks.

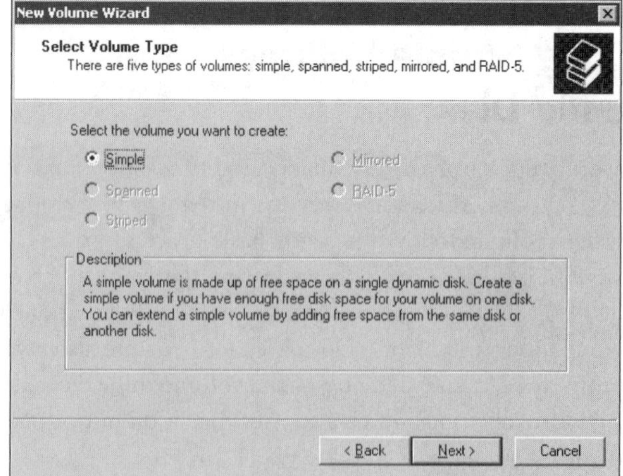

FIGURE 1.32
The New Volume Wizard, showing the types of volumes you can configure. Note that this server obviously has only one dynamic disk.

6. On the Select Disks screen shown in Figure 1.33, the disk is preselected for you because there is only one dynamic disk available. You have the option of selecting the size of the volume up to the maximum available. Click Next to continue.

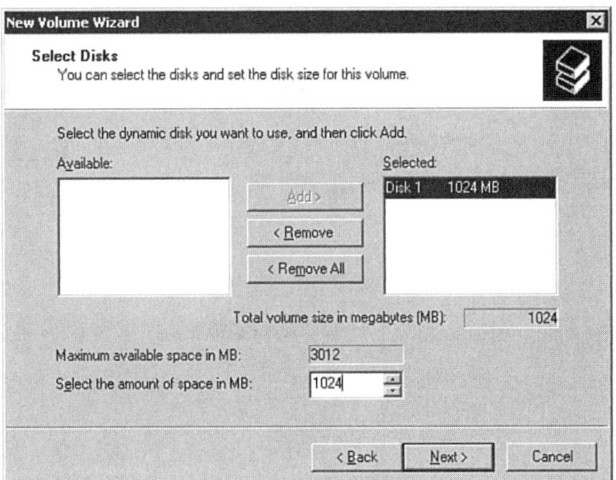

FIGURE 1.33
The partition size can be configured to be up to the maximum amount of free space.

7. The next screen allows you to select the drive letter or NTFS folder to assign the new partition to. You also have the option to not assign it, opting instead come back and do it later. Most of the time you will assign a drive letter, as shown in Figure 1.34. Click Next to continue.

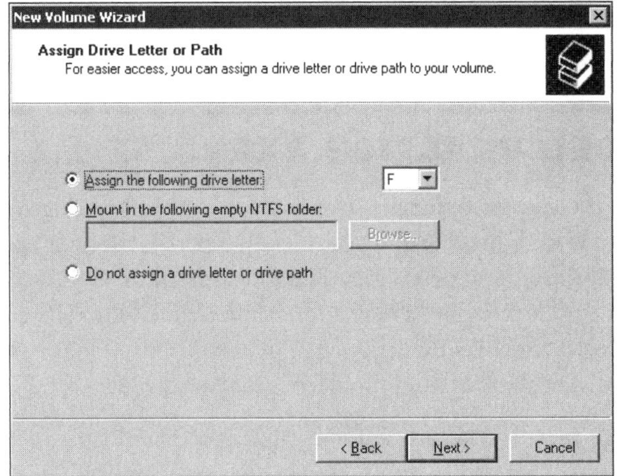

FIGURE 1.34
Assigning a drive letter to the new partition.

8. The Format Volume screen allows you to specify whether or not you want to format the volume and what cluster size to use. There is also a selection to configure the new volume for file and folder compression. Dynamic volumes in Windows Server 2003 can only be formatted as NTFS, as shown in Figure 1.35. Click Next to continue.

continues

continued

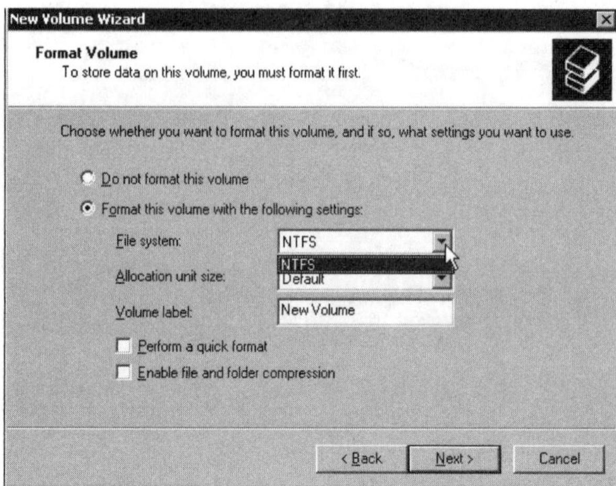

FIGURE 1.35
The Format Volume screen of the New Volume Wizard. Notice that the only formatting option available is NTFS.

> **NOTE**
> **FAT Is Dead** Although you can format a dynamic disk as FAT using the command-line format utility, or via My Computer, there is no valid reason to do so. Typically the only reason to format a drive as FAT would be to allow access to older operating systems. However, down-level operating systems cannot recognize a dynamic volume, regardless of the file format.

9. Look over the settings on the Completing the New Volume Wizard screen. Confirm that the selected settings are correct. If you need to make any changes, click the Back button. If everything is correct, click Finish.

GUIDED PRACTICE EXERCISE 1.1

You are the administrator of a network for a manufacturing company that has multiple Windows Server 2003 servers used for applications and file and print services. The Research and Development department has installed a new application on one of its servers. Unlike most intelligently designed applications, this one is hard coded to save all its files in a folder on the boot volume.

Although there is currently sufficient free space on the boot volume on this server, this application, along with other applications that might be added in the future, could easily shrink the current amount of free space.

You will need to find a way to provide more free space for this application so that other applications can be installed on the boot volume in the future.

What is the best way to solve this issue in Windows 2003? On your own, try to develop a solution that would involve the least amount of downtime and expense.

If you would like to see a possible solution, follow the procedure outlined here.

Estimated Time: 40 minutes.

This is a fairly easy solution. You can use one of the niftiest (but generally underutilized) features of NTFS—mount points. Mount points allow you to mount a volume to a folder on an existing volume, thereby adding additional space to that volume. Here are the steps to follow:

1. Shut down your server and install an additional hard drive.
2. Restart the server. From the Start menu, select All Programs, Administrative Tools, Computer Management.
3. Click the Storage entry and then select the Disk Management entry. This starts the Disk Management snap-in.
4. In the lower-right pane of the Computer Management MMC, right-click the unallocated space on the drive to which you want to add a simple volume.
5. From the pop-up menu, select New Volume. This starts the New Volume Wizard. Click Next to continue.
6. The next screen prompts you to select the type of volume to create. Select the Simple Volume radio button and then click Next to continue.
7. On the Select Disks screen, you have the option of selecting the size of the volume, up to the maximum available. Select the desired size and then click Next to continue.
8. The next screen allows you to select the drive letter or NTFS folder to assign the new partition to. Select the desired folder and then click Next to continue.
9. The Format Volume screen allows you to specify whether you want to format the volume and what cluster size to use. There is also a selection to configure the new volume for file and folder compression. Accept the defaults and then click Next to continue.

continues

continued

10. Look over the settings on the Completing the New Volume Wizard screen. Confirm that the selected settings are correct. If you need to make any changes, click the Back button. If everything is correct, click Finish.

The nice thing about the Windows Server 2003 implementation of mount points is that it allows you to add additional space to an existing volume, instead of the usual process of replacing the volume and having to back up and restore your files.

Extending Dynamic Volume Size

One of the advantages of dynamic volumes is that they can be extended after their creation to add more space. The dynamic volume can be extended using free space on the same or other disks. This can be accomplished without a reboot.

However, here are some restrictions as to which dynamic disks cannot be extended:

- The volume either must not be formatted or be formatted as NTFS.
- The volume must not be a system or boot volume.
- Dynamic volumes that were converted from basic volumes on Windows 2000 cannot be extended.
- RAID-1 (mirrored) or RAID-5 volumes cannot be extended.
- A volume that is extended onto another disk becomes a spanned volume.

Here are the types of dynamic disks that can be extended:

- Simple and spanned volumes
- Dynamic volumes that were converted from basic volumes on Windows Server 2003 or Windows XP Professional

The procedure for extending a dynamic volume is covered in Step by Step 1.14.

STEP BY STEP

1.14 Extending a Dynamic Volume

1. Open the Disk Management snap-in.
2. In the lower-right pane of the Disk Management snap-in, right-click the drive that you want to extend.
3. From the pop-up menu, select Extend Volume. This starts the Extend Volume Wizard. Click Next to continue.
4. On the Select Disks screen, shown in Figure 1.36, the disk that contains the partition you are extending is preselected for you. The free space on that disk is displayed. You have the option of adding space on the volume, up to the maximum available, and/or selecting space from another disk. Click Next to continue.

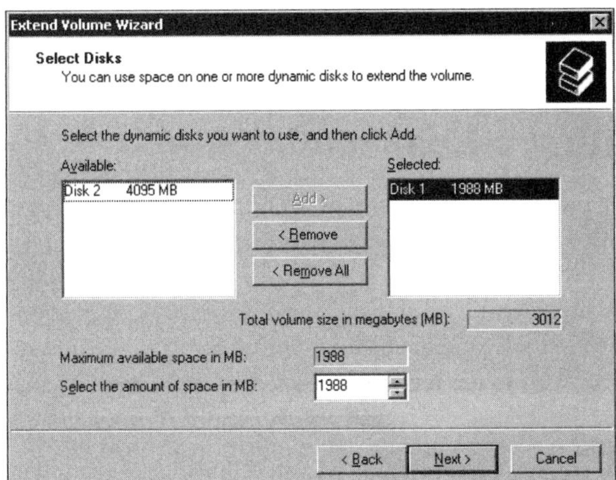

FIGURE 1.36
The partition size can be extended up to the maximum amount of the free space available on several disks.

5. Look over the settings on the Completing the Extend Volume Wizard screen. Confirm that the selected settings are correct. If you need to make any changes, click the Back button. If everything is correct, click Finish.

continues

continued

If you look at the Disk Management snap-in, as shown in Figure 1.37, you will notice that whereas a single volume is displayed in the Volume view in the top-right pane, the graphical view in the bottom-right pane shows the actual configuration—two physical drives assigned the same logical drive letter.

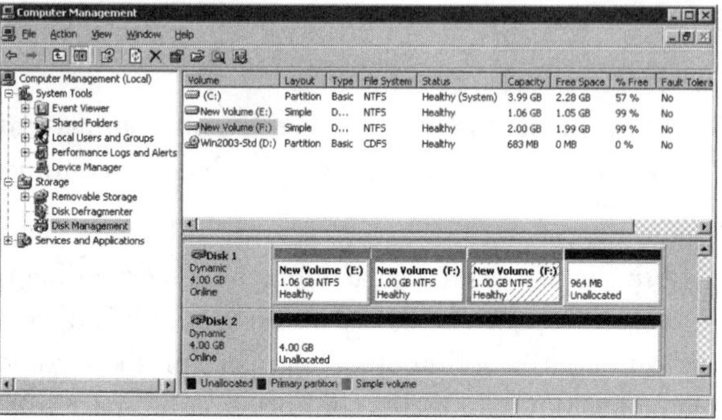

FIGURE 1.37
The graphical view shows the physical volume configuration.

Creating a Spanned Volume

Dynamic disks allow you to create spanned volumes. A spanned volume can contain up to 32 pieces of free space of various sizes from multiple physical hard disks. This allows you to create a volume that is larger than your physical disks. In addition you can create a logical drive of a useful size from smaller pieces that would be useless by themselves. Consolidating the available free space in this manner allows you to have a bigger disk represented by a single drive letter.

Unfortunately, a spanned volume is not fault tolerant. If anything, it becomes more susceptible to failure with every additional piece that is added. This is because if you lose a single hard disk or section, the entire volume is lost.

A spanned volume can be created by extending a volume across multiple disks, similar to the procedure covered in the previous section, or it can be created from scratch. Step by Step 1.15 shows how to create a new spanned volume.

STEP BY STEP

1.15 Creating a Spanned Volume

1. Open the Disk Management snap-in.
2. In the lower-right pane of the Disk Management snap-in, right-click the first section of unallocated free space that you want to use to create the volume.
3. From the pop-up menu, select New Volume. This starts the New Volume Wizard. Click Next to continue.
4. The next screen, as shown in Figure 1.38, prompts you to select the type of volume to create. Select the Spanned Volume radio button and then click Next to continue. It is important to note that in a server with a single dynamic disk, the Simple Volume entry would have been the only selection available. All the other choices require the presence of two or more dynamic disks.

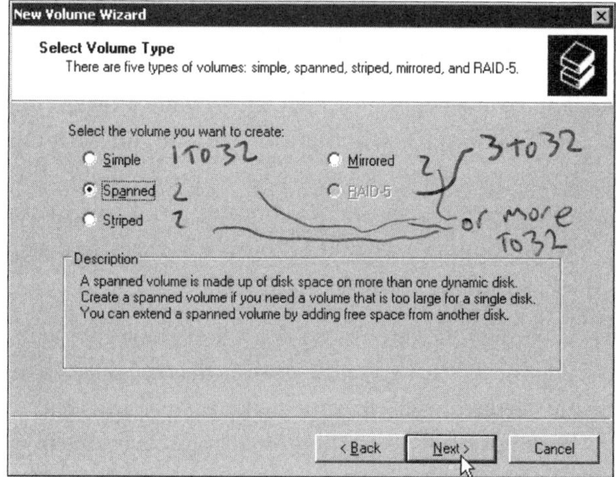

FIGURE 1.38
The New Volume Wizard, showing the types of volumes that you can configure. Note that this server obviously has multiple dynamic disks.

5. On the Select Disks screen shown in Figure 1.39, the disk you clicked is preselected for you, with all the available free space entered for you. You can highlight additional drives and click the Add button to add space from them. You have the option of selecting as much free space as you like from each disk, up to the maximum available. Make your selections and then click Next to continue.

continues

continued

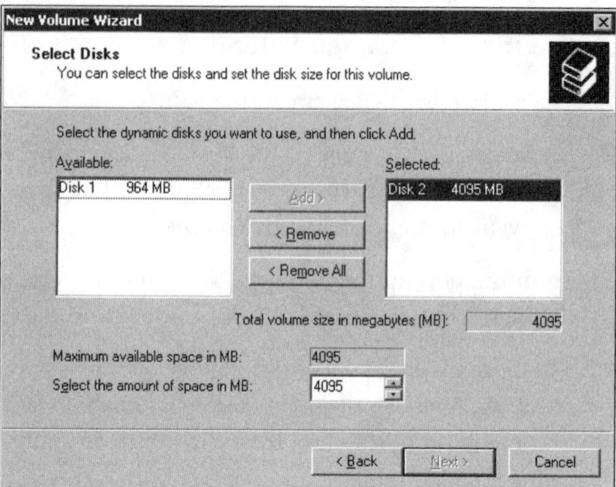

FIGURE 1.39
The size of the spanned disk can be configured to be up to the maximum of the free space available across all the selected drives.

6. The next screen allows you to select the drive letter or NTFS folder to assign the new partition to. You also have the option to not assign it, opting instead to come back and do it later. Most of the time you will assign a drive letter. Click Next to continue.
7. The Format Volume screen allows you to specify whether or not you want to format the volume and what cluster size to use. There is also a selection to configure the new volume for file and folder compression. Dynamic volumes in Windows Server 2003 can only be formatted as NTFS. Click Next to continue.
8. Look over the settings on the Completing the New Volume Wizard screen. Confirm that the selected settings are correct. If you need to make any changes, click the Back button. If everything is correct, click Finish.

Creating a Striped Volume

In theory, striped volumes are very similar to spanned volumes—they both combine space from multiple physical disks to form a larger logical drive. Striped volumes also have the same Achilles heel—if you lose one physical disk, the entire logical volume is lost.

However, there are additional benefits to striped volumes other than the ability to create a large logical disk. Windows Server 2003 writes the data alternately across the drives using a set block size (RAID-0), hence the term *striping*. This results in the best write performance of any of the volume configurations available in Windows Server 2003, as well as read performance equal to the RAID-5 configuration. Striped volumes require at least two physical disks, with the disks preferably being of the same size, manufacturer, and model. You can add up to 32 dynamic disks to the volume. Striped disks cannot be extended or mirrored.

A striped volume can be created using the procedure outlined in Step by Step 1.16.

STEP BY STEP

1.16 Creating a Striped Volume

1. Open the Disk Management snap-in.
2. In the lower-right pane of the Disk Management snap-in, right-click the first section of unallocated free space that you want to use to create the volume.
3. From the pop-up menu, select New Volume. This starts the New Volume Wizard. Click Next to continue.
4. The next screen, as shown in Figure 1.40, prompts you to select the type of volume to create. Select the Striped radio button and then click Next to continue.

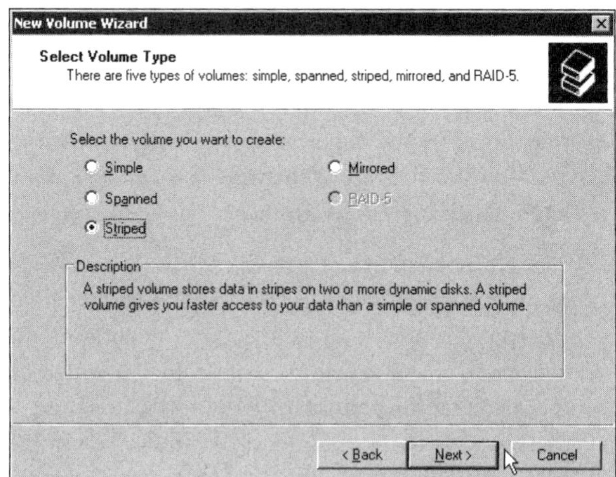

FIGURE 1.40
The New Volume Wizard, showing the types of volumes you can configure. Note that this server obviously has multiple dynamic disks.

continues

continued

5. On the Select Disks screen shown in Figure 1.41, the disk you clicked is preselected for you, with all the available free space entered for you. You can highlight additional drives and click the Add button to add space from them. You have the option of selecting as much free space as you like from each disk, up to the smallest amount of free space available on any of the disks. For example, if you have two disks, and one has 900MB of free space and the other has 800MB of free space, the maximum amount of space you can use on each disk is 800MB. The volume sizes have to be identical on each disk. Make your selections and then click Next to continue.

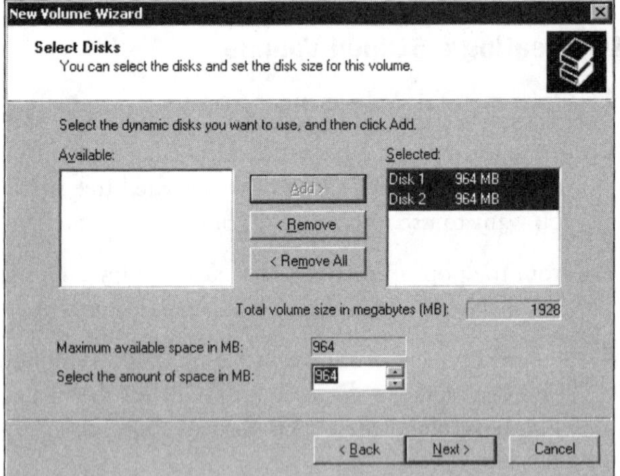

FIGURE 1.41
The size of the striped volume can be configured to be up to the maximum amount of the free space available on the smallest disk.

6. The next screen allows you to select the drive letter or NTFS folder to assign the new partition to. You also have the option to not assign it, opting instead to come back and do it later. Most of the time you will assign a drive letter. Click Next to continue.

7. The Format Volume screen allows you to specify whether or not you want to format the volume and what cluster size to use. There is also a selection to configure the new volume for file and folder compression. If you're using the stripe set for performance purposes, don't use compression. Dynamic volumes in Windows Server 2003 can only be formatted as NTFS. Click Next to continue.

8. Look over the settings on the Completing the New Volume Wizard screen. Confirm that the selected settings are correct. If you need to make any changes, click the Back button. If everything is correct, click Finish.

EXAM TIP

Know the Characteristics of Striped Volumes Remember that striped volumes require at least two disks and can contain up to 32 disks. Also remember that a striped volume is configured with equal space from each disk, even if some of the disks are larger than the others.

Creating a Mirrored Volume

A mirrored volume, also known as *RAID-1*, is one of the two fault-tolerant disk configurations available in Windows Server 2003. A mirrored volume consists of two separate physical disks that are written to simultaneously. If one of the disks fails, the system keeps running using the other disk.

It is best to use two identical disks for the mirror. For additional fault tolerance and better performance, you can install the two disks on separate disk controllers. This practice is known as *duplexing*. This configuration removes the disk controller as a potential single point of failure.

Mirrored volumes can be used as system or boot partitions. However, they cannot be extended. Refer to the previous sections in this chapter to see the restrictions that apply to having system and boot partitions on dynamic volumes.

A mirrored volume can be created using the procedure outlined in Step by Step 1.17.

NOTE

Dynamic Volume Mirroring It might be helpful to point out that Windows Server 2003 uses dynamic `volume` mirroring. This means that you are mirroring a volume, and not necessarily the physical disk, unless of course you configure the volume to be equal to the size of the physical disk. This allows you to have other volumes on the mirrored disk, if you desire. However, the other volumes will not be fault tolerant.

EXAM TIP

Usable Capacity It is important to remember that when you're using mirrored drives, a loss of 50% of the capacity of the mirrored drives occurs due to the redundancy. For example, if you mirror two 9GB drives (18GB total capacity), only 9GB will be available because you are, in effect, making two complete copies of your data.

STEP BY STEP

1.17 Creating a Mirrored Volume from Free Space

1. Open the Disk Management snap-in.
2. In the lower-right pane of the Disk Management snap-in, right-click the first section of unallocated free space that you want to use to create the mirror.
3. From the pop-up menu, select New Volume. This starts the New Volume Wizard. Click Next to continue.

continues

continued

4. The next screen prompts you to select the type of volume to create. Select the Mirrored radio button and then click Next to continue.

5. On the Select Disks screen, the disk you clicked is preselected for you, with all the available free space entered for you. Highlight an additional drive and click the Add button to add it to the mirrored set. You have the option of selecting as much free space as you like from each disk, up to the smallest amount of free space available on any of the disks. For example if you have two disks, and one has 900MB of free space and the other has 800MB of free space, the maximum space you can use on each disk is 800MB. The volume sizes have to be identical on each disk. Make your selections and then click Next to continue.

6. The next screen allows you to select the drive letter or NTFS folder to assign the new partition to. You also have the option to not assign it, opting instead to come back and do it later. Most of the time you will assign a drive letter. Click Next to continue.

7. The Format Volume screen allows you to specify whether or not you want to format the volume and what cluster size to use. There is also a selection to configure the new volume for file and folder compression. Dynamic volumes in Windows Server 2003 can only be formatted as NTFS. Click Next to continue.

8. Look over the settings on the Completing the New Volume Wizard screen. Confirm that the selected settings are correct. If you need to make any changes, click the Back button. If everything is correct, click Finish.

In addition to creating a mirrored volume from scratch, a mirrored volume can be created by mirroring an existing volume. This is how you mirror your system and boot partitions.

A mirrored volume can be created from a simple volume using the procedure outlined in Step by Step 1.18.

STEP BY STEP

1.18 Creating a Mirrored Volume from a Simple Volume

1. Open the Disk Management snap-in.
2. In the lower-right pane of the Disk Management snap-in, right-click the simple volume that you want to mirror.
3. From the pop-up menu, select Add Mirror.
4. The next screen prompts you to select the location of the drive to add to the mirror, as shown in Figure 1.42. Select a disk to add to the mirror and then click the Add Mirror button.
5. On the Disk Management screen shown in Figure 1.43, the disk you added to the mirrored set has been assigned the same drive letter as the simple volume and is synchronized with it.

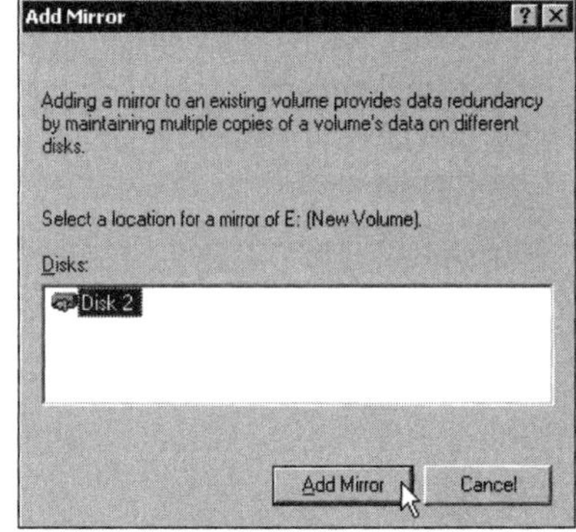

FIGURE 1.42▲
Select a disk to add to the mirrored set.

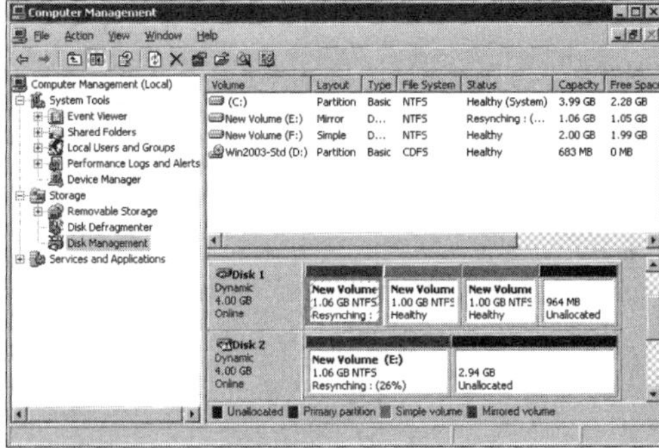

FIGURE 1.43◄
After you select the Add Mirror button, the new volume will be synchronized with the existing volume.

Creating a RAID-5 (Stripe with Parity) Volume

The RAID-5 volume, also known as *striping with parity*, is the second type of fault-tolerant disk configuration available in Windows Server 2003. A RAID-5 volume consists of 3 to 32 separate physical disks that are written to sequentially in fixed blocks, or *striped*.

Along with the data, parity information is also written across the disks. If one of the disks fails, the system keeps running using the other disks because it can re-create the missing data using the parity information.

EXAM TIP

Usable Capacity Similar to mirrored drives, when you're using RAID-5 volumes, a loss of one drive occurs due to the parity overhead. For example, if you configure five 9GB drives (45GB total capacity), only 36GB will be available because, in effect, you are dedicating one drive to containing parity information.

RAID-5 volumes have read performance equivalent to that of RAID-0, or *striped volumes*. However, because of having to generate the parity information, write performance is impacted. RAID-5 volumes cannot be extended or mirrored. In addition, they cannot contain the system or the boot volumes.

A RAID-5 volume can be created using the procedure outlined in Step by Step 1.19.

STEP BY STEP

1.19 Creating a RAID-5 Volume

1. Open the Disk Management snap-in.
2. In the lower-right pane of the Disk Management snap-in, right-click the first section of unallocated free space that you want to use to create the volume.
3. From the pop-up menu, select New Volume. This starts the New Volume Wizard. Click Next to continue.
4. The next screen prompts you to select the type of volume to create. Select the RAID-5 radio button and then click Next to continue.
5. On the Select Disks screen, the disk you clicked is preselected for you, with all the available free space entered for you. Highlight the additional drives and click the Add button to add them to the volume. You have the option of selecting as much free space from each disk as you like, up to the smallest amount of free space available on any of the disks. For example, if you have three disks, and two have 900MB of free space and the other has 800MB of free space, the maximum space you can use on each disk is 800MB. The volume sizes have to be identical on each disk. Make your selections and then click Next to continue.

6. The next screen allows you to select the drive letter or NTFS folder to assign the new partition to. You also have the option to not assign it, opting instead to come back and do it later. Most of the time you will assign a drive letter. Click Next to continue.
7. The Format Volume screen allows you to specify whether or not you want to format the volume and what cluster size to use. There is also a selection to configure the new volume for file and folder compression. Dynamic volumes in Windows Server 2003 can only be formatted as NTFS. Click Next to continue.
8. Look over the settings on the Completing the New Volume Wizard screen. Confirm that the selected settings are correct. If you need to make any changes, click the Back button. If everything is correct, click Finish.

RECOVERING FROM DISK FAILURES

Unfortunately, hard disks can and do fail. This alone is a very solid reason for ensuring that you have a well-thought-out and practiced disaster-recovery plan in place (see Chapter 7, "Managing and Implementing Disaster Recovery," for more information on using the Windows Backup utility). If your data was on a basic storage disk or a simple, spanned, or striped dynamic volume, you have no choice but to replace the disk and restore the data from the last backup. If you experience failure of a disk in a mirrored volume or a RAID-5 array, fault tolerance is in place and you can recover your data.

Recovering a Failed Mirrored Drive

If one of the drives in a mirrored set happens to fail, you will be provided with a graphical indication in Disk Management. Fortunately, because mirrored volumes are fault tolerant, your server continues to operate normally, albeit with slower read performance. You can schedule your repairs at a convenient time.

The process to repair the mirror depends on whether or not the disk that failed was part of a mirrored set that contained the system or boot partition.

If the failed disk did not contain the system or boot partition (only data), you can restore the mirror by following the procedure outlined in Step by Step 1.20.

STEP BY STEP

1.20 Repairing a Mirrored Volume

1. Open the Disk Management snap-in. You should have an error indication similar to that shown in Figure 1.44. The failed disk usually shows a status of Missing, and the volume set shows a status of Failed Redundancy.

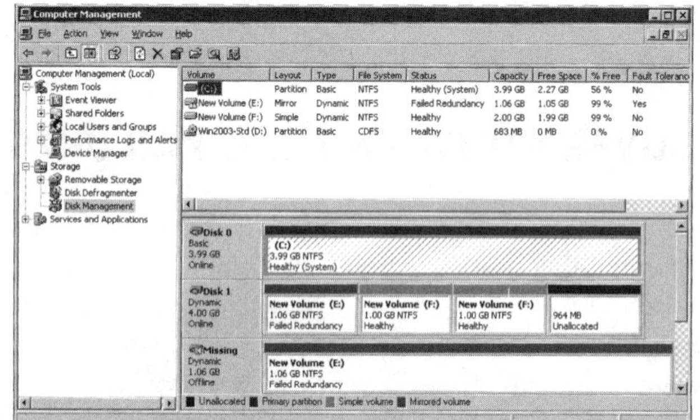

FIGURE 1.44
The Disk Manager snap-in indicates a problem with the mirrored set and flags the failed device.

2. In the lower-right pane of the Disk Management snap-in, right-click the failed mirrored volume and select Remove Mirror from the shortcut menu.
3. In the Remove Mirror dialog box, shown in Figure 1.45, select the disk that is to be removed and click Remove Mirror.

4. Confirm that you want to remove the mirror by clicking OK when prompted with a dialog box.
5. Power down the computer, replace the hard disk, and restart the computer.
6. Create a new mirrored volume using the previous mirrored disk and the replacement disk. Refer to the procedure for creating a mirror earlier in this chapter.

FIGURE 1.45
After you highlight the failed drive and select the Remove Mirror button, the volume will be removed from the mirrored set.

If the mirrored volume that contains the boot or system partition fails and it's the primary drive that has failed, you most likely will not be able to boot your server. This is because the `BOOT.INI` file is still configured to look for that drive. This will not affect the operation of your server because the server is able to access the files it needs to continue running from the other half of the mirror.

However, unless you have hot-swap drives and can replace the failed disk without shutting down the server, eventually you will need to power down, replace the failed disk, and then restart the server. The easiest way to reboot and repair the server is to create a Windows Server 2003 boot floppy that contains the system files and a copy of the `BOOT.INI` file that points to the secondary disk in the mirrored set.

Technically speaking, the floppy you are creating is not really a boot floppy because it doesn't contain the operating system. Earlier in the chapter we discussed the Windows Server 2003 boot process. When the server is started, it looks for the files in the Windows Server 2003 system partition. We will re-create the system partition on a floppy disk and edit the `BOOT.INI` file to point to the operating system files that are on the surviving secondary mirrored volume.

If the failed disk contained the system or boot partition, you can restore the mirror by following the procedure outlined in Step by Step 1.21.

STEP BY STEP

1.21 Repairing a Mirrored Boot/System Volume

1. Open the Disk Management snap-in. You should have an obvious error indication. The failed volume usually shows a status of Missing.

continues

continued

2. Determine which mirrored disk failed. If the secondary disk failed (the disk that contains the mirrored data), you can replace it as outlined previously. If the primary disk failed (the disk that contains the original data), you must proceed with these steps.

3. If you have another Windows Server 2003 computer available or if your server is still up and running, format a 3 1/2 inch floppy disk. (This disk must be formatted in Windows Server 2003 so that it has the correct MBR.) Copy the `NTLDR`, `NTDETECT.COM`, and `BOOT.INI` files to the floppy disk. You will need to edit the `BOOT.INI` file as shown in Step 6 to reflect the location of your secondary drive.

4. If you do not have another Windows Server 2003 computer available or if your server is down, copy the `NTDETECT.COM` file from the I386 folder on a Windows Server 2003 Setup CD-ROM to a blank, formatted 3-1/2 floppy. You also need to expand the `NTLDR` file from this same location by entering the following command from the command line:

```
expand Ntldr._ Ntldr
```

5. If your server uses SCSI drives that have the BIOS disabled (not common), you must include the driver `ntbootdd.sys` on your boot floppy. If used, this file is specific to your SCSI controller and will be present on your server.

6. Finally, create a `BOOT.INI` file that points to the secondary drive in your broken mirror. (For more help on working with ARC paths, see `http://support.microsoft.com/default.aspx?scid=kb;en-us;Q102873`.) Here's an example:

```
boot loader]
timeout=30
default=multi(0)disk(0)rdisk(0)
➥partition(1)\WINNT
[operating systems]
multi(0)disk(0)rdisk(0)partition(1)\
➥WINNT="Microsoft Windows Server 2003"
➥/fastdetect
```

7. Power down the computer, replace the hard disk, and restart the computer.
8. Use your boot disk to start your Windows Server 2003 computer.
9. Remove and re-create the mirror as discussed in the previous procedure.

IN THE FIELD

PREBUILD THE RECOVERY FLOPPY

When you initially configure your boot/system drives in a mirrored configuration, that's when you should build your recovery boot floppy. You should configure the boot floppy and then use it for a few test boots to make sure you have the paths configured correctly in the `BOOT.INI` file. Then make two or more copies of it and put them away in a safe place.

When the server has crashed and the phones are ringing off the hook is not the proper time to learn how to build and test a recovery floppy.

Recovering a Failed RAID-5 Drive

Recovering from a disk failure in a RAID-5 array is a fairly simple process thanks to the fault tolerance provided by the array. Remember that RAID-5 arrays can only provide fault tolerance for one failed disk, so be sure to replace the failed disk as soon as possible. While the disk is failed and not replaced, you can still use the RAID-5 array; however, I/O performance will be severely degraded because the missing data must be re-created from the parity information. Again, you should replace a failed disk in a RAID-5 array as soon as you can by performing the procedure outlined in Step by Step 1.22.

STEP BY STEP

1.22 Repairing a RAID-5 Volume

1. Open the Disk Management snap-in. The failed volume usually shows a status of Failed Redundancy.
2. Power down the server, if necessary. Replace the failed disk. Restart the server, if necessary. If the disk is hot swappable, rescan the disks.
3. In the lower-right pane of the Disk Management snap-in, right-click one of the volumes in the failed RAID-5 set (it will be marked as Failed Redundancy) and select Reactivate Volume from the shortcut menu.
4. When the confirmation prompt appears, click Yes to confirm that you want to reactivate the failed volume.
5. When prompted, select the new disk you installed and click OK to begin the rebuilding process.

FILE COMPRESSION IN WINDOWS SERVER 2003

Windows Server 2003 includes two types of file and folder compression: NTFS-based file system compression and the compressed folders feature, which is equivalent to the various Zip file utilities that have been available from sources other than Microsoft.

Using either method to compress files and folders gives you the same result: decreasing the amount of space that a file, folder, or program uses on your hard drive or removable media.

Configuring NTFS File and Folder Compression

Native file and folder compression is one of the many benefits of using NTFS; native compression is not available on the FAT file system. Unfortunately, this capability comes at a price—NTFS compression and EFS encryption are mutually exclusive. That is, you cannot both compress and encrypt a file or folder at the same time. See Chapter 4 for more information about EFS encryption in Windows Server 2003.

NTFS compression allows you to compress a single file or even the entire volume. Because compression is built in to the file system, working with compressed files and folders is invisible to the end user. When you open a file, Windows Server 2003 automatically decompresses the file, and when you close the file, it is recompressed.

Because NTFS compression is a property of a file, folder, or volume, you can have uncompressed files on a compressed volume or a compressed file in an uncompressed folder.

You can manage compression from the command line by running the `compact` command or from the Windows GUI in the applicable folder or file Properties dialog box. Step by Step 1.23 outlines how to enable NTFS compression on a folder.

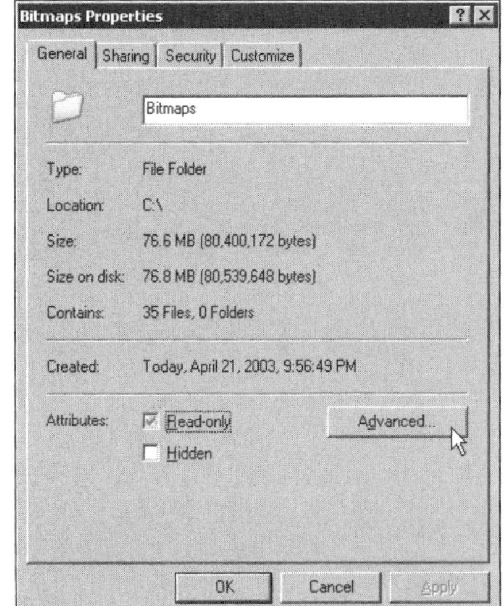

FIGURE 1.46
Compression is a property of a folder.

STEP BY STEP

1.23 Compressing a Folder on an NTFS Volume

1. Open either My Computer or Windows Explorer. Right-click the folder that you want to compress and select Properties from the pop-up menu.

2. From the folder's Properties page, click the Advanced button, as shown in Figure 1.46.

continues

continued

3. In the Advanced Attributes dialog box, shown in Figure 1.47, select the Compress Contents to Save Disk Space check box. Click OK to save.
4. Click OK on the folder's Properties page.
5. From the Confirm Attribute Changes dialog box shown in Figure 1.48, choose whether you want to apply the changes to only the selected folder or to the folder and all its subfolders and files. Click OK.

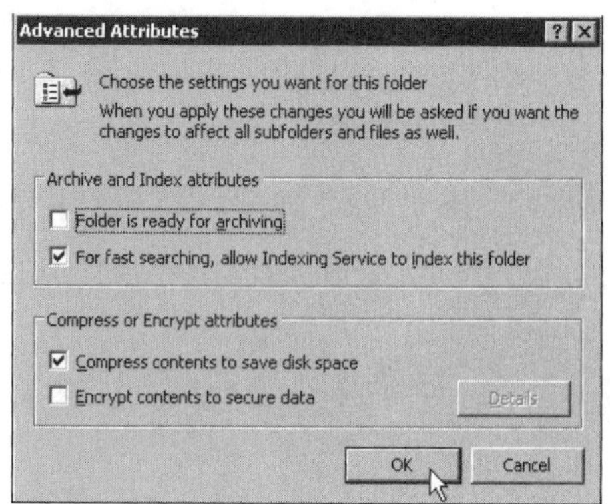

FIGURE 1.47▲
To compress a folder, select the Compress Contents to Save Disk Space check box. Notice that you can check either Compress Contents or Encrypt Contents, but not both.

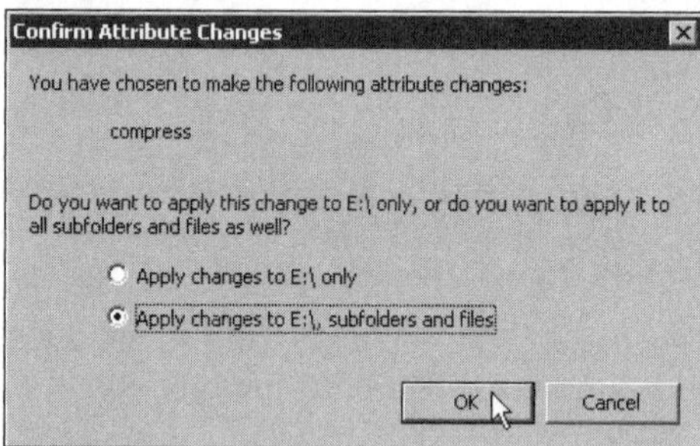

FIGURE 1.48▶
Select what you want compressed.

As mentioned earlier, you can choose to compress a single file, or a group of files, without compressing the folder or the volume that the file resides in. To compress a single file or group of files, consult Step by Step 1.24.

STEP BY STEP

1.24 Compressing a File on an NTFS Volume

1. Open either My Computer or Windows Explorer. Right-click the file that you want to compress and select Properties from the pop-up menu.
2. From the file's Properties page, click the Advanced button.

3. In the Advanced Attributes dialog box, select the Compress Contents to Save Disk Space check box. Click OK to save.
4. Click OK on the file's Properties page.

If you need to conserve a lot of space, you can choose to compress an entire NTFS volume. However, remember that it takes a certain amount of system overhead to work with compressed files, so you probably won't want to compress a volume that contains files that are frequently accessed, such as your boot drive. Also, there will always be certain files in use that cannot be compressed, such as `ntoskrnl` and `pagefile.sys`.

To compress an NTFS volume, follow the procedure outlined in Step by Step 1.25.

STEP BY STEP

1.25 Compressing an NTFS Volume

1. Open either My Computer or Windows Explorer. Right-click the drive that you want to compress and select Properties from the pop-up menu.
2. From the local disk's Properties page shown in Figure 1.49, click the Compress Drive to Save Disk Space check box.
3. From the Confirm Attribute Changes dialog box, choose whether you want to turn compression on for the volume or to compress all its subfolders and files. Click OK.
4. Click OK on the local disk's Properties page.

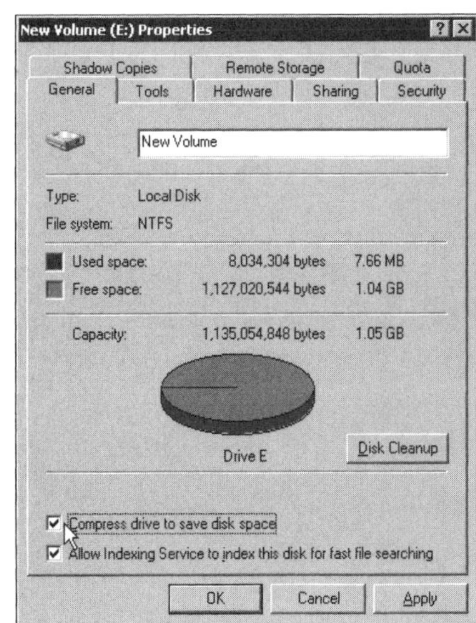

FIGURE 1.49
Compressing a volume.

By looking at the Properties page for the file or folder, you can determine how much physical space was saved by comparing the entries for Size and Size on Disk, as shown in Figure 1.46.

It's important to note that if you compress a volume or folder, you can choose to not compress the files and subfolders. However, any new files or folders created on a compressed volume or in a compressed folder will be compressed. New objects automatically inherit the compression attribute of the container in which they are created.

GUIDED PRACTICE EXERCISE 1.2

You are the administrator of a network for a manufacturing company that includes multiple Windows Server 2003 servers used for file and print services. Your company is currently having financial problems, so the hardware budget for this fiscal year is limited.

The Legal department is required to have all its documents available for at least 10 years, due to a pending wrongful-death lawsuit. Unfortunately, you are running out of drive space and the voluminous amount of data consumed by these documents isn't going away any time soon.

You must find a way to provide more free space for your users, while keeping the documents for the Legal department readily available—all without funding for new hardware!

What is the best way to solve this issue in Windows Server 2003? On your own, try to develop a solution that would involve the least amount of downtime and expense.

If you would like to see a possible solution, follow the procedure outlined here.

Estimated Time: 40 minutes.

This is a fairly straightforward decision, mainly because without a budget, you can't use features such as remote storage and offline backups, which require additional hardware. Your only option is to compress the old documents using the file and folder compression feature in Windows Server 2003. Fortunately, document files usually have a high compression ratio, so you should be able to gain a large amount of free space.

Here are the steps to follow:

1. Using either Windows Explorer or My Computer, navigate to the folder on the volume you wish to compress.

2. Right-click the folder and select Properties. From the Properties dialog box, write down the Size and the Size on Disk entries.
3. Click the Advanced box. From the Advanced Attributes dialog box, select Compress Contents to Save Space and then click OK.
4. Click OK again to close the dialog box.
5. When you are presented with the dialog box asking you whether you want to apply the changes to the selected folder or to the folder, subfolder, and all files, select the check box to apply the changes to the folder, subfolder, and all files. Click OK to save.
6. After the compression completes, right-click the folder, select Properties, and compare the Size on Disk entry with the numbers you recorded earlier.

The nice thing about the Windows Server 2003 implementation of compression is that it allows you to apply compression at the volume, folder, or file level. This allows you to selectively compress older files that are not frequently used, while leaving untouched the files that are always in use.

Copying or Moving NTFS Files or Folders

Several rules apply when you move or copy compressed files and folders. The possible outcomes of moving or copying NTFS compressed files or folders are as follows:

- Moving an uncompressed file or folder to another folder on the same NTFS volume results in the file or folder remaining uncompressed, regardless of the compression state of the target folder.
- Moving an uncompressed file or folder to another folder on a different NTFS volume results in the file or folder inheriting the compression state of the target folder.

- Moving a compressed file or folder to another folder on the same NTFS volume results in the file or folder remaining compressed after the move, regardless of the compression state of the target folder.
- Moving a compressed file or folder to another folder on a different NTFS volume results in the file or folder inheriting the compression state of the target folder.
- Copying a file to a folder causes the file to take on the compression state of the target folder, whether on the same or a different volume.
- Overwriting a file of the same name causes the copied file to take on the compression state of the target file, regardless of the compression state of the target folder.
- Copying a file from a FAT folder to an NTFS folder results in the file taking on the compression state of the target folder.
- Copying a file from an NTFS folder to a FAT folder results in all NTFS-specific properties being lost.

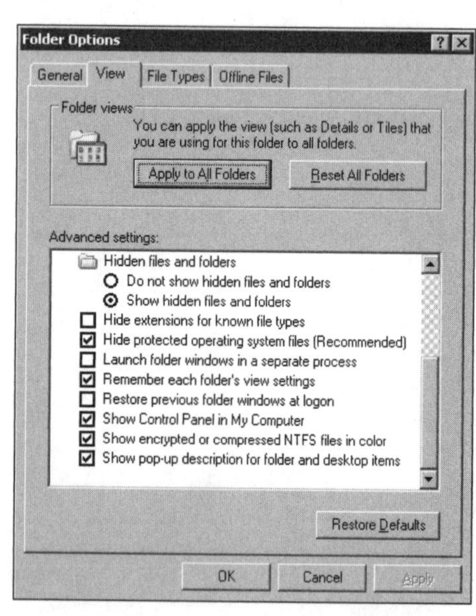

FIGURE 1.50
Turn on the View property for compressed objects.

Identifying Compressed Objects

So that you can easily identify files and folders that have been compressed, you can turn on a View property in Windows Explorer or My Computer. When this property is turned on, files and folders that are compressed are displayed in blue text. To enable this option, use the instructions in Step by Step 1.26.

STEP BY STEP

1.26 Changing the View Property to Identify Compressed Objects

1. Open either My Computer or Windows Explorer. From the system menu, click Tools, Folder Options.
2. In the Folder Options dialog box, click the View tab.
3. In the Advanced Settings window of the Folder Options dialog box, shown in Figure 1.50, select the Show Encrypted or Compressed NTFS Files in Color check box. Click OK to save.

Managing Compression from the Command Line

In addition to the GUI method of compressing files, Windows Server 2003 also has a command-line utility, COMPACT.EXE. The command-line utility is handy for use with scripting, or it can be used in those situations where you want to only compress certain types of files. For example, if you only wanted to compress the document files on your volume, you could use wildcards to specify that only those types of files should be compressed.

The compact command has the following syntax:

```
compact [{/c¦/u}] [/s[:dir]] [/a] [/i] [/f]
 [/q] [FileName[...]]
```

Table 1.1 presents the available options for use with the compact command.

TABLE 1.1

THE OPTIONS FOR THE compact COMMAND

Switch	*Description*
/c	Specifies that the directory or file is to be compressed.
/u	Specifies that the directory or file is to be decompressed.
/s	Specifies that the compression action is to be performed on all subdirectories of the specified directory.
/a	Specifies the display of hidden or system files.
/i	Specifies that errors are to be ignored during the compression process.
/f	Specifies that the compression operation is to be forced on the specified directory or file. This is useful in cases in which a directory is only partly compressed.
/q	Specifies that only the most essential information is to be reported.
FileName	Specifies the file or directory. You can use multiple filenames and wildcard characters (* and ?) .

EXAM TIP

Expect a compact Question Expect at least one exam question that deals with compressing files and folders from the command line.

Compressed (Zipped) Folders

The second form of compression available in Windows Server 2003 is compressed folders. As stated earlier, the compressed folders feature uses the industry-standard Zip format to compress files into a folder. Unlike NTFS compression, compressed folders can be copied or moved to other computers, and they retain their compressed format.

Compressed folders can be created in My Computer or Windows Explorer using the procedure outlined in Step by Step 1.27.

STEP BY STEP

1.27 Creating a Compressed Folder

1. Open either My Computer or Windows Explorer. Highlight the drive or folder that you want to create the compressed folder in. Then, select File, New, Compressed (Zipped) Folder, as shown in Figure 1.51.

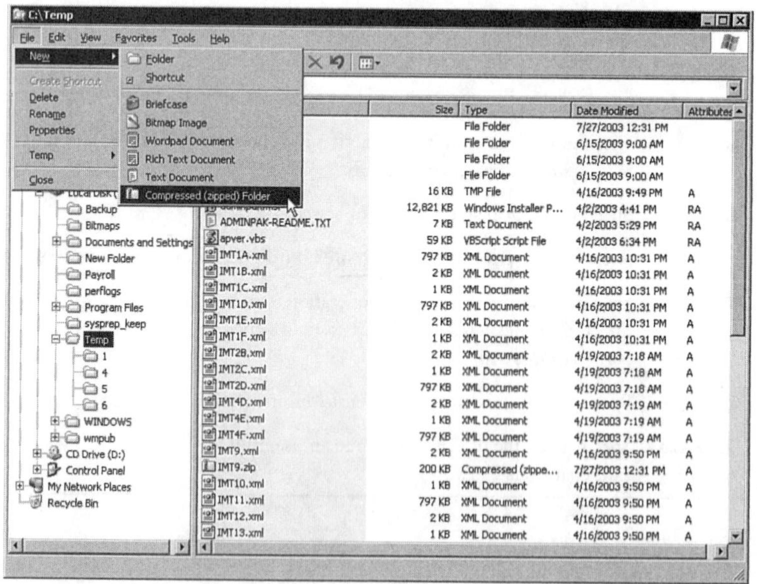

FIGURE 1.51
Creating a compressed folder.

2. Key in a name for the new folder and then press Enter to save.

After you have created the compressed folder, shown in Figure 1.52, you can add and remove files and folders to and from it by dragging and dropping, just like any other folder in Windows Server 2003. In addition, you can run most programs and open and edit files in the compressed folder. For extra security, you can password protect the compressed folders.

Because compressed folders are essentially just common Zip files, they can also be manipulated by most third-party Zip utilities.

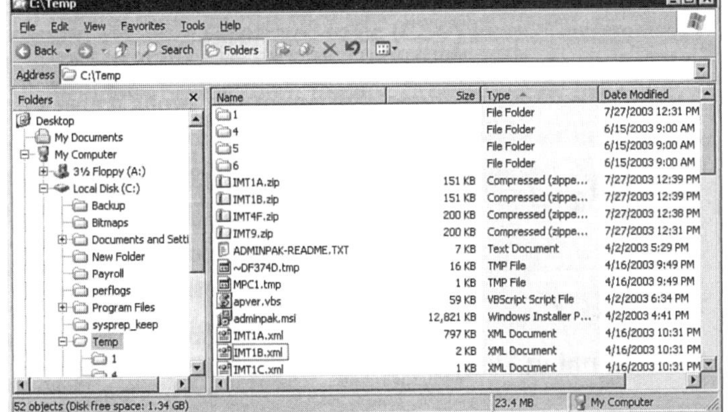

FIGURE 1.52
Compressed folders are identified by the zipper icon.

Optimizing Server Disk Performance

Windows Server 2003 comes with three fairly robust, built-in tools that you can use to perform basic troubleshooting, cleanup, and repair operations:

- **Disk Cleanup**—This utility removes temporary files and other "dead wood" that may be on your computer's disks.
- **Check Disk**—This utility checks the file and folder structure of your hard disk. You can also have Check Disk check the physical structure of your hard disk. Check Disk can perform repairs as required.
- **Disk Defragmenter**—This utility defragments your hard disks by moving all pieces of each file into a continuous section on the hard disk.

We examine each of these tools in the following subsections.

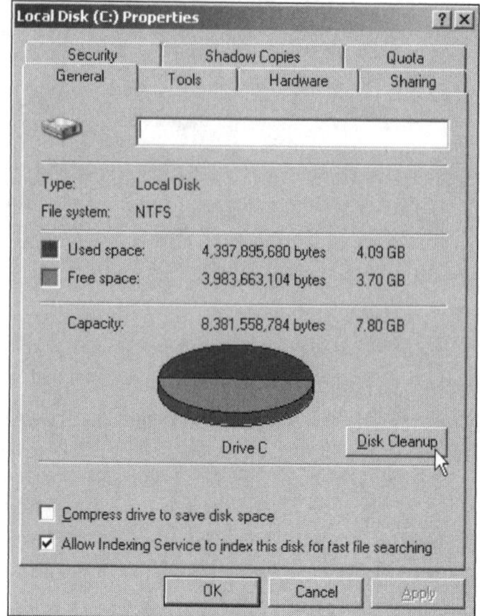

FIGURE 1.53
Starting Disk Cleanup from the Disk Properties dialog box.

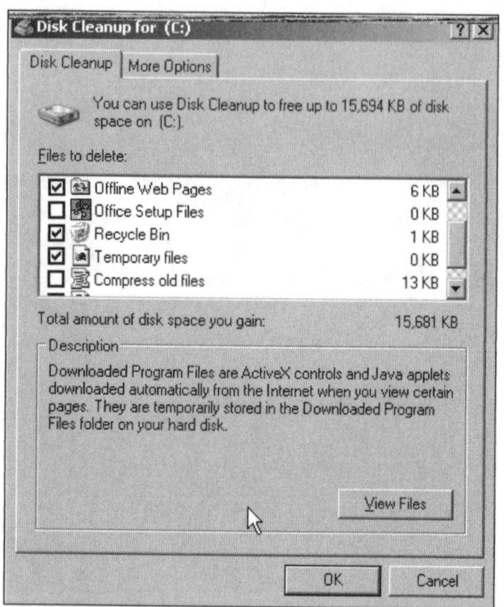

FIGURE 1.54
From the Disk Cleanup dialog box, select the files to delete or compress. To get a description of each entry, highlight it.

Using the Disk Cleanup Utility

The Disk Cleanup utility can remove temporary files, installation logs, Recycle Bin items, and other dead wood that accumulates on your volumes over time. You can start the Disk Cleanup utility in three different ways, depending on your needs:

- On the General tab of the volume's Properties dialog box, click the Disk Cleanup button (see Figure 1.53).
- From the Start menu, click All Programs, Accessories, System Tools, Disk Cleanup.
- On the command line, enter `cleanmgr /d x`, where *x* represents the volume to be cleaned. The `/d` switch is mandatory and specifies the volume to be cleaned.

Step by Step 1.28 details how to run the Disk Cleanup utility.

STEP BY STEP

1.28 Running Disk Cleanup

1. Open either My Computer or Windows Explorer. Right-click the drive that you want to run Disk Cleanup on and select Properties.
2. From the Properties page, select the General tab and click the Disk Cleanup button, as shown in Figure 1.53.
3. From the Disk Cleanup dialog box, shown in Figure 1.54, select the files to delete or compress and then click OK.
4. When the Disk Cleanup finishes, click OK.

By selecting the More Options tab in the Disk Cleanup dialog box (see Figure 1.55), you are presented with other options to create free space on your drive, such as removing Windows components or other programs that you don't use. The Disk Cleanup utility can be configured for scheduled cleaning by using the Scheduled Tasks Wizard located in the Control Panel. The Scheduled Tasks Wizard is covered later in this chapter.

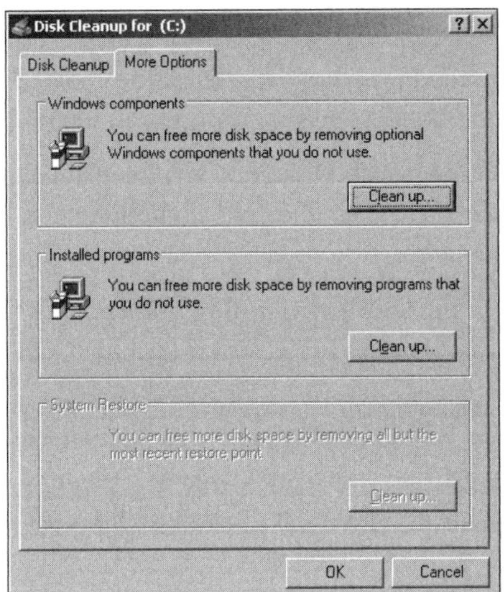

FIGURE 1.55
More options for Disk Cleanup.

Using the Check Disk Utility

The Check Disk utility can be used to check the file and folder structure of your hard disks as well as to check the physical structure of your hard disks. Check Disk can also be configured to automatically correct any errors located. Check Disk can be launched by using one of the following methods:

- As a GUI utility, Check Disk can be launched from the Tools tab of the volume's Properties dialog box.
- As a command-line utility, Check Disk can be launched by entering `chkdsk` on the command line. Table 1.2 presents the available options for use with the `chkdsk` command.

Step by Step 1.29 details how to run the GUI version of the Check Disk utility.

STEP BY STEP

1.29 Running Check Disk from the GUI

1. Open either My Computer or Windows Explorer. Right-click the drive that you want to run Check Disk on and select Properties.

continues

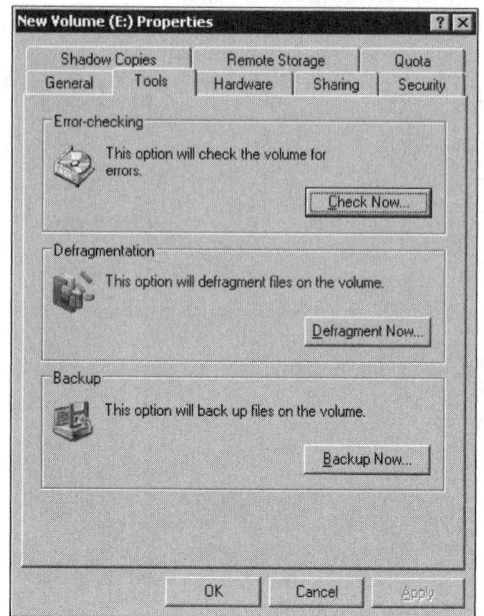

FIGURE 1.56
Click Check Now to select options for Check Disk.

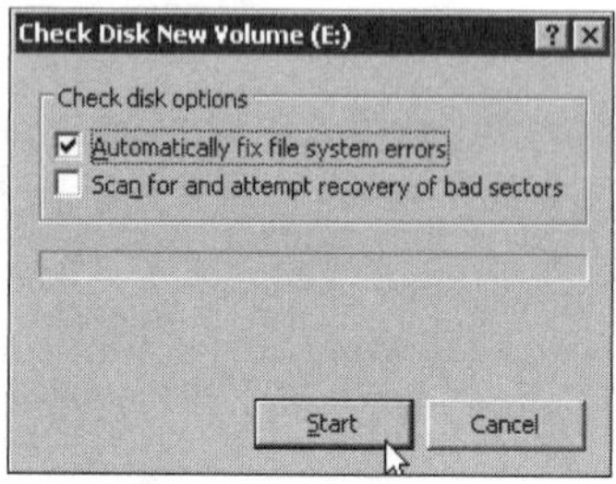

FIGURE 1.57
Select the disk tests to run.

continued

2. From the Properties page, select the Tools tab and click the Check Now button, as shown in Figure 1.56.
3. From the Check Disk New Volume dialog box, shown in Figure 1.57, select the desired checking options and then click Start.
4. When the Disk Check utility finishes, click OK.

The GUI version of Check Disk can fix most minor problems. However, there are times when you need to have more options available for checking your disks. The command-line Check Disk utility, `CHKDSK.EXE`, offers more flexibility.

The `chkdsk` command has the following syntax:

```
chkdsk [volume[[path]filename]]] [/F] [/V] [/R]
 [/X] [/I] [/C] [/L[:size]]
```

Table 1.2 presents the options for use with the `chkdsk` command.

TABLE 1.2

THE OPTIONS FOR THE chkdsk COMMAND

Switch	*Description*
`volume`	Specifies the drive letter, mount point, or volume letter.
`filename`	Specifies the files to check for fragmentation (FAT only).
`/F`	Specifies that errors are to be fixed if found on the disk.
`/V`	Specifies that cleanup messages are to be displayed.
`/R`	Specifies that bad sectors are to be recovered. Requires the `/F` switch.
`/L[:size]`	Specifies the log size to be created.
`/X`	Specifies that the selected volume is to be dismounted if required. Requires the `/F` switch.
`/I`	Specifies that less vigorous checking of index entries is to be performed.
`/C`	Specifies that checking of cycles within the folder structure is to be skipped.

Using the Disk Defragmenter Utility

It was once thought that NTFS could not become fragmented. However, it was soon discovered that NTFS becomes fragmented just as FAT and FAT32 do. Starting with Windows 2000, Microsoft includes a "light" version of Executive Software's Diskeeper, relabeled as the Disk Defragmenter utility, that is used for performing disk defragmentation.

The purpose of a defragmentation tool is to analyze a volume or partition and determine whether each file occupies a contiguous space. During the normal operation of a server, files are written, deleted, and rewritten. If a file needs to be added to, it must be given space wherever free space is available, and the free space might not necessarily be located next to the space that the file currently occupies. As a file is rewritten over and over again, parts of it may be scattered all over the volume. This can slow down the access time for the file because it has to be read from various locations. In addition, new files and programs may be installed in pieces because there is no contiguous free space left on the drive large enough to store the new program. Over time, this slows the I/O performance of the volume.

After the defragmentation program has analyzed the volume, it can then consolidate the files and folders by moving the data around until the each of the files and folders are located in contiguous space on the volume. In addition, the defragmentation program consolidates the free space at the end of the volume so that new programs and files can be installed in contiguous space. The defragmentation utility included with Windows Server 2003, Disk Defragmenter, can defrag both NTFS and FAT volumes and partitions.

> NOTE
>
> **Free Space Limitations** The GUI version of the Disk Defragmenter in Windows Server 2003 will not defragment a disk that has less than 15% free space.

NOT STRICTLY TRUE

You can access the Disk Defragmenter utility by following any one of these five methods:

- On the Tools tab of the volume's Properties dialog box, click the Defragment Now button.
- From the Start menu, click All Programs, Accessories, System Tools, Disk Defragmenter.
- From within the Computer Management console, click Disk Defragmenter, as shown in Figure 1.58.
- On the command line or from the Run dialog box, enter `dfrg.msc`.

- On the command line or from the Run dialog box, enter `MMC`. In the empty console, add the Disk Defragmenter snap-in. This can be useful for creating powerful, customized MMC consoles for a variety of management tasks.

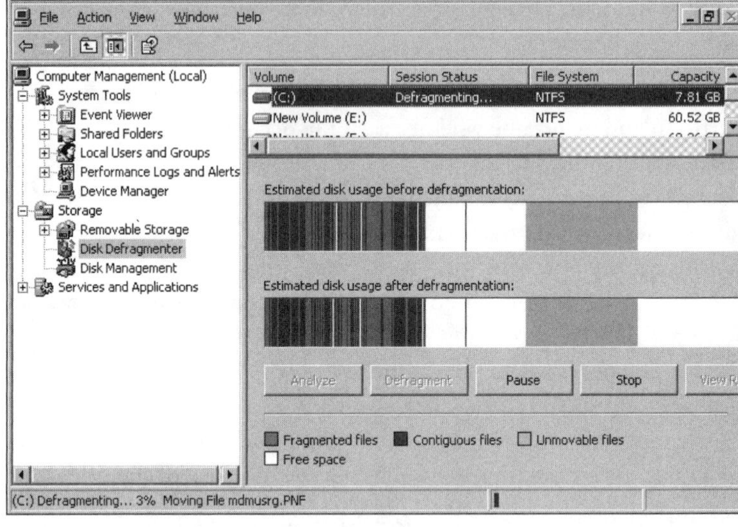

FIGURE 1.58
Disk Defragmenter in the Computer Management console.

No matter which way you start Disk Defragmenter, your options are the same. To analyze a volume, click the Analyze button. You can defragment a volume, with or without first analyzing it, by clicking the Defragment button. The View Report button shows the analysis report again. You can pause or stop a running defragmentation.

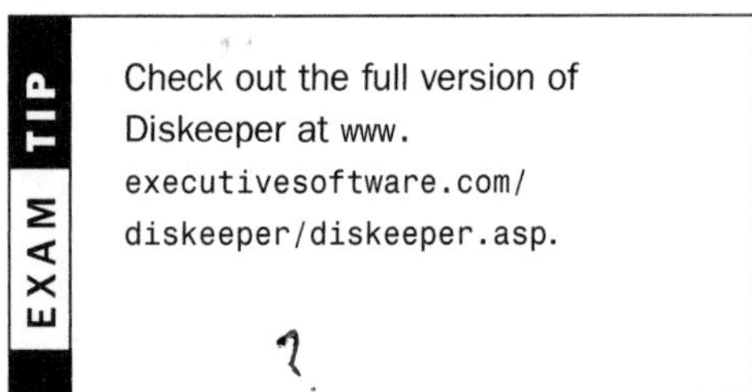
EXAM TIP

Check out the full version of Diskeeper at www.executivesoftware.com/diskeeper/diskeeper.asp.

The Disk Defragmenter utility can be configured for scheduled cleaning by using the Scheduled Tasks Wizard located in the Control Panel.

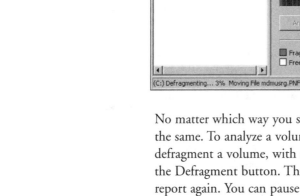

In addition to the GUI defragmentation utility, there is also a command-line utility. The command-line version of Disk Defragmenter can be used in scripts, and it also has an option to force a defragment to take place when there is less than 15% free space on the volume or partition.

When started from the command line, the `defrag.exe` command has the following syntax:

```
defrag [volume[[path]filename]]] [/A] [/V] [/F]
```

Table 1.3 presents the options for use with the `defrag` command.

TABLE 1.3

THE OPTIONS FOR THE defrag COMMAND

Switch	*Description*
volume	Specifies the drive letter, mount point, or volume letter.
filename	Specifies the files to check for fragmentation (FAT only).
/A	Performs an analysis of the volume, displays a summary report, and indicates whether a defragmentation is required.
/V	Verbose. Displays a full analysis report.
/F	Forces a defragmentation of the volume, even if the free space is less than 15%.

Using the Scheduled Tasks Utility

The Scheduled Tasks utility is a GUI interface scheduling tool that allows you to drag and drop scheduled tasks, select tasks from a menu, and save scheduled tasks in `.job` files that can be transferred to other systems. This tool is very useful for scheduling the various maintenance tasks that can be scripted or run from a command line. This tool, together with the influx of command-line–capable management utilities that Microsoft has included with Windows Server 2003, is moving the operating system closer to becoming a true enterprise-level operating system.

The versions of Windows before Windows 2000 included a command-line utility called `AT.EXE` that was used to schedule tasks. Although it is still included in Windows Server 2003, it is very limited, and it is extremely doubtful that you will see questions concerning it on the exam.

The Scheduled Tasks applet is not just a fancy interface to the `AT` command; it also adds the following features:

- The capability to modify, disable, or stop previously scheduled tasks.
- The capability to view and control tasks that are scheduled on remote computers.

- Each user can control his or her own tasks or those created by others who have granted that user permission.
- The availability of a log file that lists all scheduled activity (useful for problem determination).
- A notification feature that can send you a message when a scheduled task fails.
- All tasks scheduled using the Scheduled Tasks tool are saved as `.job` files that can be dragged and dropped or copied to the Scheduled Tasks folder of other machines.

WARNING

Using the AT Command You can view tasks that have been scheduled using the AT command in the Scheduled Tasks program. However, because of the differences in the way tasks are stored and the different options available, if you make any changes to an AT-generated task using the Scheduled Tasks program, it can no longer be viewed or manipulated using the AT command.

MOVING JOBS TO REMOTE COMPUTERS

Because of the way Windows Server 2003 handles security associated with `.job` files, when a task is moved or copied to a remote computer, you have to reenter the security account under which that task is running. This is because the security account credentials cannot be transferred between computers.

The Scheduled Tasks application is supplied with the Scheduled Task Wizard. Although you can enter tasks directly from the GUI interface, this wizard takes you step by step through the entire process.

To set up a task using the Scheduled Task Wizard, follow Step by Step 1.30.

STEP BY STEP

1.30 Configuring a Scheduled Task

1. Click Start and then select the Control Panel.
2. Double-click the Scheduled Tasks folder. The Scheduled Tasks window opens.
3. Double-click Add Scheduled Task. The Scheduled Task Wizard starts. Click Next to continue.

4. The Scheduled Task Wizard displays a list of the applications on your computer (see Figure 1.59). You can either select one of these programs or click Browse to select one that is not listed.

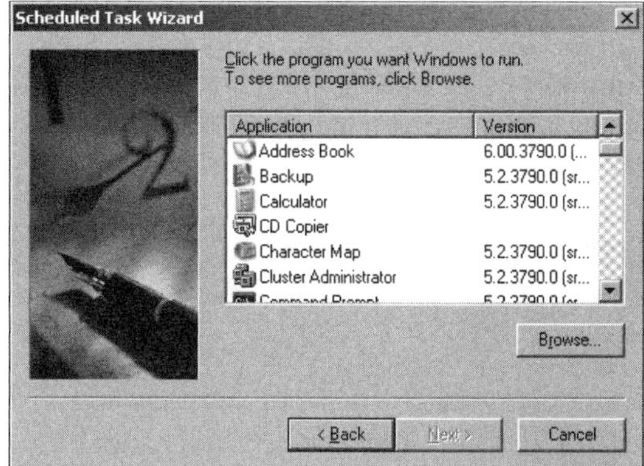

FIGURE 1.59
The Scheduled Tasks Wizard allows you to select the program to execute.

5. Select Browse.
6. The Select Program to Schedule screen appears. From this screen, you can navigate to the program, batch, or script file that you want to run.
7. Click Open to continue.
8. The Scheduled Task Wizard prompts you to type in a name for the task. A list of selections for how often to perform the task is displayed. This list includes the following selections:
    - Daily
    - Weekly
    - Monthly
    - One Time Only
    - When My Computer Starts
    - When I Log On
9. Click Next to continue.
10. On the next screen, you have options to set the time and the date for the task. Click Next to continue.

continues

continued

11. On the next screen, you enter the name of an account that has the proper authority to run the task to be scheduled and the appropriate password. Click Next to continue.

12. On the next screen, as shown in Figure 1.60, you receive a summary of the options you selected to schedule this task. If any options need to be changed, click Back to return to the previous screens.

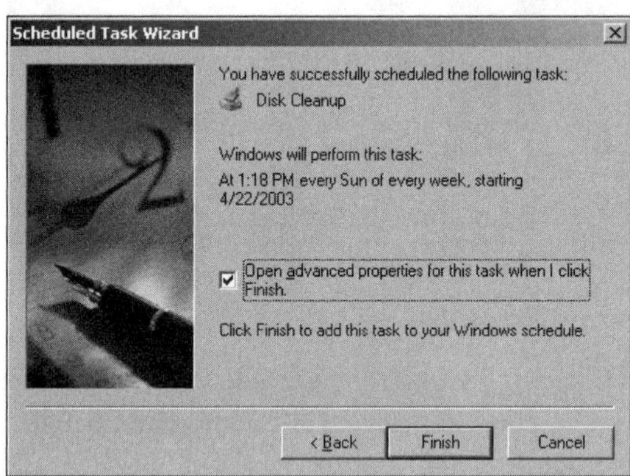

FIGURE 1.60
You can review your options and change them if necessary.

13. Select the Open Advanced Properties for This Task when I Click Finish box.

14. Click Finish.

15. The Disk Cleanup dialog box, shown in Figure 1.61, opens for this task. From here, you can change any of the options you have already configured, or you can select some new options. The following four tabs appear:

    - **Task**—This tab displays the options that were previously selected.
    - **Schedule**—This tab displays the schedule that was previously selected. However, many additional scheduling options are available from this tab. For example, you can show multiple schedules, or you can add times when you want the task to run. By selecting the Advanced button, you are presented with more scheduling options, such as running the task for a specified length of time, repeating the task every *x* minutes or hours, and scheduling a stop time for the task.

- **Settings**—The Settings tab allows you to stop the task after it has been running for a specified length of time. It also allows you to specify that the task is only to be started if the computer has been idle for a certain length of time or to stop the task if the computer is no longer idle. This tab also contains settings useful for running tasks on laptop computers. Included are options to not start the task if the computer is running on batteries, to stop the task if the computer goes into battery mode, and to wake the computer to run the task.
- **Security**—The Security tab allows you to specify the permissions that specific users and groups have for this task. This allows you to prevent users from changing the schedule of a task or deleting it.

16. Click OK when finished to save the task.

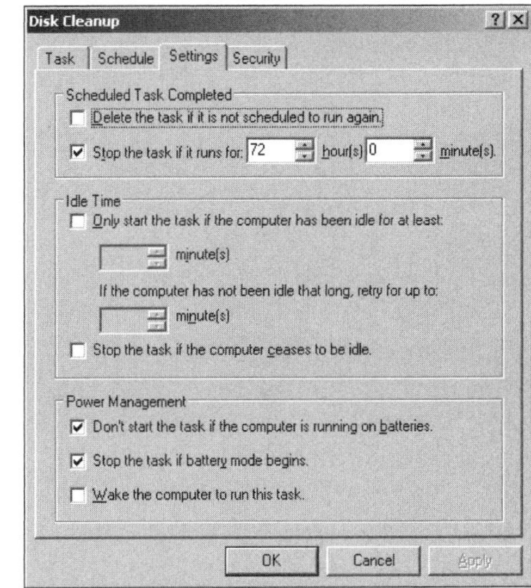

FIGURE 1.61
You can fine tune the conditions under which to run your scheduled task.

The command-line equivalent of the Scheduled Tasks GUI is the `SCHTASKS.EXE` utility. This utility is a superset of the older `AT.EXE` utility. `SCHTASKS` allows you to create or modify tasks that can be controlled and monitored via the Scheduled Tasks utility.

`SCHTASKS` is the command-line interface to the Scheduled Tasks utility. It can be used to do just about everything that can be done via the GUI interface. However, as a command-line utility, it allows you to easily script its operations.

The `Schtasks` command supports the subcommands listed in Table 1.4.

TABLE 1.4

THE Schtasks SUBCOMMANDS

Command	*Description*
`Schtasks`	Displays all scheduled tasks. Same as entering `Schtasks /Query`.
`Schtasks /Create`	Creates a new task.
`Schtasks /Change`	Allows you to modify the task.
`Schtasks /Delete`	Deletes a scheduled task.

continues

TABLE 1.4 *continued*

THE `Schtasks` SUBCOMMANDS

Command	*Description*
`Schtasks /End`	Stops a running task.
`Schtasks /Query`	Displays all scheduled tasks.
`Schtasks /Run`	Starts a scheduled task.

Because the instructions for using the `Schtasks` command are covered in the Windows Server 2003 Help files, we do not cover them here in great detail. However, here are some tips and general information that will make it easier to work with the `Schtasks` command:

- Always specify the entire path of the programs or batch files that you want to run, including the drive letter or UNC path.
- You must enter commands in quotation marks.
- Use the `/Run` command to test your tasks.
- The date and time must be specified in the format hours: minutes in 24-hour notation (00:00 [midnight] through 23:59).
- All date entries must be separated by commas.
- If the `\\computername` switch is omitted, the commands are scheduled to execute on the local computer. Remember that if you are scheduling events on remote systems, you must make sure that the Scheduled Tasks service is started on the remote system and that you have the proper rights to run this service on the remote machine. You can start this service (and even control its startup method) through the Windows Services application.
- When scheduling tasks on a remote computer, use the UNC notation for the server and share name, not a drive letter. 
- You can display or save to a file a verbose listing of all scheduled tasks in various formats, including CSV. Just use the `/v` switch with the `/fo LIST` parameter.
- The task name is assigned by you when you configure a scheduled event, and you cannot change it later. You will use this name to delete and modify scheduled events that are already in the queue.

Either the Scheduled Tasks applet or the `Schtasks` command can be used to work with scheduled tasks. It will probably be to your advantage to start using these two methods of task scheduling and limiting your use of the `AT` command. Although the `AT` command is currently supported in Windows XP and Windows Server 2003, Microsoft recommends that you use `Schtasks` instead. This is most likely Microsoft's way of saying that the `AT` command will probably not be in the next releases of Windows.

CASE STUDY: DL CRAIG

ESSENCE OF THE CASE

Here are the essential elements in this case:

- Provide a fault-tolerant database configuration.
- Provide the best performance of the database.
- Archive old data using the least amount of space.

SCENARIO

DL Craig is a wholesaler for beverages based in the Midwest. DL Craig has decided to implement a third-party order-entry and sales-analysis program that uses several separate Microsoft SQL Server databases. Because the company has been wildly successful over the past year, its old order-entry system has become slow and overburdened.

DL Craig now wants to scale the hardware supporting the SQL Server databases for the best performance of the application. In addition, the solution must be fault tolerant. Due to the popularity and the competitive nature of the beverage business, DL Craig cannot afford to have its order-entry system suffer any downtime during normal business hours.

In addition to the requirements for the new order-entry system, due to a legal settlement, DL Craig needs to maintain all its correspondence for a period of 10 years. This correspondence consists of a large number of online documents. Although daily access to the documents is not required, they still need to be reasonably accessible.

continues

CASE STUDY: DL CRAIG

continued

However, due to the enormous number of documents to be archived, DL Craig wants them to be stored as efficiently as possible.

ANALYSIS

The features in Windows Server 2003 will enable DL Craig to satisfy its fault tolerance, performance, and archival requirements. The first step is to install new Windows Server 2003 servers using a mirrored system boot partition. This will ensure that the servers will keep operating in case of a single system/boot volume failure.

The next step is to add several SCSI drives to the server in a RAID-5 configuration. This configuration will require at least three volumes, but better performance will be achieved by adding more drives to the volume set. Although a RAID-5 configuration provides excellent read performance, write performance is hindered because parity information has to be calculated and written with the data. However, this is a slight tradeoff considering the fault tolerance provided by this type of configuration.

The final requirement can be accomplished by building another Windows Server 2003 server to store the archived data. Because DL Craig did not request that the archival server provide any specific fault tolerance or performance features, any disk configuration should suffice. However, for the most efficient storage of the archived information, the data-storage volumes should be formatted with NTFS as compressed volumes. This will ensure that as documents are added to the volumes, they will automatically be compressed.

Here's an overview of the requirements and solutions in this case study:

Requirement	*Solution Provided By*
Provide a fault-tolerant data-base configuration.	Configuring Windows Server 2003 with a RAID-1 system/boot volume and a RAID-5 database volume
Provide the best performance of the database.	Configuring a RAID-5 volume
Archive old data using the least amount of space.	Configuring the data archival volumes to enable NTFS compression

CHAPTER SUMMARY

This chapter has covered a lot of ground; here are the main points:

- **Working with partitions and volumes**—This includes knowing the types of partitions available on a basic disk (primary, extended, and logical) and the types of volumes available on a dynamic disk (simple, spanned, mirrored, striped, and striped with parity). Know when and how to use them.
- **Optimizing server disk performance**—This includes knowing which of the partitions/volumes provide the best performance and how to configure and maintain them.
- **Implementing a RAID solution**—This includes knowing how to configure, troubleshoot, and repair the various RAID configurations available in Windows Server 2003.
- **Defragmenting volumes and partitions**—This is part of maintaining and optimizing server disk performance.

KEY TERMS

- Boot disk
- Boot partition
- System partition
- Basic disk
- Dynamic disk
- Mirror volume
- RAID-0
- RAID-1
- RAID-5
- `BOOT.INI`
- Extended partition
- Spanned volume
- Fault tolerant
- Defragmentation
- NTFS
- FAT32
- Striped volume

APPLY YOUR KNOWLEDGE

Exercises

1.1 Creating and Testing a Boot Disk

This exercise demonstrates how to create a boot disk. This boot disk can be used to start the server when your system files are corrupted, or when you need to boot to recover a failed mirrored set. This exercise requires a blank floppy disk.

Estimated Time: 20 minutes.

1. Format the floppy disk, either from the command line or from Windows Explorer or My Computer.
2. Using either Windows Explorer or My Computer, confirm that your view settings allow you to see hidden and system files.
3. From the system partition, copy `BOOT.INI`, `NTDETECT.COM`, `NTLDR`, and `NTBOOTDD.SYS` (if present) to your floppy disk. Remove the floppy disk.
4. Delete `NTDETECT.COM` on the system partition.
5. Reboot your server. The reboot should fail.
6. Insert your floppy disk and reboot the server. The reboot should be successful. Copy `NTDETECT.COM` from the floppy to your system partition.

1.2 Repairing a Mirrored Volume

This exercise demonstrates how to repair a mirrored volume. This exercise assumes that you are repairing the mirrored volume in a server that uses hot-plug drives. For a procedure for use in a server that does not have hot-plug drives, see Step by Step 1.20, "Repairing a Mirrored Volume."

Estimated Time: 30 minutes.

1. Create a mirrored volume using the steps outlined earlier in this chapter.
2. Remove one of the drives in the mirror volume. This will simulate a failure.
3. Open the Disk Management snap-in and check the status of the mirrored volume. It should show a status of Failed Redundancy.
4. In the Disk Management snap-in, right-click the mirrored volume and select Remove Mirror.
5. When the Remove Mirror dialog box appears, select the disk that you removed and click Remove Mirror. Select Yes to confirm.
6. Replace the drive that you removed earlier. In the Disk Management snap-in, select Re-Scan disks.
7. Right-click the remaining disk from the mirror and select Add Mirror. When the Add Mirror dialog box appears, select the disk that you just added. Click Add Mirror.

1.3 Configuring Compression on a Volume

This exercise demonstrates how to configure NTFS compression for an entire volume. This exercise requires an empty NTFS volume.

Estimated Time: 20 minutes.

1. Using either Windows Explorer or My computer, create a folder on the volume that you wish to compress.
2. Copy the contents of the `WINNT` folder to this folder. Include all files and subfolders.
3. Using either Windows Explorer or My Computer, display the root of the volume that you want to compress.

APPLY YOUR KNOWLEDGE

4. Right-click the volume and select Properties. From the Properties dialog box, write down the Size and the Size on Disk entries.
5. Click the Advanced box. From the Advanced Attributes dialog box, select Compress Contents to Save Space and then click OK.
6. Click OK again to close the dialog box.
7. When you are presented with the dialog box asking you whether you want to apply the changes to the selected folder or to the folder, subfolder, and all files, select the check box to apply the changes to the folder, subfolder, and all files. Click OK to save.
8. After the compression completes, right-click the root of the volume, select Properties, and compare the Size on Disk entry with the numbers you recorded earlier.

1.4 Defragmenting a Volume

This exercise demonstrates how to defragment a volume. This exercise is nondestructive, so it can be used on any volume.

Estimated Time: 20 minutes.

1. Using either Windows Explorer or My Computer, display the root of the volume that you want to defragment.
2. Right-click the volume and select Properties.
3. On the Tools tab of the volume's Properties dialog box, click the Defragment Now button.
4. When the Disk Defragmenter screen is displayed, select Analyze.
5. When you are presented with the dialog box asking you whether you want to view the report defragment or close, click the Defragment button.
6. After the defragmentation process completes, you can view the report.

Review Questions

1. What is a Windows Server 2003 boot disk and how is it different from a DOS boot disk?
2. What are the two types of disks available in Windows Server 2003 and how are they different?
3. What tools can you use in Windows Server 2003 to configure disks?
4. Explain the differences between a basic disk and a dynamic disk in Windows Server 2003.
5. What are the two methods for compressing files, folders, and volumes?
6. Briefly explain the method used to upgrade a Windows NT 4.0 or Windows 2000 server that contains basic disks in a RAID-5 configuration to Windows Server 2003.

Exam Questions

1. LT Bonn and Company is a publisher of cookbooks, restaurant guides, and other documents related to the restaurant industry. Because it is primarily a publishing business, it has large numbers of manuscripts stored on its servers. Even though some of the manuscripts are quite old, they are still referred to regularly.

Dave, the system administrator for LT Bonn and Company recently finished a major upgrade of the network. He upgraded all the desktops and servers from Windows NT 4.0 to Windows Server 2003 and Windows XP Professional.

Unfortunately, due to the recent recession, LT Bonn and Company has had to reduce its fee structure. Dave's IT budget has been cut, and he doesn't have any more funds for server upgrades. However, Dave is running out of space on his file servers. What can Dave do to keep his job?

Required Result:

Create additional space on the file servers.

Optional Desired Results:

All data should be easily accessible.

Achieve the required result as cheaply as possible.

Proposed Solution:

Compress the manuscript folders on the file servers using Windows Server 2003's NTFS compression. Make sure that the option is selected to compress files and subfolders.

Evaluation of Proposed Solution:

Which result(s) does the proposed solution produce?

A. The proposed solution produces the required result but neither of the optional results.

B. The proposed solution produces the required result and one of the optional results.

C. The proposed solution produces the required result and both of the optional results.

D. The proposed solution does not produce the required result.

2. You are the database administrator for a company that wants to deploy SQL Server for a new database project. The database will support your new real-time online ordering system.

Required Result:

The data in SQL Server is being updated regularly, so you need to make sure your server is configured for the best possible I/O performance.

Optional Desired Results:

All disks should be fault tolerant.

The data storage disks should be fault tolerant.

Proposed Solution:

Build a new Windows Server 2003 server. Configure a mirrored volume (RAID-1) for the system and boot partitions, and a RAID-5 volume containing five physical disks for the database.

Evaluation of Proposed Solution:

Which result(s) does the proposed solution produce?

A. The proposed solution produces the required result but neither of the optional results.

B. The proposed solution produces the required result and one of the optional results.

C. The proposed solution produces the required result and both of the optional results.

D. The proposed solution does not produce the required result.

3. You are the database administrator for a company that wants to deploy SQL Server for a new database project. The database will support your new real-time online ordering system.

APPLY YOUR KNOWLEDGE

Required Result:

The data in SQL Server is being updated regularly, so you need to make sure your server is configured for good I/O performance.

Optional Desired Results:

All disks should be fault tolerant.

Achieve the optional result with as few physical disks as possible.

Proposed Solution:

Build a new Windows Server 2003 server. Configure a mirrored volume (RAID-1) for the system and boot partitions, and a RAID-0 volume containing five physical disks for the database.

Evaluation of Proposed Solution:

Which result(s) does the proposed solution produce?

A. The proposed solution produces the required result but neither of the optional results.

B. The proposed solution produces the required result and one of the optional results.

C. The proposed solution produces the required result and both of the optional results.

D. The proposed solution does not produce the required result.

4. Jeff Harkness is the system administrator for Skelly Inc., a manufacturer of various knick-knacks and collectables. Jeff currently manages five Windows Server 2003 servers and 500 Windows XP Professional client computers.

   Due to the pending acquisition of Graham and Company, Jeff needs to add another Windows Server 2003 server to use for file storage.

Required Result:

Create additional space on the file servers.

Optional Desired Results:

The data-storage disks should be fault tolerant.

All disks should be fault tolerant.

Proposed Solution:

Build a new Windows Server 2003 server. Configure a mirrored volume (RAID-1) for the system and boot partitions, and a RAID-5 volume containing five physical disks for the file storage.

Evaluation of Proposed Solution:

Which result(s) does the proposed solution produce?

A. The proposed solution produces the required result but neither of the optional results.

B. The proposed solution produces the required result and one of the optional results.

C. The proposed solution produces the required result and both of the optional results.

D. The proposed solution does not produce the required result.

5. Mark Rein is the system administrator for Telecom Inc., a supplier of various telecommunications-related hardware and services. Mark currently manages a network comprised of 25 Windows Server 2003 servers, 30 Windows 2000 servers, 10 Windows NT 4.0 servers, 2,500 Windows XP Professional client computers, and miscellaneous Windows NT and Windows 9*x* computers.

Due to the pending end of life support of Windows NT 4.0, Mark needs to upgrade his current Windows NT 4.0 servers to either Windows 2000 or Windows Server 2003. All the Windows NT 4.0 servers utilize a mirrored volume for the system and boot partitions, and a striped volume for the data storage area.

Required Result:

Upgrade Windows NT 4.0 servers to a supported operating system.

Optional Desired Results:

The data-storage disks should be fault tolerant.

All disks should be fault tolerant.

Proposed Solution:

Upgrade the Windows NT 4.0 servers to Windows Server 2003. Keep the existing mirror volume (RAID-1) for the system and boot partitions and add a RAID-5 volume containing five physical disks for the data-storage area.

Evaluation of Proposed Solution:

Which result(s) does the proposed solution produce?

A. The proposed solution produces the required result but neither of the optional results.

B. The proposed solution produces the required result and one of the optional results.

C. The proposed solution produces the required result and both of the optional results.

D. The proposed solution does not produce the required result.

6. Davin has decided to configure a RAID-5 array on one of his servers to use for file storage. He has five 50GB SCSI hard disks available. What is the total amount of disk space that will be available after he finishes his configuration?

   A. 250GB

   B. 250MB

   C. 200GB

   D. 225GB

   E. 245GB

7. John has been assigned to build five Windows Server 2003 servers. His boss has specified that the system volume has to be fault tolerant. What type of volume can he configure in Windows Server 2003 to attain fault tolerance of the system volume?

   A. Simple volume

   B. Spanned volume

   C. Mirrored volume (RAID-1)

   D. Striped volume (RAID-0)

   E. Striped volume with parity (RAID-5)

8. Shelly is the junior system administrator for Travel, Inc. She has been assigned to compress the files and folders that contain the travel arrangements for Company B for the last quarter. She opens Windows Explorer and navigates to the necessary folders and selects the properties for the folders, but does not see the option to enable compression. What could be the possible cause of this?

   A. Shelly is not a member of the Disk Administrators group.

   B. The folders are encrypted using EFS.

APPLY YOUR KNOWLEDGE

C. Shelly is accessing a RAID-5 volume.

D. The volume is formatted using FAT32.

9. Joe wants to add fault tolerance to the storage disks on his Windows Server 2003 servers. His budget is tight this fiscal year, so he has to be able to balance fault tolerance with available storage capacity. Which of the following disk configurations will give Joe the best combination of fault tolerance and storage capacity?

    A. Striped volume

    B. Spanned volume

    C. Mirrored volume

    D. Striped with parity (RAID-5) volume

10. Jeff needs to add more space to his boot/system partition. The partition resides on a basic volume formatted with NTFS. What are Jeff's options to expand the partition?

    A. Open the Disk Management snap-in and select Extend Partition.

    B. Use the command-line utility `DISKPART.EXE` and use the commands to extend the partition.

    C. Convert the partition to a dynamic volume and then open the Disk Management snap-in and select Extend Volume.

    D. The partition cannot be expanded.

11. Jill, a junior system administrator, decided to move some old files to a new server that was purchased to hold old files. After carefully calculating the space that was needed, she created a volume to hold the old files. After moving the files, she noticed that the disk still had plenty of free space. What did Jill do wrong?

    A. She didn't calculate the needed space properly.

    B. She moved the wrong files.

    C. Compression was enabled on the new volume.

    D. The new server is more efficient than the old server.

12. Kevin, another junior system administrator, decided to move some old compressed files to a new server that was purchased to hold old files. After carefully calculating the space that was needed, he created a volume to hold the old files. Halfway through moving the files, he received the message that the disk had run out of free space. What was Kevin's problem?

    A. He didn't calculate the needed space properly.

    B. He moved the wrong files.

    C. He didn't enable compression on the new volume.

    D. The new server compressed files using a different method than the old server.

13. Joe needs to build a Windows Server 2003 server to host a mission-critical SQL database. What type of disk configuration should he use for the boot/system partition?

    A. Striped volume

    B. Spanned volume

    C. Mirrored volume (RAID-1)

    D. Striped with parity (RAID-5) volume

APPLY YOUR KNOWLEDGE

14. Joe needs to build a Windows Server 2003 server to host a mission-critical SQL database. He has already decided on the optimum configuration for his boot/system partition. However, he still needs to make a decision on the optimum configuration for the disks used to store his database. His database will be mostly read with batch updates after business hours. What type of disk configuration should he use for the database?

    A. Striped volume

    B. Spanned volume

    C. Mirrored volume (RAID-1)

    D. Striped with parity (RAID-5) volume

15. Loren is responsible for monitoring an organization that has over 2,000 Windows Server 2003 servers. While making his daily check of the servers, he discovers that one of them has suffered the failure of a mirrored volume. Because the server supports hot-plug drives, what are the first steps that he should perform to accomplish the repair?

    A. Replace the drive, open the Disk Management snap-in, and select Re-Scan drives.

    B. Power down the server, replace the drive, and then power up the server.

    C. Replace the drive and open the Add/Remove Hardware Wizard.

    D. Replace the drive, open the Disk Management snap-in, and create a new mirrored volume.

Answers to Review Questions

1. A Windows 2003 boot disk can be used to start your server if the files in the system partition become corrupted or otherwise damaged. A Windows Server 2003 boot disk must be formatted on a Windows Server 2003 server, and the files in the system partition must be copied to it. The difference between a Windows Server 2003 boot disk and a DOS boot disk is that a floppy cannot contain the Windows Server 2003 operating system, so in effect a Windows Server 2003 boot disk is just a copy of the system partition.

2. The two disk types available in Windows Server 2003 are basic and dynamic. A basic disk is the disk type that has been used since the days of MS-DOS and uses partitions and logical drives. Dynamic disks were first introduced in Windows 2000. They subdivide the physical disk into volumes and allow several different configurations, including fault tolerant.

3. In Windows Server 2003, the main tool used to configure both basic and dynamic disks is the Disk Management snap-in. The Disk Management snap-in can be started from the Computer Management MMC, or it can be started by entering the command `diskmgmt.msc`. The other tool is the command-line utility `DISKPART.EXE`, which allows you to perform all the functions that can be accomplished from the Disk Management snap-in, in addition to a few others, such as expanding basic disks. The caveat is that `DISKPART` doesn't provide error checking, and it allows you to perform actions that can be very destructive, such as deleting the system partition.

APPLY YOUR KNOWLEDGE

4. A basic disk is a legacy configuration that was used in various operating systems, including past versions of Windows and MS-DOS. It subdivides the physical disks into two types of partitions: primary and extended. Each primary partition is assigned a drive letter, whereas an extended partition can contain multiple logical drives, each assigned their own drive letter. A dynamic disk is subdivided into volumes. There are five types of volumes: simple, spanned, striped, mirrored, and striped with parity, with the last two being fault tolerant.

5. Files, folders, and volumes can be compressed by selecting the Compression option from the Properties page of the object or via the command-line utility `COMPACT.EXE`.

6. Upgrading a previous version of Windows on a server that is configured with basic disks configured as spanned, mirrored, striped, or striped with parity to Windows Server 2003 is not supported. After the upgrade, you will not be able to access these disks.

Answers to Exam Questions

1. **C.** The proposed solution produces the required result and both of the optional results. Windows Server 2003 includes the NTFS compression feature. This feature allows you to selectively compress files, folders, and volumes. This allows Dave to store more data on existing volumes. When turning on compression, you can turn it on for a volume or folder, but that will only result in new files created or copied into that volume or folder being compressed. Because the files are being left in place and are not being archived to offline storage, they are still readily accessible. In addition, the NTFS compression feature is included with Windows Server 2003, and you can't get any cheaper than free.

2. **D.** The solution does not meet the required result. Although the suggested disk configuration is certainly fault tolerant, a database that requires good write performance should not be put on a RAID-5 volume. RAID-5 achieves its fault tolerance by generating parity so that your data can be re-created if a disk is lost. This parity generation creates additional overhead when writing, so write performance is negatively impacted.

3. **A.** The suggested disk configuration meets the required results. A RAID-0 volume stripes the data across multiple volumes. This type of configuration produces the highest write performance of any of the disk configurations in Windows Server 2003. However, a RAID-0 volume is not fault tolerant; if you lose a disk, you lose the volume.

4. **C.** The suggested actions meet the required results and both optional results. Building a new server will provide more space to accommodate the new organization, and mirroring the boot/system disks and storing the data on a RAID-5 array will provide fault tolerance for all disks in the server.

5. **D.** The proposed solution will simply not work. An upgrade from Windows NT 4.0 or Windows 2000 on a computer using basic disks in a mirrored volume to Windows Server 2003 is not supported.

6. **C.** 200GB is the correct answer. A RAID-5 array will always use the equivalent space of one of the disks in the array for parity information.

APPLY YOUR KNOWLEDGE

7. **C.** The only type of volume that supports fault tolerance that can contain a system volume is a mirrored volume (RAID-1).

8. **D**. Compression is supported only on NTFS volumes. Although EFS and compression are mutually exclusive, the compression option will still be displayed.

9. **D**. The striped with parity volume will give Joe the best combination of fault tolerance and storage capacity. Of the choices available, only RAID-1 (mirrored volume) and RAID-5 offer fault tolerance. Whereas RAID-1 results in a 50% cost in disk space, RAID-5 exacts less overhead. For example, in a configuration of four drives of 10GB each, RAID-5 will require 10GB for parity, or 25%.

10. **C**. The Disk Management snap-in cannot be used to extend a partition on a basic disk. Although `DISKPART.EXE` can be used to expand a partition on a basic disk, it cannot extend the partition from which the system was booted. A basic partition must be converted to a dynamic volume before it can be extended. The Disk Management snap-in can be used to extend a volume on a dynamic disk, even the one that the system was booted from.

11. **C.** When a file is moved from an uncompressed volume to a compressed volume, it will be compressed. A file that is moved or copied to another volume will always receive the attributes of the container that it is moved or copied into.

12. **C**. When a file is moved from a compressed volume to an uncompressed volume, it will be uncompressed. A file that is moved or copied to another volume will always receive the attributes of the container that it is moved or copied into.

13. **C**. Of the choices available, only RAID-1 and RAID-5 offer fault tolerance. However, only the RAID-1 configuration can be used for boot partitions.

14. **D**. Of the choices available, only RAID-1 and RAID-5 offer fault tolerance. Of these two configurations, RAID-5 offers the best read performance because the data is striped across multiple volumes, thereby increasing read efficiency. However, because RAID-5 has to write parity information with the data, write performance is not optimal. Fortunately, updates to the database will be performed during off hours, so that should not be a problem.

15. **A**. The proper way to start the procedure on a server that uses hot-plug drives is to replace the drive and then perform a rescan in the Disk Management snap-in. This will start the Disk Initialization Wizard. Answer B would work in some circumstances. However, if the primary drive of a mirrored volume that is being used for the boot/system partition fails, you will not be able to restart your server without a fault-tolerant boot floppy.

Suggested Readings and Resources

1. Microsoft Official Curriculum Course 2275: Maintaining a Microsoft Windows Server 2003 Environment
   - Module 5: Managing Disks
   - Module 6: Managing Data Storage
2. Microsoft Official Curriculum Course 2270: Updating Support Skills from Microsoft Windows NT 4.0 to the Windows Server 2003 Family
   - Module 12: Managing File Resources
   - Module 15: Performing Disk Management
   - Module 16: Implementing Disaster Protection
3. Microsoft Official Curriculum Course 2274: Managing a Microsoft Windows Server 2003 Environment
   - Module 5: Managing Access to Resources
4. Non-Microsoft Resources
   - Boswell, William. *Inside Windows Server 2003.* New Riders, 2003. ISBN: 0735711585.
   - Matthews, Marty. *Windows Server 2003: A Beginners Guide.* McGraw-Hill, 2003. ISBN: 0072193093.
   - Minasi, Mark, et al. *Mark Minasi's Windows XP and Server 2003 Resource Kit.* Sybex, 2003. ISBN: 0782140807.
   - Minasi, Mark, et al. *Mastering Windows Server 2003 Server.* Sybex, 2003. ISBN: 0782141307.
   - Shapiro, Jeffrey, et al. *Windows Server 2003 Bible.* John Wiley and Sons, 2003. ISBN: 0764549375.

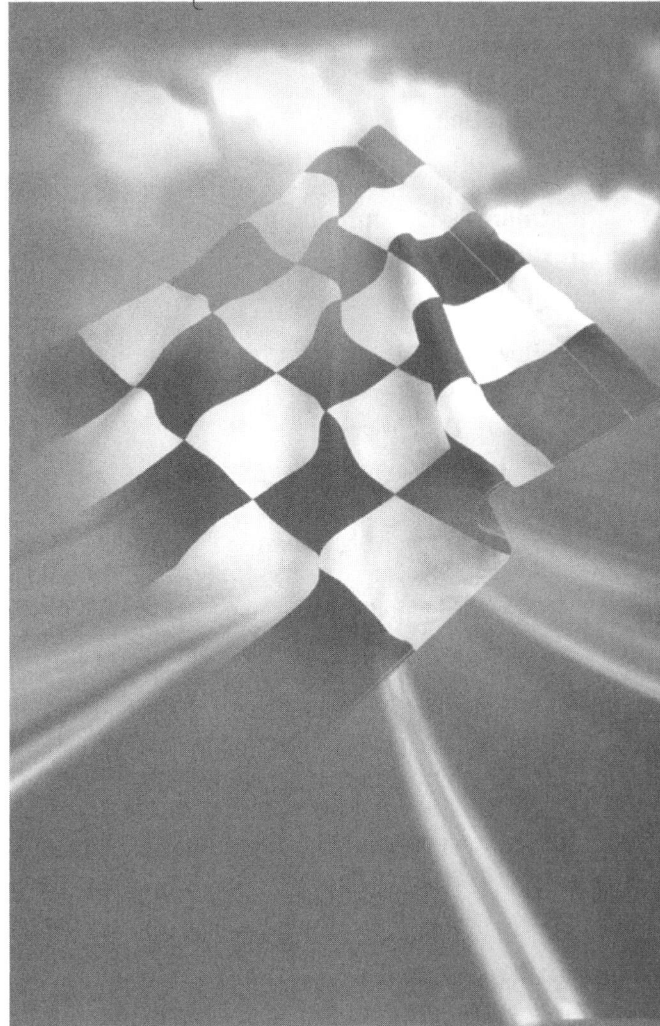

CHAPTER 2

Managing and Troubleshooting Hardware Devices

OBJECTIVES

This chapter covers the following Microsoft-specified objectives for the "Managing and Maintaining Physical and Logical Devices" section of the Managing and Maintaining a Microsoft Windows Server 2003 Environment exam:

Install and configure server hardware devices.

- **Configure driver-signing options.**
- **Configure resource settings for a device.**
- **Configure device properties and settings.**

▶ Windows Server 2003 operates much as Windows Server 2000 and Windows XP do in working with hardware devices. We explain how you control the way the system deals with unsigned device drivers and how to configure driver settings for hardware devices.

Monitor server hardware.

▶ In managing your server, you will need to monitor its hardware. We explain how to monitor your system using the Device Manager, Hardware Troubleshooting Wizard, and Control Panel items, including the Add Hardware, Mouse, and Printers and Faxes applets.

Troubleshoot server hardware devices.

- **Diagnose and resolve issues related to hardware settings.**
- **Diagnose and resolve issues related to server hardware and hardware driver upgrades.**

▶ If there's one thing sure in computing, it's that there will be problems with the computer hardware. We provide some methods for determining what devices are at fault and describe how to resolve issues due to hardware settings and hardware device drivers.

OUTLINE

STUDY STRATEGIES

- To understand hardware devices so that you can manage and troubleshoot them, you need to understand what properties and settings can be managed, as well as when manual configuration is necessary. You should have access to a Windows Server 2003 computer, but you won't be missing much if you investigate on a Windows XP computer instead.
- Make sure you are familiar with Plug and Play and how it ties in with the Advanced Configuration and Power Interface (ACPI) standard.
- Run File Signature Verification and work with the Control Panel applets to become familiar with their settings.

INTRODUCTION

The devices (or components) that make up a computer must communicate effectively, without interference. Having two or more devices trying to use the same communication channel causes errors or even system crashes, so it's critical that the devices are configured correctly.

In the early days of network administration, it was common for configuration errors to occur because these settings were performed manually, and the work was error prone. The development of the Plug and Play specification and the Advanced Configuration and Power Interface (ACPI) standard for system boards made the whole process automatic. It is very worthwhile for an administrator to insist that only devices that conform to these standards be used.

This chapter discusses installing and configuring hardware devices, ensuring that the drivers loaded to operate the devices are uncorrupted and come from reputable sources, and troubleshooting hardware issues.

INSTALLING AND CONFIGURING HARDWARE DEVICES

In an ideal world, if you wanted to install a new device in your server, you would simply power down the server, insert the new device, make sure it has power and signal cable attachments, and then power up the server. The new device would be ready immediately.

That is the goal of the people who design hardware architecture, and, actually, with modern hardware and modern operating systems, we're almost there. With a motherboard that meets the ACPI standard, Windows Server 2003 recognizes and configures all hardware that is built to the Plug and Play specification.

However, this is not an ideal world. If you have older devices, particularly devices that were built to the Industry Standard Architecture (ISA) specifications, Plug and Play won't be able to help you. (Some Plug and Play drivers were written for later ISA devices, but they don't always work effectively.) Sometimes the device is not recognized, or the device driver is corrupted or not available. That's where the skills covered in this section will come in handy.

IN THE FIELD

ISA FREE

A lot of workstations and just about all servers shipping these days are designed without ISA slots. This makes working with hardware much easier because you just have to deal with the different flavors of PCI.

What's the ACPI Standard?

ACPI is the current standard for communication with a motherboard's Basic Input/Output System (BIOS). The BIOS is the mechanism that allows an operating system to communicate with the devices on the computer. In older standards, Plug and Play negotiation and configuration was handled in hardware, but in an ACPI system, the configuration is handled by the operating system.

With ACPI, all devices that have power-management capabilities (such as sleep mode or hibernation) can be controlled by the operating system. This allows the operating system to selectively shut down devices not currently in use, to give maximum battery life to portable computing devices. ACPI is also needed for the OnNow Device Power Management initiative, which allows a computer to be started by simply touching any key on the computer's keyboard. ACPI is installed only if all components detected during setup support power management. This is because older components that do not support ACPI typically exhibit erratic behavior and could potentially cause system crashes.

How Does the Operating System Manage a Device?

A server contains many hardware devices: disk drives, network cards, display adapters, and any of a large number of peripherals. For them to be usable by the system, each must be identified by the operating system, and the appropriate device driver must be loaded.

A *device driver* is a program that passes requests between the operating system and the device. For example, the user presses the *A* key on the keyboard, and the keyboard device driver notifies the operating system that *A* has been pressed on that device. Or, the program or operating system sends data to a disk drive: The device driver receives the data from the operating system and transfers it to the disk drive.

Where Do Device Drivers Come From?

Device drivers are critical to the proper operation of hardware devices, so it's important that you understand where they come from. If the device is listed on the Hardware Compatibility List (HCL) for an operating system, the device driver may have been written by the device manufacturer, shipped to Microsoft, and supplied on the distribution CD-ROM for the operating system. Alternatively, for common devices, Microsoft may provide a generic driver, and manufacturers write additions to control specific features of their devices.

If you can't find a driver for a particular device on the Windows Server 2003 distribution CD-ROM, the device may have been produced after the Windows Server 2003 CD-ROM was made. In that case, the driver may be available on the Microsoft Web site or on the manufacturer's Web site.

IN THE FIELD

QUICK FIX

If a device is not acting properly, a possible solution is to download the latest driver from the manufacturer's Web site. This may fix the problem right away, and even if it doesn't, you can be sure the first thing the manufacturer's technical support staff will ask you is the version of the driver. However, before installing any new drivers, be sure to examine the supporting documentation for known issues.

What Drivers Are Running on My Computer?

If you want to find out what drivers are currently running on your system, the command-line utility `driverquery.exe` lists the running drivers for you nicely. At a command prompt, enter `driverquery >c:\driverquery.txt` to put the output into the `c:\driveryquery.txt` file. Then you can read it with Notepad. This utility is available only in Windows XP and Windows Server 2003.

If you use the `/fo csv` switch, the output from `driverquery.exe` will be created in comma-separated value (CSV) format, making it suitable for loading into a database or a spreadsheet for analysis. Using the `/s` switch allows you to specify a remote system, and the `/si` switch provides information about signed drivers (see the next section). The following command provides a listing in CSV format (`fo csv`) of the drivers running on the remote system MERCURY (`/s mercury`), including information about signed drivers (`/si`):

```
driverquery /fo csv /s mercury /si
```

The first few lines of the output are as follows:

```
"DeviceName","InfName","IsSigned","Manufacturer"
"Advanced Configuration and Power Interface (ACPI) PC",
➥"hal.inf","TRUE","(Standard computers)"
"Microsoft ACPI-Compliant System","acpi.inf","TRUE","Microsoft"
"Processor","cpu.inf","TRUE","(Standard processor types)"
```

What Is Driver Signing and Why Should I Care?

Device drivers are heavily used and very close to the kernel of the operating system. As a result, it is important that the device drivers in use are supplied by reputable sources. (Imagine the chaos caused by the installation of a bad driver for a backup tape drive. A seemingly perfect backup might turn out to be totally unusable!)

Microsoft requests that manufacturers submit their drivers to be tested by the Windows Hardware Quality Labs (WHQL). Drivers submitted to WHQL that pass the certification tests for Windows Server 2003 are given a Microsoft digital signature. When the driver finishes the testing phase and is approved, a catalog (`*.cat`) is created. The CAT file is a hash of the driver binary file and other relevant information. This CAT file is then digitally signed with the Microsoft private key.

When Windows Server 2003 inspects the driver, it examines the catalog file that is included. If the signature is authenticated, this is a guarantee that the driver was created by the owner of the catalog file and that the driver has not been tampered with since it was created. Signed driver files are distributed through the following methods, as well as on the Windows Server 2003 CD-ROM:

- Windows service packs
- Hotfix distributions
- Operating system upgrades
- Windows Update
- Windows Device Manager/Class Installer

For the greatest device driver security, many administrators would want to ensure that only signed device drivers are loaded. To achieve this situation, Windows Server 2003 can be configured to refuse to load unsigned drivers.

Configuring Driver-signing Options for a Single Computer

Normally, you would want to have only signed device drivers on your system. That is definitely the most secure way of operating. But what if you want to use a device driver that for some reason has not been signed? It might be a hot-off-the-press driver from the manufacturer's technical support staff, for example, that you need to try. Or it might be the only driver available for a particular device that you must use. In that case, you can change the default behavior of Windows Server 2003 to allow unsigned drivers to be loaded. Step by Step 2.1 walks you through this process.

STEP BY STEP

2.1 Configuring Windows Server 2003 to Allow Loading of Unsigned Drivers

1. Click Start, Control Panel, System and then click the Hardware tab.
2. Click Driver Signing.

3. In the Driver Signing Options dialog box, in the What Action Do You Want Windows to Take? section, click Ignore—Install the Software Anyway and Don't Ask for My Approval, as shown in Figure 2.1.

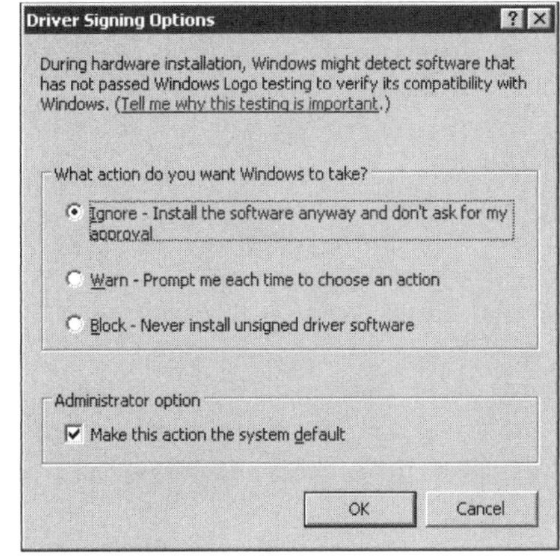

FIGURE 2.1
To instruct Windows Server 2003 to allow loading of unsigned drivers, click Ignore—Install the Software Anyway and Don't Ask for My Approval.

Of course, it's not recommended that you leave your server configured this way. This is because with this type of configuration, the operating system would allow any unsigned driver to be installed. You should check back with your hardware vendor frequently to get a signed version of the driver as soon as possible, and you should reconfigure the driver-signing options when the signed driver is installed. Alternatively, to sidestep the problem completely, consider removing the problem device from the computer and substituting a device for which signed drivers are available.

As soon as you have installed the unsigned driver, you should return to the Driver Signing Options dialog box and choose Block—Never Install Unsigned Driver Software.

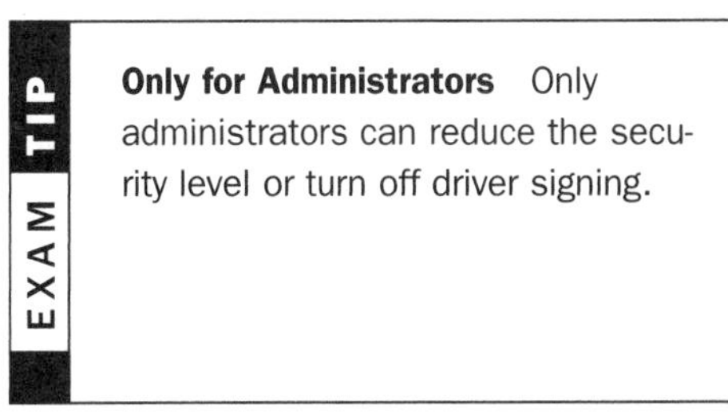

EXAM TIP

Only for Administrators Only administrators can reduce the security level or turn off driver signing.

Configuring Driver-signing Options for Several Computers at Once

What if you want to ensure that there will be no unsigned drivers at all in your network? As you have seen, it's not difficult to change the driver-signing options on a few servers by following the steps just given on each one. But if you have hundreds or thousands of Windows 2000 Professional or Windows XP Professional workstations on your network and you want to protect all of them from unsigned drivers, that would be a huge task. If you're like most administrators, you would prefer to manage all these workstations at once, instead of configuring each one individually. Not only is this faster, it's also easier than keeping track of which computers have been configured.

This is a job for Group Policies! You can create a Group Policy Object (GPO) and apply it to workstations in a given part of the Active Directory tree. For example, there is a Workstations OU (Organizational Unit) under the Calgary OU in the lantrainers.local tree (see Figure 2.2 for the structure of the lantrainers.local tree).

We can create a Group Policy Object to ensure that no unsigned drivers can be loaded. Step by Step 2.2 shows how to do this, starting with creating the necessary OU structure. Note that you must be a domain administrator, or have limited administrator rights delegated to you, to be able to create and manage GPOs.

STEP BY STEP

2.2 Creating a Group Policy Object to Prohibit the Loading of Unsigned Drivers

1. Click Start, Administrative Tools, Active Directory Users and Computers.
2. In the left pane, click the domain object (see Figure 2.2).

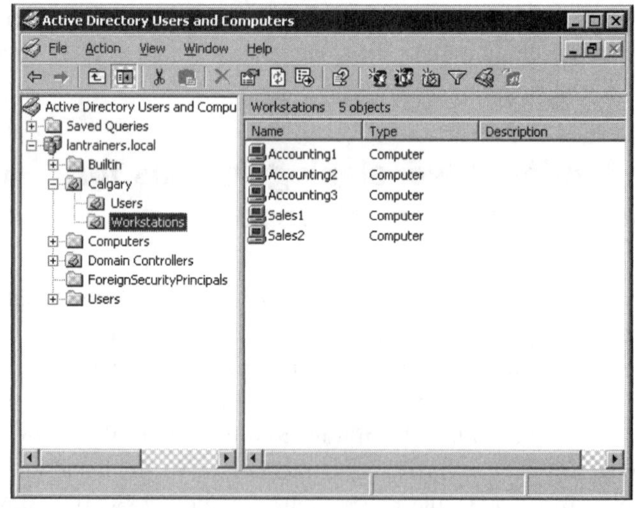

FIGURE 2.2▶
Click the domain object (Lantrainers.local in this example) to begin creating the Group Policy Object.

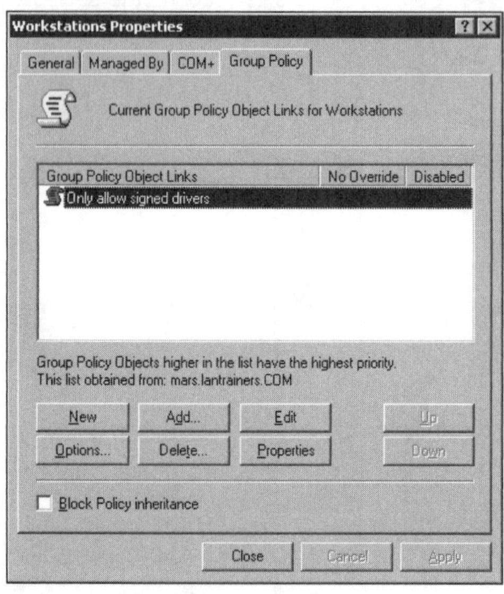

FIGURE 2.3▲
Click New to start creating a Group Policy Object and then type the policy object's name. Use a name that indicates the purpose of the policy.

3. Choose Action, New, Organizational Unit and then type **Calgary**.
4. Select the Calgary OU, choose Action, New, Organizational Unit, and type **Workstations**.
5. Now select Workstations and choose Actions, Properties. Then click the Group Policy tab.
6. Click New and then name the new Group Policy Object **Only allow signed drivers**, as shown in Figure 2.3.

7. Click Edit and navigate to Computer Configuration, Windows Settings, Security Settings, Local Policies, Security Options.
8. In the right pane, select Devices: Unsigned Driver Installation Behavior, as shown in Figure 2.4.

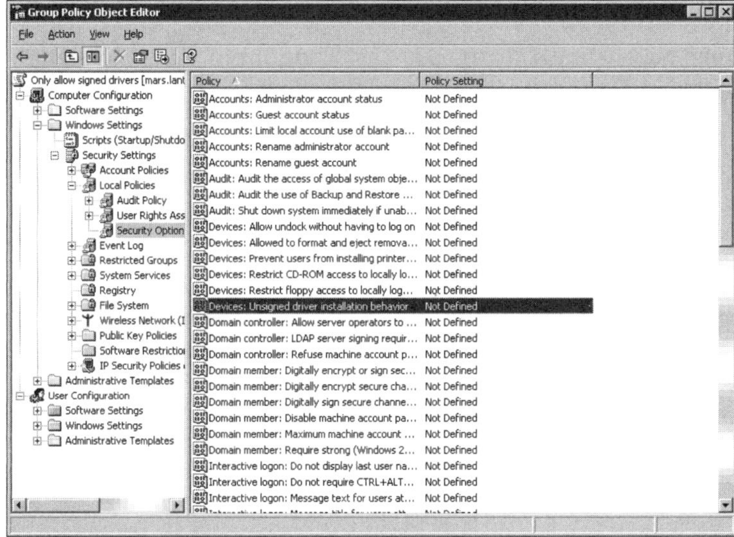

FIGURE 2.4
To control the operation of Windows Server 2003 when asked to load an unsigned driver, choose the policy Devices: Unsigned Driver Installation Behavior and get its properties.

9. Select Actions, Properties and then select Define This Policy Setting. Ensure that Do Not Allow Installation is showing in the drop-down box and then click OK. You'll see that the Policy Setting column now shows "Do Not Allow Installation" for this policy.
10. Close the Group Policy dialog boxes until you are back to the main Active Directory Users and Computers window.
11. Open a command prompt, type `GPUDATE /force`, and press Enter to apply the new policy immediately.

> NOTE
> **Group Policy Management Console** The preceding steps will be slightly different if the Group Policy Management Console is installed.

Because this policy is linked to the Workstations OU, it will be applied to each of the computers whose accounts are located in that OU or in any OUs subordinate to the Workstations OU. Also, now that the policy has been created, it can be linked to any other OU in the Active Directory, such as to the Edmonton Workstations OU when it is created.

Determining Whether a Computer Has Unsigned Drivers

Imagine you've just been made administrator of a network, and you want to know if there are any unsigned drivers on the computers you're responsible for. Microsoft has provided a tool with Windows 2003, Windows 2000, and Windows XP to check for exactly this situation. That tool is *File Signature Verification*, and you access it by using Start, Run, `sigverif.exe`. The dialog box in Figure 2.5 shows the start of this process.

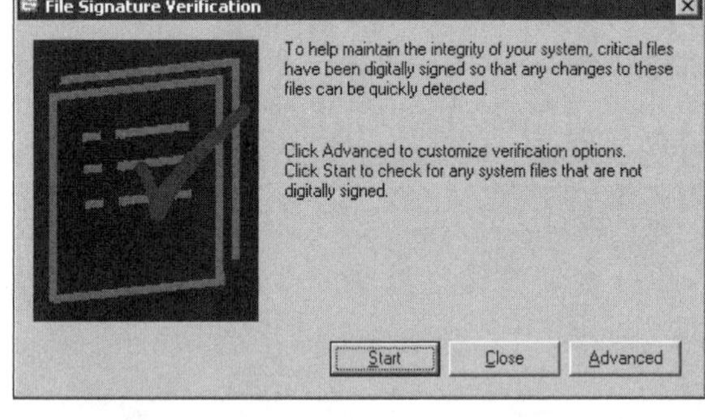

FIGURE 2.5
The starting screen for File Signature Verification. Click the Advanced button to control how the program runs.

FIGURE 2.6
Normally you would want to check the files in the Windows folder and its subdirectories, but you can choose to verify specific file types and folders.

As you can see from the Advanced dialog box, shown in Figure 2.6, you can have File Signature Verification check only system files or check the file types you specify in a folder you browse to.

When you click OK in the File Signature Verification dialog box, there will be a delay of a minute or more while every system file is checked for a signature. As you can see from Figure 2.7, several unsigned files exist on the sample Windows Server 2003 computer. These are Windows 2000 unsigned drivers for the Hewlett-Packard OfficeJet printer.

As you can see in Figure 2.6, the advanced settings allow you to narrow your search to specific file types and locations.

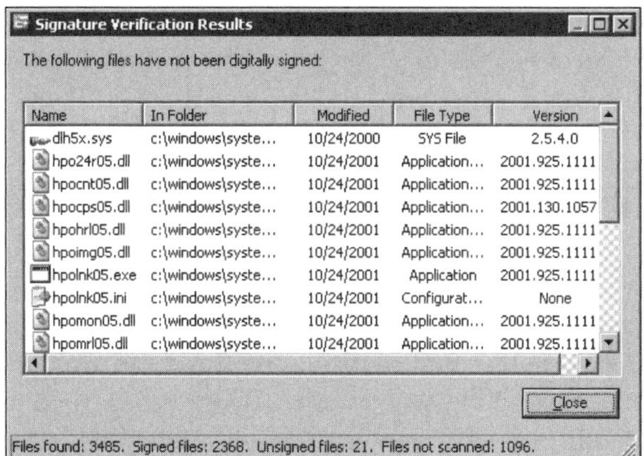

FIGURE 2.7
The sample Windows Server 2003 computer has 21 unsigned files.

Other Methods for Protecting Device Drivers

Device drivers and other system files are automatically protected against improper replacement by the Windows File Protection facility. This facility runs in the background (invisible to the user and the administrator) and is alerted whenever a file in a protected folder is changed. It determines whether the new version of the file is signed, and if not, Windows File Protection automatically rolls back the file to the version kept in the %systemroot%\system32\dllcache folder. If the desired version of the file is not in the dllcache folder, Windows File Protection asks for the Windows Server 2003 CD-ROM to be mounted, and it copies the file from there.

IN THE FIELD

WINDOWS FILE PROTECTION

For some reason, when Windows File Protection asks for the Windows Server 2003 CD, it really wants that CD! Just having a handy copy of the i386 directory on a file share doesn't seem to work.

An administrator can run the System File Checker (`sfc.exe`) to explicitly schedule a scan of the system files immediately, at the next reboot, or at every reboot. Also, if the dllcache folder is corrupted or needs to be repopulated for some other reason, the administrator can run the System File Checker (SFC) with the `/purgecache` switch to cause the folder to be emptied and reloaded.

Configuring Resource Settings for a Device

On a Windows Server 2003 machine, it is rarely necessary to configure devices manually because most hardware sold since 1995 complies with the Plug and Play specification. The operating system identifies any conflicts and configures the devices to avoid them. However, you should know how to configure settings, in case you need to resolve a conflict on non–Plug and Play devices.

What Are Resource Settings?

Resource settings are mechanisms by which the device can communicate with other hardware or the operating system. The following list describes some resources in greater detail:

- Direct memory access (DMA) allows a device to read from the computer's memory, or write to it, without using the computer's processor (CPU). Each device using DMA must have a DMA channel dedicated for its use.
- An interrupt request (IRQ) line is a hardware channel line over which a device can interrupt the CPU for service. Some devices can share an IRQ line; others must have a dedicated IRQ.
- An input/output (I/O) port is another channel through which data is transferred between a device and the CPU. It acts like an area of memory that can be read from, and written to, by the device and the CPU. I/O ports cannot be shared.

- A memory address is an area of memory allocated to the device driver, for communication between the device and the operating system.

If two devices attempt to use the same resources, and the particular resource is not sharable, one or both of the devices may be unusable.

Configuring Device Properties and Settings

In general, there is no need to change the configured settings of a device. What might require you to do so is a situation in which one or more of the communications channels used by a device is already in use by another device. This is known as a *conflict*.

To configure a device's properties and settings, the tool to use is Device Manager. Device Manager is available as a snap-in to a Microsoft Management Console (MMC), as a subentry under Computer Management, and from the Hardware tab of System Properties. If you need another way to get to Device Manager, you can create a desktop shortcut, giving `devmgmt.msc` as the location of the item.

It's a good idea to start Device Manager occasionally, to check that all devices are working properly. Figure 2.8 shows Device Manager with no devices in an error state. (Devices that are not working properly are shown with a yellow question mark icon. Devices that are disabled have a red *X* over the icon.)

To see the properties of a device, double-click its icon in the Device Manager listing. Figure 2.9 shows the General tab of the PS/2 Compatible Mouse Properties dialog box.

Click the Advanced Settings tab, if there is one, to see special settings for this type of device. See Figure 2.10 for the advanced settings for the PS/2 mouse.

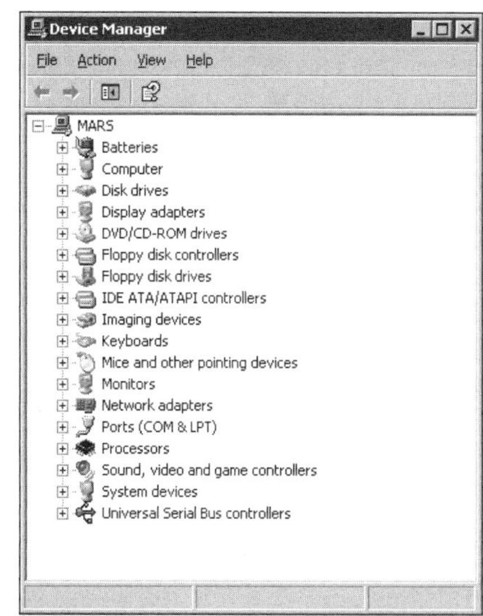

FIGURE 2.8
From within Device Manager, double-click a device's icon to see its properties.

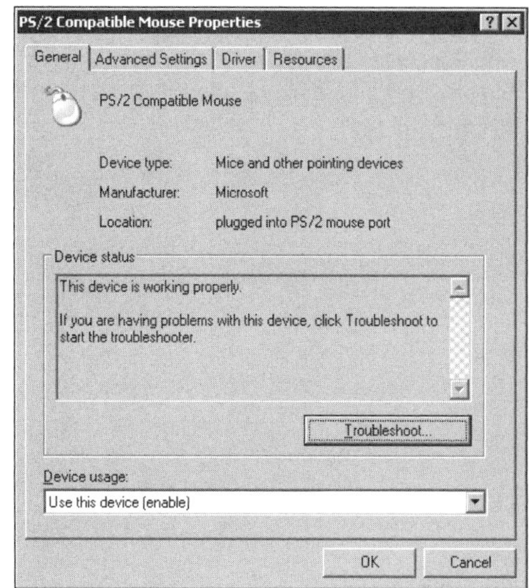

FIGURE 2.9
The General tab shows basic information about the device, has a Troubleshoot button in case there are problems, and allows you to enable or disable the device in the current configuration.

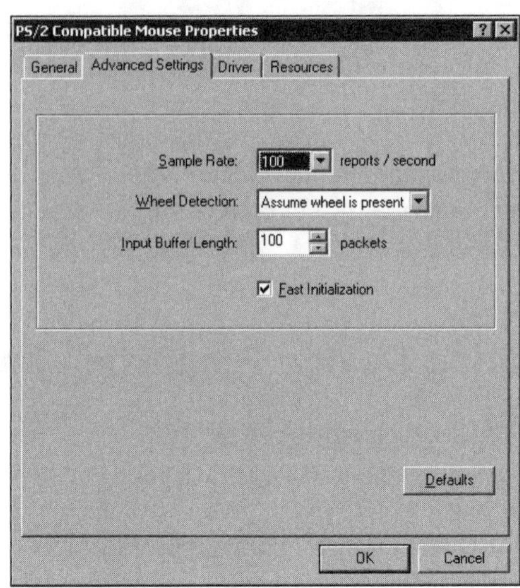

FIGURE 2.10▶
The Advanced Settings tab allows you to make changes to the special settings for a device.

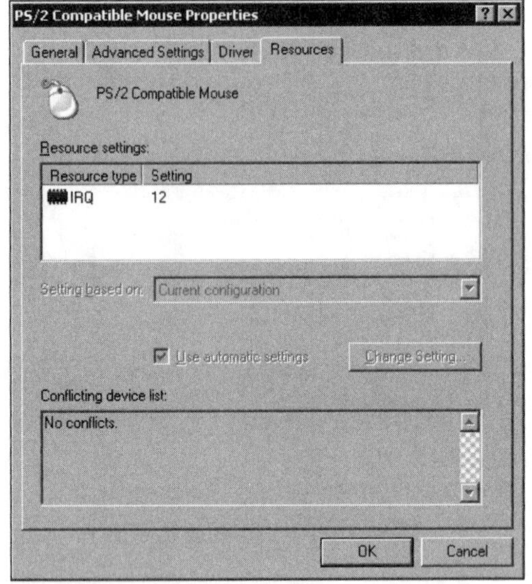

FIGURE 2.11▲
The Resources tab for the PS/2 mouse is very simple. Only one resource, the IRQ level, is used, and it cannot be changed.

Select the Resources tab to see what system resources are reserved for the device. Figure 2.11 shows this tab.

A more complex set of resources is allocated to the display driver. In Figure 2.12, you'll see that IRQ, I/O port, and memory resources are allocated.

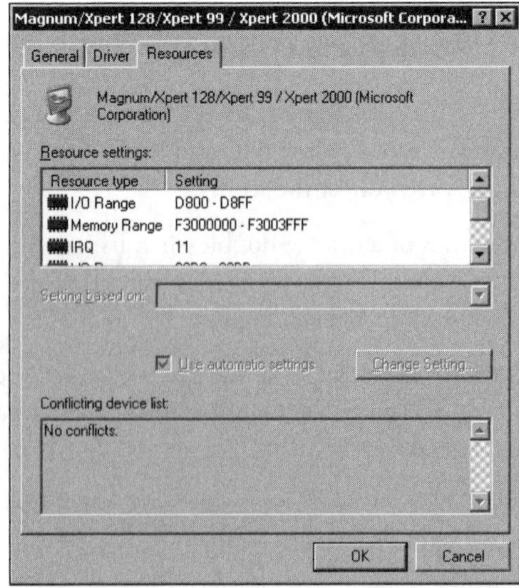

FIGURE 2.12
A display monitor is substantially more complex than a mouse. It uses several channels to communicate with the CPU.

Note the check box Use Automatic Settings, which is set by default. If this check box is enabled, it can be cleared, and then you can manually select the settings you want to use.

If all combinations of settings result in conflicts, you may find that it is impossible to use that combination of devices, and one of them will have to be removed or disabled.

To see the resources assigned on your computer, open Device Manager and on the View menu, choose Resources by Type. Then click the plus sign beside each resource type. Figure 2.13 shows the IRQ assignments on the sample server.

> NOTE
>
> **Automatic Settings** For most devices, you will find that the Use Automatic Settings check box is both checked, meaning that automatic settings will be used, and dimmed, meaning that you cannot access the check box. This happens when (a) there are no alternate settings for that resource on the device or (b) the device's resources are controlled by Plug and Play

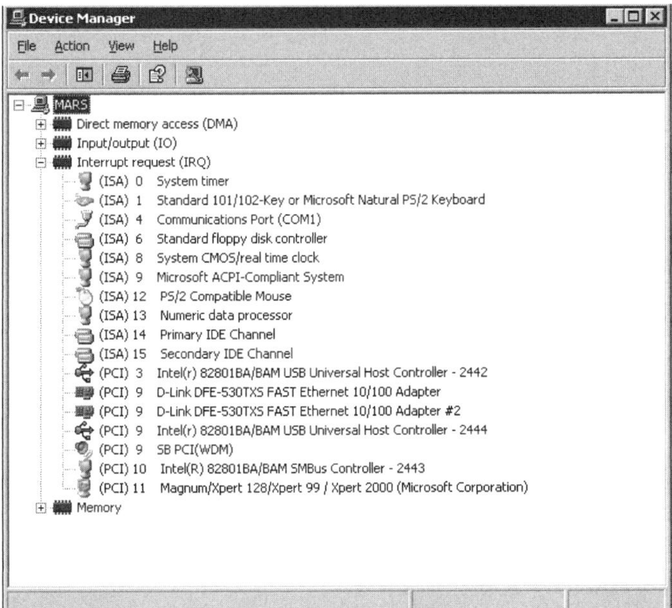

FIGURE 2.13
The assigned IRQ resources are visible by choosing View, Resources by Type.

Managing Drivers for Printers and Faxes

Device Manager does not manage device drivers for printers and fax devices. They are managed through the Printers and Faxes applet in Control Panel. When you select a printer in Printers and Faxes and then choose Set Printer Properties from the printer tasks, a dialog box like the one shown in Figure 2.14 is displayed.

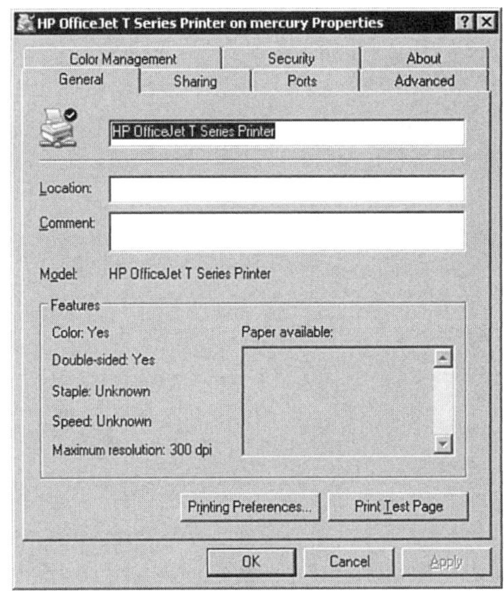

FIGURE 2.14
You can set properties for a printer via the Printers and Faxes applet of the Control Panel.

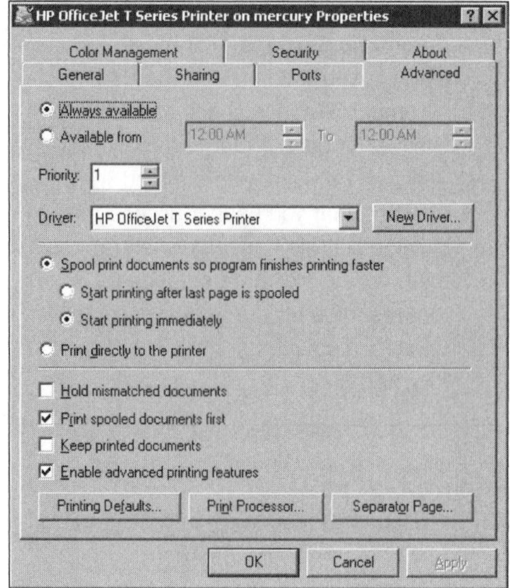

FIGURE 2.15
Click the New Driver button to start the Add Printer Driver Wizard.

When you click the Advanced tab, you will see the name of the driver currently in use. If you click the New Driver button, the Add Printer Driver Wizard starts up. See Figure 2.15 for the Advanced tab view of the Printer Properties dialog box.

Assuming you have downloaded the new driver to a location on your computer's hard drive, you can use the Have Disk button to browse to that location, and the Add Printer Driver Wizard updates your printer's driver.

Monitoring Server Hardware

The administrators of a well-run computing organization perform regularly scheduled tasks to ensure the computing infrastructure is operating properly. One of these tasks is to check that all devices on each of the servers in the organization are functional. Device Manager is the tool to use for checking the functionality of the devices on a server.

Using Device Manager

To start Device Manager, right-click My Computer, choose Manage, and in the left pane, under System Tools, select Device Manager. If any devices are not working properly, they will be identified with a yellow question mark icon, as shown in Figure 2.16.

FIGURE 2.16
Under Other Devices, you will see that the Belkin UPS has a question mark beside it. To see the reason for the question mark, we double-click the device.

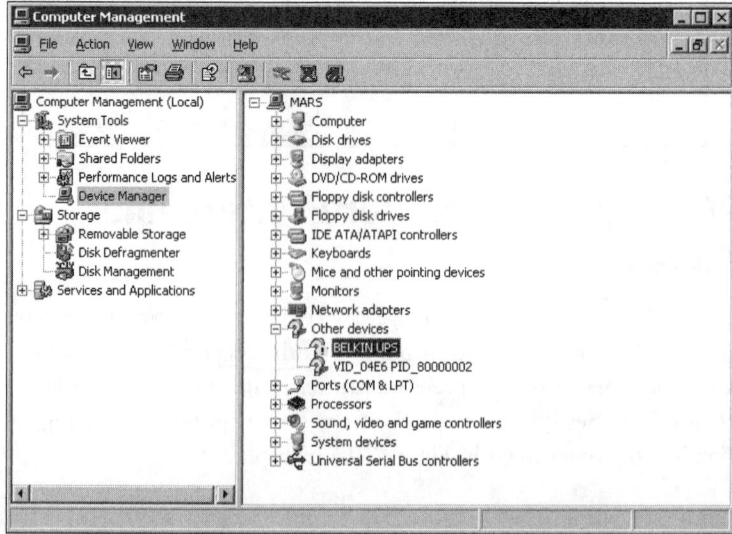

As you can see from Figure 2.17, the drivers have not been installed for the Belkin UPS. When we click Reinstall Driver, we'll be able to browse to the CD-ROM where the drivers are located.

The driver supplied is not signed, and from its name it appears that it was written for Windows 2000, not Windows Server 2003. See the warning in Figure 2.18.

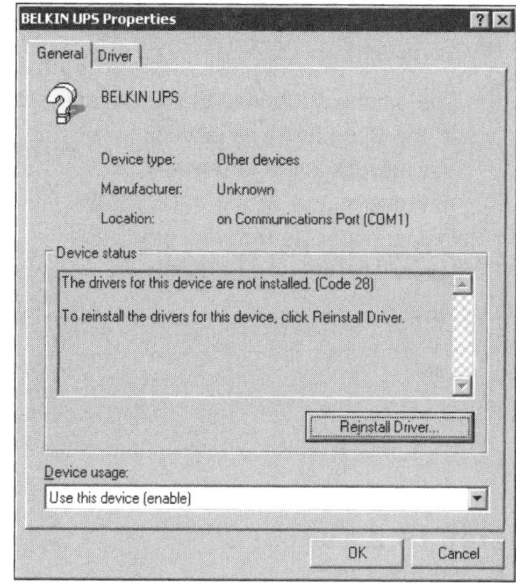

FIGURE 2.17▲
The reason for the error condition is that the drivers have not been loaded.

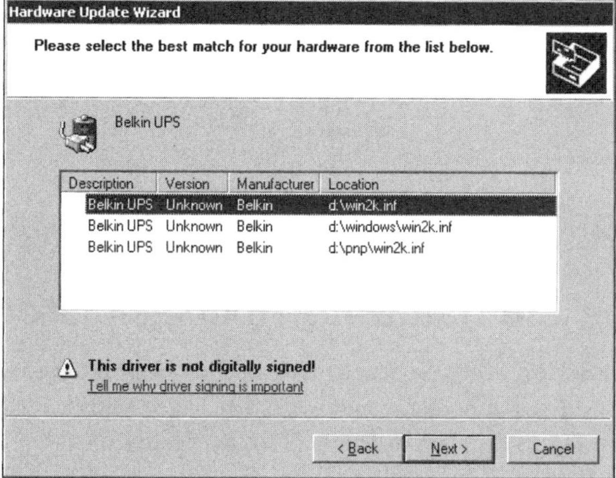

FIGURE 2.18◀
The three drivers listed are all unsigned.

Now we have a dilemma. Do we install an old driver that may not work well (or may even cause system instability), or do we work without the ability to control the UPS? Because we think control of the UPS is very important and we know the change we have just made (in case there is a problem and we need to back out the change), we decide to proceed. After a minute the driver is installed, and the Device Manager screen now appears as shown in Figure 2.19.

We should remember to go to the Belkin Web site periodically, to search for a signed driver written for Windows Server 2003.

NOTE

Nonpresent Devices An interesting problem that occurs occasionally concerns IP address conflict messages when a new network interface card (NIC) is installed on a computer and is assigned the static address of a removed NIC. In that case, the old NIC's settings are still stored in the Registry, and you can assign a different address to the new NIC. You will want to remove the old NIC, but because it is absent, the device does not show up in the list of devices, even after you choose View, Show Hidden Devices.

continues

NOTE

continued

The solution? Choose Start, Run and in the Open box type `Devmgmt.msc set DEVMGR_SHOW_NONPRESENT_DEVICES=1`. The absent NICs will be visible under Network Adapters, and you will be able to delete them.

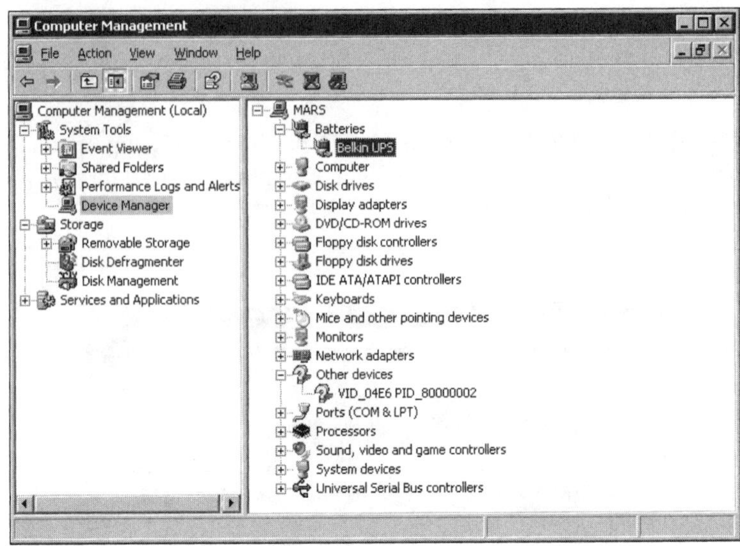

FIGURE 2.19
Belkin UPS is installed.

Using the Hardware Troubleshooter

When a device is causing problems, it is often helpful to use the Hardware Troubleshooter, which is available from within Device Manager. As you can see in Figure 2.20, the Hardware Troubleshooter offers to help you with problems with the following issues:

- Storage devices (disk drives, CD-ROMs, DVD-ROMs)
- Network adapters
- Input devices (mouse, keyboard, camera, scanner, infrared)
- Game controllers
- Universal Serial Bus (USB) devices
- Display adapters
- Modems
- Sound cards

Also, the Hardware Troubleshooter can help you resolve a hardware conflict on your computer. This is useful when two devices use the same resource (DMA channel, IRQ line, memory range, or input/output port). The wizard walks you through a series of questions aimed at determining what is wrong with the device (see Figure 2.20).

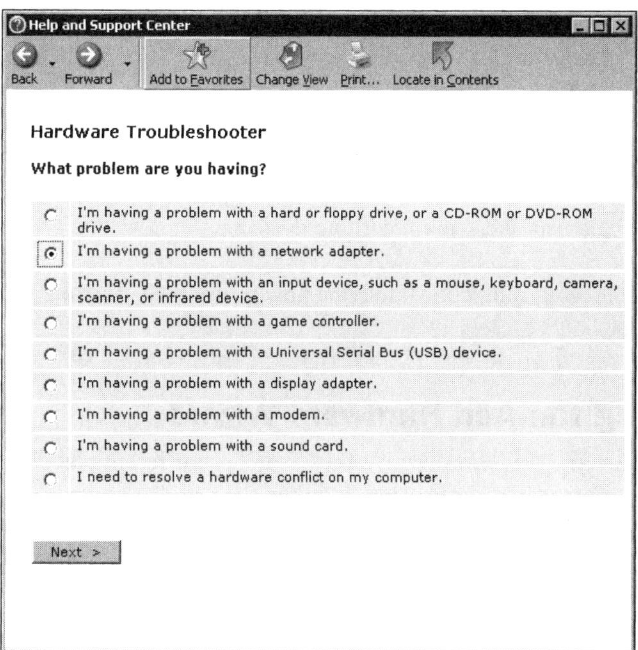

FIGURE 2.20
Choose the type of device you want to troubleshoot.

The Hardware Troubleshooter can help you solve problems that might have cost you hours of troubleshooting time, and it can help you save the money you might have spent on technical support calls.

Using Control Panel Applets

The Control Panel provides several applets (small, single-purpose applications) that can help you manage hardware; they are as follows:

- **Add Hardware**—This starts the Add Hardware Wizard, which can both help you install new hardware and help you troubleshoot existing hardware.
- **Display**—This applet allows you to control the way your display operates.
- **Game Controllers**—This applet allows you to install and configure game controller hardware.
- **Mouse**—This applet manages mouse settings.

- **Phone and Modem Options**—This applet allows you to configure phone and modem settings.
- **Printers and Faxes**—This applet is used to configure printer and fax settings.
- **Sounds and Audio Devices**—This applet enables you to configure speakers and recording devices.

The following subsections describe how to use the Control Panel applets.

NOTE

Get Some Hands-on Experience The Windows Server 2003 Control Panel applets are very close in function to the Windows XP applets, so if you're concerned that you might interfere with the operation of your Windows Server 2003 computer, you can experiment with the applets on your Windows XP system instead and get essentially the same experience.

Using the Add Hardware Wizard

Initially, the Add Hardware Wizard searches for recently added hardware that has not yet been installed. If it finds no new hardware, it asks you whether the device is installed, and if it is, shows you a list of the installed devices so that you can select the one that is having problems.

If Windows Server 2003 can recognize the problem, it will suggest remedies for it, such as reinstalling the driver, changing settings, or disabling or removing the device. If Windows Server 2003 cannot identify a problem with the device, it will offer to start the appropriate troubleshooter.

Using the Display Applet

If there are problems with the display, go directly to the Settings tab. (All the other tabs control how the display looks to the users.) You can access advanced settings from the Advanced button, or you can load the troubleshooter by selecting the Troubleshoot button. Figure 2.21 shows the Settings tab of the Display applet.

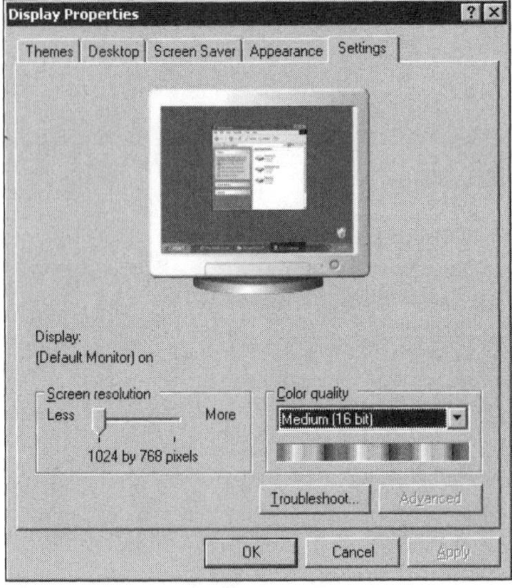

FIGURE 2.21
Select the Troubleshoot button for troubleshooting assistance or the Advanced button for more settings.

Using the Game Controllers Applet

Although it's extremely unlikely that you will be running games on a server, there may be management devices that use the game controller interfaces. To manage them, use the Game Controllers applet.

Using the Keyboard Applet

The Keyboard applet allows you to specify how the keyboard operates. You can determine how long you must hold down a key before it starts to repeat (the repeat delay), and how quickly it repeats (the repeat rate). There's a handy test area that allows you to test your settings. You can also change the rate at which the cursor blinks. See Figure 2.22 for the Keyboard applet.

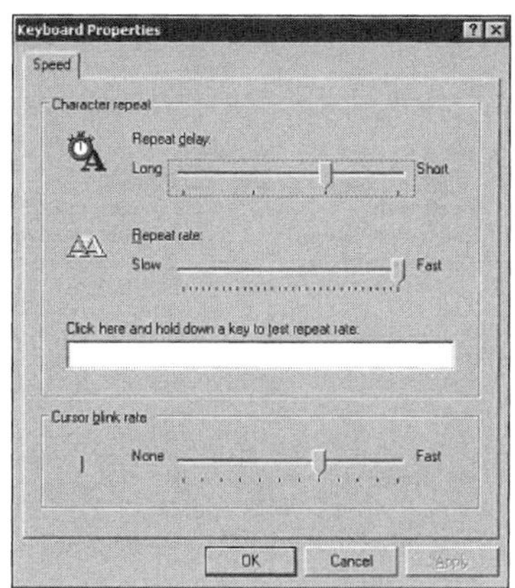

FIGURE 2.22
Use the sliders to change the repeat delay, repeat rate, or cursor blink rate.

Using the Mouse Applet

The Mouse applet lets you choose whether the left or right mouse button is the primary button. It allows you to set the double-click speed—dragging the slider to the left allows two slower clicks to be counted as a double-click. And it allows you to turn on ClickLock, which lets you highlight items, or drag selected items, without holding down the mouse button (see Figure 2.23).

The Pointer Options tab of the Mouse applet allows you to control the speed on movement of the pointer, automatically move the pointer to a dialog box's default command button, display pointer trials (particularly useful on LCD screens), hide the pointer when you are typing into a window, and (if the pointer is hidden) show where it is when you press Ctrl. See Figure 2.24 for the Pointer Options tab of the Mouse applet.

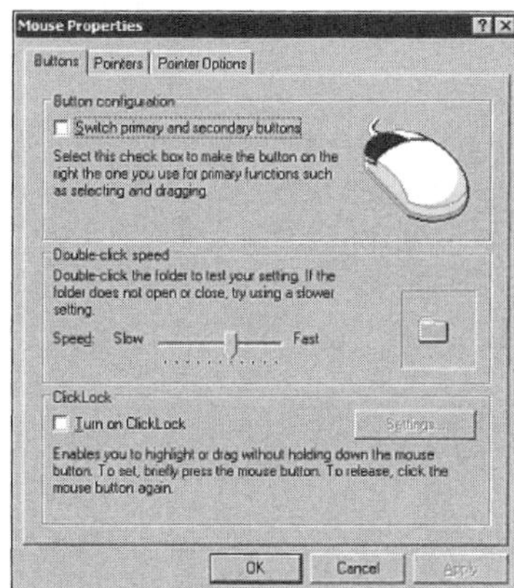

FIGURE 2.23▲
Use the Buttons tab of the Mouse applet to control button allocation, double-click speed, and ClickLock.

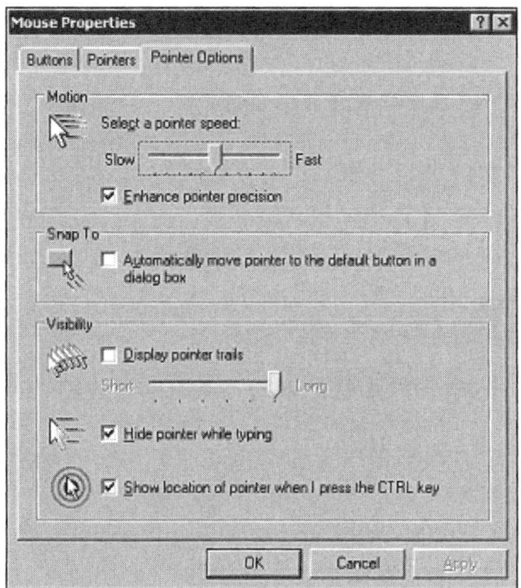

FIGURE 2.24◀
Choose the settings you want for your mouse on the Pointer Options tab.

FIGURE 2.25
Select a device in the Devices window and then click Troubleshoot or Properties.

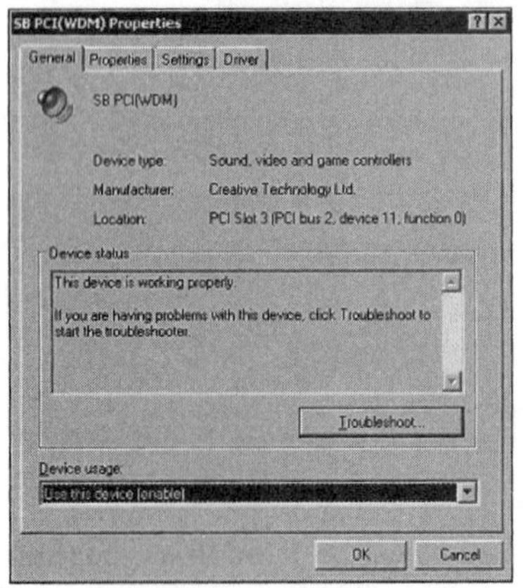

FIGURE 2.26
Invoke the Troubleshooting Wizard or select the Properties, Settings, or Driver tab.

Using the Sounds and Audio Devices Applet

On the Hardware tab of the Sounds and Audio Devices Control Panel applet, you will see a listing for any sound, video, or game controllers. This is a central management point for all such devices. If you are having problems with any of the listed devices, you can select the device and choose Troubleshoot to start the Troubleshooting Wizard for that device. Figure 2.25 shows the contents of the Hardware tab.

For example, let's say we are having trouble with the sound card on our computer. Choosing the SB PCI card and selecting Properties brings up the dialog box shown in Figure 2.26. You may choose Troubleshoot to start the Troubleshooting Wizard, or you may choose the Properties, Settings, or Driver tab to enable or disable capabilities of the device, to configure settings, or to update its driver.

TROUBLESHOOTING SERVER HARDWARE

A hardware device might stop working due to a mechanical or electronic failure, such as a disk head crash or a surge in the power. Any hardware component, especially ones with moving parts such as disk drives, will fail eventually. But it's much more common that a device will become unusable because of incorrect device settings or because of wrong or corrupted device drivers.

In this section we'll talk about issues caused by hardware settings and about issues caused by upgrades to hardware and to hardware drivers.

IN THE FIELD

SMOOTH POWER SAVES LIVES!

Hardware lives, that is! When you realize the very high speeds and fine tolerances that are used in modern computer hardware components, it's easy to see that smooth power is a must for system reliability. A small disturbance at the wrong moment in the power supplied to a disk drive can cause data corruption. And a spike in the voltage across any electronic device can damage or destroy the device.

That's why it's essential that any production computing environment be carefully protected against power fluctuations (under-voltage, over-voltage, spikes, or drops) that can damage components. An Uninterruptible Power Supply (UPS) is your first line of defense. A UPS will provide smooth power isolated from the fluctuations that exist in any power utility's service. Some production environments have power supplied from two different grids and have their own onsite emergency generators. These two steps ensure that power is available. Then they feed that power into large banks of batteries and run the data center equipment from the batteries. The result: smooth, reliable power, and hardware with a long and happy life.

Diagnosing and Resolving Issues Related to Hardware Settings

As discussed earlier, hardware devices make use of system resources to communicate with other components and with the operating system. These resources—direct memory access (DMA), interrupt request (IRQ), input/output (I/O) port, and memory address—can be shared by newer Plug and Play–compatible devices, and the devices can receive configuration settings from the operating system.

Each device responds to a query from the operating system with a list of settings it can use for each of the resources and whether the resources can be shared. The operating system then mediates between competing devices and sends configuration settings to each of them so that there is no conflict.

Some older devices, such as most Industry Standard Architecture (ISA) bus expansion cards, cannot share resources, however. And many of them, even with a Plug and Play driver, cannot have their resource settings configured by the operating system.

What happens if a computer starts up and finds two non–Plug and Play devices that both want to use IRQ 5? Although the computer might not start at all, it's more likely that one or both of the devices will not work. To resolve this situation, we would go to our friend the Device Manager and look for yellow question mark "problem" icons.

NOTE

Using Manual Settings If the check box Use Automatic Settings has been cleared, you have told Windows (or somebody else has) not to try to configure the devices. Your first action in this case should be to select that check box and see if the problem goes away. If it does, you can pat yourself on the back. If it doesn't, you will either have to find nonconflicting settings or remove one of the conflicting devices.

When you find a device with a problem icon and double-click it, you will see a statement that the device is not working due to a conflict. The Resources tab shows which resource is in conflict and usually will indicate which other device it is conflicting with. Then it's up to you to find settings for the two devices that don't result in a conflict.

Diagnosing and Resolving Server Hardware Issues

In general, if hardware issues are not caused by incorrect settings, they are caused by unsupported hardware or inappropriate device drivers.

Unsupported Hardware

As mentioned earlier, the Hardware Compatibility List (HCL) should be the first source you consult when you are looking for a new component for your production Windows Server 2003 computer. It's possible that devices not on the HCL will work without problem on your computer, but why take the chance? You're risking the reliability of your organization's computing system, and your own reputation. Just say "no" to unsupported hardware.

An efficient way to test the hardware on a computer for its suitability for use with Windows Server 2003 is to run the compatibility checker program. You can run the compatibility checker on the computer on which you intend to install Windows Server 2003 by inserting the Windows Server 2003 CD-ROM and choosing Check System Compatibility, or by executing this command from the I386 folder:

```
winnt32 /checkupgradeonly
```

The resulting report will identify devices and applications that are not compatible with Windows Server 2003. With this information, you can decide whether to remove or replace the incompatible devices. Do not overlook this situation: You will just cause yourself problems (system instability or device failures) if you do.

You can also search the online version of the HCL, which is always up-to-date at `http://www.microsoft.com/whdc/hcl/search.mspx`.

Managing Hardware Device Driver Upgrades

Let's say you have bought a new tape drive (having checked that it is listed on the HCL) and installed it on your computer, but the computer didn't recognize the tape drive when it rebooted. Chances are good that the driver installed by the operating system is not up-to-date. Device Manager should show a yellow question mark icon, and selecting Reinstall Driver from the General tab of the Device Properties dialog box, or Update Driver from the Drivers tab, will allow you to specify an updated driver.

Where do you find these updated drivers? One popular source is Windows Update, the Microsoft site from which security patches, new features, and driver updates can be manually or automatically downloaded (`http://windowsupdate.microsoft.com/`). These drivers will be digitally signed, so they will be protected by Windows File Protection. They may come from a Web site maintained by the device manufacturer, whose drivers may or may not be signed. And they might come from a third-party Web site, which makes drivers from many manufacturers available to its visitors.

By preference, you should always take the signed drivers from the Windows Update site before unsigned manufacturers' drivers, and both of these before drivers from a third-party Web site.

Dealing with a Device Driver Upgrade Problem

Occasionally, while performing maintenance on your computer, you may install a driver that causes problems. In earlier versions of the operating system, if you decided to back out a driver upgrade, you might have difficulty finding the previous version: "Where did I put that CD-ROM?"

A very useful enhancement in Windows Server 2003 is the Device Driver Roll Back facility. When you select the Driver tab on the Properties dialog box for a device in Device Manager, one of the available buttons is Roll Back Driver. Its caption describes its purpose well: "If the device fails after updating the driver, roll back to the previously installed driver." Information about the previous driver is stored by Windows Server 2003, and when Device Driver Roll Back is invoked, the current driver is uninstalled and the previous driver is reinstalled. See Figure 2.27 for the Drivers tab of the properties of one of the network cards in our test computer.

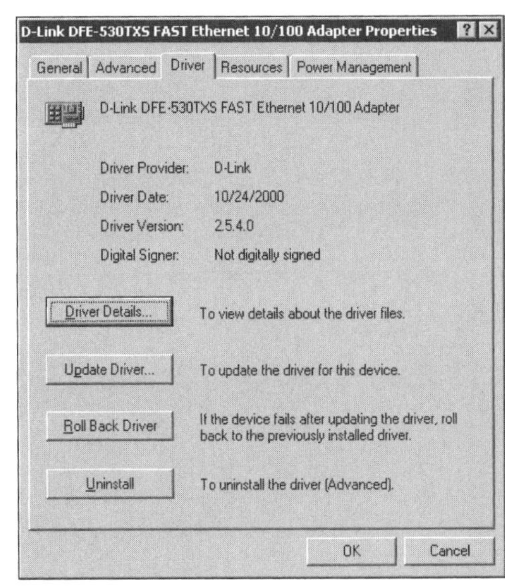

FIGURE 2.27
Select Roll Back Driver to go to the previous driver for this device.

NOTE

No Rollback for Printers Printer drivers cannot be rolled back in this way because Device Manager does not manage printers. Instead, you can select New Driver on the Advanced tab of the Printer Properties dialog box and browse to the location of the previous driver.

Also, note that you can only roll back one level of driver. To roll back two or more versions, you must uninstall the current driver and install the desired version without the help of Device Driver Roll Back.

Sometimes a driver upgrade will make the computer unable to boot up. In this case, use the F8 key during system startup and choose the option to start the system in Safe Mode. Once running in Safe Mode, run Device Manager to find the problem device and, on the Driver tab of the Properties dialog box, select Roll Back Driver.

IN THE FIELD

TRYING TO USE A NON-HCL DEVICE

When our server was first installed, there were two problem devices. The first one, the Belkin UPS, was taken care of by installing a Windows 2000 driver. That approach often works because Windows 2000 and Windows Server 2003 are similar operating systems, but you shouldn't depend on such solutions. It's much better to (a) use only devices on the Windows Server 2003 HCL and (b) find a Windows Server 2003 driver for the device.

Still, sometimes we have no choice and must try to use the out-of-date or unsupported hardware, as the following example illustrates. Figure 2.28 shows the Device Manager display with one problem device.

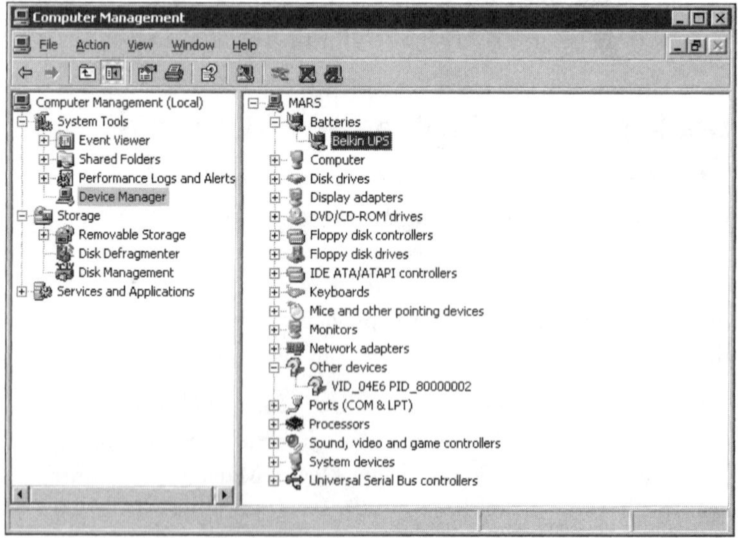

FIGURE 2.28
The yellow question mark icon shows a problem device.

Let's take a look at the cryptically identified VID_04E6 PID_80000002. A little research with a search engine establishes that this is an external HP Colorado 5GB tape drive. It's a few years old, and it's not found on the Windows Server 2003 HCL.

With that knowledge, another search discovers Windows 2000 drivers for this device on a third-party Web site, which we downloaded into C:\System management\Drivers\Colorado 5GB.

Once again we are considering whether to use a Windows 2000 driver in a Windows Server 2003 system. Again we decide that it's better to have something than nothing, so we install the driver, accepting warnings that the driver is unsigned, so Windows can't ensure that it isn't replaced improperly. In Figure 2.29 you see the dialog box in which we give the path where the drivers were downloaded.

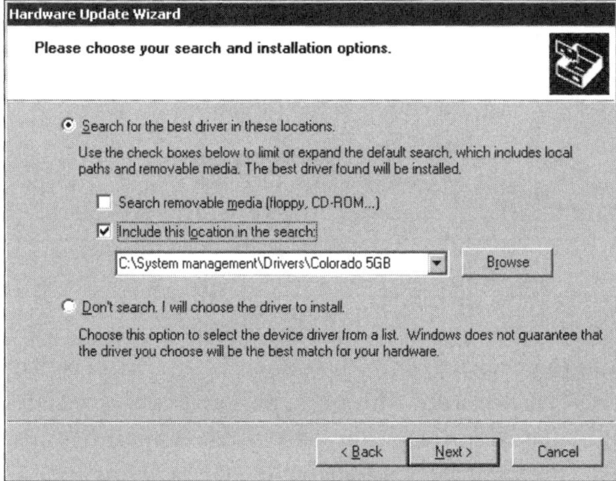

FIGURE 2.29
Specify the path where the drivers are located. Windows won't let you click OK while browsing for a path unless there is a `<driver>.inf` file in that path.

Finally, the driver for the tape drive is installed, and Device Manager has given us a clean bill of health (see Figure 2.30).

However, don't think your troubles are over just because Device Manager has no complaints. Just after this screen shot was taken, the computer was rebooted, and it would not complete the bootup. When the external tape drive was removed, bootup proceeded normally. Even Device Manager can be fooled!

continues

continued

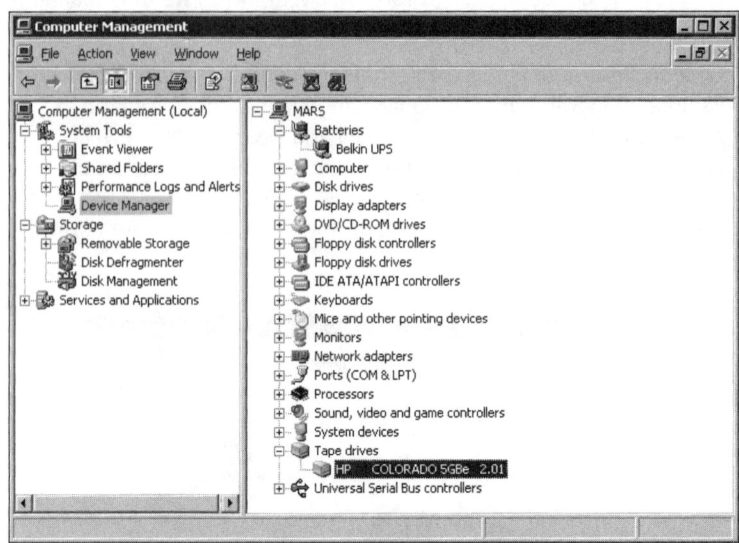

FIGURE 2.30
When there are no red or yellow icons in the Device Manager display, Windows Server 2003 is satisfied that all the devices are working fine.

The lesson to be learned from this In the Field exercise is that the decision to try to proceed with unsupported hardware was unwise. Remember that your first priority as a system administrator is to ensure that the computers you maintain are always online, and always functioning properly. Do not compromise this priority by deciding (or agreeing, even under pressure) to use unsupported hardware.

GUIDED PRACTICE EXERCISE 2.1

You are the administrator of a network that includes multiple Windows Server 2003 servers that are used for remote access and telephony services. The Customer Service department is a very heavy user of both inbound and outbound faxes, the capability of which is controlled by an older server with a set of proprietary ISA fax cards. This old server has been having hardware-related problems, and it's not cost effective for it to be repaired. Therefore, you order a new server, luckily one of the few available that still has a few ISA slots.

However, now it's up to you to make these old fax cards work with Windows Server 2003.

What is the best way to solve this issue in Windows Server 2003? On your own, try to develop a solution that would involve the least amount of downtime.

If you would like to see a possible solution, follow the procedure outlined here.

Estimated Time: 40 minutes

Unfortunately, you're going to have to work around two separate issues: older unsigned drivers and non–Plug and Play devices. First you're going to have to install the fax cards in your server and make sure they're not trying to use resources allocated to other devices. Then you're going to have to load an unsigned driver. Here are the steps to follow:

1. Consult the documentation that came with the fax boards to determine the resource configuration.
2. Click Start, Control Panel, System and then click the Hardware tab.
3. Click the Device Manager button.
4. In Device Manager, check to make sure the required resources are available. You can accomplish this by selecting the Resources by Connection entry in the View menu. If the necessary resources are not available, try to reconfigure the fax cards for some that are.
5. Power down the server.
6. Install the fax cards in the new server.
7. Boot the server.
8. Click Start, Control Panel, System and then click the Hardware tab.
9. Click the Device Manager button.
10. In Device Manager, expand the entry for the fax device.
11. Right-click the fax device and select Properties from the pop-up menu.
12. Click the Resources tab.

continues

continued

13. Select the resource setting you wish to modify.
14. Clear the Use Automatic Settings check box if it is selected.
15. Click the Change Setting button.
16. Configure the resource settings to the settings that the fax card is configured for.
17. Click OK to save. Repeat this process for the other fax cards.
18. Close Device Manager.
19. This returns you to the Hardware tab of the System Properties dialog box. Click Driver Signing.
20. In the Driver Signing Options dialog box, in the What Action Do You Want Windows to Take? section, click Ignore – Install the Software Anyway and Don't Ask for My Approval.
21. Click OK and then OK again on the System Properties dialog box to save.
22. Install the driver for the fax cards according to the manufacturer's instructions.

As soon as you have installed the unsigned driver, you should return to the Driver Signing Options dialog box and choose Block – Never Install Unsigned Driver Software.

CHAPTER SUMMARY

To ensure the stability of your servers, and to have all your devices operating properly, it is critical that the devices be compatible with Windows Server 2003 and that you use only signed drivers from reputable sources.

Modern system boards (motherboards) meet the Advanced Configuration and Power Interface (ACPI) standard, which means the operating system running in that system will be able to recognize and configure all installed hardware that is built to the Plug and Play specifications.

A device with an ACPI-compliant motherboard can have its devices selectively powered down or put into sleep mode. This allows battery-powered computers to have maximum battery life.

Older hardware, particularly devices that were built to the Industry Standard Architecture (ISA) specifications, cannot be managed by Windows Server 2003, so manual configuration is necessary to make sure the resource usage by these devices does not conflict with other devices on the computer.

Device drivers are software components that allow communication between the operating system and devices. They run very close to the kernel of the operating system, so it is crucial that they be trustworthy. Driver signing assures the administrator that the drivers running on a computer are legitimate. Running unsigned drivers compromises the stability of your computer.

You can ensure that no unsigned drivers can be installed on your computer by configuring the driver-signing options on the computer. For large numbers of computers, it's recommended that you create a Group Policy Object to automate this configuration.

To check whether there any unsigned drivers on your computer, run File Signature Verification, which you access by using Start, Run, `sigverif.exe`.

Windows Server 2003 includes an important service, Windows File Protection, that automatically removes any unsigned system files and replaces them with signed files.

continues

KEY TERMS

- Advanced Configuration and Power Interface (ACPI)
- Plug and Play
- Basic Input/Output System (BIOS)
- OnNow Device Power Management
- Device driver
- Hardware Compatibility List (HCL)
- Driver signing
- Group Policies
- File Signature Verification
- Windows File Protection
- System File Checker
- Resource settings
- Device Manager
- Hardware Troubleshooter
- Uninterruptible Power Supply (UPS)
- Direct memory access (DMA)
- Interrupt request (IRQ)
- Input/output (I/O) port
- Memory address
- Compatibility checker

CHAPTER SUMMARY *continued*

- Windows Update
- Device Driver Roll Back

For any hardware device, as many as four different resources can be defined: direct memory access (DMA), interrupt request (IRQ), input/output (I/O) port, and memory address. It is important to avoid conflicts between devices attempting to use the same settings for a given device. If the devices are Plug and Play compatible, these conflicts will not arise. If they are not, you may have to perform some manual configuration.

To determine the settings for a device, or to configure devices manually, you use the Device Manager tool. When you start Device Manager, devices that are not working properly are shown with a yellow question mark icon. Devices that are disabled have a red *X* over the icon. Device Manager does not manage device drivers for printers and fax devices.

Occasionally you will find that an error message is displayed when you attempt to assign the same IP address to a new network card, if you did not uninstall the old card before you removed it from the computer. You must start Device Manager with a special parameter to make the absent network card visible and capable of being deleted.

There are methods by which you can override the warnings that Device Manager presents if you try to install old or unsigned drivers. We don't recommend you do this, however, if you want to maintain the reliability of your computer.

Use the Add Hardware Wizard to install devices that are not automatically recognized and installed by the operating system.

You will be unable to deselect Use Automatic Settings on the Resources tab for a device's properties if the device is Plug and Play compatible and being managed by the operating system.

Use the Hardware Compatibility List (HCL) or the compatibility checker program to determine whether any devices in a computer are incompatible with Windows Server 2003.

Remember to "Just Say No" if you are tempted (or asked) to use unsupported devices or unsigned drivers on your computer.

APPLY YOUR KNOWLEDGE

Exercises

2.1 Checking for Unsigned Drivers

This exercise demonstrates how to determine whether there are any unsigned drivers on your computer. We accomplish this in two ways: by using File Signature Verification and by using driverquery.exe.

Estimated Time: 10 minutes

1. Select the Start menu, click Run, and in the Open dialog box type sigverif.
2. We want to perform the default verification, so click Start to begin the file checking. Wait while the verification program runs.
3. Review the listing of unsigned drivers. Determine the source of the drivers.
4. (Optional) Browse the Web site of the manufacturer of the device for which the unsigned drivers were loaded. See if any signed drivers exist for the devices in question.
5. Open a command prompt.
6. Enter driverquery /? and review the help information.
7. Enter driverquery /fo table /s *<computername>* /si to show a list of loaded drivers on the computer.
8. Enter driverquery /fo csv /s *<computername>* /si >c:\dr.csv to write a comma-separated values table of loaded drivers on the computer to the file c:\dr.csv.
9. (Optional) Run a spreadsheet program or a database program and load the output from Step 8. Consider how a database of driver information for each of the servers in your network might be useful.

2.2 Determining the DMA Channels in Use

This exercise demonstrates how to determine what DMA channels are in use on your computer. We'll use Device Manager.

Estimated Time: 5 minutes

1. To start Device Manager, right-click My Computer and choose Manage.
2. In the Explorer pane, click Device Manager.
3. In the View menu, choose Resources by Type.
4. Click the plus sign beside Direct Memory Access (DMA).
5. Review the channels in use on your computer.

Review Questions

1. What facilities are included with Windows Server 2003 to ensure that only legitimate drivers are running?
2. What advance in hardware architecture has made device management easier for administrators?
3. Why are digitally signed drivers important?
4. What are the disadvantages of manually configuring resources for hardware devices?
5. What tool is used to verify system files?

APPLY YOUR KNOWLEDGE

Exam Questions

1. You have been asked whether an older computer will operate properly with Windows Server 2003. What feature of the computer must be present for device resource settings to be assigned automatically by Windows Server 2003?

   A. APM

   B. SFC

   C. ACPI *

   D. PnP

2. After installing a new driver for a printer, you find that it is not functioning properly, and you decide to return to the previous driver. What procedure(s) will give you the desired results?

   * A. Uninstall the printer and then start again with the most recent functioning driver you can find.

   B. Use Device Manager to invoke Driver Roll Back.

   C. Run Driver Roll Back from Administrative Tools.

   * D. On the Advanced tab of the printer's Properties dialog box, choose New Driver and use Have Disk to select the source of the previous driver.

3. A colleague has sent you a new driver for your server's RAID controller, which he says makes the drives it controls run more efficiently. You want to ensure that the driver is from a reputable source. How do you do that?

   A. Look for the driver on the manufacturer's Web site.

   B. Run Windows File Protection to determine the creator of the driver. ?

   * C. Run `sigverif.exe`, and on the Advanced tab, choose to search on `*.sys` files in the folder where you saved the driver.

   D. Run `driverquery` with the `/fo csv` switch against the folder where you saved the file.

4. You are the administrator of a small engineering firm. Your network consists of approximately 500 workstations, consisting of a mixture of Windows 2000 and Windows XP machines. All the users and workstations are grouped into OUs depending on the department they work in. You use Group Policy to limit what the users can do on their workstations.

   However, the Materials Testing department needs to occasionally try out new hardware/driver combinations in its machines. What can you do to allow these users to do this without you being involved each time they want to test new hardware?

   Required Result:

   You want the Materials Testing department to be able to install its own hardware and drivers.

   Optional Desired Results:

   You want these users to be able install only signed drivers.

   You do not want to visit each workstation.

   Proposed Solution:

   Open the System Applet in Control Panel. Click the Hardware tab, and then click the Digital Signing button. Select the Block-Prevent Installation of Unsigned Files radio button.

APPLY YOUR KNOWLEDGE

Evaluation of Proposed Solution:

Which result(s) does the proposed solution produce?

A. The proposed solution produces the required result but neither of the optional results.

B. The proposed solution produces the required result and one of the optional results.

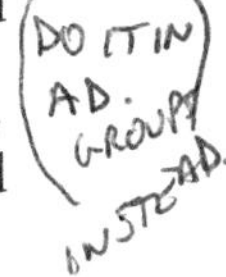

C. The proposed solution produces the required result and both the optional results.

D. The proposed solution does not produce the required result.

5. You are the administrator of a small engineering firm. Your network consists of approximately 500 workstations, consisting of a mixture of Windows 2000 and Windows XP machines. All the users and workstations are grouped into OUs depending on the department they work in. You use Group Policy to limit what the users can do on their workstations.

   However, the Materials Testing department needs to occasionally try out new hardware/driver combinations in its machines. What can you do to allow these users to do this without you being involved each time they want to test new hardware?

   Required Result:

   You want the Materials Testing department to be able to install its own hardware and drivers.

   Optional Desired Results:

   You want these users to be able install only signed drivers.

   You do not want to visit each workstation.

   Proposed Solution:

   Open the Active Directory Users and Computers MMC. Go to the OU for the Materials Testing department and add a Group Policy, or you can edit the existing policy. Configure the policy to block unsigned drivers.

   Evaluation of Proposed Solution:

   Which result(s) does the proposed solution produce?

   A. The proposed solution produces the required result but neither of the optional results.

   B. The proposed solution produces the required result and one of the optional results.

   C. The proposed solution produces the required result and both the optional results.

   D. The proposed solution does not produce the required result.

6. You are the administrator of a small network. You use Group Policy to limit what the users can do on their workstations. What action should you take to warn users about unsigned drivers, but not block the installation?

   A. Put the warning in the company policy manual and distribute it via email.

   B. Configure the driver signing policy for Notify when installing unsigned drivers.

   C. Configure the driver signing policy for Warn when installing unsigned drivers.

   D. Configure the driver signing policy for Alert when installing unsigned drivers.

7. You are the administrator of a small network. One of your junior administrators calls and says she is having a problem with one of the modems in the remote access servers. You go look at the server and open Device Manager. You notice that the entry for the modem has a question mark with a red *X*. What action should you take correct this problem?

   A. Use Device Manager to enable the device.

   B. Reinstall the drivers for the device.

   C. Reassign the resources for the device.

   D. Nothing. The device is not compatible with Windows Server 2003.

8. You are having problems getting some of the specialized hardware devices in a new server to work properly with Windows Server 2003, after installing the hardware and downloading the drivers from the Internet. You call Microsoft support, and the first thing that they ask you is whether you are using any unsigned drivers. What is the easiest way to find this out?

   A. Run `sigverif.exe` with the default options.

   B. Run `sigverif.exe` with the advanced options.

   C. Run `driverquery` with the `/fo csv` switch.

   D. Run `driverquery` with the `/fo cvs` switch.

9. One of your junior administrators inadvertently installed an older application on one of your Windows Server 2003 servers that overwrote some of the system DLLs. Fortunately, Windows Server 2003 comes with the Windows File Protection feature so that the system files are automatically replaced with the correct ones. Unfortunately, WFP can't seem to find the necessary files in the %systemroot%\system32\dllcache folder. Where can you obtain the proper files?

   A. Windows Update

   B. Windows service packs

   C. Windows Server 2003 CD-ROM

   D. Hotfix distributions

10. You are building a new print server using Windows Server 2003. All the printer drivers have loaded successfully except for an older Windows NT driver that may or may not be supported on Windows Server 2003. What utility should you use to troubleshoot this driver problem?

    A. Device Manager

    B. Computer Management

    C. Printers applet

    D. Printers and Faxes applet

Answers to Review Questions

1. To ensure that only legitimate drivers are running on a computer, Windows Server 2003 includes Windows File Protection, System File Checker, and File Signature Verification. See the "Other Methods for Protecting Device Drivers" section in this chapter.

2. The Plug and Play specification has automated a task that used to cause administrators much difficulty. Whereas earlier it was the administrator's responsibility to find a set of nonconflicting resource settings for all the devices in a computer, this task is now performed by the computer.

APPLY YOUR KNOWLEDGE

When the computer has a system BIOS that meets the Advanced Configuration and Power Interface (ACPI) standards, Windows Server 2003 performs this function. See the "Installing and Configuring Hardware Devices" section of this chapter.

3. Digitally signed drivers are important because signing indicates that they have passed stringent tests to verify that they are compatible with Windows Server 2003. Because drivers operate in the kernel in the operating system, a faulty driver could crash the server.

4. When you manually configure resources, Windows is unable to change those settings. One of the good things about Plug and Play is that Windows automatically identifies any conflicts and configures the devices to avoid them. However, if the resource is manually configured, Windows cannot adjust the configuration for that resource.

5. The System File Checker (`sfc.exe`) is used to verify that the protected system files have not been overwritten.

Answers to Exam Questions

1. **C.** ACPI must be present on the computer for Windows Server 2003 to be able to take over the configuration of devices. APM (Advanced Power Management) is a predecessor to ACPI that does not perform automatic configuration as completely as ACPI. SFC (System File Checker) is a tool for scheduling a run of the system files to identify any that are unsigned. PnP (Plug and Play) is a specification that states how devices should identify themselves and respond to configuration commands.

2. **A, D.** You must remove the existing driver and install one that you know works. You can do this explicitly, by deleting the printer and reinstalling it, or with the help of the Add Printer Driver Wizard. Device Manager does not function with printer drivers, and Driver Roll Back is not available for printer drivers.

3. **C.** File Signature Verification will inspect the files in the location you specify, and it will tell you if they are unsigned. Looking for the driver on the manufacturer's Web site is probably safer than using the one your colleague supplied, but a driver you find there may yet be unsigned. Windows File Protection replaces unsigned drivers with signed ones from the dllcache. Running `driverquery.exe` with the `/fo csv` switch shows the running drivers—it does not inspect drivers that are not running.

4. **B.** The suggested solution meets the required result but only one of the optional results. Choosing to change the option in the Control Panel means that every workstation must be visited.

5. **C.** The suggested solution meets the required result and both the optional results. By implementing the change via Group Policy, it keeps the administrator from visiting each workstation.

6. **C.** Although distributing the policy via email seems like a good idea, you will need something more reliable. By selecting the Warn option, the user will be instructed that he or she is installing an unsigned driver and will be informed of the potential consequences; however, the user will still be able to install it. The Notify and Alert options do not exist.

APPLY YOUR KNOWLEDGE

7. **B.** The icon displayed usually indicates that the drivers are either missing or corrupt. Reinstalling the drivers should correct the problem.

8. **A.** Running `sigverif.exe` with the default options generates a list of all unsigned system files and drivers on the server. Getting similar information from `driverquery.exe` requires the `/si` switch.

9. **C.** If the desired version of the file is not in the dllcache folder, Windows File Protection asks for the Windows Server 2003 CD-ROM to be mounted, and it copies the files from there.

10. **D.** Device Manager does not manage device drivers for printers and fax devices. They are managed through the Printers and Faxes applet in Control Panel.

Suggested Readings and Resources

1. OnNow Device Power Management. Microsoft Corporation white paper. `http://www.microsoft.com/whdc/hwdev/tech/onnow/devicepm.mspx`.

2. Windows Server 2003 Deployment Guide. Microsoft Corporation. `http://www.microsoft.com/windowsserver2003/techinfo/reskit/deploykit.mspx`.

3. Windows Server 2003 Resource Kit. Microsoft Corporation. Look for a link to it on the Technical Resources for Windows Server 2003 page: `http://www.microsoft.com/windowsserver2003/techinfo/default.mspx`.

OBJECTIVES

This chapter covers the following Microsoft-specified objectives for the "Managing Users, Computers, and Groups" section of the Managing and Maintaining a Microsoft Windows Server 2003 Environment exam:

Create and manage user accounts.

- **Create and modify user accounts by using the Active Directory Users and Computers console.**
- **Create and modify user accounts by using automation.**
- **Import user accounts.**

▶ A primary function of a network administrator is to create and manage user accounts because user accounts are needed for users to authenticate to the network and to determine what resources the user can access.

▶ For a small network, creating and modifying the user accounts one at a time with a management tool is not too time consuming. But on a network with hundreds or thousands of users, it makes sense to use tools that automate the process. If the data about the users exists in some other form, such as a new-hire database, you can create the user accounts by importing them from a compatible file.

Create and manage groups.

- **Create and modify groups by using the Active Directory Users and Computers console.**
- **Identify and modify the scope of a group.**
- **Manage group membership.**
- **Find domain groups in which a user is a member.**
- **Create and modify groups by using automation.**

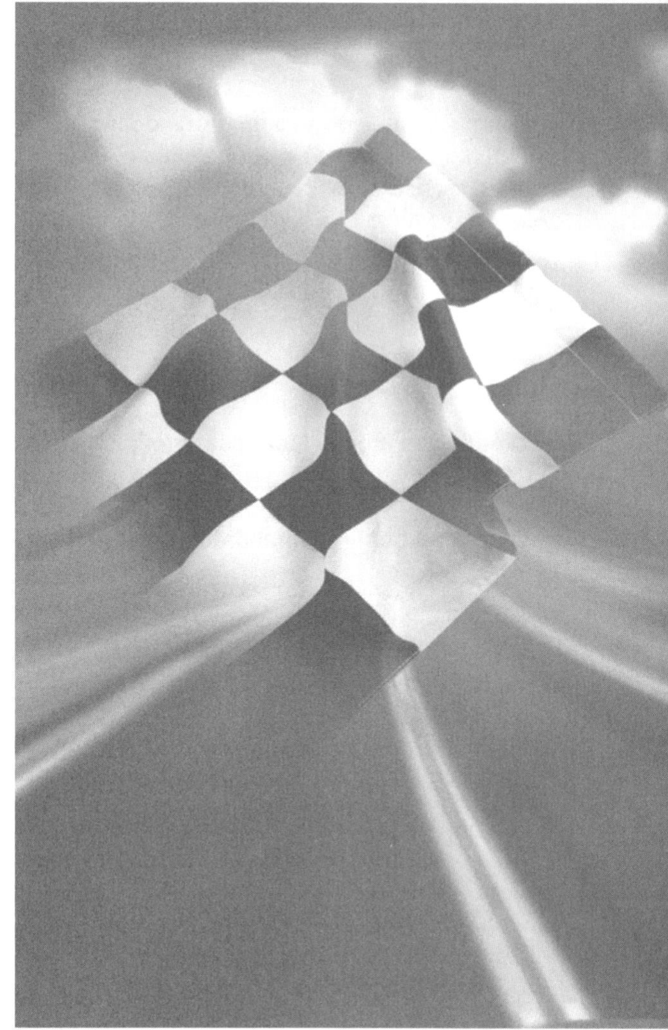

CHAPTER 3

Managing Users, Computers, and Groups

Objectives

- For simplicity of network administration, we can create group objects and allocate resource access rights to these objects. Then by making user accounts members of the group, we can grant them the access that the group objects have been assigned.

Manage local, roaming, and mandatory user profiles.

- **Create and modify local user profiles.**
- **Create and modify roaming user profiles.**
- **Create and enforce mandatory user profiles.**

- The settings for a user's work environment are stored in the user's profile. Any changes the user makes to the environment (Favorites, Start menu items, icons, colors, My Documents, Desktop, local settings, application-specific settings) are saved when the user logs off. The profile is reloaded when the user logs on again.

- It is important for administrators to know how to manage user profiles so that the users' settings are saved from session to session. If managed properly, this also ensures the users see the same desktop no matter where they log on.

Create and manage computer accounts in an Active Directory environment.

- Every computer running Windows NT, Windows 2000/2003, or Windows XP that is a member of a domain has a computer account in that domain. The computer account is a security principal, and it can be authenticated and granted permissions to access resources. A computer account is automatically created for each computer running the listed operating systems when the computer joins the domain.

Troubleshoot user accounts.

- **Troubleshoot account lockouts.**
- **Troubleshoot issues related to user account properties.**

- With a large group of users, there are sure to be trouble calls every day from users having difficulties with their accounts. One system setting that often results in trouble calls is Account Lockout—a user cannot log in because the account has been disabled after too many incorrect passwords were entered. Other problems can arise due to inappropriate settings in the user accounts.

Troubleshoot user-authentication issues.

- Sometimes a user will not be able to log on to the network. This can be caused by simple factors, such as a user error when entering a user ID and password, or by more complex issues such as the computer account being unusable. The network administrator must be able to determine what is causing the problem and to promptly correct the situation.

Troubleshoot computer accounts.

- **Diagnose and resolve issues related to computer accounts by using the Active Directory Users and Computers MMC snap-in.**
- **Reset computer accounts.**

- When a computer account is operating incorrectly, it may be impossible to log on to the domain from the computer. In this case it is necessary to reset the computer's account and rejoin the computer to the domain. This process reestablishes the secure relationship between the computer and the domain it is a member of.

OUTLINE

STUDY STRATEGIES

- In studying this section, be sure to practice all the activities described. Become very familiar with Active Directory Users and Computers, creating users and groups, resetting user and computer accounts, and defining roaming profiles and mandatory profiles. Microsoft is proud of the new command-line directory-management tools—`dsquery`, `dsadd`, `dsmod`, and `dsget`—so be sure you know what each one is for as well as how to use it. Also be sure to understand *piping*—sending the output from one command as the input to another.
- Use both `ldifde` and `csvde`, but don't spend hours making them work. Understand what they are for, and get to know the command structure. Work through the exercises until you can explain authoritatively `ldifde` and `csvde` to a colleague.
- You will need access to a Windows Server 2003 domain controller. Many of the tools are new or differ from those available in Windows 2000, so don't try to get by with a Windows 2000 domain controller.
- You don't have to buy Windows Server 2003 to try it out. You can download a free evaluation version (which expires in 180 days) from `www.microsoft.com/windowsserver2003/evaluation/trial/default.mspx`.

INTRODUCTION

Starting with this chapter, you're going to learn about some of the common daily duties of a Windows Server 2003 administrator. You can rest assured that you will be performing the tasks you learn in this chapter very often. This chapter discusses creating and managing user accounts, group accounts, and computer accounts, and setting up roaming profiles. Troubleshooting is a big part of the job, too. Troubleshooting entails helping users understand why they cannot connect to the network—whether it's because of locked-out user accounts, inoperative computer accounts, or other reasons. We'll be starting with user accounts. Let's get to it!

CREATING AND MANAGING USER ACCOUNTS

User accounts are created so that people can identify themselves to the system and receive access to the network resources they need. In Windows Server 2003 with Active Directory enabled, user accounts (often called *user IDs*) are assigned using the Active Directory Users and Computers management console. On standalone Windows Server 2003 computers, user accounts are created using the User Accounts applet in Control Panel.

Every user should have a separate account. If there are problems with system usage or a security breach, it's necessary that the administrator be able to tell who was acting incorrectly. If all the engineers in a department logged on using a single account called "Engineer," it would be impossible to tell which one of the engineers was accessing the resources. Allocating separate accounts also allows each user to have access to exactly the resources needed and no more. Also, each user account can have its own private home directory—multiple users sharing a single account would have no such private storage.

The following subsections discuss three ways of creating and managing user accounts:

- Creating and managing accounts with the Active Directory Users and Computers management console
- Creating and managing accounts with automated processes
- Creating and managing accounts using bulk Import/Export tools

Creating and Modifying User Accounts Using Active Directory Users and Computers

This section explains how to use the Active Directory Users and Computers console, first to create user accounts and then to modify user accounts.

The *Active Directory Users and Computers (ADUC)* console is the most straightforward way to create and modify user accounts. It is accessible from Start, Administrative Tools, Active Directory Users and Computers; from the Manage Your Server Wizard; or by using Start, Run and typing `dsa.msc` in the Run dialog box.

When you start Active Directory Users and Computers, as shown in Figure 3.1, you will see a familiar Explorer-like display. In the left pane is a folder containing saved queries (we'll talk about queries later on) and an icon showing the name of the domain the managing computer is attached to (`lantrainers.local`, in this case). The right pane shows the contents of the container selected in the left pane. Because we have the domain selected in the figure, we see the containers that reside in the domain.

Let's assume we're the network administrators for the Vancouver location of our organization, and we need to create some user accounts. Because the Vancouver Organizational Unit (OU) hasn't yet been created, we will need to do that. OUs are used in Active Directory to store users, groups, and resources. We'll create that OU and two more subordinate OUs below it in Step by Step 3.1.

EXAM TIP

Be Familiar with OUs

Organizational Units (OUs) are containers that the administrator creates to contain users, groups, and resources, such as computers and file shares. The administrator can then delegate authority over or assign a Group Policy to the items contained in the OU. You must have a good understanding of this for the exam.

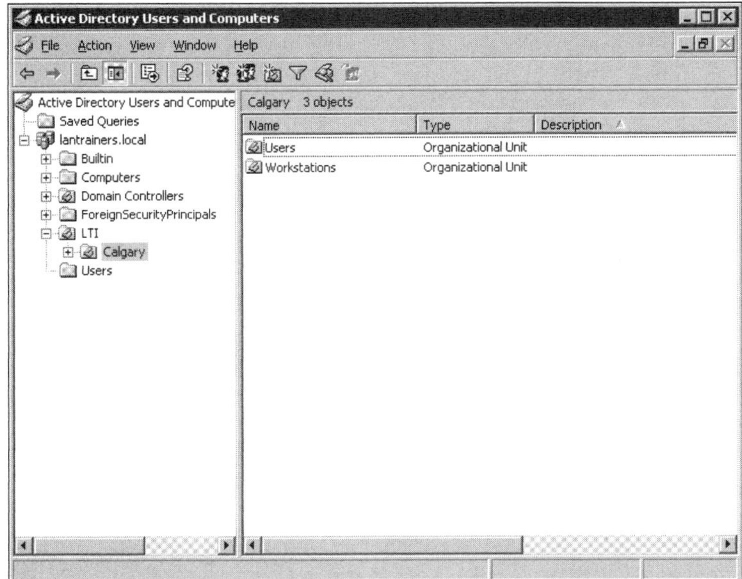

FIGURE 3.1
Selecting a container on the left pane displays its contents in the right pane.

STEP BY STEP

3.1 Creating OUs and User Accounts

1. In the left pane of the Active Directory Users and Computers console, select the top-level container in which you want to create the OU. In our example, the top-level container is `lantrainers.local`.
2. Right-click the container and choose New, Organizational Unit. Type the name `Vancouver` for the OU in the Name box.
3. Right-click the Vancouver OU and choose New, Organizational Unit. Type `Users`.
4. Repeat step 3, calling this Organizational Unit `Workstations`. We now have the organizational structure we want.
5. Right-click the Vancouver\Users container and select New, User.

continues

continued

6. Type the first and last names and the user logon name, as in Figure 3.2. In this organization, the default rule for creating the user logon name is the initial letter of the first (given) name, followed by the full last name (surname).

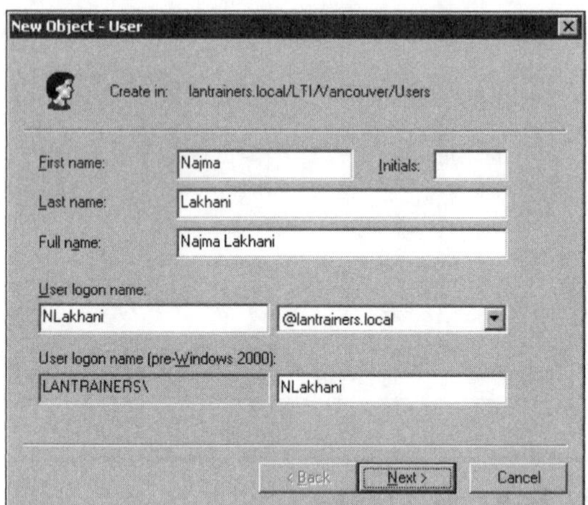

FIGURE 3.2
Fill in the name of the person for whom you are creating the user account.

7. Type the initial password for the user and repeat it in the confirmation field (see Figure 3.3). Accept the default password options.

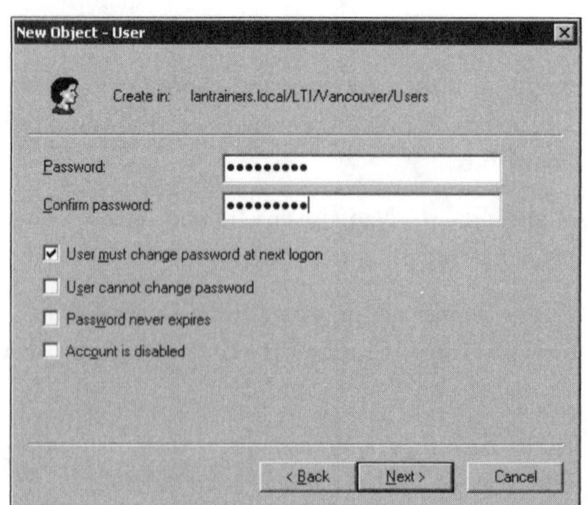

FIGURE 3.3
In most organizations, the default password settings for a new user are reasonable.

8. Review the information in the confirmation dialog box and select Finish to create the user object.

9. We need a group account for a later exercise (groups are discussed later in this chapter), so let's create one now. Start by right-clicking Users in the left pane.

10. Choose New, Group and then create a global security group called Engineers. Click OK.

The account has now been created, and at this point the user could log in. However, there are many properties of the account that we have not yet set, so let's now look at how to modify a user account with Active Directory Users and Computers.

Once the user object has been created, you can select it and review or set its properties. Simply double-clicking the object in the right panel of ADUC opens a Properties dialog box, as shown in Figure 3.4.

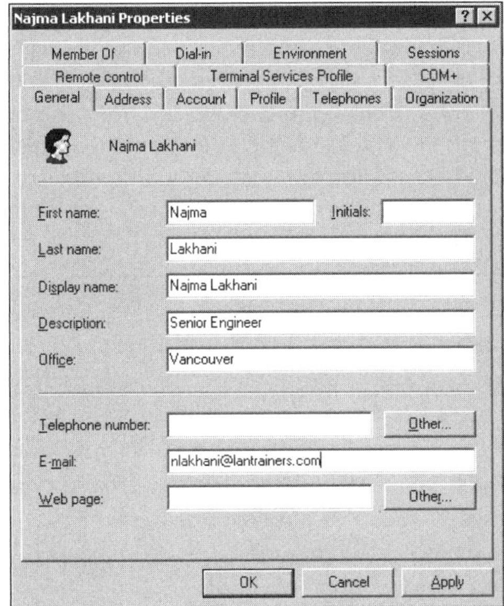

FIGURE 3.4
Change any of the properties on the General tab of the user account dialog box.

> **NOTE**
>
> **User Account Settings** In the New User Creation Wizard, the default password settings (shown in Figure 3.3) force the new user to change the password at the first successful logon. This ensures that the administrator does not know the user's credentials and therefore cannot impersonate the user. Also, forcing the user to change his password immediately makes him aware of any password complexity rules the organization has chosen, because if the password is too short or not complex enough, Windows Server 2003 will reject it and force the user's new password to comply with the complexity rules in order to log in.
>
> The second password setting is User Cannot Change Password. Typically, an organization wants users to be able to change their own passwords, but occasionally (as for a visitor account) the password should not be changed.
>
> Next is a setting that allows the administrator to exempt this account from the password-expiration rule. Most organizations want their users to change their passwords regularly (every 60 days, for example) so that if a password has been compromised, its useful period to gain access to the network is limited. The exception to this rule is for service accounts. A service account is used so that applications, such as Microsoft Exchange and Microsoft SQL Server, have access to network resources.
>
> *continues*

NOTE

continued

These applications expect the password to never be changed, or if it is changed, the change must be performed using the management tool for the application, and not through the ADUC.

Finally, the account can be disabled with the last check box, Account Is Disabled. This feature is generally used in one of two cases: when the account is created before the user is physically onsite or when the user is temporarily or permanently gone from the organization. In both cases, no one should be able to use the account, so disabling it is an appropriate security precaution.

Larger organizations generally have a list of the required information that must be entered for each user account. As an example, it may be mandatory to fill in the Office Location field, and there may be a fixed list of allowable entries. Like all fields in a user object, it is possible to search on the contents of the Office Location field. However, if one administrator enters Salt Lake, another enters SLC, and a third enters Salt Lake City, then how are users to search for that location? Requiring administrators to use office location names from a published list will resolve that problem.

IN THE FIELD

MORE ABOUT DIRECTORIES

The Active Directory is, in effect, a directory for the company, so rather than relying on a printed booklet, the users can pull all organization and contact information right from AD. Also, entry of organizational info (but not account creation) is often given to HR because they can be given the rights to only update certain properties, and usually they are aware of the changes that are happening. (For example, Bob just got promoted; he will be moving to a new office.) There are also some companies that leave it to the users to update themselves. (For example, if their extension changes, they can update that info in AD.) Microsoft is hoping that this will do away with some other internal directories that are in use (for example, printed books, email systems, databases used for printing, departmental phone lists, and so on).

The Address tab is available so that Active Directory can hold personal and business address information about the user. Most large organizations have personnel systems that carry this information, however, and these systems can use Active Directory or other database systems to store the data. Even if Active Directory is the directory system used to hold this employee data, the personnel system would update the directory programmatically, not via the Active Directory Users and Computers console.

NOTE

Beware of Interactive Logons An *interactive logon* is a logon performed at the console of the server or via a Terminal Services session. A user who can log on directly to a server is more of a risk than a user who is logged on across the network because once someone has physical access to the server, there is very little the OS can do to protect itself.

The Account tab contains several useful entry areas. The Logon Hours button allows you to specify which hours during the week the user is permitted to log on to the system. The Log On To button lets you specify the NetBIOS or the fully qualified domain name (FQDN) of the computers the user is permitted to log on to. Among the Account options is the setting Smart Card Is Required for Interactive Logon, which, if activated, requires the user to present a smart card to log on directly to a server or workstation.

In order for this to work, this smart card must be encoded with a certificate issued to the user, and a smart card reader must be installed on the computer. The smart card eliminates the need for a username and password; the user just needs the smart card and a personal identification number (PIN).

Account Expiration Date is the final entry area on the Account tab. Although we would expect most accounts to be valid indefinitely, for temporary employees, such as summer students, interns, or contractors, it is wise to specify the last date an account can be used (see Figure 3.5).

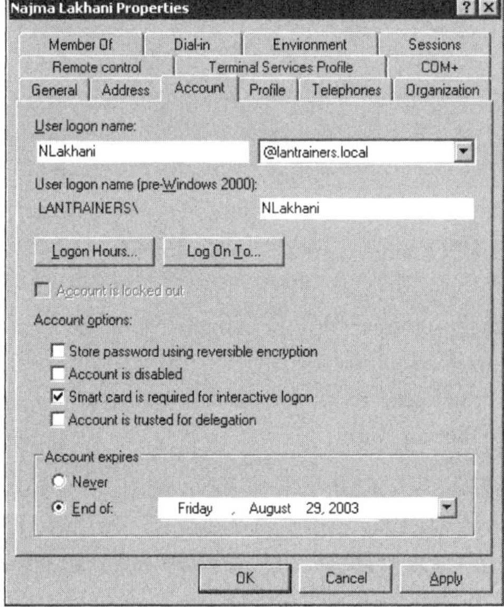

FIGURE 3.5
Use the End Of radio button to select a date after which the account will no longer be valid.

> NOTE
>
> **Managing Your Server Remotely**
> Note that you can install the Administrative Tools for Windows Server 2003 on a Windows XP workstation so that you don't have to be logged on to the server console to manage it.
>
> To install the Administrative Tools for Windows Server 2003 on a Windows XP workstation, insert the Windows Server 2003 CD-ROM in the CD-ROM drive, then choose Start, Run and in the Open Entry field type E:\I386\adminpak.msi (assuming *E* is the drive letter for the CD-ROM).
>
> If you want to manage a computer running Windows Server 2003 from a workstation that is not running Windows XP, the only available method is to start a Terminal Services session. Fortunately, Terminal Services clients are available for all Windows operating systems from Windows 95 on.

On the Profile tab, shown in Figure 3.6, in the User profile section you can specify where the user's profile data will be stored. We'll discuss profiles in depth later in this chapter, in the "Managing Local, Roaming, and Mandatory User Profiles" section. Also on the Profile tab, you can specify the name of the logon script (the scripted commands that will run on the user's behalf) when the user logs on.

In the Home Folder section of the Profile tab, you can specify the path where the user's home folder will be located. This can either be a path on the local computer or a network drive mapped to a shared folder on a server.

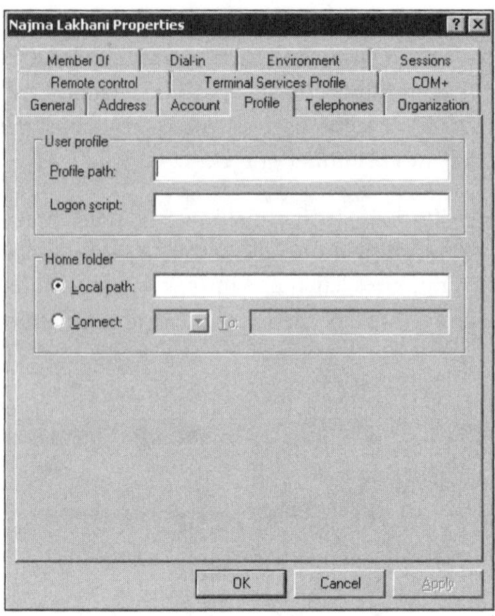

FIGURE 3.6
Enter values for profile path, logon script, and home directory location on this tab.

NOTE

Group Policy Is Preferred These methods of specifying profile, logon script, and home folder information have generally been superseded by Group Policies in Windows 2000 and Windows Server 2003. They were retained for consistency with previous versions of the operating system.

The Help and Support Center for Windows Server 2003 describes managing user profiles with Group Policies as a best practice. See "Managing Terminal Services Users with Group Policy" in Help and Support.

NOTE

Terminal Services The Terminal Services feature of Windows Server 2003 is covered in Chapter 4, "Managing and Maintaining Access to Resources."

NOTE

Remote Assistance Remote Assistance is a similar facility that allows an analyst to control a user's session remotely. Available only for Windows XP and Windows Server 2003 computers, this facility lets a user request help from a helper (typically a help desk analyst or a friend). The helper can then see the user's session and take control of it if necessary (if allowed to do so). Remote Assistance is covered in Chapter 4.

The next tabs all concern how the user interacts with *Terminal Services*—a method for having multiple users run programs in sessions that actually operate on a network server. The user can work at a low-function workstation (even one running Windows 95) and run programs that need the power and resources of a computer running Windows Server 2003.

The Remote Control tab, shown in Figure 3.7, allows the administrator to control whether a user's session can be controlled remotely. If Remote Control is enabled, the administrator can choose whether the user's permission is needed before the administrator can see the user's session. The administrator can also choose whether a session being controlled remotely can be operated by the administrator or merely viewed.

Remote Control can be a very helpful facility for help desk staff. With the appropriate authorization, a help desk analyst can connect to a user's Terminal Services session and see what the user is seeing or is having difficulties with. If needed, the analyst can take control of the session to demonstrate how a task is to be performed or to investigate program settings. This is much more efficient than having the user describe to the analyst what is on the screen, and it's much faster than having the analyst go to the user's desk to see the problem.

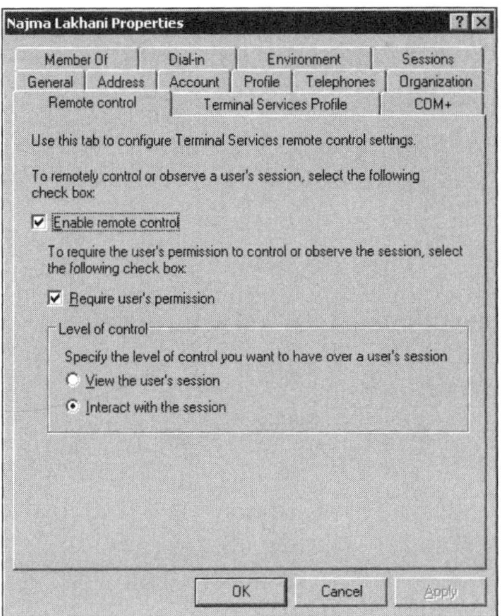

FIGURE 3.7
The Remote Control tab lets you specify whether the user's Terminal Services session can be controlled remotely.

> **NOTE** **Terminal Services** These Terminal Services settings should be changed only at the individual user-configuration level if specific functions are to be added or denied to a specific user.

The Terminal Services Profile tab allows the administrator to configure the user profile applied to the user's Terminal Services session. The administrator can specify the path of the profile to be used and the home folder location. These items can be different from the profile path and home folder location specified on the Profile tab. There is also a check box on which the administrator can determine whether the user is allowed to log on to the terminal server (see Figure 3.8).

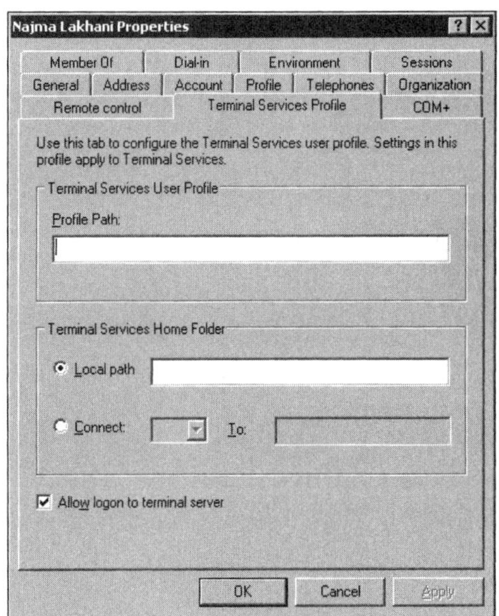

FIGURE 3.8
Use the Terminal Services Profile tab to specify the profile path and home folder location for the user's Terminal Services sessions.

On the Environment tab, shown in Figure 3.9, the administrator can configure the startup environment a Terminal Services user sees. Any setting specified here will override the setting specified by the Terminal Services client. The administrator can require that a program start automatically at logon—when the user exits the program, the session will be logged off. This is a way of limiting users to a specific application instead of presenting them with a Windows Server 2003 desktop, which is the default. In addition, the administrator can control whether drives and printers on the client computer are available from the session, as well as whether print jobs are automatically sent to the default printer of the client computer.

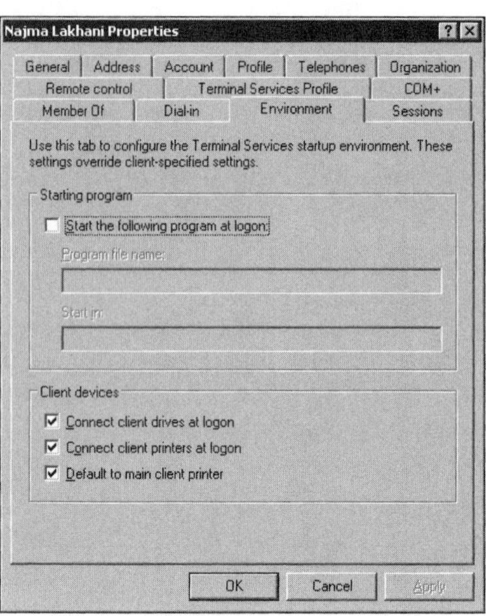

FIGURE 3.9
Control the Terminal Services user's environment through settings on the Environment tab.

> **EXAM TIP**
>
> **Be Familiar with the Added Features** Administrators who have used previous versions of Windows Terminal Services might unwittingly ignore the options for device mapping shown in Figure 3.9. However, these options are now fully supported in Windows Server 2003 Terminal Services without requiring the Citrix add-on. Expect to see questions on these added features on the exam.

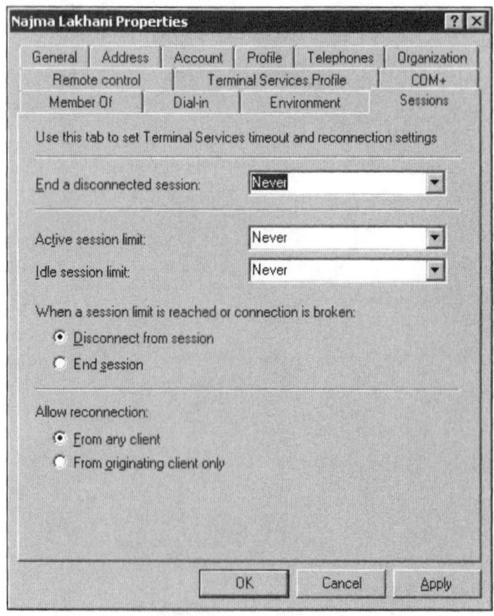

FIGURE 3.10
Specify how idle and disconnected sessions are handled on the Sessions tab.

On the Sessions tab, shown in Figure 3.10, the administrator can specify what to do with Terminal Services sessions that are disconnected or left idle. A session is disconnected when the user disconnects rather than logging off or when the communication between the client computer and the Terminal Services server is broken. The administrator can choose to leave the disconnected session running forever, or only for a fixed period (such as 3 hours). The administrator can also specify how long an active session can continue, and how long an idle session can be left connected. When either of these limits is met, the session can be disconnected or ended. Finally, when the session has been disconnected, the administrator can specify whether reconnection is allowed from any client computer, or only from the client computer with which the disconnected session was initiated.

On the Dial-In tab, shown in Figure 3.11, the administrator can determine whether a user can connect to a Windows Server 2003 machine remotely, either by a dial-in or a virtual private network (VPN) connection. When the domain is at the Windows 2000 native or Windows Server 2003 functionality level, remote access can be controlled through Remote Access Policy, which is substantially more sophisticated than a simple Allow Access or Deny Access setting. For example, a remote access policy can specify that only members of specific groups can access the network by dial-in, and then only from specific IP addresses and during stated periods in the day or week.

> **NOTE**
>
> **Terminal Services** The options on the Sessions tab are only lightly covered here. For more extensive coverage, see the section on Terminal Services in Chapter 4.

Also on the Dial-In tab, the administrator can choose to verify caller ID on the dial-in connection. The administrator can also require, for additional certainty, that only authorized locations are dialing in. By the administrator configuring the callback options, the server can break the connection as soon as authentication is complete and then call the user back at a preset telephone number. To ensure the company is paying the lowest rates for the call, the administrator can allow the server to return the call to a user-defined telephone number. Allowing the call to originate from the server location is most likely a less-expensive corporate long-distance rate package. In addition, the dial-in connection can be assigned the same static IP address each time, and TCP/IP routing can be defined.

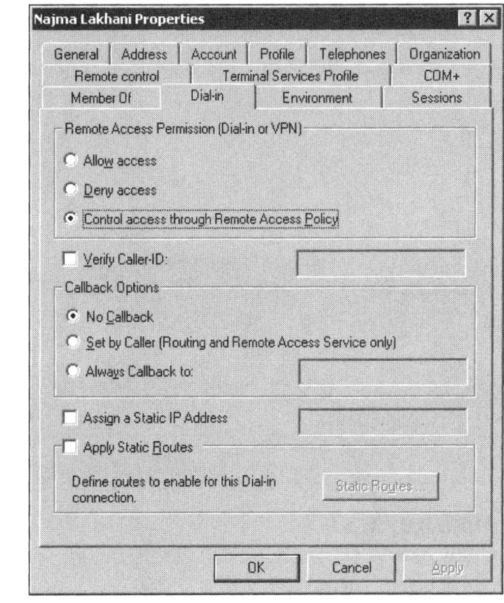

FIGURE 3.11
Control remote access on the Dial-In tab.

Adding Users to Groups

To save administrative effort, it is much easier to specify that users are members of *groups*. With users belonging to groups you can allocate resource access permissions to the group one time rather than individually to each user in that group. For example, you might have 50 members of a human resource group. You can individually grant access to human resource files and folders to the 50 members, but that obviously could take a long time and leave you open to committing an error that potentially could breach the security of highly sensitive human resource data. Now, if you create a human resource group and add the 50 human resource members to the group, you can configure all 50 access levels to human resource data at one time by configuring the proper access permissions to the group. A one-time action that takes care of 50 individuals! Therefore, it is useful to create groups, allocate members to those groups, and grant resource access permissions to the groups.

There are two ways to allocate users to groups. You can either open the Membership property of a group and add users to it, or you can open the Member Of property of a user and select the groups to which that user will belong. Step by Step 3.2 shows you how to make a user a member of a group.

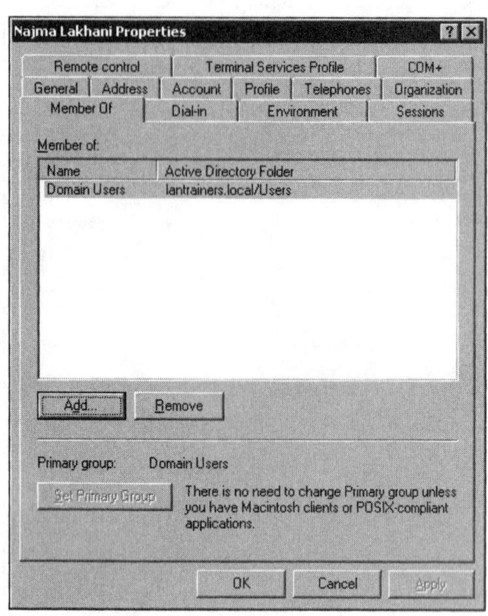

FIGURE 3.12▲
A new user is a member only of the Domain Users group.

STEP BY STEP

3.2 Adding a Member to a Group

1. In Active Directory Users and Computers, navigate to a user account object and open its properties.
2. Select the Member Of tab and view the existing memberships. By default, new users created in a domain are only members of the Domain Users group, as shown in Figure 3.12.
3. Click the Add button to bring up the Select Groups dialog box. Type the name of the group and then click the Check Names button. Figure 3.13 shows the results of typing "Engineers" and then selecting Check Names.
4. Click OK to complete the addition of the Engineers group to the user account and to see the new list of groups to which the user belongs.
5. Click OK to close the user's properties.

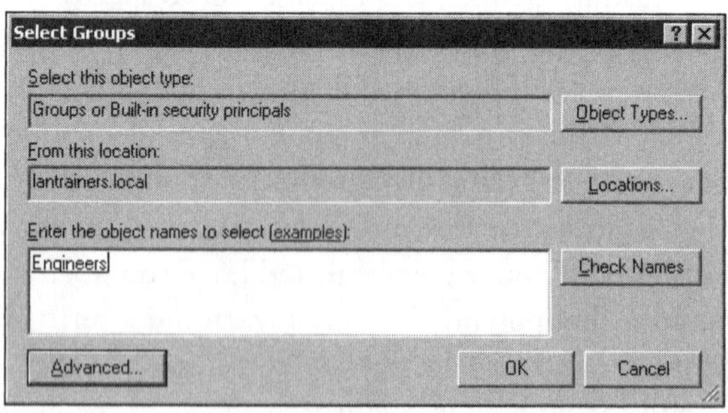

FIGURE 3.13▶
Adding a user to the Engineers group.

NOTE

New and Improved This is the first time we've used the new-and-improved Object Picker. In Figure 3.13, we could have typed "Eng" and clicked the Check Names button to find the Engineers group. We could have also selected the Advanced button and typed "Art" in the Name Starts With field and found both Arthur Lismer and Arthur Adams. Take a few minutes to play with the new Object Picker.

Saving Time with User Templates

In most organizations, many people have the same resource access needs. Perhaps all Vancouver engineers need print and management access to a particular printer, and read and write access to two shared folders. Also, staff in a particular location may have the same logon hours or other information, which is the same from person to person.

Rather than laboriously entering the same information for each user account, it's easier to create one account as a template and then copy that account whenever you need to create another user account with the same characteristics.

To do this, create a new user account and give it a display name that will cause it to be shown at the start of the username list in the container in Active Directory Users and Computers. Because special characters sort first, a name such as _Engineer or _Engineer Template would work well. Assign the account to the groups the users will be in, specify logon hours and logon computer restrictions, and enter the information on the Address, Account, Profile, and Organization tabs that you want to apply to all users. It's a good idea to disable the template account so that when new accounts are created from the template, they will be disabled also. This ensures new accounts won't be automatically available to anyone with malicious intent who knows who the new hires will be.

As an example of a user template, note the Organization page of the _Engineer account shown in Figure 3.14. This is the template account used to create the Test Engineer account.

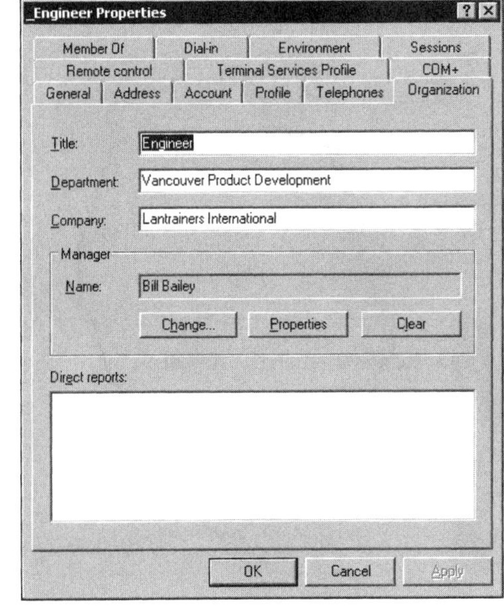

FIGURE 3.14
The template account should have commonly needed information in the fields of the Organization tab.

Once the template has been created, all you have to do to create a new user with the same characteristics is right-click the template account and choose Copy. You enter the username, user ID, and password of the specific user, and the resulting account has both the specific information for an actual user and the necessary ancillary information applicable to all users in the group because most of it was already entered into fields in the template account.

When a new account for Test Engineer was created by copying the _Engineer account, most of the information on the Organization tab was carried over, as you can see in Figure 3.15.

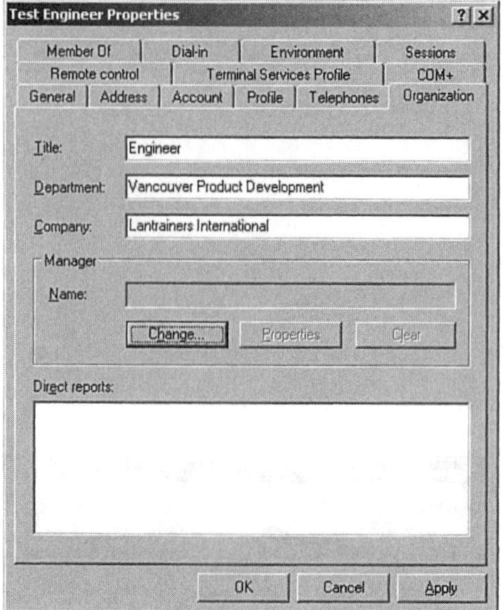

FIGURE 3.15
The Title field was not copied to the new account.

> **WARNING**
>
> **Schema Changes Are Not Reversible** You should exercise extreme caution when making changes to the Active Directory schema. Changes made to the schema are not reversible!

You might be wondering which attributes are copied to a new account created by copying a template. The values included in any attributes marked "Attribute Is Copied when Duplicating User" in the Active Directory Schema snap-in will be included in the copied account. With the necessary privileges, you can change which attributes are copied and which are not.

When creating template accounts, consider making separate templates for temporary employees. If your organization is planning to hire several summer students, set up a template with the account-expiration dates set to the end of the summer. This way, all the users created using the _Summer Intern template will have the correct expiration already set when the accounts are created.

A good rule when creating template accounts is that you want to have a new template account for every set of new user types that might have unique information prepopulated. For example, in the case of the summer interns, their accounts are unique because of the expiration date. Using the _Summer Intern template would not be appropriate for a new employee whose account will not expire, and vice versa. You might decide to create template accounts for the different departments in your company or for those who have different work hours or managers. The key thing to remember is that the template you use must match the characteristics of the user you are creating. Otherwise, information will be automatically placed in the user account properties (via the template copy) that is not relevant for that user.

Creating Accounts Using Automation

When you only have a few accounts to create or change, it's reasonable to use Active Directory Users and Computers. But for large numbers, you would want to automate the process. This section discusses using the command-line tools in conjunction with batch files to create many accounts, and we'll discuss importing user accounts as well.

Creating and Modifying User Accounts with Command-line Tools

New in Windows Server 2003 are several command-line tools that can help in automating the creation and modification of user accounts:

- **dsadd**—Used to create Active Directory objects
- **dsget**—Used to retrieve specific properties of a user account
- **dsmod**—Used to change a property in a user account
- **dsmove**—Used to move or rename an Active Directory object
- **dsrm**—Used to delete Active Directory objects

The first one we'll discuss is `dsadd`, which adds accounts to the Active Directory service.

Creating Accounts with `dsadd`

The `dsadd` command can be used to create several types of objects in Active Directory. You can consider these to be subcommands of the `dsadd` command:

- **dsadd computer**—Adds a computer to the directory
- **dsadd contact**—Adds a contact to the directory
- **dsadd group**—Adds a group to the directory
- **dsadd ou**—Adds an Organizational Unit to the directory
- **dsadd user**—Adds a user to the directory
- **dsadd quota**—Adds a quota specification to a directory partition

To learn how to use the `dsadd` command, open a command prompt and enter the following:

```
dsadd /?
```

To learn about the use of the subcommands, at the command prompt enter the following:

```
dsadd user /?
```

The `dsadd user` command can take several parameters, but the only required one is DN (distinguished name).

What's a distinguished name? It is the name assigned to an object in Active Directory, and it's made up of the object name (for example, Bill Bailey), the container it resides in, and the list of all the parent containers of that container, right up to the domain. Here's the distinguished name for Bill Bailey:

```
"CN=Bill Bailey,OU=Users,OU=Vancouver,OU=LTI,DC=lantrainers,DC=local"
```

The following list examines the parts of this name:

- **`CN=Bill Bailey`**—CN stands for *common name*. It can be used for users, groups, computers, and containers.
- **`OU=Users,OU=Vancouver,OU=LTI`**—OU stands for *Organizational Unit*, and this string lists all the containers in order, from the one the object resides in, up to the first container below the domain object.
- **`DC=lantrainers,DC=local`**—DC stands for *domain component*, and we need a DC for each part of the fully qualified domain name (FQDN) of the domain, `lantrainers.local`.

> NOTE
>
> **Know the Difference** The default Active Directory folders shown in the root of the Active Directory Users and Computers MMC—Users, Builtin, and Computers—are actually containers and not Organizational Units. When referencing these containers you have to use the `CN=` attribute and not `OU=`.

Windows Server 2003 will not permit you to create more than one object with exactly the same distinguished name so that you can be sure a distinguished name refers to a unique object. A good example of this is the Users OU we created earlier. Although its name is the same as the Users container that is created by default, the distinguished name is unique. With that knowledge in mind, you now know that we can create a new user in the same container as Bill Bailey's with the following command:

```
dsadd user "CN=Tom Thomson,OU=Users,OU=Vancouver,OU=LTI,DC=lantrainers,
➥DC=local"
```

Having run this command, we return to Active Directory Users and Computers, and after refreshing the contents of the Users container under Vancouver, we see the new user object, as shown in Figure 3.16.

If you look at the properties of the object, you will see that none of the user-defined fields have been filled in. Note that, by default, the account is shown as disabled.

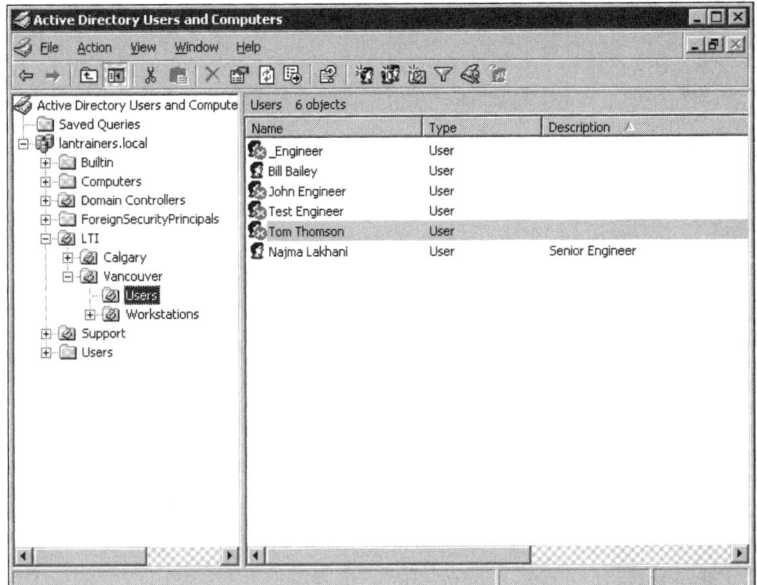

FIGURE 3.16
The user object for Tom Thomson now exists.

Obviously, using `dsadd` in this way doesn't save us much time if we later have to go into the properties of the object manually to add the user's details. However, all the usually defined properties can be included in the `dsadd` command, along with the distinguished name, so the whole object-creation process, including the user details, can be automated.

The following is a partial list of the properties that can be included with the `dsadd` command (from `dsadd user /?`):

- **`-samid`**—The user ID in a form that is usable with non–Active Directory accounts management.
- **`-upn`**—The user principal name is an alternate name that can be used for logon. In place of the usual `domain\user`, you can enter `name@domain`. For example, Bill Bailey could log on as `bbailey@lantrainers.local`.
- **`-fn`**—The user's first name.
- **`-mi`**—The user's middle initial.

- **-ln**—The user's last name.
- **-display**—The name that denotes the account in listings, such as in Active Directory Users and Computers.
- **-empid**—An EmployeeID field.
- **-pwd**—This field can contain the password to be assigned to the account. If you want to be prompted for a password when creating the account, enter `*`. This wildcard is probably not appropriate for mass-creating users because the script will stop each time a user is created asking for a password.
- **-desc**—A description of the user.
- **-memberof**—A list of distinguished names of the groups the user should be made a member of.
- **-office**—The name of the user's office.
- **-tel**—The user's main phone number.
- **-email**—The user's email address.
- **-webpg**—The user's Web page address.
- **-title**—The user's title.
- **-dept**—Department.
- **-company**—Company.
- **-mgr**—The manager of this user.
- **-hmdir**—The path to the user's home directory.
- **-hmdrv**—The drive letter assigned to the user's home directory.
- **-mustchpwd**—The user must change the password at next logon: `{yes ¦ no}`.
- **-canchpwd**—The user is able to change the password: `{yes ¦ no}`.
- **-reversiblepwd**—The password is stored with reversible encryption (used with Macintosh systems and digest authentication): `{yes ¦ no}`.
- **-pwdneverexpires**—The password does not expire: `{yes ¦ no}`.

- **-acctexpires**—The number of days until the account expires.
- **-disabled**—The account is disabled: {yes | no}.
- **-q**—The command should run with no output to the console.

Using as many of these parameters as are necessary to define the user account, the administrator can create the account with a single command, like this:

```
dsadd user "CN=Arthur Lismer,OU=Users,OU=Vancouver,OU=LTI,DC=lantrainers,
➥DC=local" -samid ALismer -upn alismer@lantrainers.local -fn Arthur
➥-ln Lismer -pwd Passw0rd -memberof "CN=Vancouver Users,OU=LTI,
➥DC=lantrainers,DC=local" -office Vancouver -disabled no
➥-mustchpwd yes
```

"But wait," you say, "that's more effort than working my way through Active Directory Users and Computers to create a user." That's true, for one user. However, if you're creating a thousand of them, and you have their names in a spreadsheet, it takes very little work to create a batch file where each line in the file creates another user.

Once you have invested the time to master `dsadd`, you can save huge amounts of time in creating large numbers of user accounts.

> **NOTE**
>
> **Using `Net User`** Another way to create users from the command line is with the `Net User` command. It works with a limited set of parameters compared to `dsadd`, but its biggest drawback is that any user account created using `Net User` is placed in the Users container. If you have any structure in your Active Directory tree (and you should, to allow administrative flexibility), you would be much better off with `dsadd` than with `Net User`.
>
> It is possible to change the default containers for newly created accounts. The command `redirusr.exe` changes the default container for users, and `redircmp.exe` changes the default container for computers. But even with these specific commands to enhance the `Net User` command, it is clear that `dsadd` is much more flexible.

Listing the Properties of User Accounts with `dsget`

If you want to get the value of some properties of a user account with a command-line tool, you use `dsget user`. The syntax of the command is as follows:

```
dsget user <dn> <list of properties>
```

The properties you can use are shown in the following list, from Windows Server 2003 Help and Support:

- **-dn**—Shows the DN of the user.
- **-samid**—Shows the SAM account name of the user.
- **-sid**—Shows the user's Security ID.
- **-upn**—Shows the user principal name of the user.
- **-fn**—Shows the first name of the user.
- **-mi**—Shows the middle initial of the user.
- **-ln**—Shows the last name of the user.

- **-display**—Shows the display name of the user.
- **-empid**—Shows the user employee ID.
- **-desc**—Shows the description of the user.
- **-office**—Shows the office location of the user.
- **-tel**—Shows the telephone number of the user.
- **-email**—Shows the email address of the user.
- **-hometel**—Shows the home telephone number of the user.
- **-pager**—Shows the pager number of the user.
- **-mobile**—Shows the mobile phone number of the user.
- **-fax**—Shows the fax number of the user.
- **-iptel**—Shows the user IP phone number.
- **-webpg**—Shows the user's Web page URL.
- **-title**—Shows the title of the user.
- **-dept**—Shows the department of the user.
- **-company**—Shows the company info of the user.
- **-mgr**—Shows the user's manager.
- **-hmdir**—Shows the user's home directory. It also displays the drive letter to which the home directory of the user is mapped (if the home directory path is a UNC path).
- **-hmdrv**—Shows the user's home drive letter (if home directory is a UNC path).
- **-profile**—Shows the user's profile path.
- **-loscr**—Shows the user's logon script path.
- **-mustchpwd**—Shows whether the user must change his or her password at the time of next logon. Displays yes or no.
- **-canchpwd**—Shows whether the user can change his or her password. Displays yes or no.

- **-pwdneverexpires**—Shows whether the user's password never expires. Displays yes or no.
- **-disabled**—Shows whether the user account is disabled for logon. Displays yes or no.
- **-acctexpires**—Shows when the user account expires. Displays a value (a date when the account expires or the string `never` if the account never expires).
- **-reversiblepwd**—Shows whether the user password is allowed to be stored using reversible encryption. Displays yes or no.

For example, the command

```
dsget user "CN=Najma Lakhani,OU=Users,OU=Vancouver,OU=LTI,DC=lantrainers,
➥DC=local" -fn -ln -desc -office
```

returns the following information:

```
desc               fn       ln         office
Senior Engineer    Najma    Lakhani    Vancouver
```

This command can be very useful in determining the values of the properties of one or several user accounts.

Modifying User Accounts with dsmod

You've probably been wondering what you would do if you had to make a change to hundreds or thousands of users. Well, just as `dsadd` allows you to automate the creation of users, `dsmod` allows you to change them.

`dsmod` uses the same parameters as `dsadd`, so you indicate the account you want to change with its distinguished name and then specify the parameter and the value it should have. For example,

```
dsmod user "CN=Arthur Lismer,OU=Users,OU=Vancouver,OU=LTI,DC=lantrainers,
➥DC=local"-office Burnaby
```

would change the value of the office parameter to `Burnaby`, while leaving all the other parameters unchanged.

Using Piping Commands

If you're like some administrators, you took one look at the `dsmod` command in the previous paragraph and said, "There's too much work in typing distinguished names! I'm sticking with Active Directory Users and Computers!"

This is where *piping* comes in. Piping allows you to use the output of one command as the input for a second command. If you can issue a dsquery command that finds the Arthur Lismer user object, you can pipe (using the ¦ symbol on the keyboard) the output from the dsquery command into the dsmod command. Let's walk through this:

```
C:\>dsquery user -name arthur*
"CN=Arthur Lismer,OU=Users,OU=Vancouver,OU=LTI,DC=lantrainers,DC=local"
"CN=Arthur Adams,OU=Users,OU=Vancouver,OU=LTI,DC=lantrainers,DC=local"
```

No, that produced too many Arthurs. Let's try this:

```
C:\>dsquery user -name *lismer
"CN=Arthur Lismer,OU=Users,OU=Vancouver,OU=LTI,DC=lantrainers,DC=local"
```

There we go, just the user we wanted. Now let's pipe the output of dsquery into dsget to find the current value of the office parameter:

```
C:\>dsquery user -name *lismer ¦ dsget user -office
  Office
  Vancouver
dsget succeeded
```

Good. Now we change the value of the office parameter with a dsmod command:

```
C:\>dsquery user -name *lismer ¦ dsmod user -office Burnaby
dsmod succeeded:CN=Arthur Lismer,OU=Users,OU=Vancouver,OU=LTI,
➥DC=lantrainers,DC=local
```

And now we can confirm that the change was made:

```
C:\>dsquery user -name *lismer ¦ dsget user -office
  Office
  Burnaby
dsget succeeded
```

This is much more efficient than typing long distinguished names! And if you use a dsquery that returns several user accounts, the dsmod command can modify the same field in all the returned accounts, all at once.

For example, as in the preceding example when we changed the office location, typing the following command changes the user's telephone number without typing the DN:

```
C:\>dsquery user -name *lismer ¦ dsmod user -tel 803-734-1122
```

You can use similar logic to change any other piece of information in the directory by simply searching for the user's name, UPN, location in the directory, or even several other parameters you can see when using `dsquery user /?`. Hopefully, you are starting to see that the power of these commands is far greater than what it first appears.

Moving or Renaming Objects with dsmove

If you need to move an object to another location within Active Directory, or you want to rename the object, you can do so with `dsmove`. The syntax of `dsmove` is as follows:

```
dsmove <ObjectDN> [-newparent <ParentDN>] [-newname <NewName>]
```

So if Najma Lakhani moves from Vancouver to Calgary, and she changes her name to Najma Larson, we could accomplish the change with the following command:

```
C:\>dsquery user -name "Najma*" ¦dsmove -newparent
"OU=Users,OU=Calgary,OU=LTI,DC=lantrainers,DC=local"
➥ -newname "Najma Larson"
```

Checking in Active Directory Users and Computers shows Najma Larson in the new OU. Note that only the object name has changed. To complete the user's name change, properties of the object such as display name, last name, and email address will still have to be modified with `dsmod` or Active Directory Users and Computers.

Removing Objects with dsrm

The final command-line tool for Active Directory is `dsrm`. It is used to delete Active Directory objects. If the object being referenced is a container, it's possible to delete the objects in the container but retain the object itself.

The syntax for `dsrm` is as follows:

```
dsrm <ObjectDN ...> [-noprompt] [-subtree [-exclude]]
```

- **`-noprompt`**—Do not prompt for confirmation before deleting object.
- **`-subtree`**—Delete the object and all objects included in it.
- **`-exclude`**—Used with `subtree`. Do not delete the object, just its contents.

For example, assume the Calgary office has just completed a Systems Analysis course and wants to delete the accounts that were created for students in the course. The accounts were in the OU called `AnalysisStudents` under the `"OU=Calgary,OU=LTI,DC=lantrainers, DC=local"` OU. The `AnalysisStudents` OU should be retained for future classes. The following command will delete all the objects in the `AnalysisStudents` OU but retain the OU:

```
C:\>dsrm "OU=AnalysisStudents,OU=Calgary,OU=LTI,DC=lantrainers,DC=local"
➥ -subtree -exclude
Are you sure you wish to delete all children of
OU=AnalysisStudents,OU=Calgary,OU=LTI,DC=lantrainers,DC=local (Y/N)? y
dsrm succeeded:OU=AnalysisStudents,OU=Calgary,OU=LTI,
➥DC=lantrainers,DC=local
```

Importing and Exporting User Accounts

Some organizations occasionally have a need to create, modify, or delete thousands of user accounts at a time. Think of a large university, with an incoming class of several thousand students at the start of each term. You certainly wouldn't want to create each of those accounts with Active Directory Users and Computers!

What saves the day here is two facts: Almost certainly there is a database somewhere in the organization that has all the information needed to define the needed accounts, and Microsoft has provided two programs with Windows Server 2003, `ldifde` and `csvde`, that can be used to import accounts into Active Directory.

To create the thousands of user accounts, you would export the necessary information from the database system, manipulate the data so that it is in the format the import program needs, and then run the import program. It may take some time to go through these steps, but that's better than many days of tedious and error-prone work with Active Directory Users and Computers.

Why are there two import utilities, and how do they differ? The next sections answer those questions. `csvde` is simpler, so we'll discuss it first.

IN THE FIELD

MORE ABOUT IMPORTING/EXPORTING

Although the utilities we discuss here are fine for small-to-medium-sized organizations, large enterprises need tools that are built to handle a large volume of changes. Hewlett-Packard offers a tool called LDAP Directory Synchronization Utility (LDSU) that can easily handle the import and export changes described here, and it's robust enough for large enterprises to rely on.

LDSU was used to synch the Digital and Compaq directories during that merger (105,000 users and mailboxes), as well as the Compaq and HP directories (165,000 user accounts and mailboxes). Both of them were completely in synch within hours after the merger was finalized.

The beauty of LDSU is that it is simple to use and can "map" fields and formatting from one side to the other and keep the directories in synch as changes occur in the future.

Some basic information on LDSU is provided at `http://h18008.www1.hp.com/services/messaging/mg_ldap_fact.html`.

The `csvde` Utility

The `csvde` (Comma Separated Value Directory Exchange) utility exports data from Active Directory, or imports data into Active Directory, in Comma Separated Value (CSV) format. In this format, each line of data represents one record, and each field is separated from the next by a comma. If any field has commas as part of the data, the whole field is enclosed by quotation marks. So that the import utility can properly allocate each value to the appropriate field, the first line of the data file lists the names of the fields in the order they will appear in the data records.

As an example, here is the output from `csvde` of the Arthur Lismer record in our sample company:

```
DN,objectClass,ou,distinguishedName,instanceType,whenCreated,whenChanged,
➥uSNCreated,uSNChanged,name,objectCategory,dSCorePropagationData,
➥cn,sn,physicalDeliveryOfficeName,givenName,displayName,
➥userAccountControl,codePage,countryCode,accountExpires,
➥sAMAccountName,userPrincipalName,description,mail,c,l,st,
```

```
➥title,postalCode,co,department,company,streetAddress,
➥userWorkstations,manager"CN=ArthurLismer,OU=Users,OU=Vancouver,
➥OU=LTI,DC=lantrainers,DC=local",user,,"CN=ArthurLismer,OU=Users,
➥OU=Vancouver,OU=LTI,DC=lantrainers,DC=local",4,20030421210344.
➥0Z,20030421210345.0Z,33732,33738,ArthurLismer,"CN=Person,
➥CN=Schema,CN=Configuration,DC=lantrainers,DC=local",
➥,ArthurLismer,Lismer,Vancouver,Arthur,
➥,512,0,0,9223372036854775807,ALismer,alismer@tlantrainers.local
➥,,,,,,,,,,,,,
```

The first line (starting `DN,objectClass`... is the header line, listing the fields in the data. The second line is the data for the Arthur Lismer record. It's hard to read, but if you load it into a spreadsheet program, each field will be in a separate column, and it's easy to work with then.

This output was created with the following command:

```
csvde -f c:\lismer.csv -r "(name=*lismer)"
```

The parameter `-f c:\lismer.csv` sends the output of the command to the file `c:\lismer.csv`, and the parameter `-r "(name=*lismer)"` tells the utility to select just those records whose name field ends in `lismer`.

To make the output of `csvde` easier to use, you can specify the fields you want to have exported. For example, the command

```
C:\>csvde -f c:\lismer.csv -r "(name=*lismer)" -l
l,company,objectclass,name,title,company,l,telephoneNumber,
➥userAccountControl,samaccountname
```

results in the simpler output file

```
DN,objectClass,title,telephoneNumber,company,name,
➥userAccountControl,sAMAccountName "CN=Arthur
➥Lismer,OU=Users,OU=Vancouver,OU=LTI,DC=lantrainers,
➥DC=local",user,Network Architect,555-5678,Thomson Associates,
➥Arthur Lismer,512,Alismer
```

It is useful to run `csvde` in output mode first, to list the names of the attributes.

Now, to import a user, we make a text file in the same format as the output files and then run `csvde` in import mode. For example, let's run the command

```
csvde -i -f c:\adams-in.csv -j c:\
```

with the following input file:

```
DN,objectClass,title,telephoneNumber,company,name,userAccountControl,
➥sAMAccountName"CN=ArthurAdams,OU=Users,OU=Vancouver,OU=LTI,
➥DC=lantrainers,DC=local",user,Network Architect,555-5678,
➥Thomson Associates,Arthur Adams,514,Aadams
```

This creates a user account for Arthur Adams, with the attributes listed. Note that we have used the `userAccountControl` value of `514`, which means the account is disabled when it is first created. This is because our work is not yet done because we haven't assigned the user to any groups and we haven't set the user's password. We can complete these tasks with the `dsmod` utility and then enable the account.

The `ldifde` Utility

The name of this utility, `ldifde`, means LDIF Directory Exchange. *LDIF (LDAP Data Interchange Format)* is a definition of how data can be exchanged between LDAP-based directories. *LDAP (Lightweight Directory Access Protocol)* is an industry-standard protocol for accessing directories. For complete information about LDAP, see RFCs 2251–2256, and for information on LDIF, see RFC 2849, which can be read at `www.ietf.org/rfc/rfc2849.txt`.

There are two primary differences between `ldifde` and `csvde`. First, whereas `csvde` can only import and export records, `ldifde` can also modify records and delete records, making it a much more powerful utility. Second, the data format is very different. Instead of a file with a header record and one record per entry, the file contains many lines per entry, with the field name as the first part of each line.

Here is what the `ldifde` output looks like for the Arthur Lismer user account. Note that an entry starts with the distinguished name (`dn`) of the entry, then a `changetype` line (the `changetype` command can be `add`, `modify`, or `delete`), and then the attributes of the entry, in alphabetical order by attribute name:

```
dn: CN=Arthur Lismer,OU=Users,OU=Vancouver,OU=LTI,DC=lantrainers,DC=local
changetype: add
accountExpires: 9223372036854775807
cn: Arthur Lismer
codePage: 0
countryCode: 0
distinguishedName:  CN=Arthur Lismer,OU=Users,OU=Vancouver,OU=LTI,
➥DC=lantrainers,DC=local
givenName: Arthur
```

```
instanceType: 4
name: Arthur Lismer
objectCategory: CN=Person,CN=Schema,CN=Configuration,DC=lantrainers,
➥DC=local
objectClass: top
objectClass: person
objectClass: organizationalPerson
objectClass: user
physicalDeliveryOfficeName: Vancouver
sAMAccountName: ALismer
sn: Lismer
userAccountControl: 512
userPrincipalName: alismer@tlantrainers.local
uSNChanged: 33738
uSNCreated: 33732
whenChanged: 20030421210345.0Z
whenCreated: 20030421210344.0Z
```

To use `ldifde` to create a series of user accounts, we'll need to build an input file of records in the format shown.

The following input file was used with the command

```
Ldifde -i -f c:\ldif-in1.txt
```

to create a new user account for Frank Carmichael:

```
dn: CN=Frank Carmichael,OU=Users,OU=Vancouver,OU=LTI,DC=lantrainers,
➥DC=local
changetype: add
cn: Frank Carmichael
codePage: 0
countryCode: 0
distinguishedName:  CN=Frank Carmichael,OU=Users,OU=Vancouver,OU=LTI,
➥DC=lantrainers,DC=local
givenName: Frank
instanceType: 4
name: Frank Carmichael
objectCategory: CN=Person,CN=Schema,CN=Configuration,DC=lantrainers,
➥DC=local
objectClass: top
objectClass: person
objectClass: organizationalPerson
objectClass: user
physicalDeliveryOfficeName: Vancouver
sAMAccountName: FCarmichael
sn: Carmichael
userAccountControl: 514
userPrincipalName: fCarmichael@tlantrainers.local
```

Using dsmod as described earlier, we can add three users' accounts to the Vancouver Users group with this command (entered as a batch file):

```
dsmod group  "CN=Vancouver Users,OU=LTI,DC=lantrainers,DC=local" -addmbr
➥ "CN=Tom Thomson,OU=Users,OU=Vancouver,OU=LTI,DC=lantrainers,DC=local"
➥ "CN=Arthur Adams,OU=Users,OU=Vancouver,OU=LTI,DC=lantrainers,DC=local"
➥ "CN=Frank Carmichael,OU=Users,OU=Vancouver,OU=LTI,DC=lantrainers,
➥DC=local" -c
```

A second dsmod command sets all these users' passwords to Secur1ty and requires them to change their passwords at the next logon:

```
dsmod user "CN=Tom Thomson,OU=Users,OU=Vancouver,OU=LTI,DC=lantrainers,
➥DC=local" "CN=Arthur Adams,OU=Users,OU=Vancouver,OU=LTI,DC=lantrainers,
➥DC=local" "CN=Frank Carmichael,OU=Users,OU=Vancouver,OU=LTI,
➥DC=lantrainers,DC=local" -pwd Secur1ty -mustchpwd yes
```

And a final dsmod command enables the three accounts:

```
dsmod user "CN=Tom Thomson,OU=Users,OU=Vancouver,OU=LTI,DC=lantrainers,
➥DC=local" "CN=Arthur Adams,OU=Users,OU=Vancouver,OU=LTI,DC=lantrainers,
➥DC=local" "CN=Frank Carmichael,OU=Users,OU=Vancouver,OU=LTI,
➥DC=lantrainers,DC=local" -disabled no
```

Using the -c Parameter

A common use for ldifde is to create a set of objects in a new directory from an existing one. For example, you might be creating a set of user accounts in a new test directory from the user accounts in a production directory.

It's a fairly simple process to use ldifde in export mode to create a file containing information about the existing user accounts. Then running ldifde in import mode will load the accounts into the new location. However, the distinguished names will all have to be changed because they will refer to the source directory.

For example, imagine that we are setting up a test domain called lantrainers.com. We want to populate the new directory with information exported from our lantrainers.local domain. All the information about the accounts will be the same, but the Active Directory paths will be different in all the distinguished names.

This is where the -c parameter is used. Using ldifde with -c <old string> <new string> causes the replacement of any occurrences of <old string> by <new string> before the data is acted on by ldifde.

Troubleshooting User Accounts

There are several reasons why users may find that they cannot use their user accounts. In this section we will look at account lockouts and at reasons why an account might not be usable.

Troubleshooting Account Lockouts

Account lockout is a Windows Server 2003 security feature designed to protect accounts from repeated attempts to guess the account's password. A policy can be set that causes a user account to be disabled if a specific number of invalid login attempts are made within the specified timeframe. The account is disabled for a specific number of minutes; if the specified timeframe passes without another invalid attempt, the count of invalid attempts is reset to zero. Figure 3.17 shows the default settings if you enable account lockout in the Group Policy Object Editor.

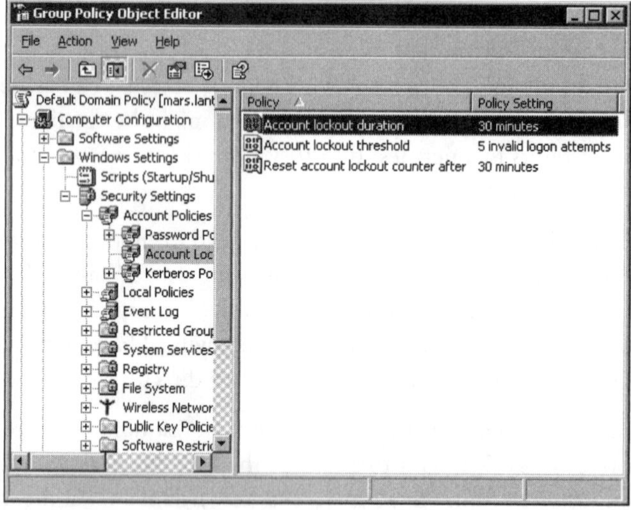

FIGURE 3.17
The default settings for account lockout.

The term *invalid logon attempt* includes attempts to guess a password that is protecting a workstation's session, whether with a password-protected screensaver, a Ctrl+Alt+Del Lock Workstation command, the initial login dialog box, or from across the network.

Table 3.1 shows the default values and the ranges of possible values for the account lockout feature.

TABLE 3.1

DEFAULT VALUES FOR ACCOUNT LOCKOUTS

Setting	*Default Value*	*Range of Values*
Account lockout duration	30 minutes	From 0–99,999 minutes. A setting of 0 means the account is locked out until an administrator unlocks it.
Account lockout threshold	Five invalid attempts	From 0–999. A setting of 0 means account lockout will not be used.
Reset lockout counter after	30 minutes	From 1–99,999 minutes.

Many administrators initially set the account lockout duration to 0 so that they will always know if an attempt was made, and this is certainly the most secure approach. However, a few irate calls from locked-out users usually results in a setting of 30 or 60 minutes!

INDEFINITE LOCKOUTS

Why is an indefinite lockout the most secure approach? If the default settings are in effect, and an intruder tries all weekend to guess an account's password, he could try dozens of times, but nobody would know about the attempts if the intruder stops 30 minutes before the actual user comes to log on.

If a user account is locked out, you can allow it to be used again with Active Directory Users and Computers. Figure 3.18 shows the location.

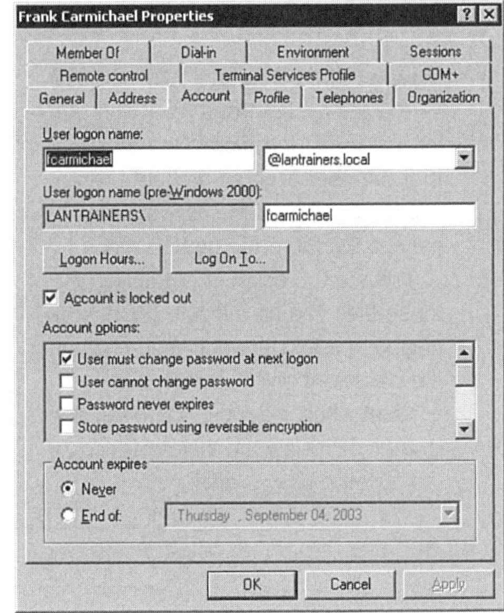

FIGURE 3.18
Allow the account to be used by clearing the Account Is Locked Out check box.

To implement account lockout, modify the Default Domain Policy (in the Group Policy tab of the domain object of Active Directory Users and Computers). The account lockout settings are found under Computer Configuration, Windows Settings, Security Setting, Account Policies, Account Lockout Policy.

Like password policies, account lockout can be defined only at the domain level. So be careful—all password policy settings will affect every user account in your domain!

Account lockout is a security feature that must be put in place for any production network to be considered secure. Be sure you have management agreement with any new account password settings, and give your user community several days' warning before you implement it.

Troubleshooting Issues Related to User Account Properties

Many help desk analysts will tell you that a large portion of the calls they receive have to do with settings on the user account. Here are several situations that arise because of settings on user account properties.

Account Disabled

It is common practice to disable the account of any user who is either on leave for an extended period or no longer with the organization. Of course, when the user returns and attempts to use the account, she will be unable to log on.

A disabled account can easily be enabled. With Active Directory Users and Computers, open the properties of the user account. On the Account tab, clear the Account Is Disabled check box. Alternatively, you can use `dsmod` and enter the following:

```
dsmod user <distinguished name> -disabled no
```

NOTE

Disable, Don't Delete! Why not just delete the account of a user who leaves an organization? One reason is that the user account probably has access to files on the network that may be useful to the organization. If you delete the account, retrieving those files can be difficult. It's best to disable the account and then change the password and reenable the account when a person has been designated to review the files to which the account has access.

Account Expired

We know that an account can have an expiration date—the date after which the account cannot be used. If a temporary worker's contract is extended and the network administrator has not been asked to adjust or remove the account expiration date, the worker will not be able to log in until the expiration date is reset.

This setting can be modified in Active Directory Users and Computers: Open the properties of the user account, then on the Account tab, in the Account Expires section, select either Never or a new date. Alternatively, with `dsmod`, you can enter

```
dsmod user <distinguished name> -acctexpires never
```

or

```
dsmod user <distinguished name> -acctexpires <number of days>
```

Dial-in Disallowed

A user might complain of being unable to connect by dial-in connection or through a virtual private network (VPN) connection. In this case, check the Dial-In tab of the user accounts properties, as shown in Figure 3.19.

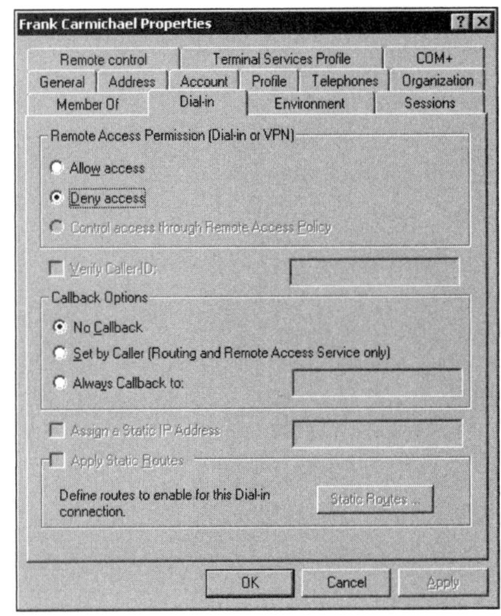

FIGURE 3.19
If the Remote Access Permission setting is Deny Access, no dial-in or VPN connections will be allowed.

To permit dial-in or VPN connections, select Allow Access or, in domains where the functional level is at least Windows 2000 native, Control Access Through Remote Access Policy.

Cannot Change Password

In some cases, users call the help desk because the operating system does not allow them to change their password. There are two possible reasons for this situation.

First, the account may have been set up with the User Cannot Change Password option. This situation is easily rectified, if appropriate, by going to the Account tab of the user account Properties dialog box and clearing the check box.

Second, a user may be unable to change the user account's password because the password entered does not meet the complexity requirements determined by the domain account policies. If enabled, this policy requires that passwords meet the following minimum requirements:

- Not contain all or part of the user's account name
- Be at least six characters in length
- Contain characters from three of the following four categories:
  - English uppercase characters (A through Z)
  - English lowercase characters (a through z)
  - Base 10 digits (0 through 9)
  - Nonalphabetic characters (for example, !, $, #, %)

If the user's password change is being denied due to password complexity requirements, minimum password age, or other restrictions, you must explain the requirements to the user.

IN THE FIELD

USING SAVED QUERIES

A very useful tool in Windows Server 2003 is *Saved Queries*, a new function under Active Directory Users and Computers. With this facility, a user can define a query that is frequently used and return to it easily whenever it is needed.

For example, assume that the administrator wants to list all disabled accounts. The administrator would right-click Saved Queries, select New Query, specify the name Disabled Accounts, select Define Query, and select the Disabled Accounts check box in the Find Common Queries dialog box. The resulting query is available for use any time the administrator returns to the Saved Queries function.

You can define quite complex queries, using the fields of the user object, and run them easily in the future.

GUIDED PRACTICE EXERCISE 3.1

You are the administrator of a network for a manufacturing company that has multiple Windows Server 2003 servers used for file and print services.

Common to most manufacturing entities is the need to protect sensitive design data from industrial espionage. The products that your company manufactures are for very price-conscious consumers—not only the design of the products, but also the manufacturing techniques, must be protected.

You need to find a way to minimize the exposure of external users hacking in to your servers.

Using the things that you have learned so far in this chapter, what is the best way to solve this issue in Windows Server 2003? On your own, try to develop a solution that would involve the least amount of downtime and expense.

If you would like to see a possible solution, follow these steps:

Estimated Time: 40 minutes

This is a fairly straightforward decision, mainly because the only security features we have discussed so far are user accounts and passwords. To increase security in your domain, you can modify the default domain policy to adjust the account-lockout settings so that hackers can't repeatedly try different passwords to access your servers. In addition, you can require complex passwords so that dictionary attacks won't be effective.

1. From the Start menu, select All Programs, Administrative Tools, Active Directory Users and Computers.
2. Right-click the domain name entry and select Properties from the pop-up menu.
3. From the Properties dialog box, click the Group Policy tab.
4. On the Group Policy tab, double-click the Default Domain Policy entry.
5. From the Group Policy MMC, navigate to Default Domain Policy, Computer Configuration, Windows Settings, Security Settings, Account Policy, Password Policy. Ensure the following settings are applied:
   - **Account Lockout Threshold**—3
   - **Account Lockout Duration**—60
   - **Passwords Must Meet Complexity Requirements**—Enabled
6. Close the MMC and then click OK on the Properties dialog box to save.

With the lockout threshold set, the account will be locked after three failed logon attempts, and it will be reenabled automatically after 1 hour. Passwords will be required to meet the complexity requirements discussed earlier in this chapter.

Managing Local, Roaming, and Mandatory User Profiles

The settings for a user's work environment are stored in a set of files and folders known as the *user profile.* The profile is automatically created the first time a user logs on to a computer running any version of Windows, and any changes to the environment (Favorites, Start menu items, icons, colors, My Documents, local settings) are saved when the user logs off. The profile is reloaded when the user logs on again. Table 3.2 lists the components of a user profile (from Windows Server 2003 Help and Support).

TABLE 3.2

USER PROFILE FOLDERS AND THEIR CONTENTS

User Profile Folder	*Contents*
Application Data	Program-specific data (for example, a custom dictionary). Program vendors decide what data to store in this user profile folder.
Cookies	Web site user information and preferences.
Desktop	Desktop items, including files, shortcuts, and folders.
Favorites	Shortcuts to favorite Internet locations.
Local Settings	History and temporary files.
My Documents	User documents and subfolders.
My Recent Documents	Shortcuts to the most recently used documents and accessed folders.
NetHood	Shortcuts to My Network Places items.
PrintHood	Shortcuts to printer folder items.
SendTo	Shortcuts to document-handling utilities.
Start Menu	Shortcuts to program items.
Templates	User template items.

The user profiles facility allows several people to use the same computer running Windows, yet each can see his or her own private desktop, and the settings will be remembered each time the user logs on.

Initially, the profile exists only on the computer where it was created: For this reason, it is called a *local user profile*. However, the profile can also be stored on a server, allowing the user to see the same desktop no matter what machine he or she is logged on to. This server-based profile is known as a *roaming user profile*. For some groups of users, we can also create mandatory user profiles, which cannot be changed by the users.

Creating and Modifying Local User Profiles

The first time a user logs on to a computer running Windows Server 2003, the folder structure shown in Figure 3.20 is created. This structure used the data and shortcuts contained in the DefaultUser profile as a template. In Figure 3.20 you see the Administrator profile.

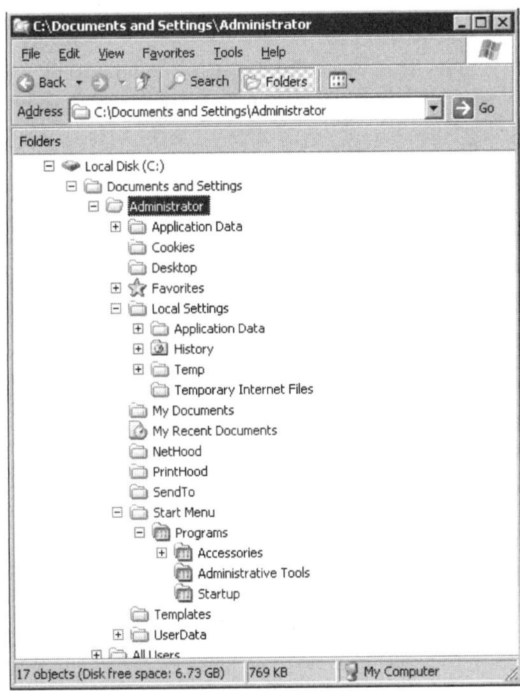

FIGURE 3.20
The folder structure of a user profile.

NOTE

For More Information For a full description of the folders, search Help and Support for "Contents of a User Profile." As you can imagine, the contents of the user profile structure can become quite large, especially because My Documents is one of the folders.

The folders of interest in the structure are *Application Data*, where software vendors store data for particular users, *Cookies*, where data about Web site preferences are stored, *Desktop*, which contains the desktop items, including any files stored there, *My Documents*, which is the default location for the storage of user data, and *Start Menu*, from which programs can be accessed that were installed for this user, but not all users of this computer.

Within the root folder of the profile, you will see a file called `NTuser.dat`. This file contains the contents of the current user-specific section of the Registry (`HKEY_CURRENT_USER`). This file is updated each time the user logs off.

Another profile structure that is used to create the user work environment is the *All Users* folder. Profile items that all users will see, such as program links that are on all users' All Programs menu, are stored in the All Users folder.

The contents and settings of the user profile are modified by working with the environment—using Control Panel applets such as Display, installing programs, and creating shortcuts on the desktop.

Creating and Modifying Roaming User Profiles

EXAM TIP

Expect a Roaming Profile Question Expect at least one exam question that deals with the topic of roaming profiles. Remember that although Windows 9x/Me and Windows NT support roaming profiles, they aren't compatible, nor can they be maintained via Group Policy the way that Windows 2000/XP/2003 can.

Because many users move from computer to computer and would like to see the same work environment each time, the *Roaming User Profiles* facility has been created. This facility allows the profile to be stored on a network server. When the user logs on, the profile is downloaded from the server, and the expected work environment is seen. When the user logs off, the profile is uploaded to the server, so any changes made are available for the next logon at that or any other computer.

To assign a roaming profile to a user using Active Directory Users and Computers, go to the Profile tab on the user accounts Properties dialog box and enter a valid path in the Profile field, as shown in Figure 3.21.

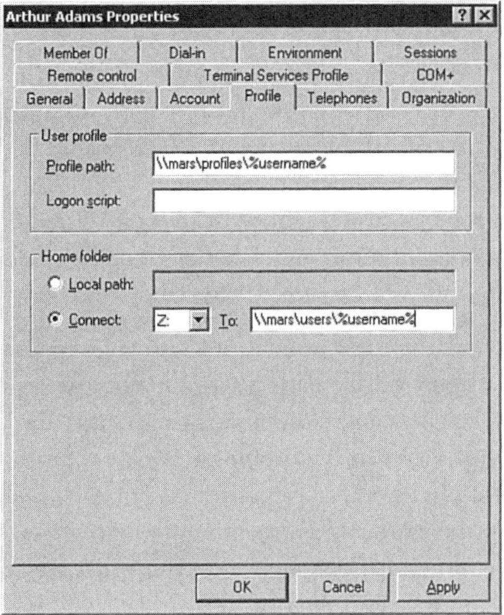

FIGURE 3.21
Use the `%username%` variable to substitute for the username.

> **EXAM TIP**
>
> **Know Your UNC Paths!** Be very familiar with the use of Universal Naming Convention (UNC) paths for the exam. For example, in the path \\mars\profiles\%username%, MARS is the NetBIOS name of the server that the PROFILES shared folder resides on. The replaceable parameter %username% refers to the name of the folder that will be created.

The next time the user logs on, the profile type will be changed to "Roaming," and after logoff the server-based profile will be updated.

Note that Active Directory Users and Computers will allow you to change some properties of multiple user accounts at once. That is, you can select multiple users and then choose Action, Properties and set the values for those properties. See Figure 3.22 for the Profile tab of the Properties on Multiple Objects dialog box.

You can also use `dsmod` to set the home folders and profile paths for multiple users. The following command entered as a batch file, for convenience, sets the profile path and the home folder path simultaneously:

```
dsmod user "CN=Tom Thomson,OU=Users,OU=Vancouver,OU=LTI,DC=lantrainers,
➥DC=local" "CN=Arthur Lismer,OU=Users,OU=Vancouver,OU=LTI,
➥DC=lantrainers,DC=local" "CN=Arthur Adams,OU=Users,OU=Vancouver,
➥OU=LTI,DC=lantrainers,DC=local" -profile "\\mars\users\
➥$username$\profile" -hmdrv x: -hmdir \\mars\users\$username$
```

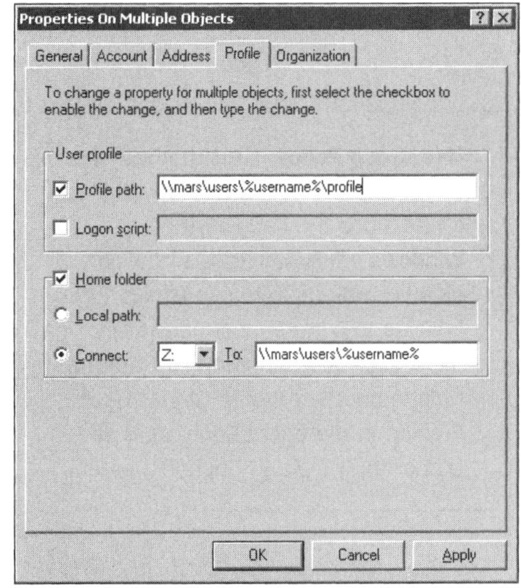

FIGURE 3.22
Changing the home folder and profile path on multiple user accounts at once.

> **NOTE**
>
> **Encrypted Files Are Not Allowed** You cannot include encrypted files in roaming user profiles.

Creating and Enforcing Mandatory User Profiles

You might want to ensure that the profiles for a specific group of users are the same for all the users and unchangeable. A preconfigured profile that is not allowed to be changed by the user is called a *mandatory user profile.* You might want to set up a mandatory user profile for a group of user accounts, all of whom do the same limited set of tasks, such as an inside sales group.

To set up a mandatory user profile, first create a temporary user account and assign a profile path (such as `\\mars\profiles\Adams`) in Active Directory Users and Computers. Ensure that the user has permissions to update files in the profile path. Once the profile path is defined, the user has a roaming profile. Log on as that user, make the changes to the work environment (appearance of the desktop, icons available, programs installed, and so on) that are appropriate for the group of users, and then log off.

Log on again as an administrator, navigate to the user's profile folder, and rename the `NTuser.dat` file to `NTuser.man`.

> NOTE
>
> **Use Group Policy** This method of controlling the user's profile works as it has since the early days of Windows NT. However, it is now considered preferable to use Group Policies to control most user environment settings. See "How to Create a Mandatory User Profile" under User Profiles in the Client Computers section of the Help and Support Center.

To test that the mandatory profile is working, log on as the temporary user, change some settings, and log off. Log on again as the same user, and you should see that the changes you made in the previous session were discarded.

The template user account now has a mandatory user profile assigned. You can assign the same mandatory user profile to any number of user accounts by adding the profile path to the Profile tab of ADUC. In addition, all users or groups who will be assigned the mandatory profile must be granted Write permissions for the folder.

CREATING AND MANAGING GROUPS

It's much easier to administer a network when you can manage several users at once. We can expect that all members of a given section of an organization will have the same needs in accessing data or using printers, and it's also likely that they should be subject to the same security restrictions. Rather than granting individual users the rights to print to a particular printer or to update files in a given folder, we can allocate those rights to a group object.

Making user accounts members of the group automatically grants them any rights that group object has.

Windows Server 2003 has a number of different ways of defining groups of user accounts. We'll describe the different methods a little later, but first you have to understand that Windows Server 2003 domains can be in four different functional levels, and those levels impact what types of groups are possible and what nesting of those groups can be done. (The functional levels have implications related to other capabilities as well, such as Active Directory replication efficiencies, but we're only interested in group behavior here.)

The Four Domain Functional Levels

When the Windows Server 2003 version of Active Directory is installed, a basic set of features is enabled that allows the new domain controller to retain backward compatibility with older domain controllers running Windows NT 4.0 or Windows 2000. As these older domain controllers are removed from the network, the administrator can enable the additional features by raising the domain functional level. The domain functional level determines what features are available and whether or not older domain controllers are supported. Here are the four domain functional levels:

> NOTE
> **Active Directory Functional Levels**
> In fact, several capabilities are only available when in the Windows Server 2003 functional level, including improved Active Directory replication and schema handling. In this section, we're only interested in the effect the domain functionality level has on groups.

- **Windows 2000 mixed**—The default level in Windows Server 2003, this level is equivalent to mixed mode in Windows 2000. At this level, a domain can contain domain controllers on computers running Windows NT, Windows 2000, or Windows Server 2003. This flexibility comes with a price, as you'll see, because at this level you cannot use the enhanced group features available in either Windows 2000 or Windows Server 2003.
- **Windows 2000 native**—Once you have removed all Windows NT domain controllers from the domain, you can increase the domain functionality level to Windows 2000 native. At the Windows 2000 native level, you get the improved group capabilities of Active Directory as delivered in Windows 2000, such as the ability to "nest" groups and the availability of groups of Universal scope.

WARNING

Raising Functional Levels This step is not reversible, so it should be initiated only on a production network by an experienced network administrator.

EXAM TIP

Expect Functional Level Questions Expect several exam questions that deal with the topic of the different features enabled at different functional levels.

- **Windows Server 2003 interim**—Both Windows NT and Windows Server 2003 domain controllers can exist in a domain at this level. As with the Windows 2000 mixed level, enhanced group functionality cannot be used.
- **Windows Server 2003**—Only domains that have no Windows 2000 or Windows NT domain controllers can be raised to this level of domain functionality. This is the most advanced level of domain functionality. Although important enhancements are achieved in upgrading from Windows 2000 to Windows Server 2003 Active Directory, there are no significant differences in group functionality between the two levels.

Figure 3.23 shows raising the domain functional level.

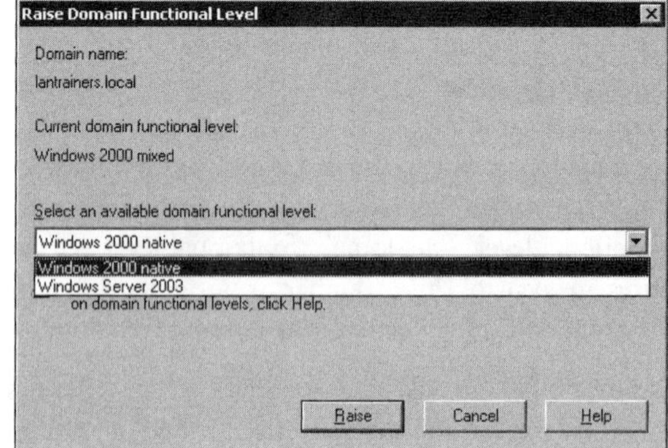

FIGURE 3.23
Raising the domain functional level.

Group Type

The two types of groups are *distribution groups*, which only are used for email lists, and *security groups*, which can be used both for email distribution and resource access. You choose the type depending on the reason you are creating the group:

- **Distribution**—Used for email distribution lists only. Cannot be assigned permissions to use resources.
- **Security**—Used both for assignment of permissions to use resources and for email distribution.

Group Scope

The second way of classifying a group is by defining its *scope*. Group scope means determining where the group members and the resources that the group can be granted access permissions to reside. Table 3.3 lists the scope of the group object in the first column (Domain Local, Global, and Universal); in the second column, the object types that can be members of this kind of group; in the third column, the locations of the resources that a group can be given access to.

Note that in several cases, the characteristics of the group object differ depending on the functionality of the domain.

TABLE 3.3

GROUP SCOPES AND APPLICABLE MEMBERS AND RIGHTS

Scope	*Can Include*	*Can Be Granted Access to Resources In*
Domain Local	Accounts, global groups, and universal groups from any domain, and, in Windows 2000 native or Windows Server 2003 functional level domains, other domain local groups from the same domain as the group object.	The local domain
Global	In domains at the Windows 2000 mixed level or at the Windows Server 2003 interim level, only accounts from the same domain as the group object. In Windows 2000 native or Windows Server 2003 functional level domains, accounts and other global groups from the same domain as the group object.	Any domain in the forest and any domain in any other forest that trusts the local domain
Universal	(Not available in domains at the Windows 2000 mixed level or the Windows Server 2003 interim level.) Accounts, global groups, and universal groups from any domain.	Any domain in the forest and any domain in any other forest that trusts the local domain

EXAM TIP

Understand Groups and Scope Expect at least one exam question that deals with the scope of groups in Windows Server 2003. Microsoft has always tested heavily on the different types of groups and their scope. This exam will probably not be any different.

NOTE

Scope of Trusts A domain trusts all other domains in its forest and any other domains that the administrator has explicitly set the domain to trust.

NOTE

Nesting Groups The ability to nest groups is very useful in administration. With nesting, you could define a G-CalgaryUsers group, whose members are groups called G-CalgaryPersonnel, G-CalgaryEngineers, and G-CalgaryHR. You would make the user accounts members of the departmental groups, with no need to also make them members of the city group.

How would you choose the scope of a group you need to create? Let's talk about each scope in turn.

Domain Local Groups

Groups of the Domain Local scope are typically used for resource access. When creating a group of this scope, you think of the resource that we're granting access to, rather than the users who might use the resource. You also name the group object after the resource. You might create a Domain Local group with the name DL-CalgaryEngineeringResources, for example. You would grant this group Read and Write access to the folders and printers that are used by engineers in Calgary. The members of the group can be (refer back to Table 3.3) user accounts, global groups, and universal groups from any domain trusted by this domain.

If the domain is at the Windows 2000 native functional level or the Windows Server 2003 functional level, the new group can also have other domain local group accounts among its members. The ability to make a group a member of another group of the same type is called *nesting*.

We have just listed the types of objects that can be members of our new domain local group, but what types are we likely to use? Typically, the member list of a domain local group includes an administrator account and one or more global group accounts. More rarely, you may also see universal group accounts in the domain local group member list.

Global Groups

A *global group* is used to collect user accounts, typically according to the function the members perform in their work. Therefore, their names reference the accounts that are on the group member list—typical global group names are G-CalgaryEngineers and G-VancouverHR. Only accounts in the same domain as the group object can be members of the global group. The reason the group is called "global" is that the group can be assigned access to any resource or made a member of any domain local group in the entire forest.

If the domain is at the Windows 2000 native functional level or the Windows Server 2003 functional level, the new group can also have other global group accounts from its domain among its members.

A good example of the use of Global groups is when users are disbursed and resources exist in few domains. For example, an engineering company has engineers in its Vancouver, Calgary, and Edmonton offices. Each location hosts its own domain in a Windows Server 2003 Active Directory forest. All engineering resources are located in the Calgary domain. Each domain administrator places his engineers in an "engineers" Global group for his domain. The Calgary domain administrator creates the EngRes Domain Local group and assigns the selected permissions to that group. He then places each Engineers Global group from each domain into the EngRes group. The Calgary administrator relies on the other administrators to determine who in their respective domains is allowed access to the resources.

Universal Groups

A *universal group*, as its name implies, has no limitations as to where its members are located, or in what domains it can be granted resource access. Its members can come from any trusted domain, and it can be a member of any group or granted access to resources in any trusted domain. These qualities make the group type seem ideal: no worrying about whether the source of members is all right or whether the group can be assigned access in another domain.

There is a cost to this universality, however: The list of members of a universal group is kept in the Global Catalog (GC) and therefore is replicated to all domain controllers designated as Global Catalog servers in the forest. However, the new link-value replication feature in Windows Server 2003 reduces the amount of replication traffic significantly, compared to Windows 2000, where the entire Universal group membership list was replicated whenever a change was made.

> NOTE
>
> **Global Catalog** The Global Catalog of a forest is a directory that contains a subset of each of the objects in every domain of the forest, though only some of the properties of each object. Although the main purpose of the Global Catalog is to provide an index for forestwide searches, it is also used during authentication (the process of ensuring that an object has the right to access the resources it is requesting) to get the list of all the groups a user object is a member of.

You create a universal group when both these conditions apply:

- The members of the group come from more than one domain.
- The group needs resource access in more than one domain.

Universal groups are useful when users and resources are disbursed in all domains. For example, when every domain has EngRes and Engineer Global groups, this might not be bad during the initial setup, but it becomes a nightmare as new domains are added. The

Universal groups make it easier, in that each domain's Engineers Global group gets added to the Engineers Universal group, and the Engineers Universal group is added to each domain's EngRes Domain Local group. As new domains come online, they only have to add their Engineers Global group to the Engineers Universal group, and the Engineers Universal group to the Domain Local group that they have assigned permissions for the shared resources to.

Recommended Sequence of Groups

In small networks (a single domain, with one domain controller), you could work exclusively with groups of global scope. Any user account within the domain can be a member of a global group, and global groups can be given access to resources anywhere within the domain.

In larger networks, the recommended usage of groups is as follows:

- Make accounts members of global groups.
- Make global groups members of domain local groups.
- Assign resource access permissions to the domain local groups.

In some cases it is helpful to make global groups members of universal groups and then to make the universal groups members of domain local groups. This is only necessary when a universal group is needed—that is, when a group will have members from multiple domains and will need access to resources in multiple domains.

This sequence is known as *AGUDLP*, which stands for Accounts, Global, Universal, Domain Local, and Permissions.

Here's the hierarchy, then: Say we have three domains (Lantrainers, Lanwriters, and Lanconsultants), and there is a global group in each domain that holds all the finance mangers in that domain (Lantrainers/G-FinanceManagers, Lanwriters/G-FinanceManagers, and Lanconsultants/G-FinanceManagers). We could make the U-FinanceManagers universal group with these three global groups as members, and then place the universal group on the member list of a domain local group in each of the domains, to give the finance managers access to the resources the domain local group provides. Finally, we could add U-FinanceManagers to the member list of the DL-FinanceResources domain local group in each domain.

You might wonder why we don't grant access to the resources directly to the universal group. We could, of course, but our assumption is that the domain local groups would exist already, to give access to the resource to groups within the local domain.

This hierarchy of groups allows very simple handling of new employees. When a new finance manager joins any of the companies, the local administrator needs only to make the finance manager's user account a member of the G-FinanceManagers global group in the new user's local domain, and that user will immediately be able to access the resources needed.

Creating and Modifying Groups by Using the Active Directory Users and Computers Console

To create a group with Active Directory Users and Computers, first select the domain or OU where you want the group object to reside. Generally you should place the group objects inside OUs because you will most likely delegate responsibility for all the objects in an OU to a subadministrator. In our sample company, it has been agreed that any domain local group that has members from outside the domain will be created at the LTI level. Also, global groups will be created at the level in the hierarchy above all the objects in the groups' member list. So the DL-FinanceResources domain local group is created at the LTI level, as is G-FinanceManagers. The G-CalgaryEngineers group would be created at the Calgary OU level.

In Step by Step 3.3, we'll create groups with Domain Local, Global, and Universal scope.

STEP BY STEP

3.3 Creating Groups with Domain Local, Global, and Universal Scope

1. Open Active Directory Users and Computers.
2. Right-click the LTI Organizational Unit.

continues

continued

3. Select New, Group from the context menu.
4. When the dialog box opens, ensure that the Domain Local and Security radio buttons are selected and then type the name **DL-FinanceResources** (see Figure 3.24).

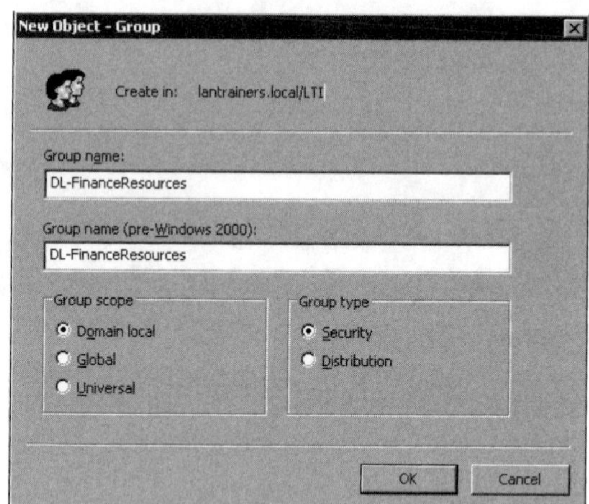

FIGURE 3.24
Give the group a name and specify its type and scope.

5. Click OK, and the group object is created.
6. Right-click the LTI Organizational Unit again and select New, Group from the context menu.
7. This time, ensure the Global and Security radio buttons are selected and then type the name **G-FinanceManagers** and click OK.
8. Right-click the LTI Organizational Unit a third time and select New, Group from the context menu.
9. This time, ensure the Universal and Security radio buttons are selected and then type the name **U-FinanceManagers** and click OK. Now we have our three groups—and in production we would create several others (see Figure 3.25).

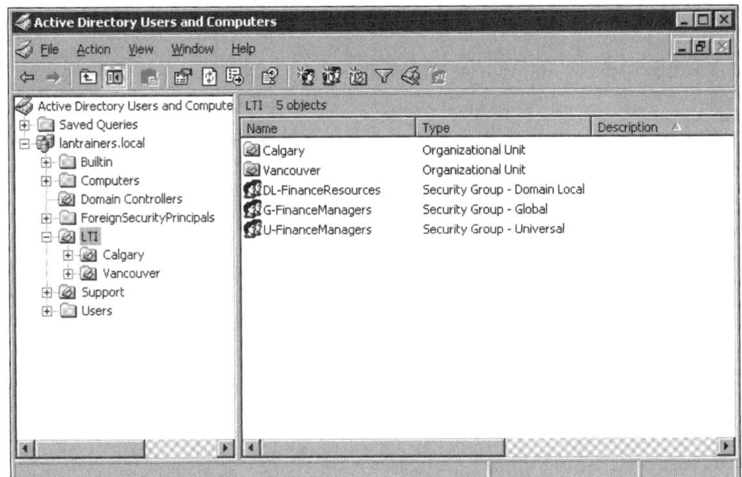

FIGURE 3.25
The group objects are shown in the details pane for the Organizational Unit in which they were created.

10. Now we want to make G-FinanceManagers a member of U-FinanceManagers, and we want to make U-FinanceManagers a member of DL-FinanceResources.
11. Right-click the U-FinanceManagers object and choose Properties. Select the Members tab.
12. Click Add. In the Select Users, Contacts, Computers or Groups dialog box (in the Enter the Object Names to Select area), type **G** and click Check Names. A dialog box appears listing all the users, contacts, computers, or groups whose names start with *G* (see Figure 3.26).

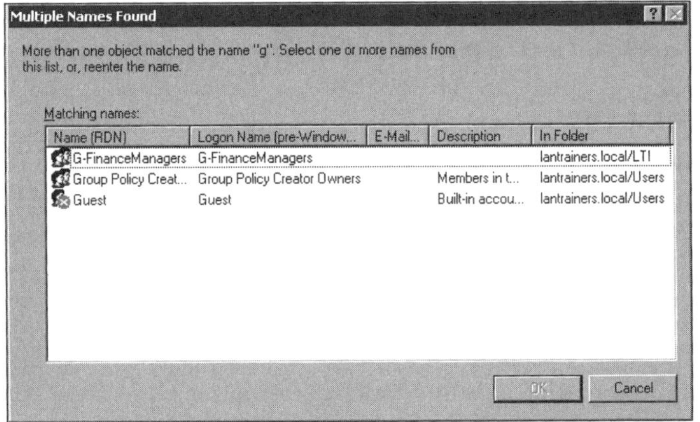

FIGURE 3.26
Select the group you want and click OK.

continues

continued

13. Select G-FinanceManagers and click OK. G-FinanceManagers is now a member of U-FinanceManagers. In production we would also add the G-FinanceManagers global groups from the other domains as well.

14. Now click the Member Of tab. Select Add, type **DL** in the Enter Object Names to Select area, and click Check Names. Select DL-FinanceResources and click OK.

15. We now want to create the `\\MARS\Finance` share and give DL-FinanceResources access rights to it. To do this, start the Share a Folder Wizard by clicking Add Shared Folder from the Manage Your Server application.

16. After selecting the folder to be shared, naming the share Finance, and assigning a share name, choose Use Custom Share and Folder Permissions, and in the dialog box click Add and browse to the DL-FinanceResources group. Assign the group Full Control rights, remove the Everyone group from the list, and click OK.

We have accomplished our task. Any member of the G-FinanceManagers global group will have the correct access to the `\\MARS\Finance` share.

Identifying and Modifying the Scope of a Group

Now you know that the scope of a group object in a domain can be Domain Local, Global, or Universal. (On a member server, stand-alone server, or workstation, local groups can also exist.) So how can you tell the scope of a group object?

The first thing to know is that it won't help you to look at the icons in the details pane of Active Directory Users and Computers. The icons used to denote group objects of all scopes are the same. However, the Type column in the details pane does indicate both the group scope and the group type. See Figure 3.25 to confirm this.

What if you want to change the scope of a group? Perhaps you have a global group, and you have realized that it would be useful to add accounts from another domain to the member list. That's not possible with a global group, but it is with a universal group. If you can change the scope to universal, you can add members from domains in different parts of the enterprise and retain the domain local memberships the existing group has.

If the domain functionality level of your domain is Windows 2000 mixed or Windows Server 2003 interim, you cannot change a group's scope. Universal groups are not available at that domain functionality level, and you cannot change a group's scope from domain local to global, or vice versa.

If the domain functionality level is Windows 2000 native or Windows Server 2003, you can change a group's scope, but only if the group is not a member of another group and has no group members that would be illegal for groups of the new scope.

Here are some examples:

- **You want to change the scope of a group from Global to Universal**—This is not allowed if the group is a member of another global group.
- **You want to change the scope of a group from Domain Local to Universal**—This is not allowed if the group has another domain local group as one of its members.
- **You want to change the scope of a group from Universal to Global**—This is not allowed if the group has another domain local group as one of its members.
- **You want to change the scope of a group from Universal to Domain Local**—This is allowed under all conditions.

Note that it is not possible to change a domain local group to a global group, or vice versa. To change a group's scope with Active Directory Users and Computers, first you have to select the group and look at its properties. Simply click the radio button beside the new scope and click OK to change the scope. If you have followed group naming conventions that indicate the scope of the group, you will probably want to rename the group to show the new scope.

To determine the scope of a group object from the command line, you can use `dsget`. This command shows the description of a group, whether its type is security, and its scope:

```
dsget group <dn> [-desc] [-secgrp] [-scope]
```

To change a group's scope from the command line, you can use `dsmod`. Its syntax in this case is very simple; you just type this:

```
dsmod group <dn> -scope <L, G, or U>
```

You need to be a member of Domain Admins, Enterprise Admins, or Account Operators, or you have to been delegated the appropriate authority to change the scope of a group by either method.

Managing Group Membership

You can make an account a member of a group in two ways:

- By starting with the properties of the account and changing the list of groups of which the account is a member
- By starting with the properties of the group object and changing the member list of the group

There are several methods for changing the group membership, both from Active Directory Users and Computers and from the command line.

In Active Directory Users and Computers, you can use the Member Of tab of the account to see the list of groups the account belongs to, or you can use the Members tab of the group to see the list of members.

Let's look at the "Member Of" method first. Choose the properties of a user, group, or computer object in Active Directory Users and Computers and then click the Member Of tab. A list of group objects is displayed. Click Add and use the Object Picker to locate the group or groups you want the account to be a member of. Click OK, and the Member Of list is updated, as shown in Figure 3.27.

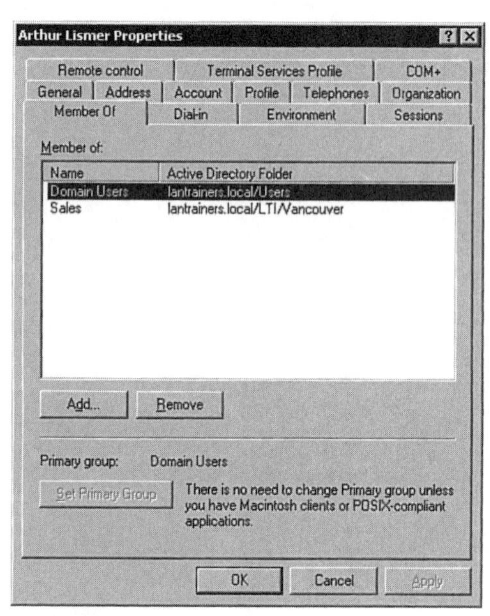

FIGURE 3.27
Click Add to make the user a member of another group.

Another way to use Active Directory Users and Computers to add accounts to a group is to select multiple accounts and then choose File, Properties and click the Member Of tab. With the Object Picker, find the group whose member list you want to add the accounts to, select it, and select OK. Alternatively, you can right-click the objects and choose Add to a Group from the shortcut menu.

Now let's try starting from the group object. Display its properties and choose Members. Use the Object Picker again, but this time the goal is to find the accounts that should be added to the member list of the group. Select the objects and click Add.

A third method (but not recommended) is to select the accounts you want to add to a group's member list and then drag them to the group object. Dropping the accounts on the group object adds them to the member list. This method is not recommended because it is too easy to drop the accounts on the wrong group object.

Adding Accounts to Groups with Command-line Tools

Naturally, a command-line tool is also available for this purpose—you can change the member list of a group with the `dsmod group` command. This command adds the accounts whose distinguished names follow `-addmbr` to the member list of the group specified:

```
dsmod group <groupdn> -addmbr <dn's of accounts to be added>
```

Note that `dsmod group` has two similar-looking parameters that can be used to alter the membership list of a group. As you can see from Table 3.4, `-chmbr` and `-addmbr` both change the membership list, but with quite different results.

TABLE 3.4

THE chmbr AND addmbr Commands

Parameter	*Member List Before*	*Member List After*
`-addmbr John`	Jack, Barbara, Gill, Catherine	Jack, Barbara, Gill, Catherine, John
`-chmbr John`	Jack, Barbara, Gill, Catherine	John

dsmod with the -addmbr parameter adds the account to the member list of the group, whereas the -chmbr parameter replaces the current member list with the accounts following -chmbr. And dsmod group with the -rmmbr parameter removes the accounts listed from the group's member list.

NOTE

Group Membership Changes As in all previous versions of the Windows server products, the group membership information is rebuilt when the user logs on. After you have changed group membership for users, be sure to tell them to log off and on again to see the effect of the group membership change.

You're probably expecting to find that there is a command-line method for adding a member to a group using dsmod user. There isn't! In the Active Directory Users and Computers interface you cannot tell whether the group membership information is a property of the user object or the group object. But because dsmod only allows group membership changes with dsmod group, it is clear that the membership information belongs to the group object.

IN THE FIELD

USERS ON THE LOCAL COMPUTER

Although we have been talking about domain users and domain groups in this section, you may find you need to create users and groups at the local computer level, too. Here are some examples:

- A member server in a domain may need a group account to provide access to the resources on that computer.
- You might need to share a printer installed on a standalone server, and you want to create a local group account to permit this.
- You have a computer running Windows Server 2003 that is not part of a domain, and you want to define users and groups to allow access to its resources.

These tasks are performed using Local Users and Groups in Computer Management or with the net localgroup command. Once the users and groups have been created, you can grant them rights to access resources on the computer.

Finding Domain Groups in Which a User Is a Member

If you want to know what groups a user belongs to, you can easily find out with Active Directory Users and Computers by looking at the properties of the user object and then selecting the Member Of tab. There you will see the groups the user belongs to.

There is a problem, however. What if the user is a member of group A, and group A is a member of group B? In that case, the user is effectively a member of group B, but that fact is not shown on the Member Of tab of the properties of the user object. In fact, there is no way within Active Directory Users and Computers to show the expanded member list. However, we can use `dsget user` to show this information.

To find all the groups the user belongs to, *not counting* those due to group nesting, use the following `dsget` command:

```
dsget user <dn> -memberof
```

To find all the groups the user belongs to, including those due to group nesting, use the following `dsget` command:

```
dsget user <dn> -memberof -expand
```

In Figure 3.28, you can see the output of these two commands for the same user.

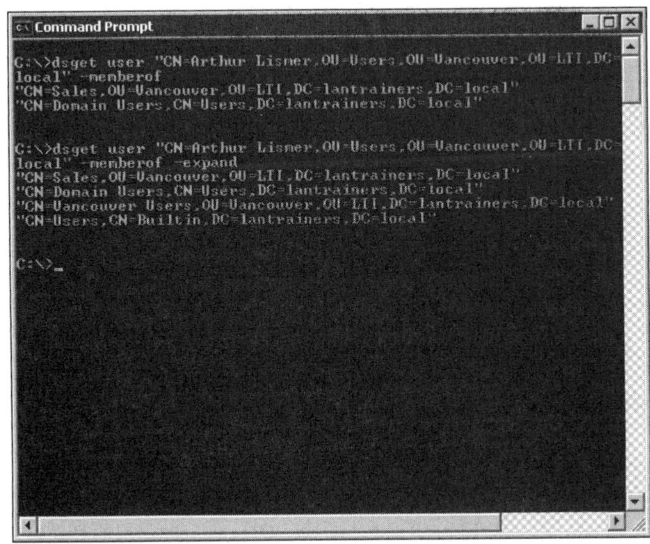

FIGURE 3.28
The first command shows the direct group memberships of the user, whereas the second shows the nested memberships as well.

Do you remember the discussion of piping earlier in this chapter? We can pipe the output of one command to another command, which will allow us to avoid having to know the distinguished name of an account in `memberof` queries. Look at Figure 3.29.

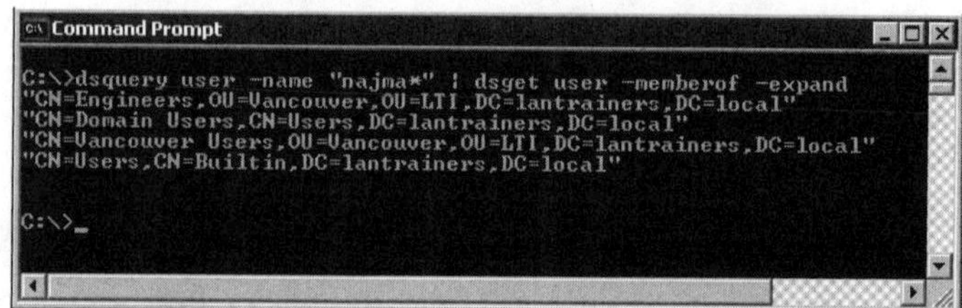

FIGURE 3.29
We only need to know enough of the user's name to make the `-name` parameter unique.

As you can see from the figure, it was sufficient to enter `najma*` to select the one user whose group memberships are wanted.

Creating and Modifying Groups by Using Automation

Earlier in this chapter, we described using `ldifde` to create and modify user accounts. `ldifde` can also be used to create and modify group accounts.

In Step by Step 3.4, we will list the group accounts in the Vancouver OU, modify the names to create new group accounts, and add user accounts to the group accounts.

STEP BY STEP

3.4 Creating Group Accounts

1. Open a command prompt and change to the root of the C: drive.

2. Type the following command:

```
ldifde -f ldifgroupout.txt -d "OU=Vancouver,OU=LTI,DC=lantrainers,
➥DC=local" -l objectclass,cn,distinguishedname,name,
➥samaccountname -r "(objectclass=group)"
```

   This command will change the OU's distinguished name appropriately, if necessary, and list the group names in the `ldifgroupout.txt` file.

3. Type `notepad ldifgroupout.txt` to open the file in Notepad.

4. Change the names of the groups to new ones—for example, `Marketing` and `Production` in place of `Sales` and `Engineering`.

5. Remove the entry for `VancouverUsers`.

6. Save the file as `ldifgroupin1.txt`.

7. Type the following command:

```
ldifde -i -f ldifgroupin1.txt -j c:\ -k
```

   `-j c:\` puts a log file called `ldif.log` on `c:\`, and `-k` tells `ldifde` to continue in case of errors. You should see the message `2 entries modified successfully`.

8. In Notepad, create a file called `ldifgroupin2.txt`, to change the member list of the Vancouver Users group, with the following content (note that `ldifde` can only replace the complete member list of a group, so you have to include all members in this file):

```
dn: CN=Vancouver Users,OU=Vancouver,OU=LTI,DC=lantrainers,DC=local
changetype: modify
replace: member
member: CN=Sales,OU=Vancouver,OU=LTI,DC=lantrainers,
➥DC=localmember: CN=Engineers,OU=Vancouver,OU=LTI,
➥DC=lantrainers,DC=localmember:CN=Marketing,OU=Vancouver,
➥OU=LTI,DC=lantrainers,DC=local
➥member: CN=Production,OU=Vancouver,OU=LTI,DC=lantrainers,DC=local
-
```

9. At the command prompt type the following command:

```
ldifde -i -f ldifgroupin2.txt -j c:\ -k
```

   You should see the message `1 entry modified successfully`.

10. In Active Directory Users and Computers, view the group objects in the Vancouver OU to see that the Marketing and Production groups have been created and that the four groups listed in `ldifgroupin2.txt` are shown as members of the Vancouver OU.

Creating and Managing Computer Accounts in an Active Directory Environment

> **NOTE**
>
> **No Account** No computer accounts are created for computers running any version of Windows 95, Windows 98, or Windows Me. They lack the advanced security features that make the computer accounts worthwhile. This is an important fact—most network administrators prefer to have no computers running these operating systems in their networks because it is difficult to manage and secure these computers.

For every computer running Windows NT, Windows 2000 Professional, or Windows XP and every server running Windows Server 2003 that is a member of a domain, a computer account must be created in the domain. The computer account is a security principal, and it can be authenticated and granted permissions to access resources. A computer account is automatically created for each computer running the listed operating systems when the computer joins the domain.

Although it is true that computer accounts are created automatically when a computer joins a domain, sometimes it is worthwhile to create computer accounts manually. Doing so allows a user to install a new computer in the appropriate location in the domain, even if that user doesn't have the necessary administrative privileges, using the name of the computer account that already exists.

When you're using Remote Installation Services (RIS), it is helpful to set up a default naming policy because this allows you to determine where in Active Directory the computer object is placed. You have three options in choosing the Organizational Unit for the computer object:

- In the default location for computer objects (Computers, under the domain object)
- In the same Organizational Unit as the object of the user installing the computer
- In a predetermined Organizational Unit

Note that even if the computer object has been pre-created, the user installing the computer must have been delegated the right to join a computer to the domain.

Creating Computer Accounts Using the Active Directory Users and Computers Console

To create a computer account using Active Directory Users and Computers, right-click the container you want the account to appear in and then choose New, Computer from the context menu. Assign the necessary values to the parameters available and click OK. Figure 3.30 shows the New Object dialog box in which you type the computer name and give a pre–Windows 2000 computer name (limited to 15 characters). You may also designate the computer as a pre–Windows 2000 computer, and you may state that the computer is to be a Windows NT 4 backup domain controller.

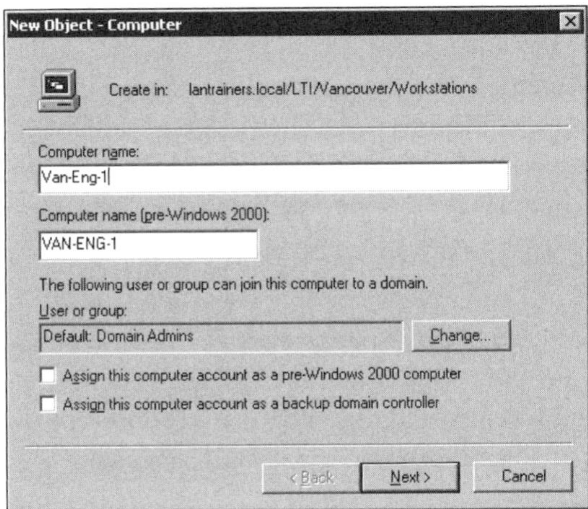

FIGURE 3.30
Type the name of the computer. Windows Server 2003 will automatically create a pre–Windows 2000 computer name.

The next dialog box you see will ask you whether this is a managed computer. If you accept this option, the computer object will be accessible for automatic operating system installation by RIS.

Creating Computer Accounts by Joining the Domain

To create a computer account by joining a domain, first log on to the computer you want to join to the domain with the credentials of a user with administrative privileges on that computer.

Choose the System applet from Control Panel, change the workgroup membership information to reference the domain the computer is to join, and click OK. The system will ask you for the credentials of a user object that has the necessary rights and, after a short pause, will show a dialog box to welcome the computer to the domain. The computer must be rebooted so that it can come up as a member of the domain.

Once the computer is a member of the domain, a user logging on to the domain has the logon request passed by the workstation through a secure channel to the domain controller. The computer must have a domain computer account for the secure channel to be created.

GUIDED PRACTICE EXERCISE 3.2

You are the administrator of a network for a manufacturing company that has multiple Windows Server 2003 servers used for applications and file and print services. The Research and Development Department has received a massive increase in funding this fiscal year, and it is purchasing all new desktop computers.

You plan to delegate the desktop replacements to the desktop support group. However, because Windows XP Professional computers are being installed, a computer account will need to be added for each computer. You do not want to grant the desktop support group the necessary access to add the computer accounts, but you cringe at the idea of adding 500 computer accounts manually.

You must find a way to automate this process.

What is the best way to solve this issue in Windows Server 2003? On your own, try to develop a solution that would involve the least amount of downtime and expense.

If you would like to see a possible solution, follow these steps:

Estimated Time: 30 minutes

This is a fairly easy solution. You can use the `dsadd` utility with the computer option to add a computer account to the domain.

The `dsadd` utility allows you to accept the computer account name from standard input (stdin) so that you can redirect the contents of a text file that contains a list of the computer names to be used in creating the accounts.

1. From the Start menu, select Run.
2. From the Run dialog box, enter **CMD** to open a command window.
3. On the command line, enter the following command, where *names.txt* is a text file that contains a listing of the computer names:

```
dsadd computer <names.txt>
```

By default, `dsadd computer` uses the user context of the currently logged on user to connect a domain controller in the logon domain. Administrative access is required.

Troubleshooting Computer Accounts

Because computers need to authenticate to one another, they need accounts and passwords. In addition to the two methods described previously, a computer account is also created when a Windows Server 2003 server is promoted to a domain controller with `dcpromo`.

Like user accounts, each computer account has a password. Passwords are created by the process that creates a computer account. On a defined interval, a process running on the local computer changes the password automatically, and the new password is communicated securely to a domain controller in the computer's domain.

What happens if a server running Windows Server 2003 changes its password, but there is no domain controller available for the new password to be written to? The next time the two computers are able to communicate, the server with the changed password, on finding that the new password is not accepted, uses the previous one instead. Once authentication is complete with the old password, the new password is stored on the domain controller and is subsequently replicated to all domain controllers in the domain.

Troubleshooting Issues Related to Computer Accounts by Using the Active Directory Users and Computers Console

When a computer account is operating incorrectly, it may be impossible to log on to the domain from the computer. You can see how, if the computer cannot authenticate to the domain controller, it will be impossible for the user to log on. In this case it is necessary to reset the computer's account and rejoin the computer to the domain. This process reestablishes the secure relationship between the computer and the domain it is a member of.

To reset a computer's account using Active Directory Users and Computers, select the folder containing the computer account and right-click the computer object. Choose Reset Account from the context menu, and click Yes from the confirmation dialog box. Reboot the workstation and then rejoin the domain as described earlier.

To reset a computer's account from the command line, you use the `dsmod` command with the `-reset` switch:

```
dsmod computer <dn of computer> -reset
```

As in the case where the computer account was reset using Active Directory Users and Computers, you will have to rejoin the computer to the domain.

CASE STUDY: T FOSTER

ESSENCE OF THE CASE

Here are the essential elements in this case:

- Export the Harshaw user accounts.
- Change the Harshaw accounts to reflect that they are now T Foster employees.
- Import the Harshaw data into the T Foster AD.

SCENARIO

T Foster is a wholesaler for farm equipment based in the Midwest. T Foster has decided to merge with Harshaw, Inc., one of its biggest rivals, located in the Upper Midwest. The mission of this newly formed conglomerate is to dominate the wholesale farm implement business in the plains states.

T Foster now wants to merge the information technology systems of the two companies as quickly as possible. Fortunately, the two companies run the same order-entry and inventory software, so there won't be any end-user training required.

T Foster has decided to give the former Harshaw employees access to resources on the T Foster network, while slowly migrating the Harshaw data over.

ANALYSIS

The features in Windows Server 2003 enable T Foster to merge the two companies with the least amount of difficulty. The first step is to export the user list from the Harshaw Active Directory using `ldifde`. This extracts the existing user accounts to a file.

The next step is to change the distinguished name in all the user records because the users are now part of T Foster. All the information about the accounts will be the same, but the Active Directory paths will be different in all the distinguished names. This can be accomplished by using `ldifde` with `-c` *<old string> <new string>* to cause the replacement of any occurrences of *<old string>* with *<new string>*.

continues

CASE STUDY: T FOSTER

continued

Here's an overview of the requirements and solutions in this case study:

Requirement	Solution Provided By
Export the Harshaw user accounts.	Exporting the user list from the Harshaw Active Directory using `ldifde`.
Change the Harshaw accounts to reflect that they are now T Foster employees.	Using `ldifde` with the `-c` switch to change the distinguished names.
Import the Harshaw data into the T Foster AD.	Importing the user list from the Harshaw AD into the T Foster AD using `ldifde`.

CHAPTER SUMMARY

KEY TERMS

- Active Directory Users and Computers
- Organizational Unit (OU)
- User accounts—domain and local
- Password
- User templates
- Command-line tools for Active Directory tasks
- `dsadd`
- `dsquery`
- `dsget`
- `dsmod`

This chapter discussed many important skills—skills that you will use every day as a network administrator.

You started with creating and modifying user accounts. You used Active Directory Users and Computers first, learning how to create user accounts in the graphical user interface (GUI). You then progressed to using the command-line tools: `dsadd` to create a user account, `dsget` to inquire into an object's properties, `dsmod` to change properties, `dsquery` to find objects of any type, and `dsrm` to remove objects from Active Directory. Then you moved on to using `csvde` and `ldifde` to create user accounts automatically, by importing information about the new user accounts from data created from other sources, such as enrollment databases or other directories.

Next you learned about Windows Server 2003 group accounts. You discovered the two types of groups—security and distribution—and the three possible scopes a group account in a domain can have: Domain Local, Global, and Universal. Once again, you started with Active Directory Users and Computers and progressed to the

CHAPTER SUMMARY

command-line tools. Then you learned about using `ldifde` to create groups.

You also covered computer accounts. There is much less that a network administrator needs to do with computer accounts compared to user and group accounts because computer accounts are typically created automatically when the computer joins the domain and are managed automatically thereafter by the operating system. The network administrator only gets involved if RIS is in use and managed computer accounts are needed, or if a computer account needs to be reset.

- `dsmove`
- `dsrm`
- `csvde`
- CSV (Comma Separated Value)
- `ldifde`
- LDAP Data Interchange Format
- Account lockout
- Disabled account
- Expired account
- Dial-in disallowed
- Complexity requirements for passwords
- User profiles—local, roaming, and mandatory
- Properties on multiple objects
- Group accounts
- Domain functionality level
- Group scope—Domain Local, Global, Universal
- Group types—distribution and security
- Nested groups
- Group expansion
- Computer accounts
- Remote installation services
- Managed computer

APPLY YOUR KNOWLEDGE

Exercises

3.1 Creating User Accounts via Automation

Imagine that our fictional company, Lantrainers, has a class starting next week, and the students registered for the class will need user accounts. Each account will need to be a member of the Students group, and we'll need the student's title, company name, and business phone number in the user account information.

We will use `dsadd`, `csvde`, and `dsmod` to make an OU called LanStudents, create user accounts, set passwords, and make the user accounts members of the Students global group.

Here is the data we'll be using:

Amell	Bernie	Trainer	555-7179	Prairie Sky Consulting
Blanchard	Verna	Systems Analyst	555-4296	Housing Associates
Bond	Dorothy	Trainer	555-7096	Prairie Sky Consulting
Clark	Cathie	Trainer	555-7028	Prairie Sky Consulting
Ducharme	Lydia	Network Administrator	555-7220	Goldenrod Developments
Emmett	Matt	Network Administrator	555-6057	Goldenrod Developments
Guyn	Karen	Network Administrator	555-1544	Goldenrod Developments
Guyn	Pat	Systems Analyst	555-6669	Goldenrod Developments
James	Robert	Systems Analyst	555-8729	Housing Associates
Jensen	Nicole	Systems Analyst	555-8849	Goldenrod Developments
Kyle	Ann	Trainer	555-8849	Prairie Sky Consulting
Magnus	Holly	Trainer	555-5295	Prairie Sky Consulting
Michell	Christine	Network Administrator	555-4755	Prairie Sky Consulting
Myers	Leslie	Network Administrator	555-1479	Goldenrod Developments
Nowlin	Patty	Systems Analyst	555-4296	Housing Associates
Poulin	Paule	Systems Analyst	555-8606	Housing Associates
Rutherford	Donna	Trainer	555-7612	Prairie Sky Consulting
Ryan	Kathleen	Network Administrator	555-5467	Goldenrod Developments
Sept	Rick	Systems Analyst	555-6057	Housing Associates
Stratton	Susan	Systems Analyst	555-6669	Housing Associates
Swenson	Kathi	Network Administrator	555-5487	Goldenrod Developments

Estimated Time: 45 minutes

1. Open a command prompt and change to the root directory of the C: drive.
2. Use `dsadd` to create an OU called `"OU=LanStudents,OU=Vancouver,OU=LTI, DC=lantrainers,DC=local"`.
3. Type a `csvde` command to create a list of the user accounts in the `OU=Users,OU=Vancouver,OU=LTI, DC=lantrainers,DC=local` OU. Use the parameter `-l l,company,objectclass,name,title,company, l,telephoneNumber,userAccountControl, samaccountname` to limit the number of fields displayed. Send the output to `csvde-out.txt`. Copy the file to `csvde-in.txt`.

APPLY YOUR KNOWLEDGE

4. Use a spreadsheet program, a database program, or Notepad to modify `csvde-in.txt`. Retain the first record (it has the field names we'll need), but replace the data lines with data from the preceding table. Ensure that the fields are in the proper columns.
5. Use `csvde` to input the data in `csvde-in.txt` into Active Directory. Confirm that the records were created with Active Directory Users and Computers (`csvde -i -f csvde-in.csv -j c:\`).
6. Use `dsquery` to display all the users in the LanTrainers OU, and pipe the result as input to a `dsmod` command that sets the password for all users to Security and enables the account (`dsquery user "OU=LanStudents,OU=Vancouver, OU=LTI,DC=lantrainers,DC=local" ¦ dsmod user -pwd Secur1ty -mustchpwd yes -disabled no`).
7. Open Active Directory Users and Computers and navigate to the LanStudents OU to see the user accounts.

3.2 Creating Users and Groups

In this exercise we will create three groups and add members to them. Then we will make the three groups members of a universal group. Because there aren't many groups to work with, we'll use Active Directory Users and Computers.

Estimated Time: 5 minutes

1. Open Active Directory Users and Computers, and navigate to the LanStudents OU.
2. Create a global security group object called AdminStudents. Add the user accounts for those users whose title is Network Administrator to the member list of the group.
3. Create a global security group object called AnalystStudents. Add the user accounts for those users whose title is Systems Analyst to the member list of the group.
4. Create a global security group object called TrainerStudents. Add the user accounts for those users whose title is Trainer to the member list of the group.
5. Create a universal security group object called AllStudents. Add the three group accounts we just created to the member list of the group.

Review Questions

1. Because you can do everything you need to do, in terms of creating and managing accounts, with Active Directory Users and Computers, why is it worthwhile to learn the command-line and automation methods?
2. What are the similarities and differences between `csvde` and `ldifde`?
3. What would be the impact of using groups of Universal scope exclusively, rather than using groups of Domain Local, Global, and Universal scope?
4. You are planning to implement Remote Installation Services. How can you ensure that the computer accounts the users create go in the right Organizational Units?
5. You are setting up instructions for help desk analysts, and you're writing a list of items for them to check when users cannot log on. What should go on that list?

APPLY YOUR KNOWLEDGE

6. Your manager has asked you to investigate Terminal Services and report on how you can control the Terminal Services sessions. What do you report?

7. Every month your manager wants you to produce a list of all accounts that have passwords that do not expire and all accounts that are disabled. How will you do this?

8. Explain how to ensure that the order-entry clerks will all see the same desktop environment each time they log on.

Exam Questions

1. You want to create a user account for Joan Myles using a command from the command prompt. The account is to be a member of the Engineers group in the Vancouver container, disabled when created, have Secur1ty as its password, and be placed in the `"ou=Users,ou=Vancouver,ou=LTI, dc=Lantrainers,dc=local"` container. Which of the following tools or combination of tools can do the job?

   A. `Net User` followed by `dsmove`

   B. `ldifde` followed by `dsmod`

   C. `dsadd`

   D. `csvde` followed by `dsmove`

   E. `dsquery` followed by `dsmod`

2. A manager tells you one of his staff has taken a job in another company. The manager wants to ensure that the user cannot access his computer or his files on the network file server. What is your best course of action?

   A. Delete the user account.

   B. Rename the user account to "Departed User."

   C. Select the Account Is Disabled check box.

   D. Change the value in the Account Expires field.

3. You are planning for resource access in a multidomain forest. Some users from all domains will need access to three continental headquarters domains. What is the recommended strategy for providing access to these resources?

   A. Users→universal groups→global groups→domain local groups→permissions to resources

   B. Users→global groups→universal groups→domain local groups→permissions to resources

   C. Users→domain local groups→universal groups→global groups→permissions to resources

   D. Users→universal groups→permissions to resources

4. You need to explain profiles to your management, and you realize that you need to start your presentation with definitions of the three profile types. Choose the three profile types.

   A. Active Directory user profile

   B. Local user profile

   C. Group profile

   D. Group policy user profile

   E. Roaming user profile

   F. Mandatory user profile

APPLY YOUR KNOWLEDGE

5. You are the network administrator for a small company that provides customer service operators for other companies. One of your users calls to complain that the photograph of her grandson that she added to her desktop yesterday wasn't there when she logged on this morning. What is the most likely cause of her problem?

   A. Her user profile is corrupted.

   B. She logged in to a different computer.

   C. She is logged on locally.

   D. She was assigned a mandatory profile.

6. Due to economic circumstances, your company had to lay off 200 people. The Human Resources department has provided you with a list of names in a text file. Which command can be used to delete these user accounts?

   A. `dsmod`

   B. `dsadd delete`

   C. `csvde`

   D. `dsrm`

7. Your company has recently purchased a small company. The other company runs Unix with an LDAP-compatible directory. Your job is to create user accounts in Active Directory for the employees from this company. What is the best tool to use for this task?

   A. `dsadd`

   B. `ldifde`

   C. `csvde`

   D. `dsrm`

8. You are the administrator for a small university. As usual for this type of environment, bored students try to hack into the university billing system every night between 10 p.m. and 2 a.m. What two steps can you take to ensure that a dictionary attack will fail, while still allowing your user to log on at 8 a.m.?

   A. Set Account Lockout Threshold to 0.

   B. Set Account Lockout Duration to 60.

   C. Set Account Lockout Duration to 0.

   D. Set Account Lockout Threshold to 3.

9. You are the network administrator for a small company that provides customer service operators for other companies. One of your users calls to complain that she can't see any files in her My Documents folder. She was able to get to them with no problem yesterday. Group Policy is not in use. What is the most likely cause of her problem?

   A. Her user profile is corrupted.

   B. She logged in to a different computer.

   C. She is logged on locally.

   D. She was assigned a mandatory profile.

10. You are the junior administrator for a large engineering firm with several locations. You read in a magazine that the best way to assign resources in a multidomain environment is to assign permissions to a Domain Local group, then add the Global groups to the Domain Local group, and then add the Global groups to a Universal group. However, the server won't let you create a Universal group. What is the most likely problem?

APPLY YOUR KNOWLEDGE

A. You don't have the proper authority.

B. The domain function level is at Windows 2000 mixed.

C. The domain functional level is at Windows 2000 native.

D. The domain functional level is *not* at Windows 2003 native.

11. You are the administrator for a small, family-owned firm. Because of the firm's size and informality, it has been tough to get users to understand the need for security. You want to change the password policy so that the users will be required to change their passwords every 30 days and can't reuse a password more than every 2 years. Which of the following choices will accomplish this?

    A. Set the password history to 730 and the maximum password age to 30.

    B. Set the password history to 365 and the maximum password age to 30.

    C. Set the password history to 25 and the maximum password age to 28.

    D. Set the password history to 24 and the maximum password age to 30.

12. A manager tells you that his administrative assistant has left the company. The manager wants to ensure that her replacement has access to her computer and her files on the network file server. What is your best course of action?

    A. Create a new user account for the replacement and grant the replacement access to the necessary files.

    B. Rename the old user account for the new user.

    C. Create a new user account for the replacement and copy the necessary files to her home directory.

    D. Give the new user the user ID and password of the departed administrative assistant.

Answers to Review Questions

1. Using Active Directory Users and Computers for creating and managing accounts is fine if you're dealing with just a few accounts. But it's time consuming and error prone if you are dealing with dozens or hundreds of accounts. The command-line and automation tools are much more efficient for dealing with large numbers of users. See "Creating and Modifying User Accounts with Command-line Tools."

2. `csvde` and `ldifde` can both be used to import or export large numbers of accounts. `csvde` uses CVS-formatted files for input and output, whereas `ldifde` uses files in the LDAP Directory Interchange Format (LDIF). Only `ldifde` can be used to modify or delete existing accounts. See "Importing and Exporting User Accounts."

3. If you used universal groups exclusively, you would lose the structure and manageability of domain local and global groups. Also, you would increase the replication traffic on your network, as the member lists of universal groups are stored in the global catalog. See "Universal Groups."

4. In the properties of Remote Installation Services (accessible on a tab of the properties of the computer running Windows Server 2003 where RIS is installed), create a default naming policy with the desired location defined. See "Creating and Managing Computer Accounts in an Active Directory Environment."

5. Here are the items to check if users cannot log on:

   - Is the account locked out due to too many logon failures?
   - Is the account disabled?
   - If the user is trying to connect via VPN or dial-up, is Remote Access Permission set to Deny Access, or is access controlled through a Remote Access Policy that denies access?
   - Has the account expired?

   See "Troubleshooting Issues Related to User Account Properties."

6. First, a Terminal Services session can be controlled. An administrator can view a user's session and control it if necessary. Second, you can specify a profile and home folder location that are different from the values set up in the user's normal profile. Third, you can configure a program to start automatically at logon and for the session to end when the program is exited. Also, you can control whether drives and printers on the client computer are available from the session.

7. You will define a saved query with the required fields selected. When the report is due, you return to Active Directory Users and Computers, select Saved Queries, and select the query you need.

8. Set up a mandatory user profile, by creating a user profile with the desired desktop environment, convert it to a roaming user profile stored on a server, and then rename the profile to `NTUser.man`. See "Creating and Enforcing Mandatory User Profiles."

Answers to Exam Questions

1. **B, C.** `ldifde` (with the appropriate data file as input) followed by `dsmod` (to change the password) does the job, as does `dsadd` by itself. `Net User` cannot create a group membership. `csvde` cannot create group memberships, and `dsmove` is unnecessary because `csvde` can create the user account in any container. `dsquery` cannot create a user account.

2. **C.** It is best to disable the account immediately and then reset the password and enable the account again when someone is ready to review the files held by the account. Deleting the user account makes the review of files very difficult. Renaming the account without changing the logon name or password does not stop the user from accessing the account. Changing the value in the Account Expires field would work, but it is inappropriate to the situation and hence would confuse other administrators.

3. **B.** This is the recommended method for providing access to resources through group membership.

4. **B, E, F.** These are the profile types.

5. **D.** Although all the other choices are possibilities, in a customer service environment, it's most likely that mandatory profiles are in use. A mandatory profile allows you to make changes; however, those changes are not saved when you log off.

6. **D.** The `dsrm` command can be used to delete Active Directory objects, using a text file as input. The `csvde` command can only be used to import or export accounts, the `dsmod` command can be used only to change the properties of accounts, and the `dsadd` command doesn't have a delete option.

Apply Your Knowledge

7. **B.** `ldifde` is the best tool to use for this task. It allows you to extract the user list from the LDAP-compatible directory on the Unix server. Next, it allows you to change the distinguished name in the exported file to match your AD structure. Then it imports the new users into AD.

8. **B, D.** Setting the lockout threshold to 3 locks the account after three failed attempts to log on. Setting the lockout duration to 60 reenables the account after 60 minutes. Setting the lockout threshold to 0 allows an indefinite number of logon attempts—definitely not what you want. Setting the lockout duration to 0 will keep the account locked until the administrator manually reenables it.

9. **B.** The most likely problem is that she logged on to a different computer, and roaming profiles are not in use.

10. **B.** Universal groups are available only at the Windows 2000 native and Windows Server 2003 functional levels. The Windows 2000 mixed and Windows Server 2003 interim levels are used to support Windows NT 4.0 domain controllers, so Global group nesting and Universal groups cannot be used.

11. **D.** With the maximum age set to 30 days, users are prompted to change their passwords every 30 days. The history setting will retain 24 passwords, approximately 2 years worth.

12. **B.** The easiest way to give the new user the proper access is to just rename the old account with the new user's name because they will be performing the same duties and need access to the same files.

Suggested Readings and Resources

1. For information about LDAP, see RFCs 2251–2256. For information on LDIF, see RFC 2849.
2. Windows Server 2003 Deployment Guide (not yet published). Microsoft Corporation.
3. Windows Server 2003 Resource Kit (not yet published). Microsoft Corporation.
4. Boswell, William. *Inside Windows Server 2003.* New Riders, 2003. ISBN 0735711585.
5. Matthews, Marty. *Windows Server 2003: A Beginners Guide.* McGraw-Hill, 2003. ISBN 0072193093.
6. Minasi, Mark, et al. *Mark Minasi's Windows XP and Server 2003 Resource Kit.* Sybex, 2003. ISBN 0782140807.
7. Minasi, Mark, et al. *Mastering Windows Server 2003.* Sybex, 2003. ISBN 0782141307.
8. Shapiro, Jeffrey, et al. *Windows Server 2003 Bible.* John Wiley & Sons, 2003. ISBN 0764549375.

OBJECTIVES

This chapter covers the following Microsoft-specified objectives for the "Managing and Maintaining Access to Resources" section of the Managing and Maintaining a Microsoft Windows Server 2003 Environment exam:

Configure file system permissions.

- **Verify effective permissions when granting permissions.**
- **Change ownership of files and folders.**

▶ The purpose of this objective is to teach you how to control the access and the type of access allowed to files and folders in the Windows Server 2003 environment. You need to know not only how to grant permissions but also what the cumulative effect is when combining file and folder permissions.

Configure access to shared folders.

- **Manage shared folder permissions.**

▶ The purpose of this objective is to teach you how to configure and manage user access to the shared folders created in Windows Server 2003.

Troubleshoot access to files and shared folders.

▶ The purpose of this objective is to teach you how to troubleshoot problems related to file and folder access in the Windows Server 2003 environment.

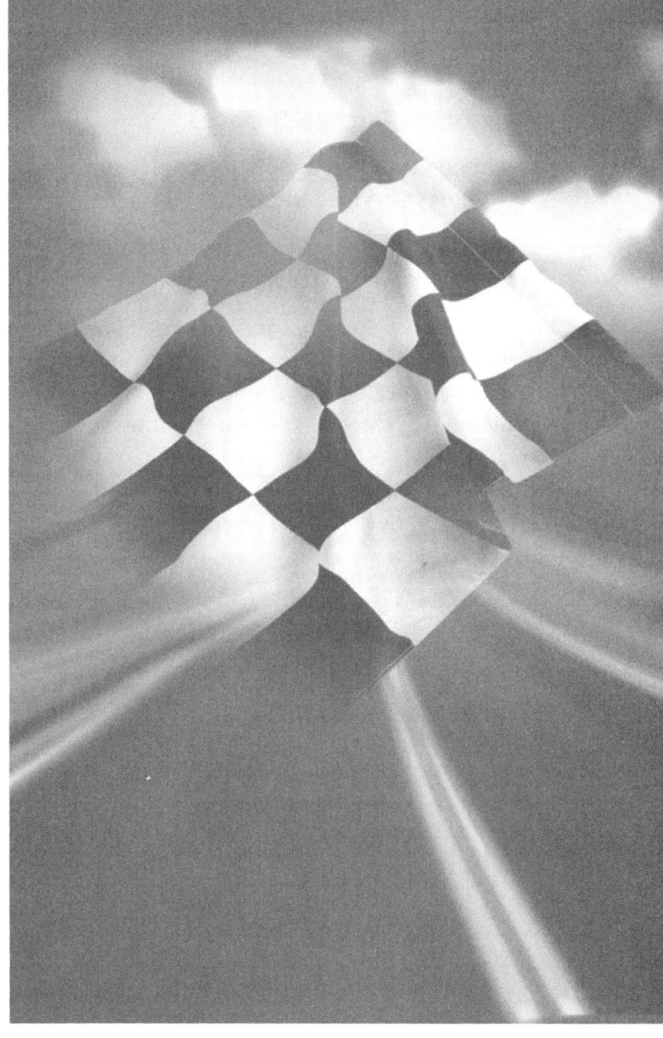

CHAPTER 4

Managing and Maintaining Access to Resources

OBJECTIVES

Troubleshoot Terminal Services.

- **Diagnose and resolve issues related to Terminal Services security.**
- **Diagnose and resolve issues related to client access to Terminal Services.**

▶ The purpose of this objective is to teach you how to work with the Windows Server 2003 version of Terminal Services. This includes both Application Server and Remote Desktop for Administration modes.

OUTLINE

OUTLINE

STUDY STRATEGIES

- The sections in this chapter outline features that are basic to using and managing a Windows Server 2003 server. A server is basically useless unless you have an easily manageable mechanism to share resources.
- A key part of this chapter is the configuration and management of shared folders. You need to know how to configure access to shared folders and how to troubleshoot shared folder access problems.
- The process of working with share and NTFS permissions has always been a major focus on Microsoft exams. Make sure you have a complete understanding of how the different permissions are applied when you access a folder over the network versus accessing it from the server console.
- This chapter covers the management and configuration of Terminal Services. In addition to knowing how to properly configure Terminal Services to access your server, you need to be able to diagnose problems in your environment that are specific to Terminal Services.

INTRODUCTION

As mentioned in previous chapters, one of the primary roles of a Windows Server 2003 server is that of a data repository or file server. The main administrative task of a file server is the management and maintenance of folder and file system permissions. This can range from deciding which users can access the files and folders on the server, to exactly what type of access they will have. In addition, the system administrator should be able to troubleshoot problems with file and folder access, not only when users are unable to access a necessary file or folder, but more importantly, when they have a higher level of access than they should.

This chapter covers the tasks and procedures required to maintain data in Windows Server 2003. This type of information is not only crucial for a job as a system administrator, it is also very important for the exam.

CONFIGURING FILE SYSTEM PERMISSIONS

In today's security-conscious environment, few items are as important as basic file system security. There are several levels and methods of protection for files and folders in Windows Server 2003. The two levels of file system security you must be familiar with for the exam are *local security* and *share security.*

Local security applies to a user who is either logged on to the server console or connected via Terminal Services. By default, the following groups have the right to log on locally on a domain controller:

- Administrators
- Account Operators
- Backup Operators
- Print Operators
- Server Operators

The following groups have logon locally rights on a workstation or member server:

- Administrators (Domain Administrators)
- Backup Operators
- Power Users
- Users
- Guest (if not disabled)

Because the members of these groups can log on to the server or workstation directly, it is always recommended that you format your volumes with the New Technology File System (NTFS). This is because you can use local security to block access for various users and groups to files and folders on an NTFS volume. On the other hand, File Allocation Table (FAT) volumes have no local security whatsoever. A user who has the necessary rights to log on to a server or workstation has unrestricted access to the files and folders contained on a FAT volume.

> NOTE
>
> **Domain Controllers** The partition of a domain controller that contains SYSVOL and the Active Directory database is required to be formatted with NTFS.

For a more detailed explanation of the various types of FAT volumes and how they differ from NTFS volumes, refer to the "Working with Basic Disks" section in Chapter 1, "Managing Server Storage Devices."

Configuring and Managing NTFS File and Folder Permissions

Although the various versions of FAT provide no local security, NTFS was created with the ability to control access to every file and folder on an NTFS volume. When a file or folder is created on an NTFS volume, an *Access Control List (ACL)* is created. The ACL contains a list of every user and group that has been granted access to the file or folder and what type of access was granted. Each user or group that has been allowed access to the resource has its own *Access Control Entry (ACE)* in the ACL. Whenever a file or folder is accessed on an NTFS volume, the operating system reads the ACE to determine whether the user or group has the necessary permissions for the type of access it is requesting.

Permissions define the type of access that is granted to a user or group for an object, such as a file or folder. Permissions can be assigned to local users or groups, or if the server is a member of a domain, permissions can be assigned to any user or group that is trusted by that domain.

The type of permission varies by object. Folders are used as containers to store files or other folders. Files are executed or written, so the permissions assigned to them apply to the amount of manipulation a user or group can perform against them.

NTFS permissions can be granted to either users or groups. By default, the Administrators group can assign permissions to all files and folders on a server.

The following permissions apply to a file:

- **Read**—This permission allows you to read the contents of a file and its attributes, including file ownership and assigned permissions.
- **Read & Execute**—This permission includes all the Read permissions, in addition to the ability to run applications.
- **Write**—This permission includes all the Read permissions, in addition to the ability to overwrite the file and change its attributes.
- **Modify**—This permission includes all the Read & Execute and the Write permissions, in addition to the ability to modify and delete the file.
- **Full Control**—This permission includes all the Modify permissions, in addition to allowing you to take ownership of a file and configure the permissions for it.

The following permissions apply to a folder and to the files and subfolders contained in that folder:

- **Read**—This permission allows you to read the contents of a folder and its attributes, including ownership and assigned permissions.
- **Read & Execute**—This permission includes all the Read permissions, in addition to the ability to run applications.

- **Write**—This permission includes all the Read permissions, in addition to the ability to create new files and subfolders and change the folder's attributes.
- **List Folder Contents**—This permission includes all the Read permissions, but for the folder only.
- **Modify**—This permission includes all the Read & Execute and the Write permissions, in addition to the ability to modify and delete the folder.
- **Full Control**—This permission includes all the Modify permissions, in addition to allowing you to take ownership of a folder and configure the permissions to it.

The creator or owner of a file or folder is able to control how permissions are set and to whom permissions are granted on that object. To configure the permissions on a file or folder, use the procedure outlined in Step by Step 4.1.

STEP BY STEP

4.1 Configuring File and Folder Permissions

1. Open either My Computer or Windows Explorer. Navigate to the object for which you want to configure permissions.
2. Right-click the object and select Properties from the pop-up menu. Click the Security tab in the resulting dialog box.
3. From the Security tab, shown in Figure 4.1, click the Add button.
4. The Select Users or Groups dialog box appears. This dialog box allows you to select either a local or domain user or group to assign permissions to. Enter the user or group and then click OK.
5. This returns you to the Folder Properties dialog box. Note that, by default, the user or group just added has been granted Read & Execute, List Folder Contents, and Read permissions for the folder.

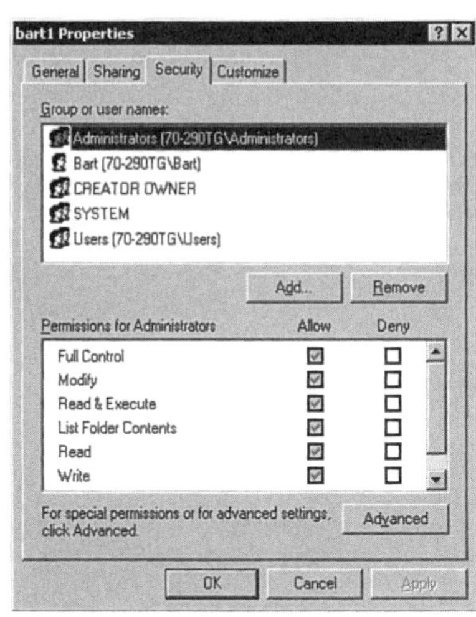

FIGURE 4.1
The Folder Properties dialog box, showing the Security tab. This dialog box allows you to see and change the permissions applied to each user or group.

continues

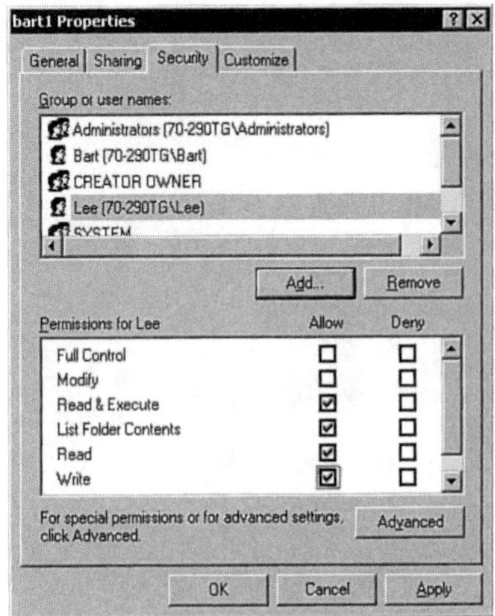

FIGURE 4.2
The Folder Properties dialog box, showing the added user and permissions. This dialog box allows you to explicitly allow or deny access to the folder.

continued

6. In the Permissions section of the Folder Properties dialog box, shown in Figure 4.2, select the check box for Write and then click the OK button to save.

This Properties dialog box allows you to add or delete users or groups that have access to a file or folder. In addition, you can explicitly select to either allow or deny the basic permissions that apply to that object.

Special Permissions

In addition to the basic permissions, NTFS also allows you to assign more granular, special permissions. Special permissions are generally a subset of the basic NTFS permissions and allow you to limit access to a file or folder to specific tasks. These special permissions apply to both files and folders and are detailed in the following list:

- **Traverse Folder/Execute File**—This permission enables a user to pass through a folder he does not have access to in order to access a file or folder to which he does have access. This permission may initially have no effect because, for it to apply, the user privilege Bypass Traverse Checking must be enabled. In the default system policy, Bypass Traverse Checking is disabled.
- **List Folder/Read Data**—This permission allows a user to list the contents of a folder. When it's applied to a file, this permission allows the file to be opened for Read access.
- **Read Attributes**—This permission allows a user to see the file or folder attributes.
- **Read Extended Attributes**—This permission allows a user to see special file or folder attributes that are created by applications. This is not commonly used.
- **Create Files/Write Data**—When applied to a folder, this permission allows a user to create new files. When applied to a file, it allows the user to edit a file.

- **Create Folders/Append Data**—When applied to a folder, this permission grants the user the ability to create new folders. When applied to a file, it allows the user to append data to the file (but not the ability to change existing data).
- **Write Attributes**—This permission allows a user to change the file or folder attributes.
- **Write Extended Attributes**—This permission allows a user to change special file or folder attributes that are created by applications. This is not commonly used.
- **Delete Subfolders and Files**—This permission allows a user to delete subfolders and files, even when the Delete permission is denied at the file and subfolder levels.
- **Delete**—This permission allows a user to delete the subfolder or file to which the permission is applied. This permission can be overruled by the Delete Subfolders and Files permission.
- **Read Permissions**—This permission allows a user to see the permissions applied to a file or folder.
- **Change Permissions**—This permission allows a user to change the permissions applied to a file or folder.
- **Take Ownership**—This permission allows a user to seize ownership of a file or folder. Once a user has ownership of a file or folder, the user will have Full Control.
- **Synchronize**—This permission applies to multithreaded, multiprocess programs and is typically used only by developers.

To configure the special permissions on a file or folder, use the procedure outlined in Step by Step 4.2.

STEP BY STEP

4.2 Configuring Special Permissions

1. Open either My Computer or Windows Explorer. Navigate to the object for which you want to configure permissions.

continues

continued

2. Right-click the object and select Properties from the pop-up menu. Click the Security tab on the resulting dialog box.

3. From the Security tab, click the Advanced button.

4. The Advanced Security Settings dialog box appears (see Figure 4.3). This dialog box allows you to select or add a user or group to assign permissions to by clicking the Add button. Alternatively, you can modify the permissions that are assigned to an existing user or group by highlighting the appropriate entry and then clicking the Edit button. Highlight a user or group and then click Edit.

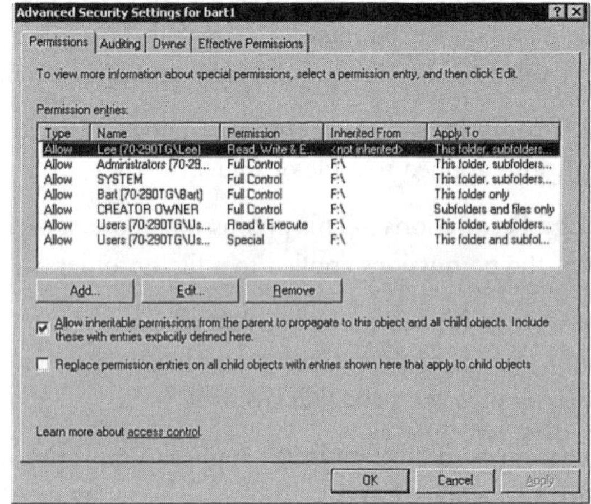

FIGURE 4.3▶
The Advanced Security Settings dialog box, which allows you to add or edit the special permissions applied to each user or group.

5. The Permissions Entry dialog box appears (see Figure 4.4). This dialog box allows you to allow or deny special permissions for the user or group selected in the Advanced Security Settings dialog box. Select the desired permissions and then click the Apply Onto drop-down list.

6. As you can see in Figure 4.5, the Apply Onto drop-down list allows you to specify where to apply the newly selected special permissions. This allows you to select various combinations of files, folders, and subfolders. At the bottom of the dialog box is a check box that prevents the permissions from being inherited by subfolders. Click OK when finished.

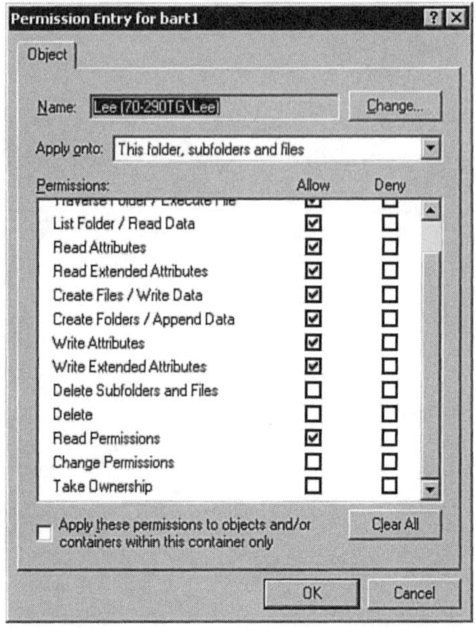

FIGURE 4.4▲
The Permissions Entry dialog box, which allows you to select the special permissions to be applied.

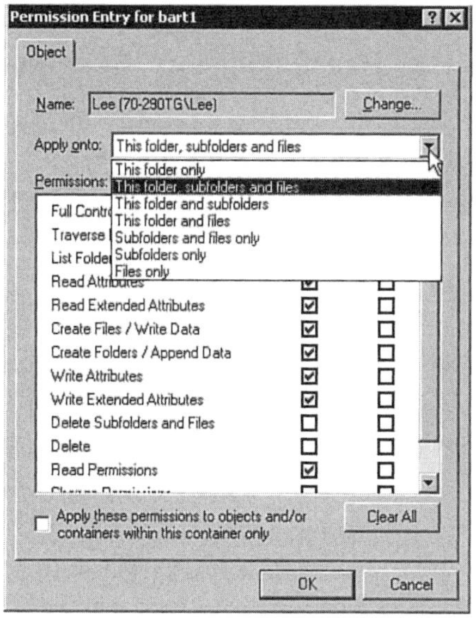

FIGURE 4.5
The Permissions Entry dialog box, showing the Apply Onto drop-down list, which allows you to select where the special permissions will be applied.

7. This returns you to the Advanced Security Settings dialog box. Click OK here and on the Folder Properties dialog box to save.

Special permissions are subsets of the basic permissions discussed earlier. To see which basic permissions the special permissions are included in, refer to Table 4.1.

TABLE 4.1

RELATING BASIC PERMISSIONS TO SPECIAL PERMISSIONS

Special Permissions	*Full Control*	*Modify*	*Read & Execute*	*List Folder Contents*	*Read*	*Write*
Traverse Folder/ Execute File	X	X	X	X		
List Folder/ Read Data	X	X	X	X	X	

continues

TABLE 4.1 *continued*

RELATING BASIC PERMISSIONS TO SPECIAL PERMISSIONS

Special Permissions	*Full Control*	*Modify*	*Read & Execute*	*List Folder Contents*	*Read*	*Write*
Read Attributes	X	X	X	X	X	
Read Extended Attributes	X	X	X	X	X	
Create Files/ Write Data	X	X				X
Create Folders/ Append Data	X	X				X
Write Attributes	X	X				X
Write Extended Attributes	X	X				X
Delete Subfolders and Files	X					
Delete	X	X				
Read Permissions	X	X	X	X	X	X
Change Permissions	X					
Take Ownership	X					
Synchronize	X	X	X	X	X	X

As you can see, the special permissions allow you to grant permission for just a specific task. This allows you to avoid giving a user Full Control access when all you want him or her to be able to do is delete files. In some cases, the basic permissions allow users to perform more tasks than you want them to have access to.

Managing Permissions Inheritance

So far we have covered *explicit* permissions—the permissions explicitly assigned on a file or folder. However, NTFS supports *inherited* permissions; these are the permissions inherited from the parent folder.

NTFS can be thought of as an upside-down tree, with the root at the top. By default, when you assign file and folder permissions, these permissions are automatically applied to the files and folders underneath them in the hierarchy. This means that any permissions applied at the root of an NTFS drive flow down to files and folders at the lowest level, unless the inheritance has been removed. In addition, if you create a file or folder in an existing folder, the permissions in effect for that folder apply to the new objects.

Unless you remove inheritance from the parent, you cannot configure the existing permissions on an object; however, you can still add new ones. As shown in Figure 4.6, the permissions are grayed out. When removing inheritance, you have the option to set the initial permissions by copying the existing inherited permissions or removing them completely. Any explicitly configured permissions remain unchanged.

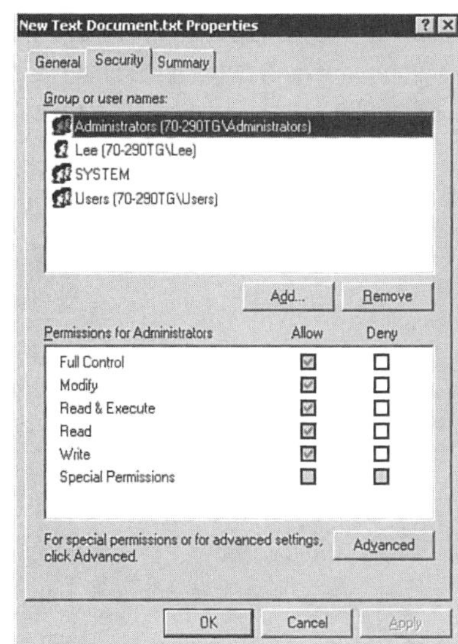

FIGURE 4.6
The File Properties dialog box, showing the inherited permissions. The grayed-out check boxes indicate that the permissions were inherited and cannot be changed.

Here are two key points to remember about inherited permissions:

- Inherited Deny permissions are overridden by an explicit Allow permission.
- Explicit permissions always take precedence over inherited permissions.

To block inheritance on a file, use the procedure outlined in Step by Step 4.3.

STEP BY STEP

4.3 Removing Inheritance for a File

1. Open either My Computer or Windows Explorer and navigate to the file for which you want to configure permissions.

continues

continued

2. Right-click the file, select Properties from the pop-up menu, and click the Security tab in the resulting dialog box.

3. From the Security tab, click the Advanced button.

4. The Advanced Security Settings dialog box appears (see Figure 4.7). Note that the Permission Entries area of the dialog box displays the permissions and where they were inherited from. Deselect the check box Allow Inheritable Permissions from the Parent to Propagate to This Object and All Child Objects.

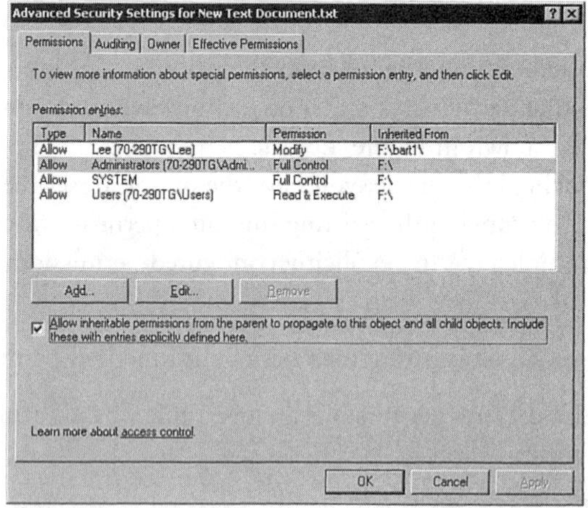

FIGURE 4.7
The Advanced Security Settings dialog box. The check box can be deselected to prevent the object from inheriting permissions from the parent containers.

5. The Security prompt appears (see Figure 4.8). This prompt allows you to either copy or remove the inherited permissions for the object. Select Copy.

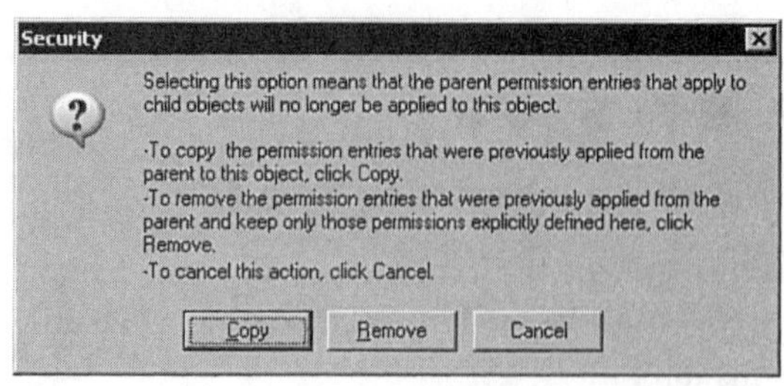

FIGURE 4.8
The Security prompt, which allows you to select whether to copy or remove the inherited permissions.

6. This returns you to the Advanced Security Settings dialog box. As you can see in Figure 4.9, the existing permissions were retained; however, notice that the Inherited From field is now empty. Click OK.

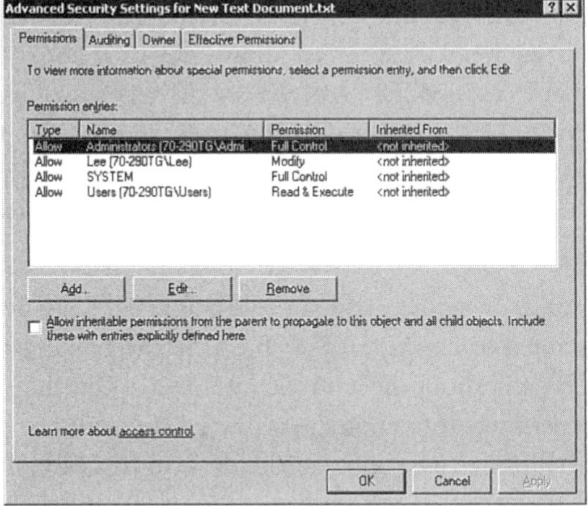

FIGURE 4.9
The Advanced Security Settings dialog box. Notice that the permissions are no longer displayed as inherited.

7. The File Properties dialog box appears, as shown in Figure 4.10. Click OK to save.

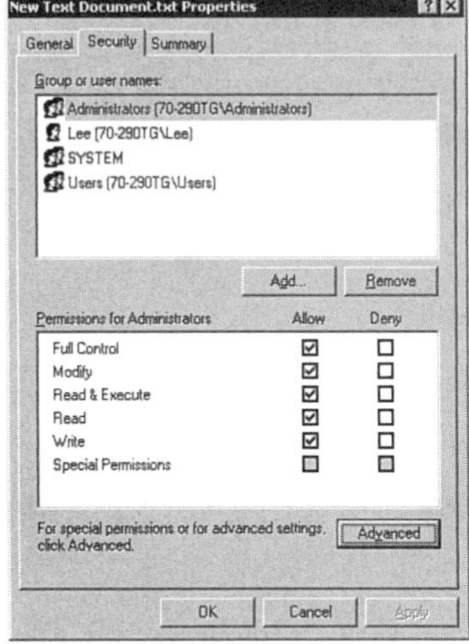

FIGURE 4.10
The File Properties dialog box. Notice that the permissions entries are no longer grayed out and can be changed.

> **NOTE**
>
> **Be Careful with Remove** If you choose to remove the inherited permissions, the only permissions that remain are those that were explicitly added. If there are no added permissions, no one can access the object. The administrator must take ownership of the object and assign permissions to it.

Changing Ownership of Files and Folders

So what happens when the owner of a file or folder leaves the company? How do you regain access to the data she controls? As an administrator, you have the option of resetting the password and logging on using her user account. However, this is not a viable option in many cases because security restrictions may not allow the administrator to be the owner of secure user files. Instead, to ensure the audit trail is intact and not interrupted by the administrator accessing the files, the administrator must transfer the ownership to the new user responsible for the files.

As mentioned earlier, when a file or folder is created, by default the creator is granted ownership of the object. In the case of someone leaving the organization, the administrator can assign the Take Ownership permission to another user or group so that it can take control of the former user's files and folders. In this case, the user or group must then take ownership of the files to complete the process. In Windows Server 2003, however, the administrator also has the option to assign ownership to the new user or group. Either method of transferring ownership allows the administrator to pass control to the new user or group responsible for the files without himself having ownership and disrupting the auditing trail.

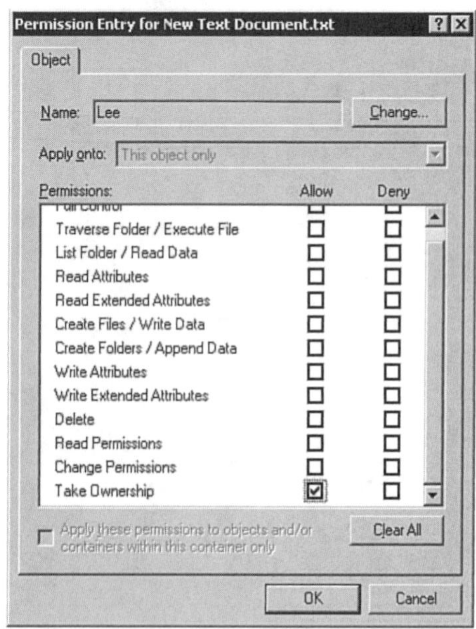

FIGURE 4.11
The Permission Entry dialog box, showing the Take Ownership permission.

The Take Ownership setting is configured on the Permission Entry dialog box for the object, as shown in Figure 4.11.

Ownership of an object can be taken by the following users and groups:

- Administrators
- A user or group that has been assigned the Take Ownership permission
- A user or group that has the Restore Files and Directories privilege

> **EXAM TIP**
>
> **You Can Assign Ownership** Unlike in previous versions of Windows, where the administrator could take ownership, in Windows Server 2003, you can assign ownership of a file or folder to another user.

To assign ownership of a file or folder, use the procedure outlined in Step by Step 4.4.

STEP BY STEP

4.4 Assigning Ownership of a File or Folder

1. Log on as an administrator.
2. Open either My Computer or Windows Explorer. Navigate to the object for which you want to configure permissions.
3. Right-click the object, select Properties from the pop-up menu, and click the Security tab in the resulting dialog box.
4. From the Security tab, click the Advanced button.
5. The Advanced Security Settings dialog box appears. Select the Owner tab.
6. The Owner tab, shown in Figure 4.12, allows you to assign ownership of the object to a user or group. Click the Other Users or Groups button.

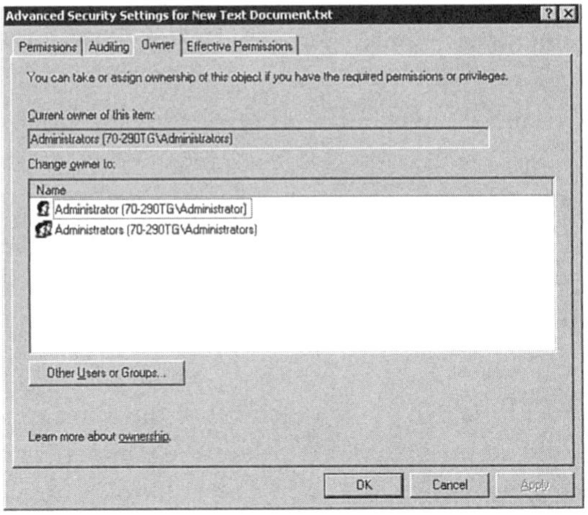

FIGURE 4.12
The Advanced Security Settings dialog box, showing the Owner tab.

7. The Select User or Group dialog box appears, as shown in Figure 4.13. Enter the desired user or group and then click the OK button.

continues

continued

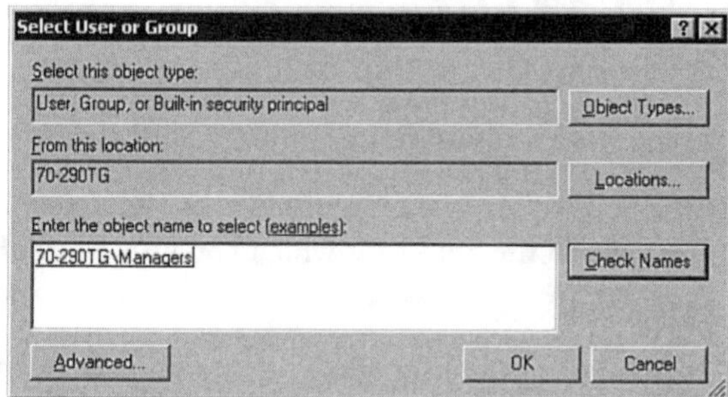

FIGURE 4.13
The Select User or Group dialog box. Click the Advanced button to search for a user or group.

8. This returns you to the Advanced Security Settings dialog box. Click OK here and in the Object Properties dialog box to save.

Verifying Effective Permissions when Granting Permissions

NTFS file and folder permissions are cumulative. This means that the effective permissions are a combination of the permissions granted to the user and those permissions granted to any group to which the user belongs. For example, Dave is a member of the Accounting group, and the Accounting group has Read access to the ACCT folder. However, Dave is also a member of the Managers group. The Managers group has Write access to the ACCT folder. In this case, Dave would have Read and Write access to the ACCT folder.

Let's look at another example. Joe has been granted Full Control access to the EOY folder. Joe is a member of the Managers group, which has Read access to the EOY folder. Joe is also a member of the Planning group, which has Deny Full Control permission on the EOY folder. Joe's effective permission is Deny Full Control.

Another important point to remember is that the least-restrictive permissions apply. For example, if Mary is a member of the HR group, which has Read access to a folder, and she's also a member of the Managers group, which has Full Control access, her effective permission for the folder is Full Control.

All NTFS permissions are cumulative, except in the case of Deny, which overrules everything else. Even if the user has been granted Full Control in several groups, being a member of one group that has been assigned the Deny permission negates everything else.

Windows Server 2003 includes the Effective Permissions tool. This tool automatically looks at a user's permissions and the permissions of the groups of which the user is a member to calculate the effective permissions for an object on an NTFS volume.

To view the effective permissions for an object, follow the procedure outlined in Step by Step 4.5.

STEP BY STEP

4.5 Viewing the Effective Permissions of a File or Folder

1. Open either My Computer or Windows Explorer and navigate to the object for which you want to view permissions.
2. Right-click the object, select Properties from the pop-up menu, and click the Security tab in the resulting dialog box.
3. From the Security tab, click the Advanced button.
4. The Advanced Security Settings dialog box appears. Select the Effective Permissions tab.
5. The Effective Permissions tab appears, as shown in Figure 4.14. This page allows you to display the effective permissions of the object for a user or group. Click the Select button.
6. The Select User or Group dialog box appears. Enter the desired user or group and then click the OK button.

continues

continued

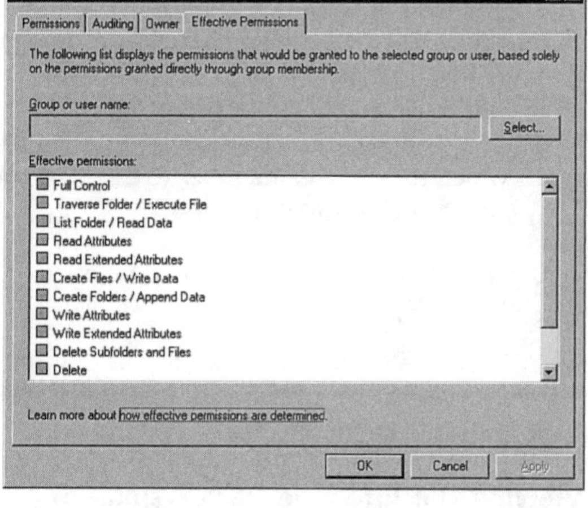

FIGURE 4.14
The Advanced Security Settings dialog box, showing the Effective Permissions tab.

7. This returns you to the Advanced Security Settings dialog box, shown in Figure 4.15. The effective permissions for the user are shown. Click OK here and in the Object Properties dialog box to quit.

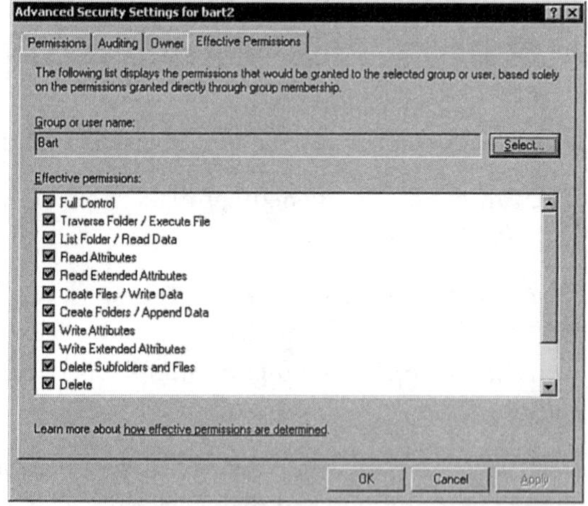

FIGURE 4.15
The Advanced Security Settings dialog box, showing the effective permissions.

NOTE

Share Permissions Share permissions are not included in the effective permissions calculations.

Copying and Moving Files and Folders

When files and folders are copied or moved on an NTFS partition, the configured permissions may change. This depends on whether the file or folder was copied or moved, and where it was moved to. Several rules apply when you move or copy NTFS files and folders. The possible outcomes of moving or copying NTFS files and folders are as follows:

- ▶ Moving a file or folder to another folder on the same NTFS volume results in the file or folder retaining its permissions, regardless of the permissions configured on the target folder.
- ▶ Moving a file or folder to a different NTFS volume results in the file or folder assuming the permissions of the target folder.
- ▶ Moving a file or folder from a FAT volume to an NTFS volume results in the file or folder assuming the permissions of the target folder.
- ▶ Moving a file or folder from an NTFS volume to a FAT volume results in all NTFS-specific properties (including permissions) being lost.
- ▶ Copying a file to another folder on the same NTFS volume results in the file assuming the permissions of the target folder.
- ▶ Copying a file or folder to a different NTFS volume results in the file or folder assuming the permissions of the target folder.
- ▶ Copying a file or folder from a FAT volume to an NTFS volume results in the file or folder assuming the permissions of the target folder.
- ▶ Copying a file or folder from an NTFS volume to a FAT volume results in all NTFS-specific properties being lost.

It's important to note that if you configure permissions on a folder, you can choose whether or not to propagate the permissions to the existing files and subfolders contained within that folder. However, any new files or subfolders created within that folder automatically inherit the permissions of the container.

CONFIGURING AND MANAGING SHARED FOLDERS

Now that we have examined the properties of local security, let's take a look at share security. As previously discussed, one of the main roles of a computer running Windows Server 2003 is that of a file server. The role of a file server is to provide centralized access to files over a network. Regardless of whether the server is serving files to a workgroup or a domain, this is an important role.

Unfortunately, without the proper security in place, just having physical access to the network allows any user to access any file on the file server. In this section, we examine not only how to share files and folders over a network but also how to assign permissions to restrict access to the appropriate users.

Creating and Managing Shared Folders

EXAM TIP

Better Security in Windows Server 2003 In previous versions of Windows, when a folder was shared, the Everyone group was granted Full Control permissions.

NOTE

Be Careful with Deny If you want to remove the permissions for the Everyone group for an object, remove the Everyone entry from the Permissions dialog box. Do not assign the Deny permission to the Everyone group because the Everyone group includes all users, including administrators.

Users on other computers can connect to a file server via shares. The term *share* is shorthand for *shared folder*. Sharing a folder allows the contents of the folder to be available to multiple concurrent users on a network. When a folder is shared, any user with the proper permissions can access it.

A shared folder can contain applications, data, or a user's personal data. Using shares allows an administrator to centralize the management, security, and backup of applications and data. Shared folders can be implemented on either workstations or servers.

When a folder is shared, the Everyone group is granted Read access by default. As additional users or groups are added to the share, they are also given Read permission initially. Unless there is a good reason not to do so, you should always remove the permissions from the Everyone group and assign the proper permissions directly to other groups.

Only members of the Administrators, Server Operators, or Power Users group are permitted to share folders. To share a folder on a local volume, follow the procedure outlined in Step by Step 4.6.

STEP BY STEP

4.6 Creating a Shared Folder on a Local Volume

1. Open either My Computer or Windows Explorer. Navigate to the folder that you want to share.
2. Right-click the folder and select Sharing and Security from the pop-up menu. The Folder Properties dialog box appears, as shown in Figure 4.16. Click the Share This Folder radio button.
3. Enter a share name. This is the name that users will use to access this folder over the network. It does not have to be the same as the folder name. The description is optional; some user interfaces display this field, whereas others do not. The User Limit field allows you to specify the maximum number of users that can concurrently access the share.
4. Select the desired options and then click OK to save.
5. The shared folder appears in Windows Explorer or My Computer as an icon of a hand holding a folder, as shown in Figure 4.17.

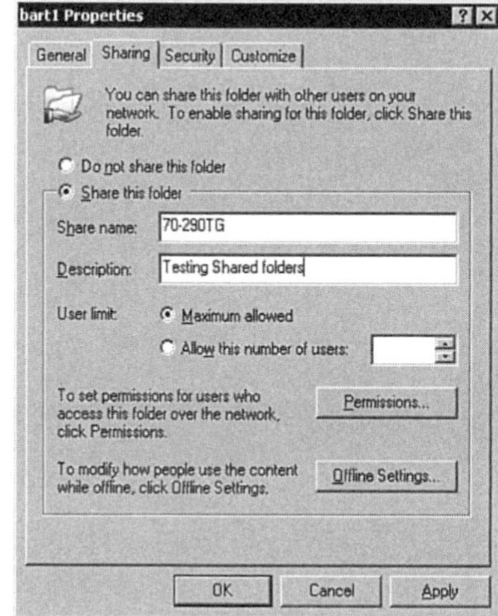

FIGURE 4.16
The Folder Properties dialog box, showing the Sharing tab.

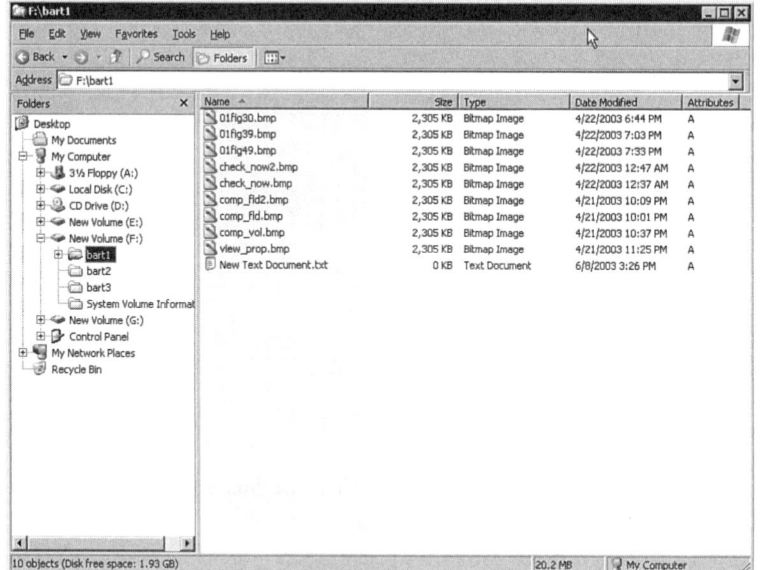

FIGURE 4.17
Windows Explorer, showing the shared folder icon.

A share can also be created on a remote computer. This is accomplished using the Shared Folders snap-in of the Computer Management MMC.

To share a folder on a remote volume, follow the procedure outlined in Step by Step 4.7.

STEP BY STEP

4.7 Creating a Shared Folder on a Remote Volume

1. Click Start, All Programs, Administrative Tools, Computer Management.
2. From the Computer Management MMC, in the left pane right-click the Computer Management (Local) entry. From the pop-up menu, select Connect to Another Computer.
3. From the Select Computer dialog box, enter the name of the remote computer and then click the OK button.
4. From the Computer Management MMC, shown in Figure 4.18, click the System Tools entry in the left pane.

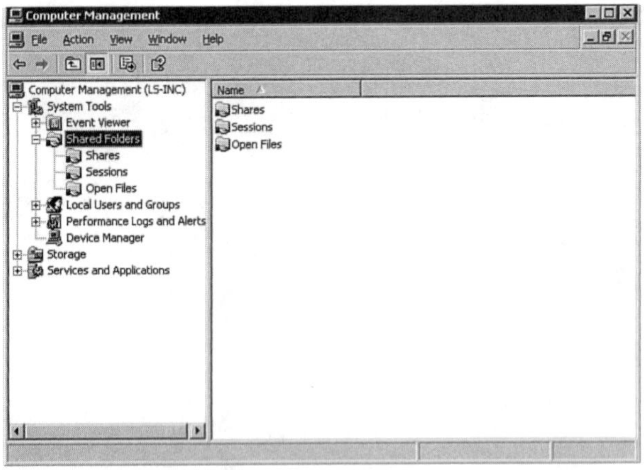

FIGURE 4.18
The Computer Management MMC, showing the Shared Folders snap-in.

5. From the expanded tree, click the Shared Folders entry. Under Shared Folders, right-click Shares and select New Share from the pop-up menu.
6. This starts the Share a Folder Wizard. Click Next on the opening screen of the wizard.

7. From the Folder Path screen of the Share a Folder Wizard, shown in Figure 4.19, enter the path of the folder to be shared. If desired, you can click the Browse button to search for it. Click Next to continue.

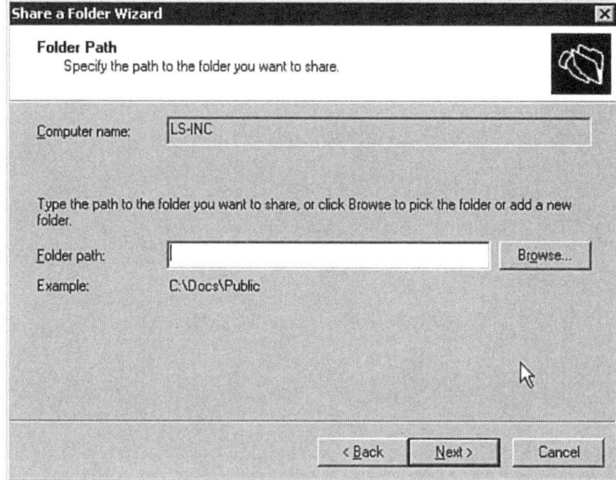

FIGURE 4.19
The Share a Folder Wizard's Folder Path screen. Enter the path for the shared folder.

8. From the Name, Description, and Settings screen, shown in Figure 4.20, enter a share name. This is the name users will use to access this folder over the network. It does not have to be the same as the folder name. The description is optional; some user interfaces display this field, whereas others do not. Click Next to continue.

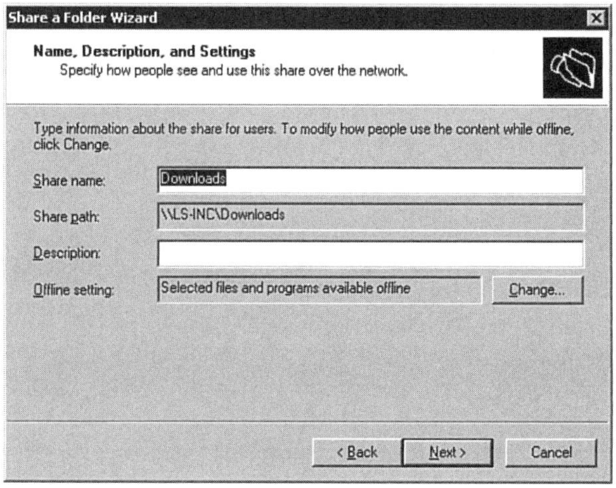

Share a Folder Wizard
Name, Description, and Settings
Specify how people see and use this share over the network.
Type information about the share for users. To modify how people use the content while offline, click Change.
Share name: Downloads
Share path: \\LS-INC\Downloads
Description:
Offline setting: Selected files and programs available offline
Change...
< Back
Next >
Cancel

FIGURE 4.20
Enter a share name and description.

continues

continued

9. From the Permissions screen, shown in Figure 4.21, select the desired permissions and then click the Finish button.

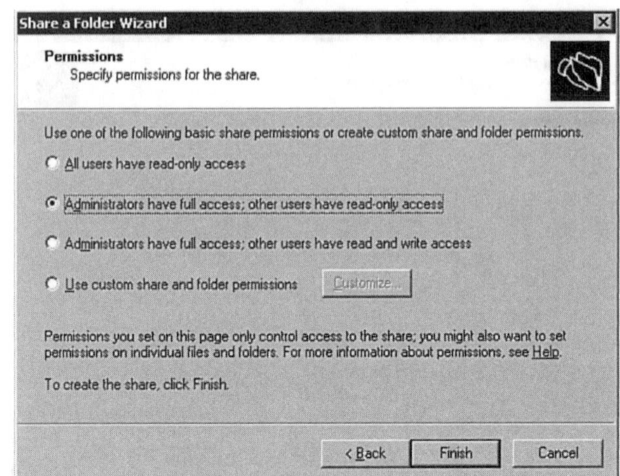

FIGURE 4.21
Enter the desired permissions. The default is for everyone to have Read access.

10. Select the desired options and then click OK to save.

11. The shared folder appears in the right pane of the Shared Folders snap-in as an icon of a hand holding a folder, as shown in Figure 4.22.

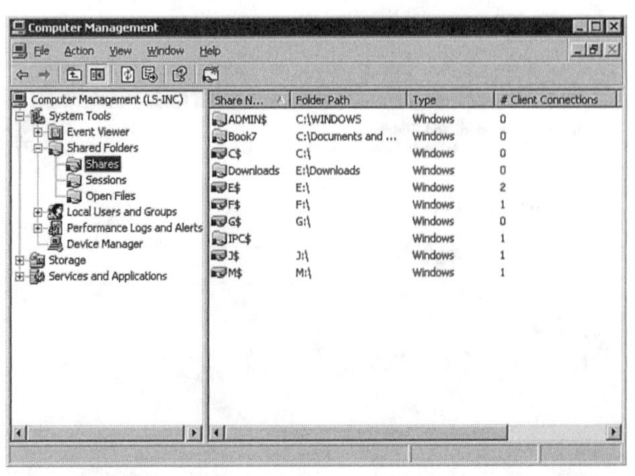

FIGURE 4.22
The Shared Folders snap-in, showing the shared folder icon.

As you might have noticed in Figure 4.22, when the new share was created, several shares were already present—most of which have a dollar sign ($) after their name. These shares are Administrative Shared folders. These folders are shared during the default installation of Windows Server 2003. They are used for the convenience of administrators and the operating system to administer files and folders on remote computers.

The permissions for Administrative Shared folders cannot be changed. By default, members of the Administrators group are granted Full Control access. The names and purposes of the folders are as follows:

- **C$, D$, E$, and so on**—The root of every volume is automatically shared.
- **Admin$**—This is a shortcut to the `%systemroot%` folder. This is handy because the systemroot folder can be on any volume, and depending on whether your installation of Windows Server 2003 is an upgrade or a clean installation, the systemroot could either be in a `\winnt` or `\windows` folder.
- **Print$**—This folder contains the installed print drivers. In addition to the Administrators group, the Server Operators and Print Operators groups have Full Control permissions to this folder. The Everyone group has Read permission.
- **IPC$**—This is a system folder that is used for interprocess communications (IPC). It is used by most of the Windows Server 2003 administrative tools.
- **FAX$**—This shared folder is used as temporary storage for the Windows Server 2003 Fax application.

The dollar sign after the name tells Windows Server 2003 not to display the folder in My Network Places or when the server is being browsed. You can create your own hidden shares by simply adding the trailing dollar sign at the end of the share name.

Publishing a Shared Folder in Active Directory

In Windows Server 2003, you can publish a shared folder as a shared folder object in Active Directory using the Active Directory Users and Computers snap-in. This allows users to query Active Directory for the shared folder instead of browsing to locate it. Just creating a shared folder is not enough; it must be also be published to be visible in Active Directory.

To publish a shared folder in Active Directory, use the procedure outlined in Step by Step 4.8.

STEP BY STEP

4.8 Publishing a Shared Folder in Active Directory

1. Click Start, All Programs, Administrative Tools, Active Directory Users and Computers.
2. From the Active Directory Users and Computers MMC, in the left pane click the domain entry to expand the tree. Then navigate to the container of the OU that you want to publish the folder in.
3. Right-click the desired container. From the pop-up menu, select New, Shared Folder.
4. The New Object - Shared Folder dialog box appears.
5. In the New Object - Shared Folder dialog box, type in the Fully Qualified Domain Name (FQDN) path of the shared folder that you would like to publish (`\\`*`servername.domainname`*`.com\`*`sharename`*).
6. Type in the name you want to use to refer to the shared folder within Active Directory.
7. Click OK to save.

NOTE

Use the Fully Qualified Domain Name Notice in the previous Step by Step that the fully qualified domain name was used to refer to the network path for the shared folder. If you use the NetBIOS name, only users within the domain can access the share.

Managing Shared Folder Permissions

Shared folder permissions are important, especially when the share is hosted on a FAT volume. Because the objects on FAT volumes can't be assigned permissions at the file or folder level, share permissions are the only type of file security available.

Share permissions, as you might have guessed from the name, apply only when a file or folder is accessed over the network through a shared folder. Permissions assigned to a share have no effect on a user logged on to the server console or logged on to a Terminal Services session on that server.

When a share is created, the Everyone group is granted Read access by default. Obviously, this isn't appropriate for many circumstances, so you should make adjustments. Only three types of access permissions can be configured on a share. The default permission is Read, and it allows you to perform the following:

- View file and subfolder names.
- View the contents of files.
- Execute applications.

The second permission is Change. It allows you to do everything that the Read permission allows and also the following:

- Add files and subfolders.
- Change the contents of files.
- Delete files and subfolders.

The last permission is Full Control. It allows you to perform all of the Read and Change tasks in addition to allowing you to change the permissions on NTFS files and subfolders in the share.

To share a folder on a local volume, follow the procedure outlined in Step by Step 4.9.

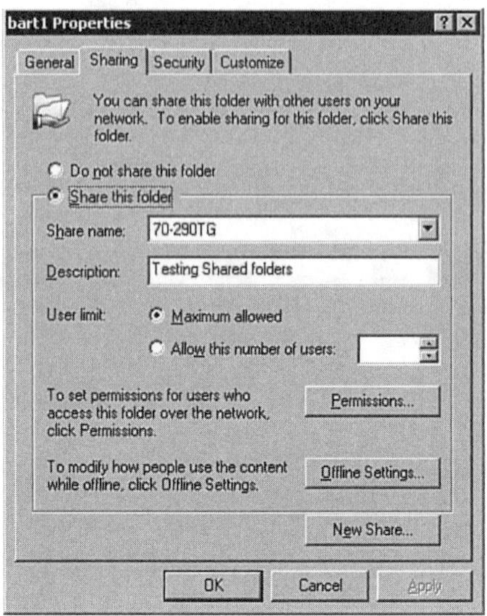

FIGURE 4.23
The Folder Properties dialog box, showing the Sharing tab.

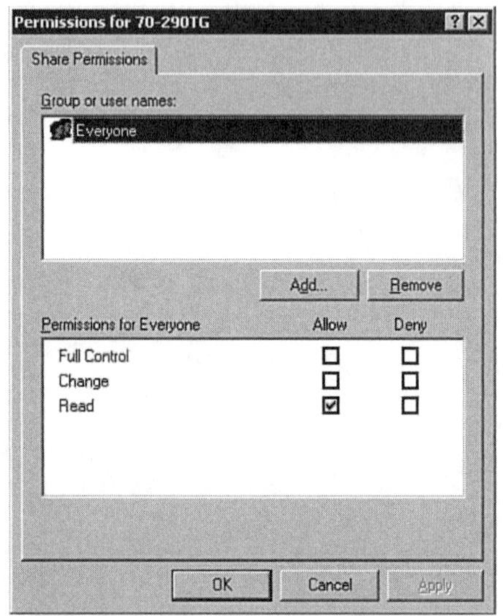

FIGURE 4.24
The Share Permissions dialog box, showing the default settings.

STEP BY STEP

4.9 Configuring Shared Folder Permissions

1. Open either My Computer or Windows Explorer and navigate to the shared folder that you want to configure.
2. Right-click the folder and select Sharing and Security from the pop-up menu. The Folder Properties dialog box appears (see Figure 4.23). Click the Permissions button.
3. The Share Permissions dialog box appears, as shown in Figure 4.24. By default, the Everyone group is granted Read permission. Click the Remove button; this deletes the entry for the Everyone group. Click the Add button; this opens the Select Users or Groups dialog box. Add a user or group and then click the OK button to save.
4. This returns you to the Share Permissions dialog box. Select the desired permissions for the user or group that was added. Then click OK here and in the Folder Properties dialog to save.

COMBINING SHARE AND NTFS PERMISSIONS

When you're accessing the contents of a shared folder on an NTFS volume, the effective permissions for the object that you are trying to access is a combination of the share and the NTFS permissions applied to the object. The effective permission is always the most restrictive of the two.

For a real-world example, think about it in this way: John has just been named Employee of the Month. As part of this award, he gets a party in his department's break room. Sitting around a table in the break room are several employees from John's department. Sitting on the table is a cake and in John's pocket is the bonus check John received with the award. Think of the people sitting around the table as users sitting at the console of a workstation or server.

The check in John's pocket has his name on it, so effectively he has Full Control permissions on the check. Because the check was explicitly made out to John, no other users have access to it, even if they are sitting at the console, or in our example, the table in the break room.

On the other hand, the cake is for everybody in the department, so imagine that the Everyone group has Full Control permissions to the cake. This means that anyone sitting at the table has full access to the cake.

Being a good friend of John, you of course wouldn't miss his celebration, even though you work in another department. However, as usual, you're running late. You approach the door of the break room and discover that you need a card key or access code to get in, which you do not have. Even though you are a member of the Everyone group, and you have permissions to access the cake, you can't get to it because you don't have the proper level of access to get through the door.

A shared folder is similar to the door in our example. If you don't have the necessary access rights for a folder, you can't get to its contents, even if you have been granted the necessary rights at the object level.

To carry the example a little further, say that the door to the break room is made of glass. In this case, because you can see through the door, you have permission to look around (Read), but you can't eat any of the cake (Change). Although the cake still has the permission of Everyone Full Control, because you can only see through the door, you have only the rights that were granted through it.

This, in a nutshell, is how combined file and share permissions work. If you are sitting at the server or workstation console, only the NTFS file and folder access permissions apply to you. However, if you are trying to access the files across the network via a shared folder, both the file and the share permissions apply. And the most restrictive permission applies.

Let's use our previous example again. Say that Mary, a member of John's department, is also late for the party. She is able to enter the break room because she has full access rights as a member of John's department (that is, she has the necessary card key or access code to get in). However, she still does not have access to John's bonus check because she doesn't have the proper permissions.

So as you can see, when combining file and share permissions, the most restrictive permissions apply.

TROUBLESHOOTING ACCESS TO FILES AND SHARED FOLDERS

As you saw in the previous section, share permissions, not just NTFS permissions, can prevent access to a file or folder. However, the problem of a user having too much access to data can be an even more severe problem. For example, how many people in your organization need to know the salaries of the IT staff?

Most access problems are caused by simple things, such as bad passwords or incorrectly configured permissions. For example, does the user who is having problems accessing the file or shared folder have the necessary permissions for proper access? Is the user a member of a group that has been denied access to the file or shared folder? Remember that Deny has precedence over a granted permission.

When you're tracking down permissions problems, sometimes creating a new user account can be a good troubleshooting aid. Does the new user account fail in the same way as the existing ones? The Effective Permissions tool can be helpful—up to a point. Because share permissions are not included in effective permissions calculations, the Effective Permissions tool can be used to verify that you are obtaining the desired results from the NTFS permissions, but you will still need to analyze the combination of share and NTFS permissions.

GUIDED PRACTICE EXERCISE 4.1

You are the administrator of a network that includes multiple servers running Windows Server 2003 for file and print services. The Human Resources department wants to have its files stored on one of your servers, but it doesn't want anyone outside the group to have access to them. The users in the HR department will not be logging on to the server, but they need to access the files over the network. They want you to set this up for them.

What is the best way to solve this issue in Windows Server 2003? On your own, try to develop a solution that would involve the least amount of downtime.

If you would like to see a possible solution, follow these steps:

Estimated Time: 20 minutes

1. Open either My Computer or Windows Explorer. Navigate to the volume where you want to create a folder.
2. Create a folder and name it HR.
3. Right-click the folder and select Sharing and Security from the pop-up menu.
4. On the Sharing tab of the HR Properties dialog box, select the Share This Folder option, and accept the default share name of HR.
5. Click the Permissions button. The Permissions for HR dialog box appears.
6. Click the Add button. From the Select Users, Computers, or Groups dialog box, enter the HR group. Click the OK button to save.
7. Back at the Permissions for HR dialog box, make sure the HR group entry is highlighted and then click the Full Control check box.
8. Highlight the Everyone entry and then click the Remove button.
9. Click OK. Then click OK again on the HR Properties dialog box to save.

One of the key things to remember when creating a shared folder is that the Everyone group is given Read permission by default. For greater security, you should always remove this group as you add permissions for specific groups.

Using Windows Server 2003 Terminal Services

Windows Server 2003 Terminal Services is designed to provide a multiuser environment, which makes it possible for several users to connect to a server and run applications concurrently.

Terminal Services consists of three major components:

- **Multiuser server core**—This is a modified version of the Windows Server 2003 kernel that allows the operating system to support multiple concurrent users and share resources.
- **Client software**—The Remote Desktop Connection (RDC) client software provides the user interface. It can be installed on a PC, Windows terminal, or handheld device. It provides the look and feel of the standard Windows interface.
- **Remote Desktop Protocol (RDP)**—This is the protocol that provides communication between the server and the client software. It runs only on TCP/IP.

Windows Terminal Services is designed to distribute the Windows 32-bit desktop to clients that are usually not able to run it. Although for the client it appears that the application is running locally, all processing actually occurs on the server. The only processing that occurs at the client involves displaying the user interface and accepting input from the keyboard and mouse.

> NOTE
>
> **Additional Clients** Not included on the Windows Server 2003 CD-ROM, but available for download from the Microsoft Web site, are clients for the Macintosh (`http://www.microsoft.com/downloads/details.aspx?FamilyID=c669fcf7-c868-4d45-95f3-f75ddd969232&displaylang=en`) and a Terminal Services (not RDC) client for the Pocket PC (`http://www.microsoft.com/windowsmobile/resources/downloads/pocketpc/tsc.mspx`).

Although the application is run on the server, the information needed to control the user interface, such as keystrokes and mouse clicks, is sent over the connection to the client. The data rate of the connection is very small, generally less than 16Kbps. This makes Terminal Services well suited for low-bandwidth connections, such as low-speed dial-up lines.

The RDP clients supplied with Windows Server 2003 Terminal Services can be used on most Windows PCs and Windows terminals. A 32-bit client is used with Windows 9x, NT, 2000, and XP.

IN THE FIELD

LINUX

An open-source RDP client is available for the Linux platform called Rdesktop. It is available from `www.rdesktop.org`.

The RDC client provides the standard Win32 desktop to users. It is a Windows-based application and runs only on Windows platforms. However, it is a very small application (generally less than 2MB in size) and can run on machines with very limited processor and memory resources.

This client provides the following features:

- **Roaming disconnect support**—This allows a user to disconnect her session and then reconnect to the server—either from the same PC or terminal or from any other PC or terminal—and her session resumes just where she left it, without any data loss.
- **Multiple login support**—This allows a user to be connected to multiple sessions simultaneously.
- **Local resources are available**—The RDC 5.1 client allows you to connect to most of the resources attached to the local PC that is running the RDC client. This includes drives, smart cards, printers, and the Clipboard. For instance, files can be opened, saved, and printed to the user's local PC, regardless of whether the application is running locally or remotely.
- **Automatic session reconnection**—If a user is disconnected from the server due to a local problem, such as a communications line failure, the RDC client automatically attempts to reconnect to the user's session on the Terminal Services server.

Terminal Services Advantages and Disadvantages

Terminal Services offers many advantages. Here are a few of them:

- **Windows Terminal Services runs Windows applications**—Most Windows and DOS applications run on Terminal Services without any modifications.

- **The client is very small**—This allows the client to run on low-powered terminals or PCs.
- **The client can be used with older technology**—This allows older machines to be used as clients that would normally be sent to the scrap heap.
- **The responsibility for processing is put in the server room**—Everything to do with the support of the server and applications is directly controlled by the system administrator in the server room. Users have fewer opportunities to "help" the administrator. This results in fewer problems. In addition, because just about everything is controlled from a centralized location, expensive, time-consuming visits to the desktop are rare.

Terminal Services also has a couple disadvantages, as follows:

- **Hardware**—Terminal Services requires much more hardware than the typical file and print server needs. You can use lower-end systems for the client, but you have to spend more money on the server.
- **Security**—You must be aware of the security weaknesses introduced with Terminal Services. For example, Terminal Services users are, in effect, given the equivalent of Log On Locally access to your server, so you need to be especially vigilant in limiting access to sensitive files and folders. In addition, because of this Log On Locally access, you should never install Terminal Services in Application Server mode on a domain controller.

Environments for Which Terminal Services Is Recommended

Terminal Services is recommended for use in a variety of environments. The following are some examples:

- **Harsh environments**—Terminal Services is very good for harsh environments, such as manufacturing facilities. This allows you to utilize a low-cost Windows terminal that has no moving parts and would normally be susceptible to damage or contamination.

- **Remote access**—Because of the low-bandwidth requirements, a remote Terminal Services user usually sees the same relative performance as if he were running applications locally. In addition, the remote user doesn't have to have frequent software and hardware updates because all updates are performed on the server by the administrator(s).
- **Public access terminals**—A Windows terminal used as a kiosk is very secure because Terminal Services allows administrators to lock down applications and system access.
- **Customer service**—Users running a single or a few task-based applications are ideal candidates for Terminal Services because they can be supplied with a low-cost Windows terminal for far less money than a PC, which would likely be overkill for their needs.
- **Wireless applications**—Because of the low-bandwidth requirements, Terminal Services is especially good for providing server applications to wireless users, especially users of handheld devices.

Terminal Services Is Not Recommended For...

Here are some applications for which the use of Windows Terminal Services is not recommended:

- **Applications requiring heavy calculations**—Typical examples are Computer Aided Drafting (CAD) applications.
- **Applications that identify users or sessions by IP address or machine name**—Examples include some terminal-emulator applications.
- **Applications with memory leaks or that perform constant keyboard polling**—These problems are common with older DOS applications.
- **Applications using animation**—Passing screen updates for large, detailed bitmaps uses a lot of bandwidth and takes time for the user to see the painted bitmap.

- **Publishing and drawing programs**—Although the Terminal Services clients supported in Windows Server 2003 can support more than 256 colors, the excess color depth requires more processing and network bandwidth. In addition, all graphics screen updates have to be passed over the connection, which can get pretty slow.

Working with Terminal Services

Terminal Services is available in two modes: Remote Desktop for Administration (formerly called Remote Administration mode) and Application Server mode. Application Server mode configures Windows Server 2003 to operate similar to the previous version of Windows NT Terminal Server 4.0. Remote Desktop for Administration mode is used to provide remote server management. Unlike in Windows 2000, where the Remote Administration mode was an option, the Remote Desktop for Administration mode is automatically installed in Windows Server 2003. However, incoming connections are disabled by default.

Using Terminal Services in Remote Desktop for Administration Mode

The Terminal Services (TS) Remote Administration mode was first available in Windows 2000. The previous version of Windows NT 4.0 Terminal Server did not have this feature. With Windows Server 2003 Terminal Services in Remote Desktop for Administration mode, you are allowed two concurrent sessions, plus a console session to the Windows server. These sessions can be used to remotely access any programs or data on the server.

Using the Terminal Services client is just like working on the server console. The Remote Desktop for Administration mode allows you to have two concurrent TS sessions without any additional Client Access Licenses required. The beauty of the Remote Desktop for Administration mode is that it allows you to manage your server from just about anywhere and from just about any computer. Because the TS client is supported on a variety of Windows platforms, including Windows CE and Pocket PC 2002 and later, you can load the client on any Windows box that you have available and manage your server. Imagine managing your server from your Pocket PC!

In addition, because the RDC connection between the server and the client requires a minimum of bandwidth, you are not limited to a high-speed LAN connection. The Terminal Services client can access the servers via a dial-up connection, the Internet, or even a wireless connection. Again, think about managing your servers from your Pocket PC while sitting on a warm, sandy beach.

NOTE

Switching Between Terminal Services Modes Although it is possible to switch from one mode to another, it is necessary to reinstall all applications.

In addition to the two virtual sessions, a new feature in Windows Server 2003 provides the ability to connect to the real console of the server. In the past, a lot of tools and applications could not be run remotely because they were written to interact directly with "session 0," or the physical server console. Also, most system messages are routed to the console automatically, so if you were trying to manage the server remotely and a pop-up error message was sent, you wouldn't be able to see it.

Working with Terminal Services in Remote Desktop for Administration mode is covered at length in the "Managing Servers Remotely" section of Chapter 5, "Managing and Troubleshooting Servers."

Terminal Services in Application Server Mode

The purpose of Application Server mode in Windows Server 2003 Terminal Services is to enable applications to be shared and managed from a central location. The Terminal Services Application Server mode changes the characteristics of the server. Normally, a server is tuned to give best performance to the background processes that are running. This enables server-type applications, such as databases and mail servers, to perform better. However, when Windows is configured for Terminal Services Application Server mode, the server is tuned to give the best performance to the foreground processes. This is similar to the way a workstation operating system is tuned because those are the types of tasks the operating system is now handling. With Terminal Services, each user is assigned his own session of 2GB of virtual memory on the server. Performance depends on the capacity of the server, how many users are logged on, and what applications are running.

The Application Server mode of Terminal Services allows the system administrator to load common applications that can be shared by multiple users. The users can be granted the ability to connect to a specific application or a complete desktop environment.

This can greatly decrease the support costs associated with an organization because there are fewer visits to the end user. There is no need for upgrade visits, and there are fewer visits for application issues because everything is located and controlled centrally.

Unlike Remote Desktop for Administration mode, in which there are only two concurrent connections plus the console allowed, Application Server mode allows you to have an unlimited number of concurrent connections, subject to server capacity and licensing. The number of users supported varies widely, depending on the type of applications in use and the hardware configuration of the server. Typically, on the same hardware, you can support far more users running terminal emulator–type applications than users who are using CAD applications.

To install Terminal Services in Application Server mode, follow the procedure outlined in Step by Step 4.10.

STEP BY STEP

4.10 Installing Terminal Services in Application Server Mode

1. Click Start, All Programs, Control Panel, Add or Remove Programs.
2. Click the Add/Remove Windows Components button in the left pane of the Add or Remove Programs dialog box, as shown in Figure 4.25.
3. The Windows Components Wizard appears, as shown in Figure 4.26. Select the Terminal Server check box.
4. If Internet Explorer Enhanced Security Configuration is enabled (it is enabled by default), you will receive the Configuration Warning prompt shown in Figure 4.27. After you read and understand this warning, click the Yes button to continue.

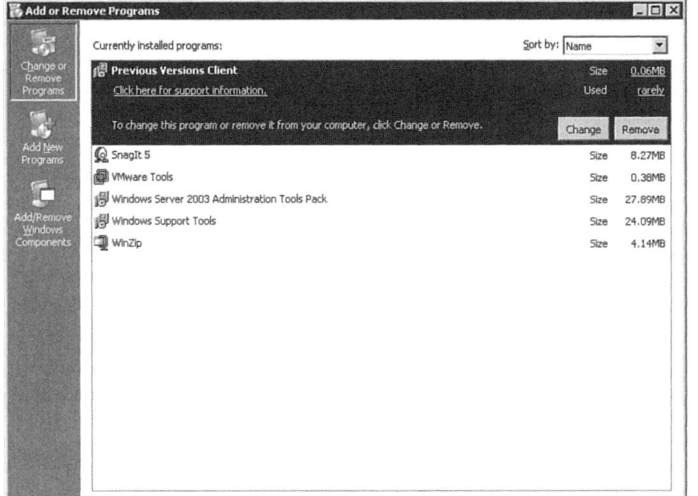

FIGURE 4.25
The Add or Remove Programs dialog box is used to install Terminal Services in Application Server mode.

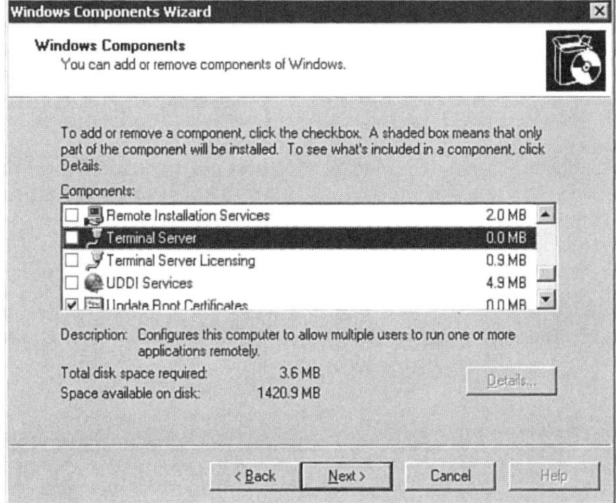

FIGURE 4.26
The Windows Components Wizard is where you select to install Terminal Services.

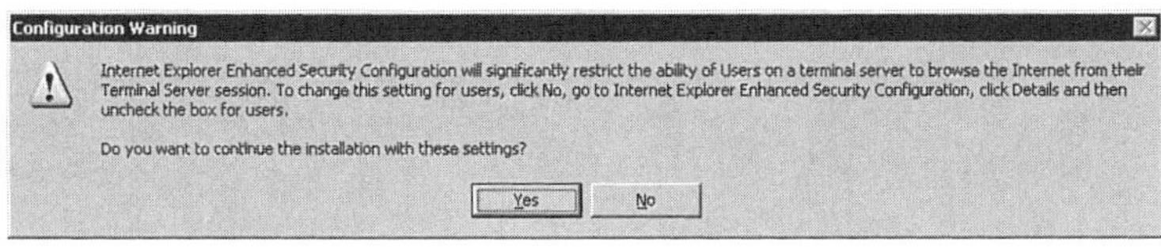

FIGURE 4.27
The Configuration Warning prompt—you must click the Yes button to continue installing Terminal Services.

5. This returns you to the Windows Components Wizard. Click the Next button to continue.

continues

continued

6. The Terminal Server Setup warning appears, as shown in Figure 4.28. Read and understand the warnings before clicking the Next button to continue.

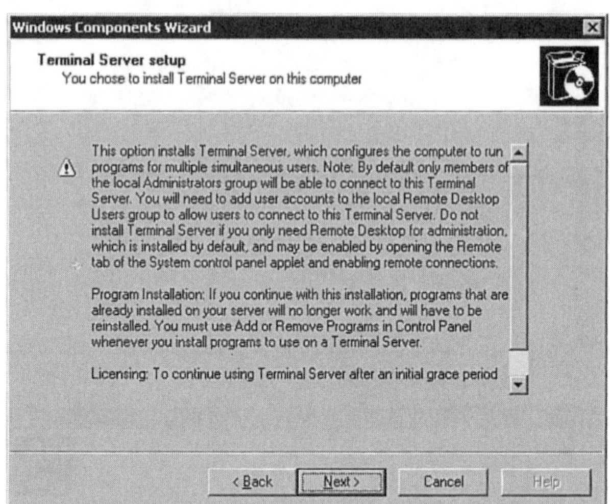

FIGURE 4.28
The Terminal Server Setup warning prompt alerts you to the requirements of a Terminal Server.

7. The Terminal Server Setup screen appears, as shown in Figure 4.29. This screen allows you to select the Full Security mode, which is new to Windows Server 2003, or the Relaxed Security mode, which is roughly equivalent to the security on a Windows 2000 Terminal Services server. Click the desired option button and then click the Next button to continue.

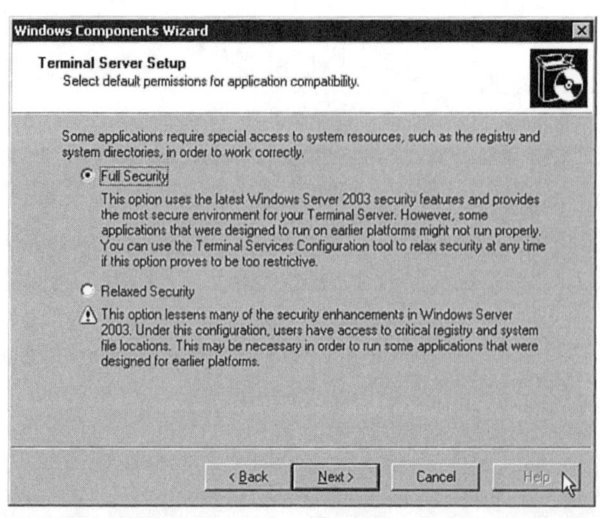

FIGURE 4.29
The Terminal Server Setup screen allows you to configure Terminal Services security.

8. When the Completing the Windows Components Wizard screen appears, click the Finish button. You will be prompted to reboot the server.

Application Server mode requires that each remote connection have a Windows Server 2003 Terminal Services user or device Client Access License (TS CAL). These licenses are separate from the normal Windows Client Access Licenses (CALs) and must be installed and managed using a Terminal Services licensing server. Terminal Server Licensing is an option that is installed from the Add/Remove Programs applet in the Control Panel.

Windows Server 2003 offers two types of Terminal Services licensing servers:

- **Enterprise license server**—An enterprise license server should be used when you have Windows Server 2003 Terminal Services servers located in several domains. This is the default.
- **Domain license server**—A domain license server is used if you want to segregate licensing by domain, or if you're supporting a Windows NT 4.0 domain or a workgroup.

To install a Terminal Services licensing server, follow the procedure outlined in Step by Step 4.11.

STEP BY STEP

4.11 Installing a Terminal Services Licensing Server

1. Click Start, All Programs, Control Panel, Add or Remove Programs.
2. Click the Add/Remove Windows Components button in the left pane of the Add or Remove Programs dialog box.
3. The Windows Components Wizard appears, as shown in Figure 4.30. Select the Terminal Server Licensing check box.

continues

continued

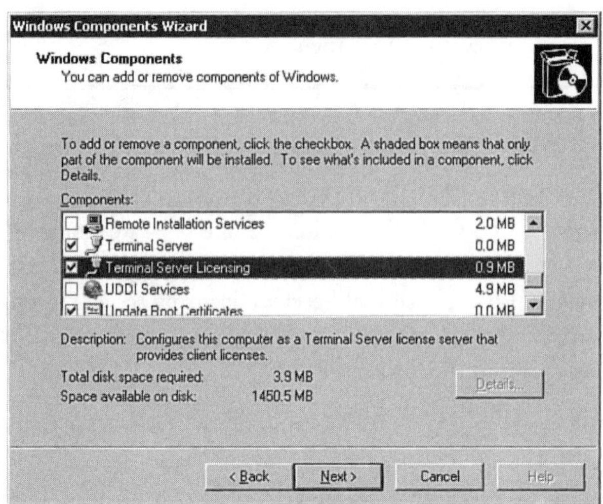

FIGURE 4.30
Use the Windows Components Wizard to install a Terminal Services licensing server.

4. The Terminal Server Licensing Setup screen appears (see Figure 4.31). This screen allows you to choose the type of licensing server to install and the location of the license database. Make a selection and then click the Next button to continue.

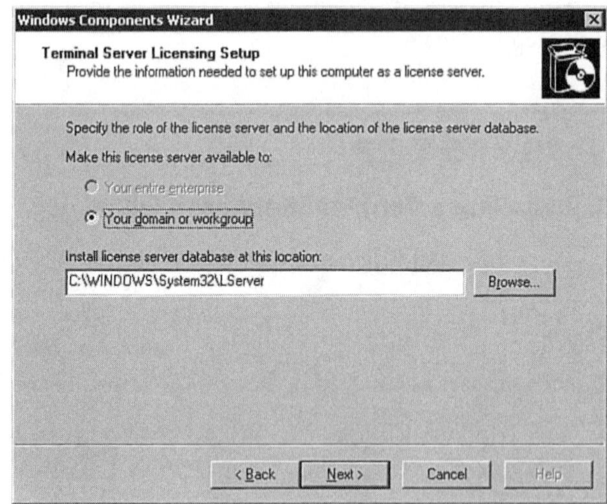

FIGURE 4.31
Choose the type of licensing server to install on the Terminal Server Licensing Setup screen.

5. When the Completing the Windows Component Wizard screen appears, click the Finish button.

NOTE

TS CALS New with Windows Server 2003 are the concepts of a user Client Access License and a device Client Access License. Separating licensing in this way allows organizations additional license options. For example, if a Terminal Services user connects via multiple devices, such as a PC and a handheld device, the organization would need to purchase a user license instead of a device license. The standard TS CAL is only valid for connections to Windows 2000 Terminal Services servers.

Unlike the Windows 2000 license server, which had to be installed on a domain controller in an Active Directory environment, the Windows Server 2003 Terminal Services license server can be installed on any domain controller, member server, or standalone server. This license server can support an unlimited number of Terminal Services servers, and it can issue Terminal Services 2000 Internet Connector licenses, TS 2003 user CALs, TS 2003 device CALs, and temporary TS CALs. The Internet Connector CALs are for nonemployees who connect to your Windows 2000 Terminal Services servers over the Internet. A temporary TS CAL is issued when there are no TS user or device CALs available on the license server. A temporary TS CAL allows the client to connect to the Terminal Services server for 120 days. A Terminal Services server can initially operate for up to 120 days without being serviced by a TS licensing server. However, after this grace period expires, the server no longer accepts any TS connections until it is associated with a valid licensing server.

The new licensing setup is only for Windows Server 2003 Terminal Services. As you can see, it is somewhat different from Microsoft's previous Terminal Services licensing methods. Fortunately, Microsoft has provided a whitepaper that gives an overview of the new licensing rules and processes. It can be obtained from the Microsoft Web site at `www.microsoft.com/windowsserver2003/techinfo/overview/termservlic.mspx`.

> NOTE
>
> **TS External Connector** Another new licensing feature is the Windows Server 2003 Terminal Server External Connector license. This is a license that is purchased to allow an unlimited number of external users access to your Terminal Services server. This replaces the Internet Connector license that was available for Windows 2000 Terminal Services.

Installing Applications

For each user to have his own application configurations, Terminal Services monitors the changes that the application makes to the Registry as the program is being installed, and it watches for changes to the `%windir%` folder. Once captured, these changes are copied to a home folder that Terminal Services maintains for each user. When the user logs on to Terminal Services, these Registry settings are transferred to the user-specific Registry keys.

To install applications on a Terminal Services server, you must be in Install mode. This can be accomplished by installing programs via the Add/Remove Programs applet in the Control Panel or via the `Change User` command.

The `Change User /install` command places Terminal Services in Install mode so that all user-specific mapping is turned off, and the system can monitor the installation process. After the application is installed, use the `Change User /execute` command to restore user-specific mapping. This also moves any newly installed user-specific files to the user's home folder.

To install an application on a Terminal Services server in Application Server mode, follow the procedure outlined in Step by Step 4.12.

STEP BY STEP

4.12 Installing an Application on a Terminal Services Server

1. Click Start, All Programs, Control Panel, Add or Remove Programs.
2. Click the Add New Programs button in the left pane of the Add or Remove Programs dialog box.
3. Click the CD or Floppy button, as shown in Figure 4.32.

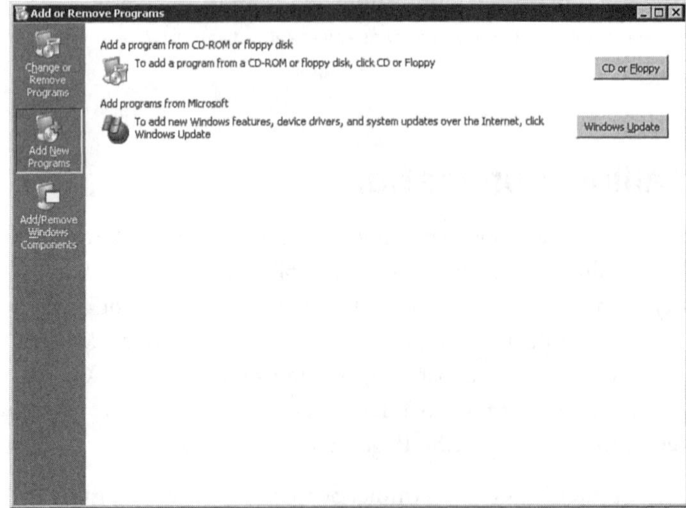

FIGURE 4.32
Use the Add or Remove Programs dialog box to install an application on a Terminal Services server.

4. When prompted, insert the CD-ROM or floppy disk and click the Next button to continue.

5. If the application isn't found automatically, as shown in Figure 4.33, you can click the Browse button on the Run Installation Program screen to search for it. Click the Next button when you're finished.

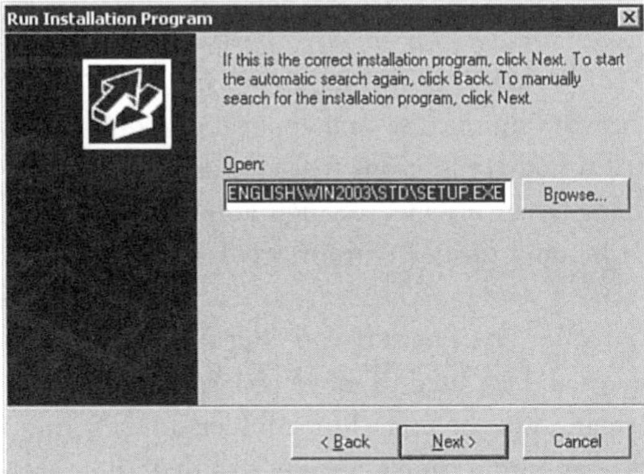

FIGURE 4.33
Use the Run Installation Program screen to install an application on a Terminal Services server.

6. As the installation starts, the screen shown in Figure 4.34 appears. Do not click the Next button until the application's installation procedure has been completed.

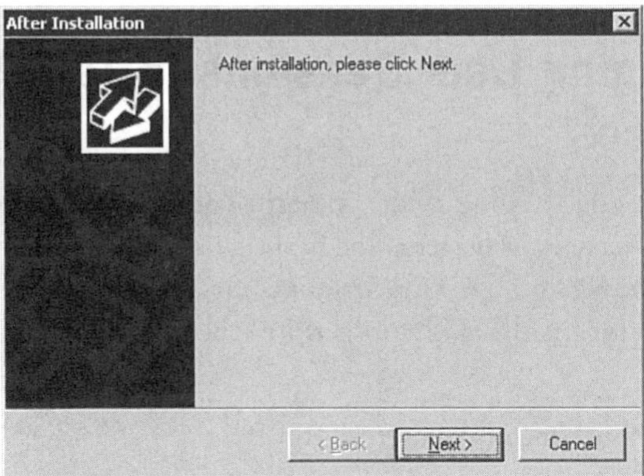

FIGURE 4.34
The After Installation Program screen. Click the Next button once the installation is complete.

7. When the Finish Admin Install screen appears, click the Finish button.

NOTE

Terminal Services–Aware Applications Current applications may be Terminal Services aware. For example, Office XP no longer needs either compatibility scripts or transform files to be installed in Windows Server 2003 Terminal Services.

NOTE

Application Installation in Remote Desktop for Administration Mode There are no special steps necessary to install applications in Windows Server 2003 TS Remote Desktop for Administration mode.

Although not all applications install or run properly in a multiuser environment, some manufacturers are supplying Terminal Services configuration files so that their applications install properly. An example is Microsoft, which has supplied a transform file with Office 2000 so that it can be properly installed on Terminal Services. This file is named `TERMSRVR.MST` and is available in the Office 2000 Resource Kit.

Microsoft has also supplied several application-compatibility scripts for several common applications that are run after application installation to change their installed configuration to allow them to operate properly in a multiuser environment. These scripts are located in the `%systemroot%\Application Compatibility Scripts\Install` folder. These scripts are typically run after the initial installation of the application and are used to move user-specific files and configuration information to the user's home folder. These scripts can be run at every logon by adding a reference to them in `USRLOGON.CMD`, which is run whenever a user logs on to Terminal Services, or via an individual user's Terminal Services logon script. A close examination of these scripts can give you ideas on how to create compatibility scripts for your own applications.

Managing User Sessions in Terminal Services

Terminal Services comes with a variety of administrative tools. The Terminal Services Manager is the tool that is used to monitor and manage the Remote Desktop sessions. From this tool, the system administrator has the ability to perform the following tasks on a user session:

- Remote control the user session.
- Observe and terminate user processes.
- Reset the session.
- Disconnect the session.
- Connect to the user session.
- Send messages to the user.

As shown in Figure 4.35, when a user connects to a Remote Desktop session, this connection is displayed in the Terminal Services Manager MMC. This view shows the status for all the connections, including the following:

- **User**—The user ID of the user who started the session.
- **Session**—The type of session. This will be either RDP-TCP# or Console. Note that the special listener port is designated as just RDP-TCP.
- **State**—The current state of the connection. This will be Active, Disconnected, or, in the case of the listener session, Listening.
- **Type**—This is the type of connection. It will be either Console or the client version.
- **Client Name**—This is the name of the client machine on which the connection software is running.
- **Idle Time**—This is the time since there was any activity on the connection.
- **Logon Time**—This is the time and date of the initial connection.

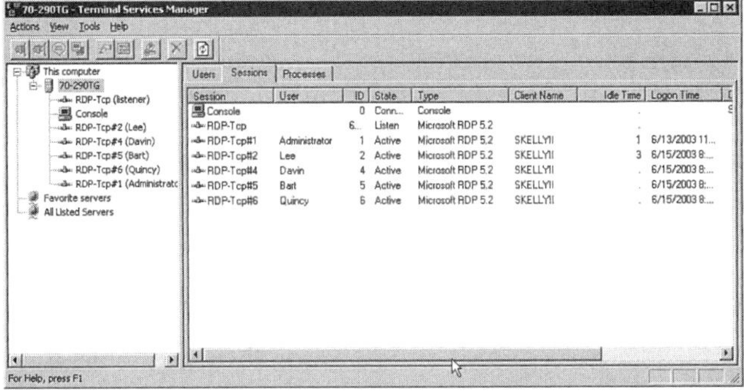

FIGURE 4.35
The Terminal Service Manager MMC, showing the connected sessions.

To manage a user session, right-click the connection from the Sessions tab and select an option from the pop-up menu, as shown in Figure 4.36. Descriptions of the various options are listed in the following sections.

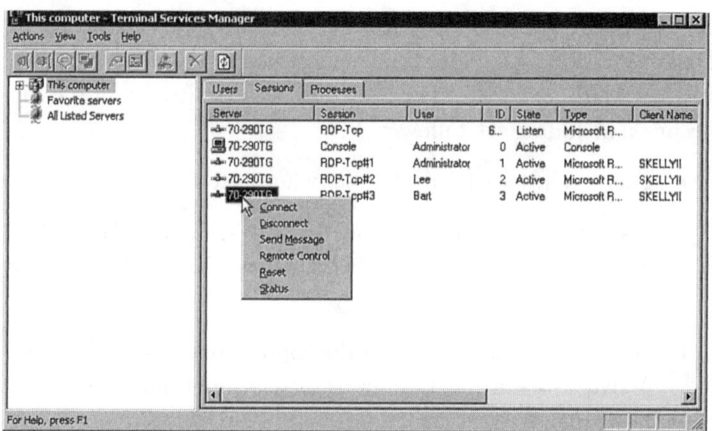

FIGURE 4.36
The Terminal Service Manager MMC, showing the session-management options.

NOTE

Terminal Services Manager Restrictions The Remote Control and Connect to Session features of the Terminal Services Manager tool are available only when the tool is run in a Terminal Services session. These features are not available when the Terminal Services Manager is run from the server console.

Disconnecting and Reconnecting a Session

To disconnect a session, click Disconnect on the Action menu. Disconnecting a session closes the connection between the server and client; however, the user is not logged off and all running programs remain. If the user logs on to the server again, the disconnected session is reconnected to the client. A disconnected session shows Disc in the State field.

To connect to the disconnected session, click the session in Terminal Services Manager and select Connect from the Action menu. The current session is disconnected, and the selected session is connected to your terminal.

Your session must be capable of supporting the video resolution used by the disconnected session. If the session does not support the required video resolution, the operation fails.

Sending Messages

You can send a message to users informing them of problems or asking them to log off the server. To send a message, right-click an active session and then select Send Message from the Action menu. If you select multiple users, the message is sent to each user.

Remote Controlling a User's Session

You can monitor the actions of users by remote controlling their sessions. The remote-controlled session is displayed in the controller's session, and it can be controlled by the mouse and keyboard of the remote control terminal. By default, the user being controlled is asked to allow or deny session remote control. Keyboards, mice, and notification options can be controlled from the Active Directory Users and Computers MMC.

To remote control a session, right-click the session from the Sessions tab and then select Remote Control from the Action menu.

The remote control session must be capable of supporting the video resolution used by the shadowed session. If the remote control session does not support the required video resolution, the operation fails.

Resetting a Session or Connection

You can reset a session in case of an error. Resetting the session terminates all processes running on that session. To reset a user session, right-click the user from the Users tab of the Terminal Services Manager MMC and then select Reset from the Action menu. If you select multiple users, each user session is reset.

Resetting a session may cause applications to close without saving data. If you reset the special RDP-TCP Listener session, all sessions for that server are reset.

> WARNING
>
> **Data Loss!** Logging off or resetting a user's session without giving her a chance to close her applications can result in data loss.

Logging Users off the Server

You can forcefully end a user's session by right-clicking the user from within the Users tab and then selecting Logoff from the Action menu. If you select multiple users, each user is logged off.

Terminating Processes

To end a user or system process, right-click the process from the Process tab and then select Terminate from the Action menu. If you select multiple processes, each process is terminated.

> WARNING
>
> **Termination Instability!** Terminating a user process can result in the loss of data and can also cause the server to become unstable.

Using the Remote Desktop Connection Client

The Remote Desktop Connection client is installed by default on Windows Server 2003. You can open an RDC session by clicking Start, All Programs, Accessories, Communications, Remote Desktop Connection.

This opens the RDC client, as shown in Figure 4.37. In the Computer field, you can type either the IP address or the name of the remote computer to which you want to connect. If you have previously connected to this computer, you can click the drop-down list, and you will see a list of the computers to which you have made connections.

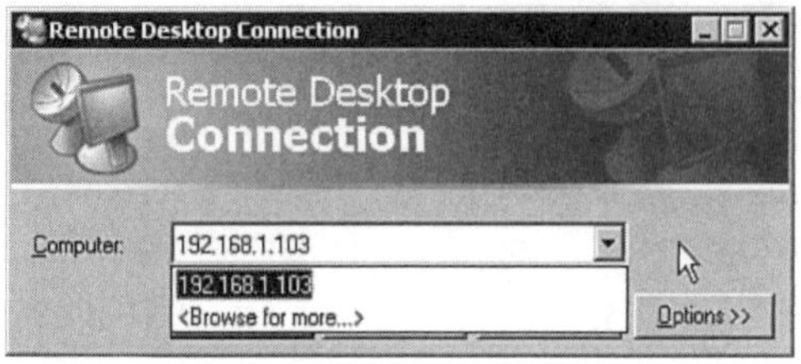

FIGURE 4.37
You can select a previous RDC connection via the drop-down list in the Remote Desktop Connection dialog box.

If you do not see the name or IP address listed, and you cannot remember it, you can click <Browse for more…>, and all the Terminal Services servers you are able to connect to will be listed.

After selecting a connection, click Connect and you will see the logon prompt for the remote server. Enter the proper credentials, and you will log on to a desktop from the remote server (see Figure 4.38).

> **NOTE**
>
> **Remote Desktop for Administration Mode Doesn't Advertise** By default, only Windows Server 2003 computers running Terminal Services in Application Server mode advertise their presence to the browse list. To enable a Windows Server 2003 server running in Remote Desktop for Administration mode to advertise itself as a Terminal Services server in the browse list, change the value of the `HKEY_LOCAL_MACHINE\System\CurrentControlSet\Control\Terminal Server\TSADVERTISE` key from `0` to `1`.

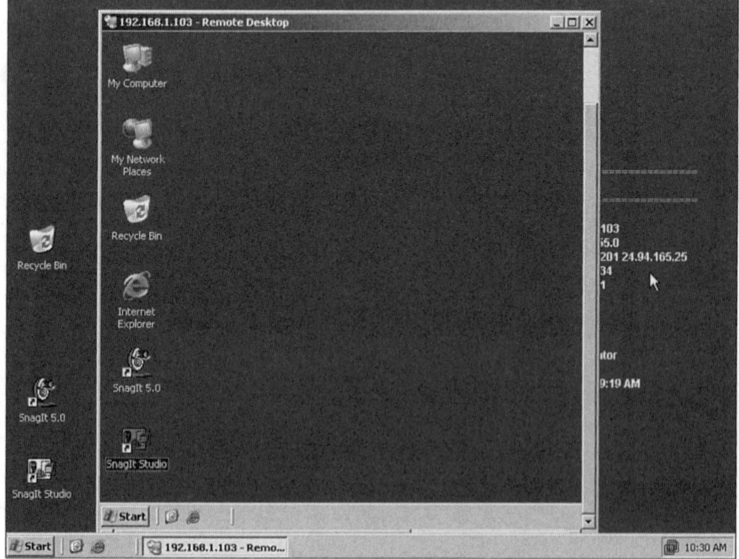

FIGURE 4.38
Once you successfully connect remotely, you will see a Remote Desktop window.

From this window, you can run the programs on the remote server, just as if you were sitting in front of the server console. If you would prefer to see the remote desktop in full-screen mode, just click the Maximize button in the upper-right corner of the window. When running RDC in full-screen mode, as shown in Figure 4.39, it is hard to tell that this is a virtual session.

FIGURE 4.39
You can run Remote Desktop in full-screen mode.

When it's time to end your session, you have two choices: You can either log off or disconnect the session. You log off the session by clicking Start, Shutdown, then Logoff from the Security dialog box. To disconnect the session, select Disconnect from the Security dialog box or just click the Close button in the upper-right corner of the window. If you log off a session, any programs running are automatically shut down for you, just as if you were using your own computer. However, if you disconnect a session, any programs that are running remain running. The next time you log on to the server, the session will be just as you left it.

> NOTE
>
> **Terminal Services Etiquette** The default configuration of a Terminal Services server is to maintain disconnected sessions indefinitely. However, even when a session is disconnected, it still uses resources on the server. Unless you have a good reason for leaving a session running, such as running a batch job or a long-running database function, it is usually best to log off when you are finished. Logging off allows the server to release the session, and the resources associated with keeping it active will be available for other processes.

Using the Remote Desktop Client

In the previous section, we logged on to a Remote Desktop session using the default settings. However, the RDC client has many configuration options available that allow you to configure it for the optimum performance in many different situations.

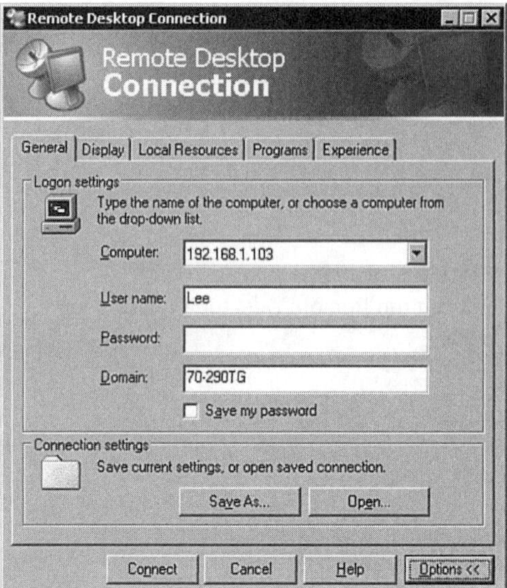

FIGURE 4.40
You can configure connection options for Remote Desktop Connection via the General tab.

To access these settings, open the RDC client and click the Options button. The settings on the General tab allow you to preconfigure the server, username, password, and domain to connect to (see Figure 4.40).

The RDC client also allows you to export your client configuration settings to a file that can be used on other machines. Just click Save As under Connection Settings.

The display settings are available from the Display tab (see Figure 4.41). The screen display can be configured in the following resolutions:

- 640 × 480
- 800 × 600
- 1024 × 768
- 1152 × 864
- 1280 × 1024
- 1600 × 1200

You can also set the color resolution, up to a maximum of True Color (24 Bit); however, the higher the resolution, the more data that has to go over the link between the client and the remote server. You will probably want to keep this as low as possible over low-speed links. It's important to remember that the settings on the Terminal Services server always override the RDC client settings.

> **NOTE**
>
> **Display Characteristics** The maximum values that you can configure the display resolution to will be equal to the settings on your client computer. For example, if the client is configured for 800 × 600 with 256 colors, you won't be able to configure the RDC session to 1024 × 768 with 16-bit resolution. The client has to have a desktop resolution either equal to or higher than the RDC session.

There is also an option to display the connection bar when you are in full-screen mode. The icons on the connection bar allow you to quickly minimize or maximize your session. The connection bar appears when you move your mouse to the top of the screen. To always display the connection bar, click the push pin. The connection bar was shown earlier in Figure 4.39.

The Local Resources tab, shown in Figure 4.42, allows you to configure the interface characteristics of the session, such as sound, keyboard, and device mapping. The Remote Computer Sound option allows you to hear the sounds generated by the remote server session through your local computer. Although this is useful for applications that use sounds as prompts, it's not a good idea to play MP3s over a low-speed connection because sound uses a significant amount of bandwidth. For slow connections, it's recommended that you set this to Do Not Play.

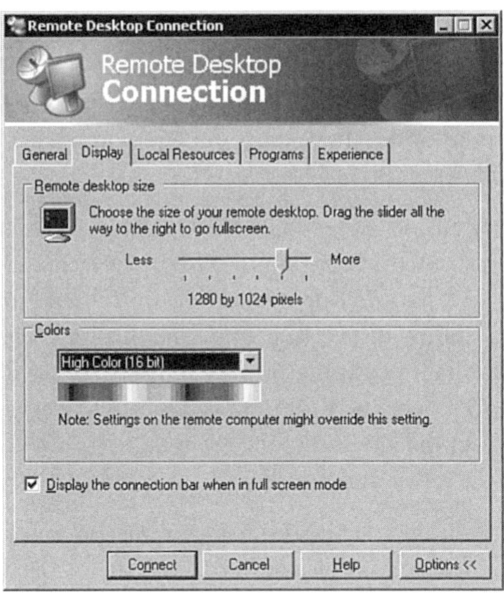

FIGURE 4.41◀
You configure display settings for Remote Desktop Connection via the Display tab.

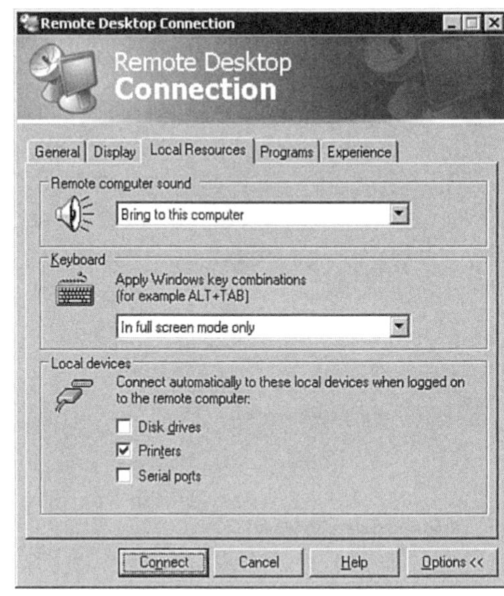

FIGURE 4.42▲
You can configure interface characteristics for the Remote Desktop connection via the Local Resources tab.

The Local Devices option allows you to specify which of the devices attached to your local computer will be available in your RDC session. This allows you to access your local drives, printers, the Clipboard, or any devices attached to your serial port.

For example, you can cut and paste data from the RDC session to the local computer, and vice versa. You can also copy files from the local drives to the drives of the Windows Server 2003 Terminal Services server, if you have the proper NTFS permissions.

The Keyboard option allows you to specify how the standard Windows key combinations are handled while you are in a remote session. For example, if you are running a remote session and you select the Alt+Tab key combination, the local computer will respond to the keystrokes. You can choose to have the Windows keys assigned to one of the following:

- ▶ The local computer
- ▶ The remote computer
- ▶ The remote computer, only when the session is in full-screen mode

The Programs tab allows you to specify the name and location of a program to run when you connect to the remote session. You will have access only to the program and will not get the Windows desktop. When you close the application, your session will be automatically logged off.

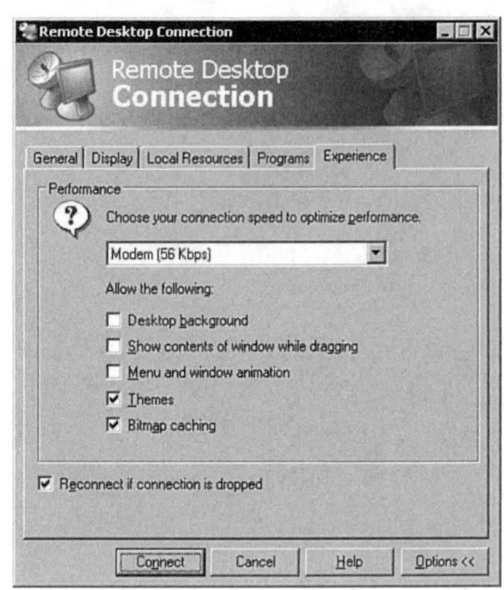

FIGURE 4.43
You can configure additional options for Remote Desktop Connection via the Experience tab.

The Experience tab, shown in Figure 4.43, allows you to tailor the performance of your RDC session to the speed of your connection. For example, on a slow dial-up connection, you should turn off all the options except for Bitmap Caching. The Bitmap Caching feature improves performance by using your local disk to cache frequently used bitmaps to reduce the RDP traffic. The visual features listed here greatly affect the amount of data that has to be carried over the link between the server and the client.

You will notice as you select the different connection speeds, different options are selected. These are Microsoft's recommendations for each link speed. You can create your own configuration by selecting Custom. Unless you are connecting locally via a LAN, it's usually best to turn off all the options except for Bitmap Caching.

Configuring Terminal Services Connections

Although the default Terminal Services configuration settings are fine for the average installation, the Terminal Services Configuration MMC allows you to fine tune Terminal Services to provide the best combination of performance and features for your installation. The Terminal Services Connection MMC is used to configure the Remote Desktop Protocol–Transmission Control Protocol (RDP-TCP) used to communicate between the Windows Server 2003 server and the RDC client.

The RDP-TCP connection can be configured by right-clicking the connection entry in the Terminal Services Connection MMC and selecting Properties from the pop-up menu, as shown in Figure 4.44.

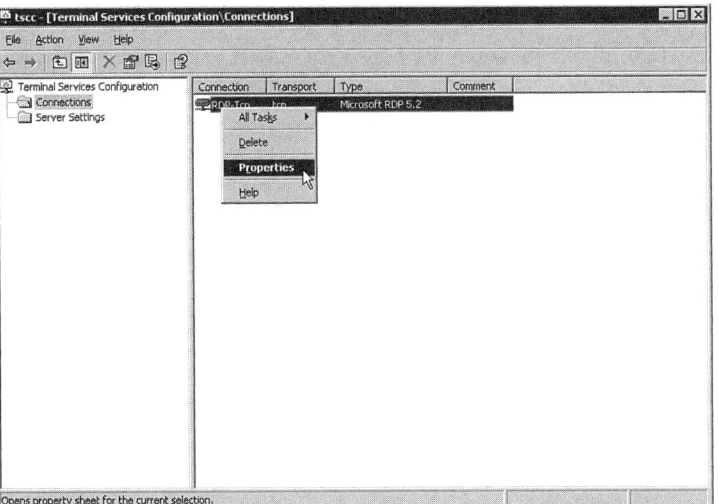

FIGURE 4.44◀
You configure the RDP-TCP connection via the Terminal Services Connection MMC.

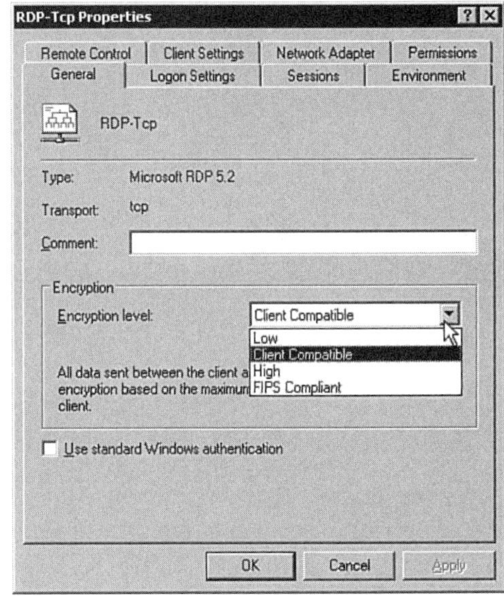

FIGURE 4.45▲
The RDP-TCP Properties dialog box, showing the options on the General tab.

From the General tab, shown in Figure 4.45, you can add a comment to describe the connection, configure the encryption level of the connection, or select whether or not to use Windows authentication. The settings for encryption are as follows:

- **Low**—This setting encrypts the data traveling over the connection using 56-bit encryption. However, only the data sent from the client to the server is encrypted; data sent from the server to the client is not. This option is useful because it encrypts the user password as it is sent from the client to the server.
- **Client Compatible**—This option automatically encrypts all data sent between the client and the server at the maximum key strength supported by the client. This option is useful in an environment where different types of clients are supported.
- **High**—This option encrypts all data using 128-bit encryption. This option can be used in an environment that supports only the RDC client; all other connections will be refused.
- **FIPS Compliant**—This option encrypts all data using the Federal Information Processing Standard (FIPS) encryption algorithms.

> **NOTE**
>
> **Per User Settings** The settings described in this section apply to all users. The settings for an individual user can be configured via the Terminal Services tab of the user object in the Active Directory Users and Computers MMC.

The Use Standard Windows Authentication option needs to be selected only in those cases where a third-party authentication mechanism has been installed and you want to use the Windows Standard Authentication method for RDP connections.

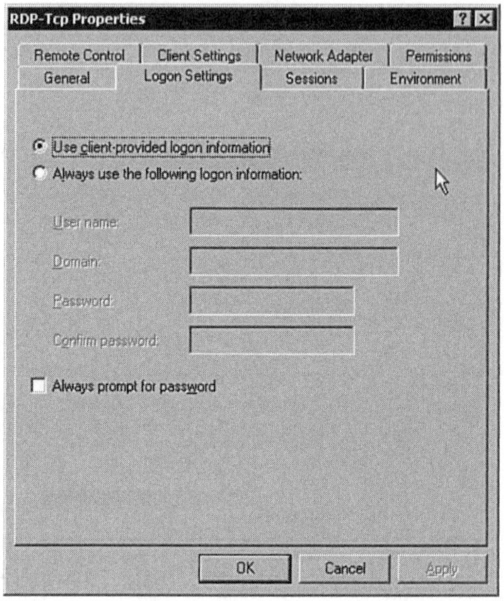

FIGURE 4.46
You can configure user logon settings via the RDP-TCP Properties dialog box's Logon Settings tab.

From the Logon Settings tab, shown in Figure 4.46, you can select to have all users automatically log on to the Terminal Services server by using a common username and password that you enter here. In addition, you can select to prompt them for a password when using this common account by selecting the Always Prompt for Password option. The default is for the user to provide logon credentials.

From the Sessions tab, shown in Figure 4.47, you can select the default session timeout and reconnection settings. These settings are used to determine what action, if any, to take for sessions that have been connected longer than a specified time or have been disconnected. The options are as follows:

- **End a Disconnected Session**—This option determines what to do with a disconnected session. A session can become disconnected by a user or because of a communication failure between the server and the RDC client. Even though a session is in the disconnected state, any applications that were running will continue to run. However, these applications will continue to use resources on the server. This option can be used to automatically terminate sessions that remain in a disconnected state for a configured period of time. After the disconnected session is terminated, any resources it was using will be available for other sessions. However, this option can cause the loss of user data if any user files are open when the session is terminated.

- **Active Session Limit**—This setting allows you to configure the maximum time that a session can be active before it is either terminated or disconnected, depending on the setting of the When Session Limit Is Reached or Connection Is Broken option.

- **Idle Session Limit**—This setting allows you to configure the maximum time a session can be idle before it is either terminated or disconnected, depending on the setting of the When Session Limit Is Reached or Connection Is Broken option.
- **When Session Limit Is Reached or Connection Is Broken**—This option allows you to configure the action to take when a session is disconnected or when a session limit is reached. In the case of the session limit being reached, the session is either disconnected or terminated, depending on this setting. When this option is selected, a disconnected session will automatically be terminated.
- **Allow Reconnection**—This option is used only with the Citrix-ICA connection. The default for the RDP-TCP connection in Windows Server 2003 is to allow reconnection from any client when a session is in the disconnected state.

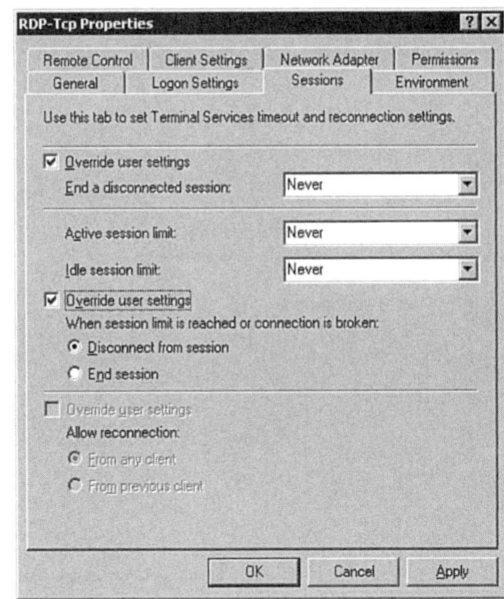

FIGURE 4.47
The RDP-TCP Properties dialog box, showing the options on the Sessions tab.

The Environment tab, shown in Figure 4.48, allows you to override any configuration settings that were made in the user profile, RDC, or Terminal Services client using the options on the tabs of the RDP-TCP Properties dialog box. There is also the option to start an application, instead of the Windows Server 2003 desktop, when logging on.

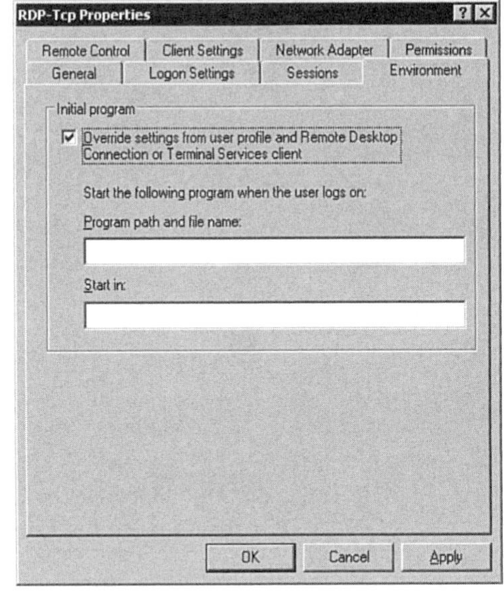

FIGURE 4.48
You can override user settings via the RDP-TCP Properties dialog box's Environment tab.

The Remote Control tab, shown in Figure 4.49, allows you to configure the Remote Control feature of Windows Server 2003 Terminal Services. The available options are as follows:

- **Use Remote Control with Default User Settings**—This is the default option, and it uses the configuration from the user account to determine whether or not Remote Control is allowed and how it is configured.
- **Do Not Allow Remote Control**—This option turns off Remote Control for all sessions.
- **Use Remote Control with the Following Settings**—This option turns on Remote Control and is used to select whether or not the user will be prompted when the administrator attempts to control a remote session, and what level of control the administrator will have.

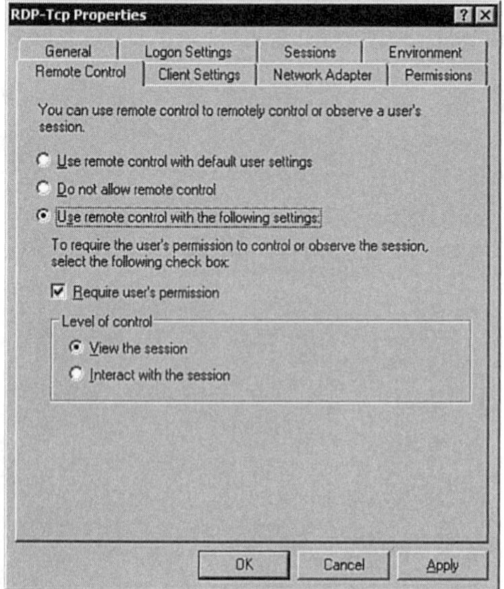

FIGURE 4.49
You control the settings for Remote Control via the RDP-TCP Properties dialog box's Remote Control tab.

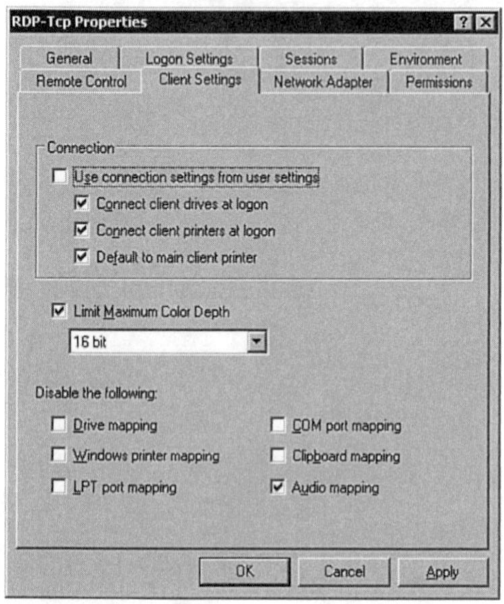

FIGURE 4.50
You configure the client experience feature via the RDP-TCP Properties dialog box's Client Settings tab.

The Client Settings tab, shown in Figure 4.50, allows you to configure the client experience features of Windows Server 2003 Terminal Services.

The Connection area allows you either to use the connection settings chosen on the Local Resources tab of the RDC client (the default) or to configure the settings individually. These options control whether the various devices configured on the computer that the RDC client is installed on will be available in the RDC session.

The options in the Disable the Following area allow you to enable/disable various actions, such as printing from the RDC session to the printers attached to the client computer on which you are running the RDC client. As shown in Figure 4.51, when drive mapping is enabled, the drives on the local client are available within an RDC session, listed under the Other section.

The Network Adapter tab allows you to limit the number of concurrent RDC client connections by network adapter.

The Permissions tab, shown in Figure 4.52, allows you to configure which users or groups are allowed to connect to Windows Server 2003 Terminal Services and what permissions they will have. The recommended method of allowing users to connect to Windows Server 2003 Terminal Services is to add their user accounts to the Remote Desktop Users group. This group has already been granted the necessary permissions, including the Allow Logon Through Terminal Services, which is necessary to connect via a Terminal Services or RDC client.

In addition to the settings available from the property pages of the RDP-TCP connection are the configuration options listed under the Server Settings folder, as shown in Figure 4.53.

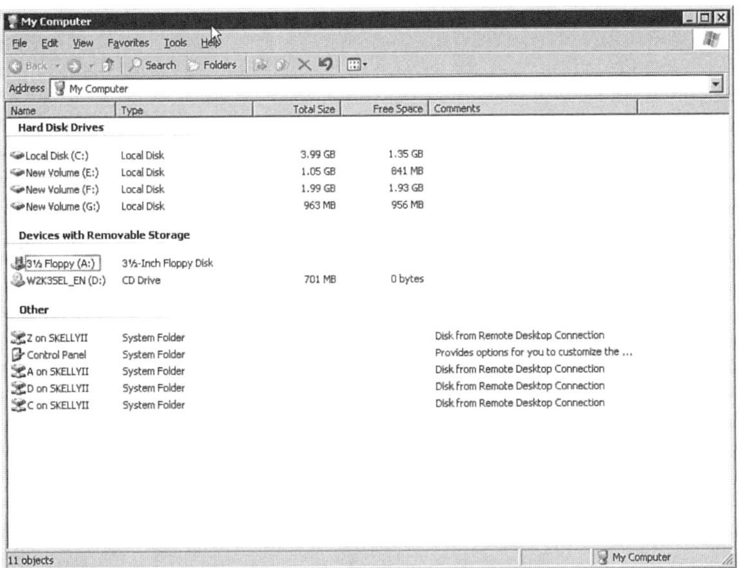

FIGURE 4.51◀
My Computer, showing the mapped client devices listed under Other.

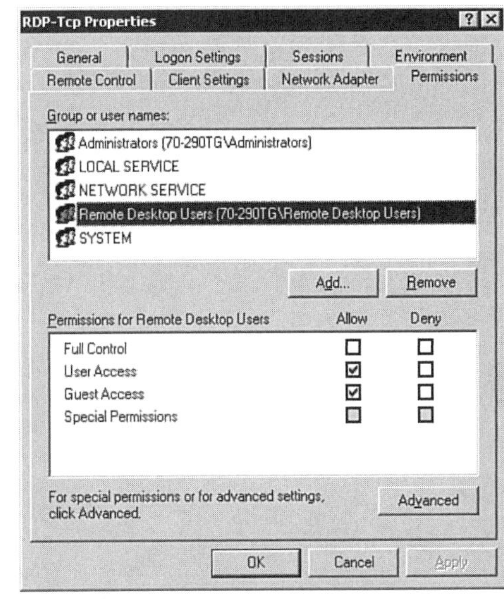

FIGURE 4.52▲
You can configure user and group access to Terminal Services via the RDP-TCP Properties dialog box's Permissions tab.

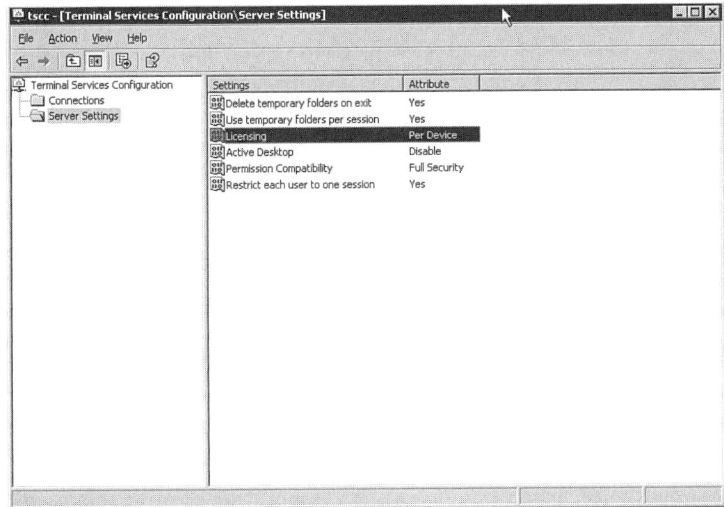

FIGURE 4.53◀
You can configure additional server settings via the Terminal Services Connection MMC, in the Server Settings folder.

These settings are as follows:

- **Delete Temporary Folders on Exit**—This option deletes all temporary folders created by RDC sessions as they are exited. This option is turned on by default.
- **Use Temporary Folders Per Session**—This option allows you to create a temporary folder for each session. This option is turned on by default.

- **Licensing**—This option allows you to select either per-device or per-user licensing. This option is set to Per Device by default. On a Terminal Services server in Remote Administration for Desktops mode, this attribute is displayed as Remote Desktop and is not configurable.
- **Active Desktop**—This option is used to enable/disable the Active Desktop in RDC sessions. It is disabled by default. This option should not be enabled because the additional overhead required to support Active Desktop in RDC sessions impacts performance.
- **Permission Compatibility**—This option is set to Full Security by default. Full Security is equivalent to the default security settings present on Windows Server 2003. Because most folders and the Registry are locked down, a lot of older applications cannot be installed or run in this configuration. The other option provided is Relaxed Security, which is equivalent to running on a Windows 2000 Terminal Server. For the best security, set this option to Full Security and use only Windows Server 2003–compatible applications.
- **Restrict Each User to One Session**—This option keeps users from connecting to multiple sessions via multiple RDC clients. This option is enabled by default.

GUIDED PRACTICE EXERCISE 4.2

You are the administrator of a network that includes a Windows Server 2003 server configured for Terminal Services Application Server mode. The programming staff has just finished loading a new application on the Terminal Services server. However, the staff needs your assistance. It seems that this new application requires the users to respond to audio signals that are output through their PC speakers. Unfortunately, although the program is running fine on client workstations, the staff has never tested it on a Terminal Services server before and doesn't know the proper way to configure sound.

What is the best way to solve this issue in Windows Server 2003 Terminal Services? On your own, try to develop a solution that would involve the least amount of configuration changes.

If you would like to see a possible solution, follow these steps:

Estimated Time: 20 minutes

1. On the Windows Server 2003 Terminal Services server, click Start, All Programs, Administrative Tools, Terminal Services Configuration.
2. In the right pane of the Terminal Services Configuration MMC, double-click the Connections folder.
3. Right-click the RDP-TCP connection and then select Properties from the pop-up menu.
4. Click the Client Settings tab of the RDP-TCP Properties dialog box.
5. On the Client Settings tab, deselect the Audio Mapping check box under Disable the Following in the lower-right section of the dialog box.
6. Click the OK button to Save. Close the MMC.
7. On the client computer, start the RDC client.
8. From the RDC client prompt, click the Options button.
9. From the Options dialog box, click the Local Resources tab.
10. Change the Remote Computer Sound drop-down list to Bring to This Computer.
11. Click Connect.

Audio mapping is turned off by default in Windows Server 2003 Terminal Services, so you have to enable it on the server and on the client. In addition, there must be a sound card with the proper drivers loaded on both the server and the client. Typically, sound is not used in Terminal Services sessions because it can demand a lot of bandwidth over the RDP connection.

Managing Windows Server 2003 Terminal Services via Group Policy

Although Windows Server 2003 Terminal Services can be managed using the Terminal Services Connection MMC, if you have multiple Terminal Services servers, this can become a nightmare. Fortunately, Microsoft has included some additions to Group Policy in Windows Server 2003 to support Terminal Services configuration. These policies can be found under the Computer Configuration section of Group Policy, as shown in Figure 4.54.

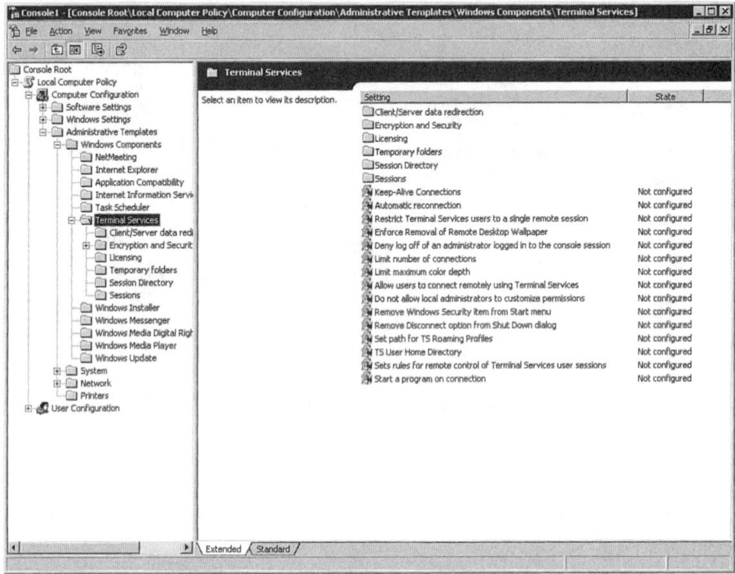

FIGURE 4.54
You can configure settings for multiple Terminal Services servers via the Group Policy MMC's Terminal Services folder.

The options available include not only the options from the Terminal Services Manager and the Terminal Services Connection MMC but also various user interface options applicable in the Terminal Services environment. This simplifies Terminal Services configuration by putting the majority of configuration options in a centralized location.

You should create an Organizational Unit (OU) to hold all of your Windows Server 2003 Terminal Services servers and then configure the Computer Configuration settings in the Group Policy object, instead of configuring each individual server. Group Polices override the settings configured with the Terminal Services Configuration tool.

NOTE

Only for Windows Server 2003
Group Policy can be used to manage only Windows Server 2003 Terminal Services servers. Windows 2000 and Windows NT Terminal Services are not supported.

GUIDED PRACTICE EXERCISE 4.3

You are the administrator of a network that includes a Windows Server 2003 server configured for Terminal Services Application Server mode. The server is configured properly and should have enough capacity for the projected number of users. However, lately you have noticed that performance seems to decrease toward the end of the day. After some checking around, you discover that some of the users are disconnecting their sessions instead of properly logging off. This results in their disconnected sessions using valuable system resources.

What is the best way to solve this issue in Windows Server 2003 Terminal Services? On your own, try to develop a solution that would involve the least amount of configuration changes.

If you would like to see a possible solution, follow these steps:

Estimated Time: 20 minutes

1. Click Start, All Programs, Administrative Tools, Terminal Services Configuration.
2. In the right pane of the Terminal Services Configuration MMC, double-click the Connections folder.
3. Right-click the RDP-TCP connection and then select Properties from the pop-up menu.
4. Click the Sessions tab of the RDP-TCP Properties dialog box.
5. On the Sessions tab, click the Override User Settings check box in the upper-left section of the dialog box.
6. From the End a Disconnection Session drop-down list, select the length of time you want Terminal Services to wait before terminating a disconnected session.
7. Click the OK button to Save. Close the MMC.

Because there is only one Windows Server 2003 Terminal Services server, it's just as easy to set the disconnection settings in the Terminal Services Configuration MMC as it would be to accomplish the same thing via Group Policy.

Terminal Services Session Directory

Even though you can support quite a few user sessions per processor using Windows Server 2003 Terminal Services, there will always be certain applications that are CPU hogs or that need to be available to a large number of users. You can set up multiple Windows Server 2003 Terminal Services machines and assign groups of users to each one, but this doesn't provide any redundancy. In addition, what if one server has 200 users and is starting to slow down under the load, while another server is loafing along with only 10?

You can use a process called *load balancing* to spread the application load across two or more servers. This prevents one server from becoming overloaded while another is loafing. This also provides redundancy for your applications because the failure of a single server does not prevent your users from completing their work.

Windows Server 2003 Network Load Balancing is a feature included in all the Microsoft Windows Server 2003 operating systems. The Network Load Balancing (NLB) feature is used to enhance the scalability and availability of mission-critical, TCP/IP-based services such as Web, Terminal Services, virtual private networking, and streaming media servers. NLB requires no additional hardware or software components.

NLB works by distributing IP traffic across multiple Windows Server 2003 servers. Load balancing works on the principle that if a server is busy or unavailable, a client connection is routed to the next available server. Unlike clustering, load balancing does not require that you have identical servers. It also does not require any special disk units or other hardware, so it is an economical configuration. However, you are required to install identical applications in exactly the same manner on each server that is to be balanced.

To the client, it looks like a single server is handling requests because the client sees a single virtual IP address and hostname. NLB is also capable of detecting host server failures and automatically redistributing traffic to the surviving servers. NLB can support up to 32 servers in a balanced configuration.

When you set up an NLB configuration, you can either allow the load to be equally distributed among the servers or specify the load percentages for individual servers. By specifying individual load percentages, you can use dissimilar servers in your balanced configuration. Incoming client requests are distributed among the servers according to this configuration.

All the servers in the balanced configuration exchange heartbeat messages, so they know when a server enters or leaves the configuration. When a server is added or leaves the configuration by either configuration change or failure, the other servers automatically adjust and redistribute the workload. In the current version of Windows Server 2003 Network Load Balancing, the load balance is a static percentage and does not change in response to the actual load of the server, as determined by CPU or memory usage.

Most server failures are detected within 5 seconds, and the recovery and redistribution of the workload are accomplished within 10 seconds. However, the RDC client loses its connection and must reconnect. As long as IP affinity, which automatically redirects a client session to the last server it was connected to, is turned on in NLB, this isn't a problem. Because NLB uses the IP address of the client when routing, it can reconnect to a disconnected session. However, in those situations where the user has moved to another computer or received a different IP address via DHCP, the user receives a new session chosen at random from the group of servers.

To solve this dilemma, Microsoft has included the Terminal Services Session Directory Service as a new feature in the Windows Server 2003 Enterprise and Datacenter editions. The Session Directory Service creates a database on a server that contains a record of the current sessions being hosted by a load-balanced cluster of Windows Server 2003 Terminal Services servers. This database indexes the sessions using the username instead of the IP address. This database allows disconnected sessions to be reconnected using the username to look up the location of a disconnected session when the user is trying to log on to the Terminal Services server again. After it is determined which server is hosting the session that the user was disconnected from, his logon is routed to that server.

The Session Directory (SD) doesn't have to be on a server that has Terminal Services installed. In large Windows Server 2003 Terminal Services installations, it's recommended that SD be hosted on a separate high-availability server.

The Session Directory Service is not enabled by default. To enable it, use the procedure outlined in Step by Step 4.13.

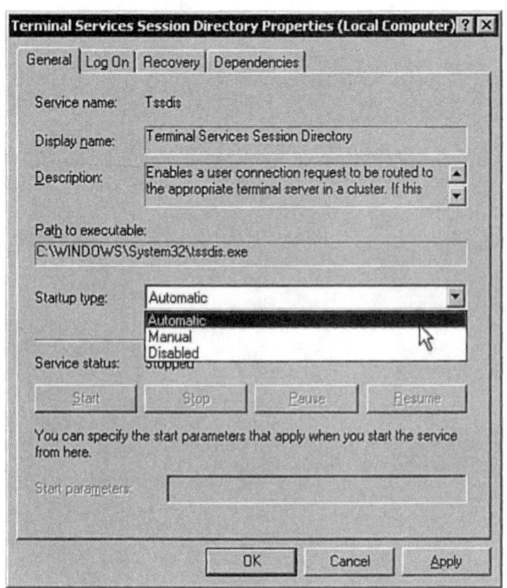

FIGURE 4.55

You enable the Session Directory Service via the Terminal Services Session Directory dialog box.

STEP BY STEP

4.13 Enabling the Session Directory Service

1. Click Start, All Programs, Administrative Tools, Services.
2. Right-click the Terminal Services Session Directory entry in the right pane and select Properties from the pop-up menu.
3. Click the Start button. As shown in Figure 4.55, select Automatic from the Startup Type drop-down list.
4. Click OK to save.

After the Session Directory Service is started, you will have to add the Windows Server 2003 Terminal Services servers that you want to use with the service to an OU. After the servers are added to this OU, you will need to use Group Policy to enable SD for the Terminal Services servers in this OU.

To enable SD for a group of servers, use the procedure outlined in Step by Step 4.14.

STEP BY STEP

4.14 Enabling the Session Directory for a Group of Servers

1. Click Start, All Programs, Administrative Tools, Active Directory Users and Computers.
2. In the right pane, right-click the OU that contains the Windows Server 2003 Terminal Services servers that you want to be controlled by the Session Directory Service. Then select Properties from the pop-up menu.
3. From the Properties dialog box, select the Group Policy tab. Click the Add button to add a new policy.
4. From the Group Policy MMC, shown in Figure 4.56, navigate to the Administrative Templates, Windows Components, Terminal Services, Session Directory folder.

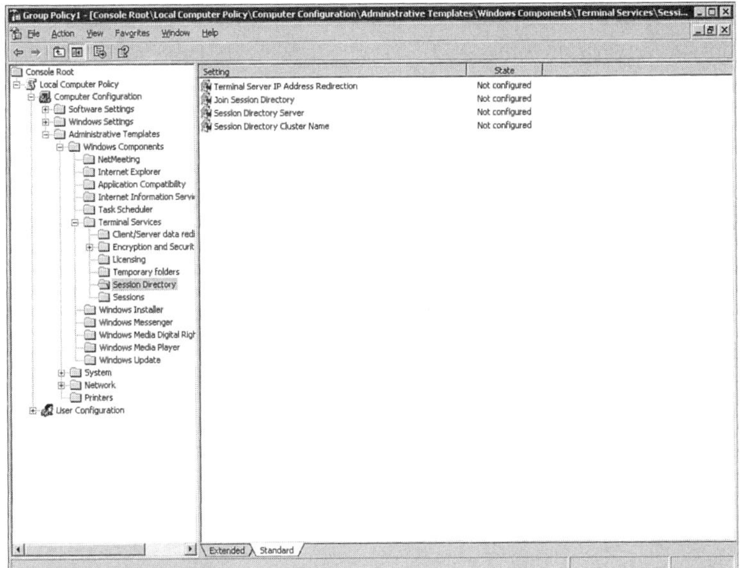

FIGURE 4.56
The Group Policy MMC, showing the options available for the Terminal Services Session Directory.

5. Double-click the Join Session Directory entry, and then select the Enabled option from the Properties dialog box. Click OK.
6. Double-click the Session Directory Server entry and then type in the name of the SD server in the Properties dialog box. Click OK.
7. Double-click the Session Directory Cluster Name entry and then type in a name for the SD cluster in the Properties dialog box. Click OK.
8. Close the Group Policy MMC.

TROUBLESHOOTING TERMINAL SERVICES

Windows Terminal Services is dependent on the common services on the network, such as TCP/IP and domain services. If you are having problems with Terminal Services, make sure no other functions on the network are failing.

A common problem with Terminal Services involves connecting to the server with the older RDP 4.0 client instead of the RDC 5.0 client, which is included with Windows 2000, or the RDC 5.1 client, which is included with Windows XP and Windows Server 2003. The clients look and function in a similar manner; however, the advanced functionality that is enabled in RDC 5.1, such as improved encryption, audio support, and keyboard mapping, are not available with the older RDP clients.

The multiple-monitor support in Windows XP/2003 can cause problems when you're connecting to one of these machines. If the application that you want to work with was last displayed or is currently displayed on the secondary monitor, you will not be able to see it.

To move the application to your RDC session, use the procedure outlined in Step by Step 4.15.

STEP BY STEP

4.15 Moving an Application to Your RDC Session

1. Select the application's icon on the Taskbar.
2. Hold down the Alt key and press the spacebar to open the Window menu. (You won't be able to see it.)
3. Press the M key (Move) and use the arrow keys to move the application window into your RDC session, as shown in Figure 4.57.
4. After the application window is within your session window, press the Enter key to lock it down.

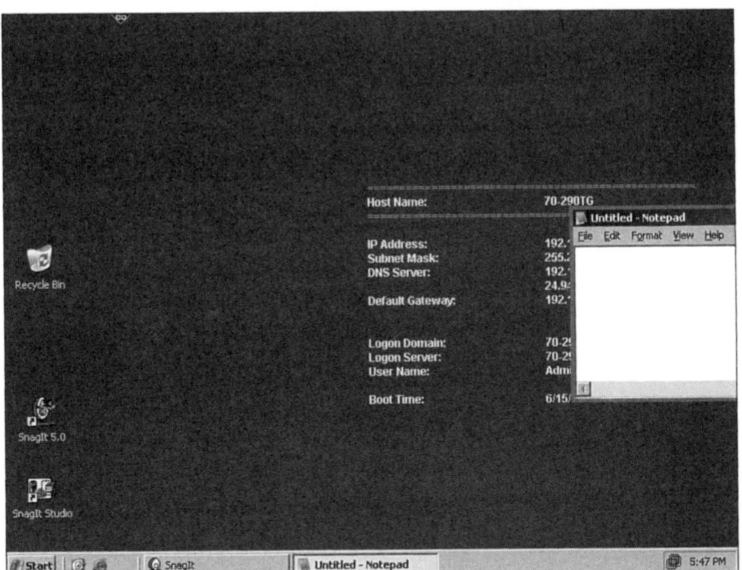

FIGURE 4.57
Moving a window back onto the viewable desktop.

When trying to diagnose a possible Terminal Services problem, sometimes you need to know what mode the server is in. To determine which mode a Terminal Services server is using, follow the procedure outlined in Step by Step 4.16.

STEP BY STEP

4.16 Determining the Terminal Services Mode

1. Select Start, All Programs and then click Administrative Tools.
2. Select Terminal Services Configuration.
3. Select Server Settings.
4. Locate the Licensing entry in the right pane. The mode is listed in the Attribute column, as shown in Figure 4. 58.

continues

continued

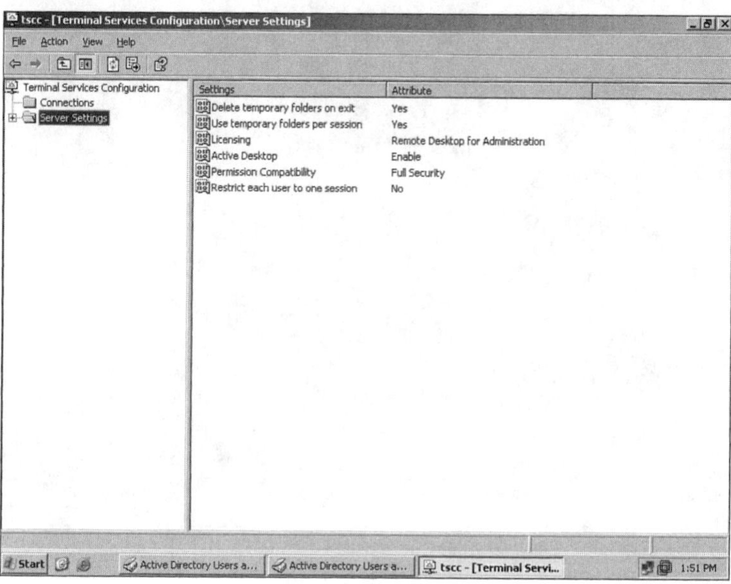

FIGURE 4.58
Identifying the Terminal Services mode.

There are many applications, including some from Microsoft, that you cannot install on the Terminal Services computer from a Remote Desktop session. You have to install these programs from the server console connection. This includes SQL, most of the service packs for Windows, and other Microsoft applications.

CASE STUDY: SOUTHERN WINDS

ESSENCE OF THE CASE

Here are the essential elements in this case:

- Secure all data.
- Provide reliable access to applications.

SCENARIO

Frank is putting together a business plan for a startup company. He wants to run a small application service provider (ASP) that caters to several local small businesses that can't afford to have their own server farm and IT staff. Frank plans for all his clients to access his server farm over the Internet either through a VPN or via one of the Web servers.

CASE STUDY: SOUTHERN WINDS

Because he is in effect running the business for a number of small companies, Frank realizes that it is essential he provide the companies reliable access to their data as well as ensure that their data is not accessible by other companies, both those sharing his resources and those external to his network.

ANALYSIS

After a close examination of the needs for Frank's business, it should be possible to address these needs using the built-in Windows Server 2003 security features, along with Windows Terminal Services.

Frank should set up a cluster of load-balanced Windows Server 2003 Terminal Services servers, with identical applications installed on each server. These load-balanced Terminal Services servers should have the Session Directory Service enabled so that a disconnected user (common over Internet connections) will be automatically routed back to his existing session.

To ensure that users from one company cannot access the data of another, Frank should set up different user groups for each company. Each company should be configured with its own file shares and folders. Each company's file shares should grant Deny Read permission to the groups from the other companies.

OVERVIEW OF THE REQUIREMENTS AND SOLUTIONS IN THIS CASE STUDY

Requirement	Solution Provided By
Secure all data.	Using a combination of Windows share and NTFS permissions
Provide reliable access to applications.	Creating a group of load-balanced Windows Server 2003 Terminal Services servers, using the Session Directory Service to ensure that disconnected users are automatically reconnected to their existing session

CHAPTER SUMMARY

KEY TERMS

- Remote Desktop Protocol (RDP)
- Remote Administration for Desktop mode
- Application Server mode
- Session Directory
- Remote Control
- File share
- Permissions

This chapter covered the main features in Windows Server 2003 used for sharing and protecting data. In addition, this chapter highlighted the capability for supporting the Windows Server 2003 desktop on devices that would not normally be able to run Windows Server 2003 applications. To summarize, this chapter contained the following main points:

- **Securing files**—This includes planning for and implementing both local and remote security.
- **Publishing resources**—This includes creating and maintaining network shares.
- **Using Terminal Services**—This includes installing, configuring, and maintaining the two Windows Server 2003 Terminal Services modes.

APPLY YOUR KNOWLEDGE

Exercises

4.1 Installing Terminal Services in Application Server Mode

In this exercise, you will install Terminal Services in Application Server mode and install a sample application.

Estimated Time: 40 minutes

1. Click Start, All Programs, Control Panel, Add or Remove Programs.
2. Click the Add/Remove Windows Components button in the left pane of the Add or Remove Programs dialog box.
3. The Windows Components Wizard appears. Select the Terminal Server check box.
4. If Internet Explorer Enhanced Security Configuration is enabled (it is enabled by default), you will receive the Configuration Warning prompt. After you read and understand this warning, click the Yes button to continue.
5. This returns you to the Windows Components Wizard. Click the Next button to continue.
6. The Terminal Server Setup warning appears. Read and understand the warning and then click the Next button to continue.
7. The Terminal Server Setup screen appears. This screen allows you to select Full Security mode, which is new to Windows Server 2003, or Relaxed Security mode, which is roughly equivalent to the security on a Windows 2000 Terminal Services server. Click the desired option button and then click the Next button to continue.
8. When the Completing the Windows Component Wizard screen appears, click the Finish button. You will be prompted to reboot the server.
9. After the server has rebooted, log on as a member of the Administrators group.
10. Click Start, All Programs, Control Panel, Add or Remove Programs.
11. Click the Add New Programs button in the left pane of the Add or Remove Programs dialog box.
12. Click the CD or Floppy button.
13. When prompted, insert the CD-ROM or floppy disk and click the Next button to continue.
14. If the application isn't automatically found, click the Browse button and search for it. Click the Next button when finished.
15. As the installation starts, a screen appears. Do not click the Next button until the application's installation procedure has been completed.
16. When the Finish Admin Install screen appears, click the Finish button.

4.2 Securing a Local Folder

Because all users accessing a Windows Server 2003 Terminal Services in Application Server mode server will have been granted the Log On Locally right, you will need to use local security to prevent them from accessing certain folders. In this exercise, you will secure a local folder so that only selected users can access its contents.

Estimated Time: 40 minutes

1. Verify that the volume the desired folder is on is an NTFS volume. If it is not, use the `CONVERT` command to change it to NTFS.

APPLY YOUR KNOWLEDGE

2. Open either My Computer or Windows Explorer. Navigate to the folder on which you want to configure security.
3. Right-click the object and select Properties from the pop-up menu. Click the Security tab on the resulting dialog box.
4. From the Security tab, click the Add button.
5. The Select Users or Groups dialog box appears. This dialog box allows you to select either a local or domain user or group to assign permissions to. Enter the user or group and then click OK.
6. This returns you to the Folder Properties dialog box. Note that, by default, the user or group just added has been granted Read & Execute, List Folder Contents, and Read permissions for the folder.
7. In the Permissions section of the Folder Properties dialog box, select the desired permissions and then click the OK button to save.

4.3 Configuring the Disconnect Timeout via Group Policy

In this exercise, you will use Group Policy to set the Windows Server 2003 Terminal Services client disconnect timeout.

Estimated Time: 20 minutes

1. Click Start, All Programs, Administrative Tools, Active Directory Users and Computers.
2. In the right pane, right-click the OU that contains the Windows Server 2003 Terminal Servers that you want to be controlled by the Session Directory Service. Then select Properties from the pop-up menu.
3. From the Properties dialog box, select the Group Policy tab. Click the Add button to add a new policy.
4. From the Group Policy MMC, navigate to the Administrative Templates, Windows Components, Terminal Services, Sessions folder.
5. Double-click the item Set Time Limit for Disconnected Sessions in the right pane of the MMC.
6. From the Properties dialog box, select the Enabled radio button and then select a time from the End a Disconnected Session drop-down list.
7. Click OK to save. Close the MMC.

Review Questions

1. What are the two Terminal Services modes available in Windows Server 2003?
2. Which operating systems is the RDP client available for?
3. What is required to provide local security for files and folders on a Windows Server 2003 server?
4. If you have both NTFS and share permissions applied to the contents of a folder, what are the effective permissions over the network?
5. What tool can be used to assist in determining permissions?
6. What tool is used to create and manage shares on remote computers?

APPLY YOUR KNOWLEDGE

Exam Questions

1. You are the administrator of a Windows Server 2003 computer named Server1. You create a share named Public. You add a folder named Docs under Public. The share and NTFS permissions for Public and Docs are as shown.

   Public Share Permissions:

   Everyone: Read

   Domain Admins: Full Control

   Training: Full Control

   Doc Folder Permissions:

   User: Read

   Domain Admins: Full Control

   A user named Maria is a member of the User and Training user groups. When Maria attempts to save the file `\Server1\Public\Docs\memo.doc`, she receives an "Access denied" error message.

   Required Result:

   You want Maria to be able to change and delete all files in the Docs folder.

   Optional Desired Results:

   You do not want to change the share permissions.

   You do not want her to have more access than necessary.

   Proposed Solution:

   Set the NTFS permissions for the Docs folder and its subobjects to grant Maria Full Control permission.

   Evaluation of Proposed Solution:

   Which result(s) does the proposed solution produce?

   A. The proposed solution produces the required result but neither of the optional results.

   B. The proposed solution produces the required result and one of the optional results.

   C. The proposed solution produces the required result and both the optional results.

   D. The proposed solution does not produce the required result.

2. You are the administrator of a Windows Server 2003 computer named Server1. You create a share named Public. You add a folder named Docs under Public. The share and NTFS permissions for Public and Docs are as shown.

   Public Share Permissions:

   Everyone: Read

   Domain Admins: Full Control

   Training: Full Control

   Doc Folder Permissions:

   User: Read

   Domain Admins: Full Control

   A user named Maria is a member of the Users and Training user groups. When Maria attempts to save the file `\Server1\Public\Docs\memo.doc`, she receives an "Access denied" error message.

   Required Result:

   You want Maria to be able to change and delete all files in the Docs folder.

APPLY YOUR KNOWLEDGE

Optional Desired Results:

You do not want to change the share permissions.

You do not want her to have more access than necessary.

Proposed Solution:

Set the permissions for the Docs folder to grant Maria the Modify permission.

Evaluation of Proposed Solution:

Which result(s) does the proposed solution produce?

A. The proposed solution produces the required result but neither of the optional results.

B. The proposed solution produces the required result and one of the optional results.

C. The proposed solution produces the required result and both the optional results.

D. The proposed solution does not produce the required result.

3. You are the administrator of a Windows Server 2003 computer named Server1. You create a share named Public. You add a folder named Docs under Public. The share and NTFS permissions for Public and Docs are as shown.

Public Share Permissions:

Everyone: Deny Full Control

Domain Admins: Full Control

Training: Full Control

Doc Folder Permissions:

User: Read

Domain Admins: Full Control

A user named Maria is a member of the Users and Training user groups. When Maria attempts to save the file `\Server1\Public\Docs\memo.doc`, she receives an "Access denied" error message.

Required Result:

You want Maria to be able to change and delete all files in the Docs folder.

Optional Desired Results:

You do not want to change the share permissions.

You do not want her to have more access than necessary.

Proposed Solution:

Set the permissions for the Docs folder to grant Maria the Modify permission.

Evaluation of Proposed Solution:

Which result(s) does the proposed solution produce?

A. The proposed solution produces the required result but neither of the optional results.

B. The proposed solution produces the required result and one of the optional results.

C. The proposed solution produces the required result and both the optional results.

D. The proposed solution does not produce the required result.

4. You are the administrator for a small sporting goods company. The Human Resources manager of your company creates several files in a shared folder called HR-Data on a Windows Server 2003 server. The share and the files have the permissions shown.

APPLY YOUR KNOWLEDGE

HR-Data Share Permissions:

Users: Read

Administrators: Read

HR Managers: Full Control

HR-Data NTFS Permissions:

Users: Read

Administrators: Read

HR Managers: Full Control

While the HR manager is on vacation, you receive a call from one of your users. It seems that one of the files in the HR-Data folder contains some very sensitive information, and it should be removed. How can you accomplish this without disrupting normal operations, using the minimum amount of authority necessary to delete the file?

A. Grant yourself Full Control permission for the HR-Data folder. Delete the file. Remove Full Control permission for the HR-Data folder.

B. Take ownership of the HR-Data folder. When prompted, take ownership of existing files. Grant yourself Full Control permission for the file. Delete the file.

C. Take ownership of the file. Grant yourself Modify permission for the file. Delete the file.

D. Grant yourself Modify permission for the HR-Data folder and its contents. Delete the file. Remove Modify permission for the HR-Data folder.

5. Mary is the network administrator for a loan company. As part of her duties, she has built a new Windows Server 2003 server and configured Terminal Services in Application Server mode. Users report that when they try to connect to the Terminal Services server, they receive the following error message: "The local policy of this system does not allow you to log on interactively." When Mary attempts to log on to the Terminal Services server from a user's computer, she is able to log on successfully. How can Mary enable the users to log on to the Terminal Services server?

   A. Grant the users the right to log on locally.

   B. Add the users to the TSUsers group.

   C. Grant the users the right to log on over the network.

   D. Add the users to the Remote Desktop Users group.

6. As part of a server consolidation, you are moving a group of shared folders to a new Windows Server 2003 server. After moving the folders and their contents using `XCOPY`, you turn the server back over to the users. Soon, your telephone rings with users complaining that they can't see the file shares. What steps will you need to perform to fix the problem?

   A. You need to reconfigure the NTFS permissions.

   B. You need to reconfigure the share permissions.

   C. You need to restart the Server service on the new server.

APPLY YOUR KNOWLEDGE

D. You need to reshare the shares.

E. You need to give the shares unique names.

7. You are the administrator of a small network. You have configured a Windows Server 2003 server to run Terminal Services in Application Server mode. What is the maximum number of users that can be supported?

   A. The same amount as the number of Terminal Server licenses that were purchased

   B. Two, plus one for the console

   C. About 100 on Windows Server 2003 Standard Edition and 200 on Windows Server 2003 Enterprise edition

   D. As many as the performance of the server will support

8. You are the administrator of a small network. You have configured a Windows Server 2003 server to run Terminal Services in Application Server mode. What is the proper way to install applications?

   A. Open Windows Explorer, navigate to the folder where the installation files are stored, and then double-click the MSI file.

   B. Open Add/Remove Programs, navigate to the folder where the installation files are stored, and then double-click the MSI file.

   C. Open a command prompt and navigate to the folder where the installation files are stored. Enter the command `install`. Run the MSI file from the command line.

   D. Open Windows Explorer and navigate to the folder where the installation files are stored. Open a command prompt, enter the command `change mode /install`. Then double-click the MSI file in Windows Explorer.

9. You are the administrator of a small network. You have configured a Windows Server 2003 server to run Terminal Services in Remote Desktop for Administration mode. What is the proper way to install applications?

   A. Open Windows Explorer, navigate to the folder where the installation files are stored, and then double-click the MSI file.

   B. Open Add/Remove Programs, navigate to the folder where the installation files are stored, and then double-click the MSI file.

   C. Install the applications just like on any other server.

   D. Open Windows Explorer and navigate to the folder where the installation files are stored. Open a command prompt, enter the command `change user /install`. Then double-click the MSI file in Windows Explorer.

10. You have just finished building a new Windows Server 2003 server. Your plan is to manage it remotely using Terminal Services Remote Desktop for Administration mode, just like you've been doing with your Windows 2000 servers. However, when you open the RDC client and try to browse to the new server, you don't see it in the list. What is the most likely cause of the problem?

    A. A bad network interface card.

    B. The personal firewall is blocking the ports for the browse list.

    C. Remote Desktop for Administration mode has not been enabled.

    D. Windows Server 2003 in Terminal Services Remote Desktop for Administration mode doesn't advertise to the browse list.

APPLY YOUR KNOWLEDGE

11. You are the administrator for a small network. The data partitions on your file server are formatted with FAT32. The Director of Payroll wants you to set up a file share so that users will be able to view their timesheets.

    Required Result:

    You want users to be able to view their timesheets from a common share.

    Optional Desired Results:

    You do not want users to be able to change their timesheets.

    You do not want users to have more access than necessary.

    Proposed Solution:

    Create a share on the file server and accept the defaults.

    Evaluation of Proposed Solution:

    Which result(s) does the proposed solution produce?

    A. The proposed solution produces the required result but neither of the optional results.

    B. The proposed solution produces the required result and one of the optional results.

    C. The proposed solution produces the required result and both the optional results.

    D. The proposed solution does not produce the required result.

12. The administrative assistant for the CIO of your company resigns without warning. The assistant's personal folders contain several files that the CIO needs access to. The folders have the following permission:

    Admin Assistant: Full Control

    All the user folders are located on a server formatted with NTFS. What's the quickest way to give the CIO access to these files?

    A. Reset the password on the administrative assistant's account and give the CIO the user ID and the new password.

    B. Assign ownership of the files to the CIO.

    C. Take ownership of the files and give the CIO Full Control permission.

    D. Move the files to the CIO's folders.

13. You are the administrator for a small network. The Director of Human Resources is extremely security conscious. She wants you to set up a file share so that users will not have access to it or be able to browse it. However, specified users in the HR department should be able to access it easily.

    Required Result:

    Set up a secure file share for Human Resources.

    Optional Desired Results:

    Users should not be able to browse it.

    Specified users in the HR department should be able to access it easily.

    Proposed Solution:

    Create a file share named HRSecure. Set the share permissions for the HRSecure folder to grant the specified HR users Full Control permission. No permissions are specified for any other user or group.

APPLY YOUR KNOWLEDGE

Evaluation of Proposed Solution:

Which result(s) does the proposed solution produce?

A. The proposed solution produces the required result but neither of the optional results.

B. The proposed solution produces the required result and one of the optional results.

C. The proposed solution produces the required result and both the optional results.

D. The proposed solution does not produce the required result.

14. You are the administrator for a small network. The Director of Human Resources is extremely security conscious. She wants you to set up a file share so that users will not have access to it or be able to browse it. However, specified users in the HR department should be able to access it easily.

Required Result:

Set up a secure file share for Human Resources.

Optional Desired Results:

Users should not be able to browse it.

Specified users in the HR department should be able to access it easily.

Proposed Solution:

Create a file share named HRSecure$. Set the share permissions for the HR folder to grant the specified HR users Full Control permission. No permissions are specified for any other user or group.

Evaluation of Proposed Solution:

Which result(s) does the proposed solution produce?

A. The proposed solution produces the required result but neither of the optional results.

B. The proposed solution produces the required result and one of the optional results.

C. The proposed solution produces the required result and both the optional results.

D. The proposed solution does not produce the required result.

15. The Contracts folder is configured with the following permissions:

Share Permissions:

Managers: Full Control

Legal department: Change

HR: Read

NTFS Permissions:

Managers: Full Control

Legal department: Modify

HR: Read

If Bill is a member of the legal department and the HR group, what is his effective permission over the network?

A. Change

B. Modify

C. Read

D. Full Control

APPLY YOUR KNOWLEDGE

Answers to Review Questions

1. The Windows Server 2003 Remote Desktop for Administration and Application Server modes. Remote Desktop for Administration only supports two concurrent remote sessions, plus the remote console session, whereas Application Server mode supports an unlimited number of remote sessions.
2. Windows Server 2003 includes RDP clients for all 32-bit versions of Windows (from Windows 9x to Windows Server 2003), Windows for Workgroups, and Windows CE clients. Also, a client for the iPAQ and one for the Macintosh are available for download from the Microsoft Web site.
3. The volume must be formatted with NTFS to provide local file system security.
4. When both NTFS and share permissions are applied, the most restrictive permission is applied.
5. The Effective Permissions tool can be used to analyze the resulting permissions when combining file, folder, and group permissions.
6. The Shared Folders snap-in in the Computer Management MMC is used to create and manage shared folders on remote computers.

Answers to Exam Questions

1. **B.** The solution satisfies the required result and one of the optional results. Although the solution allows Maria to make the necessary changes, and the share permissions were not changed, granting her Full Control permissions gives her more authority than is necessary.
2. **C.** The solution satisfies the required result and both the optional results. The Modify permission allows Maria to create, change, and delete files and folders contained in the Docs folder.
3. **D.** The solution will not work. Because Deny Full Control overrides all other permissions, Maria and all other users will have no access to the share or to any files and folders under the share. This question points out a common problem in the real world: All users, including administrators, are members of the Everyone group. Even if the user is a member of another group with Full Control permissions to the share, Deny Full Control will override that permission.
4. **C.** You must take ownership of the file and then give yourself the Modify permission. Then you can delete the file. Modify is the minimum permission needed to delete a file.
5. **D.** Although granting the users the right to log on locally will work, this can get unwieldy if there are a large number of users. The proper way is to add the users that need to log on to the Terminal Services server to the Remote Desktop Users group.
6. **A, B, D.** When a shared folder is moved, it is no longer shared. When it is moved to a different server, it will assume the NTFS permissions of the target folder, which probably won't be the same as the original folder.
7. **A.** The number of concurrent Terminal Services connections on all versions of Windows Server 2003 is limited to the number of licenses that are installed. However, performance will suffer as the hardware capacity is reached.

APPLY YOUR KNOWLEDGE

8. **B.** Applications can be installed on a Windows Server 2003 server running in Terminal Services Application Server mode in two ways: From Add/Remove Programs and, after setting the server in Install mode, by entering the command `change user /install`.

9. **C.** Applications can be installed on a Windows Server 2003 server running in Terminal Services Remote Desktop for Administration mode just like they would on any other server. This is because it is not a multiuser environment.

10. **D.** Unlike in Windows 2000 Server, Windows Server 2003 Terminal Services servers in Remote Desktop for Administration mode will not be advertised, so they can't be browsed using the RDC client. You will either need to enter the IP address or server name.

11. **C.** The solution satisfies the required result and both the optional results. When a share is created on a Windows Server 2003 server, the default permission is Read for Everyone.

12. **B.** Unlike in previous versions of Windows, in Windows Server 2003, the administrator can assign the ownership of files and folders. Moving the files would not work because files moved to a different folder on an NTFS partition will retain their existing permissions. The other options would work, but they involve more steps.

13. **B.** The solution satisfies the required result and one of the optional results. Although the solution allows HR easy access to the share and blocks other users, all network users will know that it exists.

14. **B.** The solution satisfies the required result and one of the optional results. Although the solution prevents casual access to the share, because it will not appear in the browse list, and other users are blocked via share permissions, the HR users will have to be taught how to manually map to the share.

15. **A.** Because Bill is accessing the folder through a share, his permissions will be the more restrictive of the combined share and NTFS permissions.

Suggested Readings and Resources

1. Microsoft Official Curriculum Course 2274: Managing a Microsoft Windows Server 2003 Environment
   - Module 4: Managing Access to Resources
2. Microsoft Official Curriculum Course 2275: Maintaining a Microsoft Windows Server 2003 Environment
   - Module 1: Preparing to Administer a Server
3. Microsoft Official Curriculum Course 2270: Updating Support Skills from Microsoft Windows NT 4.0 to the Windows Server 2003 Family
   - Module 12: Managing File Resources
4. Boswell, William. *Inside Windows Server 2003.* New Riders, 2003. ISBN 0735711585.
5. Matthews, Marty. *Windows Server 2003: A Beginners Guide.* McGraw-Hill, 2003. ISBN 0072193093.
6. Minasi, Mark, et al. *Mark Minasi's Windows XP and Server 2003 Resource Kit.* Sybex, 2003. ISBN 0782140807.
7. Minasi, Mark, et al. *Mastering Windows Server 2003 Server.* Sybex, 2003. ISBN 0782141307.
8. Shapiro, Jeffrey, et al. *Windows Server 2003 Bible.* John Wiley & Sons, 2003. ISBN 0764549375.
9. Microsoft Session Directory Whitepaper: `http://www.microsoft.com/windowsserver2003/docs/SessionDirectory.doc`
10. Microsoft Terminal Services Overview Whitepaper: `http://www.microsoft.com/windowsserver2003/docs/TerminalServerOverview.doc`
11. Microsoft Windows 2003 File Server Best Practices: `http://www.microsoft.com/technet/treeview/default.asp?url=/technet/prodtechnol/windowsserver2003/proddocs/entserver/file_srv_bestpractice.asp?frame=true`

Objectives

This chapter covers the following Microsoft-specified objectives for the "Managing and Troubleshooting Servers" section of the Managing and Maintaining a Microsoft Windows Server 2003 Environment exam:

Manage servers remotely.

- **Manage a server by using Remote Assistance.**
- **Manage a server by using Terminal Services Remote Desktop for Administration mode.**
- **Manage a server by using available support tools.**

▶ The purpose of this objective is to teach you how to use the various tools available in Windows Server 2003 to remotely manage your servers.

Manage a Web server.

- **Manage Internet Information Services (IIS).**
- **Manage security for IIS.**

▶ Now more than ever, it is very important that you properly install and manage Internet Information Services (IIS) in the Windows Server 2003 environment. With all the exploits targeted at IIS, it is essential that you keep your IIS 6.0 server locked down so that it doesn't become an easy target for hackers or viruses.

Manage a software update infrastructure.

▶ With new security exploits announced what seems to be weekly, with corresponding patches that need to be applied, it is important that you automate as much of this process as possible. Microsoft has made available Software Update Services (SUS) to allow you to control the patches and updates applied to the Windows platform.

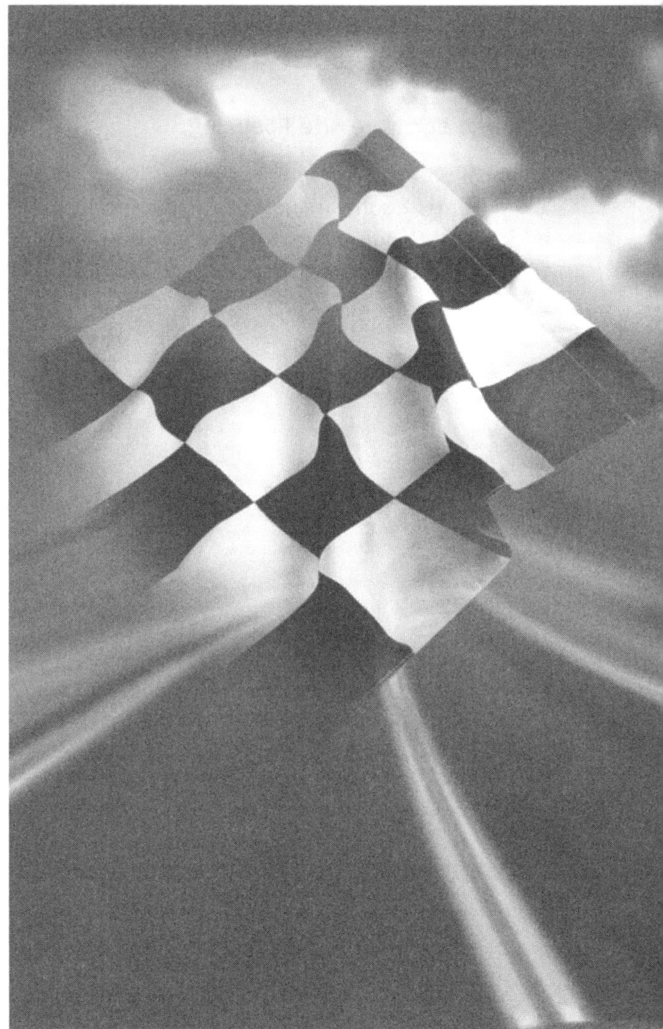

CHAPTER 5

Managing and Troubleshooting Servers

Objectives

Manage software site licensing.

- Each Microsoft server and workstation must have an appropriate software license. It's important to understand the different licensing modes so that you don't purchase licenses that you don't need.

Outline

Outline

Study Strategies

- The sections in this chapter outline features that are essential to managing a Windows Server 2003 environment.
- Expect to see a number of questions on two areas that are being heavily emphasized in Windows Server 2003: Software Update Services (SUS) and the various types of remote server management. Know how these features work, under what circumstances they should be used, and how to implement them.
- Know how to configure IIS and its various features. A lot of different options and scenarios are available in IIS 6.0. The best strategy is to install it, set up several test Web sites to get a feel for how IIS works, and try some of the various configuration options.
- Know and understand the different licensing modes, and understand which one is more advantageous in specific environments.

INTRODUCTION

Windows Server 2003 system administration is a task-based responsibility that requires you to rely on the tools and utilities at your disposal. If you are unfamiliar with your tools, you cannot perform the required tasks.

Just as a handyman needs the right tool for a particular job, you need to know which tools can perform which functions. In the following sections, we walk through some of the management tools included with Windows Server 2003. In addition to reviewing the discussion in this chapter, you should take the time to work with the tools themselves. Hands-on experience is invaluable and cannot be substituted. Plus, you may want to review the online help documentation included in the tools, as well as the following material:

- **Microsoft Technical Information Network (TechNet)—** A monthly CD-based publication that delivers numerous electronic titles on Windows products. Its offerings include all the Microsoft Resource Kits (see next bullet), product facts, technical notes, tools, utilities, the entire Microsoft Knowledge Base, as well as service packs, drivers, and patches. A single-user license to TechNet costs $299 per year (TechNet Plus, which includes Beta versions of Microsoft products, costs $429), but it is well worth the price. For more details, visit `www.microsoft.com/technet/` and check out the information under the TechNet Subscription heading in the About TechNet menu entry.
- **Microsoft Press Resource Kits**—Available on nearly all major products from Microsoft. The Microsoft Windows Server 2003 Resource Kit and the Microsoft Windows XP Professional Resource Kit are essential references for Windows information. Both book sets come with CD-ROMs that contain useful tools. Visit `http://mspress.microsoft.com` for additional information on the resource kits.

Additional resources that provide information about Windows Server 2003 are also available. For instance, a quick search at `www.amazon.com` using the phrase "Windows Server 2003" should turn up a list of additional references on this subject.

MANAGING SERVERS REMOTELY

There are always situations in which the system administrator must perform a task on a Windows Server 2003 server but is currently not physically located near the server console. In some cases, the system administrator is not located in the same part of the building as the server room, or for that matter, may even be located in a different country!

Microsoft has included several tools for remotely managing servers with Windows Server 2003. These tools allow the system administrator to perform system management tasks as though he or she were physically sitting in front of the console of each server in the organization. Knowing which tool to use in specific situations allows you to be more effective as a system administrator.

The Microsoft Management Console: Where Management Begins

When Microsoft released the Windows NT Option Pack for Windows NT 4.0, it introduced a new tool known as the *Microsoft Management Console (MMC)*. Microsoft's vision was that this tool would become the de facto tool for administering anything and everything in future versions of Windows NT.

What makes the MMC different from earlier Windows NT administration tools is that the MMC itself does none of the administration. Instead, it is simply a shell into which administration tools can be added, modified, and removed. As you can see in Figure 5.1, when the MMC is launched (by running the `MMC.EXE` command), it brings up a blank window.

FIGURE 5.1
The Microsoft Management Console.

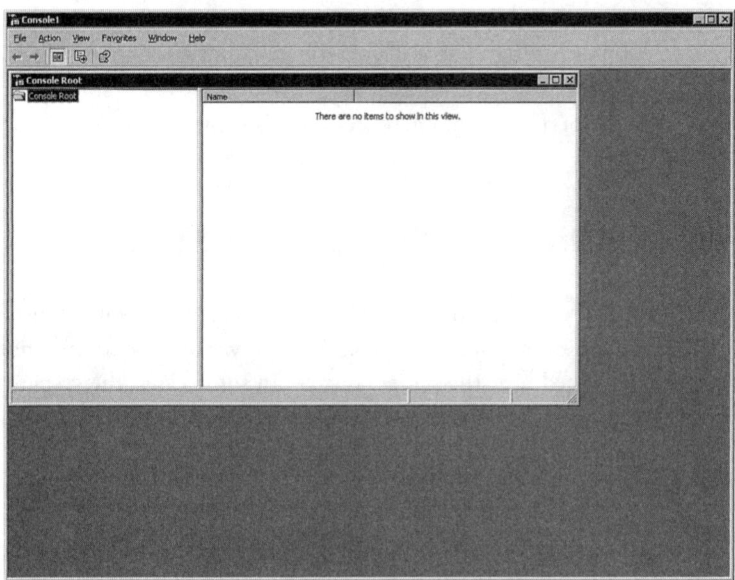

If the MMC looks familiar to you, that is because the majority of the tools we worked with in previous chapters, such as Disk Management and Computer Management, are preconfigured versions of the MMC. These Microsoft-supplied MMCs have been configured with a selection of administrative tools.

The administrative tools that can be added to the MMC are known as *snap-ins*. The capability to pick and choose which administrative tools are included in an MMC is an extremely flexible feature, especially in an environment in which several administrators perform different tasks. Each administrator can create (or have created for him by the system administrator) an MMC that has only the tools he requires. For example, Sue may be responsible for monitoring server performance, the event logs, and the Domain Name Service, whereas Joe's job may be to create users and groups and set security policies for each user. To create Joe's MMC, follow the procedure in Step by Step 5.1.

STEP BY STEP

5.1 Creating a Custom MMC

1. From the Start menu, select Start, Run. Type **MMC** in the field and click OK.

2. The MMC appears, as shown previously in Figure 5.1. Select File, Add/Remove Snap-In from the Console menu.

FIGURE 5.2◀
The Add/Remove Snap-In dialog box.

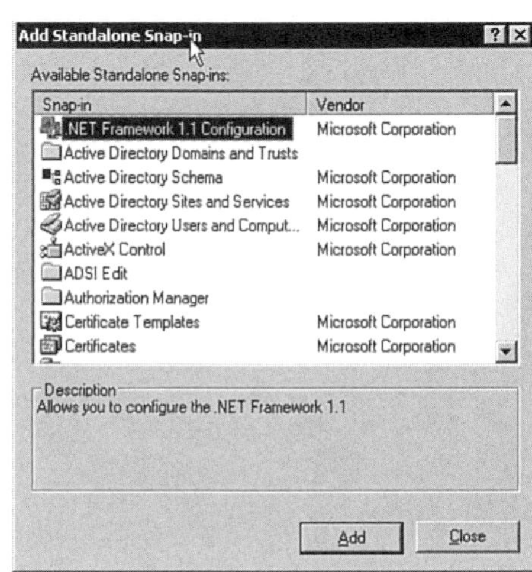

FIGURE 5.3▲
The Add Standalone Snap-In dialog box allows you to select the desired snap-ins.

3. The Add/Remove Snap-In dialog box appears, as shown in Figure 5.2. Click the Add button.

4. The Add Standalone Snap-In dialog box appears, as shown in Figure 5.3. Select the Group Policy snap-in and then click the Add button. From the Group Policy Wizard dialog box, accept the defaults by clicking the Finish button.

5. Select the Local Users and Groups snap-in and then click the Add button. The Choose Target Machine dialog box appears, as shown in Figure 5.4. Click the Finish button to accept the defaults.

continues

continued

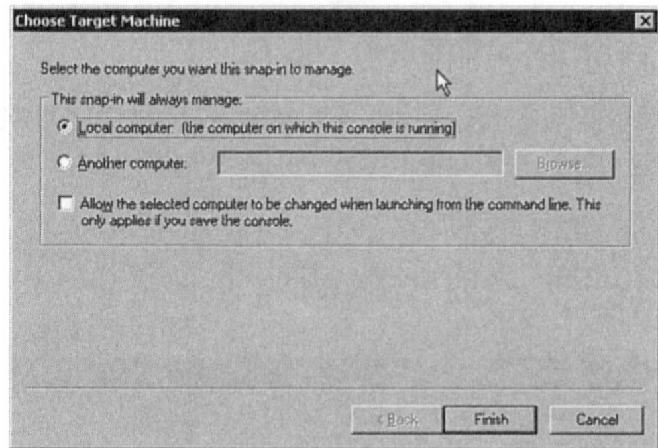

FIGURE 5.4
The Choose Target Machine dialog box allows you to select the focus of the add-in—either the local computer or another computer.

6. Back at the Add Standalone Snap-In dialog box, click the Close button. This returns you to the Add/Remove Snap-In dialog box. If the selections are correct, click the OK button.
7. This returns you to the custom MMC.

The real beauty of the MMC snap-in administrative tools are that they don't limit you to managing only the local machine you are working on. By selecting Connect to Another Computer, you can connect the tool to a remote computer and perform the administrative tasks as though you were sitting at the system console. This allows you not only to manage all your servers from one server but to manage either servers or workstations from any Windows 2000 or later computer by starting the appropriate MMC and snap-ins.

Step by Step 5.2 walks you through connecting to a remote computer to perform management tasks.

STEP BY STEP

5.2 Connecting to a Remote Computer to Perform Management Tasks

1. From the Start menu, select All Programs, Administrative Tools, Computer Management.

2. In the left pane of the Computer Management MMC, right-click the Computer Management (Local) entry and then select Connect to Another Computer from the pop-up menu. This opens the Select Computer dialog box.
3. From the Select Computer dialog box, you can either browse for or enter the name of the remote computer to manage. Enter the name of the computer and then click the OK button.
4. The Computer Management MMC opens with the focus assigned to the remote computer.

If the user has the proper permissions, she can use any computer in the Windows 2000/2003/XP family to manage other family members via the Computer Management MMC. For example, a Windows 2000 Professional computer can be used to manage a Windows Server 2003 or Windows XP Professional computer. Only the features supported on the remote computer are available in the Computer Management MMC. For example, if you are using a Windows Server 2003 computer to manage a Windows XP Professional computer, the selection for RAID-5 is not available because it is not supported on the remote computer, which in this case is Windows XP Professional.

You can access the rest of the tools that appear in this book either through their own administrative tools or by creating a custom MMC and adding their respective snap-ins. A good example of an MMC with a variety of snap-ins included is the Computer Management MMC. The purpose of the Computer Management MMC is to group together a selection of Windows utilities in a single MMC that can be connected to either the local computer or a remote computer. We have used the Computer Management MMC to access a variety of management tools in the previous chapters.

The Computer Management MMC comes prepopulated with the most commonly used administrative tools:

- Event Viewer
- Shared Folders
- Local Users and Groups

- Performance Logs and Alerts
- Device Manager
- Removable Storage
- Disk Defragmenter
- Disk Management
- Services
- WMI Control
- Indexing Service

Using the Computer Management MMC, you can perform tasks such as adding and managing disks, adding shared folders, and stopping and starting services on local or remote computers.

In addition to the capabilities mentioned previously, the MMC can be used to manage tasks simultaneously on multiple remote computers. That is the scenario used in Guided Practice Exercise 5.1.

GUIDED PRACTICE EXERCISE 5.1

In this scenario, you must log the performance of four Windows Server 2003 servers from a remote computer. You should do this using as few steps as possible.

How would you set this up?

You should try working through this problem on your own first. If you get stuck, or if you'd like to see one possible solution, follow these steps:

1. From the Start menu, select Start, Run. Type **MMC** in the field and click OK.
2. The MMC appears. Select File, Add/Remove Snap-In from the Console menu.
3. The Add/Remove Snap-In dialog box appears. Click the Add button.
4. The Add Standalone Snap-In dialog box appears. Select the Performance Logs and Alerts snap-in and then click the Add button.

5. Repeat the previous step three more times to add additional instances of the Performance Logs and Alerts snap-in.
6. At the Add Standalone Snap-In dialog box, click the Close button. This returns you to the Add/Remove Snap-In dialog box. If the selections are correct, click the OK button.
7. From the custom MMC, you can right-click each instance of Performance Logs and Alerts and add objects and counters from different servers on the General tab of the Properties dialog box.

There are many advantages to using the MMC for server management. For example, as you have seen in this Guided Practice Exercise, you can manage multiple instances of the same or different tools connected to multiple servers, all within a single MMC. Moving from server to server or tool to tool is as simple as clicking the mouse to change the focus.

Remote Desktop for Administration

The basic functionality of the Remote Desktop for Administration feature has actually been available for some time from other vendors, such as Citrix, and even Microsoft as Windows Terminal Services.

As discussed previously in Chapter 4, "Managing and Maintaining Access to Resources," Terminal Services is available in two modes: Remote Desktop for Administration (formerly called Remote Administration mode) and Application Server mode. Application Server mode configures the Windows Server 2003 machine to operate similar to the previous version of Windows NT Terminal Server 4.0. Remote Desktop for Administration mode is used to provide remote server management. Unlike in Windows 2000, where the Remote Administration mode was an option, the Remote Desktop for Administration mode is automatically installed in Windows Server 2003. However, incoming connections are disabled by default.

NOTE

More Info on Terminal Services Modes For a detailed discussion of Windows Server 2003 Terminal Services in Application Server mode, see Chapter 4, "Managing and Maintaining Access to Resources."

Terminal Services in Remote Desktop for Administration Mode

The Terminal Services (TS) Remote Administration mode was first available in Windows 2000. The previous versions of Windows Terminal Services did not have this feature.

With Windows 2003 Terminal Services in Remote Desktop for Administration mode, you are allowed two concurrent sessions, plus a console session to the Windows server. These sessions can be used to remotely access any programs or data on the server. The console session actually takes over the physical console of the server. In the past, a lot of tools and applications could not be run via a Terminal Services session because they were written to interact directly with "session 0," the physical server console. Also, most system messages are automatically routed to the console, so if you are trying to manage the server remotely and receive a pop-up error message, you won't be able to see it.

Using the Terminal Services client is just like working on the server console. The Remote Desktop for Administration mode allows you to have two concurrent TS sessions without any additional Client Access Licenses required. The beauty of the Remote Desktop for Administration mode is that it allows you to manage your server from just about anywhere and from just about any computer. Because the TS client is supported on a variety of Windows clients, including Windows CE, you can load the client on any Windows box that you have available and manage your server. Imagine managing your server from your Pocket PC!

Like the tools discussed in the previous section, Remote Desktop enables you to open a session on a remote Windows Server 2003 machine and run applications as though you were physically sitting at the console of the remote machine. In addition, because the RDP connection between the server and the client requires a minimum of bandwidth, you are not limited to having a high-speed LAN connection. The Terminal Services client can access the servers via a dial-up connection, the Internet, or even a wireless connection. With this feature, you can connect to your Windows Server 2003 servers from home or a hotel room and have full access to all your applications, files, and other network resources.

To use Remote Desktop, you must enable it on your server and grant access to the appropriate users and groups by following the procedure in Step by Step 5.3.

STEP BY STEP

5.3 Enabling the Remote Desktop for Administration Feature

1. Log on to the Windows Server 2003 server as a member of the local Administrators group.
2. Open Control Panel and select the System applet.
3. In the System Properties dialog box, select the Remote tab.
4. From the Remote tab, shown in Figure 5.5, select the Allow Users to Connect Remotely to This Computer check box.

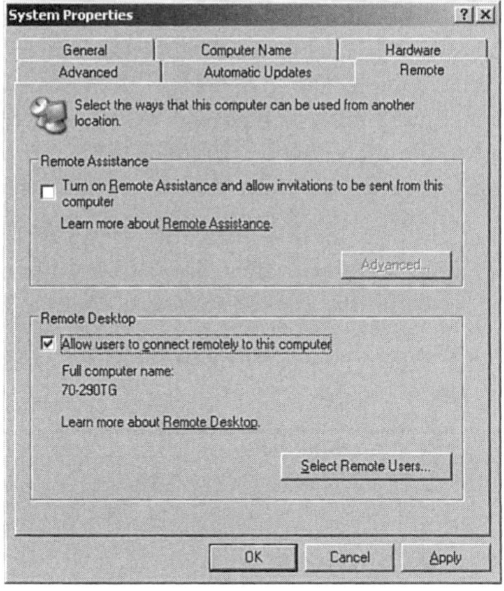

FIGURE 5.5
Remote Desktop must be manually enabled on Windows Server 2003.

5. When the Remote Sessions information prompt appears, read the information and then click the OK button to continue.

continues

continued

6. Click the Select Remote Users button. By default, members of the local Administrators group have been granted access.
7. The Remote Desktop Users dialog box appears.
8. Click the Add button. The Select Users dialog box appears, as shown in Figure 5.6.

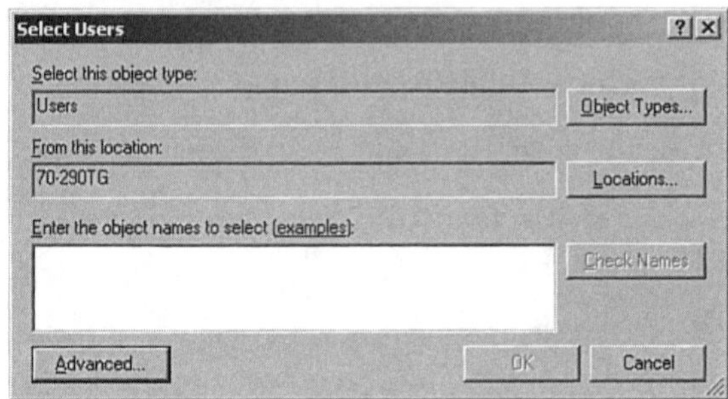

FIGURE 5.6
Controlling RDP access using the Remote Desktop Users dialog box.

9. In the Select Users dialog box, you are given the opportunity to select the users and/or groups that are granted access to your machine via Remote Desktop for Administration. The terminology can be somewhat confusing. Just remember that users and groups are objects, and the location is either the individual server or a domain. Table 5.1 defines the terms used in this interface.
10. After making your other selections, if you click the Advanced button, a search dialog box opens, where you can search for the users or groups you want to add.
11. When you're finished, click OK three times to save your settings.

TABLE 5.1

OBJECT TYPE DEFINITIONS

Prompt	*Meaning*
Object Types	Users or groups.
Locations	This can show users or groups from an individual machine. If you're connected to a domain, you can select the domain directory.
Object Names	User or group names.

These steps configure Windows Server 2003 to accept incoming connections. The Windows 2003 Remote Desktop Connection (RDC) client can be installed on any version of Windows from Windows 95 on up. To install the client, insert the Windows Server 2003 CD-ROM into the client machine's CD-ROM drive. When the Welcome page appears, click Perform Additional Tasks and then click Set Up Remote Desktop Connection.

To connect to your Windows Server 2003 server remotely, start the RDP client on the remote computer. This computer must have a connection of some kind to the other computer—LAN, WAN, VPN, or dial-up. Enter the IP address or the name of the remote computer and then click the Connect button. Enter the username and password, and you're in!

NOTE

Using Older Clients Windows Server 2003 also supports connections from the older Windows Terminal Services clients, so you can use the 16-bit client from a Windows 3.1 machine, if you still have one. However, some of the newer features, such as device redirection, are not available. Citrix clients are not supported because they use the Independent Computing Architecture (ICA) protocol instead of the Remote Desktop Protocol (RDP) used with the RDC client.

Remote Desktops Snap-In

The Remote Desktops snap-in is useful for those situations when you need to remotely manage or monitor several Windows Server 2003 servers. This snap-in allows you to be connected concurrently to the RDC sessions of multiple servers. Each session can be given focus by selecting it via a navigable tree interface.

Step by Step 5.4 walks you through connecting to multiple remote computers using the Remote Desktops snap-in.

STEP BY STEP

5.4 Connecting to a Remote Computer to Perform Management Tasks

1. From the Start menu, select All Programs, Administrative Tools, Remote Desktop.
2. If this is the first time that Remote Desktop has been selected, the MSI file is loaded. In the left pane of the Remote Desktops MMC, right-click the Remote Desktops entry and then select Add New Connection from the pop-up menu.
3. This opens the Add New Connection dialog box, which allows you to either browse for or enter the name or IP address of a remote computer to manage. Notice that you are given the option to connect to the console session.

continues

continued

4. Enter the name or the IP address of the remote server and then click the OK button.
5. The Remote Desktops MMC lists all configured connections.
6. To connect to a remote server, right-click the appropriate entry in the left pane of the Remote Desktops MMC and select Connect from the pop-up menu.
7. The remote session now appears in the right pane of the MMC.

You can switch between multiple remote sessions by clicking the entry in the left pane of the MMC. By creating multiple custom MMCs, you can have several Remote Desktops MMCs that are preconfigured to connect to different groups of servers.

Remote Assistance

Diagnosing a computer problem can be difficult if you are not sitting in front of the computer. The Windows Server 2003 Remote Assistance feature enables you to grant a friend or a help desk operator permission to connect to your computer and assist you with a problem. Your computer must have a connection of some kind to the other computer, such as a LAN, WAN, VPN, or dial-up connection.

The Remote Assistance function is similar to the Remote Desktop function in that it allows a remote user to connect to your Windows Server 2003 machine. Remote Desktop, however, is designed to allow you to run applications remotely on your computer, whereas the Remote Assistance function is designed to allow a remote user to log in to your running session and assist you in determining a problem with a currently running session. Remote Assistance is more of a remote-control tool, similar to PCAnywhere.

Remote Assistance allows you to exchange messages via a chat session, or you can talk to another user if you both have the required sound cards and microphones. You can even grant a remote user the ability to take over your desktop to make changes and run programs.

The Remote Assistance feature was first available on Windows XP Professional and XP Home Edition. Unlike in the versions of Windows XP, it is disabled by default in Windows Server 2003.

To use Remote Assistance, you must enable it on your server by following the procedure in Step by Step 5.5.

STEP BY STEP

5.5 Enabling the Remote Assistance Feature

1. Log on to the Windows Server 2003 server as a member of the local Administrators group.
2. Open Control Panel and select the System applet.
3. In the System Properties dialog box, select the Remote tab.
4. From the Remote tab, shown in Figure 5.7, select the Turn On Remote Assistance and Allow Invitations to Be Sent from This Computer check box.

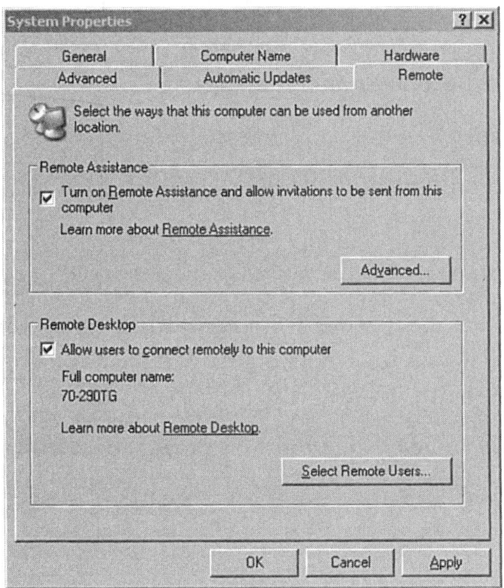

FIGURE 5.7
Remote Assistance must be manually enabled on Windows Server 2003.

5. Click the OK button to save this setting.

After enabling Remote Assistance, you must issue an invitation before another user can connect to your machine. This invitation can be sent to the other user via one of the following methods:

- Windows Messenger (the preferred method)
- Email
- Disk

The invitation is an encrypted ticket used to grant the remote user access to the Windows Server 2003 server. The remote user must have the ticket and a password to be permitted access. You can send the password separately by email (not recommended), instant messaging, or telephone.

By default, the invitation is good for 30 days, but you should probably change it to 24 hours or less. To change the invitation time, perform the procedure in Step by Step 5.6.

STEP BY STEP

5.6 Changing the Invitation Duration

1. Log on to the Windows Server 2003 server as a member of the local Administrators group.
2. Open Control Panel and select the System applet.
3. In the System Properties dialog box, select the Remote tab.
4. From the Remote tab, click the Advanced button.
5. From the Remote Assistance Settings dialog box, set the invitation time to 24 hours. The default setting is 30 days, as shown in Figure 5.8.
6. Click the OK button twice to save your settings.

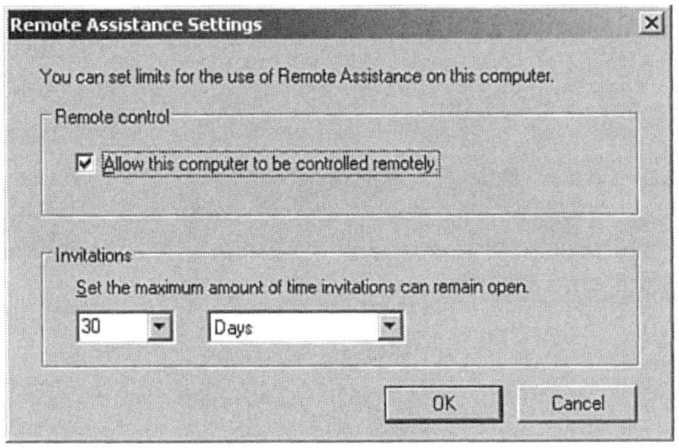

FIGURE 5.8
The Remote Assistance Settings dialog box allows you to control whether or not the server can be remote controlled and how long an invitation is valid.

An example of when the Remote Assistance feature comes in handy is if you are having a problem on a Windows Server 2003 server and you require assistance from a support person. You can allow the support person to view your activities on the server console. The first step in this process is to create an invitation for the support person.

To create an invitation, perform the procedure outlined in Step by Step 5.7.

STEP BY STEP

5.7 Creating an Invitation

1. Click Start, All Programs, Remote Assistance.
2. Click the Invite Someone to Help You button, shown in Figure 5.9.
3. In the next window, you can elect to send the invitation via Windows Messenger or email, or you can save it as a file. Click the Save Invitation As a File button.
4. The Remote Assistance - Save Invitation window appears. Enter your name. Note that the default invitation duration for a file is 1 hour.

continues

continued

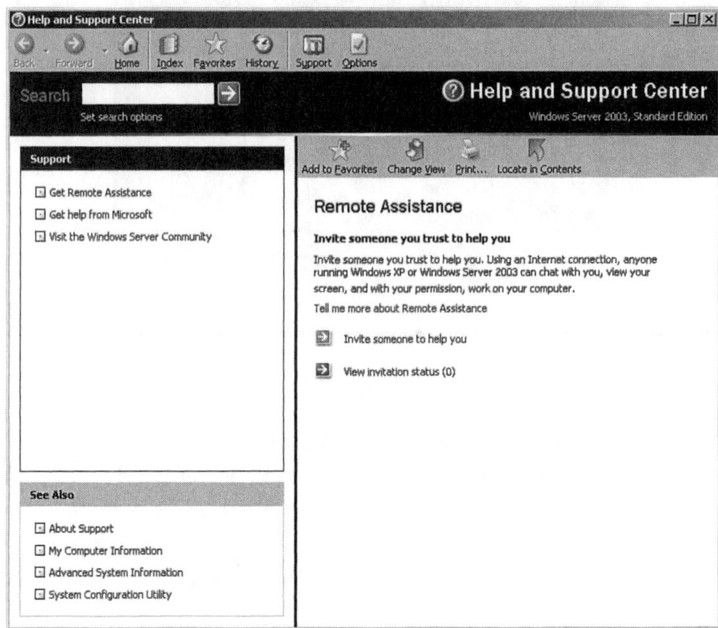

FIGURE 5.9
The Remote Assistance page in the Help and Support Center allows you to generate invitations or check on the status of existing invitations.

5. The next window allows you to specify a password for the support person to use to connect to your server. Enter a password and then click the Save Invitation button to continue.

6. From the Save As dialog box, save the invitation file to an appropriate location. You are returned to the opening Remote Assistance page.

The invitation has been saved to a file. This file can be emailed, saved to a disk and carried to a remote user, or copied to a network share. The user from whom you have requested assistance must be running a version of Windows XP or Windows Server 2003.

To respond to an invitation, perform the procedure outlined in Step by Step 5.8.

STEP BY STEP

5.8 Responding to an Invitation

1. On the remote machine, the assisting user must locate the invitation and double-click it.
2. The Remote Assistance dialog box opens, and the assisting user will see this message: "Do you want to connect to user's computer now?" (see Figure 5.10). The assisting user will need to enter the password and then click the Yes button.

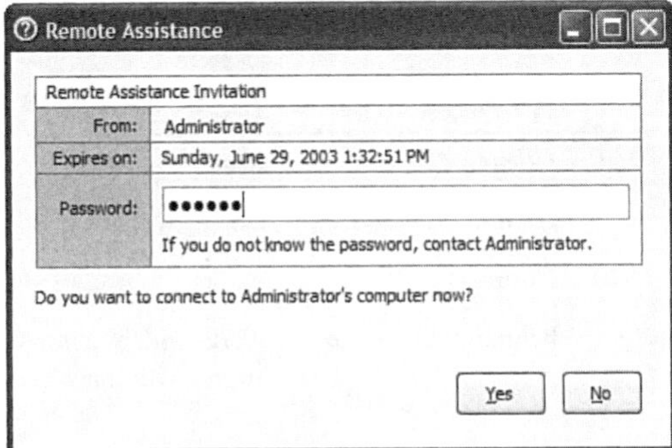

FIGURE 5.10◀
Enter the Remote Assistance password.

3. On the computer requesting assistance (your computer), a dialog box appears asking whether you want to accept the connection. Click the Yes button.
4. The assisting user is now able to see your desktop and communicate with you via chat.

If the assisting user needs to take over your machine, he can click the Take Control icon on his toolbar. You are prompted as to whether you want this to happen. You can both share control of the desktop until you press the Esc key. When finished, just click the Disconnect button on the Remote Assistance dialog box (see Figure 5.11).

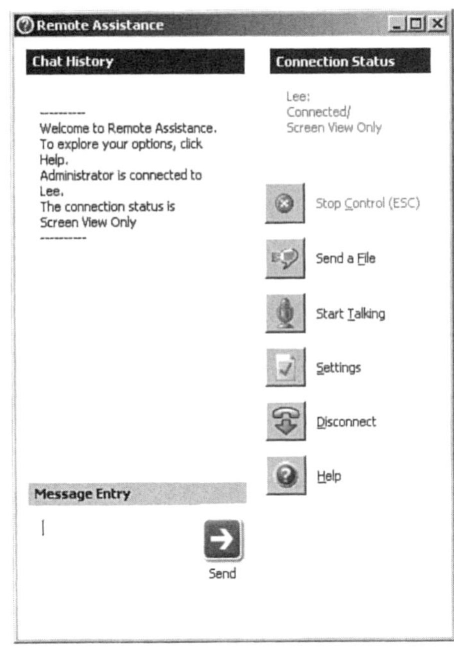

FIGURE 5.11▲
Remote Assistance, showing the view from the assisted desktop.

Of course, allowing someone to take over your machine requires a great amount of trust. Don't open this feature to anyone you don't know! Make sure your invitations always require a password, which should *not* be sent with the invitations, and keep your invitation durations as short as possible.

Problems with Remote Assistance

If you are accessing a Remote Assistance computer that is behind a firewall, port 3389 must be open. Table 5.2 lists some common connection scenarios.

TABLE 5.2

REMOTE ASSISTANCE CONNECTION SCENARIOS

Assistant	*Client*	*Result*
Behind NAT device	Behind NAT device	Doesn't work.
Behind NAT device	Normal	Works.
Normal	Behind NAT device	Works with Windows Messenger, but not with file or email invitations.
Behind proxy server	Behind proxy server	Doesn't work.
Behind proxy server	Normal	Must install proxy software on Assistant.
Normal	Behind proxy server	Doesn't work.

For more information on the Remote Assistance feature, consult Microsoft Knowledge Base Article Q301529, "Supported Connection Scenarios for Remote Assistance," or Article Q306298, "Description of the Windows Messenger Reverse Connection Process Used by Remote Assistance."

MANAGING INTERNET INFORMATION SERVICES (IIS) 6.0

Of all the components in Windows Server 2003, Internet Information Services 6.0 has received the most attention. It has been completely reworked so that it retains very little of the basic architecture from previous versions. The majority of the improvements have been in the following areas:

- Security
- Reliability
- Management

Security

In previous versions of Windows, IIS was installed and enabled by default. This vulnerability was displayed multiple times over the past few years as various viruses and exploits targeting IIS were distributed, and administrators who had applied only IIS patches to their "Web servers" were presented with a rude awakening. Countless servers that were not intended to perform any Web-serving role were brought to their knees, mainly because a lot of administrators did not realize that they had installed IIS on their servers.

As part of the overall Microsoft Security Initiative, in Windows Server 2003, Microsoft has made IIS an optional component. It is no longer installed as a default component. In addition, even after it is installed, it presents only static pages. If your Web site requires the use of ASP or other dynamic content, you must manually enable the support for each feature.

In addition, during an upgrade from a previous version of Windows, IIS is installed; however, the service is disabled, and you must start it manually. This prevents administrators from carrying over vulnerabilities from previous versions of Windows. Microsoft's intention is for administrators to run only IIS on those servers that require it, and only with the bare minimum of features, thereby reducing the overall vulnerability to attack.

To install IIS, follow the procedure outlined in Step by Step 5.9.

STEP BY STEP

5.9 Installing Internet Information Services (IIS) 6.0

1. Click Start, All Programs, Control Panel, Add or Remove Programs.
2. Click the Add/Remove Windows Components button in the left pane of the Add or Remove Programs dialog box.
3. The Windows Components Wizard appears. Select the Application Server check box, as shown in Figure 5.12. Click the Next button to continue.

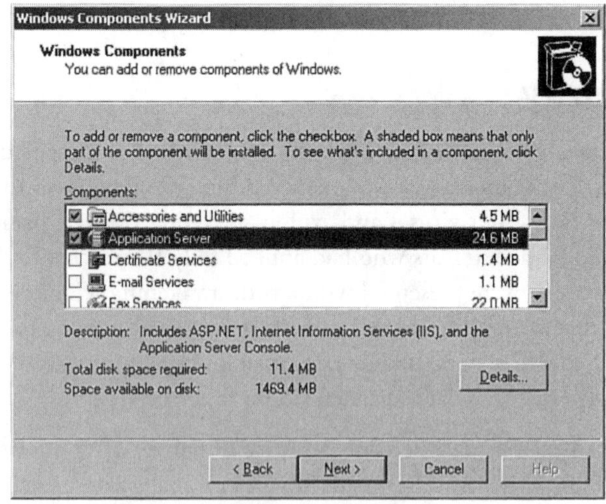

FIGURE 5.12
The Windows Components Wizard.

4. The Configuring Components screen appears. When prompted, insert the Windows Server 2003 CD-ROM and then click the OK button to continue.
5. When the Completing the Windows Component Wizard screen appears, click the Finish button. You are prompted to reboot the server.

The previous steps install the default components of IIS 6.0. As we discussed earlier, the default installation for IIS 6.0 is in "locked down" mode. In locked down mode, only pages containing static content are displayed. All other pages return a 404 error when they are accessed.

IN THE FIELD

DEFAULT INSTALLATION OF IIS 6.0

In the previous Step by Step, we covered installing a basic installation of IIS 6.0. If you click the Details button, as shown in Figure 5.12, you can select or deselect the various components of IIS, including the IIS Services Manager, FrontPage Server Extensions, and the FTP server.

The following features can be enabled using the Web Service Extensions node in the IIS Manager snap-in:

- ASP
- ASP.NET
- Server-Side Includes
- WebDAV Publishing
- FrontPage Server Extensions
- ISAPI Extensions
- CGI Extensions

Using IIS Manager, you can allow, prohibit, or add additional Web Service Extensions to allow different types of dynamic content to be used on your Web sites.

To enable the Web Service Extensions in IIS, follow the procedure outlined in Step by Step 5.10.

STEP BY STEP

5.10 Enabling Web Service Extensions in IIS 6.0

1. Click Start, Administrative Tools, Internet Information Services Manager.
2. The IIS Manager MMC opens with the default status of the Web Service Extensions, as shown in Figure 5.13.

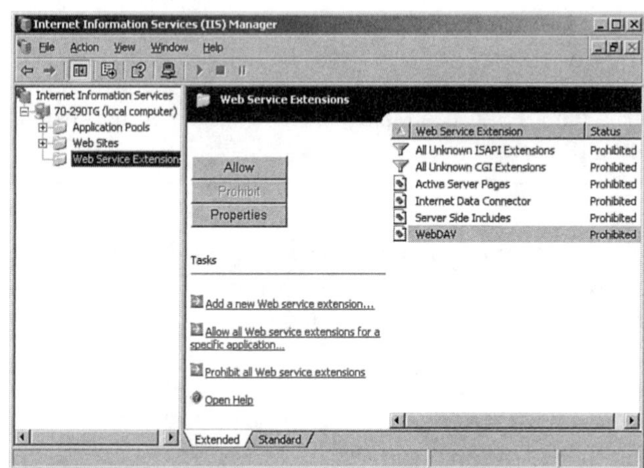

FIGURE 5.13
The IIS Manager MMC, showing the default status of the Web Service Extensions. The list varies, depending on what extensions are installed.

3. Highlight the desired extensions in the right pane of the MMC and then click the Allow button. The setting listed in the Status column for the extension is changed from Prohibited to Allowed.

Web Service Extensions are just a group of EXE and DLL files that are required for the specific function being enabled. For example, for Active Server Pages to be used, the `asp.dll` file must be enabled. To get a list of the files required for each Web Service Extension, in the IIS Manager MMC, highlight the desired extension and click the Properties button. The files are displayed on the Required Files tab of the Properties page.

If you need to add a custom extension, you can click the Add a New Web Service Extension link, which opens the New Web Service Extension dialog box, shown in Figure 5.14. This dialog box allows you to enter a name for the extension, add the required files, and set the status of the extension to Allowed.

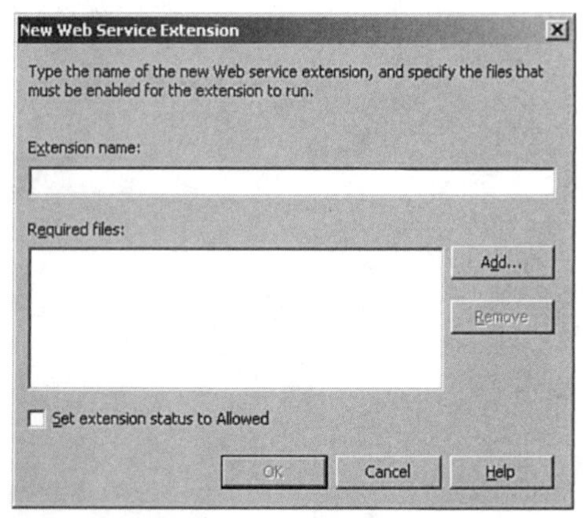

FIGURE 5.14
The New Web Service Extension dialog box, where you enter the required configuration for a custom extension.

Reliability

IIS 6.0 allows you to run your Web applications in either of two different modes:

- IIS 5.0 Isolation mode
- Worker Process Isolation mode

IIS 5.0 Isolation mode is used to run older IIS 5.0–compatible applications that do not run natively in IIS 6.0. By default, a Web server that is upgraded from a previous version of IIS is enabled in IIS 5.0 Isolation mode to ensure that the application installed continues to run. IIS 5.0 Isolation mode manages applications in a similar manner to the way that they were managed in IIS 5.0: All in-process applications are run inside a single instance of `inetinfo.exe`, whereas all out-of-process applications are run in separate DLL hosts. Unfortunately, this mode brings along all the problems that were inherent in IIS 5.0, such as a single application bringing the entire Web service down, and memory leaks that require the server to be restarted.

These problems are fixed in the native mode of IIS 6.0, Worker Process Isolation mode. In this mode, applications and processes can be separated into *application pools*. An application pool is a set of one or more applications that are assigned to a set of one or more worker processes. An application pool can contain Web sites, applications, and virtual directories. Each application pool is isolated from the others. Because of this, a failure or memory leak affects only the processes running in that application pool and has no effect on any of the other functions in other application pools.

In Windows Server 2003, you can run in either IIS 5.0 Isolation mode or Worker Process Isolation mode, but not both simultaneously on the same server.

To change the application mode in IIS, follow the procedure outlined in Step by Step 5.11.

STEP BY STEP

5.11 Changing the Application Mode in IIS 6.0

1. Click Start, Administrative Tools, Internet Information Services Manager.

2. The IIS Manager MMC opens with the current isolation mode indicated by the presence or absence of the Application Pools folder, as shown in Figure 5.15.

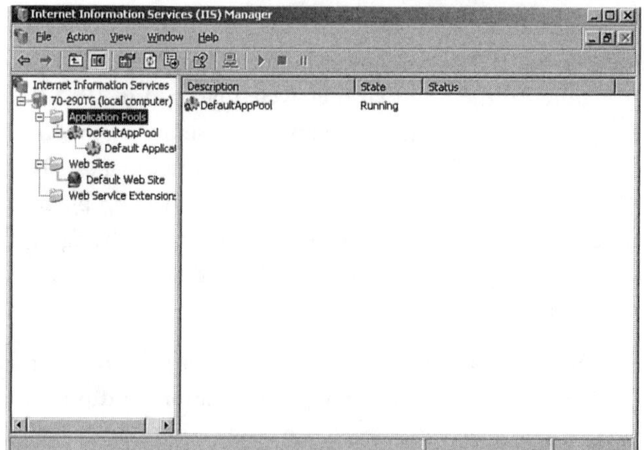

FIGURE 5.15
The IIS Manager MMC, showing the current isolation mode. The server must be in Worker Process Isolation mode because the Application Pools folder is displayed.

3. In the left pane of the MMC, right-click the Web Sites entry and then select Properties from the pop-up menu.

4. From the Web Sites Properties dialog box, click the Service tab. From the Service tab, shown in Figure 5.16, click the Run WWW Service in IIS 5.0 Isolation Mode check box.

5. Click OK to save this setting.

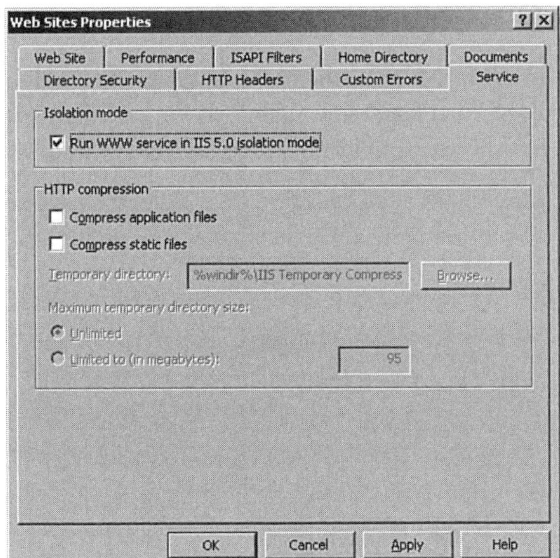

FIGURE 5.16
The Web Sites Properties dialog box, where you can change the isolation mode of the Web server.

When IIS is running in the default Worker Process Isolation mode, all processes are assigned to the default pool, named DefaultAppPool. To take advantage of Worker Process Isolation mode, you should create multiple pools and separate your applications.

To add application pools in IIS, follow the procedure outlined in Step by Step 5.12.

STEP BY STEP

5.12 Adding Application Pools in IIS 6.0

1. Click Start, Administrative Tools, Internet Information Services Manager.
2. The IIS Manager MMC opens with the Worker Process Isolation mode indicated by the presence of the Application Pools folder. If the folder is not present, use the previous procedure to enable Worker Process Isolation mode.

continues

continued

3. In the left pane of the MMC, expand the Application Pools entry and then right-click the DefaultAppPool entry. Select New, Application Pool from the pop-up menu.

4. The Add New Application Pool dialog box appears, as shown in Figure 5.17. Select the configuration settings to use and then click the OK button to save them.

FIGURE 5.17
The Add New Application Pool dialog box. You can use the system defaults or an existing application pool as a template for the configuration.

5. The new application pool entry appears in the MMC.

Management

IIS 6.0 can be managed via the following four methods:

- IIS Manager MMC
- Administration scripting
- Manually editing the configuration file
- Remote Administration Web site

These management options give you greater flexibility in that you can use whatever method of administration makes sense for a particular environment. For example, if you are managing only one or two Web servers, it might not be worth the trouble to write administrative scripts to make configuration changes. In this situation, either making a couple quick changes using the IIS Manager MMC or manually editing the configuration file might be the most efficient way to accomplish the changes. However, in a larger environment, possibly hosting 10 or more Web servers, automating changes via scripting is the only way to go!

IIS Management Using Administrative Scripting

IIS 6.0 installs with a selection of Visual Basic–based scripts that allow you to perform the following functions:

- Starting and stopping Web services
- Creating default Web sites
- Backing up and restoring Web sites
- Configuring Web Extensions
- Managing FTP sites
- Managing IIS configuration

These scripts allow you to automate common tasks from the command line, and to even generate a new Web site from a backup so that a failed server can be replaced. These scripts are stored in the `%systemroot%\System32` folder. All the scripts are ready to be used; just enter the name of the script on the command line to see the required parameters. For additional details on scripting, refer to the IIS online help.

EXAM TIP

Administrative Scripting Although the ability to perform administrative scripting is becoming more essential in most environments, you probably will not see it covered at length on the exam.

IIS Management Through Manually Editing the Metabase

In previous versions of IIS, the configuration information was stored in a binary file called the *Metabase*. Starting in IIS 6.0, this file is no longer stored in a binary format. It is now stored as a plain-text file that can be directly edited via Notepad or a similar text-editing program. This allows you to quickly make changes to the configuration of IIS, even when it is running. You no longer have to start and stop the WWW service to apply configuration changes. The `Metabase.xml` file is stored in the `%systemroot%\System32\inetsrv` folder.

To edit the `Metabase.xml` file without stopping the IIS service, you must ensure that two items are enabled:

- **The Metabase History feature**—This feature saves the last 10 changes to the Metabase file. It is enabled by default.
- **The Enable Direct Metabase Edit feature**—This item is turned on via the Local Computer Properties dialog box in the IIS Manager.

To make configuration changes in IIS by editing the `Metabase.xml` file, follow the procedure outlined in Step by Step 5.13.

STEP BY STEP

5.13 Configuring IIS 6.0 by Editing the Metabase File

1. Click Start, Administrative Tools, Internet Information Services Manager.
2. From the IIS Manager MMC, right-click the Local Computer entry and then select Properties from the pop-up menu.
3. In the Local Computer Properties dialog box, select the Enable Direct Metabase Edit check box, as shown in Figure 5.18.
4. Click OK to save this setting.
5. Click Start, All Programs, Accessories, Notepad.
6. Click File, Open and then navigate to the `%systemroot%\System32\inetsrv` folder and select the `Metabase.xml` file.
7. Click Edit, Find and then enter **IIs5IsolationMode** in the Find dialog box.
8. The entry for IIs5IsolationMode should be highlighted, as shown in Figure 5.19.

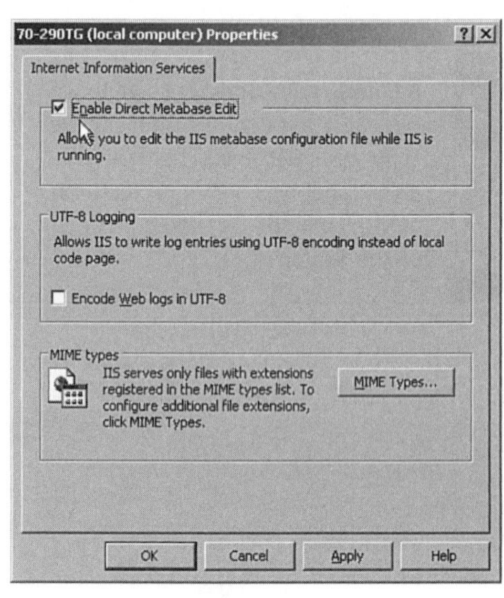

FIGURE 5.18▲
The IIS Manager MMC, showing how to enable direct Metabase editing.

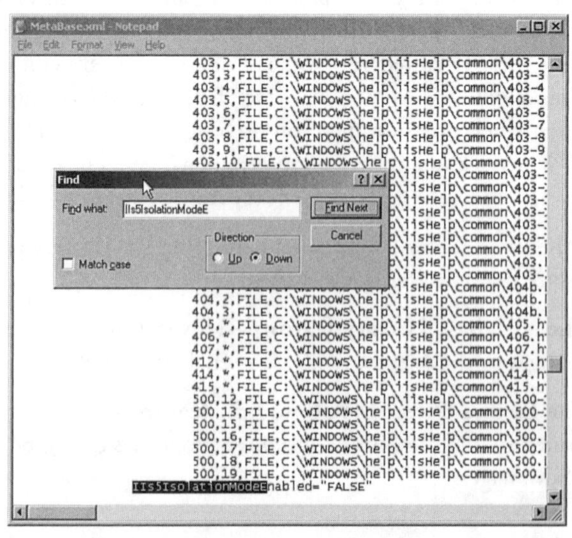

FIGURE 5.19▶
Manually editing the `Metabase.xml` file.

9. Change the entry from FALSE to TRUE and then save the file.
10. In the left pane of the IIS Manager MMC, right-click the Web Sites entry and then select Properties from the pop-up menu.
11. From the Web Sites Properties dialog box, click the Service tab. From the Service tab, notice that the Run WWW Service in IIS 5.0 Isolation Mode check box has been selected.

WARNING

Manually Editing the Metabase Although Microsoft has made it easier to manually edit the Metabase, and even allows you to do it while your Web site is up and running, you should always use extreme caution when doing so.

IIS Management Using the IIS Manager MMC

The IIS Manager MMC, first introduced with the Windows NT 4.0 Option Pack, is still with us, and although the basic operations haven't really changed that much, there have been additional options added to support the new features in IIS 6.0. The IIS snap-in can be added to other MMCs using the methods covered in the beginning of this chapter.

EXAM TIP

Know IIS Manager All the configuration options available in IIS 6.0 can be configured via the IIS Manager MMC, so it is important to become very familiar with its operation, both for your day-to-day administration tasks and for the exam.

You should already be somewhat familiar with the IIS Manager MMC because we have used it in previous examples in this chapter. In the field, the IIS Manager is the most commonly used administrative tool for IIS. It is still the quickest and easiest method of creating and configuring IIS in small-to-medium-sized environments.

The IIS Manager MMC is just like the other MMCs covered in this chapter in that it can be used to configure either the local computer or a remote computer by right-clicking on the Local Computer entry and selecting Connect from the pop-up menu.

Managing the Default Web Site

Unlike previous versions of IIS, which were installed with multiple virtual directories and lots of sample pages that could be exploited by hackers, the default installation of IIS 6.0 is set up with a minimum of files. Basically only enough content is installed to present an Under Construction page, as shown in Figure 5.20.

FIGURE 5.20
The IIS 6.0 default page.

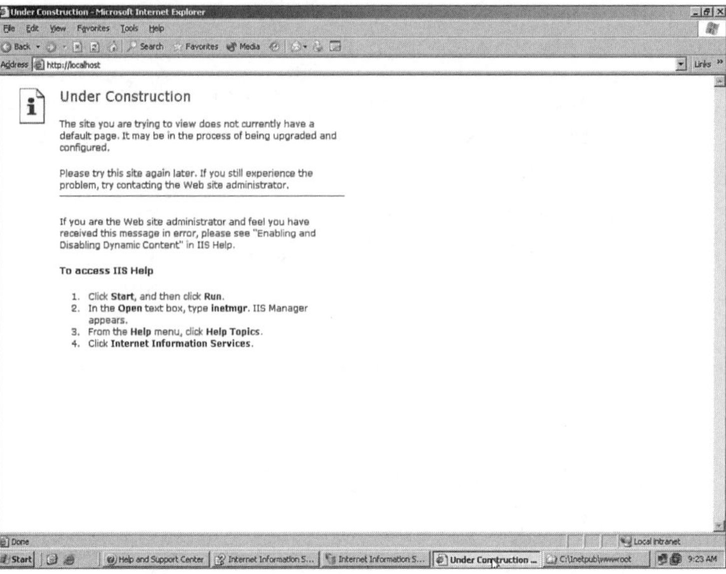

From the IIS Manager MMC, you can set the properties for each Web site, or you can set the defaults for all Web sites hosted on the server. To view and set the defaults for all Web sites, right-click the Web Sites entry in the IIS Manager MMC and then select Properties from the pop-up menu. The default Web Sites Properties dialog box appears with the Web Site tab selected, as shown in Figure 5.21.

FIGURE 5.21
The Web Sites Properties dialog box's Web Site tab.

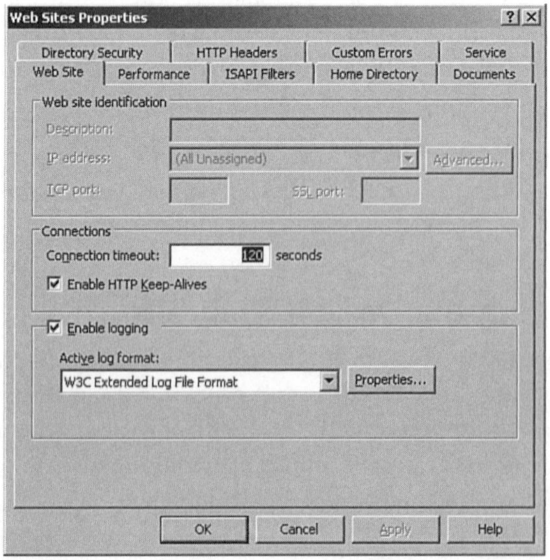

NOTE

Scope of Settings Unless otherwise indicated, the settings shown on the Properties pages can be applied either globally to all Web sites or uniquely to each individual Web site.

From the Web Site tab, you can select the timeout settings, whether to log Web site activity, and the format and the location for the log files. Notice that certain settings, such as the IP Address field, are grayed out. This is because those settings are unique to each individual Web site.

Click the Performance tab, and you are presented with the settings displayed in Figure 5.22.

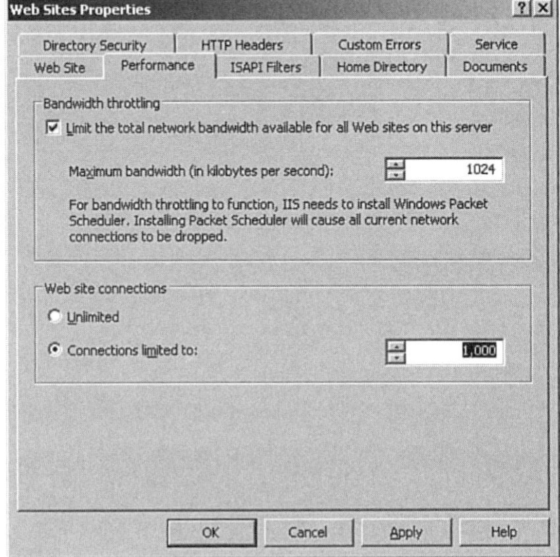

FIGURE 5.22
The Performance tab.

From this tab, you can adjust the settings that determine the overall performance of your Web server. The Bandwidth Throttling setting, along with the Web Site Connections setting, is used to control the amount of bandwidth that is consumed by the Web server, and it also limits the amount of memory that is preallocated to caching. This allows you to prioritize the amount of bandwidth consumed by each Web server over a shared connection. This can be used to ensure that a higher availability Web site is granted more bandwidth than a less significant site.

The ISAPI Filters tab, shown in Figure 5.23, allows you to add custom-written filters that respond to specific events during an HTTP request.

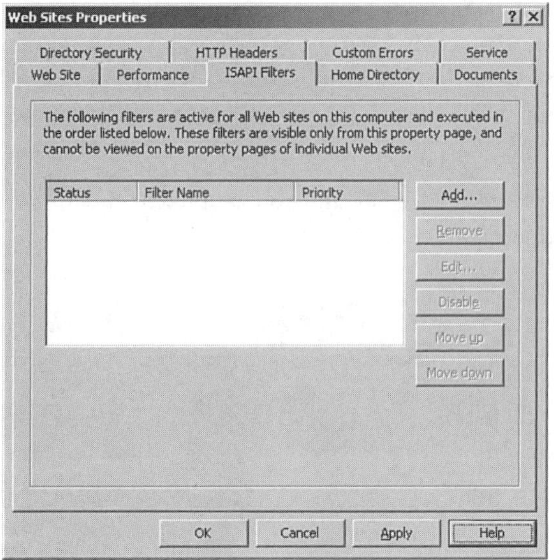

FIGURE 5.23
The ISAPI Filters tab.

The Home Directory tab, shown in Figure 5.24, allows you to specify the location of the files used for your Web sites. This tab is used for individual sites.

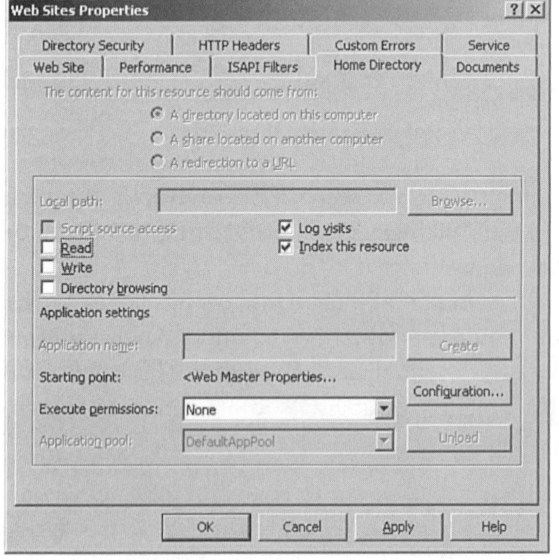

FIGURE 5.24
The Home Directory tab.

The Home Directory tab allows you to assign content for your Web site from the following locations:

- **A directory located on this computer**—This is the default. Enter a local path, or select one by clicking the Browse button and navigating to it.
- **A share located on another computer**—This option allows you to specify a server and share name where the necessary resources are stored. After entering the share name, you have the option of entering a specific user ID and password if needed to access the share by clicking the Connect As button.
- **A redirection to a URL**—This option allows you to specify a Web site or virtual directory that will provide content.

In addition to controlling access via NTFS or share permissions, the Home Directory tab allows you to specify what visitors to the site can do.

The options are as follows:

- **Script Source Access**—If either Read or Write access is selected, this option allows visitors to see the source code of the pages that they are viewing. This option should be selected only for development sites.
- **Read**—This option allows visitors to view the Web pages and to download files. If this option is not selected, the Web site cannot be viewed.
- **Write**—This option allows visitors to upload files to the Web site and to edit the content of a file that they have the necessary permissions for. This option requires a browser that supports HTTP 1.1 or later.
- **Directory Browsing**—This option allows users to see a listing of the files and subdirectories.
- **Log Visits**—This option allows you to select to log all user interaction with the site. This option requires logging to be enabled on the Web Site tab.
- **Index This Resource**—If the Indexing service was installed, this option allows the site to be indexed for faster searching.

The Execute Permissions field allows you to select what type of scripts or executable files can be invoked by a browser:

- **None**—With this option, only static HTML pages or image files will be displayed.
- **Scripts Only**—This option allows ASP scripts to run; however, executables such as ASAPI DLLs and CGIBIN applications cannot be run.
- **Scripts and Executables**—This option allows any file type to be run.

> **WARNING**
>
> **Invitation to Disaster** Allowing both Execute and Write access allows visitors to upload and execute any code that they want on your site.

The Application Pool drop-down list allows you to specify which of the application pools you have created the Web site is to be a member of.

The Documents tab, shown in Figure 5.25, is used to specify the default document that is sent to the browser when no specific document is requested. This can be either a home page or an index page. The Enable Document Footer option allows you to attach a footer to every document that is displayed.

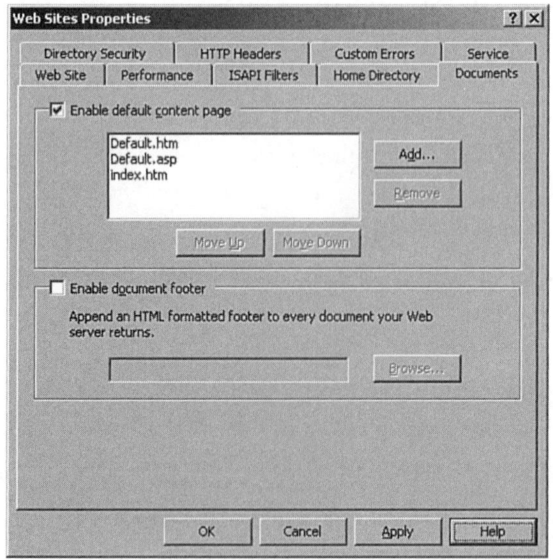

FIGURE 5.25
The Documents tab.

The Directory Security tab, shown in Figure 5.26, allows you to control the access to your Web site. This tab is covered at length in the section "Managing Security for IIS."

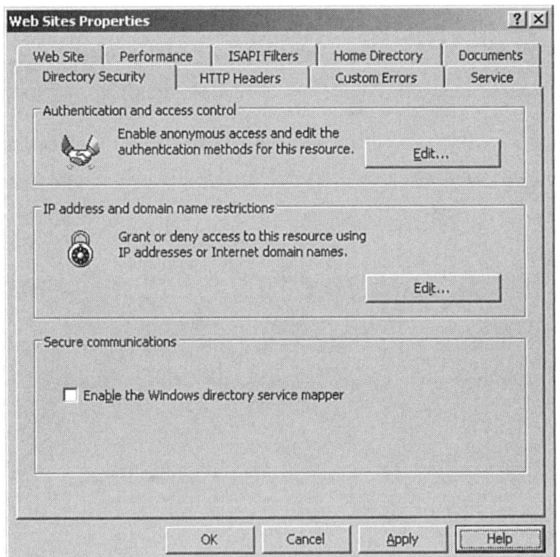

FIGURE 5.26
The Directory Security tab.

The HTTP Headers tab, shown in Figure 5.27, allows you to configure the values returned to the browser via the header included in the HTML page. These values include Content Expiration, which tells the browser when to refresh cached pages, Content Rating, which identifies the type of content provided by the site, and the Mime Types setting, which maps a file extension to a file type.

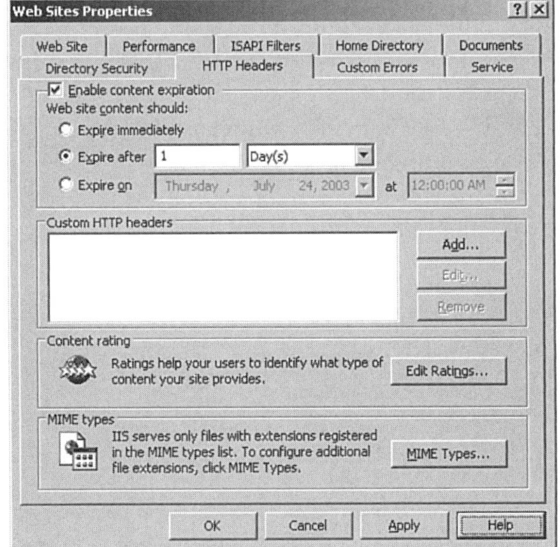

FIGURE 5.27
The HTTP Headers tab.

The Custom HTTP Headers option allows you to send custom HTTP headers to a client browser. These can be used to support browser features that the Web site does not yet officially support.

The Custom Errors tab, shown in Figure 5.28, allows you to define replacement error messages. Instead of the default numerical messages, you can define something more informative.

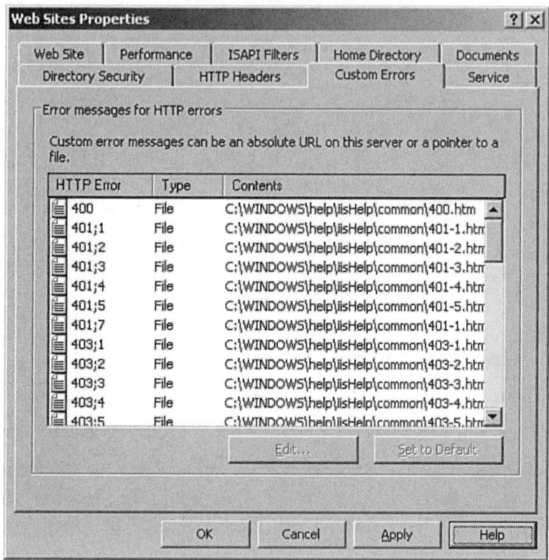

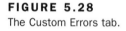

FIGURE 5.28
The Custom Errors tab.

The Service tab, shown in Figure 5.29, allows you to set the mode in which the Web server is run—either IIS 5.0 Isolation mode or Worker Process Isolation mode. There are also settings for HTTP Compression. HTTP Compression mode allows you to compress static files or dynamic content, or both, to be sent to the browser. Sending compressed files consumes less bandwidth, and this feature can be very useful in limited-bandwidth situations.

However, compressing and uncompressing the files consumes additional processing cycles, both on the Web server and the client, so the HTTP Compression options should not be enabled if the Web server is already processor starved.

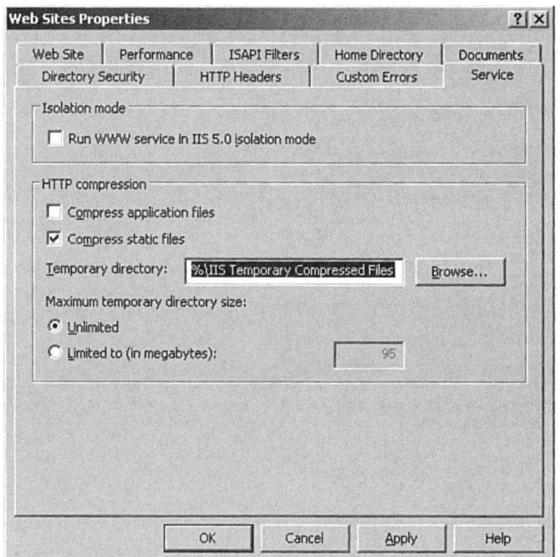

FIGURE 5.29
The Service tab.

Creating a Web Site

Like most other functions in Windows Server 2003, a wizard is supplied to make creating a Web site easier. To create a new Web site, follow the procedure outlined in Step by Step 5.14.

STEP BY STEP

5.14 Creating a New Web Site

1. Click Start, Administrative Tools, Internet Information Services Manager.
2. From the IIS Manager MMC, right-click the Web Sites entry and then select New, Web Site from the pop-up menu.
3. On the Welcome to the Web Site Creation Wizard screen, click the Next button to continue.

continues

continued

4. On the Web Site Description screen, type in a descriptive name for the Web site. Click the Next button to continue.

5. The IP Address and Port Settings screen appears, as shown in Figure 5.30. From this screen, you can select the IP address, TCP port, or host header to which this Web site will respond. Make the appropriate choices, and then click the Next button to continue.

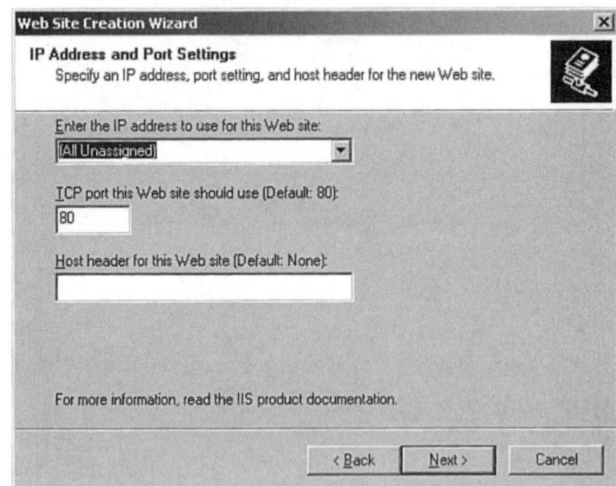

FIGURE 5.30
Specify the IP or port settings for the new Web site.

6. The Web Site Home Directory screen appears. From this screen, you can select the folder that contains the files for your Web site. You can also specify that you want to allow anonymous access to your site. Make the appropriate choices and then click the Next button to continue.

7. The Web Site Access Permissions screen appears, as shown in Figure 5.31. From this screen, you can specify the permissions you are granting visitors to your Web site. You should always specify the minimum permissions needed. Make the appropriate choices and then click the Next button to continue.

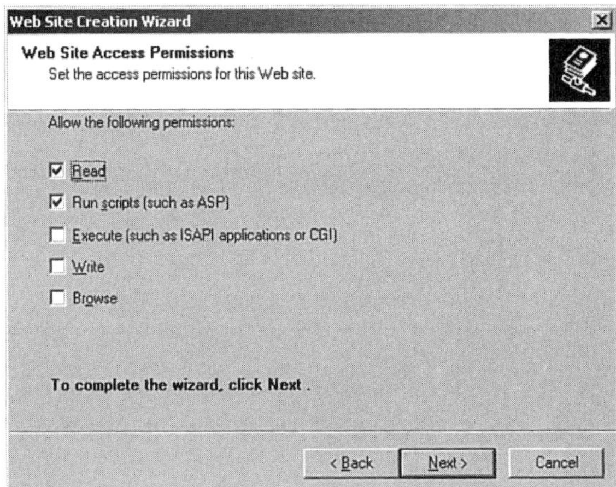

FIGURE 5.31
Specify the permissions for the files for the new Web site.

8. When the Finishing the Web Site Creation Wizard screen appears, click the Finish button to save your settings. The new Web site appears in the IIS Manager console, listed under the Default Web Site entry.

Hosting Multiple Web Sites

In the previous Step by Step, you learned how to add an additional Web site to a Web server, but we left out one small detail. If a Web server is hosting multiple Web sites, how do you determine which Web site is presented to the browser?

When you're hosting multiple Web sites on a single server, each Web site must have a unique identity. This is accomplished by using the following identifiers:

- **Unique IP address**—Commonly used for Web sites accessed over the Internet. This is required when Secure Sockets Layer (SSL) is used.
- **Host header name**—Also commonly used, both over the Internet and within intranets.
- **Nonstandard port number**—Nonstandard port numbers, such as TCP port numbers, are rarely used on production Web servers.

By configuring one or more of these identifiers, you can uniquely identify each Web site on your server. When using multiple IP addresses to identify the Web sites on your server, you can either install multiple network interface cards (NICs), each with a unique IP address, or just assign multiple IP addresses to a single NIC.

To identify a new Web site by IP address, use the procedure outlined in Step by Step 5.15.

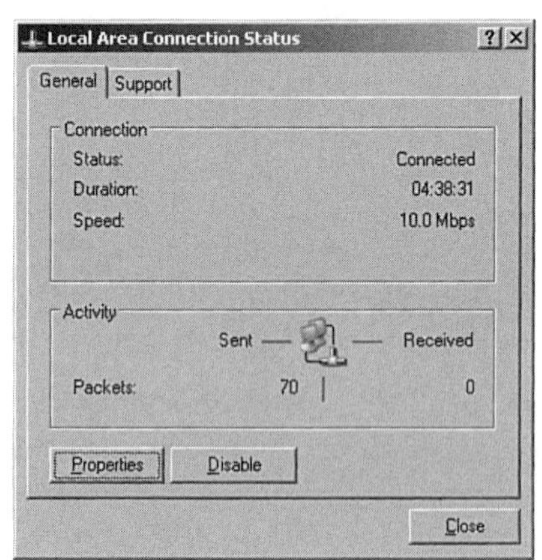

FIGURE 5.32
The Local Area Connection Status dialog box.

STEP BY STEP

5.15 Identifying a New Web Site by IP Address

1. Click Start, Control Panel, Network Connections, Local Area Connection.
2. From the Local Area Connection Status dialog box, shown in Figure 5.32, click the Properties button.
3. From the Local Area Connection Properties dialog box, highlight the Internet Protocol (TCP/IP) entry and then click the Properties button.
4. When the Internet Protocol (TCP/IP) Properties dialog box appears, click the Advanced button.
5. From the Advanced TCP/IP Settings dialog box, click the Add button.
6. From the Advanced TCP/IP Address dialog box, enter the new IP address and subnet mask. When you're finished, click the Add button. Repeat this process for additional addresses.
7. Click OK twice and then click the Close button on the Local Area Connection Properties dialog box and the Local Area Connection Status dialog box to save your settings.
8. Click Start, Administrative Tools, Internet Information Services Manager.
9. From the IIS Manager MMC, right-click the Web Sites entry and then select New, Web Site from the pop-up menu.
10. On the Welcome to the Web Site Creation Wizard screen, click the Next button to continue.

11. On the Web Site Description screen, type in a descriptive name for the Web site. Click the Next button to continue.

12. The IP Address and Port Settings screen appears, as shown in Figure 5.33. Notice that if you click the drop-down list for the IP Address field, the new IP address you entered in the previous steps is available. Select the new IP address for your Web site and then refer to the information in Step by Step 5.14 to complete the Web site configuration.

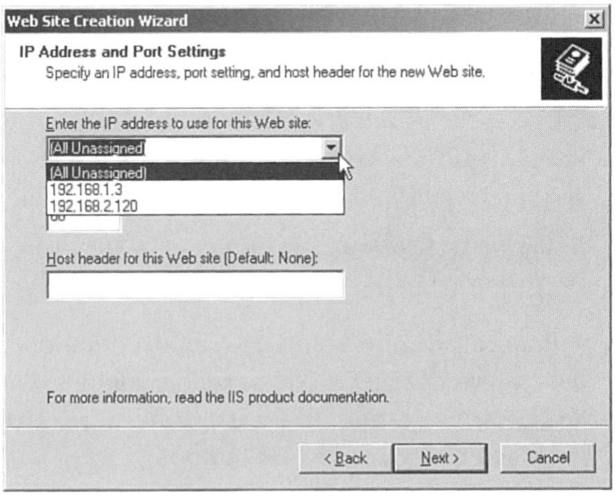

FIGURE 5.33
The IP Address and Port Settings screen.

With the explosion in popularity of the Internet and the slow adoption of IPv6, the number of available IP addresses is dwindling rapidly. This means that it's not always possible or feasible to lease multiple IP addresses from an ISP to host multiple Web sites. Fortunately, Web sites can also be configured to respond to a unique host header.

A *host header* is nothing more than a unique DNS name that is used to identify one of the additional Web sites. The site that is using the host header shares the same port and IP address, but when the browser connects to the default Web site, it asks for the site using the host header entry. The server reads the request from the browser and directs it to the requested site. This allows you to host multiple sites at the same IP address; they just have to have unique header names, such as `www.abc.com`, `www.xyz.com`, and so on.

Host headers require that you use a browser that supports HTTP 1.1 or later. If your browser does not support HTTP 1.1, you will be connected to the default Web site.

To identify a Web site by host header, use the procedure outlined in Step by Step 5.16.

STEP BY STEP

5.16 Identifying a Web Site by Host Header

1. Click Start, Administrative Tools, Internet Information Services Manager.
2. From the IIS Manager MMC, right-click a Web site entry and then select Properties from the pop-up menu.
3. From the Web Site tab of the Properties dialog box, click the Advanced button.
4. This opens the Advanced Web Site Identification dialog box, shown in Figure 5.34. To add an additional host header to the existing IP address, highlight the IP address entry and then click the Add button.

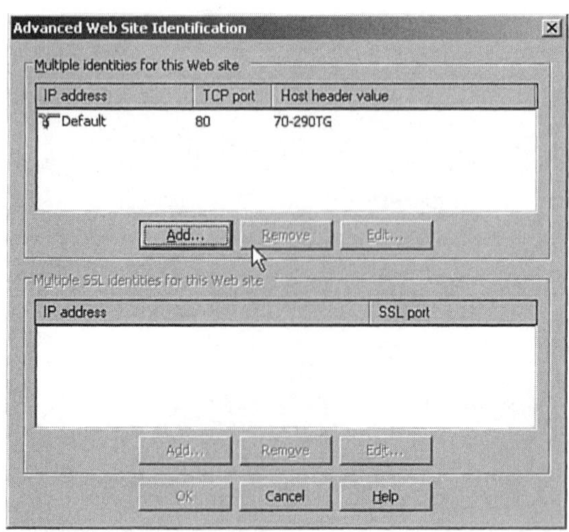

FIGURE 5.34
The Advanced Web Site Identification dialog box.

NOTE **Additional Security** Because all the sites now have host headers, you will not be able to connect to the Web site by IP address, giving an additional layer of security.

5. This opens the Add/Edit Web Site Identification dialog box, shown in Figure 5.35. Enter the desired host header name and assign it to port 80. Then click the OK button to save your settings. Repeat this for any additional host headers.

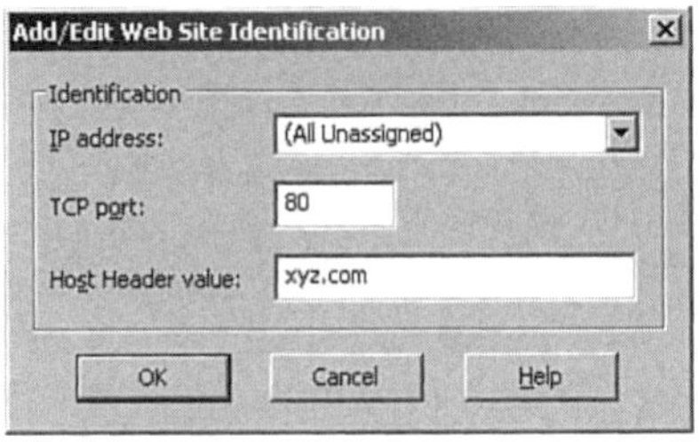

FIGURE 5.35
The Add/Edit Web Site Identification dialog box. Note that you can enter unique port numbers using this dialog box.

As noted in the previous procedure, the port number can be changed as well. When you're using a unique port number, it has to be entered in the URL as follows:

```
www.abc.com:60
```

A port number can be any number from 1 to 65535. Port numbers are rarely used, except for testing purposes.

NOTE

Port Numbers Although it is technically true that any port to 65K can be used, it is not the best idea to use any well-known ports for this purpose. Ports such as 25 (SMTP), 110 (POP), 3268 (LDAP), and 443 (SSL), among many others, would not make sense to serve Web pages from.

GUIDED PRACTICE EXERCISE 5.2

When new Web sites and applications are added to a Web server, by default they are placed in the DefaultAppPool application pool. To obtain the maximum benefit from running IIS 6.0, you should assign your applications to separate application pools.

In this scenario, you are required to create a new Web site and then assign it to a new application pool. You should do this using as few steps as possible.

How would you set this up?

You should try working through this problem on your own first. If you get stuck, or if you'd like to see one possible solution, follow these steps:

1. Click Start, Administrative Tools, Internet Information Services Manager.
2. From the IIS Manager MMC, right-click the Web Sites entry and then select New, Web Site from the pop-up menu.
3. On the Welcome to the Web Site Creation Wizard screen, click the Next button to continue.

EXAM TIP

SSL and Host Headers Don't Mix Host headers cannot be used with SSL because the domain name is encoded in the certificate, and the browser is able to see only the IP address. When using SSL, you must use unique IP addresses.

continues

continued

4. On the Web Site Description screen, type in a descriptive name for the Web site. Click the Next button to continue.
5. The IP Address and Port Settings screen appears. From this screen, you can select the IP address, TCP port, or host header to which this Web site will respond. Make the appropriate choices and then click the Next button to continue.
6. The Web Site Home Directory screen appears. From this screen, you can select the folder that contains the files for your Web site. You can also specify that you want to allow anonymous access to your site. Make the appropriate choices and then click the Next button to continue.
7. The Web Site Access Permissions screen appears. From this screen, you can specify the permissions you are granting visitors to your Web site. You should always specify the minimum permissions needed. Make the appropriate choices and then click the Next button to continue.
8. When the Finishing the Web Site Creation Wizard screen appears, click the Finish button to save your settings.
9. From the IIS Manager MMC, expand the Web Sites entry, right-click the name of the Web site you just created, and then select Properties from the pop-up menu.
10. This opens the Web Sites Properties dialog box. Click the Home Directory tab.
11. From the Home Directory tab, shown in Figure 5.36, select the application pool you want to assign the Web site to. Click the OK button to save this setting.
12. The Web site is listed in the assigned application pool.

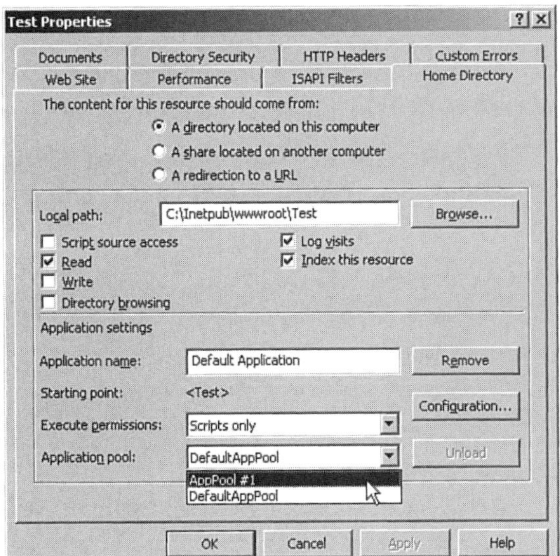

FIGURE 5.36

The Home Directory tab, where you select the application pool to which to assign the Web site.

IIS Management Using the Remote Administration Console

The Remote Administration Console can be used to configure IIS 6.0 from a browser—either via the local LAN or from the Internet. Unlike in previous versions of IIS, which installed the Remote Administration Console by default, in IIS 6.0, it must be installed manually.

To install the IIS Remote Administration Console, use the procedure outlined in Step by Step 5.17.

STEP BY STEP

5.17 Installing the IIS Remote Administration Console

1. Click Start, All Programs, Control Panel, Add or Remove Programs.

continues

continued

2. Click the Add/Remove Windows Components button in the left pane of the Add or Remove Programs dialog box.
3. The Windows Components Wizard appears. Select the Application Server check box. Click the Details button to continue.
4. The Application Server dialog box appears. Select the Internet Information Services entry. Click the Details button to continue.
5. The Internet Information Services dialog box appears. Select the World Wide Web Service entry. Click the Details button to continue.
6. The World Wide Web Service dialog box appears, as shown in Figure 5.37. Select the Remote Administration check box. Click the OK button three times to continue.

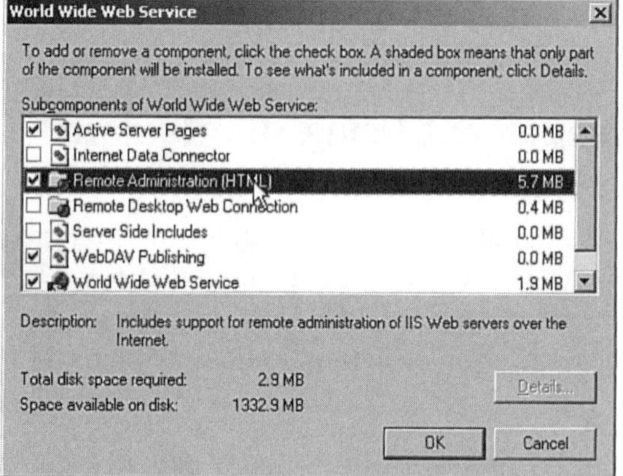

FIGURE 5.37
The World Wide Web Service dialog box.

7. This returns you to the Windows Components Wizard. Click the Next button to continue.
8. The Configuring Components screen appears. When prompted, insert the Windows Server 2003 CD-ROM and then click the OK button to continue.
9. When the Completing the Windows Component Wizard screen appears, click the Finish button.

After the Remote Administration Console is installed, it appears listed as the Administration Web site in the IIS Manager MMC.

By default, the Administration Web site can be reached via a Web browser using SSL on port 8098, but this can be changed at any time. To access it, use the following syntax:

`https://servername:8098`

From the opening screen, shown in Figure 5.38, you can use the various wizards to perform most of the common administrative tasks.

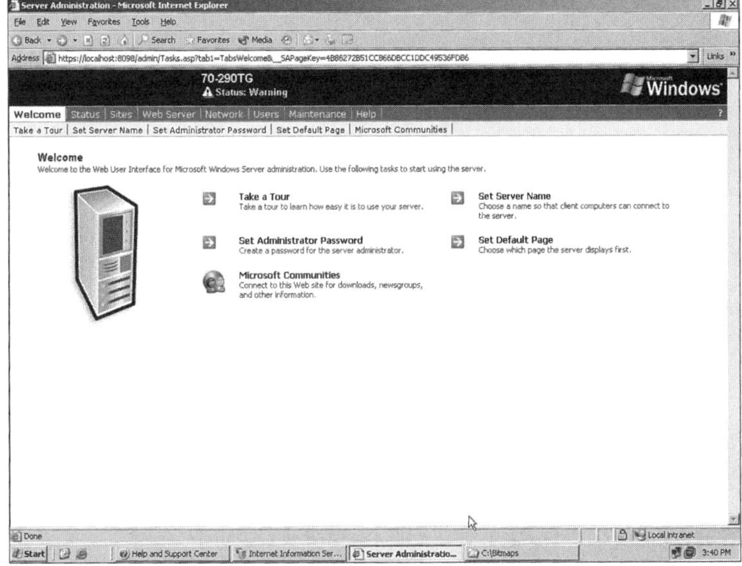

FIGURE 5.38
The Administration Web site.

Unlike previous versions of IIS, which upon installation restricted access to the Remote Administration Console to localhost, in Windows Server 2003, the Remote Administration Console can be reached from any IP address. This seems strange considering Microsoft has locked down so many other areas of Windows Server 2003. However, it is a simple task to restrict access to a specified range of IP addresses using the procedure in Step by Step 5.18.

STEP BY STEP

5.18 Restricting the Remote Administration Console

1. Click Start, Administrative Tools, Internet Information Services Manager.
2. From the IIS Manager MMC, right-click the Administration Web site entry and then select Properties from the pop-up menu.
3. From the Directory Security tab of the Administration Properties dialog box, shown in Figure 5.39, click the Edit button in the IP Address and Domain Name Restrictions area.

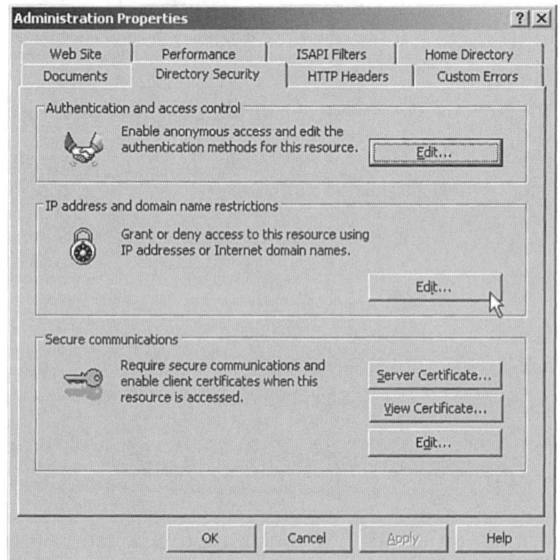

FIGURE 5.39
Configuring security for the Remote Administration Console.

4. This opens the IP Address and Domain Name Restrictions dialog box, shown in Figure 5.40. This dialog box requires some explanation. The IP addresses and domain names that you enter here are the *exceptions.* For example, if you select the Granted Access radio button, the IP addresses or domains you enter will be denied access to the Web site because the logic indicates that all IP addresses and domains will be granted access *except* those listed. To add a specific IP subnet to accept connections from, select the Denied Access radio button and then click the Add button.

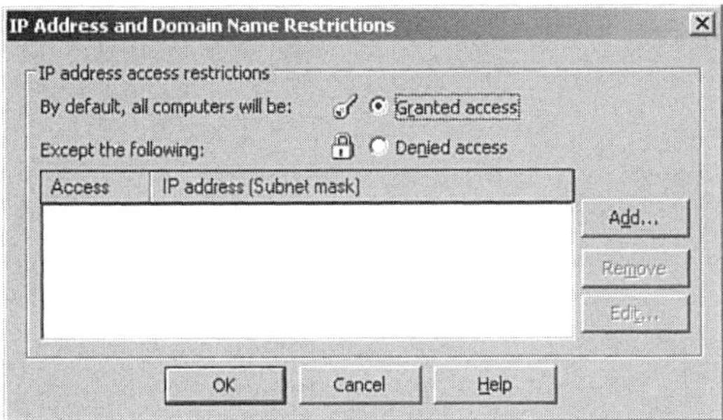

FIGURE 5.40◀
The IP Address and Domain Name Restrictions dialog box.

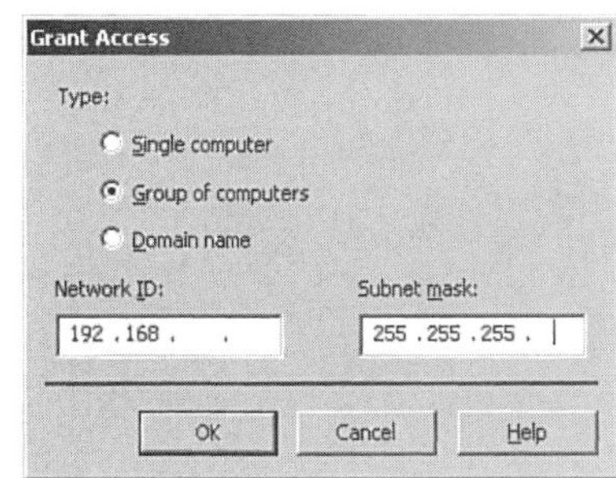

FIGURE 5.41▲
The Grant Access dialog box. Note that you can enter IP addresses or domain names using this dialog box.

5. This opens the Grant Access dialog box, shown in Figure 5.41. Enter the desired IP address(es) or domain names and then click the OK button to save your settings. Repeat this for any additional IP addresses or domain names.

6. This returns you to the IP Address and Domain Name Restrictions dialog box. Confirm that the settings are correct and then click the OK button twice to save.

> NOTE
>
> **Performance Hit** Selecting Domain Name restrictions impacts the performance of your server as reverse DNS lookups are performed.

Managing Security for IIS

As mentioned earlier in the chapter, IIS is probably the subsystem of Windows Server 2003 that has received the most attention, especially related to security. In IIS 6.0, the worker processes and most of the ASP functions run in the Network Service security context, which is a low-privileged context. In addition, each of these worker processes can exist in separate application pools, thereby isolating them from other processes. This lessens the exposure to poorly written code or of hackers inserting malicious code that would crash the entire Web server.

In addition, when a buffer overflow occurs, previously a favorite exploit, the worker processes automatically terminate. With these low-level changes and the refusal to accept requests for files with unknown extensions, in addition to preventing the execution of command-line tools, IIS 6.0 is far more secure than any previous version.

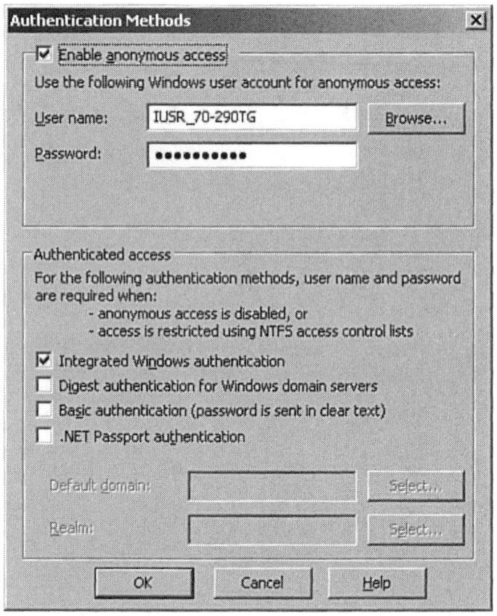

FIGURE 5.42
Multiple authentication methods are available from this dialog box.

We partially covered the contents of the Directory Security tab when configuring restrictions for access to the Remote Administration Console. We have already examined how to restrict access to a Web site by IP address and domain name. However, several other settings are important to IIS security.

If you select the Edit button in the Authentication and Access Control section of the Directory Security tab, you open the Authentication Methods dialog box, shown in Figure 5.42.

When IIS is installed, two accounts are created: IUSR_*servername* and IWAM_*servername*. IWAM_*servername* is run in the Network Service security context and is used to start and run most applications. The IUSR_*servername* account is a member of the GUEST local group and is used to control anonymous access to published resources on IIS. For example, if you have a Web site that you want to publish so that anyone on the Internet can access it without authentication, you would use the IUSR_*servername* account to assign read access to the necessary resources. You have the ability to change the account used for anonymous access, or you can disable anonymous access completely.

The second half of the dialog box controls authenticated access. Authenticated access is used to integrate the Web server with Windows security. The user is required to present a user ID and password to access Web site resources. These user IDs and passwords are stored either as a local account on the Web server or in the Active Directory domain database. When anonymous access is disabled, all users who attempt to access the Web site are prompted for a user ID and password. Authentication is also required when the Web site resources are protected via NTFS permissions.

Four types of authenticated access are available:

- **Integrated Windows Authentication**—If the Web server and the client are members of trusted domains, the browser passes the user ID and password to the Web server automatically and the user is not prompted for a password. This method does not work through some firewalls, but it's fine for intranets. The password is transmitted as a hash value.
- **Digest Authentication**—This method is supported only if the client is using Internet Explorer 5 or later, in an Active Directory domain, and the password is stored in clear text.

However, this method works through most firewalls. The password is transmitted as an MD5 hash value.

- **Basic Authentication**—This is the least secure method because it transmits the password as clear text. However, it is supported by just about any browser available. Basic Authentication is usually used in combination with SSL so that the passwords are encrypted.
- **.NET Passport Authentication**—This is a new feature in Windows Server 2003. This method uses the Passport Authentication system that Microsoft is marketing to e-commerce Web sites. It allows a user to create a single sign-on that is honored across various Passport-enabled sites. Authentication is performed by a central Passport Authentication server. When Passport Authentication is selected, a default domain must be specified.

The final two options available from the Authentication Methods dialog box are as follows:

- **Default Domain**—By entering the name of the default domain, users who are members of that domain will not need to enter the domain name when logging on to the Web site.
- **Realm**—This field allows you to specify the name of an alternate authentication service, such as a Remote Authentication Dial-Up User Service (RADIUS) server or Microsoft's Internet Authentication Server (IAS).

As mentioned briefly in the previous paragraphs, NTFS can be used to control access to resources on the Web server. For example, if anonymous access is enabled, but there are sensitive areas on your Web server, you can control access to those areas using NTFS security. You can simply exclude or deny access for those resources to the Anonymous user account. The user is prompted for a user ID and password when she attempts to access those resources.

Another method of securing access to a Web server is via Secure Sockets Layer (SSL). We mentioned SSL briefly in this chapter, but we haven't taken the time to explain it yet. SSL is used with HTTP to encrypt all traffic between the browser and the Web server. This is especially critical for e-commerce sites because the last thing you want to do is to transmit your credit card number in clear text over the Internet!

SSL works by using encryption keys—in this case, certificates that are distributed by a trusted source. These certificates are used to encrypt the data that passes between the client and the Web server. Certificates are issued by Certificate Authorities (CAs), of which VeriSign is the most prominent. Web site administrators apply to the CA for a certificate, and they have to provide the proper credentials to prove their identity. After the CA is satisfied that they are who they say they are, the CA issues the certificates, and the Web site administrators install them on their Web servers.

This same process can be used by enterprises using their own CAs to issue certificates to employees or contractors wishing to access Web content from outside the boundaries of these organizations' LANs. In this case, the CA issuing the certificates is not a public CA (like VeriSign) but rather a private one controlled internally. In many cases, organizations choose to run Microsoft Certificate Services to issue and manage these certificates. Other CA software vendors also exist, but Microsoft's CA is the most common because the software is included as part of Windows Server 2003 for no additional charge.

When clients try to access the Web site, they might be presented with a prompt asking whether they trust the source of the certificate. This normally does not occur if the Web server is using a certificate issued by VeriSign or one of the other common CAs. The client and the Web server then negotiate a connection, and all traffic between them is encrypted.

In addition to server certificates, clients can be issued certificates also. This enables a password-free logon because the certificate serves as both the user ID and password. Three steps are involved in setting up SSL on a Web server:

1. Generate a certificate request.
2. Install the certificate.
3. Configure the server to use certificates.

To generate a certificate request, use the procedure in Step by Step 5.19.

STEP BY STEP

5.19 Generating a Certificate Request

1. Click Start, Administrative Tools, Internet Information Services Manager.
2. From the IIS Manager MMC, right-click the Web site entry and then select Properties from the pop-up menu.
3. From the Directory Security tab of the Properties dialog box, click the Server Certificate button.
4. This opens the IIS Certificate Wizard. Click the Next Button to Continue.
5. The Server Certificate screen appears, as shown in Figure 5.43. Select the Create a New Certificate radio button and then click the Next button.

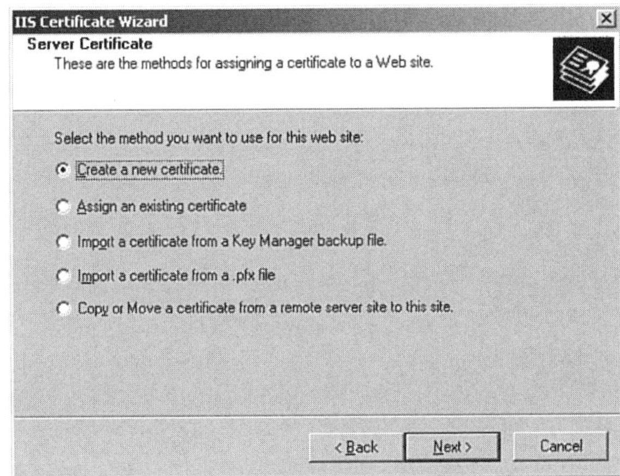

FIGURE 5.43
The Server Certificate screen presents various options to use with certificates.

6. The Delayed or Immediate Request screen appears. Select the Prepare the Request Now, but Send It Later radio button. Click the Next button to continue.
7. The Name and Security Settings screen appears. Enter a descriptive name for the Web site, and provide the length of the key. A long key is more secure. Click the Next button to continue.

continues

continued

8. The Organization Information screen appears. Enter a descriptive name for your organization. Click the Next button to continue.
9. The Site Common Name screen appears. Enter the DNS name for your Web site. Click the Next button to continue.
10. The Geographical Information screen appears. Enter the appropriate information for your organization. Click the Next button to continue.
11. The Certificate Request File Name screen appears. Enter the location where you want to save the certificate request file. Click the Next button to continue.
12. The Request File Summary screen appears, as shown in Figure 5.44. Confirm that the settings are correct and then click the Next button to continue.

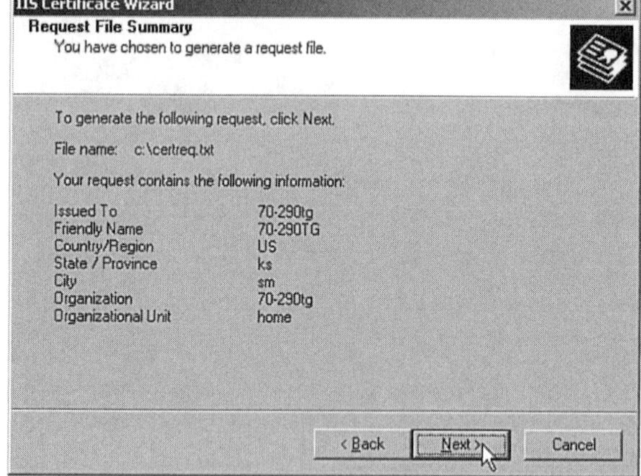

FIGURE 5.44
Verify the settings.

13. Click Finish to save the request file.

After the request file has been created, it must be sent to the Certificate Authority for approval. After the CA has processed your request, you receive a certificate from the CA. To install the received certificate, follow the procedure outlined in Step by Step 5.20.

STEP BY STEP

5.20 Installing a Certificate

1. Click Start, Administrative Tools, Internet Information Services Manager.
2. From the IIS Manager MMC, right-click the Web site entry and then select Properties from the pop-up menu.
3. From the Directory Security tab of the Properties dialog box, click the Server Certificate button.
4. This opens the IIS Certificate Wizard. Click the Next Button to Continue.
5. The Pending Certificate Request screen appears, as shown in Figure 5.45. Select the Process the Pending Request and Install the Certificate radio button and then click the Next button.

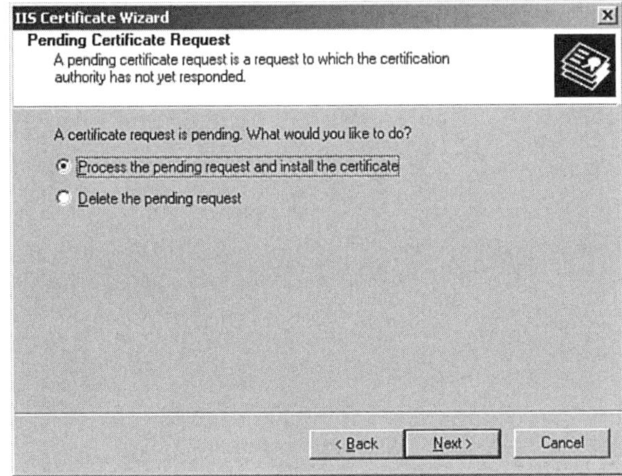

FIGURE 5.45
The Pending Certificate Request screen allows you to process the request or delete it.

6. The Process a Pending Request screen appears. Select the path and filename of the certificate. Click the Next button to continue.
7. The certificate is loaded, and you are presented with the Certification Summary screen. If the displayed configuration is correct, click the Next button to continue.
8. Click the Finish button.

After the certificate is installed, the final step is to configure the settings on the Web site to use SSL. To configure the Web site to support SSL, follow the procedure outlined in Step by Step 5.21.

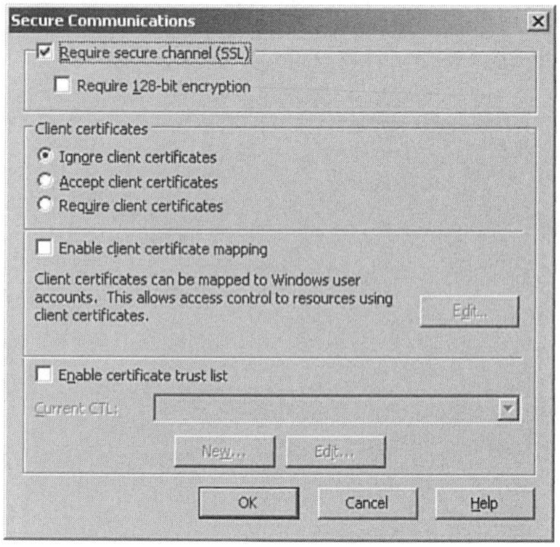

FIGURE 5.46
SSL can be used with 40-bit encryption (the default) or 128-bit encryption.

STEP BY STEP

5.21 Configuring the Web Site to Support SSL

1. Click Start, Administrative Tools, Internet Information Services Manager.
2. From the IIS Manager MMC, right-click the Web site entry and then select Properties from the pop-up menu.
3. From the Directory Security tab of the Properties dialog box, click the Edit button in the Secure Communications area.
4. This opens the Secure Communications dialog box, shown in Figure 5.46. Select the Require Secure Channel (SSL) check box. Then click the OK button.

Managing security for IIS 6.0 is an important topic, especially in light of all the attention IIS has received as a favored target for hackers. It is important to understand that one of the best strategies to secure IIS is to enable only the minimal features required to support the applications being run on IIS. Also, never grant more authority to any users than they will ever possibly require.

MANAGING A SOFTWARE UPDATE INFRASTRUCTURE

No matter how well it seems that software is written, there is always a need for bug fixes and security patches. In addition, there never seems to be an end to the need for updated drivers and minor feature upgrades. Sometimes it seems that the system administrator's job never ends.

The later versions of Windows include the Windows Update feature. Windows Update is used to keep your Windows system up to date by connecting to the Microsoft Windows Update Web site over the Internet and automatically downloading and installing security fixes, critical updates, and new drivers. These updates are used to resolve known security and stability issues with the Windows operating system.

Although relying on Windows Update is fine if you have only a few computers, in an enterprise environment, it leaves much to be desired. Consider the following:

- Most of the updates require the user to have administrative rights on the computer. This is rarely allowed in an enterprise environment.
- The updates have not been tested in the user's specific environment. If an update has a conflict with other software on the network, it can bring the company to its knees.
- Each computer is responsible for downloading its own updates. This can be bandwidth intensive if you have a large environment.

Fortunately, Microsoft has provided Software Update Services (SUS) to assist the system administrator in managing updates in the small-to-medium-sized enterprise environment.

Microsoft SUS is a service that can be installed on an internal Windows 2000 or Windows Server 2003 server that can download all critical updates as they are posted to Windows Update. Administrators can also receive email notification when new critical updates have been posted.

The client computers and servers can be configured through Group Policy or the Registry to contact the internal SUS server for updates, instead of going out over the Internet to the Microsoft servers. SUS is basically an internal version of the Windows Update service, with the exception that the network administrator has the option to control which updates get downloaded from Microsoft and which ones get installed on the computers in the environment.

SUS allows administrators to quickly and easily deploy most updates to Windows 2000 or Windows Server 2003 servers as well as desktop computers running Windows 2000 Professional or Windows XP Professional.

You can install multiple SUS servers in your environment, both for load balancing or for test purposes. For example, you can set up an SUS server to automatically download all of the latest updates from Microsoft. After they have been downloaded, you can distribute the updates to test computers to verify compatibility with the existing software. After the updates have been tested, they can be published to the production environment.

The SUS servers can be set up in a hierarchy, as shown in Figure 5.47. In this example, the SUS server in the headquarters is configured to run a scheduled synchronization with the Microsoft Windows Update Web site. The administrator then publishes the updates to a group of test computers. After testing has been completed, the approved updates on the HQ server are synchronized with the other SUS servers in the enterprise.

FIGURE 5.47
A sample SUS infrastructure.

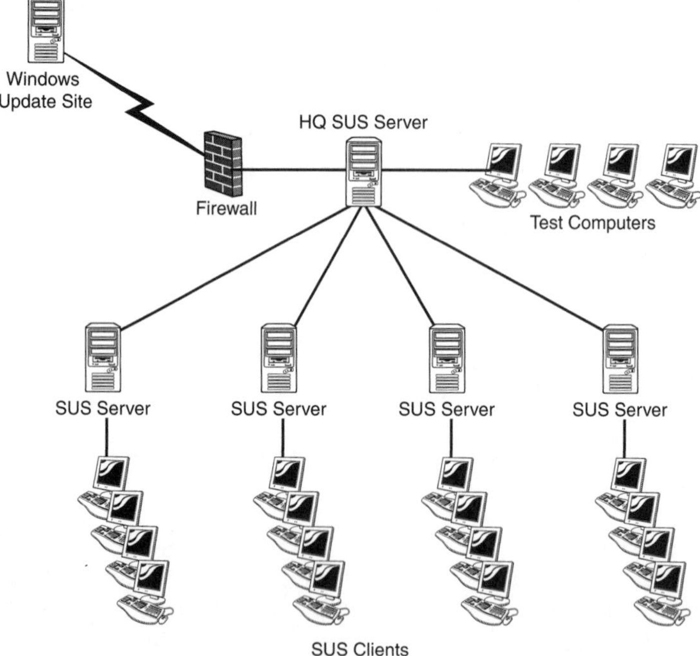

The SUS clients can be configured to point to a specific SUS server so that, in a WAN environment, they always receive updates from the server that is closest to them. You can also configure how often the clients should check their local SUS server for updates.

Installing Software Update Services

SUS is not included with Windows Server 2003; instead, it must be downloaded from the Microsoft Web site at `www.microsoft.com/windows2000/windowsupdate/sus/default.asp`. The requirements for SUS are as follows:

- Windows 2000 Service Pack 2 or later
- IIS 5.0 or later
- Internet Explorer 6.0 or later
- Pentium III 700MHz or higher
- 512MB RAM
- 6GB of hard drive space formatted as NTFS

To install SUS, use the procedure in Step by Step 5.22.

STEP BY STEP

5.22 Installing SUS

1. Locate the downloaded SUS install file and then double-click it to start the installation.
2. From the Setup Wizard screen, click the Next button to continue.
3. Select the I Accept the Terms in the License Agreement radio button and click the Next button to continue.
4. From the Choose Setup Type screen, click the Custom button.
5. The Choose File Locations screen appears. Select the folders in which to store the Web site files and the updates. Then click the Next button.
6. The Language Settings screen appears. You can select English, another specific language, or all available languages. The more languages you select, the more content you must download. Make a selection and then click the Next button to continue.

continues

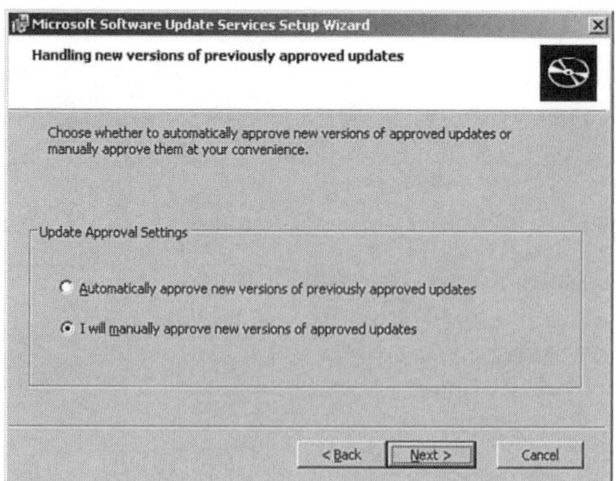

FIGURE 5.48
Choose how to handle updated versions of previously approved updates.

continued

7. The Handling New Versions of Previously Approved Updates screen appears, as shown in Figure 5.48. The Update Approval Settings area of this screen allows you to specify how to handle updated versions of updates. Make a choice and then click the Next button to continue.
8. The Ready to Install screen appears. Review the URL and then click the Install button to continue.
9. When the wizard completes, click the Finish button to end the procedure.
10. From the Directory Security tab of the Properties dialog box, click the Edit button in the Secure Communications area.

After the installation procedure has completed, you can connect to the SUS Administration page by entering `http://servername/SUSAdmin`. From the SUS Administration page, you can synchronize the server with the Microsoft Windows Update site and configure various options.

To synchronize SUS with the Microsoft Windows Update site, use the procedure in Step by Step 5.23.

STEP BY STEP

5.23 Synchronizing SUS

1. Enter `http://servername/SUSAdmin` in your Web browser. This opens the SUS Administration Web page.
2. In the left pane of the Web page, click the Set Options entry.
3. From the Set Options page, shown in Figure 5.49, you can change the options you selected during the installation of SUS, in addition to other options to configure the SUS server to operate behind a proxy server. Notice that there is an option to specify a local SUS server to synchronize with.

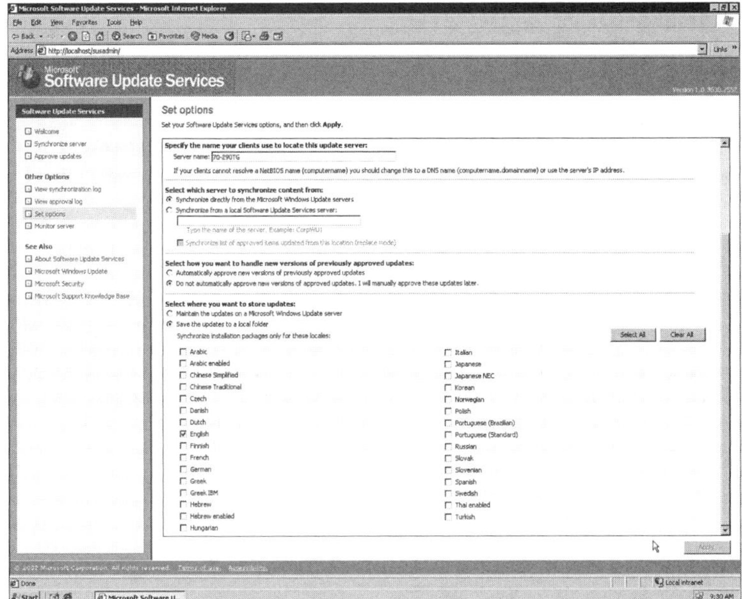

FIGURE 5.49

The Set Options page allows you to control the configuration of your SUS server.

4. In the left pane of the Web page, click the Synchronize Server entry.

5. From the Synchronize Server page, you have the option to synchronize immediately or to synchronize on a scheduled basis. Click the Synchronize Now button to continue.

6. The updates are downloaded to your SUS server. This might take a while depending on the options you've selected and the number of updates currently available. A progress bar is displayed to indicate the progress.

7. When the synchronization with the Microsoft Windows Update site is complete, click the OK button.

There is also an option to specify a local SUS server to synchronize with. Along with this option is a check box that specifies that only approved items should be synchronized. These options are used in the scenario with multiple SUS servers that we covered earlier. Using these options allows you to download updates only to a single server. The updates are tested and approved by the HQ SUS server. By configuring your other SUS servers to point to this central server and to synchronize only approved updates, you can reduce the traffic on your network.

Approving Updates

Not all the updates apply to the computers on your network. Also, there is the possibility that one of the fixes might actually break something in your environment. Fortunately, SUS can be configured to not make any updates available until after you have approved them. This gives you the opportunity to select which updates you want to distribute and to test them before you release them to your production environment.

You are sent to the Approve Updates page after you have completed your initial synchronization, or you can select Approve Updates from the SUS menu.

To approve SUS updates so that they can be distributed to your clients, use the procedure in Step by Step 5.24.

STEP BY STEP

5.24 Approving SUS Updates

1. Open the SUS Administration Web page.
2. In the left pane of the Web page, click the Approve Updates entry.
3. From the Approve Updates page, shown in Figure 5.50, you can select the updates you wish to make available to your clients. After selecting the desired updates, click the Approve button.
4. You receive a warning prompt telling you that the selected list will replace all previously approved updates. Click the Yes button to continue.
5. If a license agreement is required for any of the updates, it is displayed. Read the agreement and then click the Yes button. Click the Synchronize Now button to continue.
6. When prompted, click the OK button to save the list.

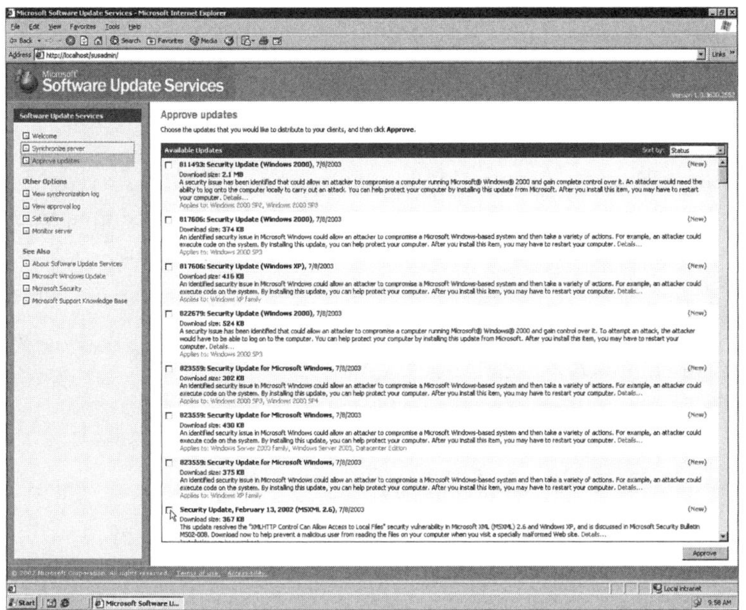

FIGURE 5.50
The Approve Updates page allows you to control which updates are made available to your clients. A brief description of each update is supplied, along with any prerequisites. For more information, you can click the Details hyperlink supplied with each entry.

Configuring Clients for Automatic Updates

After the updates have been synchronized and approved, they are ready to be distributed to the clients. To connect to the SUS server, the client should have the Automatic Update software installed. The correct version is included with the following:

- Windows XP Service Pack 1 or later
- Windows 2000 Service Pack 3 or later
- All versions of Windows Server 2003

Older versions of the Windows Update client do not support SUS. The updated client can be downloaded from the SUS Web page at `www.microsoft.com/windows2000/windowsupdate/sus/default.asp`.

By default, the Microsoft Windows client and server operating systems are configured to obtain updates from the Microsoft Windows Update site; they must be reconfigured to obtain updates from an SUS server.

Although you can manually edit the Registry of Windows servers and clients to use an SUS server, that process is time consuming and error prone. The most efficient way to make this change is via Group Policy.

To enable updates via SUS for a group of computers, follow the procedure outlined in Step by Step 5.25.

STEP BY STEP

5.25 Enabling Updates via SUS for a Group of Computers

1. Click Start, All Programs, Administrative Tools, Active Directory Users and Computers.
2. In the right pane, right-click the OU that contains the Windows computers you want to be controlled by Software Update Services and then select Properties from the pop-up menu.
3. From the Properties dialog box, select the Group Policy tab. Click the Add button to add a new policy.
4. From the Group Policy MMC, navigate to the Administrative Templates, Windows Components, Windows Update folder.
5. Double-click the Specify Intranet Microsoft Update Service Location entry and then select the Enabled option from the Properties dialog box and enter the name of your SUS server in both fields. Click the OK button to save these settings.

6. Double-click the Configure Automatic Updates entry, and then select the Enabled option from the Properties dialog box (see Figure 5.51). Configure an appropriate schedule and then click the OK button to save.
7. Close the Group Policy MMC.

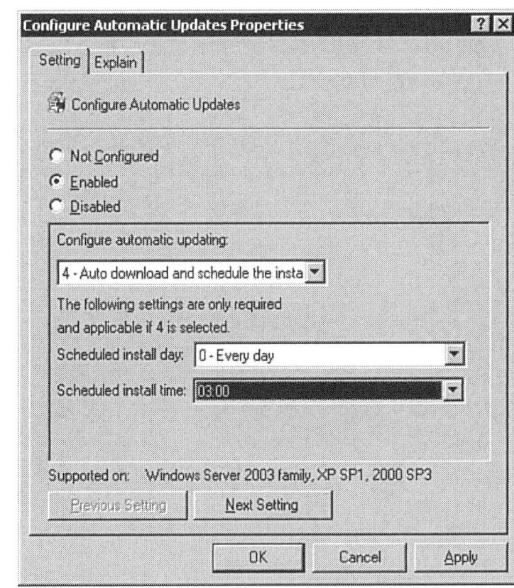

FIGURE 5.51
The Configure Automatic Updates policy, showing the options available for scheduling. The default is every day at 3:00 a.m.

The other Group Policy options are used to control whether the computer performs an auto-restart after it installs an update that requires a reboot or waits until a scheduled reboot. The last option controls whether the updates are automatically installed when the computer is first started after it has missed an update window (for example, if the computer was scheduled for an update at 3:00 a.m. but was turned off).

Managing Updates

Unfortunately, Microsoft doesn't provide much in the way of tools to manage SUS. SUS is intended for the small-to-medium-sized enterprise. For larger enterprises, Microsoft recommends that you implement the System Management Server (SMS) product. SMS provides much more powerful update capabilities, including expanded operating system support, hardware and software inventory, and remote control management capabilities. Most important, SMS also provides a reporting function so that you know when updates are applied to systems and which updates are still pending.

The tools that Microsoft does include are the Approval Log, shown in Figure 5.52, and the Monitor Server tool, shown in Figure 5.53. The Approval Log provides a list of all the available updates, along with those that have been approved and by whom. The Monitor Server tool displays a summary of updates grouped by operating system or product. Clicking the individual entry provides a list of the packages available for the product, along with various statistics.

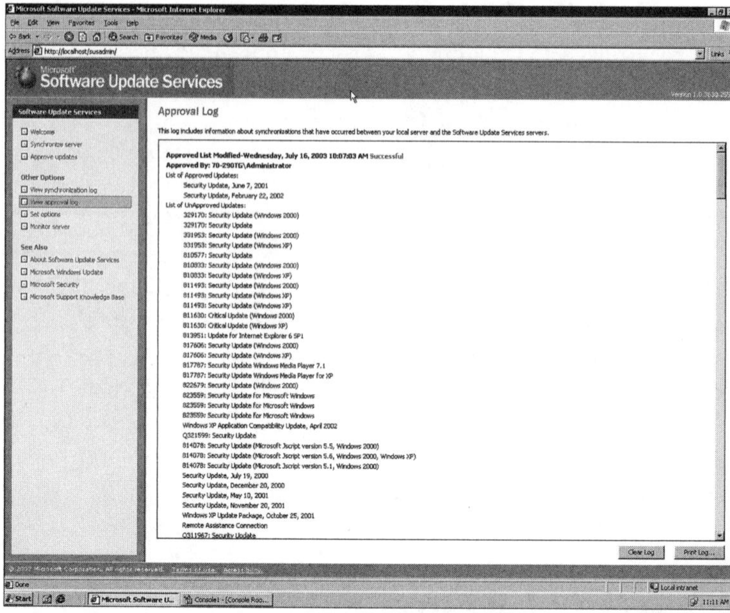

FIGURE 5.52
The Approval Log, showing the status of all downloaded updates.

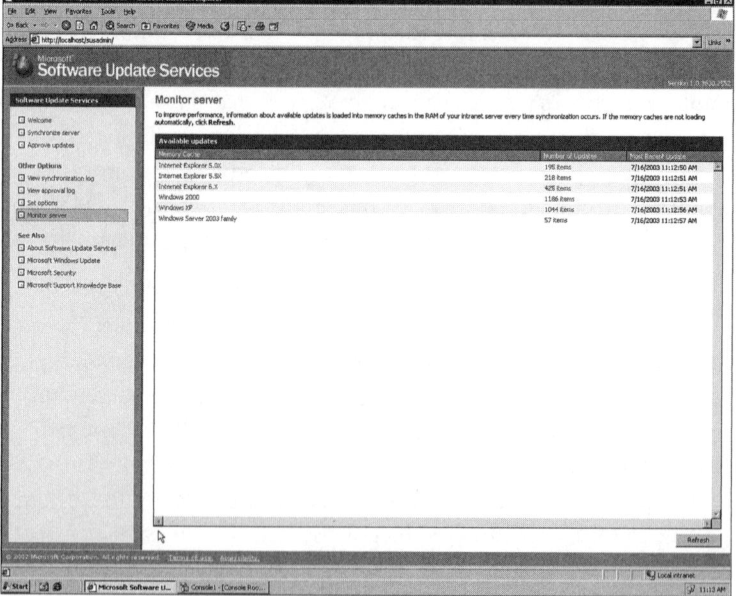

FIGURE 5.53
The Monitor Server tool, showing a summary of the updates available sorted by product and operating system.

MANAGING SOFTWARE SITE LICENSING

One of the lesser-known, but extremely important, responsibilities of a network administrator is software licensing. It is important to ensure that your company has the correct number of licenses for the software in use in your organization. Not only because it saves your company money by purchasing only the number of licenses needed, but more importantly, you avoid lawsuits by software publishers that discover you are using their software illegally.

Microsoft requires that every Windows client computer have a client license. This is obtained automatically when you buy a copy of the client operating system over the counter, or when you make a volume purchase via one of Microsoft's volume licensing programs, such as Open or Select Licensing.

In addition to the client licenses, Microsoft also requires that every user or device that connects to a Microsoft server obtain a Client Access License (CAL).

There are two methods of licensing for Windows Server 2003 servers:

- Per seat
- Per server

In the *per-server* licensing method, the server is licensed for a specific amount of concurrent connections. The connections are allowed on a first-come-first-served basis. For example, if your server is licensed for 100 CALs, the 101st client that attempts to connect to your server would be refused.

In the *per-seat* licensing method, each user or device is required to obtain a CAL. This CAL allows the user or device to connect to multiple servers. The default licensing mode in Windows Server 2003 is per server.

Typically, per-server licensing is used in environments where there is only one server. The per-seat licensing mode is more economical for enterprise environments where each client needs to access multiple servers.

For example, if you have 100 clients and a single server, you would be required to purchase 100 CALs under the per-server licensing. In this case, you are licensing the number of connections to the server.

However, if you have two servers, and your clients need to access both servers, under the per-server licensing mode, you would have to purchase 200 CALs. This is because each server would need to be licensed for 100 connections each.

Using the per-seat licensing mode, you would only have to purchase 100 CALs because the licensing is by the number of clients, not by the number of connections to the server.

Administering Licenses

Two tools are used to administer Microsoft licenses, depending on the scope of your enterprise:

- **Licensing applet**—This applet is found in the Control Panel and is used to manage per-server licensing on the server that the applet is run on.
- **Licensing utility**—This utility is found in the Administrative Tools folder and is used to manage per-seat licensing for the enterprise.

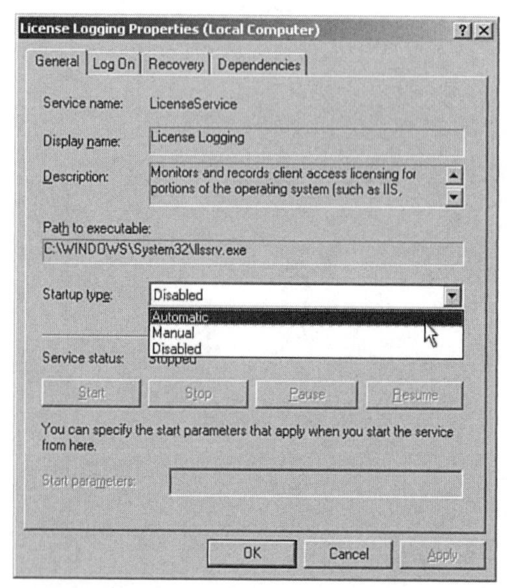

FIGURE 5.54
The Services tool, showing how to change the Startup type of the License Logging service to Automatic.

By default, licensing is enforced; however, it is not tracked or monitored. Before you can manage and track licensing, you must enable the License Logging service. The service is disabled by default in Windows Server 2003. To enable the License Logging service, change the Startup type to Automatic using the Services utility in the Administrative Tools folder, as shown in Figure 5.54. After the startup type is set, click the Start button to start the service.

After the Licensing service is started, you can use either of the two licensing tools to manage your licenses.

Licensing Applet

The Licensing applet in Control Panel can be used to do the following:

- Add or remove client licenses for the per-server mode.
- Change the licensing mode from per server to per seat.

- Configure the replication of the server's licensing information to the Site License Server.

To add per-server licenses, follow the procedure in Step by Step 5.26.

STEP BY STEP

5.26 Adding Per-Server Licenses

1. Click Start, Control Panel, Licensing.
2. The Choose Licensing Mode dialog box appears. If this is the first time you have run the Licensing applet, you will need to select a licensing mode and then click the OK button. If this is not the first time that you have run the Licensing applet, go to step 6.
3. Select the Per Server radio button and then click the OK button.
4. From the Terms and Conditions dialog box, select the I Agree check box to accept the terms and conditions. Then click the OK button.
5. Click Start, Control Panel, Licensing.
6. The Choose Licensing Mode dialog box appears, as shown in Figure 5.55. Click the Add Licenses button.

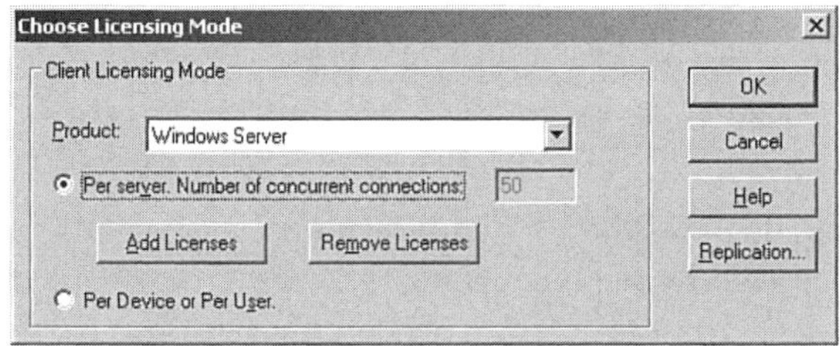

FIGURE 5.55
The Choose Licensing Mode dialog box allows you to add or remove licenses or to change the licensing mode.

7. The New Client Access License dialog box appears, as shown in Figure 5.56. This dialog box allows you to enter the number of Client Access Licenses to add. After entering the desired number of licenses, click the OK button.

continues

continued

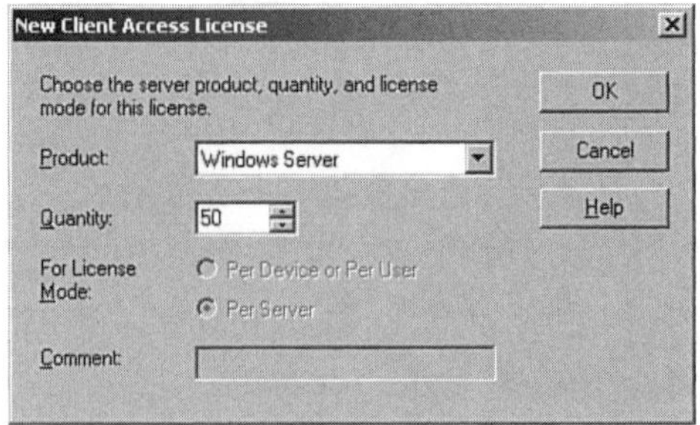

FIGURE 5.56
The New Client Access License dialog box allows you to add licenses.

8. The Per Server Licensing Terms and Conditions dialog box appears. Read the text and click the I Agree check box. Then click the OK button twice to save.

9. Close the Group Policy MMC.

Removing licenses can be accomplished by following the procedure in the previous Step by Step and selecting the Remove Licenses button.

Changing Licensing Modes

The licensing mode can be changed from per server to per seat using the Licensing applet. This is a one-time change, so you should always confirm that this is what you really want to do. This can be accomplished by clicking the Per Device or Per User radio button on the Choose Licensing Mode dialog box, as shown in Figure 5.55. When the License Violation dialog box appears, read the warning and then click the No button to change the mode.

Configuring License Replication

In an enterprise environment, you will configure a Site License Server to collect all the licensing data for that site. The Licensing applet allows you to configure the replication time and frequency to send the licensing data to the Site License Server. This can be configured by starting the Licensing applet and clicking the Replication button on the Choose Licensing Mode dialog box, as shown in Figure 5.55. When the Replication Configuration dialog box appears, as shown in Figure 5.57, enter appropriate values for the start time or the replication frequency.

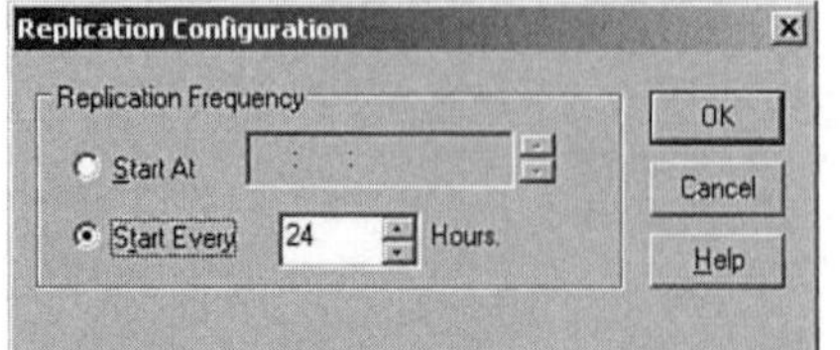

FIGURE 5.57
The Licensing applet, showing how to change the replication frequency of the license information to the Site License Server.

Licensing Utility

The Licensing utility, available in the Administrative Tools folder, allows you to manage licensing at the site or the enterprise level.

The Licensing utility can be used to perform the following:

- Add or remove client licenses for the servers in the site or enterprise.
- View all per-server, per-device, and per-user licenses for the site or enterprise.
- Manage the replication of the server licensing information on the network.
- View user usage statistics.

Before you can administer the Site License Server, you must determine what server is currently holding that role. By default, the Site License Server is the first domain controller installed in a site. Although the Site License Server is not required to be a domain controller, it should reside within the site that is being managed.

To display or change the server used as the Site License Server, follow the procedure in Step by Step 5.27.

STEP BY STEP

5.27 Displaying or Changing the Server Used As the Site License Server

1. Click Start, All Programs, Administrative Tools, Active Directory Sites and Services.
2. In the left pane, click the site that you want to display. The Licensing Site Settings icon will be displayed in the right pane, as shown in Figure 5.58.
3. In the right pane, double-click the Licensing Site Settings entry. In the Licensing Site Settings Properties dialog box, the licensing server is displayed in the Computer field, as shown in Figure 5.59.

continues

continued

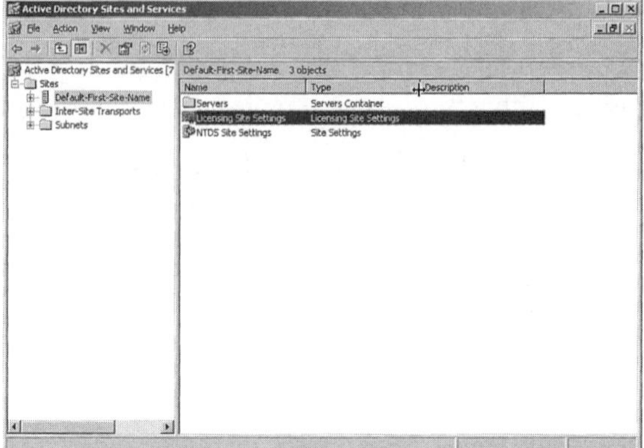

FIGURE 5.58▶
The Active Directory Sites and Service MMC, showing the location of the Licensing Site Settings icon.

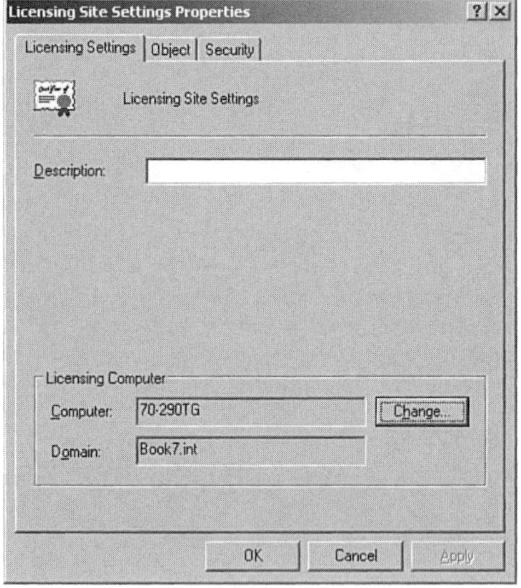

FIGURE 5.59▲
The Licensing Site Settings Properties dialog box, showing the server that is assigned the Site License Server role.

4. If desired, click the Change button to assign the Site License Server role to another server. Select a server then click OK twice to save.

5. Close the Group Policy MMC.

After you determine which server is the Site License Server, you can open the Licensing utility by clicking Start, Administrative Tools, Licensing on that server. The Licensing utility defaults to the Purchase History tab, as shown in Figure 5.60. The Purchase History tab shows you when, how many, and what type of licenses were added or deleted.

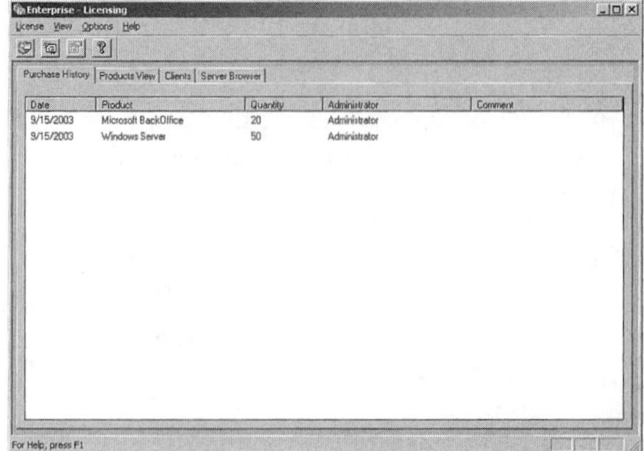

FIGURE 5.60▶
The Licensing utility, showing the Purchase History tab.

The Products View tab, shown in Figure 5.61, displays the following information for each product on the server:

- The number of per-device or per-user licenses purchased
- The number of per-device or per-user licenses allocated
- The number of per-server licenses purchased
- The number of connections for per-server mode that have been reached

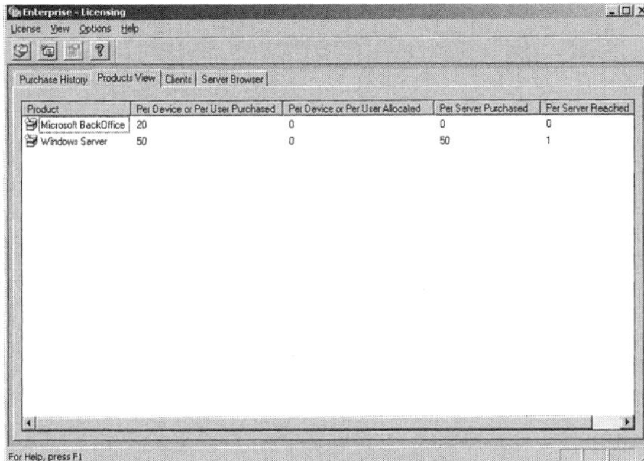

FIGURE 5.61
The Licensing utility, showing the Products View tab.

The Clients tab, shown in Figure 5.62, displays the following information for each client that has accessed the server:

- The username
- The licensed usage to the server
- The unlicensed usage to the server
- The product that was accessed by the user (for example, Microsoft BackOffice or Windows Server)

The Server Browser tab, shown in Figure 5.63, displays the servers, sites, and domains in Active Directory.

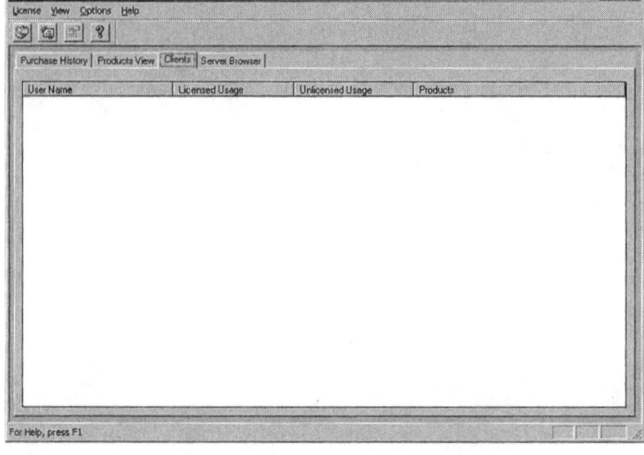

FIGURE 5.62
The Licensing utility, showing the Clients tab.

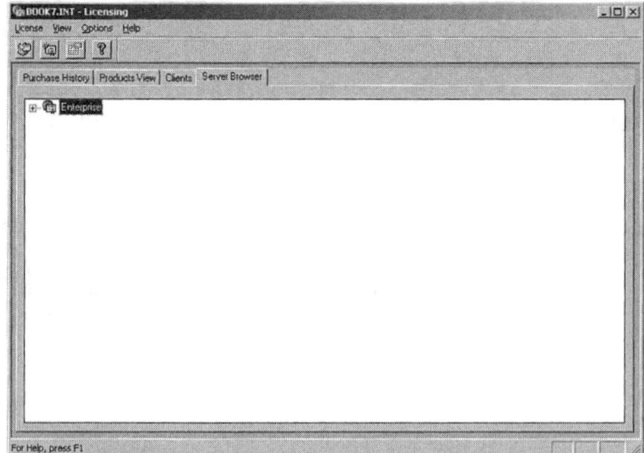

FIGURE 5.63
The Licensing utility, showing the Server Browser tab.

License Groups

License groups are created in special circumstances in which the basic per-seat or per-server licensing may not be the best fit. A good example of this is a situation where several users share a computer. The License Logging service tracks licenses by username. So even though the server is accessed only from a single computer, several licenses are consumed because every user will need a license, even though they will never all be connected to the server concurrently.

To create a license group, follow the procedure in Step by Step 5.28.

STEP BY STEP

5.28 Creating a License Group

1. Click Start, All Programs, Administrative Tools, Licensing.
2. From the system menu of the Licensing utility, select Options, Advanced, New License Group.
3. From the New License Group dialog box, shown in Figure 5.64, enter a group name.
4. Enter the number of licenses to be assigned to the group. Click the Add button.
5. The Add Users dialog box appears, as shown in Figure 5.65. Click the Add button to add the desired users. When you're finished, click OK twice to save.

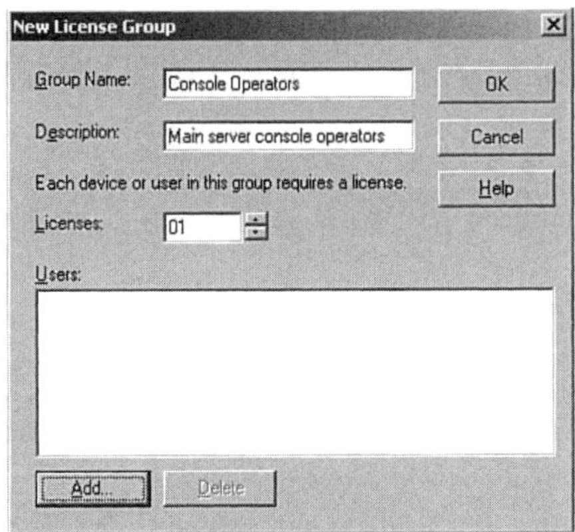

FIGURE 5.64▲
The New License Group dialog box.

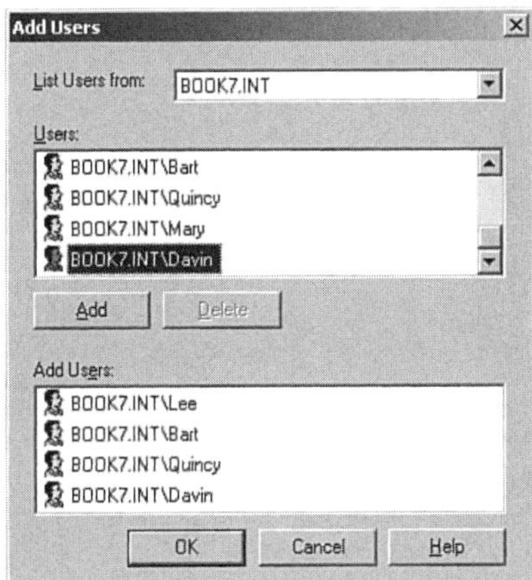

FIGURE 5.65◄
The Add Users dialog box.

When you create a license group and add users to it, the Licensing service will treat the members of the group as a single entity, so they will only consume one license.

CASE STUDY: WEBS R US

ESSENCE OF THE CASE

Here are the essential elements in this case:

- Secure all data.
- Manage servers remotely.
- Keep data safe from hackers.

SCENARIO

Mary is a full-time system administrator for a mid-sized company in the Midwest. Due to the imminent downsizing of her company, Mary will soon be unemployed. Because of her background in system administration and Web site development, Mary is putting together a business plan for a startup company. She wants to run a small Web site–hosting company that caters to several local small businesses that can't afford to develop and support their own Web sites. These Web sites should be able to accept online transactions.

Mary plans to purchase her own servers and to co-locate them at a local Internet service provider (ISP). Although the ISP will handle the backups for her servers, she is still responsible for the administration and maintenance.

Because she is in effect managing the Web presence for a number of small companies, Mary realizes that not only is it essential that she be able to provide reliable service, she must also ensure that the data from one company is not accessible by other companies and that the data is not vulnerable to viruses and hackers.

ANALYSIS

After a close examination of the needs for Mary's business, it should be possible to address these needs using the built-in Windows Server 2003 security features, IIS 6.0, and the Windows Remote Desktop feature.

Mary should set up an appropriate number of Windows Server 2003 servers running IIS 6.0. These IIS 6.0 servers should have only the necessary features enabled.

CASE STUDY: WEBS R US

To ensure that users from one company cannot access the data of another, anonymous access should be disabled. Mary should use Basic Authentication, with Secure Sockets Layer (SSL), and obtain the certificate from a reputable Certificate Authority. Mary should set up different user groups for each company. Mary should obtain multiple IP addresses from her ISP so that each Web site will have its own address. Each Web server will be assigned multiple IP addresses because each one will host multiple Web sites. Each company should be configured with its own Web site, file shares, and folders. Each company's Web resources should be granted Deny Access permission to the groups from the other companies.

OVERVIEW OF THE REQUIREMENTS AND SOLUTIONS IN THIS CASE STUDY

Requirement	Solution Provided By
Secure all data.	Using a combination of SSL, Web site, and NTFS permissions.
Manage servers remotely.	Using the Remote Desktop for Administration feature of Windows Server 2003 to manage the servers. In addition, the Web sites can be managed using the IIS Remote Administration Console.
Keep data safe from hackers.	Using SSL to encrypt all traffic between the browser and the Web server.

CHAPTER SUMMARY

This chapter has covered a lot of ground. We started with a discussion of the remote management capabilities of Windows Server 2003, both using custom MMCs and with the Remote Desktop for Administration feature.

That was followed by a discussion of the new features in IIS 6.0. It is important to remember that, unlike previous versions of Windows, in Windows Server 2003 IIS is not installed by default. In addition, when IIS 6.0 is installed, it is installed in "lockdown mode." In this mode, only static pages can be served, and the support for dynamic content such as ASP or CGI has to be manually configured. These default settings present a far smaller "attack surface" for viruses and hackers.

KEY TERMS

- Remote Desktop Protocol
- Remote Desktop for Administration
- Software Update Services (SUS)
- Microsoft Management Console (MMC)
- Application pool
- Remote Assistance

continues

CHAPTER SUMMARY *continued*

- Windows Update
- Secure Sockets Layer (SSL)
- Internet Information Services (IIS)

Managing security for IIS 6.0 is an important topic, especially in light of all the attention that IIS has received as a favorite target for hackers. It is important to understand that the best way to secure IIS is to enable only the minimal features required to support the applications being run on IIS. Also, you should never grant more authority to any users than they can ever possibly require.

It is important to remember that no matter how much work is put into it, no software is perfect. That's where Microsoft Software Update Services (SUS) comes in. SUS allows the system administrator to set up, control, and monitor an internal version of the Microsoft Windows Update Web site. This provides the administrator greater control over the patches, security fixes, and other updates that are to be distributed to both servers and client computers.

APPLY YOUR KNOWLEDGE

Exercises

5.1 Creating a Custom MMC

In this exercise, you create a custom MMC. This MMC is for an enterprise administrator responsible for managing the configuration of sites, domains, and trusts.

Estimated Time: 20 minutes

1. From the Start menu, select Start, Run. Type **MMC** in the field and click OK.
2. The MMC appears. Select File and then Add/Remove Snap-In from the Console menu.
3. The Add/Remove Snap-in dialog box appears. Click the Add button.
4. The Add Standalone Snap-In dialog box appears. Select the Active Directory Sites and Services snap-in and then click the Add button.
5. Select the Active Directory Domain and Trusts snap-in and then click the Add button.
6. Back at the Add Standalone Snap-In dialog box, click the Close button. This returns you to the Add/Remove Snap-In dialog box. If the selections are correct, click the OK button.
7. This returns you to the custom MMC. To save it, select File, Save As from the system menu. Enter an appropriate name and location and then click the Save button.

5.2 Creating a Web Site

In this exercise, you use the Web Site Creation Wizard to create a Web site to serve some Active Server Pages. Because only static content is allowed with the default installation of IIS 6.0, you must configure IIS to use Active Server Pages manually.

Estimated Time: 20 minutes

Additional Requirements: A folder containing a sample Web site.

1. Click Start, Administrative Tools, Internet Information Services Manager.
2. From the IIS Manager MMC, right-click the Web Sites entry and then select New, Web Site from the pop-up menu.
3. On the Welcome to the Web Site Creation Wizard screen, click the Next button to continue.
4. On the Web Site Description screen, type in a descriptive name for the Web site. Click the Next button to continue.
5. The IP Address and Port Settings screen appears. From this screen, you can select the IP address, TCP port, or host header to which this Web site will respond. Make the appropriate choices and then click the Next button to continue.
6. The Web Site Home Directory screen appears. From this screen, you can select the folder that contains the files for your Web site. You can also specify that you want to allow anonymous access to your site. Make the appropriate choices and then click the Next button to continue.
7. The Web Site Access Permissions screen appears. From this screen, you can specify the permissions you are granting visitors to your Web site. You should always specify the minimum permissions needed. Make the appropriate choices and then click the Next button to continue.
8. When the Finishing the Web Site Creation Wizard screen appears, click the Finish button to save.

APPLY YOUR KNOWLEDGE

9. The new Web site appears in the IIS Manager console, listed under the Default Web Site entry.
10. In the left pane of the IIS Manager, click the Web Service Extensions folder.
11. Highlight the Active Server Pages entry in the right pane of the MMC and then click the Allow button. The status of the extension is changed to Allowed.
12. Close IIS Manager.

Review Questions

1. What are the two Terminal Services modes available in Windows Server 2003?
2. Which operating systems are supported by Microsoft Software Update Services?
3. What are the three methods of sending an invitation to a user for a Remote Assistance session on a Windows Server 2003 server?
4. What is the preferred method of configuring the Automatic Updates client?
5. What tool(s) does Microsoft supply to work with SUS?

Exam Questions

1. You are the administrator of a Web site based on a Windows Server 2003 computer named Server1. The Web site contains company profit projections, salary data, and other sensitive items. Although the Web server is behind a firewall, the company president wants you to make the Web site available on the Internet so that executives can access the information while traveling.

   Required Result:

   You want executives to be able to access the data on the Web site while traveling.

   Optional Desired Results:

   You do not want casual users to access the data.

   You do not want the data to be accessible to hackers.

   Proposed Solution:

   Open the necessary ports on the firewall so that the Web site is accessible from the Internet. Turn anonymous access off. Configure the Web site to support Integrated Windows Authentication.

   Evaluation of Proposed Solution:

   Which result(s) does the proposed solution produce?

   A. The proposed solution produces the required result but neither of the optional results.

   B. The proposed solution produces the required result and one of the optional results.

   C. The proposed solution produces the required result and both the optional results.

   D. The proposed solution does not produce the required result.

2. You are the administrator of a Web site based on a Windows Server 2003 computer named Server1. The Web site contains company profit projections, salary data, and other sensitive items. Although the Web server is behind a firewall, the company president wants you to make the Web site available on the Internet so that executives can access the information while traveling.

APPLY YOUR KNOWLEDGE

Required Result:

You want executives to be able to access the data on the Web site while traveling.

Optional Desired Results:

You do not want casual users to access the data.

You do not want the data to be accessible to hackers.

Proposed Solution:

Open the necessary ports on the firewall so that the Web site is accessible from the Internet. Turn anonymous access off. Configure the Web site to support Basic Authentication.

Evaluation of Proposed Solution:

Which result(s) does the proposed solution produce?

A. The proposed solution produces the required result but neither of the optional results.

B. The proposed solution produces the required result and one of the optional results.

C. The proposed solution produces the required result and both the optional results.

D. The proposed solution does not produce the required result.

3. You are the administrator of a Web site based on a Windows Server 2003 computer named Server1. The Web site contains company profit projections, salary data, and other sensitive items. Although the Web server is behind a firewall, the company president wants you to make the Web site available on the Internet so that executives can access the information while traveling.

Required Result:

You want executives to be able to access the data on the Web site while traveling.

Optional Desired Results:

You do not want casual users to access the data.

You do not want the data to be accessible to hackers.

Proposed Solution:

Open the necessary ports on the firewall so that the Web site is accessible from the Internet. Turn anonymous access off. Configure the Web site to support Basic Authentication. Obtain and install a certificate from a trusted Certificate Authority. Enable SSL. Select the option to require SSL.

Evaluation of Proposed Solution:

Which result(s) does the proposed solution produce?

A. The proposed solution produces the required result but neither of the optional results.

B. The proposed solution produces the required result and one of the optional results.

C. The proposed solution produces the required result and both the optional results.

D. The proposed solution does not produce the required result.

APPLY YOUR KNOWLEDGE

4. You are the lead administrator for a large manufacturer of farm machinery and related parts based in the Upper Midwest. Your company has several small manufacturing plants spread out over a five-state area. Most of the end users are not computer savvy, so the client computers are somewhat locked down. All clients are running Windows XP, and all servers are running Windows Server 2003. The manufacturing plants are connected to headquarters via T1 lines in a hub-and-spoke configuration.

   Due to the large number of updates and security fixes that Microsoft is releasing on a regular basis, your staff is becoming overwhelmed with the workload of updating the client computers in the remote locations. You need to identify an automated solution to assist you in keeping your clients up to date.

   Required Result:

   You want to apply patches and updates supplied by the Microsoft Windows Update Web site in a timely manner.

   Optional Desired Results:

   You want an automated solution to apply patches and updates supplied by the Microsoft Windows Update Web site.

   You want to minimize the bandwidth used.

   Proposed Solution:

   Install the latest version of the Windows Update client on the Windows XP client computers. Instruct the users on how to click the Windows Update icon weekly to install the latest fixes and updates.

   Evaluation of Proposed Solution:

   Which result(s) does the proposed solution produce?

   A. The proposed solution produces the required result but neither of the optional results.

   B. The proposed solution produces the required result and one of the optional results.

   C. The proposed solution produces the required result and both the optional results.

   D. The proposed solution does not produce the required result.

5. You are the lead administrator for a large manufacturer of farm machinery and related parts based in the Upper Midwest. Your company has several small manufacturing plants spread out over a five-state area. Most of the end users are not computer savvy, so the client computers are somewhat locked down. All clients are running Windows XP, and all servers are running Windows Server 2003. The manufacturing plants are connected to headquarters via T1 lines in a hub-and-spoke configuration.

   Due to the large number of updates and security fixes that Microsoft is releasing on a regular basis, your staff is becoming overwhelmed with the workload of updating the client computers in the remote locations. You need to identify an automated solution to assist you in keeping your clients up to date.

   Required Result:

   You want to apply patches and updates supplied by the Microsoft Windows Update Web site in a timely manner.

APPLY YOUR KNOWLEDGE

Optional Desired Results:

You want an automated solution to apply patches and updates supplied by the Microsoft Windows Update Web site.

You want to minimize the bandwidth used.

Proposed Solution:

Install the latest version of the Windows Update client on the Windows XP client computers. Install a Software Update Services (SUS) server in the HQ location. Configure the SUS server at HQ to synchronize with the Microsoft Windows Update Web site. Configure the clients to receive and install updates from the SUS server.

Evaluation of Proposed Solution:

Which result(s) does the proposed solution produce?

A. The proposed solution produces the required result but neither of the optional results.

B. The proposed solution produces the required result and one of the optional results.

C. The proposed solution produces the required result and both the optional results.

D. The proposed solution does not produce the required result.

6. As part of a server consolidation, you are moving several Web sites on your intranet from Windows 2000 Servers to a new Windows Server 2003 server. After moving the Web sites, you turn the server back over to the users. Soon, your telephone rings with users complaining that they are receiving 404 errors when they try to access any of the Web sites. What steps will you need to perform to fix the problem?

   A. You need to reconfigure the NTFS permissions.

   B. You need to reconfigure the share permissions.

   C. You need to restart the Server service on the new server.

   D. You need to enable the Web Service Extensions.

7. You are the administrator of a small network. You have configured a Windows Server 2003 server to run in Remote Desktop for Administration mode. What is the maximum number of users that can be supported?

   A. The same amount as the number of Terminal Server licenses that were purchased.

   B. Two, plus one for the console.

   C. About 100 on Windows Server 2003 Standard Edition and 200 on Windows Server 2003 Enterprise edition.

   D. As many as the performance of the server supports.

8. After reading about how much improved IIS 6.0 is over IIS 5.0, you decide to perform an in-place upgrade of one of the Windows 2000 servers for your intranet. After the upgrade has completed, you check all the install logs and the Event Viewer and don't see any problems. After you turn the Web server back over to the users, your telephone rings with users complaining that they cannot access the Web site. What step must you perform to fix the problem?

   A. Replace the network interface card.

   B. Start the Web service.

Apply Your Knowledge

C. Rewrite the Web apps to be compatible with IIS 6.0.

D. Reconfigure the Web service in IIS 5.0 Isolation mode.

E. Reconfigure the Web service in Worker Process Isolation mode.

9. You are the administrator for Widgets, Inc. The Director of Human Resources is extremely security conscious. She wants you to set up an intranet site in such a way that users will not have access to it or be able to browse it. However, specified users in the HR department should be able to access it easily, without requiring additional user IDs and passwords.

   Required Result:

   Set up a secure intranet site for Human Resources.

   Optional Desired Results:

   Users should not be able to browse it.

   Specified users in the HR department should be able to access it easily without requiring additional user IDs and passwords.

   Proposed Solution:

   Create a Web site named HRSecure. Set the NTFS permissions for the HRSecure folder to grant the specified HR users Full Control permission. No other permissions are changed.

   Evaluation of Proposed Solution:

   Which result(s) does the proposed solution produce?

   A. The proposed solution produces the required result but neither of the optional results.

   B. The proposed solution produces the required result and one of the optional results.

   C. The proposed solution produces the required result and both the optional results.

   D. The proposed solution does not produce the required result.

10. You are the administrator for Widgets, Inc. The Director of Human Resources is extremely security conscious. She wants you to set up an intranet site in such a way that users will not have access to it or be able to browse it. However, specified users in the HR department should be able to access it easily, without requiring additional user IDs and passwords.

   Required Result:

   Set up a secure intranet site for Human Resources.

   Optional Desired Results:

   Users should not be able to browse it.

   Specified users in the HR department should be able to access it easily without requiring additional user IDs and passwords.

   Proposed Solution:

   Create a Web site named HRSecure. Set the NTFS permissions for the HRSecure folder to grant the specified HR users Full Control permission. Delete the permissions for any other user or group.

   Evaluation of Proposed Solution:

   Which result(s) does the proposed solution produce?

   A. The proposed solution produces the required result but neither of the optional results.

APPLY YOUR KNOWLEDGE

B. The proposed solution produces the required result and one of the optional results.

C. The proposed solution produces the required result and both the optional results.

D. The proposed solution does not produce the required result.

11. You have just finished building a new Windows Server 2003 server. Your plan is to manage it remotely using Remote Desktop for Administration mode, just like you've been doing with your Windows 2000 servers. However, when you open the RDP client and try to connect to the new server, you can't seem to get connected. What is the most likely cause of the problem?

    A. A bad network interface card.

    B. The personal firewall is blocking the ports for the browse list.

    C. Remote Desktop for Administration mode has not been enabled.

    D. Remote Desktop for Administration mode has not been installed.

12. You are the administrator for Widgets, Inc. The Director of Information Security is extremely security conscious. She wants you to agree to install all Microsoft security patches within 48 hours of their release to the Windows Update site. On which of the following clients can this *not* be accomplished using SUS?

    A. Windows Server 2003

    B. Windows XP

    C. Windows 2000

    D. Windows NT 4.0 Service Pack 6

13. You are the administrator for a Windows Server 2003 server running IIS 6.0. The CIO is extremely security conscious. She wants you to set up an intranet site in such a way that only authorized users can access it. All users on your network are running Windows XP. What is the easiest way to accomplish this?

    A. Turn off anonymous access for the site and configure it for Digest Authentication.

    B. Turn off anonymous access for the site and configure it for Basic Authentication in combination with SSL.

    C. Turn off anonymous access for the site and configure it for Integrated Authentication.

    D. Turn off anonymous access for the site and configure it for Basic Authentication.

14. You are the administrator for a Windows Server 2003 server running IIS 6.0. The CIO is extremely security conscious. She wants you to set up a site on the Internet in such a way that only authorized users can access it. The Web site should support all types of browsers. What is the easiest way to accomplish this?

    A. Turn off anonymous access for the site and configure it for Digest Authentication.

    B. Turn off anonymous access for the site and configure it for Basic Authentication in combination with SSL.

    C. Turn off anonymous access for the site and configure it for Integrated Authentication.

    D. Turn off anonymous access for the site and configure it for Basic Authentication.

APPLY YOUR KNOWLEDGE

15. Bill is the lead administrator for BigCO, Inc. An associate administrator in one of the branch offices calls Bill and requests his help on a server problem. Bill attempts to assist the associate administrator, but the associate is fairly green, and he is having trouble describing what he is seeing on his screen. What technology in Windows Server 2003 can Bill use to show the associate how to fix his problem?

    A. Remote Desktop for Administration

    B. Terminal Services

    C. Remote Assistance

    D. Remote Administrator

Answers to Review Questions

1. Windows Server 2003 Remote Desktop for Administration mode and Application Server mode. Remote Desktop for Administration mode supports only two concurrent remote sessions, plus the remote console session, whereas Application Server mode supports an unlimited number of remote sessions.
2. SUS supports Windows XP Service Pack 1 or later, Windows 2000 Service Pack 3 or later, and all versions of Windows Server 2003.
3. Although sending an invitation via Windows Messenger is the preferred method, sending it via email and via a disk or network share are also supported.
4. Although the client can be configured in the Registry, the recommended method is to configure it via Group Policy.
5. The tools that Microsoft includes are the Approval Log and the Monitor Server tool. The Approval Log provides a list of all the available updates, along with those that have been approved and by whom. The Monitor Server tool displays a summary of updates grouped by operating system or product.

Answers to Exam Questions

1. **D.** The solution does not satisfy the required result. Although turning off anonymous access and turning on Integrated Authentication protects the Web site from unauthorized users, Integrated Authentication does not work through most firewalls.
2. **B.** The solution satisfies the required result and one of the optional results. Although turning off anonymous access and turning on Basic Authentication protects the Web site from unauthorized users, Basic Authentication transmits the password as clear text—a hackers dream!
3. **C.** The solution satisfies the required result and both the optional results. Although turning off anonymous access and turning on Basic Authentication protects the Web site from unauthorized users, Basic Authentication transmits the password as clear text. The final step is to use SSL to encrypt all data that passes between the browser and the Web site.
4. **D.** The solution does not satisfy the required result. Although instructing the end users on how to click the Windows Update icon periodically seems like a good idea, in practice, it probably won't work. Most security patches and updates require the end user to have local administrative

APPLY YOUR KNOWLEDGE

rights on the computer, and the scenario indicates that the computers are at least partially locked down.

5. **B.** The solution satisfies the required result and one of the optional results. Software Update Services can be configured to automatically download fixes and updates from the Microsoft Windows Update Web site and distribute them to clients. The Windows XP Service Pack 1 (and later) Windows Update client is required for connectivity to an SUS server. However, to cut down on bandwidth usage, an SUS server should be placed in each remote location.

6. **D.** In Windows Server 2003, the default for IIS 6.0 is to install in "locked down" mode. In locked down mode, only pages containing static content are displayed. All other pages return a 404 error when they are accessed. Enabling the Web Service Extensions allows you to use pages containing dynamic content.

7. **B.** The number of concurrent Remote Desktop for Administration sessions on Windows Server 2003 is two RDP sessions, plus the console. Terminal Services connections on all versions of Windows Server 2003 are unlimited.

8. **B.** During an upgrade from a previous version of Windows, IIS is installed; however, the service is disabled, and you must start it manually. This prevents administrators from carrying over vulnerabilities from previous versions of Windows. A Web server that is upgraded from a previous version of IIS is enabled in IIS 5.0 Isolation mode, by default, to ensure that the application installed continues to run.

9. **D.** The solution does not satisfy the required result. When a share is created on a Windows Server 2003 server, the default permissions are Read for Everyone.

10. **C.** The solution satisfies the required result and both the optional results. By granting permissions solely to the HR group, only they can access the content on the Web site.

11. **C.** Unlike in Windows 2000 Server, Windows Server 2003 Remote Desktop for Administration mode is installed by default; however, it is not enabled.

12. **B, C, D.** To support SUS, client computers must be running the updated Automatic Updates client and Windows 2000 (Service Pack 2), Windows XP (Service Pack 1), or Window Server 2003.

13. **C.** Integrated Authentication is the best answer. Although the other options would work, they all have limitations. Basic Authentication would work, but it transmits the password in clear text. Anyone with a Sniffer utility could discover the passwords. Adding SSL would be fine, but you would either have to purchase a certificate or set up your own CA. Digest Authentication requires that the passwords are stored unencrypted in the Active Directory.

14. **B.** The only correct answer for this situation is Basic Authentication in combination with SSL. Basic Authentication is the only option that supports all browsers, and SSL is required to encrypt the traffic between the browser and the Web site.

15. **C.** The Remote Assistance feature allows both Bill and the associate administrator to see and control the console on the server.

Suggested Readings and Resources

1. Microsoft Official Curriculum Course 2274: Managing a Microsoft Windows Server 2003 Environment
    - Module 9: Managing the User Environment by Using Group Policy
2. Microsoft Official Curriculum Course 2275: Maintaining a Microsoft Windows Server 2003 Environment
    - Module 1: Preparing to Administer a Server
    - Module 8: Maintaining Software by Using Microsoft Software Update Services
3. *Windows Server 2003 Deployment Guide.* Microsoft Corporation. `http://www.microsoft.com/windowsserver2003/techinfo/reskit/deploykit.mspx`.
4. *Windows Server 2003 Resource Kit.* Microsoft Corporation. Look for a link to it on the Technical Resources for Windows Server 2003 page. `http://www.microsoft.com/windowsserver2003/techinfo/default.mspx`.
5. Boswell, William. *Inside Windows Server 2003.* New Riders, 2003. ISBN 0735711585.
6. Matthews, Marty. *Windows Server 2003: A Beginners Guide.* McGraw-Hill, 2003. ISBN 0072193093.
7. Minasi, Mark, et al. *Mark Minasi's Windows XP and Server 2003 Resource Kit.* Sybex, 2003. ISBN 0782140807.
8. Minasi, Mark, et al. *Mastering Windows Server 2003 Server.* Sybex, 2003. ISBN 0782141307.
9. Shapiro, Jeffrey, et al. *Windows Server 2003 Bible.* John Wiley & Sons, 2003. ISBN 0764549375.

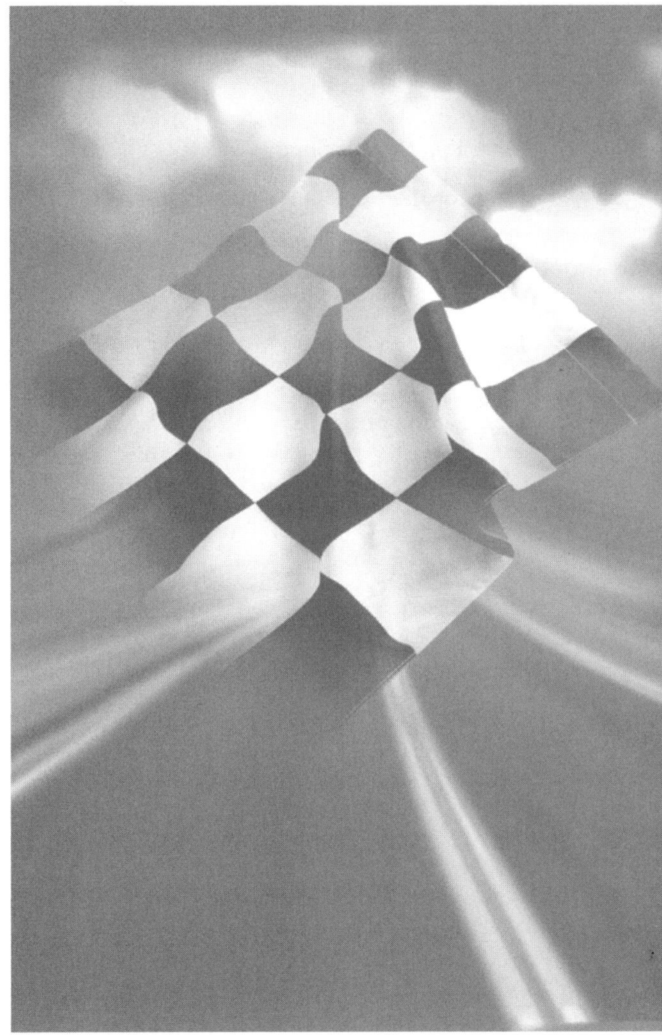

CHAPTER 6

Monitoring and Optimizing Server Performance

OBJECTIVES

This chapter covers the following Microsoft-specified objectives for the "Monitoring and Optimizing Server Performance" section of the Managing and Maintaining a Microsoft Windows Server 2003 Environment exam:

Monitor and analyze events. Tools might include Event Viewer and System Monitor.

- The purpose of this objective is to teach you how to use the System Monitor to track the performance of your Windows Server 2003 computer. In addition, you should be familiar with locating and identifying errors using the Event Viewer logs.

Monitor file and print servers. Tools might include Task Manager, Event Viewer, and System Monitor.

- **Monitor disk quotas.**
- **Monitor print queues.**
- **Monitor server hardware for bottlenecks.**

- The purpose of this objective is to teach you how to monitor file and print usage using the various tools available in Windows Server 2003. In addition, you should be familiar with the process of identifying performance bottlenecks.

Troubleshoot print queues.

- When working in a Windows Server 2003 environment, it is important that you have a thorough understanding of troubleshooting print problems. Printing is one of the major roles of a Windows Server 2003 server.

Monitor system performance.

- When working in a Windows Server 2003 environment, it is important that you have a thorough understanding of the performance characteristics of your servers. This makes it easier to identify potential problems before they cause outages.

OBJECTIVES

Monitor and optimize a server environment for application performance.

- **Monitor memory performance objects.**
- **Monitor network performance objects.**
- **Monitor process performance objects.**
- **Monitor disk performance objects.**

▶ The purpose of this objective is to teach you how to monitor and optimize your Windows 2003 server by monitoring the four basic performance objects.

OUTLINE

OUTLINE

STUDY STRATEGIES

- The sections in this chapter outline features that are basic to using and managing a Windows Server 2003 server. The File and Print server roles are common to just about every network, so they are areas you can expect to be heavily emphasized. The proper use of the performance-monitoring tools to identify problems with and to optimize server subsystems has always been a major point on Microsoft exams. Expect the Windows Server 2003 exams to continue that tradition. Make sure that you have a complete understanding of the capabilities of both the System Monitor and the Performance Logs and Alerts tool. In addition, you should be very familiar with Task Manager, especially as far as how it is similar to System Monitor and how it is different.
- Most of the Event Viewer questions will probably be related to the use of the Security log and auditing. Although auditing is turned on by default in Windows Server 2003, you still have to configure auditing on the individual objects. Make sure you understand the various auditing capabilities, how to enable auditing for an object, and how to configure and archive the event logs.
- The disk quota questions will probably be related to how quotas are applied to users and what happens when a file is moved or copied. Make sure you understand the limitations of the Microsoft version of disk quotas and how to monitor and configure them.

INTRODUCTION

No matter what role your Windows Server 2003 server has in your network, if it does not perform well, you're not doing your job as a system administrator. A good system administrator can use the monitoring and troubleshooting tools included in the operating system to identify and diagnose problems.

This chapter covers the tools, tasks, and procedures required to monitor, collect, and review operational and performance data on a Windows Server 2003 server. This type of information is not only crucial for a job as a system administrator, it is also very important for the exam.

USING THE EVENT LOGS

The Event Viewer, shown in Figure 6.1, in Windows Server 2003 is available in the Computer Management MMC or as a standalone MMC snap-in. This Windows Server 2003 utility records information about various system occurrences. The Event Viewer is not only the first place you should look when you're having problems, you must also review it regularly to monitor regular server operations and events.

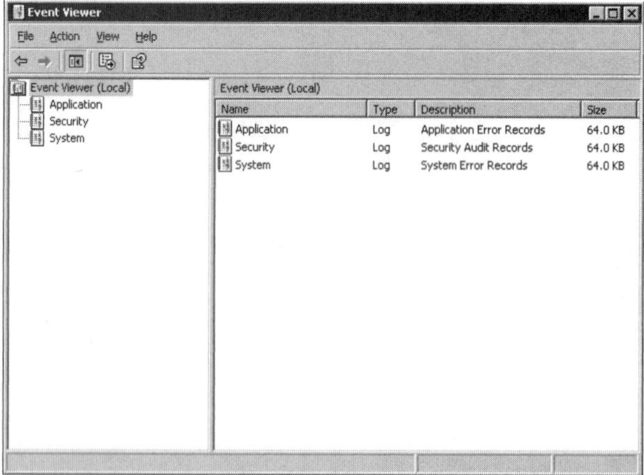

FIGURE 6.1
The Windows Server 2003 Event Viewer.

The Event Viewer is used to view event log files that are updated by the operating system and various services and applications running on your server. Typically, events are written to the logs for any significant occurrence that a user or administrator should be aware of. Reading the contents of these log files can assist you in determining the status of your server and as a first step in diagnosing problems.

As in previous versions of Windows, all servers have the following three log files: System, Security, and Application. Although these three logs have been carried over from previous versions of Windows, the Event Viewer has been expanded to allow other components or third-party applications to use it as the global location for log files. The logs that appear in your installation of Windows Server 2003 vary depending on the components installed. For example, the Domain Name Service maintains its own log in the Event Viewer. All Windows Server 2003 systems have at the very least the following three logs:

- **System log**—This file records events related to system operation, most often associated with device drivers and services such as DHCP and WINS. Most of the information here relates to the stopping and starting of services or the failure of a system component.
- **Application log**—This file records events related to applications, programs, and utilities, usually not native Windows Server 2003 components. Examples are database programs, email servers, and print messages. The information that is recorded here is determined by the application developer, and it usually consists of informational messages, errors, or warnings. This log is also used to store the alerts generated by the Performance Logs and Alerts tool.
- **Security log**—This file records events related to security and auditing. Typical events include valid or invalid logon attempts and the accessing of resources such as the opening, reading, or deleting of a file or folder. The types of events recorded in this log can be configured via the audit policy. In previous versions of Windows, the Security log would not record any information until an audit policy was enabled. In Windows 2003, security logging is enabled by default.

If the DNS service is installed on your server, the *DNS log* is also available. It records events related to the operation of the DNS service. If you're having name-resolution problems on your network, this is the first place to look.

In addition, Active Directory domain controllers have the following logs:

- **Directory Service log**—This file records events related to the operation of the Active Directory service. Typical events in this log are related to communication between domain controllers and Global Catalog servers.
- **File Replication Service log**—This file records events related to replication of the SYSVOL and the DFS tree, as well as other applications that use FRS, such as DFS.

Understanding the Event Logs

As mentioned earlier, event logs can be very useful, not only for monitoring server operations but also as a first step in diagnosing a problem. It is helpful to become familiar with the normal events that occur on a daily basis because some errors normally reoccur and are not an indication of a problem.

The event logs contain five main types of events that range from informational messages that do not require any action to serious events, such as hardware or service failures, that require your immediate attention. As shown in Figure 6.2, each type of event is visually cued by an icon. This allows you to quickly recognize events that require your attention.

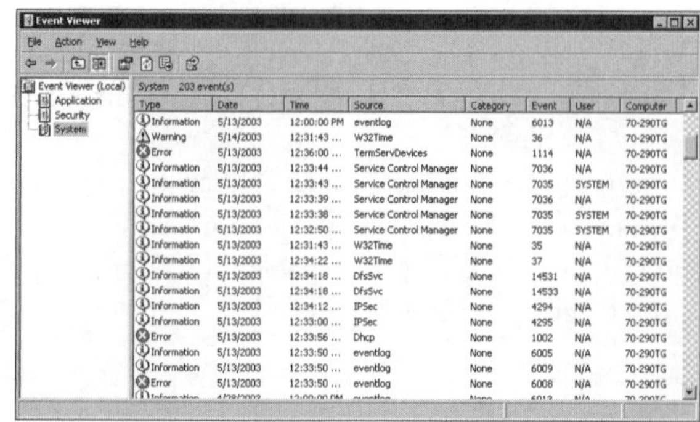

FIGURE 6.2
The Windows Server 2003 Event Viewer, showing the icons for various types of events.

The five types of events and their related icons are as follows:

- **Error events**—These are displayed as an *X* in a red circle. An error event is usually serious and can lead to data loss or a loss of functionality. Typical examples of error events are services that have stopped or failed to load on system startup and disk read or write failures.
- **Warning events**—These are displayed as an exclamation point on a yellow triangle. A warning event is usually not critical but indicates that you might have to take action in the future. Typical examples of warning events are low disk space conditions or failures in synchronization of the time service.
- **Information events**—These are displayed as a lowercase *i* on a bubble. Most information events are just to let you know that a task has been completed successfully. For example, when a service is started, it might write an information event to the log. Although the majority of informational events are benign, if you have Alert Logging turned on, that service writes an information message to the log when an alert has been triggered, which is a condition that requires follow-up.
- **Success audits**—These are displayed as a key icon. Successfully logging on to the server or accessing an audited resource are examples of things that would generate a success audit event.
- **Failure audits**—These are displayed as a padlock icon. If a user tries and fails to log on to a server or access an audited resource that he or she has not been granted access to, a failure audit event is generated.

Each entry in the event log, regardless of type, contains the following information:

- A description of the event (usually, but not always)
- The date and time that the event was logged
- The type of event (one of the five types we discussed earlier)
- The source of the event—usually the service, component, or application that posted the event to the log
- The username—either the user ID of the logged-on user for a security event or the process name for system events

- The name of the server where the event occurred
- The category of the event, which is typically used only in the Security log for events such as logon/logoff, object access, and policy changes
- The event ID, which is used to identify the event type, which is a number that can be used to aid in the troubleshooting of server problems

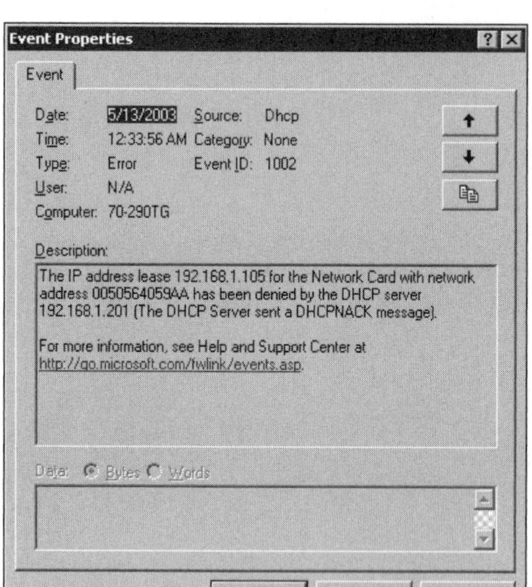

FIGURE 6.3
Log entries aren't always as clear as this one, so you will sometimes be able to click a URL for more information.

As shown in Figure 6.3, some events provide a URL that you can click. This URL links you to the Microsoft Web site. If there is more information available for your event, it is displayed. If you don't understand an error message and there is no URL, write down the event ID. The event ID can be used to perform a search using the Microsoft Knowledge Base at `http://support.microsoft.com`. The articles in the Knowledge Base can sometimes be useful in figuring out a problem, or at least giving you more information to work with.

IN THE FIELD

EVENTID.NET

EventID.net is a third-party Web site that collects definitions for most of the common events. Basic searches and information are free. This site also provides troubleshooting information and extra documentation for subscribers. This is a good reference if you can't locate any useful information on an event in the Microsoft Knowledge Base. The site is accessible at `www.eventid.net`.

Working with the Event Logs

Although the System and Application logs can be viewed by anyone, the Security log is restricted to administrators. To open and view an event log, perform the procedure outlined in Step by Step 6.1.

STEP BY STEP

6.1 Opening the Event Viewer and Viewing the System Log

1. Click Start, All Programs, Administrative Tools, Event Viewer.
2. In the left pane of the Event Viewer MMC, click the entry for the System log.
3. Find an event with a source of EventLog and an Event ID of 6005. Double-click the entry to open it.

As you can see in Figure 6.4, an event is written to the System log when the event log service is started. The event log service is started every time the server is started, so that gives you a good starting point when you want to look for errors that have occurred since the last system restart.

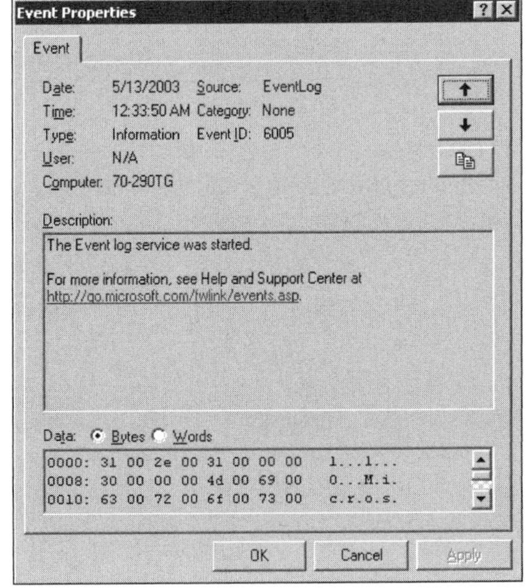

FIGURE 6.4
A System log event is recorded every time the server is started.

Viewing Logs on Another Computer

You can view the log files from a remote system on your network using the Connect to Another Computer command from the Event Viewer menu. This feature simplifies administrative tasks by allowing you to diagnose a system remotely via Event Viewer rather than requiring you to sit at that computer's keyboard. You must be a member of the Administrators group on the remote computer to view its event logs.

To open and view an event log on a remote computer, perform the procedure outlined in Step by Step 6.2.

STEP BY STEP

6.2 Opening the Event Viewer on a Remote Computer

1. From the Start menu, click Start, All Programs, Administrative Tools, Event Viewer.

continues

continued

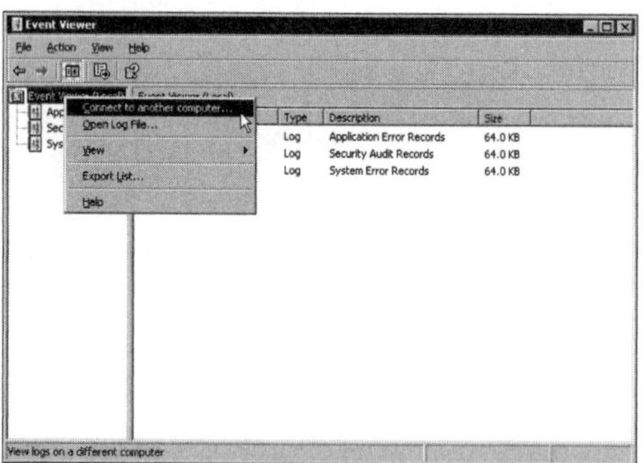

FIGURE 6.5▲
Using the Event Viewer to connect to another computer.

2. In the left pane of the Event Viewer MMC, right-click the Event Viewer (Local) entry. Select Connect to Another Computer from the pop-up menu, as shown in Figure 6.5.

3. From the Select Computer dialog box shown in Figure 6.6, you can either enter the name of the remote computer (without the leading \\) or click the Browse button to locate it on your network if you're not sure of the computer name. Click the Browse button to continue.

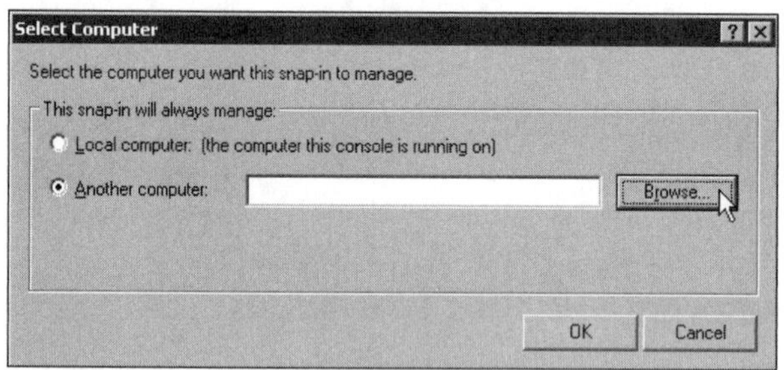

FIGURE 6.6▶
Remember to enter the computer name without the leading backslashes.

4. From the next Select Computer dialog box, shown in Figure 6.7, click the Advanced button.

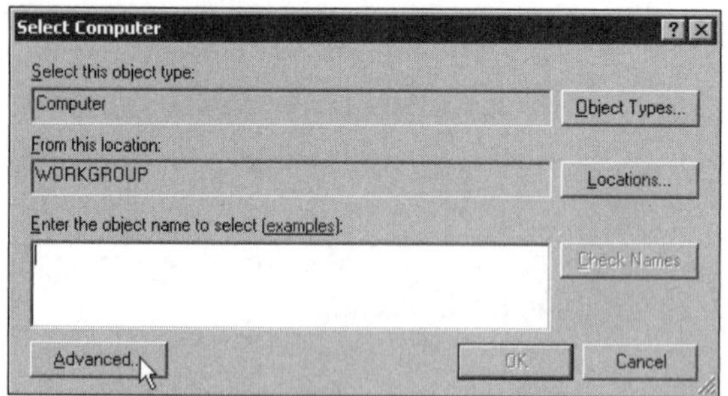

FIGURE 6.7
Click the Advanced button to search the Active Directory for the computer to connect to.

5. From the Select Computer dialog box shown in Figure 6.8, click the Locations button to select the domain to browse. Then click the Find Now button to search for computers.

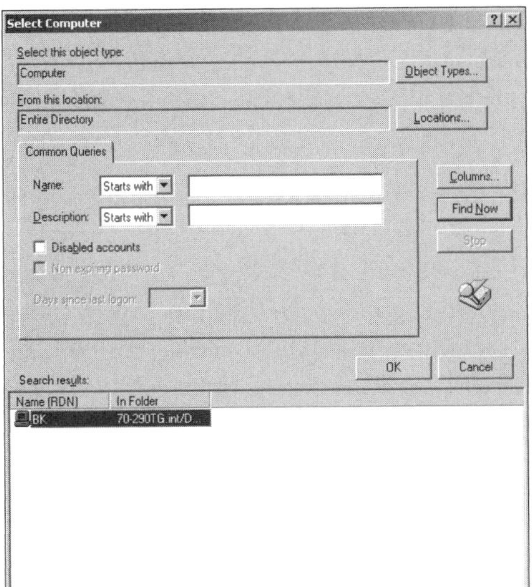

FIGURE 6.8
Locating the remote computer by searching the Active Directory.

6. Select a computer and then click OK twice to connect.

Configuring Log Properties

When you open a log in the Event Viewer, a snapshot of the log is displayed. Any new information that is written to the log as you are viewing it is not displayed until you click the Refresh icon on the Toolbar. When you switch between logs, the view is refreshed automatically.

Several configuration settings determine how much information can be stored in the event logs and how long the information is retained before it is overwritten. You can change the event log retention options through the Event Log Properties dialog box, shown in Figure 6.9, accessed from the Log menu. Each log file has its own size and day limit settings.

In addition to the setting for log size, three additional settings determine the retention properties of the logs:

- **Overwrite Events As Needed**—When the log is full, new events overwrite the oldest events.

- **Overwrite Events Older Than X Days**—This prevents the information in the logs from being overwritten until the specified time has elapsed. If the log becomes full, no events are recorded until there are events older than the specified period.
- **Do Not Overwrite Events**—This option prevents the logs from ever being overwritten, even if they become full. It should be used only if you clear or archive the logs on a regular basis. This option is typically used for the Security logs on highly secure networks, where access records must be maintained indefinitely. Increasing the maximum size of the log file is a good idea to ensure the server does not stop functioning in the event the log reaches its maximum size and is set to avoid overwriting older events.

WARNING

Be Careful when Setting Retention Time If you are not careful when configuring your event log retention settings, you could configure your logs so that important events are missed. For example, if you set the overwrite period too short, or turn on Overwrite Events As Needed with too small of a log size, as the log fills up, events will be overwritten. In addition, if you set the log size too small and then turn on Do Not Overwrite Events, after the log fills up, no events will be logged.

The default settings for the logs restrict each log file to a maximum of 16,384KB. When the fixed file size is reached, the oldest events are overwritten by new events, if the events are at least 7 days old. If you need to retain events for longer time periods, you should increase the file size and the retention time.

To configure the retention settings for an event log, perform the procedure outlined in Step by Step 6.3.

EXAM TIP

Event Log Defaults The event logs in Windows 2000 defaulted to 512KB and would overwrite events older than 7 days. The Windows Server 2003 defaults, however, are a much more practical 16,384KB and remain set to overwrite events older than 7 days. The change in size is a significant difference, and it's something you might get to see on the exam.

STEP BY STEP

6.3 Configuring the Event Log Retention Settings

1. From the Start menu, click Start, All Programs, Administrative Tools, Event Viewer.
2. In the left pane of the Event Viewer MMC, right-click the desired event log. From the pop-up menu, select Properties.
3. From the Event Log Properties dialog box shown in Figure 6.9, you can adjust the log size, set the retention time, or clear the log manually. After making the desired changes, click the OK button to save.

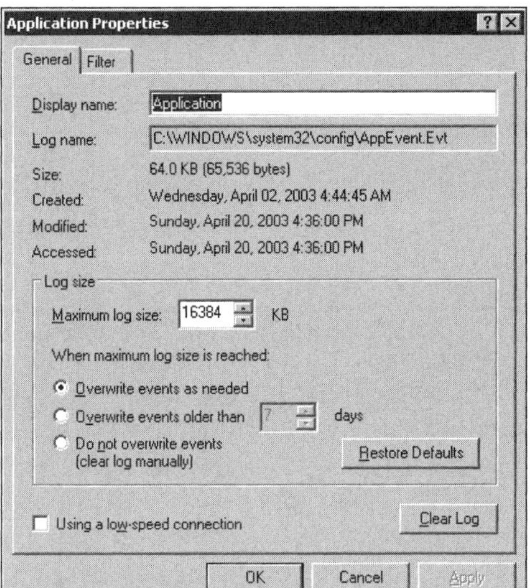

FIGURE 6.9
Changing the event log retention settings.

Clearing and Saving Logs

In addition to the retention settings, the Event Log Properties dialog box has an option to clear the log files. This option allows you to clear all entries from the selected log file. The option is also available from the pop-up menu when you right-click a log file in the Event Viewer MMC.

To clear a log file from the Event Viewer MMC, perform the steps outlined in Step by Step 6.4.

STEP BY STEP

6.4 Clearing an Event Log

1. From the Start menu, click Start, All Programs, Administrative Tools, Event Viewer.
2. In the left pane of the Event Viewer MMC, right-click the desired event log. From the pop-up menu, select Clear All Events, as shown in Figure 6.10.

continues

continued

3. After you elect to clear events, the confirmation dialog box shown in Figure 6.11 appears.

4. From the Save Log As dialog box shown in Figure 6.12, specify a name and location for the saved log and then click the Save button.

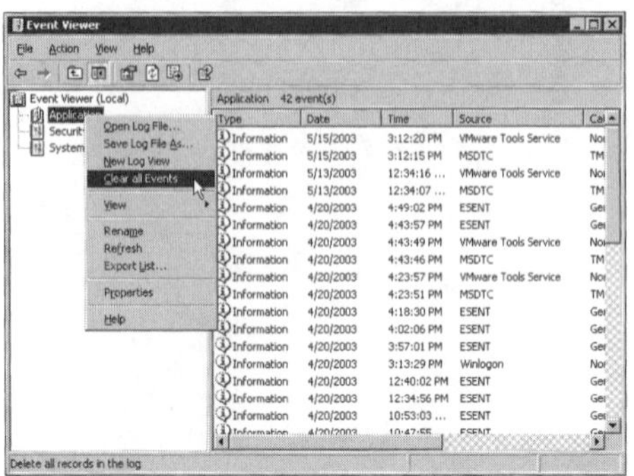

FIGURE 6.10
Select Clear All Events from the pop-up menu.

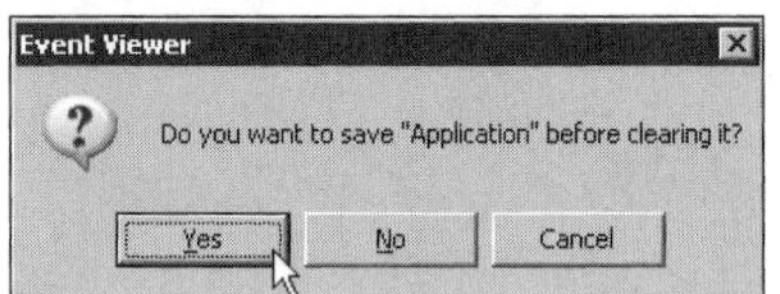

FIGURE 6.11
Select Yes to save the event log to a file.

FIGURE 6.12▲
Specify the name, path, and type to save the log file as.

As part of your regular maintenance, even if you have the logs set to overwrite as needed, you can manually archive them without clearing them. You can save the logs by right-clicking a log file entry in Event Viewer and selecting Save Log File As. You can save logs to an event file (`.evt`) or in a format that can be used with other applications (`.txt`). You can load the EVT file type into another Event Viewer. The log's TXT file can be saved in either standard monospace-columned or comma-delimited format. These formats can be used in common word processing or spreadsheet programs.

Log Viewing Options

The default view of the Event Viewer is to display the newest entry at the top. A handy feature of the Windows Server 2003 Event Viewer is its capability to sort the logs based on the columns displayed in the utility. For example, to sort the logs based on event ID, simply click the Event column heading, and the information is sorted in either ascending or descending order, depending on whether you click the column heading once or twice (see Figure 6.13).

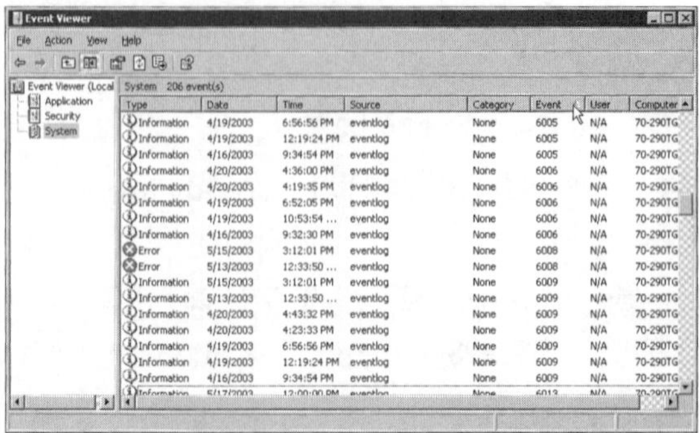

FIGURE 6.13▶
Click one of the column headings to sort the event files.

Filtering Events

By default, the Event Viewer shows the entire contents of the log file. This can be quite overwhelming, especially on a busy server, because a lot of informational messages are usually irrelevant when you are searching for the cause of a problem.

In these situations, you can use the Filter command from the View menu to quickly locate events of a certain type or pertaining to a particular source, category, user, computer, event ID, or date range. For example, you might want to see how many warnings have been recorded.

To filter a log file from the Event Viewer MMC, perform the steps outlined in Step by Step 6.5.

STEP BY STEP

6.5 Filtering an Event Log

1. From the Start menu, click Start, All Programs, Administrative Tools, Event Viewer.
2. In the left pane of the Event Viewer MMC, right-click the desired event log. From the system menu, select View, Filter, as shown in Figure 6.14.

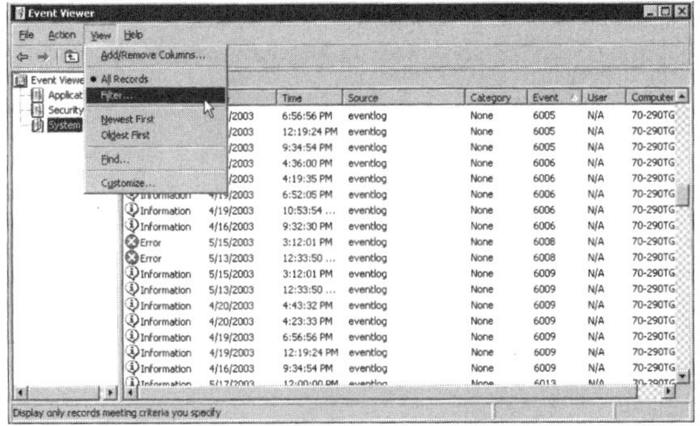

FIGURE 6.14
Select View, Filter from the system menu.

3. After you select Filter, the Properties dialog box shown in Figure 6.15 appears.

continues

continued

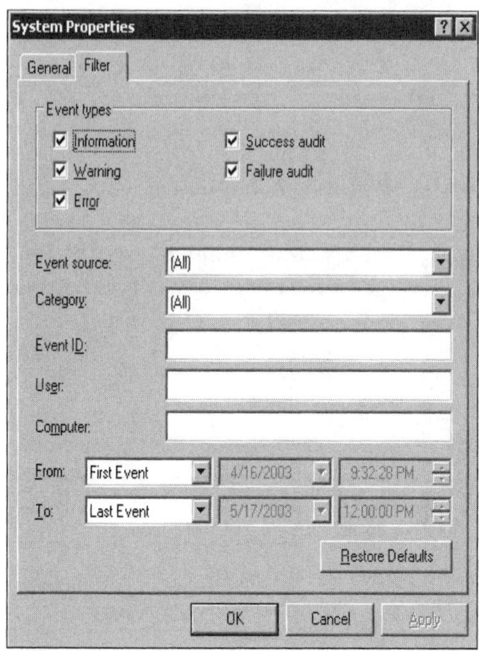

FIGURE 6.15
Select the desired filtering options, and then click OK.

4. From the Event Log Properties dialog box shown in Figure 6.15, deselect all the event types, except for Warning, and then click OK. The results after filtering are shown in Figure 6.16.

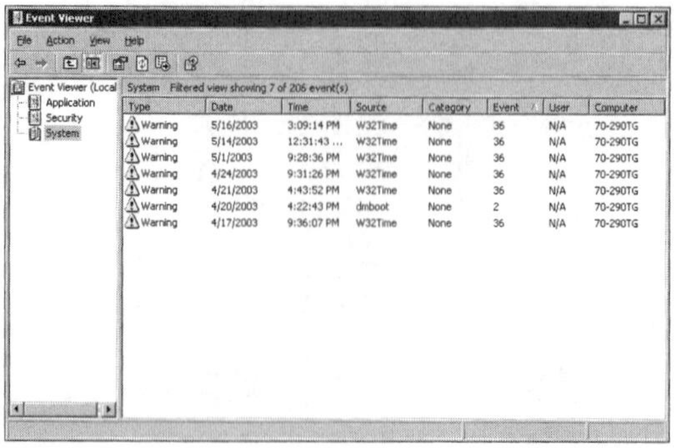

FIGURE 6.16
The log file after filtering.

5. To return to the default view that shows all events, from the system menu select View, All Records, as shown in Figure 6.17.

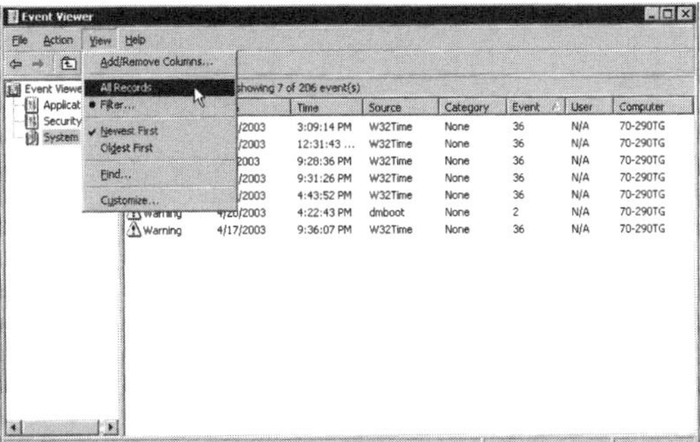

FIGURE 6.17
Resetting the event log to the default view.

The filtering options are very flexible; you can select either one or multiple filters to display only those entries that apply to the area you are working on.

The available filters are as follows:

- **Event Types**—This allows you to filter based on the type of events. For example, you might want to just see events that relate to a problem, such as warnings or errors. If you're working with Security logs, you would be more interested in success or failure audits, such as multiple failed logons, which might indicate an intrusion attempt.
- **Event Source**—This option allows you to filter events from a specific source, such as a driver, system component, or service.
- **Category**—This option allows you to filter events from a specific category. This filter is mostly useful with the Security log because it uses the category field more than the other logs do. This allows you to quickly filter the user logon type events from resource access and system events. Typical categories for the Security log are Account Logon, Logon/Logoff, System Event, and Policy Change.
- **Event ID**—Filters the log to display only a single event ID.
- **User**—Filters the log to show events that are associated with a particular user. Not all events have a user entry.

- **Computer**—Filters the log to show events that are associated with a particular computer. Because the initial release of Windows Server 2003 lets you display the log from only one computer at a time, this option is not commonly used.
- **From and To**—Filters the log to show only events that are included in the specified time/date range.

New Log View

As discussed in the previous section, sometimes a specific view of the logs makes it easier for you to do your job. Microsoft has supplied an option for the Event Viewer named New Log View. Using this option, you can customize a view of any of the logs, including filtering, size, and so on. You can then save this view under another name. This allows you to customize your view of the event logs, without affecting the default views or the logs themselves.

A new view can be added for any log by highlighting the log, and then right-clicking it. From the pop-up menu, select New Log View. The new log entry will appear in Event Viewer and can be renamed and configured like any other log.

Finding Specific Events

There might be times when you must find a specific event, or series of events, that can't be easily grouped using filtering. For example, if you want to see how many and what types of disk errors have been occurring on your server, filtering might not find all the events you are searching for due to the specific nature of filters. In cases like these, it is useful to search the logs using the options available for filtering with the added ability to search using keywords.

To search through the contents of the selected log for an event by keywords, use the Find command from the View menu. As you can see in the Find dialog box shown in Figure 6.18, you have similar options to those you used for filtering, in addition to the option to search for specific keywords in the Description field. Because the Find command does not allow you to search using a specific date range, it allows you to search backward and forward in a log. It displays a single entry at a time; use the Find Next button to move to the next entry.

To find a specific log entry, perform the procedure outlined in Step by Step 6.6.

STEP BY STEP

6.6 Finding an Event

1. From the Start menu, click Start, All Programs, Administrative Tools, Event Viewer.
2. In the left pane of the Event Viewer MMC, right-click the desired event log. From the system menu, select View, Find.
3. After you select Find, the Find dialog box shown in Figure 6.18 appears.
4. From the Find dialog box, deselect all the event types except for Failure Audit and then click OK.
5. The first log entry that matches the Find criteria is highlighted. You can double-click the entry to display it, or you can click Find Next to move to the next matching entry.

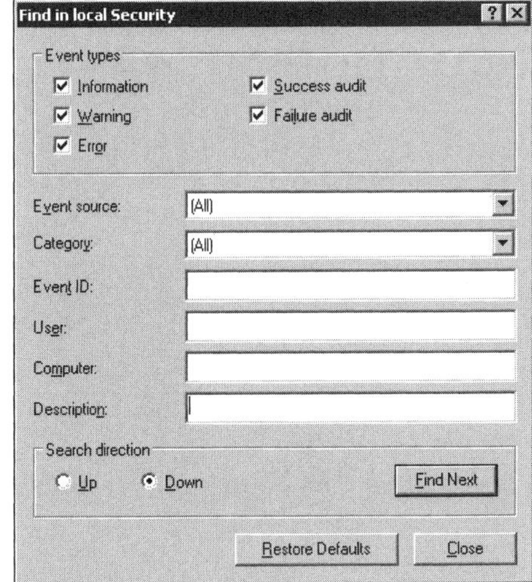

FIGURE 6.18
Select the desired Find options and then click Find Next.

Loading a Saved Event Log

In most high-security environments, archiving the Security log is required. This is so that a record is maintained of previous security and auditing events. In addition, there might be situations where you will archive other logs for error-tracking purposes. After a log is archived, it can be imported into the Event Viewer on any Windows 2000/2003/XP computer.

To load a saved log file, perform the procedure outlined in Step by Step 6.7.

STEP BY STEP

6.7 Loading a Saved Event Log

1. From the Start menu, click Start, All Programs, Administrative Tools, Event Viewer.
2. In the left pane of the Event Viewer MMC, right-click Event Viewer (Local). From the pop-up menu, select Open Log File.
3. In the Open dialog box shown in Figure 6.19, select the file to open. Saved event logs have an `*.evt` filename.

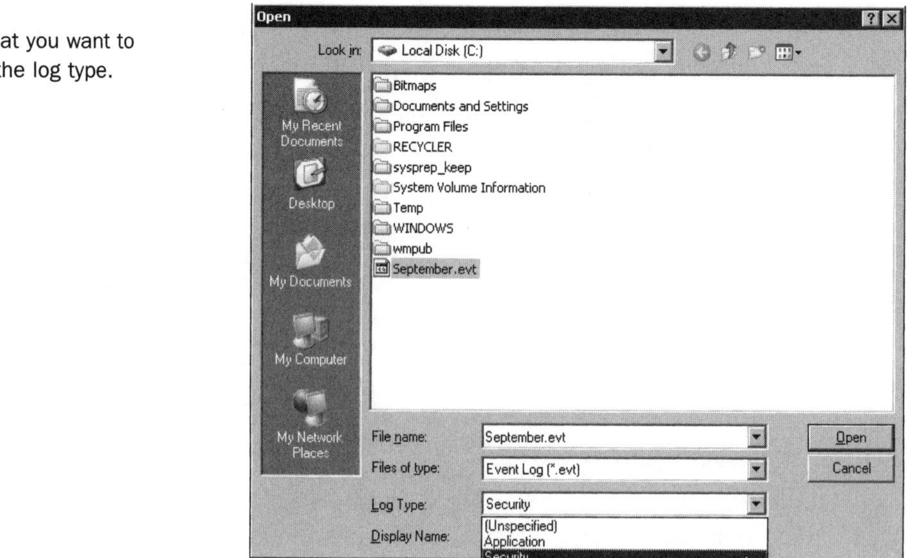

FIGURE 6.19
Select the saved event log that you want to view. Make sure you specify the log type.

4. Click Open to load the saved log file. As you can see in Figure 6.20, the saved file is added as an additional entry in the Event Viewer.

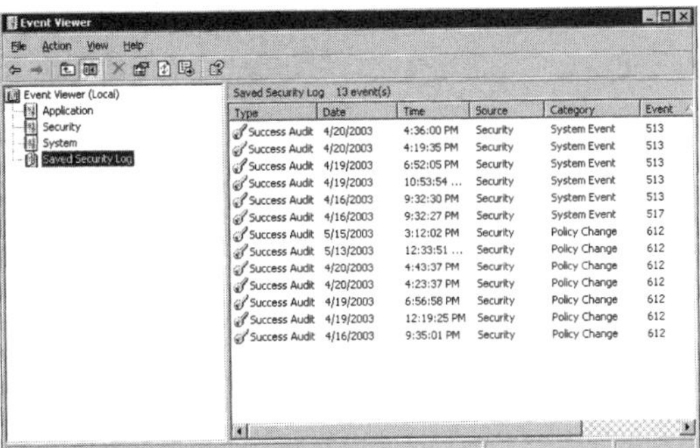

FIGURE 6.20
The log file is displayed as an additional entry. It does not replace the existing logs.

IN THE FIELD

THIRD-PARTY SOLUTIONS

Event Viewer can record a significant amount of useful, if not vital, information, but extracting or even locating the data within the log files can be a daunting task. You may want to invest in an event-consolidation and -reporting utility that can automatically and semi-intelligently scan Event Viewer. These tools look for patterns of failure, intrusion, or degradation of the system and then report the findings to you in a concise format.

Microsoft included a useful tool in the Windows 2000 Resource Kit, called `dumpel.exe`, that filters the event logs for specific events using a variety of search criteria. For some reason, it was left out of the Windows 2003 Resource Kit. However, it can still be downloaded from `http://www.microsoft.com/downloads/details.aspx?FamilyID=c9c31b3d-c3a9-4a73-86a3-630a3c475c1a&DisplayLang=en`.

AUDITING

Now that we've covered the basics of using the Event Viewer, we are going to put this knowledge to use. One of the primary uses of the event logs, specifically the Security log, is to monitor the access of server resources by users and processes. In the current climate of security breaches and what seems like weekly security exploits, it's very important to know who is using your servers and for what purposes.

Auditing is the process of recording user and system activities on the network. These events are recorded in the Windows Server 2003 Security Log, which is one of the logs contained in the event log we examined earlier in this chapter.

Just about any activity involving a Windows Server 2003 object can be recorded in the Security log. When you configure auditing, you decide what activities, called *events*, you want to track and against what object. Typical activities that can be tracked are valid or invalid logon attempts, creating or opening files, and changes in user rights. After the audited events are recorded in the Security log, you can use the Event Viewer utility to view and analyze them.

In Windows Server 2003, the *security descriptor* is used to control access to objects. In addition to storing permissions information, a security descriptor also contains auditing information. The portion of the security descriptor that contains this auditing information is known as a *System Access Control List (SACL)*. The SACL is used to specify what attributes of the object are audited and what events associated with the attributes are audited.

It is just as important to audit user account–management tasks as it is to audit the accesses of important network resources. The entries saved to the Security log provide the network administrator with a summary of network operations, showing what tasks were attempted and by whom. Not only does this help to detect intrusions by malicious invaders, but the logs can also show more mundane problems, such as careless users who inadvertently delete important files.

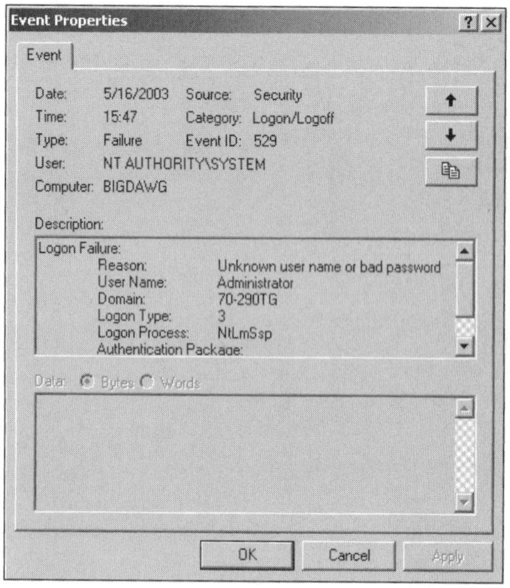

FIGURE 6.21
A typical Security log entry showing a failed logon.

As shown in Figure 6.21, a typical entry in the Security log shows the following:

- The time and date the event occurred
- The event performed
- The user account that performed the event
- The success or failure of the event

Using Audit Policies

To simplify the configuration of auditing, Windows Server 2003 allows you to create an *audit policy*, which is used to define the events that are recorded in the Windows Server 2003 Security logs. Audit policies are created and applied similar to the other types of policies using the Group Policy snap-ins. Unlike previous versions of Windows, when Windows Server 2003 is first installed, auditing is turned on. By turning on various auditing event categories, you can implement an auditing policy that suits the security needs of your organization.

The first step in creating an audit policy is deciding which events and users should be audited and on which computers. Generally, the audit policies are different depending on the role, or type of computer, that is being audited. For example, the audit policy would most likely be more extensive for a domain controller than for a workstation. In addition, audit policies can be applied at different levels, so you need to decide whether to apply them at the site, Organizational Unit, or domain level.

> NOTE
>
> **Check for Inheritance** Auditing policies are subject to policy inheritance, so the policies that you set on your local computer could be overshadowed by policies set for the domain as a whole.

The next step is to decide what attributes of the events you are auditing you want to track. For example, if you are tracking logon attempts, you must decide if you want to record successful logons, failed logons, or both. As part of this step, you must consider the fact that the more events that are audited, the larger the Security logs become. Although you can configure the Security logs to be larger, this makes it more difficult to find specific events.

After you have decided what events to audit, and how you want them audited, you must specify your choices using the Audit Policy container in the Group Policy snap-in. After you have made your choices, you can use the Group Policy snap-in to apply the audit policy to the desired objects.

The type of events that can be audited by Windows Server 2003 are separated into the following event categories:

- **Account Logon Events**—This event is recorded when a domain controller receives a request to validate a user account. This provides the network administrator with a record of user accounts that have logged on to the network, when they logged on, and what privileges they were given.

- **Account Management**—This event monitors the actions of the network administrator. It records any changes that the administrator makes to the attributes of a user, a group, or a computer account. It also records an event when the administrator creates or deletes an account. This option is of the most use in networks with multiple administrators, especially when you have inexperienced administrators that need to be monitored closely.
- **Directory Service Access**—This event monitors user access to the Directory Service objects. Auditing has to be turned on for the specific object for this activity to be logged.
- **Logon Events**—This event monitors logons and logoffs at the local console as well as network connections to the computer.
- **Object Access**—This event monitors user access to objects on the network, such as files, folders, or printers. Auditing has to be turned on for the specific object for this activity to be logged.
- **Policy Change**—This event monitors changes in any of the policies that have been applied in the domain. This includes changes to user security options, user rights, and audit policies. This option can be very handy when certain permissions-related operations stop working. You can search back through the log to see if any policies have been changed inadvertently.
- **Privilege Use**—This event monitors the use of user rights. Typical examples are the administrator viewing or working with the Security log, or a user changing the system time. The entry in the log shows the account name, the time, and exactly which right was used.
- **Process Tracking**—This event is used to monitor executable files, such as EXE, DLL, and OCX files, and is generally used by programmers who want to track program execution. It can also be used for virus detection. In most cases, better tools are available for doing both tasks.
- **System Events**—This is a catchall event monitor. It is used to track events such as users restarting or shutting down computers, services starting and stopping, and any events that affect overall Windows Server 2003 security. An example of this would be if the audit log fills up.

NOTE

Auditing Is Object Specific The types of events that can be audited for an object are determined by the type of object to be audited. For example, the auditing features for files and directories require the use of an NTFS file system.

Creating an Audit Policy

Audit policies are created using the Group Policy snap-in or from the Active Directory Users and Computers snap-in, if your server is a member of a domain.

To create an Audit policy, perform the procedure outlined in Step by Step 6.8.

STEP BY STEP

6.8 Creating an Audit Policy for Logon Failure Events

1. From the Start menu, click Start, All Programs, Administrative Tools, Active Directory Users and Computers.
2. From the Active Directory Users and Computers console, right-click the Domain Controllers folder and then click Properties. From the Domain Controllers Properties dialog box, click the Group Policy tab.
3. The policies in effect for the object are displayed. Double-click the desired policy. This opens the Group Policy console shown in Figure 6.22.

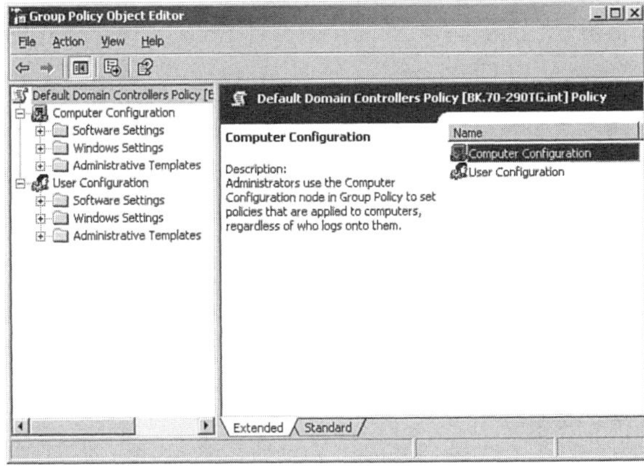

FIGURE 6.22
The Group Policy console for the default Domain Controllers policy.

continues

continued

4. Click Computer Configuration, Windows Settings, Security Settings, Local Policy, Audit Policy. The Audit Policy settings are displayed in the right pane, as you can see in Figure 6.23.

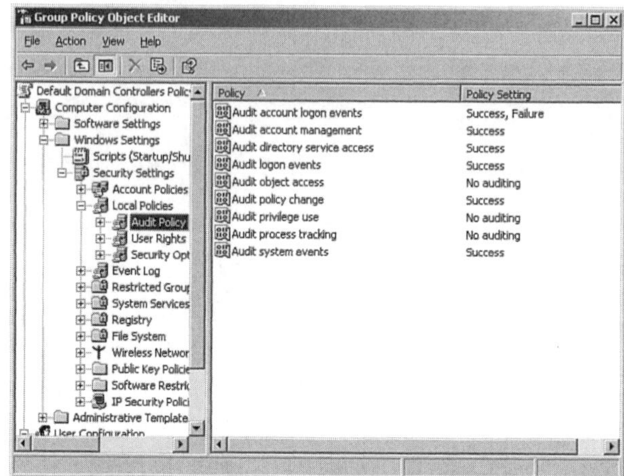

FIGURE 6.23
The default audit policies available for the domain controller. Note that several are turned on by default.

5. Right-click the Audit Account Logon Events audit policy.
6. The Audit Policy Properties dialog box appears, as shown in Figure 6.24. Select the Define These Policy Settings check box and then select both the Success and the Failure check boxes. This turns on auditing for any logon event.
7. Click OK to save.

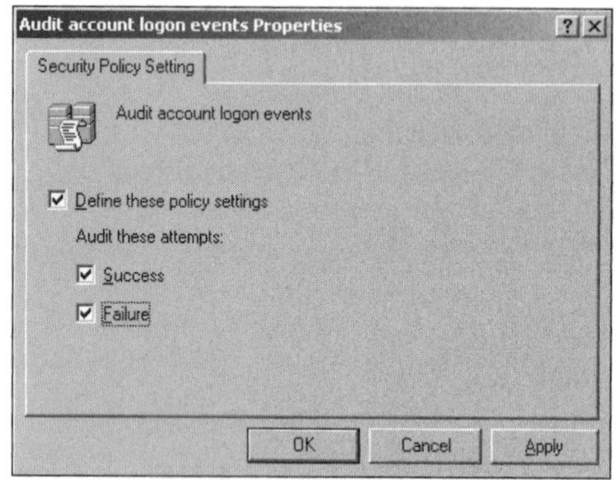

FIGURE 6.24
Auditing successful logons is turned on by default. Turn on failure auditing for this exercise.

It is important to remember that for objects, auditing is a two-step project. First, you have to enable the specific auditing category that includes the object you want to audit. Second, you have to enable auditing of specific events on this object, from the properties page of the object itself.

For example, if you want to audit the access of the Payroll folder on one of your file servers, you must turn on auditing for object access, either at the site, domain, Organization Unit, or local level. Next, select the properties page of the folder and enable auditing for that folder.

In Step by Step 6.9, we first turn on auditing for object access using the Local Security Policy MMC; then we enable auditing on the Payroll folder.

STEP BY STEP

6.9 Creating an Audit Policy for Object Access

1. From the Start menu, click Start, All Programs, Administrative Tools, Local Security Policy.
2. From the Local Security Policy MMC, shown in Figure 6.25, click Local Properties, Audit Policy.

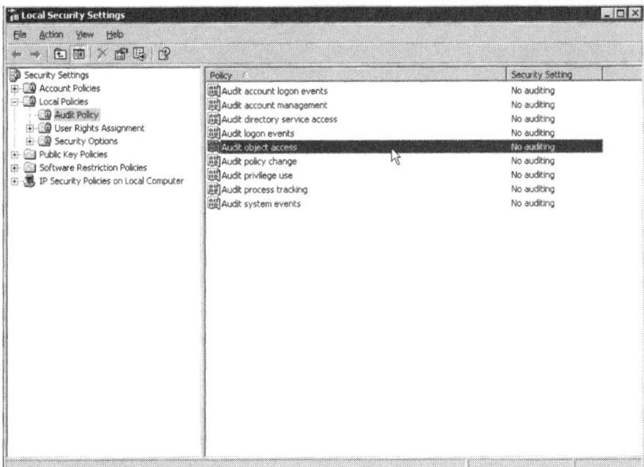

FIGURE 6.25
Double-click the desired Audit Policy to configure it.

3. The policies in effect for the object are displayed. Double-click the Audit Object Access policy. This opens the Properties dialog box shown in Figure 6.26.
4. Under Audit these Attempts, select the Failure check box. Click OK to save.
5. Close the Local Security Policy MMC.
6. Open either Windows Explorer or My Computer and navigate to the Payroll folder. Right-click the Payroll folder and select Properties.
7. From the resulting Properties dialog box, select the Security tab. From the Security tab, click the Advanced button.

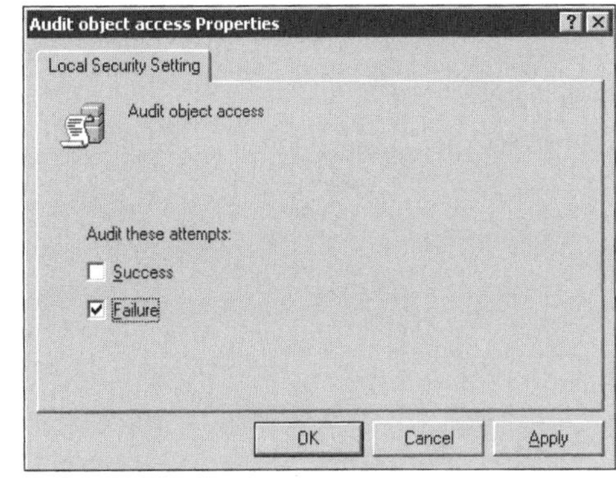

FIGURE 6.26
Select the Failure check box to record an entry in the Security log anytime an unauthorized attempt to access an object is made.

continues

continued

8. This opens the Advanced Security Settings dialog box shown in Figure 6.27. Select the Auditing tab.

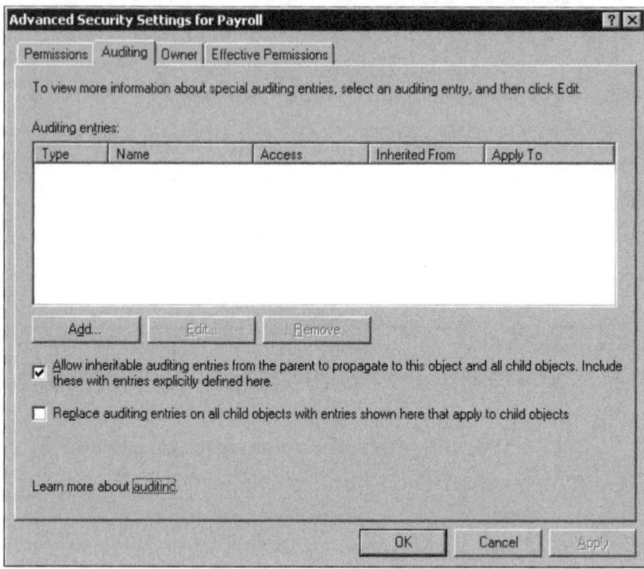

FIGURE 6.27
The Auditing tab displays the type of auditing enabled, whom it applies to, whether or not it was inherited, and from where.

9. On the Auditing tab, click the Add button. From the Select User or Group dialog box that appears, enter the user or group for which you would like to track access to the resource. If you don't know the exact name, you can click the Advanced button to browse for a user or group name (see Figure 6.28). Click OK when you're finished.

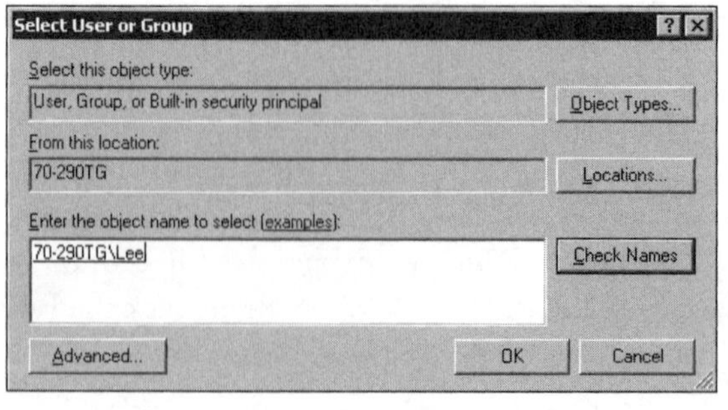

FIGURE 6.28
Select the user or group from which you want to track access to the resource.

10. The Auditing Entry dialog box appears, as shown in Figure 6.29. Notice that you can select from a variety of events for success, failure, or both. In addition, you have the option to apply the auditing settings to the folder only, the folder and its files, and a variety of other options. This turns on auditing for any logon event.

11. Click OK three times to save.

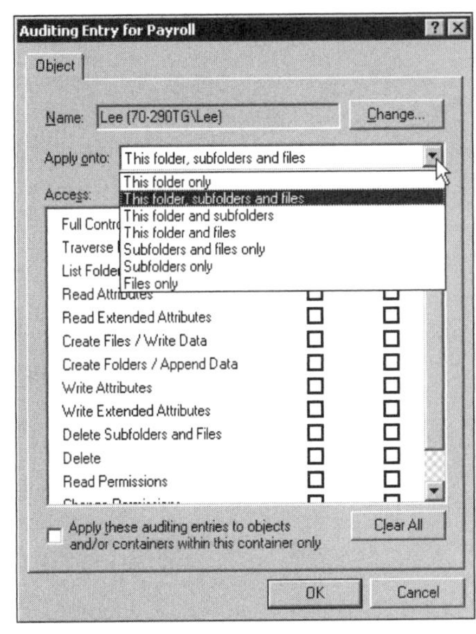

FIGURE 6.29
The Auditing Entry dialog box allows you to select both the events and the objects on which to enable auditing.

When you're defining your audit policy, it is important to know what you plan to do with all the data that is collected. If you are using the audit policy for resource planning, you might want to increase the log size so that you can store data for a longer length of time, or you can archive logs from time to time so that you can keep an ongoing record of system and resource usage.

Always audit the files and folders that contain sensitive data, while ignoring common files that most users access regularly. Quantity of data does not always equal quality of data. In addition, auditing does create overhead, both in processing time and disk space.

The Everyone group should be used to audit resource access instead of using the Users group. Certain user accounts are not members of the Users group that are members of the Everyone group. Remember that *all* user accounts are added to the Everyone group by default. Note that in Windows Server 2003, the Everyone group no longer includes anonymous users.

Don't forget to audit all administrative tasks performed by the administrative groups. This allows you to spot problems created by inexperienced administrators. In addition, the Administrator account is a favorite target for intruders. By monitoring the administrative accounts, you should be able to spot the erratic activity that is common to an improperly trained or unauthorized user.

> **EXAM TIP**
>
> **Have a Good Understanding of Auditing** With the heavy emphasis that Microsoft has been putting on security, you should expect to see at least one, if not more, security-related auditing questions on the exam.

Monitoring and Analyzing Security Events

Earlier in the chapter, we examined how to use the Event Viewer to work with various log files. Most of the other log files, such as the Application and System log files, can be viewed by all users. However, the Security log can be viewed only by administrators.

You can make various configuration changes to the Security log, the most important of which is to increase the size of the log. The default size is 16,384KB, which is sufficient for light logging in small-to-medium-sized organizations but becomes quickly filled in larger organizations that perform a lot of auditing.

Although we covered how to manually increase the size of the event logs earlier in the chapter, it would be time consuming to make this change on every server in your enterprise. To make the configuration of the event logs consistent on the computers in your organization, you can create an Event Log Settings policy. This policy can be created via the Group Policy snap-in. After the policy is configured, it can be applied to the desired computers just like any other policy.

To configure the Security log size for all computers in the domain, perform the procedure outlined in Step by Step 6.10.

STEP BY STEP

6.10 Creating a Security Log Policy

1. From the Start menu, click Start, All Programs, Administrative Tools, Domain Security Policy.
2. From the Default Domain Security Settings MMC, shown in Figure 6.30, click Security Settings, Event Log.

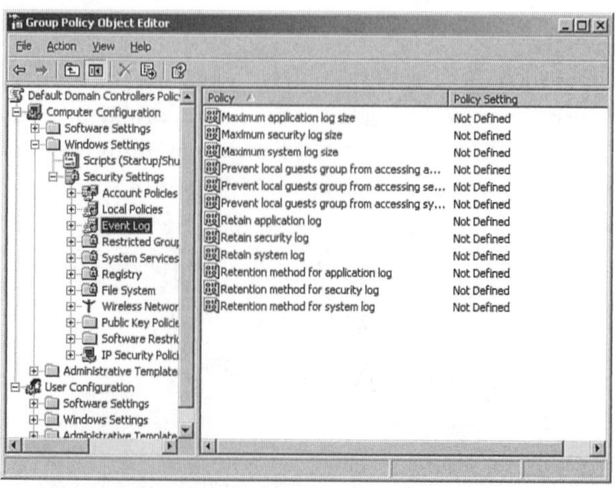

FIGURE 6.30
The Default Domain Security Settings MMC.

3. The policies available for the object are displayed. Double-click the Maximum Security Log Size policy. This opens the Properties dialog box shown in Figure 6.31.
4. Set the log size to 30,000. Note that the settings are in kilobytes. Click OK to save.
5. Close the Default Domain Security Settings MMC.

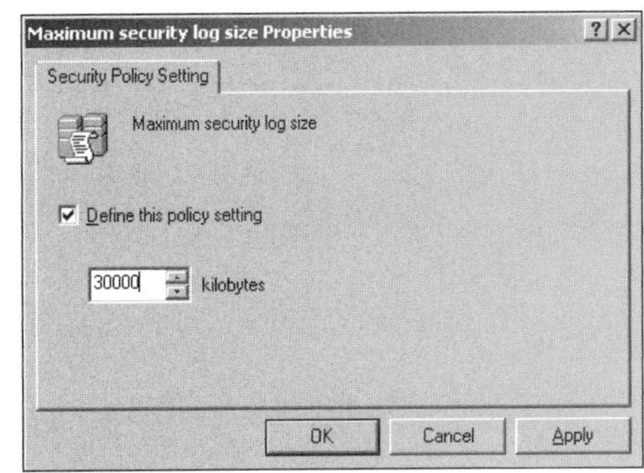

FIGURE 6.31
Select Define This Policy Setting, and then increase the default value to 30,000.

Recording security events is used as a form of intrusion detection. When security auditing and the Security logs are configured properly, it is possible to detect some types of network break-ins before they succeed. An example of this would be a password attack, which in a network with a good password policy can take some time to perform successfully. The Security log is also invaluable after a break-in has occurred, so you can track the movements and actions of the intruder, and how he was able to enter your system. Above all, security logging is effective only if the network administrator takes the time to review it frequently.

IN THE FIELD

BEST PRACTICES

It is important to realize that a good security implementation involves the coordination of many network functions. Above all, it is imperative that the user is able to log on to the network and locate and use the appropriate resources without an undue level of difficulty.

Critical network servers should always be kept in a secure area. The odds of a system break-in are greatly increased if a skilled intruder has physical access to a server console. In addition, having critical servers in an open area can make them vulnerable to a disgruntled employee with nothing more sophisticated than a baseball bat or a bucket of water. Attacks do not have to be sophisticated to be damaging, and historically most losses occur from inside the company versus from the outside.

One of the best security policies is proper user education. Users should be aware of how important it is to protect company resources and the implications of what could happen if critical information falls into the wrong hands. Users should be educated about how to keep their passwords confidential and secure. A good idea is to publish a clearly worded security policy and require everyone, including network administrators, to review it periodically.

GUIDED PRACTICE EXERCISE 6.1

In the world we live in today, security has become a major concern. A good system administrator must not only be wary of threats from the outside, but must also guard against inside threats. Recent statistics have shown that a server is more likely to be attacked from inside the firewall than from the outside.

Some parts of your network need to be more secure than others. For example, anything that has to do with trade secrets, proprietary company information, or employee data should have the strongest security applied.

But how do you know whether your security measures are effective? Are you suffering from a false sense of security? (No pun intended!) What types of tools are included in Windows Server 2003 that can reassure you? On your own, try to develop a strategy to address this type of issue.

If you would like to see a possible solution, follow the upcoming steps.

Estimated Time: 20 minutes

One way to attack this problem would be to turn auditing on for specific files and folders. A good practice would be to always audit the files and folders that contain sensitive data, while ignoring common files that most users access regularly.

On the server that contains the objects you want to audit, follow these steps:

1. From the Start menu, click Start, All Programs, Administrative Tools, Local Security Policy.
2. From the Local Security Policy MMC, click Local Properties, Audit Policy.
3. The policies in effect for the object are displayed. Double-click the Audit Object Access policy; this opens a Properties dialog box.
4. Under Audit These Attempts, select the Failure check box. Click OK to save.
5. Close the Local Security Policy MMC.

6. Open either Windows Explorer or My Computer and navigate to the folder that you want to audit. Right-click the folder and select Properties.
7. From the resulting Properties dialog, select the Security tab. From the Security tab, click the Advanced button.
8. This opens the Advanced Security Settings dialog box. Select the Auditing tab.
9. The Auditing tab displays the type of auditing enabled, who it applies to, whether it was inherited, and from where. On the Auditing tab, click the Add button.
10. From the Select User or Group dialog box that appears, enter the user or group for which you want to track access to the resource. For security auditing, select the Everyone group. Click OK when you're finished.
11. The Auditing Entry dialog box appears. Notice that you can select from a variety of events for success, failure, or both. In addition, you have the option to apply the auditing settings to the folder only, to the folder and its files, and a variety of other options.
12. Click OK three times to save.

USING TASK MANAGER

The Task Manager utility is included in Windows Server 2003 to give administrators a way to monitor and manage the state of currently running applications and processes. Almost a mini Performance utility, this tool provides a quick glance into a system's health. In addition, Task Manager provides the administrator with a summarized view of the basic system resources in use.

The Task Manager can be used to monitor the state of active applications, including a real-time view of the system resources assigned to each application. Task Manager also allows you to observe applications that have stopped responding and to terminate them.

Task Manager can be started in several ways:

- Right-clicking the Taskbar and clicking Task Manager on the pop-up menu.
- Pressing Ctrl+Shift+Esc.
- Pressing Ctrl+Alt+Del to open the Windows Security dialog box and clicking the Task Manager button.

The Task Manager window has five tabs: Applications, Processes, Performance, Networking, and Users. Each tab is discussed in the sections that follow.

Applications Tab

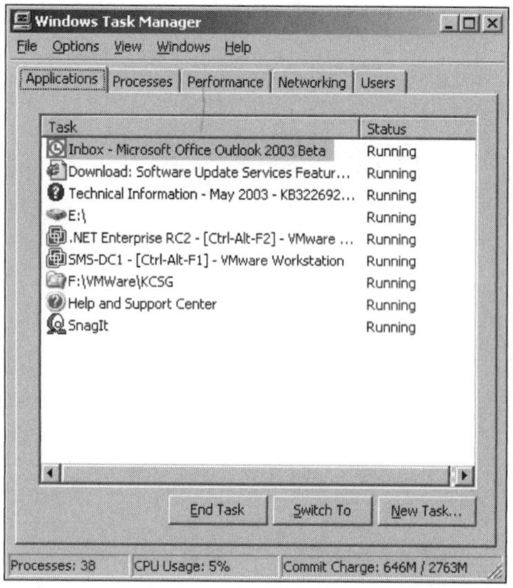

FIGURE 6.32
The Task Manager's Applications tab, showing running applications.

The Applications tab, shown in Figure 6.32, displays a list of the currently active applications, along with their status—either Running or Not Responding. The default status for a program is Running; however, there are times when a program temporarily displays a status of Not Responding. This usually occurs when another program or programs have a higher priority and receive the bulk of the system resources, or if a program is performing a computationally heavy task and is too busy to acknowledge any requests.

If the application not responding is not automatically restored to Running status after the other applications have completed, you probably need to terminate it manually. This can be accomplished by right-clicking the application and selecting End Task from the pop-up menu or by clicking the End Task button at the bottom of the Task Manager window. Unfortunately, if the application has any files open, your data will not be saved. Task Manager also allows you to terminate running applications.

There are also three methods to start applications using Task Manager:

- From the Task Manager window menu bar, select File, New Task (Run).
- Select Start, Run and then type **taskmgr**.
- From the Task Manager's Applications tab, click the New Task button in the lower-right corner of the window.

Processes Tab

The Processes tab, shown in Figure 6.33, displays a list of the currently active processes, along with the resources they are using. Even on a system that is displaying few applications running, there will always be multiple processes running in the background.

There are two reasons for this. First, operating system processes won't be displayed on the Applications tab. The second reason is that if you start an application called `go.exe`, for example, odds are the application will start multiple background processes. This is where the Processes tab can actually be pretty handy because the main application might not be using a lot of resources, but one of the background processes could be maxing out the CPU!

The default view shows the processes running for the currently logged-on user, but the processes for all users can be shown by selecting the Show Processes from All Users check box in the lower-left corner of the dialog box. The default resources displayed are CPU % (abbreviated as CPU) and Memory Usage. However, additional items, such as Page Faults, I/O Writes, and Peak Memory Usage, can be added by selecting View, Set Columns from the Task Manager menu bar.

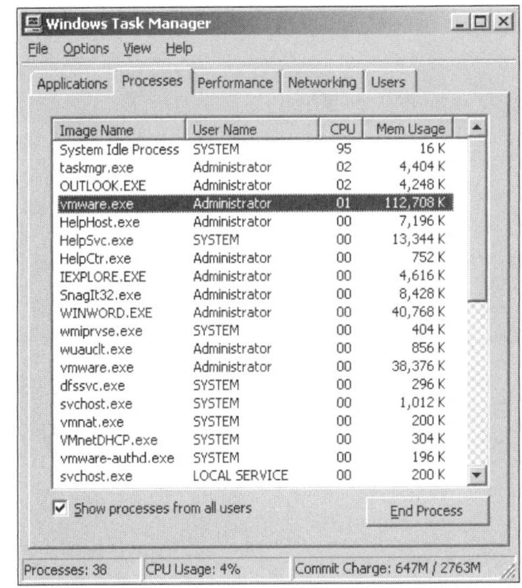

FIGURE 6.33
The Task Manager's Processes tab, showing processes sorted by CPU Time.

Using the Processes tab, you can immediately see which processes are using the majority of the system resources. In the default view, you can sort the processes by name (Image Name), username, CPU percentage used (CPU), or memory used (Mem Usage).

For example, to sort the processes by the amount of CPU percentage used, click the CPU heading twice. This allows you to identify a process that is hogging the resources and starving the other processes. This can indicate a process that is having a problem and needs to either be terminated or set to a lower priority. Under normal conditions, the System Idle Process should have the highest percentage in the CPU column.

Understanding Priority

Windows Server 2003 provides a fast, reliable, multitasking environment that supports preemptive multitasking and the execution of applications in separate address spaces. In preemptive multitasking, the operating system controls which application has access to the CPU and for how long. The operating system is free to switch resources at any time to an application with a higher priority.

This also allows the operating system to revoke resources from a defective or a poorly designed program that tries to dominate resources.

Windows Server 2003 supports multiple units of execution for a single process, using a process called *multithreading*. In a multithreaded environment, a process can be broken up into subtasks, called *threads*, that can execute independently of the main process. This allows a program to perform multiple tasks simultaneously instead of sequentially. For example, when you are using Microsoft Outlook, you can read messages or create a new message while downloading or sending messages. Multithreading means one process does not have to wait for another to finish.

In a preemptive multitasking system, individual tasks cannot dictate how long they use the system resources. This means that some type of priority system is necessary to ensure that critical tasks get a larger share of the processor's time. The priority system is part of the operating system, but the individual tasks can tell the OS what priority they need. This works well in theory, but there are always situations in which a system might get loaded with high-priority tasks that keep the low-priority tasks from getting any system resources at all.

Windows Server 2003 uses a dynamic priority system that allows it to adjust the priority of tasks to reflect constantly changing system conditions. For example, if a low-priority task is passed over in favor of a high-priority task, Windows Server 2003 increases the priority of the low-priority task until it gets some system resources. After a high-priority task runs for a while, Windows Server 2003 lowers that task's priority. The dynamic priority system ensures that some tasks get more system resources than others and that every task gets at least some system resources.

A *foreground application* is one that is made active by selecting it on the Windows Server 2003 desktop, thus bringing it to the foreground. All other applications running are then termed *background applications*, with respect to the foreground application. By default, Windows Server 2003 assigns more resources and a higher priority to a background application than to foreground applications in the same priority class. This is, of course, because Windows Server 2003 is a server operating system, and servers typically host background operations such as file sharing and print services.

Windows Server 2003 uses priority to allocate processor time in small chunks to applications. This is called *time slicing*. Windows Server 2003 allocates multiple, short, variable-length time slices to foreground applications, while allocating longer, fixed-length, but less-frequent time slices to background applications or services.

To change the default behavior, open the System applet in the Control Panel (see Figure 6.34). From the Advanced tab, click the Settings button in the Performance area. From the Performance Options dialog box, you can select the Advanced tab to optimize the responsiveness of your system. Two choices are available: Programs and Background Services. The default is Background Services, in which the server assigns more resources to applications running in background sessions, such as mail or database servers. This results in a more responsive system, and it's recommended for servers that are not running foreground applications.

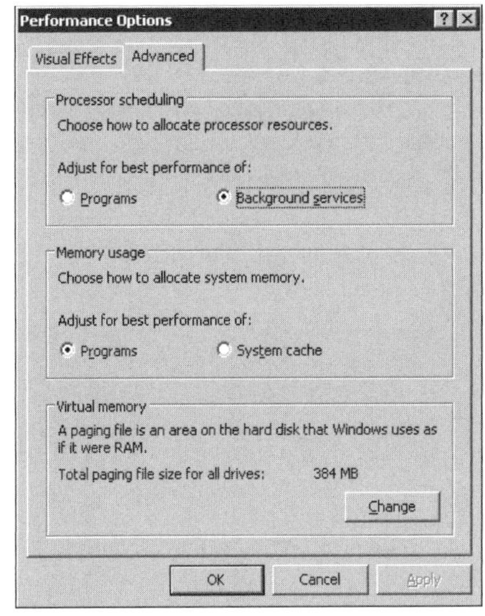

FIGURE 6.34
The Advanced tab of System Properties, showing performance options.

> **NOTE**
> **Processor Scheduling** On a server, there is rarely a good reason to change the configuration to adjust performance for programs, except on Terminal Servers running in Application mode.

Windows Server 2003 further subdivides processing time to applications using different classes of priority levels. Priority levels are assigned numbers from 0 to 31. Applications and noncritical operating system functions are assigned levels of 0 to 15, whereas real-time functions, such as the operating system kernel, are assigned levels of 16 to 31. The normal base priority is 8.

By default, priority levels are not displayed in the Task Manager window. To configure Task Manager to display the priority level of running applications, perform the procedure outlined in Step by Step 6.11.

STEP BY STEP

6.11 Configuring Task Manager to Display Priority Levels

1. Right-click the Taskbar and then click Task Manager in the pop-up menu.
2. From the Task Manager window, select the Processes tab.
3. On the Task Manager system menu, select View, Select Columns. This opens the Select Columns dialog box shown in Figure 6.35.

continues

continued

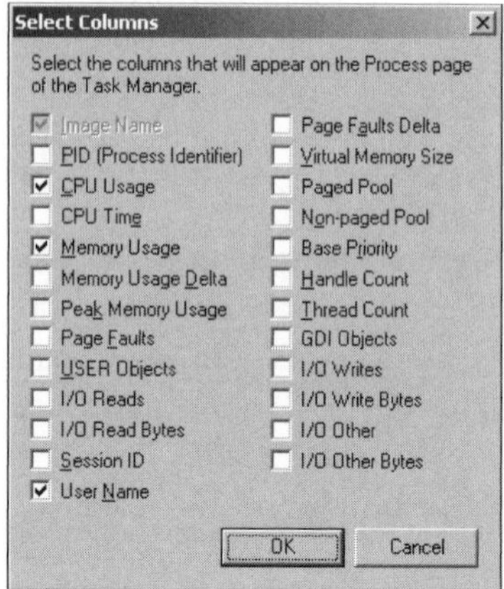

FIGURE 6.35
The Select Columns dialog box allows you to select the information you want displayed on the Processes tab of Task Manager.

4. Click the Base Priority check box shown in Figure 6.35. Click OK to save. The result is shown in Figure 6.36.

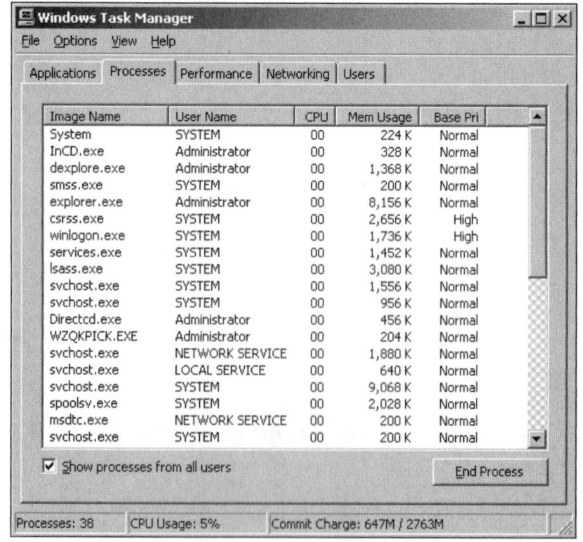

FIGURE 6.36
Task Manager reconfigured to display the priority of all processes.

If a process is running at a low priority, and a real-time process is started, the real-time process receives more system resources than the process running at low priority. This can sometimes cause the application that the lower-priority process is controlled by to show a status of Not Responding on the Task Manager's Applications tab.

To keep a real-time process from starving a lower-priority process, you can manually set the priority of the lower-priority process to a higher value.

To set a process to a higher priority, perform the procedure outlined in Step by Step 6.12.

STEP BY STEP

6.12 Setting a Process to a Higher Priority

1. Right-click the Taskbar and then click Task Manager in the pop-up menu.
2. From the Task Manager window, select the Processes tab.
3. On the Task Manager system menu, right-click the process that you want to change the priority of (in this case, `InCD.exe`) and select Set Priority from the pop-up menu, as shown in Figure 6.37.

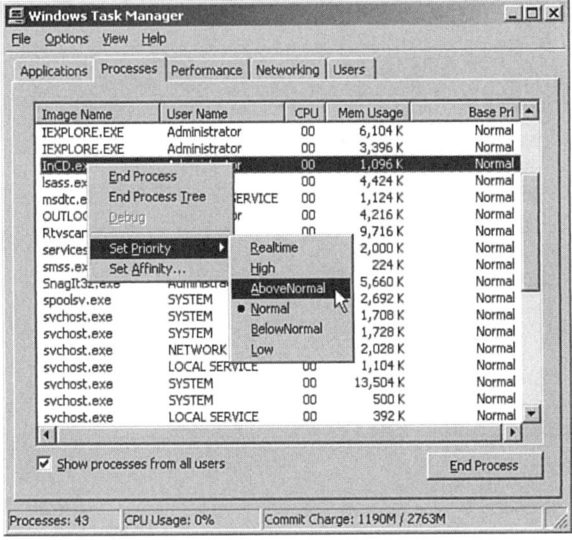

FIGURE 6.37
Select the desired priority from the pop-up menu.

continues

continued

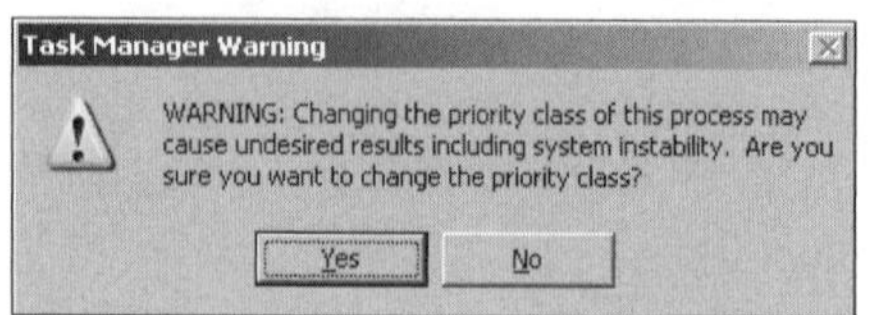

FIGURE 6.38▲
Be sure you understand the implications of changing priorities of running processes before you select Yes.

4. After selecting a priority, you receive the warning message shown in Figure 6.38. Click Yes if you're sure that this is what you want to do.

5. As shown in Figure 6.39, the priority of the process has been successfully changed.

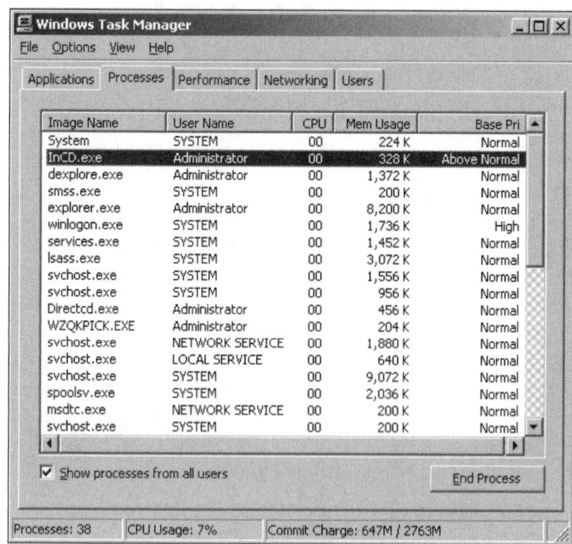

FIGURE 6.39
The selected process now is running at Above Normal priority.

Task Manager does not allow you to set a process to a specific number: It allows you only to set priority classes. The priority classes are as follows:

- **Realtime**—Priority 24
- **High**—Priority 13
- **AboveNormal**—Priority 9
- **Normal**—Priority 8
- **BelowNormal**—Priority 7
- **Low**—Priority 4

Using Task Manager to tune an application in this manner is a temporary fix because after you reboot your system or stop and start the application, you lose the priority properties.

Normally, there should be no need to change the priority of processes. However, suppose you have a database query process that cannot complete because the process is not getting enough CPU time. In this case, you can temporarily change the priority of the process to High to enable the task to complete successfully. Be warned that if you run applications at High priority, this can slow overall performance because other applications get less I/O time.

In some situations, a process must be terminated. You can either terminate a specific process or terminate the process and all other processes linked to it. This is accomplished by right-clicking the process entry in the Processes tab of the Task Manager and selecting End Process to terminate a specific process or by selecting End Process Tree to terminate that process and any other processes it has started. For example, if you terminate the process for a word processing program, you can select End Process Tree to additionally terminate the spell checker and grammar processes started by the word processor process.

On a multiprocessor server, an additional menu item called Set Affinity appears on the pop-up menu on the Processes tab. The Set Affinity command allows you to limit a process to a specific CPU.

To set a process to use a specific CPU, perform the procedure outlined in Step by Step 6.13.

NOTE

Realtime Rights To use the Realtime option, you have to be logged on as a user with Administrator rights.

WARNING

Be Careful with Realtime Changing the base priority of an application to Realtime makes the priority of the application higher than the process that monitors and responds to keyboard input. If the process you set to Realtime completes successfully, fine. However, if it requires any input for processing or recovery, your only option is to reboot the system.

EXAM TIP

Not all processes can be terminated using Task Manager. The Kill utility, included in the Windows Server 2003 Resource Kit, terminates most processes, including services or system processes. Use it very carefully because terminating system processes can cause your server to become unstable.

STEP BY STEP

6.13 Setting Processor Affinity

1. Right-click the Taskbar and then click Task Manager in the pop-up menu.
2. From the Task Manager window, select the Processes tab.
3. On the Task Manager system menu, right-click the process that you want to assign to a specific processor and select Set Affinity from the pop-up menu.

continues

continued

4. From the Processor Affinity dialog box shown in Figure 6.40, select the processor you want to run the process on. Click OK to save.

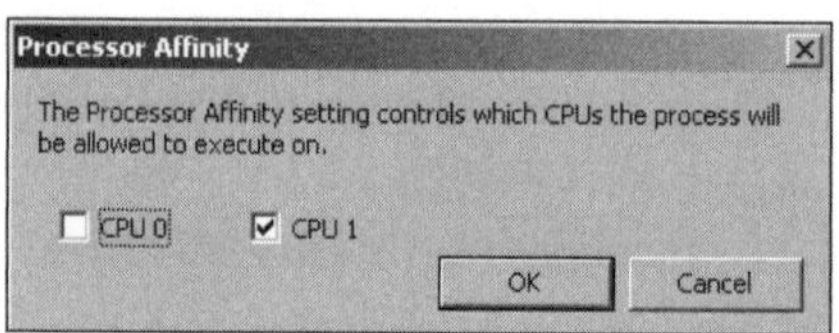

FIGURE 6.40
Make sure you understand the implications of setting Processor Affinity before you select OK.

> **WARNING**
>
> **Processor Affinity** This option should be used with care because it could potentially decrease the performance of the process. This can occur in a situation where the processor that you have selected starts to get overloaded. Unlike other processes that can use time slices from other processors, your process is locked onto the overloaded processor.

Performance Tab

The Performance tab, shown in Figure 6.41, displays the CPU and memory usage for your server. The display includes graphs of the current usage, plus additional histograms showing recent usage. Below the graphs are numerical statistics for the CPU and memory usage.

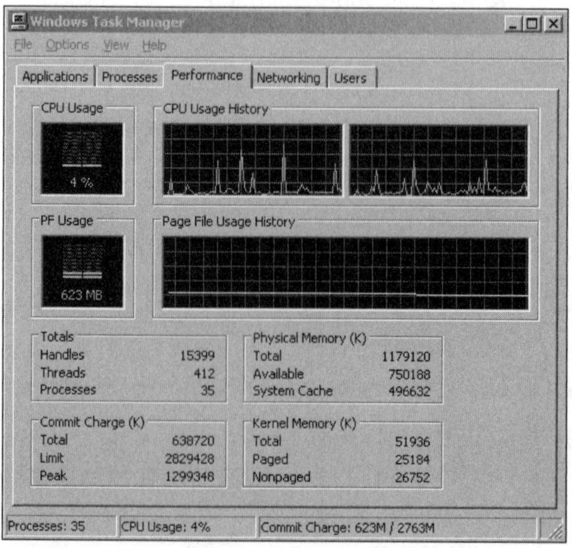

FIGURE 6.41
The Task Manager's Performance tab, showing server-usage statistics.

The information shown here can give you a quick overview of the performance characteristics of your server. Any abnormalities displayed here indicate that you should investigate further using some of the other Windows Server 2003 utilities.

Networking Tab

The Networking tab is displayed if you have a NIC installed. The default view displays the state, link speed, and network utilization of each NIC, as shown in Figure 6.42.

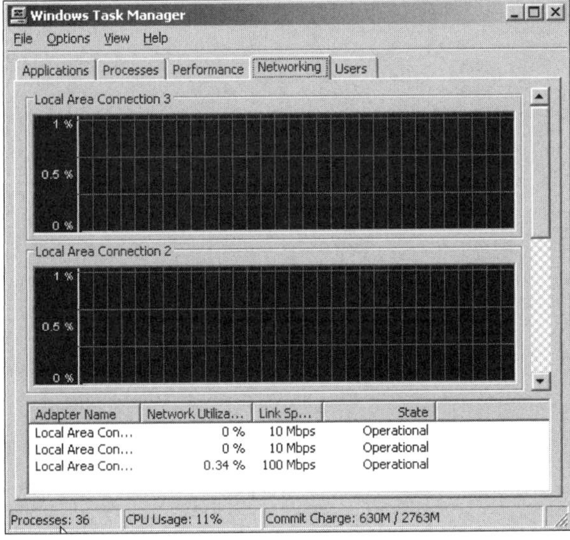

FIGURE 6.42
The Task Manager's Networking tab, showing network-utilization statistics.

The information available on the Networking tab gives you an overview of the performance of your network connections. At a glance, you can see what connections are active, how much bandwidth is being consumed, and which connection is seeing the most traffic. This information can be helpful in your initial problem determination because you can immediately see how your network connections are performing.

As with the other tabs in Task Manager, a multitude of additional items can be displayed. For a complete listing, from the System menu click View, Select Columns.

Users Tab

The Users tab displays the users currently logged on to your server. This includes users logged on to the console, users connected via the Remote Desktop Protocol (RDP) client in Remote Administration Mode, and Terminal Services users connected in Application Mode. Each session is assigned a session ID, with session 0 always representing the console session. In addition to the username session ID and session type, the status of the session and the name of the client computer are displayed, as shown in Figure 6.43.

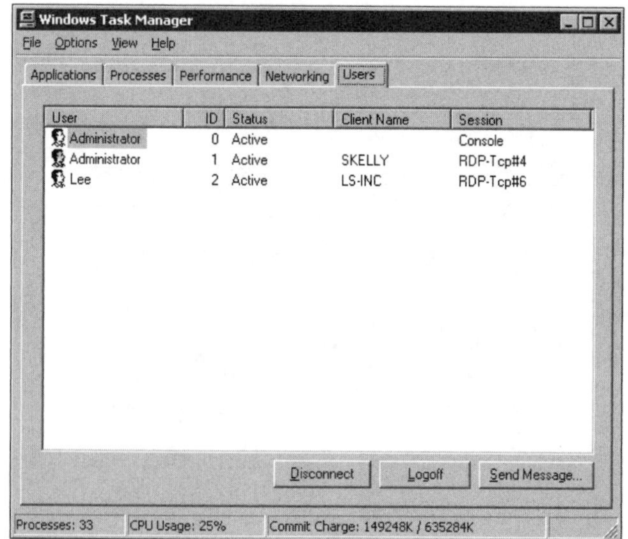

FIGURE 6.43
The Task Manager's Users tab, showing the users who are logged onto the server. You have the option to Logoff, disconnect, or send messages to the user sessions.

It is important to remember that if your Windows Server 2003 server is not running in Terminal Services Application Mode, only three connections are allowed into your server. Two of these are remote administrative sessions, and the third is the console session, which can be either local or connected via RDP. If an administrator logs on to one of the sessions, then goes off to lunch (or otherwise keeps the session active), other administrators are prevented from connecting to that server. From this interface, you have the option to send the administrator a message asking him to log off. Alternatively, if he is away from his workstation, you can either log him off or disconnect his session.

MONITORING AND OPTIMIZING A SERVER ENVIRONMENT FOR APPLICATION PERFORMANCE

In Windows Server 2003, Microsoft has included the Configure Your Server Wizard, which tunes your server for specific roles on your network. Even though Microsoft has done a fairly good job with defining the server roles and configuring the performance options for each role, you can always do better. In this section, we examine the tools and utilities you can use to optimize your server's performance.

EXAM TIP

Configure Your Server Wizard The Configure Your Server Wizard is not included in the Windows Server 2003 Web Edition operating system. This is logical because that version is intended to be used only for Web servers, and it comes optimized for that role out of the box. As an administrator, you should be familiar with the capabilities of all versions of Windows Server 2003 for the exam.

Monitoring System Resources

Although Task Manager can give you a quick overview of system performance, there are situations in which a more thorough investigation is needed. This is where the Performance tool comes in handy. The Performance tool is actually made up of two separate Microsoft Management Console (MMC) snap-ins: System Monitor and Performance Logs and Alerts.

The Performance tool is started by following the procedure outlined in Step by Step 6.14.

STEP BY STEP

6.14 Starting the Performance Tool in System Monitor View

1. From the Start menu, click Start, All Programs, Administrative Tools, Performance.

2. As shown in Figure 6.44, the Performance tool opens with the System Monitor view displayed.

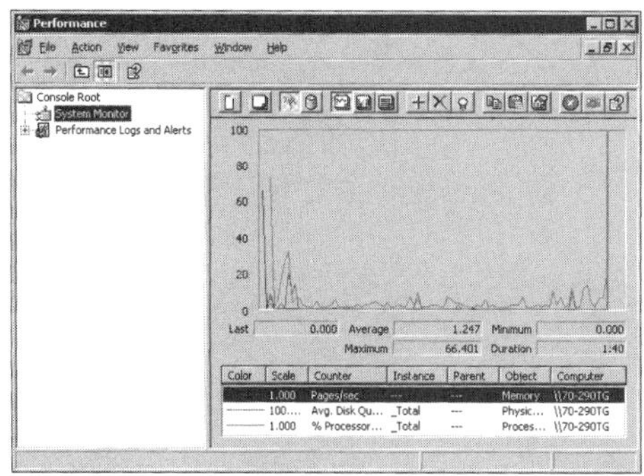

FIGURE 6.44
The Windows Server 2003 Performance tool showing the System Monitor view.

System Monitor

The System Monitor snap-in allows you to view real-time performance data contained in the counters from your domain controllers, member servers, or workstations on your network. In addition, System Monitor allows you to review performance data that is stored in a log file created with the Performance Logs and Alerts snap-in.

Windows Server 2003 is a modular, object-oriented operating system. Each subsystem within Windows Server 2003 is an object. For example, the CPU is an object, the memory is an object, the storage subsystem is an object, and so on. As your computer performs various tasks, each of these objects generate performance data.

Each object has several monitoring functions called *counters*. Each counter offers insight into a different aspect or function of the object. For example, the memory object has counters that measure % Committed Bytes in Use, Available Bytes, Page Faults/sec, and more. System Monitor takes the readings from these counters and presents the information to you in a human-readable format (numbers or graphs). Each counter is displayed as a colored line. Multiple counters from the same system or from remote systems can be viewed simultaneously.

In addition, objects can be separated by instance. *Instance* is the terminology used to refer to multiple occurrences of the same type of object, such as in a multiprocessor server. A separate instance exists for each processor.

By default, System Monitor is started with the following counters displayed:

- Memory: Pages per Second
- Physical Disk: Average Disk Queue Length
- Processor: % Processor Time

Numerous other counters can be added to give you a more thorough view of your server's performance. To add additional counters to be monitored, perform the procedure outlined in Step by Step 6.15.

STEP BY STEP

6.15 Adding Additional Performance Counters

1. From the Start menu, click Start, All Programs, Administrative Tools, Performance.
2. The Performance tool opens with the System Monitor view displayed. As shown in Figure 6.45, right-click anywhere on the graph in the System Monitor view. Select Add Counters from the pop-up menu.
3. From the Add Counters dialog box shown in Figure 6.46, select Processor from the Performance Object drop-down list and then select % Processor Time from the Select Counters from List area.
4. Click the Add button to add the object and counter to the view. Repeat for any additional counters as desired. Then click the Close button to save.

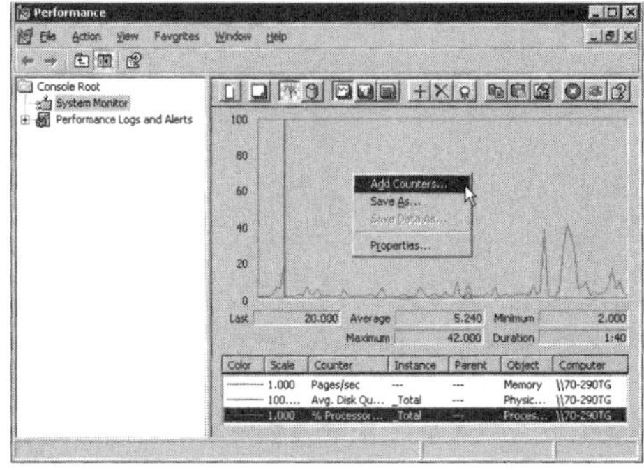

FIGURE 6.45
Select Add Counters from the pop-up menu or click the + icon in the Toolbar.

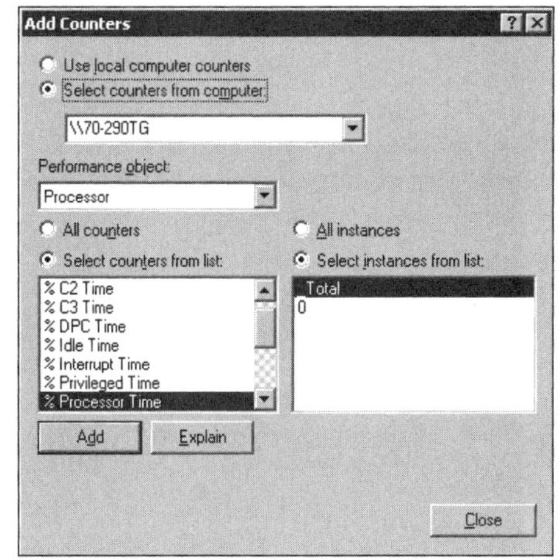

FIGURE 6.46
Select the desired Performance object and then select the counters and instance to monitor. Clicking the Explain button provides an explanation of what each counter records.

As you saw in this Step by Step procedure, the Add Counters dialog box allows you to make choices from several areas to customize your monitoring needs. The choices found in this dialog box are as follows:

- **Computer**—This option allows you to select whether to add counters from the local computer or any remote computer on your network. You add remote computers using their Universal Naming Convention (UNC) computer name.
- **Performance Object**—This is a drop-down list that displays all the objects available for monitoring.
- **Counters**—This option allows you to select either all counters or individual counters from a list. Hold down the Shift or Ctrl key and click to select multiple items.
- **Instance**—If an object has multiple instances (for example, your server might have multiple network cards), you can select each individual instance or all instances.

After selecting each counter, click the Add button to add the counter to the System Monitor display. For a description of each counter, highlight the counter and click the Explain button. When finished, click the Close button.

The number of objects available for monitoring vary by system. Most server services and applications, such as DNS, DHCP, and mail servers, install their own counters that can be used to monitor the performance of those functions.

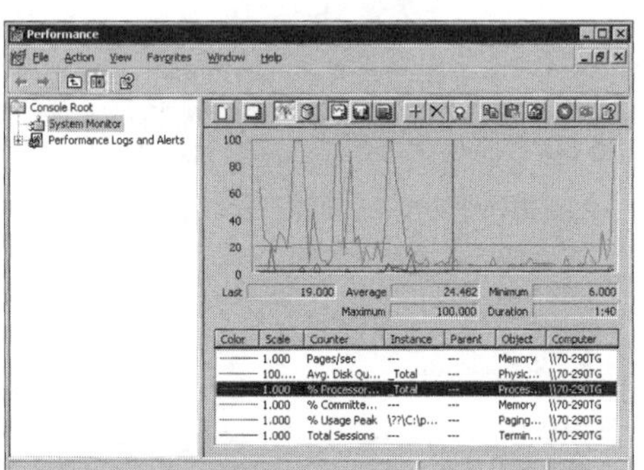

FIGURE 6.47
The Windows Server 2003 System Monitor showing several additional server-usage counters.

Each counter can be displayed as a colored line in one of the graph views. Multiple counters from the same system or from remote systems can be viewed simultaneously. Figure 6.47 shows you an example of what one of the graph views, of which there are several, may look like on your system.

Of all the items you can monitor on a typical server, here are the objects you need to monitor closely for performance issues:

- Memory
- Processor
- Physical disk
- Network

These counters provide instant insight into the overall performance on a system. When these counters get too high, it's a good indication that you need to upgrade the system or segment the network.

The Performance Logs and Alerts Snap-In

Although System Monitor provides far more system-monitoring information than Task Manager, it still only provides a snapshot view of system performance. To perform a more thorough evaluation of system performance, you need to view the system statistics over a period of time. You can find these statistics in the Performance Logs and Alerts tool, located under System Monitor in the Performance tool MMC. The following two subsections detail the logging and alert features you can use to capture performance data over an extended time period.

Performance Logs

The Performance Logs and Alerts MMC snap-in allows you to log performance data over a period of time and save it to a log file for later viewing. Two logging options are available: Counter Logs and Trace Logs. Counter logs allow you to record data about hardware usage and the activity of system services from local or remote computers. You can configure logging to occur manually or automatically based on a defined schedule. Trace logs record data as certain activity, such as disk I/O or a page fault, occurs. When the event occurs, the provider sends the data to the log service.

NOTE

Trace Logs Trace logs are commonly used for developers to trace an application's interaction with the operating system. It will probably not be covered on the exam.

The snap-in allows you to save log data in the following file formats:

- **Text file (CSV)**—Comma-delimited format, for import into spreadsheet or database programs.
- **Text file (TSV)**—Tab-delimited format, for import into spreadsheet or database programs.
- **Binary file**—This is the default for use with the System Monitor snap-in. Data is logged into this file until it reaches the maximum limit. The default maximum file size is 1MB, but this can be changed when you configure settings for the file from the Log Files tab of the Log Properties dialog box by clicking the Configure button.
- **Binary circular file**—Data is logged into this file until it reaches the maximum limit. Then the file is overwritten, starting at the beginning of the file. The default maximum file size is 1MB, but this can be changed when you configure settings for the file from the Log Files tab of the Log Properties dialog box by clicking the Configure button.
- **SQL**—Data is logged directly into an existing SQL database.

Because the data is available in so many common formats, you have the option of analyzing the data using the default Microsoft tools or importing it into the tool of your choice.

NOTE

Establishing a Baseline You should take a measurement of your system during its normal operation to establish a baseline. This baseline provides something to compare counters to when the system experiences problems. A baseline comparison provides a quick way to pinpoint problem areas.

The Performance utility allows you to log on an object basis and on a counter basis. This means you can configure a log to record all the data for an object instead of using individual counters. Therefore, after a log file is recorded, you can select any counter from an object to examine. After you determine what to record, you need to determine two time-related issues: the measurement interval and the length of time to record the log file. These issues are detailed as follows:

- The measurement interval determines how often a performance reading is taken. Too short an interval can produce spurious results and can cause additional workload on your system. Too long an interval might hide performance changes. Although most readings are insignificant, frequent readings can cause significant performance degradations.
- The length of time over which a log file is recorded should be long enough to capture all the normal operational activities. This typically means recording a log file for at least a week. A shorter time period might not offer you a complete picture of your system's normal weekly performance.

The sample log is defined with the following basic counters:

- Memory: Pages per Second
- Physical Disk: Average Disk Queue Length
- Processor: % Processor Time

Note that these are the same counters that appear in the initial System Monitor view. You can create your own logs with the counters you specify.

To create a new counter log, perform the procedure outlined in Step by Step 6.16.

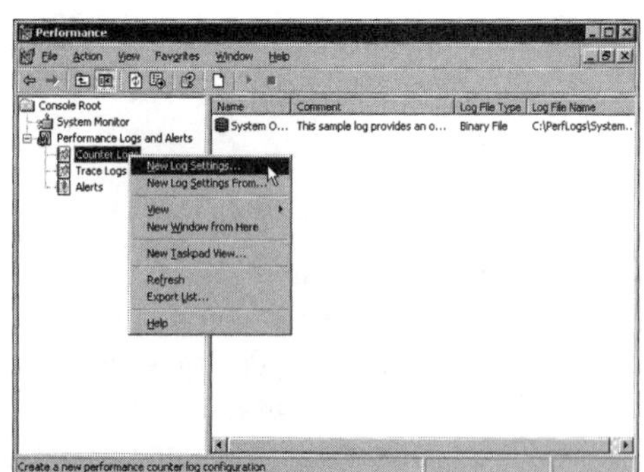

FIGURE 6.48
Right-click Counter Logs and then select New Log Settings from the pop-up menu.

STEP BY STEP

6.16 Creating a New Counter Log

1. From the Start menu, click Start, All Programs, Administrative Tools, Performance.
2. The Performance tool opens with the System Monitor view displayed. Right-click Counter Logs under Performance Logs and Alerts in the left pane and then select New Log Settings from the pop-up menu (see Figure 6.48) .

3. In the New Log Settings dialog box, shown in Figure 6.49, enter the name for the new log and then click OK.

4. In the Log Properties dialog box, shown in Figure 6.50, click the Add Objects button or the Add Counters button to add the desired objects and counters to the log. Repeat this step for any additional counters desired. Notice that an option is available that allows you to run the logs using a different user ID and password.

5. Click the Log Files tab.

6. On the Log Files tab. Enter the desired log file name, type, and location, if the defaults are not what you want. Change the maximum log file size if desired (see Figure 6.51).

FIGURE 6.49▲
Enter the name of the new log.

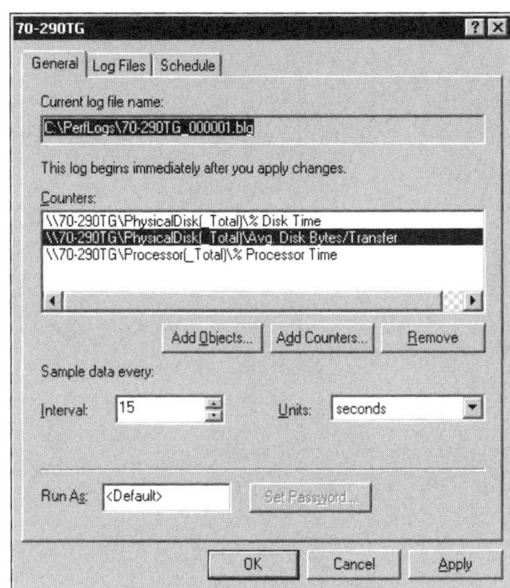

FIGURE 6.50▲
Adding counters and objects to the new log. The procedure is similar to adding counters in System Monitor.

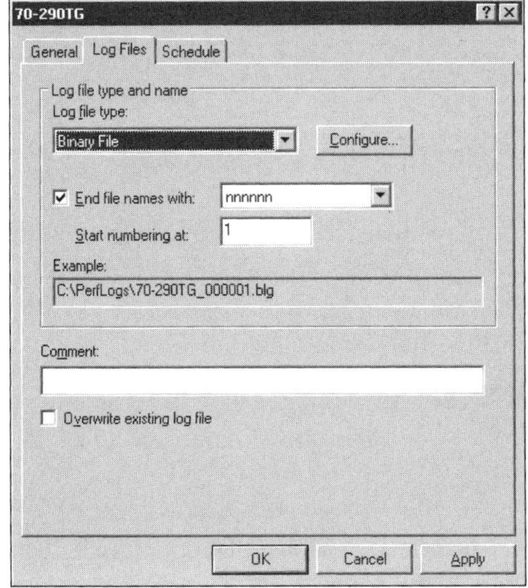

FIGURE 6.51◄
The Logs Files tab showing counter log file configuration.

7. Click the Schedule tab. On the Schedule tab, you can select the start and stop times for logging or select to manually start and stop the log (see Figure 6.52).

continues

continued

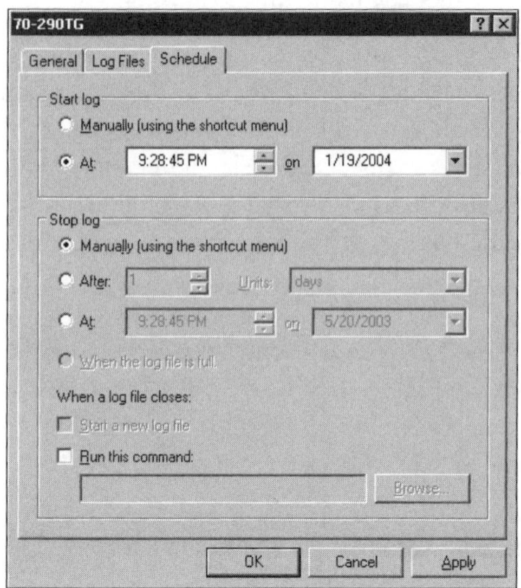

FIGURE 6.52
The Schedule tab showing the counter log schedule.

8. Click OK to save the log.

If you selected to manually start the counter log, you can start it by right-clicking the log entry in the right pane of the Performance Logs and Alerts snap-in and selecting Start. The icon for the log is *green* when running and *red* when stopped.

After you have recorded data in your log file, you can view it within System Monitor. To open your log file, use the procedure outlined in Step by Step 6.17.

STEP BY STEP

6.17 Viewing Counter Logs

1. From the Start menu, click Start, All Programs, Administrative Tools, Performance.
2. The Performance tool opens with the System Monitor view displayed. Right-click anywhere in the right pane and select Properties from the pop-up menu.

3. In the System Monitor Properties dialog box, select the Source tab. On the Source tab, shown in Figure 6.53, select the Log Files radio button and then click the Add button to browse for the log file. After locating the file, click the Open button.

4. In the System Monitor Properties dialog box, click the Time Range button to adjust the time window that you want to view within the log file. Click OK when finished.

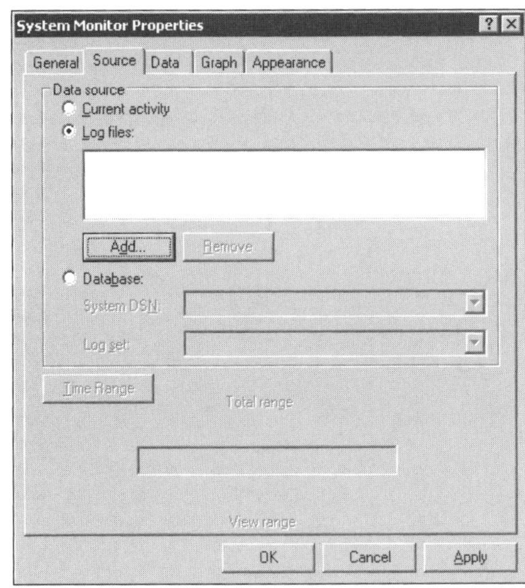

FIGURE 6.53
The System Monitor Properties dialog box showing the Source tab.

A *time window* is a selected block of time from a log file. When a log file is used as the source of data, the System Monitor utility automatically sets every data point within the log file as active—that is, it views the data from the start to the end of the log file. Through the use of a time window, you can shorten or otherwise alter the data in use. The Source tab from the Log Properties dialog box reveals the Time Range settings. From this dialog box, you can slide the start and end points manually to select your start or stop points. Only the data in the selected time frame (between the start and stop points and shaded gray) is used by the System Monitor utility.

While it is being recorded, don't try to view a log file from the same instance of the Performance utility that is performing the logging. If you need to view the contents of the open log file, use another instance of the Performance utility. You can view all data points up to the point when you opened the log file, and new data continues to be recorded into the file by the first instance of the Performance utility.

After a log file is recorded, you can append and resample the file to combine multiple files or to remove spurious readings. To record new data into an existing log file, just specify the path to the existing file in the Log Options dialog box.

The only limitation to log file recording is the free disk space on the destination drive; if your hard disk is full, the log file cannot record unless it is emptied or deleted.

IN THE FIELD

NAMING LOG FILES

You should always name your log files with as much description as possible within the 255-character filename limitation. Try to include the name of the system, the start and end date/time, and the object names recorded. A properly labeled log file is easy to use and locate.

Performance Alerts

The Alerts container is used to define threshold alerts. These can be used with real-time measurements or with historical log files. An alert is issued when a specific counter crosses a defined threshold value. When this occurs, a trigger event is initiated.

Creating an alert is similar to configuring a counter log. To create an alert, perform the procedure outlined in Step by Step 6.18.

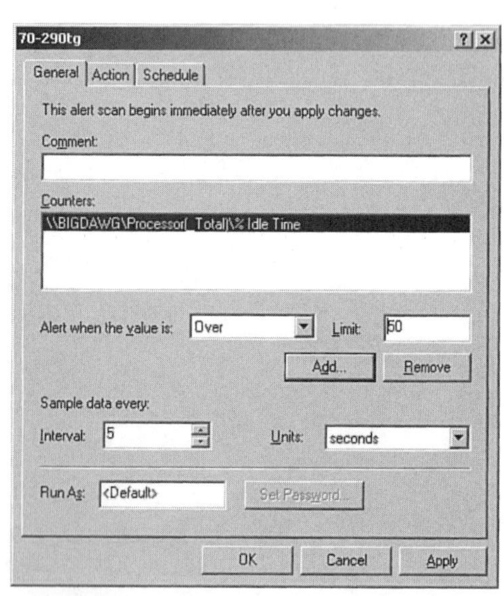

FIGURE 6.54
Add or remove counters.

STEP BY STEP

6.18 Creating an Alert

1. From the Start menu, click Start, All Programs, Administrative Tools, Performance.
2. The Performance tool opens with the System Monitor view displayed. Right-click the Alerts entry under Performance Logs and Alerts in the left pane of the snap-in and select New Alert Settings from the pop-up menu.
3. In the New Alert Settings dialog box, enter the name for the new alert.
4. In the Alert Properties dialog box, shown in Figure 6.54, click the Add button to add additional objects and counters or click the Remove button if the wrong counters have been selected.
5. After you have selected the desired counters to monitor, set the alert condition using the Alert Value drop-down field. Notice that an option is available that allows you to monitor the alerts using a different user ID and password.

6. If you click the Action tab, shown in Figure 6.55, you can select the action to take when the threshold is reached.

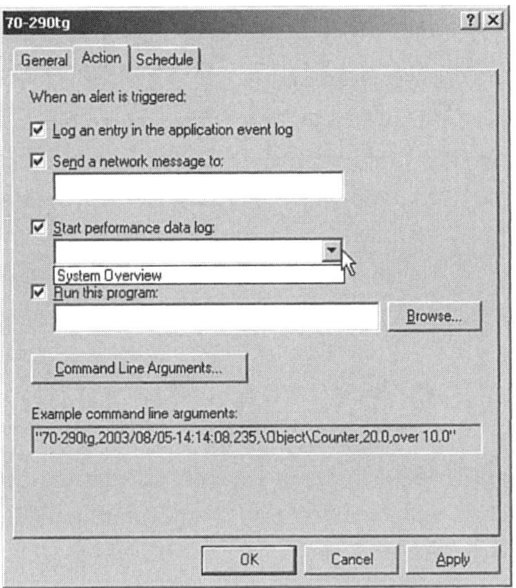

FIGURE 6.55
Alert properties showing the Action tab.

7. Click the Schedule tab. On the Schedule tab, you can select the start and stop times for monitoring or select to manually start and stop the log, as shown in Figure 6.56.

8. Click OK to save the log.

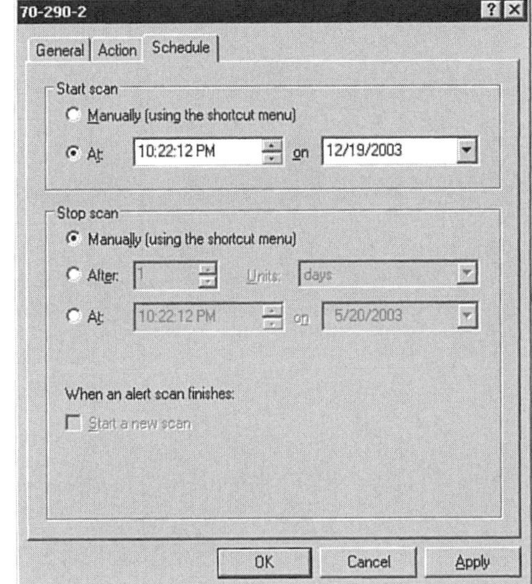

FIGURE 6.56
Showing the Alerts Log schedule.

You can select several actions to be performed when an alert threshold is reached, as follows:

- **Log an entry in the application event log**—If a threshold is reached, Windows Server 2003 creates an entry in this log, and you can view it in the Application event log found in the Event Viewer.
- **Send a network message to**—This allows you to send a message to a user via the Messenger service.
- **Start performance data log**—This starts logging to a predefined counter log. This is useful if you are trying to see what happens to system performance when a specific event occurs.

- **Run this program**—This can be any program that can be run from a command line. For example, it might be a program that performs some type of system maintenance, such as compressing files.

Alerts are most often used to monitor systems in real time. You can set an alert to notify you when a specific event occurs. Some of the conditions that you might want to configure an alert for are low disk space, swap file usage, and task queues for network cards and CPUs. Any of these items can point to a current or potential system problem.

Optimizing System Resources

Before you can optimize a server, you must understand its characteristics, including how it operates under a normal load and what areas are stressed when the load increases. This has a lot to do with the application type and load of the server. For example, a Web server reacts differently to a load condition than a server that is hosting Terminal Services.

The first step in optimization should be to establish a *baseline.* To establish a baseline for a server, you should log performance data for the server when it is under a normal load for an established period of time. You typically want to log at least a day, and sometimes even a week or more. This allows you to observe the various components of your server under normal load and stress circumstances. You should have a large enough sample so that you can observe all the highs and lows and determine what figures are averages for your server.

After you establish this baseline, the next step is to observe your server under load and to identify any components that are limiting the overall performance of your server. As mentioned earlier in this chapter, the main four components that cause the majority of the bottlenecks in a server are the memory, disk, processor, and network interface. The following four subsections discuss optimizing resources associated with these vital server objects.

Monitoring Memory Performance Objects

The Windows Server 2003 memory system uses a combination of physical memory and a swap file stored on the hard disk to provide space for the applications to run. Data in memory is written to the swap file through a process called *paging*. Paging is used to increase the amount of memory available to applications. Windows Server 2003 performs paging to make it seem to applications that the computer has more physical memory than is installed. The amount of virtual memory available on a computer is equal to its physical memory plus whatever hard disk space is configured for use as paging files.

Because accessing data from a hard disk is many times slower than accessing it from memory, you want to minimize the frequency with which the server has to swap data to the hard drive. This can usually be accomplished simply by adding more physical memory.

Here are some counters to watch to monitor memory performance:

- **Memory: Pages Input/sec**—When this counter remains at a low value (2 or less), it indicates that all operations are occurring within physical RAM. This means that paging is not occurring and therefore is not the cause of the performance degradation.
- **Memory: Cache Faults/sec**—Indicates how frequently the system is unable to locate data in the cache and must search for it on disk. If this number grows steadily over time, your system is headed into constant thrashing. This means every bit of information required by the system must be retrieved directly from the disk. This condition usually indicates an insufficient amount of RAM on your system. However, it can also be caused by running a combination of applications, such as a read-intensive application (typically a database that is performing a large number of queries) at the same time as an application that is using an excessive amount of memory. In this case, you can either schedule the applications to not run at the same time or move one of them to another system.

- **Memory: Page Faults/sec**—Similar to Cache Faults/sec, except that it also measures faults when a requested memory page is in use by another application. If this counter averages above 200 for low-end systems or above 600 for high-end systems, excess paging is occurring.
- **Memory: Available Bytes**—Indicates the amount of free memory available for use. If this number is less than 4MB, you do not have sufficient RAM on your system, so the system performs excessive paging.
- **Paging File: % Usage Peak**—Indicates the level of paging file usage. If this number nears 100% during normal operations, the maximum size of your paging file is too small, and you probably need more RAM. If you have multiple drives with multiple paging files, be sure to view the Total instance of this counter.

Monitoring Disk Performance Objects

> NOTE
>
> **No more DISKPERF** In previous versions of Windows, you were required to use the DISKPERF utility to enable the disk counters. Windows Server 2003 enables the counters by default.

The disk subsystem can be a bottleneck, either directly or indirectly. If the access speed of the disk is slow, it negatively affects the load time of applications and the read and write time of application data. In addition, because Windows Server 2003 relies on virtual memory, a slow disk subsystem indirectly affects memory performance.

Here are some key performance counters for the disk subsystem:

- **PhysicalDisk: Avg. Disk Queue Length**—Tracks the number of system requests waiting for disk access. The number of queued requests should not exceed the number of spindles in use plus 2. Most drives have only a single spindle, but RAID arrays have more (and Performance Monitor views RAID arrays as a single logical drive). A large number of waiting items indicates that a drive or an array is not operating fast enough to support the system's demands for input and output. When this occurs, you need a faster drive system.
- **PhysicalDisk: % Disk Time**—Represents the percentage of time that the disk is actively handling read and write requests. It is not uncommon for this counter to regularly hit 100% on active servers. Sustained percentages of 90% or better, however, might indicate that a storage device is too slow.

This usually is true when its Avg. Disk Queue Length counter is constantly above 2.

- **PhysicalDisk: Avg. Disk sec/Transfer**—Indicates the average time in seconds of a disk transfer.

NOTE

Keep Your Data Accurate When you're recording a log file for the Disk objects, be sure not to record the file to the same drive being measured. You are not recording accurate values if you do because the act of reading the object and writing to the drive adds a significant amount of workload.

Monitoring Process Performance Objects

The processor is the heart of your server. Most operations in the server are controlled either directly or indirectly by the processor. Most processor bottlenecks are caused by multiple processes running at the same time, requiring more cycles than the processor can deliver efficiently. This can be alleviated by replacing the processor with a faster model or by adding an additional processor in a multiprocessor-capable server.

To identify problems with the processor, monitor the following counters:

- **Processor: % Processor Time**—Indicates the amount of time the CPU spends on non-idle work. It's common for this counter to reach 100% during application launches or kernel-intensive operations (such as SAM synchronization). If this counter remains above 80% for an extended period, you should suspect a CPU bottleneck. (There will be an instance of this counter for each processor in a multiprocessor system.)
- **Processor: % Total Processor Time**—Applies only to multiprocessor systems. This counter should be used the same way as the single CPU counter. If any value remains consistently higher than 80%, at least one of your CPUs is a bottleneck.
- **System: Processor Queue Length**—Indicates the number of threads waiting for processor time. A sustained value of 2 or higher for this counter indicates processor congestion. This counter is a snapshot of the time of measurement, not an average value over time.

Monitoring Network Performance Objects

Although not as common as processor, disk, or memory bottlenecks, thanks to the preponderance of high-performance 100MB and even 1,000MB NICs, there are occasions when the network card is a bottleneck. This is most likely to occur on Web servers or terminal servers.

To identify performance problems with the network interface, monitor the following counters:

- **Network Interface: Bytes Total/sec**—Indicates the rate at which data is sent to and received by a NIC (including framing characters). Compare this value with the expected capacity of the device. If the highest observed average is less than 75% of the expected value, communication errors or slowdowns might be occurring that limit the NIC's rated speed.
- **Network Interface: Current Bandwidth**—Estimates a NIC's current bandwidth, measured in bits per second (bps). This counter is useful only for NICs with variable bandwidth.
- **Network Interface: Output Queue Length**—Indicates the number of packets waiting to be transmitted by a NIC. If this averages above 2, you are experiencing delays.
- **Network Interface: Packets/sec**—Indicates the number of packets handled by a NIC. Watch this counter over a long interval of constant or normal activity. Sharp declines that occur while the queue length remains nonzero can indicate protocol-related or NIC-related problems.

Other network-related counters that may be worth monitoring include protocol-specific objects, such as ICMP, IP, TCP, and UDP.

Make sure you understand the common performance counters and their meanings. In addition, know what ranges are normal and what values indicate that a specific hardware component needs to be upgraded.

Monitoring Server Hardware for Bottlenecks

As you know, a *bottleneck* is a component in a computer system that is preventing some other part of the system from operating at its optimum performance level. However, a bottleneck does not necessarily refer to components operating at 100% of their capability. It is possible for components operating at only 60% to slow down other components. Bottlenecks can never be fully eliminated; there *always* is a slowest or limiting component. The goal of removing bottlenecks is to attempt to make the user the most significant bottleneck rather than having a computer component as the bottleneck. This way, the system is faster than its user.

Bottleneck discovery and elimination is not an exact science. In fact, it's not even an automated process. Through a comparison of a baseline and current or recorded activity, you need to decipher the clues that might indicate a bottleneck. The objects and counters discussed in the previous sections of this chapter are a good start to monitor for conditions that can indicate a bottleneck.

Every system is different. You need to use the methods discussed in this chapter and learn to apply them to your own unique situation. A measurement value that indicates a bottleneck on one system might not be a bottleneck on another. Typically, you want to look for areas of your computer that are operating outside of your normal baseline measurements or that are affecting other components adversely. After you identify a trouble spot, you need to take action through software configuration or hardware replacement to improve the performance of the suspect area. Don't just look for low-throughput measurements. Table 6.1 shows some common counters and the settings that indicate there might be a potential problem.

TABLE 6.1

COMMON PERFORMANCE INDICATORS

Component	*Counter*	*Measurement*
Memory	Pages Input/sec	A measure of 2 or more indicates that paging is occurring.
Memory	Available Bytes	Less than 4MB indicates that you need to increase RAM.

continues

TABLE 6.1 *continued*

COMMON PERFORMANCE INDICATORS

Component	*Counter*	*Measurement*
Paging File	% Usage Peak	A measure of 80% or more indicates that you need to increase the size of the paging file.
PhysicalDisk	Avg. Disk Queue Length	The number of queued requests should not exceed the number of spindles in use plus 2.
PhysicalDisk	% Disk Time	Sustained percentages of 90% or better might indicate that the disk is too slow.
Processor	% Processor Time	If this counter remains above 80% for an extended period, you should suspect a CPU bottleneck.
System	Processor Queue Length	A sustained value of 2 or higher indicates processor congestion.
Network Interface	Bytes Total/sec	If the highest observed average is less than 75% of the expected value, communication errors or slowdowns might be occurring that limit the NIC's rated speed.
Network Interface	Output Queue Length	If this averages above 2, you are experiencing delays.

EXAM TIP

Know the Common Performance Counters A common scenario question on the exam tests your knowledge of determining bottlenecks. A typical question will present you with a specific set of counters, and you will need to determine the problem area.

Other common telltale signs of bottlenecks include long task queues, resource request patterns, task frequency, task duration, task failures, retransmissions or re-requests, and system interrupts. With a little practice and by using some of our suggestions, you are sure to get a feel for bottleneck discovery.

IN THE FIELD

WINDOWS MANAGEMENT INSTRUMENTATION

All the performance counters can also be accessed via the Windows Management Instrumentation (WMI) interface using any of the scripting languages supported in Windows Server 2003. This allows you to create your own custom monitoring applications.

GUIDED PRACTICE EXERCISE 6.2

As a system administrator, you must monitor and manage various servers and workstations. Most of your job consists of fielding questions and requests, as well as troubleshooting common problems and complaints, such as not being able to print, resetting passwords, and so on.

However, the real challenging part of your job occurs when fielding ambiguous complaints, such as the server seems slow or the database takes forever to update.

How would you address this type of concern? What types of tools are included in Windows Server 2003 that can assist you? On your own, try to develop a strategy to address this type of issue.

If you would like to see a possible solution, follow these steps:

Estimated Time: 20 minutes

1. From the Start menu, click Start, All Programs, Administrative Tools, Performance.
2. The Performance tool opens with the System Monitor view displayed. By default, the following counters are displayed:
   - Memory: Pages per Second
   - Physical Disk: Average Disk Queue Length
   - Processor: % Processor Time
3. The default counters can help you to quickly determine if one or more of the monitored areas are a bottleneck. For more in-depth study, you can add more counters.
4. Right-click anywhere on the graph in the System Monitor view. From the pop-up menu, select Add Counters.
5. From the Add Counters dialog box, select additional counters from the Performance Object drop-down list, using the guidelines in the chapter. At the very least, add one of the suggested network objects because the default counters do not include a network object.

continues

continued

6. Click the Add button to add the object and counter to the view. Repeat this step for any additional counters desired. Finally, click the Close button to save.

MONITORING FILE AND PRINT SERVERS

One of the primary roles of a Windows Server 2003 server is that of a data repository or file server. Right behind that is the use of your Windows Server 2003 server as a print server. Even though people have been talking about the advent of a paperless society for at least the last 40 years, we're still nowhere near attaining that goal.

As an administrator, you must be able to monitor the performance of file and print servers as well as configuring and managing user access to printers. All the performance-optimization information covered to this point in the chapter applies as well to servers in file and print roles.

In addition, you must be able to set user quotas on your file servers so that users won't have the opportunity to misuse space on the server. In this section, you'll work with some of the tools that system administrators use to manage and monitor file and print servers.

Implementing and Monitoring Disk Quotas

No matter how much storage you have on your file servers, users always manage to fill it up. Even if you restrict Internet access so that they can't download their favorite games and pictures, they still pack your servers with various documents and other assorted business-related files that they just can't live without. Is it really necessary to retain WordPerfect 5.0–formatted documents from 1993?

In most environments there needs to be a mechanism for the administrator to be able to monitor and control the amount of space that users are allocated. Although there have always been third-party utilities available to control disk usage, Microsoft has included the Disk Quota feature in its operating systems starting with Windows 2000. The Disk Quota feature in Windows Server 2003 is largely unchanged since the initial version.

Disk quotas are a method of controlling the amount of space a user has access to on a file server. You can also use the Disk Quota feature to monitor the space in use by your users.

In Windows Server 2003, quotas are set on a per-volume basis and are assigned to each user, but unfortunately they cannot be assigned by group. Similar to encryption and compression, quotas can be used only on NTFS-formatted partitions and volumes. When you enable disk quotas for a volume, volume usage is automatically tracked for all users from that point on.

Quotas can be configured in one of two ways: as a monitoring tool so that the administrator can track disk usage by user or as a tool to prevent the user from saving files to the disk when a specified limit is reached.

Quotas can be configured so that when users reach a preset warning level, they get a warning message telling them that they are running out of space. The users can continue to save files to the volume until they reach their quota limit. At that time, they will be unable to save any more files to the volume. Both of these actions not only generate a message to the users, they also record an event in the event log.

Here are some of the key points to remember about disk quotas:

- Disk quotas do not apply to members of the local Administrators account.
- The files contained on a volume converted from FAT to NTFS do not count against user quotas because they are initially owned by the local administrator. Files created or moved to the volume after the conversion has been completed are owned by the user.
- Disk quotas cannot be applied on a per-folder basis. They can only be applied per volume.

- If a physical disk has multiple volumes, a quota can be applied separately to each volume.
- Even if a volume consists of multiple physical disks, the quota for the volume applies to the entire volume.
- Disk usage is based on all files that the user creates, copies, or takes ownership of.
- File compression cannot be used to prevent users from exceeding their quota. Disk quotas are based on the actual file size, not the compressed file size.
- Disk quotas affect the free size that an installed application sees during the installation process.
- Disk quotas can be enabled on local or network volumes and removable drives formatted with NTFS.
- Disk quotas are not available on any volume or partition formatted using a version of Windows prior to Windows 2000. Disk quotas are available only on NTFS volumes or partitions formatted by Windows 2000 or later.

Implementing Disk Quotas

Quotas are applied at the volume level from the Volume Properties dialog box of the NTFS volume. In addition to turning quotas on or off, the following options are available on the Quota Properties tab:

- **Deny disk space to users exceeding quota limit**—This option causes users who have exceeded their limit to receive an "insufficient disk space" message when they try to save a file. They will be unable to add any more data to the volume until they free up space by moving or deleting some existing files.
- **Limit disk space to**—This setting is used to configure the amount of space to which new users are limited.
- **Log event when a user exceeds their quota limit**—When a user exceeds his or her quota, an event is written to the System log. These events are queued and written hourly.
- **Log event when a user exceeds their warning level**—When a user exceeds his or her warning level, an event is written to the System log. These events are queued and written hourly.

The default in Windows Server 2003 is for quotas to be turned off. To set quota limits on a volume, perform the procedure outlined in Step by Step 6.19.

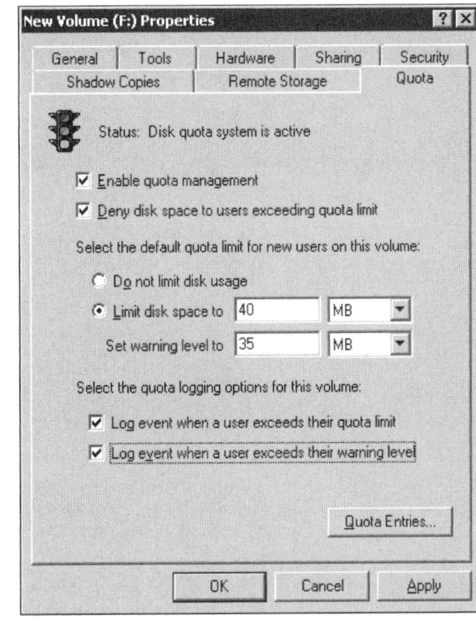

FIGURE 6.57
You can configure quotas from the Quota tab.

STEP BY STEP

6.19 Setting Quota Limits on a Volume

1. From My Computer or Windows Explorer, right-click the volume you want to enable quotas on and select Properties from the pop-up menu.
2. On the Volume Properties dialog box, select the Quota tab.
3. On the Quota tab, select the check box Enable Quota Management, as shown in Figure 6.57.
4. In the Volume Properties dialog box shown in Figure 6.57, select the Limit Disk Space To radio button and add limit and warning levels.
5. Click OK.
6. When you receive the warning dialog box shown in Figure 6.58, read it and then click OK.

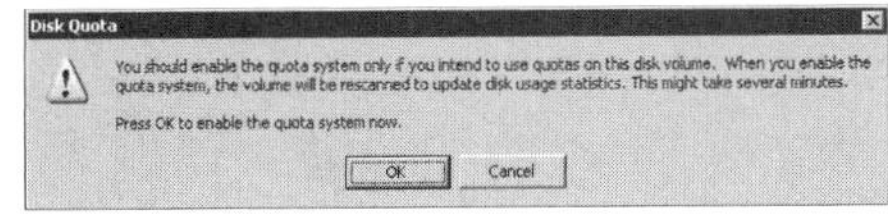

FIGURE 6.58
This warning dialog box tells you that the drive will be scanned so that the file ownership can be inventoried and the disk usage can be credited to each user.

After you turn on disk quotas, the volume is scanned and the file space is calculated, depending on the Creator Owner of each file. Although all new users are assigned, by default, the quota limit you just configured, users with files already residing on the volume will not be affected. However, you can manually assign a quota to users, or you can change the quota configuration of an existing user.

To add quota users, perform the procedure outlined in Step by Step 6.20.

STEP BY STEP

6.20 Adding Users to the Quota List

1. From My Computer or Windows Explorer, right-click the volume you want to add quota users to and select Properties from the pop-up menu.
2. On the Properties dialog box, select the Quota tab.
3. On the Quota tab, select the Quota Entries button, as shown previously in Figure 6.57.
4. In the Quota Entries window shown in Figure 6.59, from the system menu select Quota and then click New Quota Entry from the drop-down menu.
5. The Select Users dialog box appears, as shown in Figure 6.60. From here you can select one or more users from the local or domain database. Add a user and then click OK to save.

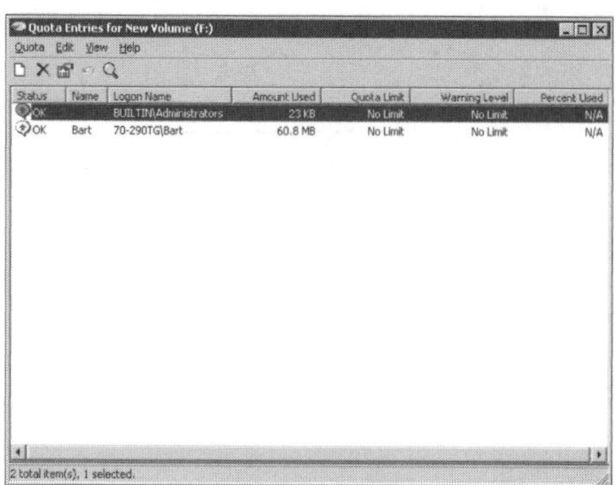

FIGURE 6.59▲
The Quota Entries window from a drive that just had quotas enabled. Note that there is no limit on either of the administrators account, or the account of a user who had allocated space on the drive before quotas were enabled.

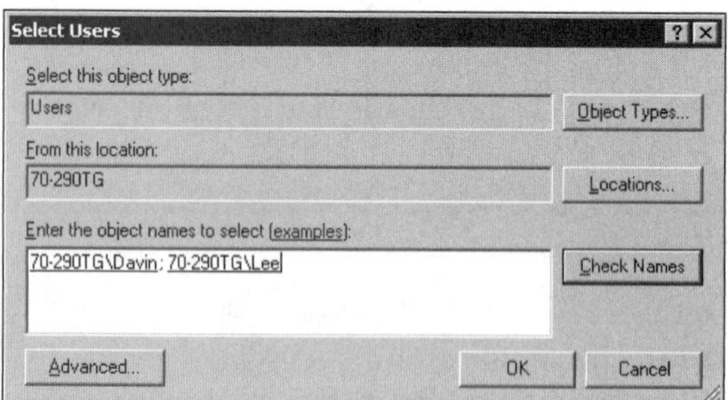

FIGURE 6.60▶
The Select Users dialog box lets you select users from the local or domain database. Notice that you can click the Advanced button to search the user database if you're not sure of the exact name.

6. The Add New Quota Entry dialog box shown in Figure 6.61 appears. Set the desired limits and then click OK.
7. The new users are added with the configured settings, as shown in Figure 6.62.

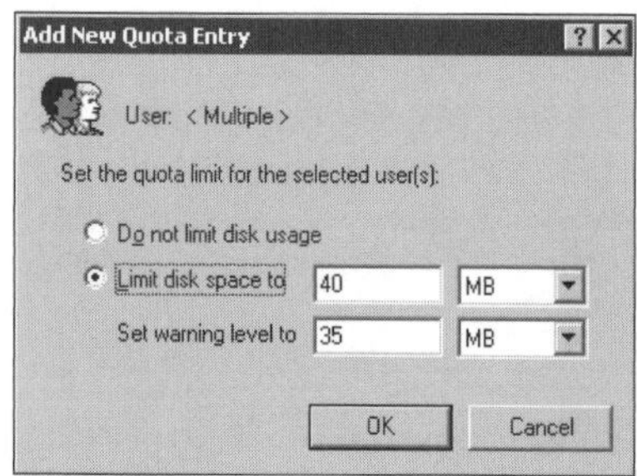

FIGURE 6.61▲
The Add New Quota Entry dialog box allows you to set the quota for new users.

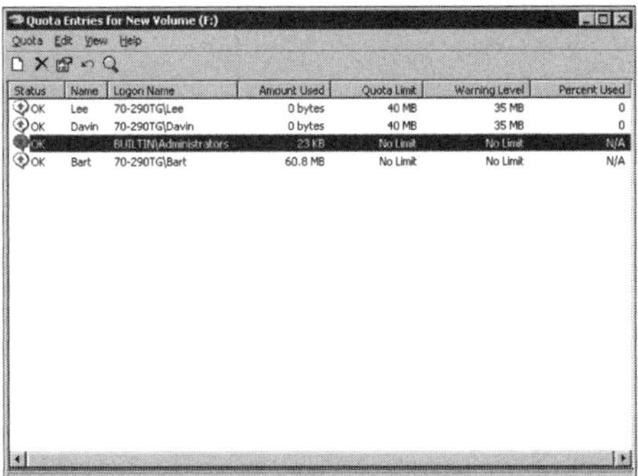

FIGURE 6.62
The Quota Entries window with the new users added.

Managing Disk Quotas

After disk quotas have been implemented on your server, most of the work required in managing them involves monitoring the disk space that the users have allocated and making adjustments when a user has a good reason to receive more disk space.

A lot of this monitoring can be performed from Event Viewer if you selected the option to write an entry in the event logs when a user crosses the warning threshold or exceeds the hard limit. The applicable entries in the event logs can be found by performing a search or filtering for the event IDs 36 (for warning threshold) and 37 (for over the limit), with a source entry of NTFS.

To locate disk quota events in the System log, use the procedure outlined in Step by Step 6.21.

STEP BY STEP

6.21 Filtering an Event Log to Find Quota Entries

1. From the Start menu, click Start, All Programs, Administrative Tools, Event Viewer.
2. In the left pane of the Event Viewer MMC, right-click the System log. From the system menu, select View, Filter.

continues

continued

3. After you select Filter, the Log Properties dialog box, shown in Figure 6.63, appears.

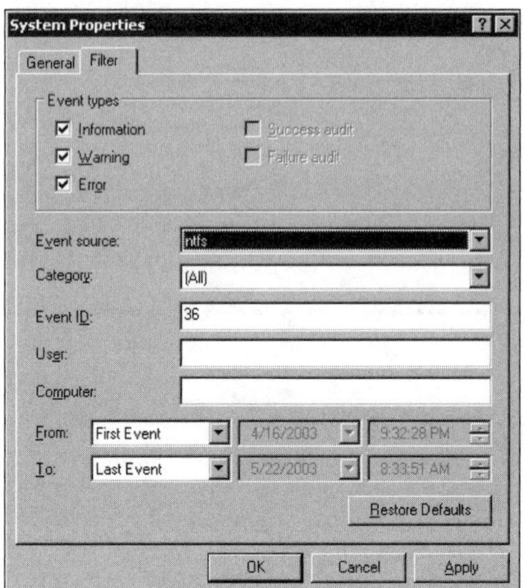

FIGURE 6.63
Enter the event ID 36, with an Event Source entry of NTFS.

4. From the Log Properties dialog box, select the event ID and the source and then click OK. The results after filtering are shown in Figure 6.64.

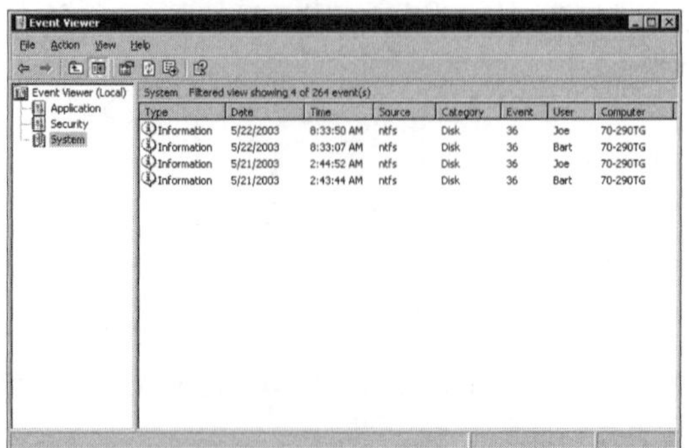

FIGURE 6.64
The log file after filtering.

The second major task associated with disk quotas involves monitoring the space each user has available. This can be accomplished by opening the Quota Entries window and sorting the space entries to find out which users have exceeded their limits and which users are near their limits, as shown in Figure 6.65.

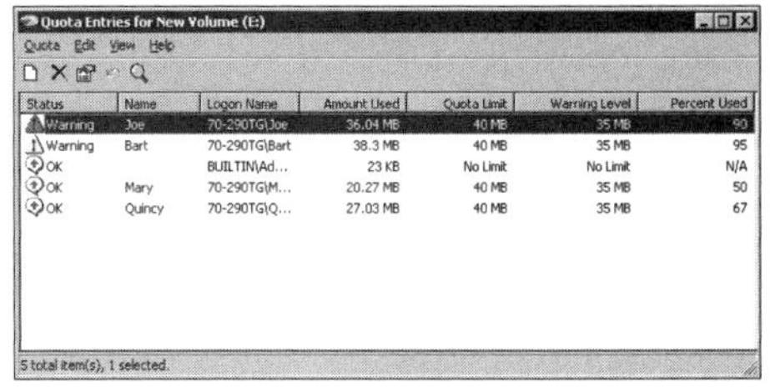

FIGURE 6.65
The Quota Entries window supplies all the quota information at a glance.

This is made easier by referring to the icons to the left of the entries. The following icons are used so that you can see the status at a glance:

- **Green**—This means the user is below the warning threshold.
- **Yellow triangle with exclamation point**—This means the user is over the warning threshold but under the limit.
- **Red circle with exclamation point**—The user has exceeded the limit.

> **EXAM TIP**
>
> **Expect a Question Related to Copying/Moving Files and Disk Quotas** Expect at least one exam question that deals with how quotas are affected when a file is copied or moved between folders or volumes. Remember that moving files on the same volume retains ownership, whereas copying does not.

Managing and Monitoring Print Queues

Just behind file server, print server is the most common role for a Windows Server 2003 server. Having a printer directly connected to each user's computer is impractical for most organizations, so most networks have a variety of printers connected to a Windows Server 2003 server that is acting as a print server. When a Windows Server 2003 server is configured as a print server, it allows clients on a variety of operating systems to submit print jobs to printers attached to it.

Having a centralized print server offers several advantages, including but not limited to the following:

- A central point of administration. The system administrator has only to be concerned with configuring and updating printer drivers on a single computer.
- The print server manages the printer driver settings for all clients.
- Having to purchase fewer printers means you can purchase better printers.

- Depending on the configuration, a single print queue is shared by multiple users. This allows the users to see where their print job is in the queue in relation to other print jobs; it also allows the administrator or print operator to manage the print jobs from a single queue. The administrator or print operator can centrally hold, resume, or cancel print jobs.
- Error messages are optionally sent to all users so that everyone knows the status of the printer.
- Most of the processing of the print job is passed off to the server, allowing the client computer to continue on with other tasks.
- There is a single event log for the administrator and/or printer operator to manage.
- Drivers can be automatically downloaded for Windows NT/XP/200x client computers the first time they connect to the print server. In addition, drivers can be updated on the server and then updated on the client the next time it connects to the print server.
- Drivers can be automatically downloaded for Windows 9x client computers the first time they connect to the print server. However, they are not automatically updateable.
- A dedicated computer is not required, except for the largest of organizations. Typically, a print server has another role on the network, such as also serving the role of a file server.

One of the hardest parts of understanding Microsoft's printing process is keeping the technology clear. As mentioned earlier, a *print server* is a server we install the print drivers on. The role of the print server is to accept the print jobs or instructions from the applications running on the client computers. The print server routes this information to the print drivers.

Print drivers are the software that enables the operating system to communicate to the printing device. The role of the print driver is to accept commands from the operating system and translate them into commands that the print device understands. The *print device* is that piece of hardware that most people refer to as a printer.

The intermediate step between the print driver and the print device is the *spooler*, which is also known as the *spool file*. It's a file on the print server that contains the data to be printed. This file contains the print data and the print device–specific commands needed to format the printed output. Most print jobs do not go directly to the print device, especially on a print device that is heavily used. Because a print device usually prints slower than the print job can be processed, the file is stored in the spool file so that the user can continue on with his or her work while the print server manages the print job. This has additional benefits. Printers, being mechanical devices, tend to jam and run out of paper. Because the print job is stored in a file, it can be resumed when the print device is repaired. In addition, the print job can be restarted, if some of the pages were damaged or lost.

The content of the spool file is referred to as the *print queue*. Users have the ability to view the print queue, using the Print Manager applet. Users can hold or cancel their own print jobs, or the print jobs of other users if they are granted the appropriate permissions. After the print device finishes printing the job, the print job is deleted.

Each model of print device usually requires a unique printer driver to support the differences in hardware and features supported. In addition, there might be different drivers to support each version of the client operating system. Typically, Windows NT/XP/200x drivers are somewhat interchangeable, whereas DOS and Windows 9x drivers are more specific to the version of the operating system.

In addition, there are two types of printers: local and network. A *local* printer is defined as a printer directly attached to and managed by the print server, either via a LPT or serial port, a USB interface, or a network connection. Network attached printers are print devices that have their own network interface card (NIC), IP address, and attach to the network like any other device. Their configuration and management is handled by the print server.

To summarize, here's a list of important terms:

- **Print job**—The sequence of data and print device commands sent to the print device.
- **Spooler (spool file)**—This is the file that stores the print data while it's waiting to be printed.
- **Print queue**—The list of print jobs currently in the spooler.
- **Print server**—A computer, usually a Windows Server 2003 server, that you install the print drivers on.
- **Printer driver**—The software that enables the operating system to communicate to the printing device.
- **Print device**—The physical printer.
- **Local printer**—Any print device that is directly attached and controlled by the print server.
- **Network printer**—Any print device that is directly attached to the network.

EXAM TIP

It's important that you thoroughly understand the terms Microsoft uses to describe the print system because that's the terminology used for the exam questions.

Managing and Configuring Printers

One of the basic steps of working with a Windows Server 2003 print server is installing a printer. Local printers can be installed only by members of the Administrators or Printer Operators group.

To install a printer, perform the procedure outlined in Step by Step 6.22.

STEP BY STEP

6.22 Installing and Configuring a Printer

1. From the Start menu, click Start, Printers and Faxes.
2. In the left pane of the Printers and Faxes window, under Printer Tasks, click Add a Printer. This starts the Add Printer Wizard.
3. Click Next. The Local or Network Printer screen shown in Figure 6.66 appears.

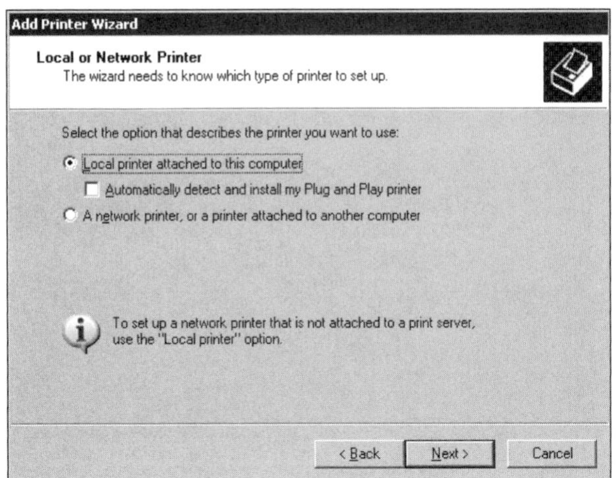

FIGURE 6.66
The Local or Network Printer screen allows you to select to install a printer to be controlled either by this computer or by a remote computer.

4. Select Local Printer Attached to This Computer and then click Next. The Select a Printer Port screen appears, as shown in Figure 6.67.

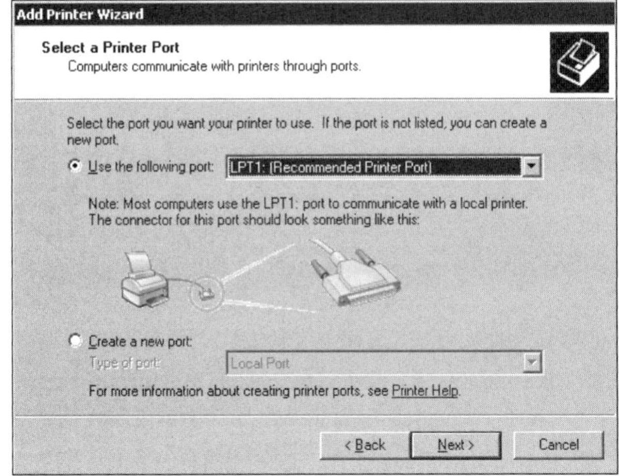

FIGURE 6.67
The Select a Printer Port screen allows you to specify what port the printer is connected to. This can be anything from the standard LPT1, a Terminal Services logical port, or a new TCP/IP port you create.

5. Select the desired port and then click Next. The Install Printer Software screen appears, as shown in Figure 6.68. Select the appropriate drives and then click Next. In this screen, you have the option of selecting drivers included on the Windows Server 2003 CD-ROM, or you can click the Windows Update button to download drivers for your printer from the Windows Update Web site. In addition, if you have a driver disk, you can click the Have Disk button.

continues

continued

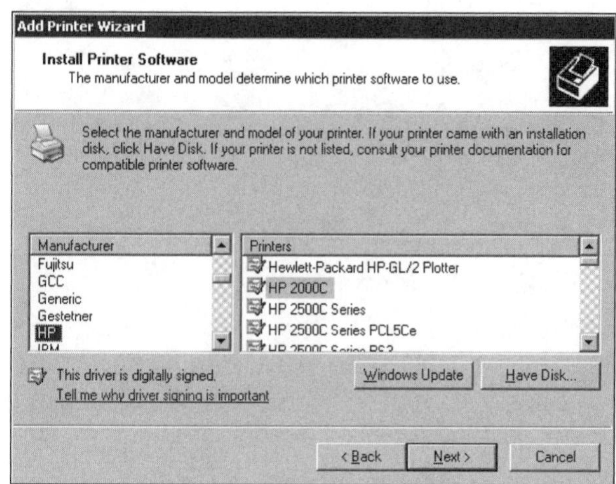

FIGURE 6.68
The Install Printer Software screen allows you to load the necessary printer drivers.

6. The Name Your Printer screen appears, as shown in Figure 6.69. You can leave the default name assigned by Windows, or you can enter your own. Make sure the name is something recognizable because it is the name you'll use to refer to the printer. Click Next.

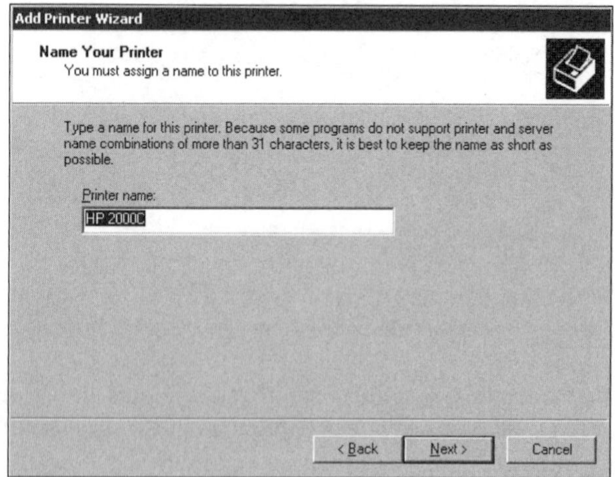

FIGURE 6.69
Give the printer a name that describes its location or function.

7. The Printer Sharing screen appears, as shown in Figure 6.70. This is the name that other users on the network see. You can leave the default name assigned by Windows, or you can enter your own. Click Next.

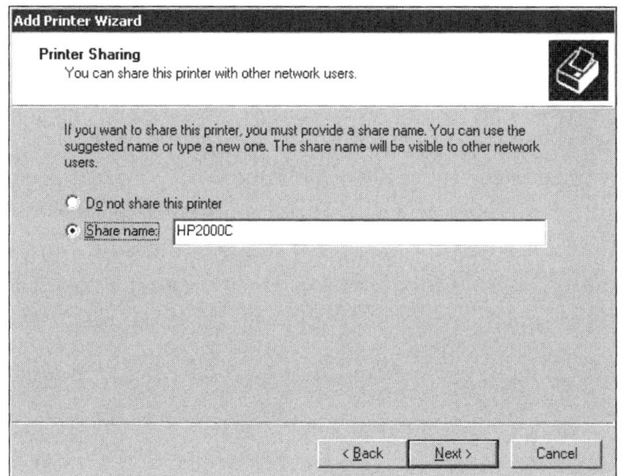

FIGURE 6.70
This name is visible to other users on the network of your selected share.

8. The Location and Comment screen appears, as shown in Figure 6.71. These fields help to identify the printer to other users. They can also be used to locate the printer when searching in Active Directory. Click Next.

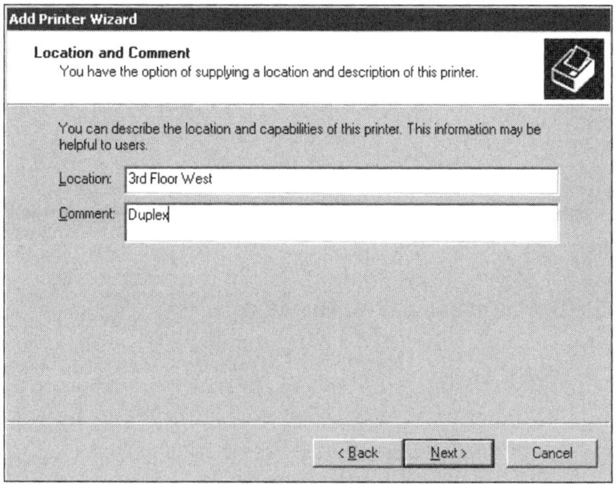

FIGURE 6.71
Add a location and comments to make identification of this printer easier for your end users.

9. The Print Test Page screen allows you to test your configuration by sending a test print job to the printer. Click Next.

10. From the Completing the Add Printer Wizard screen, check the printer settings. Click the Back button to redo a setting, or click the Finish button if you're done.

Printer Pooling

Printer pooling is a form of load balancing in that two or more print devices are represented by a single printer. The users send their print jobs to what looks like a single printer. The print server then queues the print jobs in the order they were submitted. When a print device finishes a print job, it receives the next job in the queue. This is a very efficient way to print because it balances the load. You never have multiple jobs waiting for a specific printer while another printer is idle.

For printer pooling to work successfully, the following conditions must be met:

- The printers must use the same print driver. They don't all have to be the same exact model, just as long as they give the same results using a common printer driver.
- They must all be configured on the same print server because they have to share the same driver and print queue.
- They should be located in close proximity to each other. The user has no way of knowing which printer the print job ended up on, so it's best to have them all in the same room.

To configure a printer pool, use the procedure outlined in Step by Step 6.23.

STEP BY STEP

6.23 Configuring a Printer Pool

1. From the Start menu, click Start, Printers and Faxes.
2. In the left pane of the Printers and Faxes window, under Printer Tasks, click Add a Printer. This starts the Add Printer Wizard. Follow the procedure in Step by Step 6.22 to install the appropriate printer device, if it's not already present.
3. In the Printers and Faxes window, as shown in Figure 6.72, right-click the printer you want to set up in a pool and select Properties from the pop-up menu.

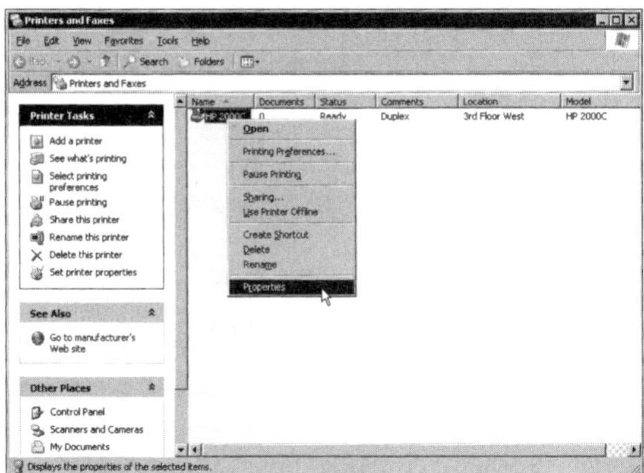

FIGURE 6.72◄
Select Properties for the printer you are setting up in a printer pool.

4. In the Printer Properties dialog box, select the Ports tab, as shown in Figure 6.73.
5. Select the Enable Printer Pooling check box and then select the desired ports. Click OK when you're finished.

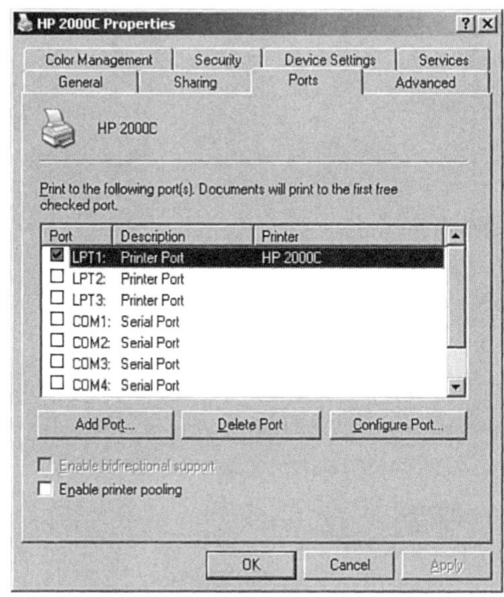

FIGURE 6.73▲
The Ports tab allows you to select the ports that the printers for your pool are connected to.

After the procedure has been completed, if you look at the Ports tab, you will see that several ports have the identical printer name assigned to them, as shown in Figure 6.74.

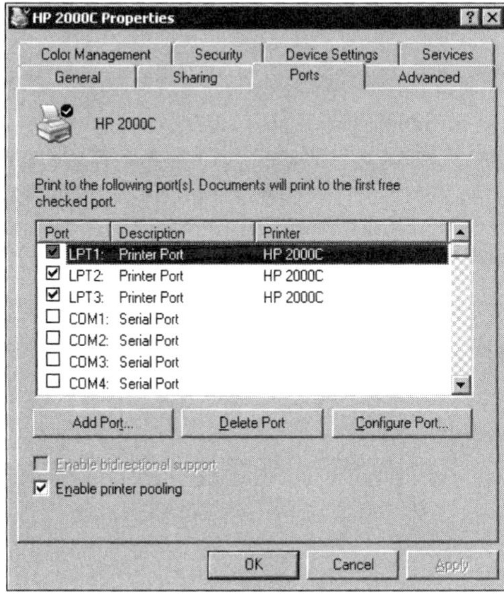

FIGURE 6.74◄
The Ports tab showing the completed configuration.

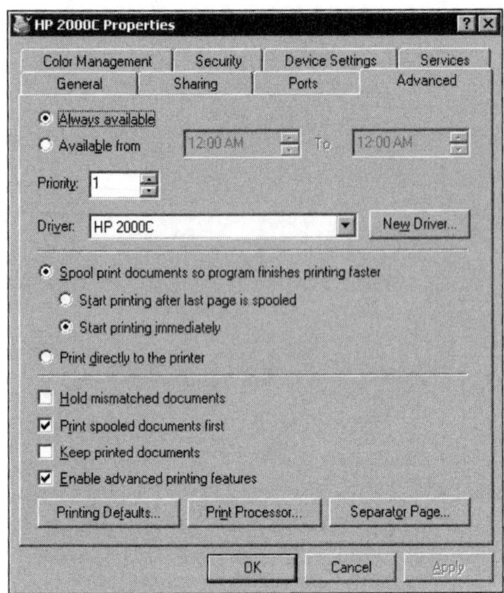

FIGURE 6.75
The Printer Properties dialog box's Advanced tab.

Multiple Logical Printers

Now that you've seen how to use one logical printer to represent several physical print devices, let's set up several logical printers to represent one physical print device. You can set up several logical printers, each with slightly different configurations (but using the same print driver) and assigned to different people. For example, take a look at the Advanced tab of the Printer Properties dialog box shown in Figure 6.75. There are two areas here that are of interest.

The first area is the Always Available and Available From radio buttons. The default is for the printer to always be available. However, suppose the Accounting department has a weekly job that prints a 500-page report. Unless you have a very fast printer, you wouldn't want to print that during normal business hours because no one else would be able to print. You could create an additional logical printer and name it After Hours. The Advanced tab of the Printer Properties dialog box for the After Hours printer might say that it is available only from 6:00 p.m. to 6:00 a.m. Then, whenever users need to print a huge print job, they would print to the After Hours logical print device. The job would sit in the print queue for that logical device until 6:00 p.m., and then start printing when everyone has gone home.

The other area is the Priority entry, which sets the default importance of the print jobs in the queue. Priority can be set from 1 to 99. The job assigned the higher numerical number is printed first. For example, suppose you have a department with 30 employees and 2 managers. The managers feel that their print jobs should be printed before the employee print jobs. In this case, you would create two logical printers, one for the managers and one for the employees. The manager printer would have a priority of 99, whereas the employee's printer could be left at 1.

Assigning Print Permissions

On the surface, setting different print priorities for different logical devices sounds like a great idea. However, what's to stop some devious employee from trying to print using the manager's logical printer?

Like any Windows resource, the printing environment in Windows Server 2003 is highly secure and configurable. Access to printer objects is controlled in the same manner as access to objects such as files and folders—they are defined on a user and group basis. For printer objects, three basic roles are granted the permissions shown in Table 6.2. These permissions allow users who are assigned these predefined roles to print, manage documents, or manage printers.

TABLE 6.2

PRINTER-SPECIFIC PERMISSIONS

Permission	*Print*	*Manage Documents*	*Manage Printer*
Print documents	X	X	X
Pause, restart, and cancel own documents	X	X	X
Connect to a printer	X	X	X
Control job settings for all documents		X	X
Pause, restart, and cancel all documents		X	X
Share a printer			X
Change printer properties			X
Delete printers			X
Change printer permissions			X

The permissions are broken down by the default groups that are granted the predefined roles, as shown in Table 6.3.

TABLE 6.3

GROUP-SPECIFIC ROLES

Group	*Print*	*Manage Documents*	*Manage Printer*
Administrators	X	X	X
Creator Owner		X	
Everyone	X		
Power Users	X	X	X
Print Operators	X	X	X
Server Operators	X	X	X

The previous two tables outline the default permissions and roles. However, these can be changed to provide more granularity. For example, let's configure a logical printer for the managers group referred to in the previous example.

To configure a logical printer that grants a higher priority to print jobs submitted by managers, perform the procedure outlined in Step by Step 6.24.

STEP BY STEP

6.24 Configuring the Security Settings on a Printer

1. From the Start menu, click Start, Printers and Faxes.
2. In the Printers and Faxes window, right-click the printer you want to configure and select Properties from the pop-up menu.
3. In the Printer Properties dialog box, select the Advanced tab. Change the Priority setting to 99, as shown in Figure 6.76.
4. Select the Security tab. Click the Add button to open the Select Users or Groups dialog box, as shown in Figure 6.77. Enter the Managers and Employees groups. Click OK.

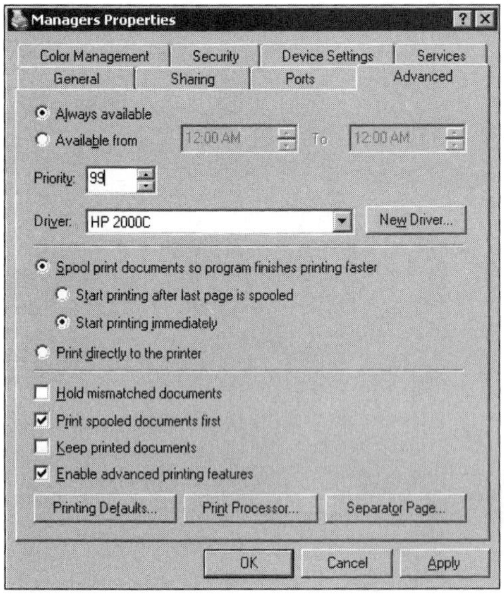

FIGURE 6.76▲
Set the Priority to 99.

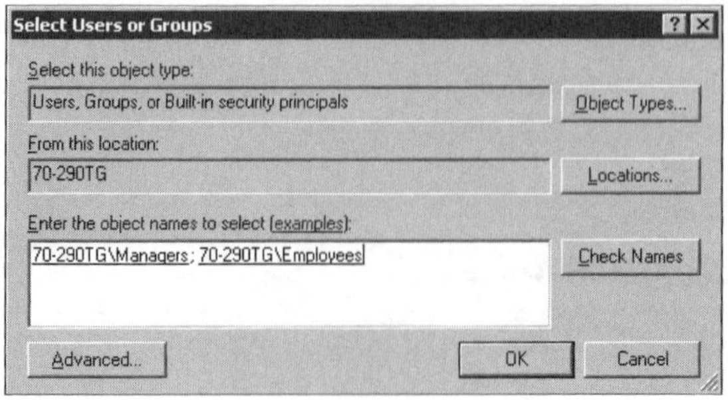

FIGURE 6.77▶
Enter the Managers and Employees groups.

5. From the Security tab of the Managers print object's Properties dialog box, shown in Figure 6.78, highlight the Employees group and select Deny for all entries. If desired, you can add the Manage Printers and Documents roles to the Managers group.
6. Click OK when you're finished.

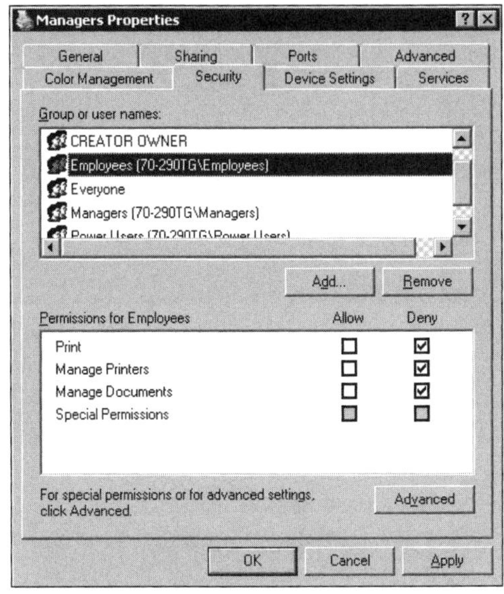

FIGURE 6.78
Deny access to the Employees group.

This works unless the managers are also members of the Employees group. Review the rules on Deny Access from Chapter 4, "Managing and Maintaining Access to Resources."

Monitoring Printers

To monitor print server performance, Windows Server 2003 includes the Print Queue performance object, which is used with the System Monitor applet covered earlier in this chapter. This object allows you to monitor counters such as bytes printed per second, job errors, and total pages printed. In addition to the Print Server object, the areas you need to monitor for print performance are the standard four areas: disk, memory, NIC, and, to a lesser extent, processor.

CASE STUDY: DM WILKINSON

ESSENCE OF THE CASE

Here are the essential elements in this case:

- Conserve disk space.
- Provide the best performance for the file and print servers.
- Archive a record of intrusion attempts.

SCENARIO

DM Wilkinson is a wholesaler for a wide variety of electronic goods and supplies that it primarily imports for the Far East. Because of the current economic slowdown, DM Wilkinson is going to be unable to refresh its server hardware as it had planned. However, the company is still experiencing slow but steady growth, so it is adding more employees on a regular basis. Because the company was wildly successful over the previous years, although its servers are a couple of years

continues

Case Study: DM Wilkinson

continued

old, when purchased they were top of the line. DM Wilkinson only has enough money in its current budget to upgrade the server operating systems.

DM Wilkinson now wants to optimize its servers that support its file and print services to handle more users, without upgrading the server hardware. The company also needs to conserve disk space because it is starting to get low on free space for its users.

In addition to the previous requirements, due to the fiercely competitive nature of the electronics business, DM Wilkinson is constantly seeing hacking attempts from "professional" hackers and suspicious insiders. DM Wilkinson needs to maintain a record of all these intrusion attempts for its legal department to use in prosecutions. Although daily access to these records is not required, they still need to be reasonably accessible. However, due to the potentially enormous number of records to be archived, the company wants them to be stored as efficiently as possible.

ANALYSIS

The features in Windows Server 2003 enable DM Wilkinson to satisfy its disk space, performance, and archival requirements. The first step is to update the servers to Windows Server 2003 and then turn on disk quotas for all users, allowing them a reasonable amount of disk space to perform their duties, but not allowing them enough space for extraneous items such as MP3s, pictures, and games.

The next step is to use the performance-monitoring tools to baseline the server performance. Using this baseline information, the company should examine the performance logs that are generated to identify bottlenecks in the various subsystems. Then it can configure the servers so that they are achieving the maximum performance from their existing hardware.

The final requirement can be accomplished by turning on auditing for logon attempts. This provides a record of attempted intrusions by recording logon failures in the Security log. The company can archive the log data by periodically saving and clearing the Security log when it approaches the maximum size.

Table 6.4 provides an overview of the requirements and solutions in this case study.

TABLE 6.4

Overview of the Requirements and Solutions in This Case Study

Requirement	*Solution Provided By*
Conserve disk space	Configuring Windows Server 2003 to use disk quotas on volumes where the users store their files.
Provide the best performance for the file and print servers	Recording a baseline using the Performance Monitor tools. The company will use this baseline to identify performance bottlenecks and to configure the server for best performance.
Archive a record of intrusion attempts	Configuring auditing to track failed logon attempts. The company should periodically save and clear the Security log.

CHAPTER SUMMARY

This chapter has covered a lot of ground; here are the main points:

- **Using the event logs**—This includes knowing the types of event logs available on both a domain controller and a member server. This also includes knowing how to configure, search, filter, delete, and archive the data contained in the event logs.
- **Optimizing server performance**—This includes knowing what tools are available to monitor and optimize performance on your Windows Server 2003 server and how to use them.
- **Implementing and monitoring disk quotas**—This includes knowing how to enable, configure, and troubleshoot the Disk Quota feature available in Windows Server 2003.
- **Managing and monitoring print queues**—This includes knowing how to manage the queue and delegate authority to users.

KEY TERMS

- Security descriptor
- Print queue
- Disk quota
- Audit policy
- Security log
- Quota limit
- Counters
- Instance
- Event ID
- Printer
- Print device

APPLY YOUR KNOWLEDGE

Exercises

6.1 Configuring User Disk Quotas

A common problem when managing file servers is running out of free space. Users typically have to be reminded that the amount of space available is not infinite. As a system administrator, it is your job to allocate disk space to users and make sure they don't use more space than they should.

To simplify this task, as the administrator, you should put some of the onus of managing disk space constraints back on the users. After all, they know more about which files need to be deleted than you do.

What is the best way to accomplish this in Windows Server 2003? On your own, try to develop a solution that involves limited on-going management by the system administrator.

If you would like to see a possible solution, follow these steps:

Estimated Time: 20 minutes

1. From My Computer or Windows Explorer, right-click the volume you want to enable quotas on and select Properties from the pop-up menu.
2. In the Properties dialog box, select the Quota tab.
3. On the Quota tab, select the check box Enable Quota Management.
4. In the Quota Properties dialog box, select the Limit Disk Space To radio button and add limit and warning levels. Click OK.
5. A warning dialog box appears. It tells you that the drive will be scanned so that the file ownership will be inventoried and the disk usage can be credited to each user. Click OK.
6. In the Quota Entries window, from the system menu, select Quota and then click New Quota Entry from the drop-down menu.
7. The Select Users dialog box appears. From here you can select one or more users from the local or domain database. Add a user and then click OK.
8. The Add New Quota Entry dialog box appears. Set the desired limits and then click OK.
9. The new users are added with the configured settings.

6.2 Creating a New Log View

It can be helpful to have a custom view of the event logs so that you can easily find specific events. For example, to quickly find quota events, you can filter the event logs. By saving a custom view of the logs, you can easily identify these events without having to reconfigure the filter on the logs every time you want to monitor quotas.

What is the best way to accomplish this in Windows Server 2003? On your own, try to develop a solution that involves limited on-going management by the system administrator.

If you would like to see a possible solution, follow these steps:

Estimated Time: 20 minutes

1. From the Start menu, click Start, All Programs, Administrative Tools, Event Viewer.
2. In the left pane of the Event Viewer MMC, right-click the System log. From the pop-up menu, select New Log View.

APPLY YOUR KNOWLEDGE

3. A new log entry appears in the left pane of the Event Viewer MMC. Right-click the entry and select Rename from the pop-up menu. Change the name to Quota.
4. Right-click the Quota log. From the system menu, select View, Filter.
5. After you select Filter, the Properties dialog box appears. From the Log Properties dialog box, select the event ID 36 and a source of NTFS and then click OK.

This gives you a custom log that can be used to track Quota events.

Review Questions

1. Which event logs are present on all versions of Windows Server 2003?
2. Discuss which users will and will not have quotas applied when disk quotas are turned on for an existing volume.
3. Discuss the difference between a printer and a print device.
4. What is the major difference in auditing between Windows 2000 and Windows Server 2003?
5. What is the major difference in the configuration of the event logs between Windows 2000 and Windows Server 2003?
6. Discuss the purpose of the Users tab that has been added to the Windows Server 2003 version of Task Manager.
7. What permissions are required to view the event logs?

Exam Questions

1. Joe is the system administrator for a small trucking company. He is running short on space on one of his servers, and he needs to make sure the server doesn't crash because it has run out of disk space. However, the server contains user files, and the users always want their files available, even though some of their files might not have been accessed for years.

   Joe wants to be notified when his server is low on disk space so that he can surreptitiously move some of the user files off of the server.

   Required Result:

   Joe wants to be notified when disk space is running low on his server.

   Optional Results:

   The users' space on the volume must be limited.

   Notify users when they are running out of space.

   Proposed Solution:

   Turn on Disk Quotas for all users; configure the quotas so that they send out a notification when the users reach their warning threshold.

   Evaluation of Proposed Solution:

   Which result(s) does the proposed solution produce?

   A. The proposed solution produces the required result but neither of the optional results.

   B. The proposed solution produces the required result and one of the optional results.

   C. The proposed solution produces the required result and both of the optional results.

APPLY YOUR KNOWLEDGE

D. The proposed solution does not produce the required result.

2. Joe is the system administrator for a small trucking company. He is running short on space on one of his servers, and he needs to make sure the server doesn't crash because it has run out of disk space. However, the server contains user files, and the users always want their files available, even though some of their files might not have been accessed for years.

   Joe wants to be notified when his server is low on disk space so that he can surreptitiously move some of the user files off of the server.

   Required Result:

   Joe wants to be notified when disk space is running low on his server.

   Optional Results:

   The users' space on the volume must be limited.

   Notify users when they are running out of space.

   Proposed Solution:

   Turn on Disk Quotas for all users, configure the quotas so that they send out a notification when the users reach their warning threshold. Configure an alert in Performance Monitor to warn Joe when the instance of LogicalDisk\%FreeSpace falls below 10%.

   Evaluation of Proposed Solution:

   Which result(s) does the proposed solution produce?

   A. The proposed solution produces the required result but neither of the optional results.

   B. The proposed solution produces the required result and one of the optional results.

   C. The proposed solution produces the required result and both of the optional results.

   D. The proposed solution does not produce the required result.

3. Mary is a developer for a small software firm. She is testing a new server-based product that updates a SQL database and then prompts the administrator for information that it then sends to an email server. Because Mary is running Windows Server 2003 on a desktop computer, the performance is not very good. She wants to increase the performance of the database update so that it finishes faster.

   Required Result:

   Increase the performance of the database update.

   Optional Results:

   Increase the performance of the entire procedure.

   Make the entire procedure finish faster.

   Proposed solution:

   Mary starts the test application. She then opens Task Manager to the Processes tab. She changes the priority of her test application from Normal to Realtime.

   Evaluation of Proposed Solution:

   Which result(s) does the proposed solution produce?

   A. The proposed solution produces the required result but neither of the optional results.

   B. The proposed solution produces the required result and one of the optional results.

APPLY YOUR KNOWLEDGE

C. The proposed solution produces the required result and both of the optional results.

D. The proposed solution does not produce the required result.

4. Davin is a new system administrator for an engineering firm. The engineering firm recently fired its previous system administrator because the performance of the firm's file server was always poor. The server is configured with a hardware RAID-5 array with three disks. The disk cabinet has space available for three more disks. Davin decides that he is going to retain his job, so he fires up System Monitor and observes the performance of his file server.

   The first thing that he notices is that the PhysicalDisk: %Disk Time and the Paging File: %Usage Peak counters are both pegged at 100%.

   Required Result:

   Improve the performance of the file server.

   Optional Results:

   Add more free space to the file server.

   Davin gets to keep his job.

   Proposed Solution:

   Add two more drives to the drive array.

   Evaluation of Proposed Solution:

   Which result(s) does the proposed solution produce?

   A. The proposed solution produces the required result but neither of the optional results.

   B. The proposed solution produces the required result and one of the optional results.

   C. The proposed solution produces the required result and both of the optional results.

   D. The proposed solution does not produce the required result.

5. John is having what he thinks are disk performance problems on his new Windows Server 2003 server. He decides to use System Monitor to look at the disk counters to see how everything is performing. What must he do to enable the counters for the logical disks?

   A. At the command line, type `DISKPERF -y` and then restart the server.

   B. At the command line, type `DISKPERF -yd` and then restart the server.

   C. At the command line, type `DISKPERF -y`.

   D. Nothing, the counters are already enabled.

6. Davin is a new system administrator for an engineering firm. The engineering firm recently fired its previous system administrator because the performance of the firm's file server was always poor. The server is configured with a hardware RAID-5 array with three disks. The disk cabinet has space available for three more disks. Davin decides that he is going to retain his job, so he fires up System Monitor and observes the performance of his file server.

   The first thing he notices is that the PhysicalDisk: %Disk Time counter is pegged at 100%. In addition, the Memory: Pages Input/sec is at 1.

   Required Result:

   Improve the performance of the file server.

   Optional Results:

   Add more free space to the file server.

   Davin gets to keep his job.

APPLY YOUR KNOWLEDGE

Proposed Solution:

Add two more drives to the drive array.

Evaluation of Proposed Solution:

Which result(s) does the proposed solution produce?

A. The proposed solution produces the required result but neither of the optional results.

B. The proposed solution produces the required result and one of the optional results.

C. The proposed solution produces the required result and both of the optional results.

D. The proposed solution does not produce the required result.

7. Dave is the system administrator for a large law firm. He has to manage 20 servers and 10 print servers in addition to 400 desktops. To streamline the printing of large documents, Dave has set up an empty office as a print center and installed four Behemoth 2000 printers. All four printers are similarly configured. Unfortunately, one of the printers is heavily used while the other three see little usage.

   Because the contract from Behemoth has a rider that charges Dave extra for exceeding a certain amount of use, he wants to balance the usage across the four printers as closely as possible.

   Required Result:

   Balance the workload across all four printers.

   Optional Results:

   Accomplish the result with minimal user training.

   Accomplish the result with minimal intervention by Dave.

   Proposed Solution:

   Connect the printers to the same print server. Configure the four printers in a printer pool.

   Evaluation of Proposed Solution:

   Which result(s) does the proposed solution produce?

   A. The proposed solution produces the required result but neither of the optional results.

   B. The proposed solution produces the required result and one of the optional results.

   C. The proposed solution produces the required result and both of the optional results.

   D. The proposed solution does not produce the required result.

8. You work in a mid-sized advertising agency. You have a color printer that is lightly used, but it should always be available for the account managers to use because they sometimes need brochures in a hurry. What's the best way to accomplish this?

   A. Configure two logical printers that are assigned to the same printing device. Assign different priorities and groups to each printer.

   B. Buy another identical printer. Set up a printer pool that contains both printers.

   C. Configure the printer so that only the account managers have access to it.

   D. Instruct the other users on how to kill their print jobs when an account manager needs the printer.

9. Shelly is starting to run out of space on one of her file servers, so she decides to turn on Disk

Apply Your Knowledge

Quotas. She starts monitoring the System log for the warning messages that indicate users are crossing the warning threshold. After she has been running with Disk Quotas for a couple of weeks, she still hasn't received any notification messages. However, one day the file server locks up. After she reboots it, she notices that the user drive has zero free space. What is the most likely problem?

A. Because quotas don't apply to administrators, one of the administrators saved too many files to the server.

B. After Shelly turned on Disk Quotas, she forgot to turn on System log notification.

C. Shelly forgot to configure a hard limit, so the users were able to keep saving additional files after exceeding their quotas.

D. Shelly didn't manually assign quotas to the existing users.

10. Don is the system administrator for a mid-sized company. He needs to delegate some of his trivial duties so that he can get more of his important work done. He decides to delegate some of the document-management duties to some of the administration assistants. What default group can he make them a member of so that they can manage print documents without giving them too much authority?

A. Server Operators

B. Power Users

C. Print Operators

D. Printer Operators

11. Jason is the system administrator for a small bank. The bank requires that he maintain a log of all logon events in the domain and retain it for a period of no less than 7 years. What must Jason do to obtain and archive this data?

A. Auditing is automatically turned on in Windows Server 2003. He must clear and archive the Security logs weekly.

B. In the domain GPO, he must turn on the option Audit Account Logon Events for both success and failure. He must also clear and archive the Security logs weekly.

C. In the domain GPO, he must turn on the option Audit Logon Events for both success and failure. He must also clear and archive the Security logs weekly.

D. In the domain GPO, he must turn on the option Audit Account Logon Events and the option Audit Logon Events for both success and failure. He must also clear and archive the security logs weekly.

12. James is having performance problems on one of his database servers. He ran System Monitor for a couple of days and came up with the following average values:

- Processor: %Processor Time: 80%
- System Processor Queue Length: 5
- PhysicalDisk: Avg. Disk Queue Length: 2
- Memory: Pages Input/sec: 2

What should James do?

A. Add more RAM.

B. Add a faster disk.

Apply Your Knowledge

C. Add an additional processor.

D. Get a better NIC.

13. The legal department of your company has a monthly print job that details the company's efforts to correct past human rights violations in Third World countries. This monthly print job is over 1,000 pages, so it needs to be printed outside of normal business hours. What is the best way to accomplish this?

    A. Create two logical printers for a print device. Assign one with a priority of 99 and name it Overnight. Leave the other with the default settings. Use the Overnight printer for the monthly report.

    B. Create two logical printers for a print device. Assign one with a priority of 1 and name it Overnight. Configure the other with a priority of 99. Use the Overnight printer for the monthly report.

    C. Create two logical printers for a print device. Assign one with a priority of 1 and name it Overnight. Set the hours available on the Overnight Printer to 6:00 p.m. to 6:00 a.m. Configure the other with a priority of 99. Use the Overnight printer for the monthly report.

    D. Buy another printer and dedicate it to the monthly print job.

14. Stuart is running a database application that runs in the background but requires a lot of processor time. He is running this application on a server with several other applications, but they are neither critical nor time sensitive. What can Stuart do to improve the performance of his database application?

    A. Install more memory in his server.

    B. Install a faster disk subsystem in his server.

    C. Install a faster NIC in his server.

    D. Use Task Manager to set his application to a higher priority.

15. Frank works for a manufacturing company that has 30 servers running Windows Server 2003, 600 Windows NT workstations, 700 Windows XP Professional workstations, and 200 Windows 98 computers. The main print server is running Windows Server 2003 and is used to support several color printers. The printers are shared from the print server, with drivers loaded for all the client machines.

    The manufacturer of the color printers releases new drivers with more features. Frank installs the updated drivers on the print server. After getting everything set up, Frank tests printing from the clients and notices that whereas the Windows NT and XP clients seem to support the new features, the Windows 98 clients do not. What is the most likely cause of the problem?

    A. Frank installed the wrong drivers on the print server.

    B. Frank did not install the Windows 98 drivers on the print server.

    C. Frank needs to install the drivers on the Windows 98 clients.

    D. Frank needs to restart the Spooler service so that the Windows 98 clients are recognized.

APPLY YOUR KNOWLEDGE

Answers to Review Questions

1. The Security, System, and Application logs are available on all versions of Windows Server 2003. The DNS Server log is present on a server running the DNS service, whereas the File Replication Service log and the Directory Service log are present on domain controllers.

2. When disk quotas are turned on for an existing volume, quotas are applied to any new users who create a file on that volume. However, quotas are not applied to members of the local Administrators group.

3. Microsoft defines a *printer* as the software interface on the print server, whereas a *print device* is the actual hardware device that produces the printed output.

4. In Windows 2000, you had to specifically turn auditing on, and then you could configure auditing on an object. In Windows Server 2003, auditing is turned on by default; you just have to select the objects to be audited.

5. In Windows 2000, the default size of the event logs was 512KB, which was usually inadequate for all but the least busy servers. In Windows Server 2003, the default is 16,384KB, with the ability to overwrite events as needed, which is a far more practical configuration for most small and medium networks.

6. The Users tab displays the users currently logged on to your server. This includes users logged on to the console, users connected via the RDP client in Remote Administration Mode, or Terminal Services users connected in Application Mode.

7. Although ordinary users can view the System and Application logs, a user must be a member of the local Administrators group to view the Security log. In addition, to view any log on a remote machine, the user must be a member of the local Administrators group on the remote machine.

Answers to Exam Questions

1. **D.** This solution does not meet the required result. Although it may help the users to limit their use of space on the server, the only notification is when a user is running out of space, not when the volume is.

2. **C.** This produces the desired result and both optional results. Joe uses Performance Monitor to issue an alert that he can receive in various ways when disk space is low. Turning on Disk Quotas limits the space that the users have available, and it's configured to warn them when they are running low on space.

3. **D.** This solution does not meet the required results. When a process is set to Realtime, it is unable to respond to external input. Changing the base priority of an application to Realtime makes the priority of an application higher than the process that monitors and responds to keyboard input. The second step in Mary's application test requires keyboard input. The application, therefore, will hang, and Mary will be required to reboot.

4. **D.** The proposed solution does not meet the required results. Although the Disk Time counter is excessively high, so is the Paging File usage. When the paging file usage is extremely high, that means that the server is constantly swapping to disk, which is a pretty good indication that the server is running out of physical memory.

Apply Your Knowledge

5. **D.** Nothing, all of the disk counters are enabled by default in Windows Server 2003.

6. **C.** The proposed solution should meet the required result and also both optional results. Because the Disk Time counter is excessively high, but the Memory: Pages Input/sec value is less than 2, this indicates a disk problem because there doesn't seem to be a significant amount of pages swapped into memory. Adding additional drives to the array spreads I/O across more spindles, which should increase performance, add additional file space, and allow Davin to keep his job.

7. **C.** The solution meets the required and both optional results. To use a printer pool, all the printers must be capable of using the same printer driver, must be connected to the same print server, and should (for the convenience of the users) be located in close proximity to each other.

8. **A.** You should configure two logical printers assigned to the same printing device and then assign the Account Managers group a priority of 99 on one logical printer and leave the defaults on the other.

9. **A.** Quotas do not apply to members of the Administrators group.

10. **C.** Print Operators is the best choice. It gives them the ability to manage both documents and printers without giving them any additional administrative rights. The Server Operators and Power Users groups would give them more authority than they need. The Printer Operators group does not exist.

11. **D.** For all logon events on all workstations to be collected in the Security logs on the domain controllers, both Audit Account Logon and Audit Logon Events must be turned on. Although auditing is turned on by default in Windows Server 2003, Audit Account Logon and Audit Logon Events are turned on only for success events, not failure events.

12. **C.** Both the processor time and the processor queue length are suspect. An average processor time of 80% by itself would be a problem, but the processor queue length should never get above 2 for an extended period of time.

13. **C.** Windows Server 2003 allows you to create multiple logical printers that point to a single print device. Each of these logical printers can be configured differently and assigned to different users via permissions. In this case, when you print to the Overnight printer, it will hold the print job in its queue until its time window begins.

14. **D.** Because you weren't given any performance measurements in this question, you have no way of knowing whether any of the components mentioned are being stressed. However, because the database application is a background process and is running with other applications, setting Stuart's database application to a higher priority should give it a little more processing time.

15. **C.** Frank has to manually update the appropriate drivers on the Windows 98 clients. Unlike Windows NT and above, which automatically download new and updated drivers when they connect to the print server, Windows 98 clients must have the print drivers updated manually.

Suggested Readings and Resources

1. Microsoft Official Curriculum Course 2274: Managing a Microsoft Windows Server 2003 Environment
   - Module 5: Implementing Printing
   - Module 6: Managing Printing
2. Microsoft Official Curriculum Course 2275: Maintaining a Microsoft Windows Server 2003 Environment
   - Module 1: Preparing to Administer a Server
   - Module 2: Preparing to Monitor Server Performance
   - Module 3: Monitoring Server Performance
   - Module 6: Managing Data Storage
3. Microsoft Official Curriculum Course 2270: Updating Support Skills from Microsoft Windows 4.0 to the Windows Server 2003 Family
   - Module 13: Configuring Printing
4. Microsoft Official Curriculum Course 2279: Planning, Implementing, and Maintaining a Microsoft Windows Server 2003 Active Directory Infrastructure
   - Module 4: Implementing User, Group, and Computer Accounts (Auditing)

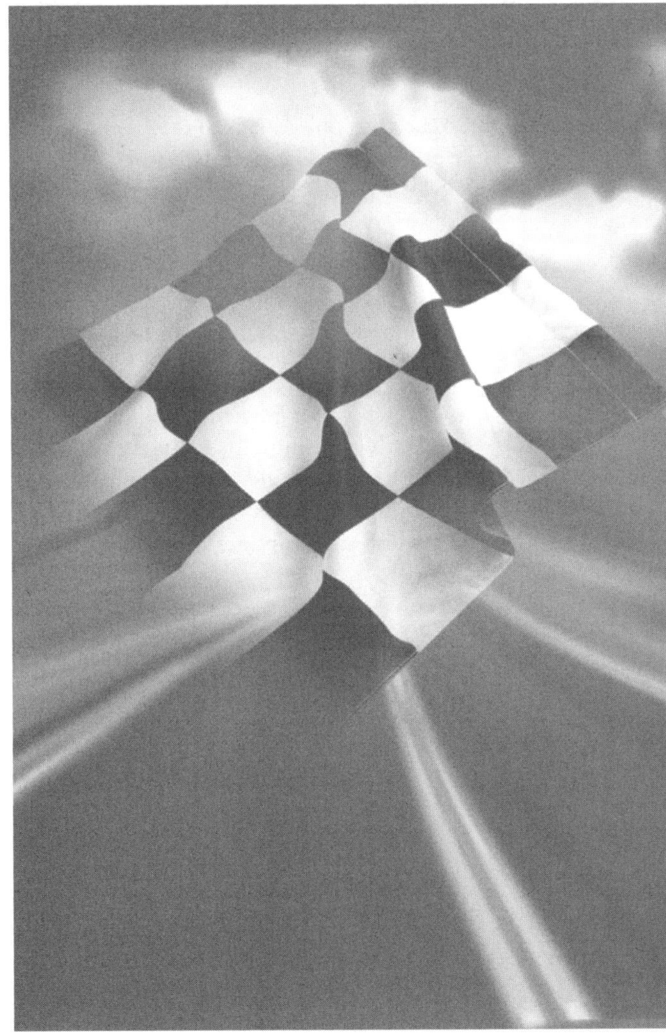

CHAPTER 7

Managing and Implementing Disaster Recovery

Objectives

This chapter covers the following Microsoft-specified objectives for the "Managing and Implementing Disaster Recovery" section of the Managing and Maintaining a Microsoft Windows Server 2003 Environment exam:

Manage backup procedures.

- **Verify the successful completion of backup jobs.**
- **Manage backup storage media.**

▶ The purpose of this objective is to teach you how to use the various tools available in Windows Server 2003 to back up your server. In addition, you should be familiar with the various strategies for dealing with backup media rotations.

Restore backup data.

▶ When working in a Windows Server 2003 environment, it is important that you not only have a thorough understanding of backup procedures but also of restoring the data on a server.

Schedule backup jobs.

▶ When working in a Windows Server 2003 environment, it is important that you have a thorough understanding of the performance characteristics of your servers. This way, it is easier to identify potential problems before they cause outages.

Perform system recovery for a server.

- **Implement Automated System Recovery (ASR).**
- **Restore data from shadow copy volumes.**
- **Back up files and system state data to media.**
- **Configure security for backup operations.**

Objectives

- The purpose of this objective is to teach you how to recover both system and user data to your Windows Server 2003 server. You must be able to use the built-in tools to ensure that your data is available at all times.

Recover from server hardware failure.

- Although not as common as it once was, due to the improvements in server hardware reliability over the years, server hardware failure is still an event that you must plan for. This could be something as simple as a disk failure, or a completely destroyed server due to a natural catastrophe.

Outline

Outline

Study Strategies

- The sections in this chapter outline features that are essential to using and managing a Windows Server 2003 environment. The backup and restoration of data are common tasks you can expect to be heavily emphasized on the test.
- Expect to see a number of questions on two new features introduced in Windows Server 2003: *Automated System Recovery (ASR)* and the *Volume Shadow Copy Service (VSS)*. Know how both these features work, under what circumstances they should be used, and how to implement them.
- Understand the different types of system recovery available and under what circumstances each one should be used. Know the differences between Safe Mode, the Recovery Console, and Last Known Good Configuration, as well as when each should be used.
- Know how to use the Windows Server 2003 Backup utility, including how to back up and restore both user data and the system state information. Know what data is saved as system state data on domain controllers and member servers. In addition, know how to schedule the backup to run unattended.

INTRODUCTION

Managing and maintaining the performance of a Windows Server 2003 environment is only part of the typical duties a system administrator will perform. No matter how well maintained the environment remains, the system administrator must eventually deal with the inevitability of a situation that causes data loss.

The system administrator needs to know how to handle these situations by preparing for them in advance and knowing what steps to perform when the inevitable occurs.

This chapter covers the tools, tasks, and procedures required to back up, restore, and recover both system and user data on Windows Server 2003. This type of information is not only crucial for a job as a system administrator, it is very important for the exam.

USING WINDOWS BACKUP

Backing up data is the simple process of copying the files and folders located on a server to another location. This provides a safety blanket of sorts in the event of a drive or server failure, power outage, virus infection, or user error. With a proper backup you can rest assured that important files are still available in the event something catastrophic happens.

Windows Server 2003 provides a more advanced backup program than what was included with Windows NT. Starting with Windows 2000, Microsoft opted to license backup software from VERITAS Software (formerly Seagate Software). Compared to the Windows NT backup utility, this tool is a big step forward.

Windows Server 2003 Backup allows you to create backup jobs that you can run manually or schedule to run unattended. Unlike the Windows NT 4.0 Server backup, which could only back up to tape, you can now back up to disk, Zip drives, CD-R/RW, or any other media available via the Windows Server 2003 file system.

Windows Backup also allows you to back up files from other computers. However, it cannot back up the Registry or system state data from other computers. The Backup utility allows you to back up a single file, a folder, a drive, or multiple drives. Also, all the backup and restore functions can be performed manually or via wizards.

IN THE FIELD

MORE ABOUT WINDOWS BACKUP

Although using the Windows Backup utility to back up the Registry and system state data on remote computers is not supported, there is an unofficial workaround. Just use the Windows Backup program on the remote computer to back up the Registry and system state data to disk. Then the backup file can be backed up remotely.

Windows Backup allows you to back up files and folders on FAT16, FAT32, or NTFS volumes. However, if you have backed-up data on an NTFS volume restoring to either type of FAT volume, this results in loss of configured file and folder permissions, in addition to the loss of encryption and compression attributes.

To perform a backup or restore on a Windows Server 2003 server, you must be a member of the local Administrators or Backup Operators group. If you are a member of the local Administrators or Backup Operators group on a domain controller, you can back up and restore files on any computer that is a member of the domain or has a two-way trust relationship with the domain. If you are not a member of either of these groups, you can back up only the files you are the owner of or that you have at least Read permissions for. To restore a file or folder, you must have Write permission. In addition, administrators and backup operators can back up and restore encrypted files and folders. The files and folders will not be decrypted during the backup and restore process.

NOTE

User Rights You can grant other users and/or groups the ability to back up and restore files using user rights. Assigning user rights is covered later in the chapter in the section "Configuring Security for Backup Operations."

Volume Shadow Copy

Using Volume Shadow Copy, you are now able to back up most open files. In previous versions of Windows, including Windows 2000, open-file backup was only available using third-party utilities. For example, most database programs (such as Microsoft SQL Server and Microsoft Access), user files (such as Word documents and Excel spreadsheets), and even common files (such as the WINS and DHCP databases) would not be backed up by the Windows Backup utility. This is because most programs lock access to files that they are updating to prevent data corruption.

Therefore, when the backup program attempted to open these files, its request would be rejected. Most of the time, the Backup utility would keep trying until it either received access to the file or the retry timeout period expired. This would slow down the backup procedure, or in the case of some unattended backup procedures, the backup process would terminate without completing a full backup.

Using Volume Shadow Copy during a backup, when an open file is encountered, a snapshot is taken of the file. This is an exact copy of the file that is saved to another area on the disk. This copy is then saved via the Backup utility.

Volume Shadow Copy has the following advantages:

- Users cannot be locked out by the backup program.
- Open files are not skipped.
- The backup completes faster.
- Applications can write data to a file during a backup.
- It eliminates the need for additional third-party software in most cases.
- Backups can be performed during business hours.

Volume Shadow Copy is enabled by default in the Windows Backup program and is part of the Volume Shadow Copy Service feature covered in depth later in this chapter.

Types of Backups

Windows Server 2003 has five backup options: Normal, Copy, Daily, Differential, and Incremental. Each type varies as to what is backed up and whether or not the archive bit is set. The *archive bit* is a file attribute that is turned on when a file is created or modified, and can be cleared, depending on the type of backup, whenever a file is successfully backed up. It is used to let the backup software know what files need to be backed up based on whether the file has just been created or whether modifications to a previously backed-up file have happened since the last backup.

Normal

A *normal* (sometimes referred to as a *full* backup) backup is used to back up all of the files and folders that you select, regardless of the setting of the archive bit. It then clears the archive bit of the files to show that they were backed up. The disadvantage of a normal backup is that it takes longer than some of the other backup types because it backs up all of the files and folders. However, it does have the advantage of only requiring a single media (or set of media) for a full restore. To minimize backup time, the normal backup is typically used in a rotation with incremental or differential backups.

Copy

A *copy backup* is typically used to make an archival copy of data and does not interrupt your current backup set. It does not read or change the archive bit.

Daily

A *daily backup* is used to back up only the files and folders that have been created or modified on that day. It does not read or change the archive bit. A daily backup is typically used to make a quick snapshot of the daily activity. This is useful when you need to perform a task on the server and want to have a current backup available.

Differential

A *differential backup* is used to back up only the files and folders that have been created or modified since the last normal or incremental backup. It does not change the archive bit. However, it reads the archive bit to determine which files need to be backed up. A differential backup is typically used between instances of a normal backup. For example, if you perform a normal backup on Monday, you can perform differential backups the rest of the week. The differential backup takes longer and longer each day because it backs up all the files and folders that have been created and modified since the last normal backup. A differential backup has the advantage that it takes less time than a normal backup but more than an incremental backup. When you perform a full restore, it requires the media for both the last normal backup and the last differential backup.

Incremental

An *incremental backup* is used to back up only the files and folders that have been created or modified since the last normal or incremental backup. It reads the archive bit to determine which files have been changed and need to be backed up. It then changes the archive bit of the files that were backed up so that the next time the backup program is run, these files will not be backed up again unless they were changed. An incremental backup is typically used between instances of a normal backup. Unlike the differential backup, the backup times typically do not get longer each day because the incremental backup only backs up the files and folders that were modified since the last incremental backup. An incremental backup has the advantage of taking less time than a normal backup, but when you perform a full restore, it requires the media for the normal backup and all the incremental backups performed since the normal backup (which can be time consuming, depending on how many incremental backups you must restore).

EXAM TIP

Know Your Backups! You should be familiar with the various types of backups, when each one should be used, and what data is restored during a recovery procedure.

Although in some situations you might perform a normal backup daily, this is not common except for the smallest of organizations. Typically, most organizations perform a normal backup once a week and then an incremental or differential backup on the other days.

To back up data files using the Backup or Restore Wizard, perform the procedure outlined in Step by Step 7.1.

STEP BY STEP

7.1 Backing Up Data Using the Backup or Restore Wizard

1. From the Start menu, click Start, All Programs, Accessories, System Tools, Backup.

2. The Backup or Restore Wizard appears, as shown in Figure 7.1.

FIGURE 7.1
The Backup or Restore Wizard's opening screen. You can switch to Advanced mode and deselect the option to start in Wizard mode from this screen.

3. From the Backup or Restore screen, shown in Figure 7.2, you can select to either back up or restore files and settings. Select Backup Files and Settings and then click the Next button to continue.

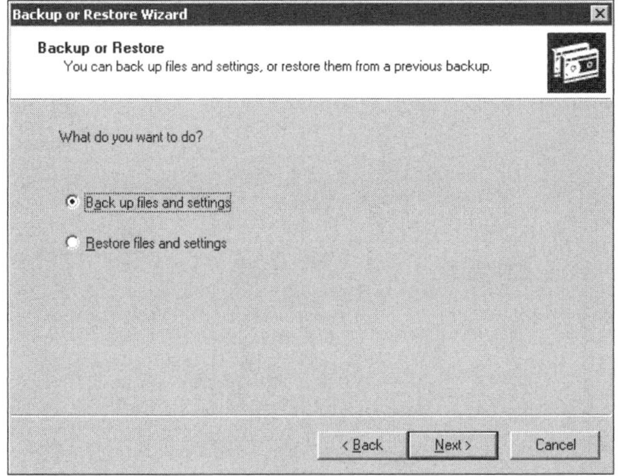

FIGURE 7.2
Select to either back up or restore.

4. From the What to Back Up screen, shown in Figure 7.3, you can select to back up all the information on the computer, or you can choose what to back up. Select the option to choose what to back up and then click the Next button to continue.

continues

continued

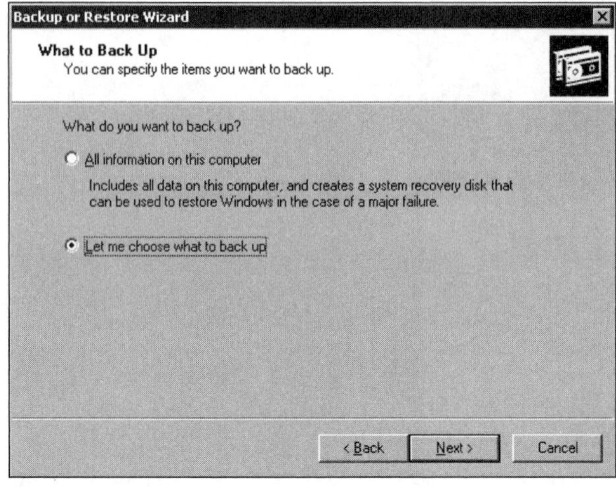

FIGURE 7.3
The What to Back Up screen allows you to select the option to back up all information on the computer, which includes a system recovery disk, or you can choose what to back up.

5. From the Items to Back Up screen, shown in Figure 7.4, you can select the files and folders to back up. Select the desired files and folders and then click the Next button to continue.

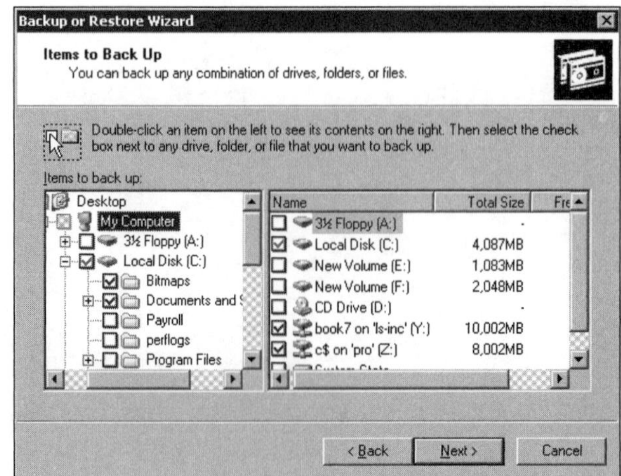

FIGURE 7.4
You can select files and folders on remote computers if you have a connection to them.

6. From the Backup Type, Destination, and Name screen, shown in Figure 7.5, you can select to back up to a tape or file, specify where to save the backup, and provide a name for the backup. Select the desired options and then click the Next button to continue.

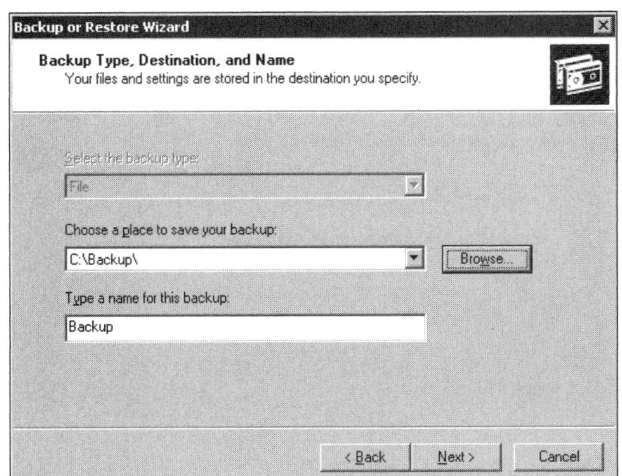

FIGURE 7.5
Select the type of backup.

7. From the Completing the Backup or Restore Wizard screen, shown in Figure 7.6, examine the selected backup settings. If any settings are not correct, click the Back button to reconfigure them. If everything is correct, click the Finish button.

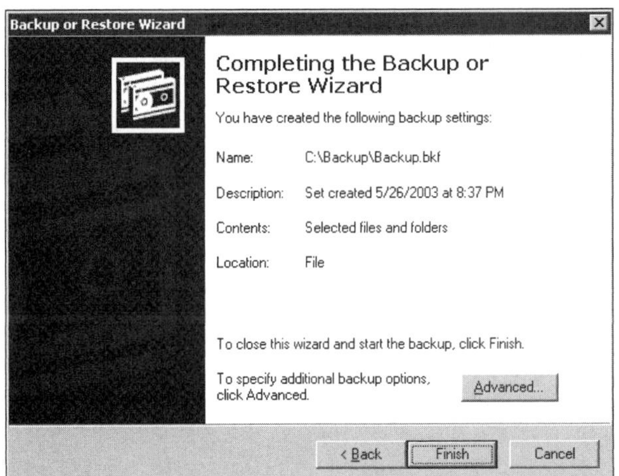

FIGURE 7.6
The Completing the Backup or Restore Wizard summary screen. If you want to specify additional backup options, click the Advanced button.

8. If you clicked the Advanced button, you will see the Type of Backup screen, shown in Figure 7.7. This screen allows you to select from the following types of backups: Normal, Copy, Incremental, Differential, and Daily. Select the desired type of backup and then click the Next button to continue.

continues

continued

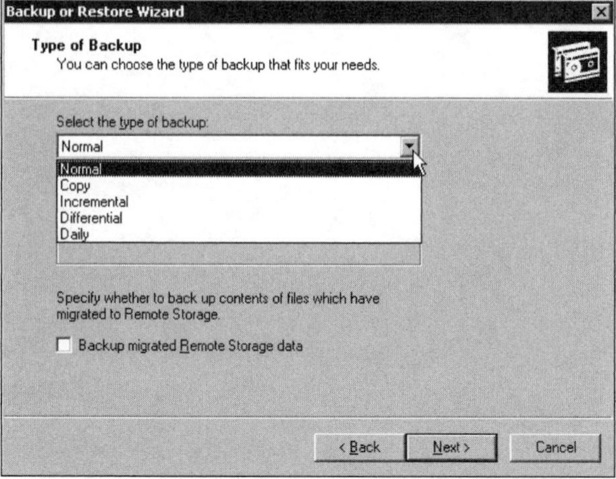

FIGURE 7.7
The Type of Backup screen. The default is a normal backup.

9. From the How to Back Up screen, shown in Figure 7.8, you can select verification, hardware compression, and Volume Shadow Copy options. Select the desired options and then click the Next button to continue.

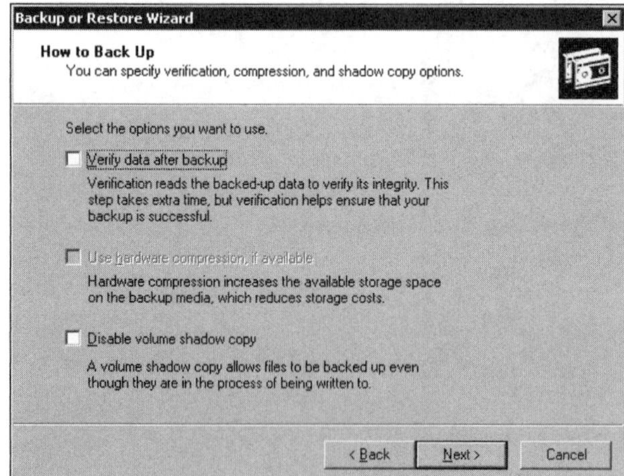

FIGURE 7.8
The How to Back Up screen. This screen allows you to select whether to use Volume Shadow Copy and hardware compression and whether to verify the data after the backup.

10. From the Backup Options screen, shown in Figure 7.9, you can select to overwrite or append to an existing backup. From this screen, you have the additional option of setting more security for the backup. Select the desired options and then click the Next button to continue.

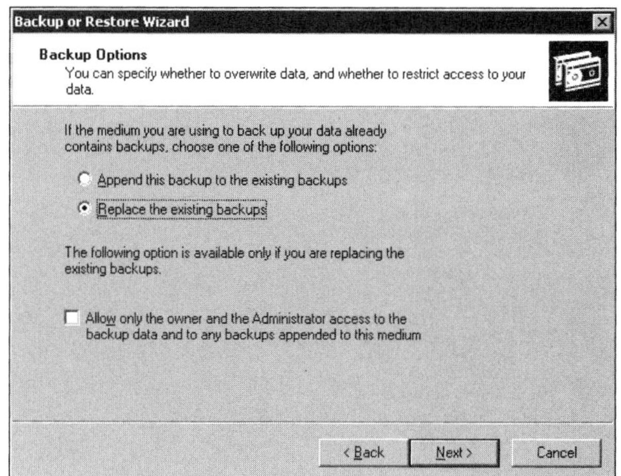

FIGURE 7.9
The Backup Options screen. This screen allows you to select whether to append to an existing backup set or overwrite it. Additionally, you can specify to restrict access to the backup set to the administrator and the owner.

11. From the When to Back Up screen, shown in Figure 7.10, you can select to run the backup job immediately or schedule it to run later. Select the desired option and then click the Next button to continue.

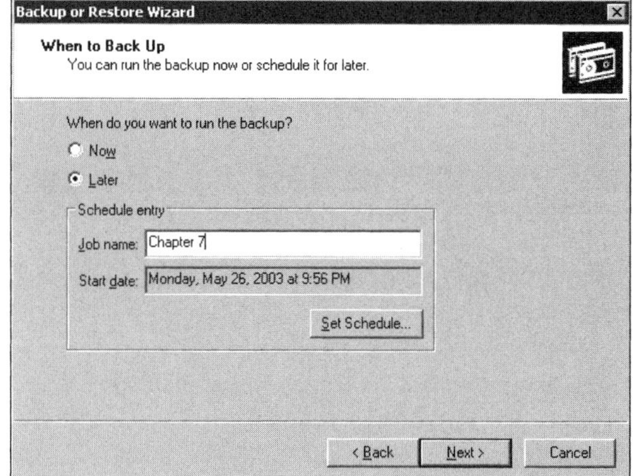

FIGURE 7.10
The When to Back Up options screen. This screen allows you to select a backup job to run immediately, or you can set a schedule by clicking the Set Schedule button.

12. From the Completing the Backup or Restore Wizard screen, shown in Figure 7.11, examine the selected backup settings. If any settings are not correct, click the Back button to reconfigure them. If everything is correct, click the Finish button.

continues

continued

FIGURE 7.11
The Completing the Backup or Restore Wizard summary screen. If you need to make changes, click the Back button.

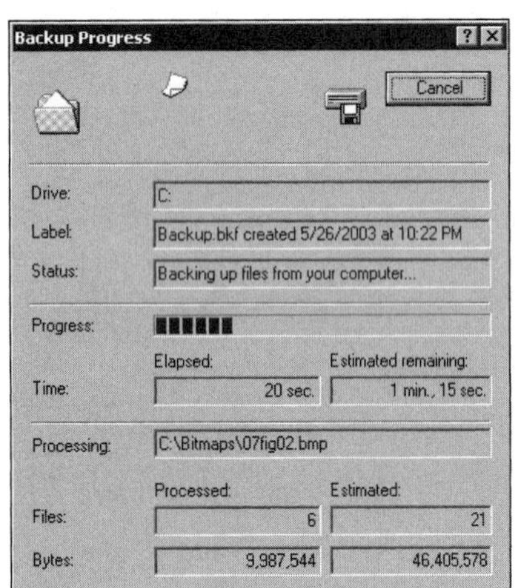

FIGURE 7.12▲
The Backup Progress window.

13. The backup starts and the Backup Progress window appears, as shown in Figure 7.12. When the backup completes, the Report button will appear.

14. Click the Report button to open the backup report, shown in Figure 7.13, which displays the progress of the backup.

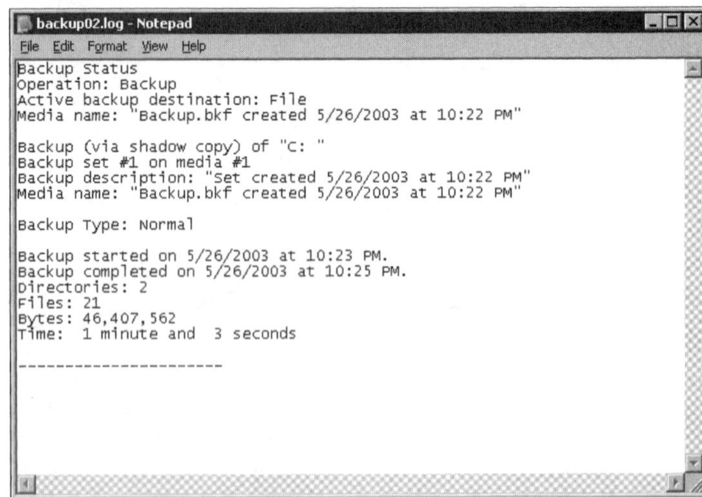

FIGURE 7.13▶
The backup log, showing the backup process.

15. Close all windows when finished.

To shorten the steps required for backups in the future, you can preconfigure most of the settings configured after selecting the Advanced button. These settings are located on the Options tab in the Backup program.

To configure the default options for a backup, perform the procedure outlined in Step by Step 7.2.

STEP BY STEP

7.2 Configuring the Default Options for the Backup Program

1. From the Start menu, click Start, All Programs, Accessories, System Tools, Backup.
2. The Backup or Restore Wizard appears, as shown in Figure 7.14.

FIGURE 7.14
The Backup or Restore Wizard's opening screen. Click the highlighted Advanced Mode link to open the Backup screen.

3. From the Backup Utility Advanced Mode screen, shown in Figure 7.15, select Tools, Options.
4. The Options dialog box appears. From here, you can set the defaults for your backups and restores (see Figure 7.16).

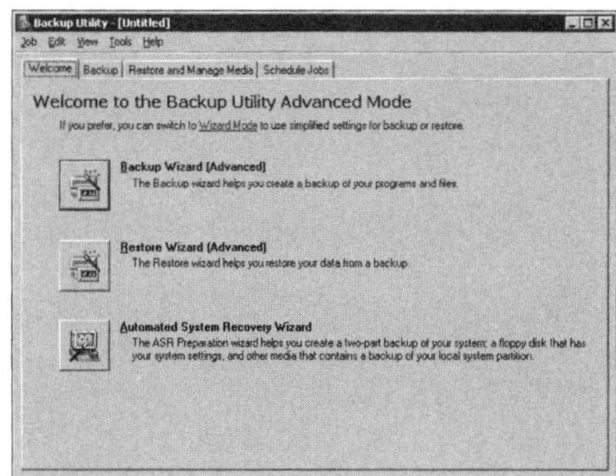

FIGURE 7.15
The Backup Utility Advanced Mode screen.

continues

continued

FIGURE 7.16
The Options dialog box's Backup Type tab.

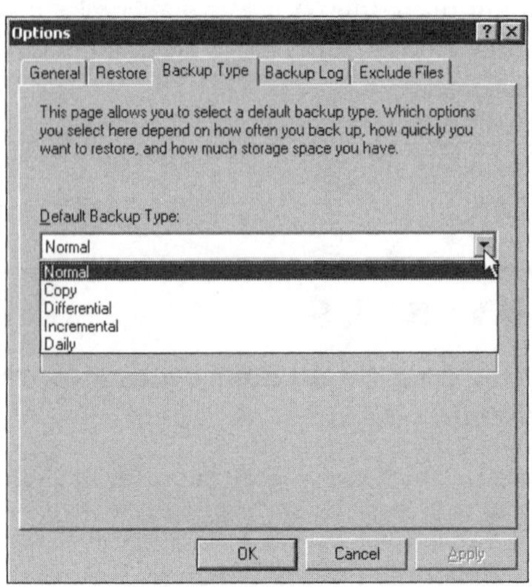

The five tabs on the Options dialog box allow you to set the defaults for your backup and restore jobs. This way, you can use the wizard to quickly set up a backup or restore job with the preconfigured settings.

The Backup Type tab shown in Figure 7.16 allows you to select the default type of backup to perform. The selections are the standard five types of backups: Normal, Copy, Differential, Incremental, and Daily.

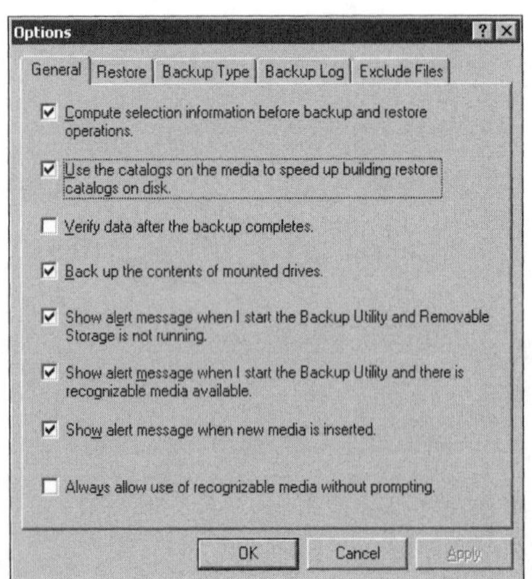

FIGURE 7.17
The Options dialog box's General tab.

The General tab, shown in Figure 7.17, allows you to set the default actions for the backup procedure, as well as the alerts presented for various conditions.

Here's a list of the options and their explanations:

- **Compute selection information before backup and restore operations**—This option displays the number of files and the total size of the files and folders selected.
- **Use the catalogs on the media to speed up building restore catalogs on disk**—This option forces the restore to use the catalog saved with the media. A *catalog* is an inventory of the files and folders that were backed up, along with their locations.

This file is normally saved on the last volume of the backup media. This option should only be deselected if the catalog is damaged or missing because rebuilding the catalog can take a long time for a large backup.

- **Verify data after the backup completes**—This option is not selected by default. If it is selected, after the completion of the backup, Windows Backup compares the information on the backup media to the files on the hard drive to verify that they were backed up properly. This can double the length of the backup procedure, but it is good insurance for important files.
- **Back up the contents of mounted drives**—This option tells Windows Backup to back up the contents of drives that are mounted as folders on an NTFS volume.
- **Show alert message when I start the Backup utility and Removable Storage is not running**—This option should only be checked if you are using a tape drive for backup. The Removable Storage service manages the tape drives for you. If it is not running, the backup will fail.
- **Show alert message when I start the Backup utility and there is recognizable media available**—This option should only be checked if you are using a tape drive for backup. This message option generates an alert if a compatible tape is mounted when you start the backup utility.
- **Show alert message when new media is inserted**—This option should only be checked if you are using a tape drive for backup that is managed by Removable Storage. This message option generates an alert if a compatible tape is mounted when you start the backup utility.
- **Always allow use of recognizable media without prompting**—Does just what it states. If the proper media is in place, the backup starts automatically.

The Restore tab, shown in Figure 7.18, allows you to set the default actions for the restore procedure to take when restoring a file that is already present. Here are the available options:

- Do not replace the file on my computer (recommended).
- Replace the file on disk only if the file on disk is older.
- Always replace the file on my computer.

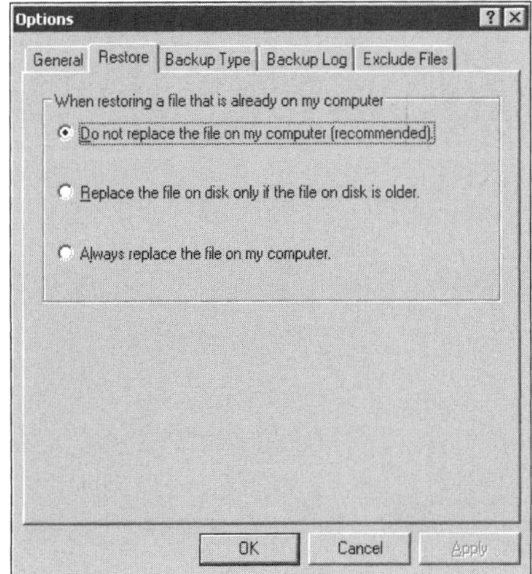

FIGURE 7.18
The Options dialog box's Restore tab.

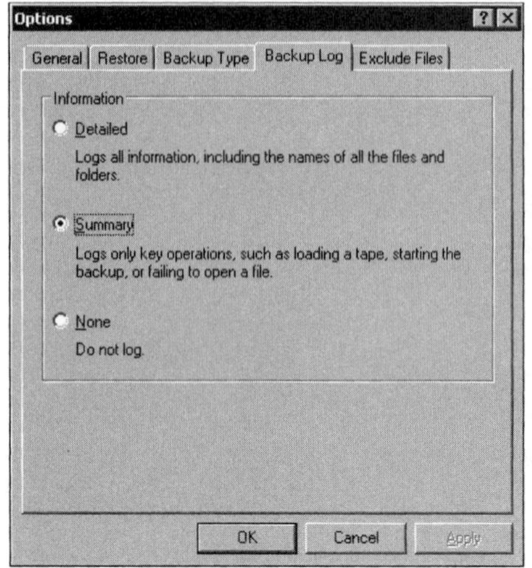

FIGURE 7.19▲
The Options dialog box's Backup Log tab.

The Backup Log tab, shown in Figure 7.19, allows you to set the amount of information that is to be recorded in the backup log. The default is to create a summary log that only records the actions taken. The other options available are to keep a detailed log that includes the names of all files and folders that were backed up, and to not create a backup log at all.

The Exclude Files tab, shown in Figure 7.20, allows you to define the files that should not be backed up, both for all users (top window) and the current user (bottom window). By default, files such as the page and hibernate files are excluded.

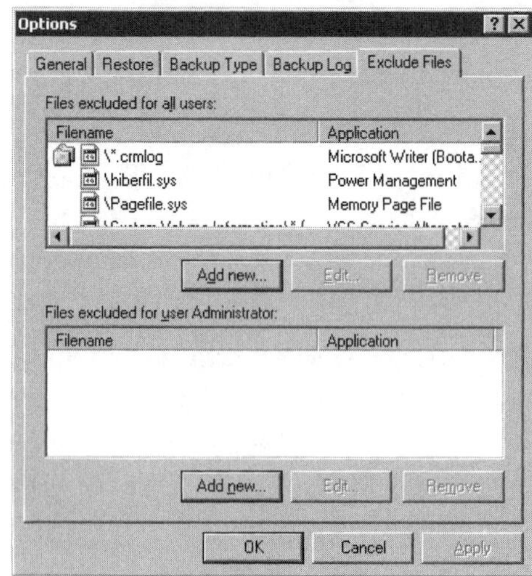

FIGURE 7.20▶
The Options dialog box's Exclude Files tab.

System State Backups

All backups of a Windows Server 2003 server should include the *system state data*. System state data is a collection of data that contains the operating system configuration of the server. For all Windows Server 2003 operating systems, the system state data includes the following:

- Registry
- COM+ class registration database
- System boot files
- The system files included in the Windows File Protection area

For Windows Server 2003, the system state data also includes the Certificate Services database (if the server is operating as a certificate server). If the server is a domain controller, the system state data also includes the Active Directory services database and the SYSVOL directory. In addition, the system state data includes the IIS Metabase or the Cluster Service configuration if these features are installed on the server.

EXAM TIP

System State You should be familiar with the contents of the system state data and on which type of server it will be present.

The system state backup procedure automatically backs up all the system state data relevant to your server configuration. Due to their interdependencies, these components cannot be backed up or restored separately.

It's important to back up the system state data for each server and domain controller. The system state backup from one server or domain controller cannot be restored to a different server or domain controller.

There are two types of system state backup/restore procedures: local and remote. A *local* backup/restore is used when the backup media is hosted on the server being restored. A *remote* restore is performed when the backup media is located on another machine. The Windows Server 2003 Backup program is only capable of backing up and restoring the system state data on the local server.

To back up system state data on a Windows Server 2003 server, perform the procedure outlined in Step by Step 7.3.

STEP BY STEP

7.3 Backing Up System State Data

1. From the Start menu, click Start, All Programs, Accessories, System Tools, Backup.
2. The Backup or Restore Wizard appears.
3. From the Backup or Restore screen, you can select to either back up or restore files and settings. Select Backup Files and Settings and then click the Next button to continue.

continues

continued

4. From the What to Back Up screen, you can select to back up all the information on the computer, or you can choose what to back up. Select the option to choose what to back up and then click the Next button to continue.

5. From the Items to Back Up screen, shown in Figure 7.21, click the My Computer entry to expand the tree. Select the System State entry and then click the Next button to continue.

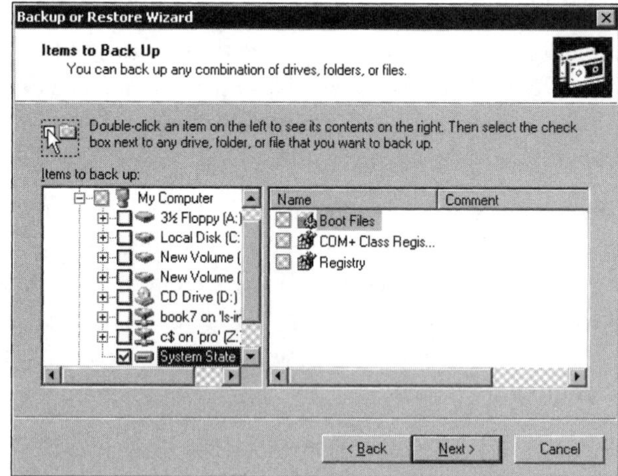

FIGURE 7.21
The Backup or Restore Wizard showing the System State check box selected. Note that on the right, the items present indicate that this is a member server.

6. From the Backup Type, Destination, and Name screen, you can select to back up to a tape or file, specify where to save the backup, and provide a name for the backup. Select the desired options and then click the Next button to continue.

7. From the Completing the Backup or Restore Wizard dialog box, examine the selected backup settings. If any settings are not correct, click the Back button to reconfigure them. If everything is correct, click the Finish button.

The system state data can be backed up separately or as part of a complete server backup.

Scheduling Backup Jobs

A backup job runs faster and more efficiently when fewer users are on the server. In addition, even with the Volume Shadow Copy service, it's better to back up a closed file rather than an open one. This ensures that the most current version of the file is backed up. Unfortunately, in most environments the period of least usage is either in the middle of the night or on weekends. Most system administrators would prefer to work more conventional hours.

Fortunately, Windows Backup includes a built-in scheduling service. This feature allows the administrator to schedule backups to run unattended at anytime in the future. Jobs can be scheduled to run once, or they can be repeated using the following options:

- Daily
- Weekly
- Monthly
- At System Startup
- At Logon
- When Idle

Scheduling backups with the native Backup utility no longer requires the use of the Task Scheduler service. You no longer need to use the `AT.EXE` utility to schedule the backup (although you still can if you really want to). Instead, you simply click the Set Schedule button when creating a backup job using the advanced backup options of the Backup or Restore Wizard (see Figure 7.22), or you use the Schedule Jobs tab of the Backup utility (shown later in Figure 7.24).

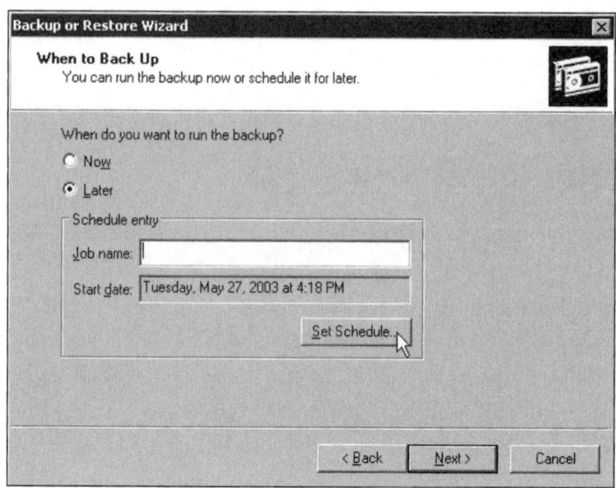

FIGURE 7.22
The When to Back Up screen. This screen is part of the advanced tasks of the Backup or Restore Wizard. From this screen you can set a backup schedule by clicking the Set Schedule button.

To configure an unattended backup, perform the procedure outlined in Step by Step 7.4.

STEP BY STEP

7.4 Scheduling an Unattended Backup Job

1. From the Start menu, click Start, All Programs, Accessories, System Tools, Backup.
2. The Backup or Restore Wizard appears, as shown in Figure 7.23.

FIGURE 7.23
The Backup or Restore Wizard's opening screen. Click the highlighted Advanced Mode link to open the Backup utility.

3. From the Backup utility's Advanced Mode screen, shown in Figure 7.24, select the Schedule Jobs tab.

4. From the Schedule Jobs tab, double-click the data for which you want to run a backup job. This starts the Backup Wizard. On the Backup Wizard's opening screen, click Next to continue.

5. The What to Back Up screen appears, as shown in Figure 7.25. Select one of the options and then click Next to continue.

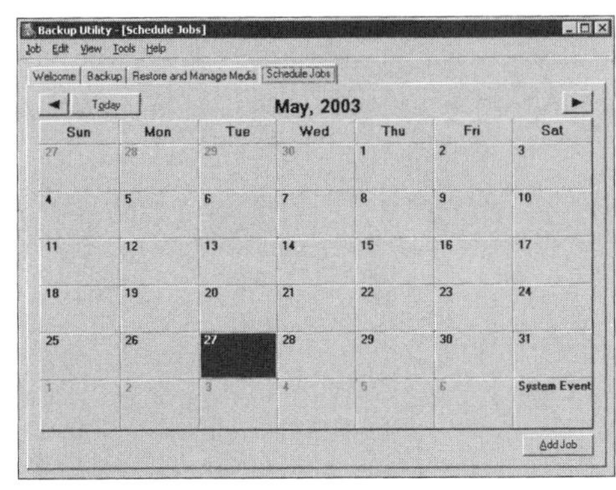

FIGURE 7.24▲
The Backup utility's Advanced Mode screen displaying the Schedule Jobs tab.

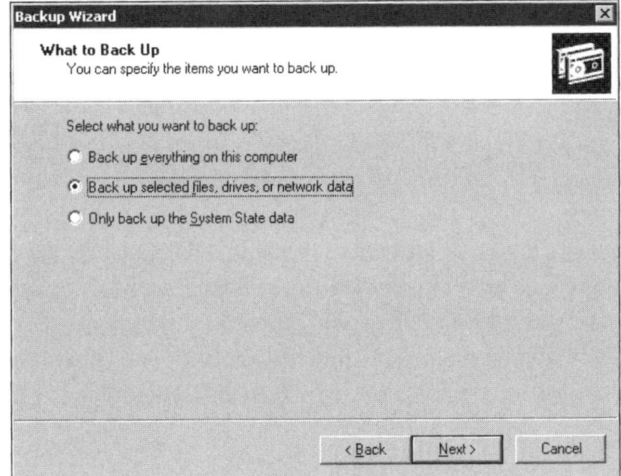

FIGURE 7.25◄
Select what you want to back up. You can choose to back up everything, selected files and folders, or system state data.

6. The Items to Back Up screen appears. Select the files and folders to be backed up and then click Next to continue.

7. The Backup Type, Destination, and Name screen appears. Select the backup type and where to save it and then give it a job name. Click Next to continue.

8. The Type of Backup screen appears. This screen allows you to select from the following types of backups: Normal, Copy, Differential, Incremental, and Daily. Select the desired type of backup and then click the Next button to continue.

9. The How to Back Up screen appears. You can select verification, hardware compression, and Volume Shadow Copy options. Select the desired options and then click the Next button to continue.

continues

continued

10. From the Backup Options screen, you can select to overwrite or append to an existing backup. From this screen, you have the additional option of setting more security for the backup. Select the desired options and then click the Next button to continue.

11. From the When to Back Up screen, you can select to run the backup job immediately or schedule it to run later. Click the Set Schedule button.

12. The Schedule Job dialog box appears, as shown in Figure 7.26. Select the desired options and then click the Advanced button.

13. The Advanced Schedule Options dialog box appears, as shown in Figure 7.27. Select the desired options and then click the OK button.

14. Back on the Schedule Job dialog box, click the Settings tab, as shown in Figure 7.28. Here, you can specify additional options, such as what to do if the task runs longer than a certain time, and only start the task if the computer is idle. Select the desired options and then click the OK button.

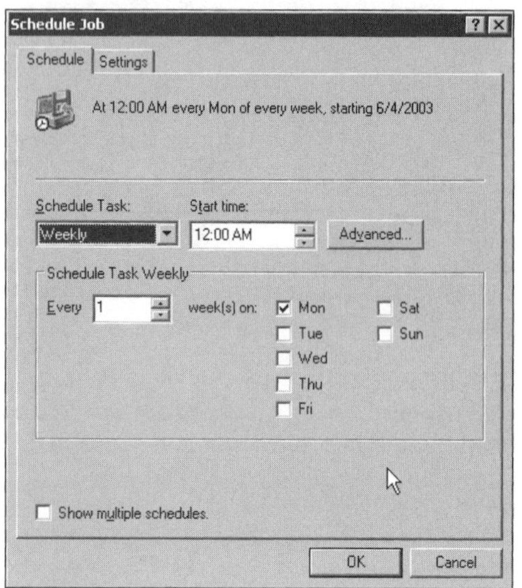

FIGURE 7.26
Select when you want the backup to run. You can choose a recurring schedule and/or a specific date.

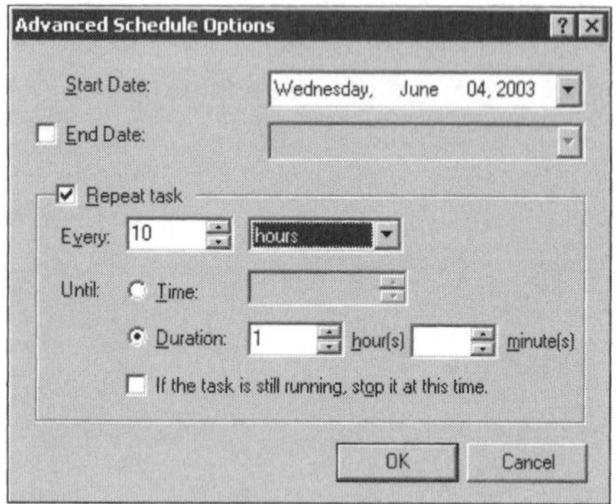

FIGURE 7.27▲
The Advance Schedule Options dialog box presents you with more granular scheduling parameters.

FIGURE 7.28▶
Select additional parameters for your scheduled task.

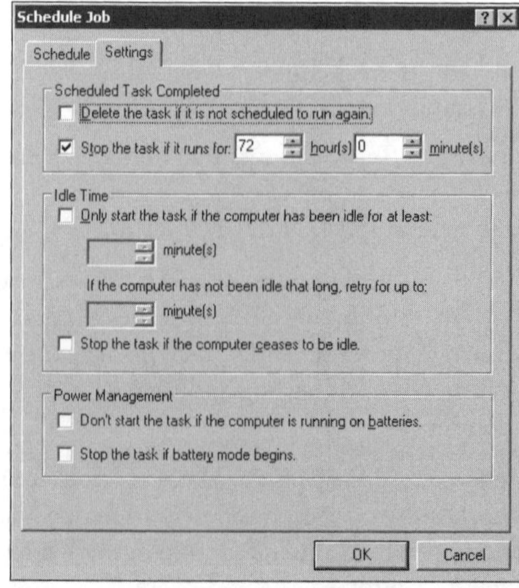

15. The Set Account Information dialog box appears, as shown in Figure 7.29. Enter the user account and password that you want the backup job to run as. Then click the OK button.

16. Back at the When to Back Up screen, click Next to continue.

17. From the Completing the Wizard screen, examine the selected backup settings. If any settings are not correct, click the Back button to reconfigure them. If everything is correct, click the Finish button.

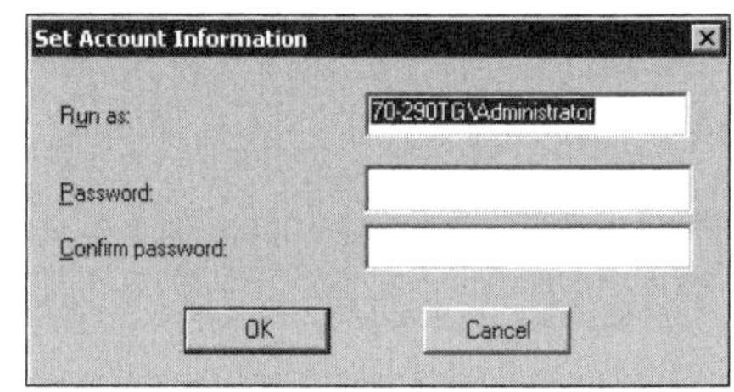

FIGURE 7.29
Enter a user account and password with the appropriate rights.

Back Up from the Command Line

In addition to the GUI we have been working with, Windows Server 2003 has a command-line version of the Backup program called `ntbackup.exe`. The command-line version allows you to schedule a backup either from the command line or in a batch file or script. Prior to Windows 2000, this method was very popular because at that time Windows Backup did not have the built-in scheduler service it has now.

There will always be a use for command-line utilities. For example, if you need to run a backup as part of another process, and this process requires automation, it is simple to include the command-line Backup utility in a batch file or script.

Here is the syntax for the `ntbackup` command:

```
ntbackup backup [systemstate] "@FileName.bks" /J {"JobName"}
➥[/P {"PoolName"}] [/G {"GUIDName"}] [/T { "TapeName"}]
➥ [/N {"MediaName"}] [/F {"FileName"}] [/D {"SetDescription"}]
 [/DS {"ServerName"}]  [/IS {"ServerName"}] [/A] [/V:{yes ¦ no}]
➥ [/R:{yes ¦ no}] [/L:{f ¦ s ¦ n}] [/M {BackupType}]
➥[/RS:{yes ¦ no}] [/HC:{on ¦ off}][/SNAP:{on ¦ off}]
```

Table 7.1 defines the command-line parameters available for a command-line backup.

TABLE 7.1

COMMAND-LINE PARAMETERS FOR ntbackup.exe

Parameter	*Description*
`systemstate`	Backs up the system state data. This option forces the backup to be either a normal or a copy type.
`@`*`FileName`*`.bks`	Specifies the name of the backup selection file. The selection file contains the names of the files and folders you want to be backed up. The selection file must be created using the GUI version of Windows Backup.
`/J {"`*`JobName`*`"}`	The name of the job to be recorded in the log file.
`/P {"`*`PoolName`*`"}`	The media pool from which to use media.
`/G {"`*`GUIDName`*`"}`	The tape, referred to by its Globally Unique Identifier (GUID). Do not use this switch with `/P`.
`/T {"`*`TapeName`*`"}`	The tape, referred to by its name. Do not use this switch with `/P`.
`/N {"`*`MediaName`*`"}`	Specifies a new name for the tape. Do not use with `/A`.
`/F {"`*`FileName`*`"}`	The logical path and filename. Do not use with `/P`, `/G`, or `/T`.
`/D {"`*`SetDescription`*`"}`	Specifies a label for each backup set.
`/DS {"`*`ServerName`*`"}`	Backs up the Directory Service database for the specified Exchange Server.
`/IS {"`*`ServerName`*`"}`	Backs up the Information Service database for the specified Exchange Server.
`/A`	Appends to an existing backup. Must be used with either `/G` or `/T`. Cannot be used with `/P`.
`/V:{yes¦no}`	Verifies the backup.
`/R:{yes¦no}`	Restricts access to the tape to members of the Administrators group or the owner.
`/L:{f ¦ s ¦ n}`	Specifies the type of log file, either `f` (full), `s` (summary), or `n` (none).
`/M {`*`BackupType`*`}`	Specifies the type of backup: `Normal`, `Copy`, `Differential`, `Incremental`, or `Daily`.
`/RS:{yes ¦ no}`	Backs up the Remote Storage database.
`/HC:{on ¦ off}`	Turns on/off hardware compression, if supported.
`/SNAP:{on ¦ off}`	Enables or disables Volume Shadow Copy.
`/?`	Display help.

The command-line options automatically default to whatever is configured via the GUI version of Backup. Any options specified override the GUI settings for that instance only.

The following is a sample ntbackup command with the parameters explained:

```
Ntbackup backup "@c:\full.bks" /J "Full Backup" /t "Week1Full"
➥ /V:yes /L:f /HC:on
```

This command line specifies that ntbackup will back up the file and folders specified in the backup selection file `c:\full.bks`. The job name will be Full Backup, and the tape used is Week1Full. The data will be verified after the backup is complete, the log type is full, and hardware compression is turned on for the tape drive.

To create a backup selection file to be used with the command-line version of Backup, perform the procedure outlined in Step by Step 7.5.

STEP BY STEP

7.5 Creating a Backup Selection File

1. From the Start menu, click Start, All Programs, Accessories, System Tools, Backup.
2. The Backup or Restore Wizard appears. Click the highlighted Advanced Mode link to open the Backup utility.
3. From the Backup utility's Advanced Mode window, shown in Figure 7.30, select the Backup tab.
4. From the Backup tab, select the files and folders you want to include in the backup job. This starts the Backup Wizard. On the Backup Wizard's opening screen, click Next to continue.
5. From the system menu, select Job, Save Selections. From the Save As dialog box, enter a file and path for the selection file. It must have an extension of `*.bks`.
6. Click Save.

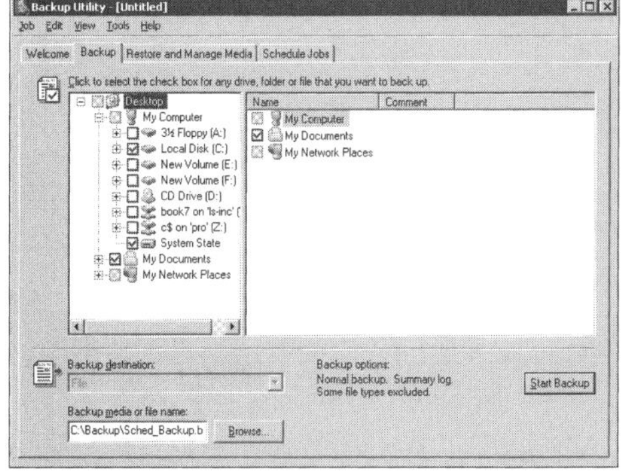

FIGURE 7.30
The Backup utility's Advanced Mode window, displaying the Backup tab. From here, select the files and folders you want to back up.

Know the Capabilities You probably do not need to memorize the various command-line parameters for the test. However, you should have a general idea of the capabilities of ntbackup from the command line and how to create the backup selection file.

Configuring Security for Backup Operations

Earlier in this chapter, we discussed that to back up and restore a Windows Server 2003 server, you must be a member of the Administrators or the Backup Operators group. If you are not a member of one of these groups, you can back up only the files that you own or that you have at least Read permissions for. To restore a file or folder, you must have Write permission.

These permissions are assigned via the Backup Files and Directories and the Restore Files and Directories user rights. These rights can be assigned via Group Policy.

To assign other users the Backup Files and Directories right, follow the procedure outlined in Step by Step 7.6.

STEP BY STEP

7.6 Assigning Other Users the Backup Right

1. From the Start menu, click Start, All Programs, Administrative Tools, Local Security Policy.

2. From the Local Security Settings MMC, shown in Figure 7.31, click Local Policies and then User Rights Assignment.

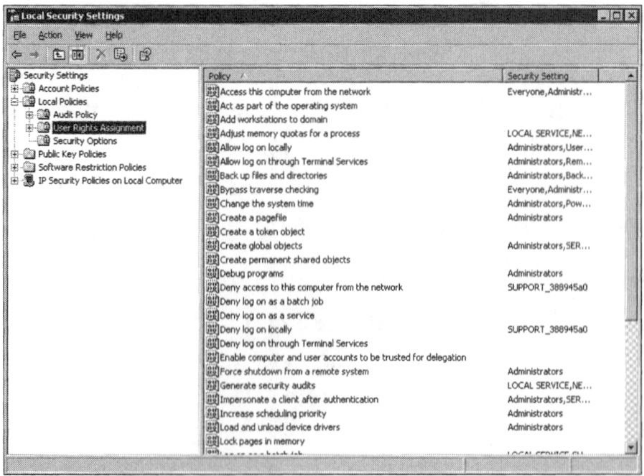

FIGURE 7.31
Double-click the desired user right to configure it.

3. The users and groups that possess Backup rights are displayed in Figure 7.32.

4. Click the Add User or Group button. This opens the Select Users or Groups dialog box shown in Figure 7.33. Add users or groups from the local or domain accounts database. Click OK to save.

5. Click OK to save.

6. Close the Local Security Settings MMC.

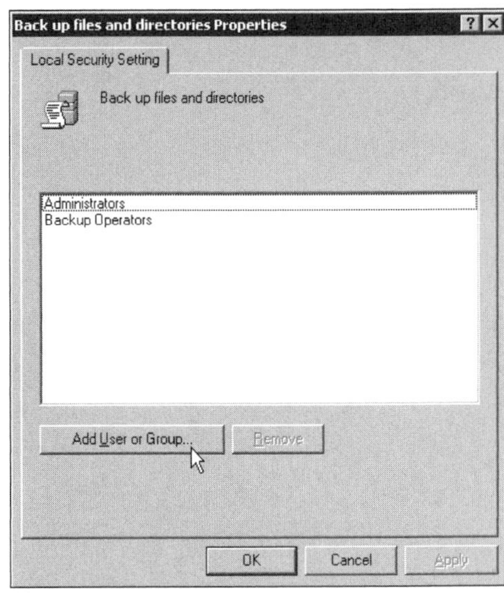

FIGURE 7.32▲
The users and groups with Backup rights are displayed.

FIGURE 7.33◀
Add the desired users or groups.

The Restore Files and Directories right can be configured using the same procedure. In addition to restricting backup and restore access to files and folders via Group Policy, you can also control who has the ability to restore backed-up files during the backup process. This is accomplished by selecting the Allow Only the Owner and the Administrator Access to the Backup Data option from the Backup Options dialog box, shown in Figure 7.34, during the backup configuration. This option prevents anyone other than an administrator or the person performing the backup from restoring the information that is being backed up.

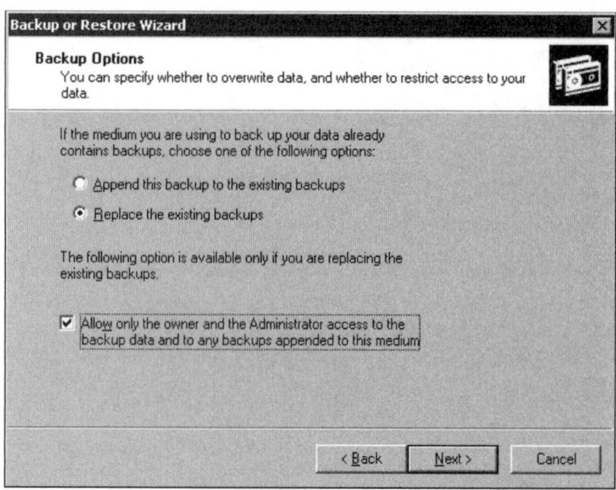

FIGURE 7.34
The option to restrict restore rights is displayed.

Verifying the Successful Completion of Backup Jobs

After a backup or restore job completes, you can verify its completion by clicking the Report button that appears on the Backup Progress dialog box at the completion of a backup or restore, as shown in Figure 7.35.

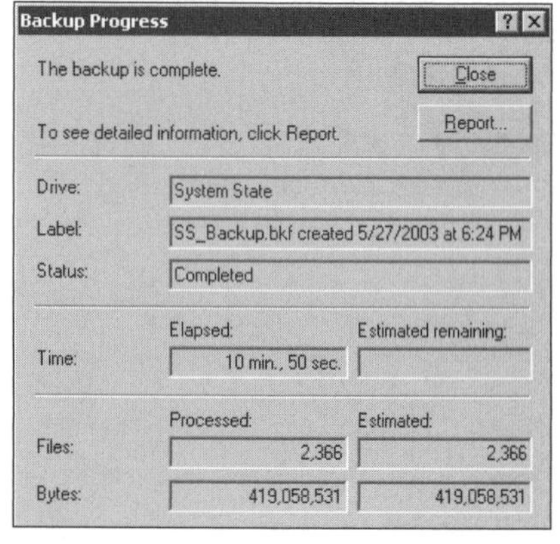

FIGURE 7.35
Click Report to open the backup log.

Clicking the Report button opens the backup log, as shown in Figure 7.36. This is a sample log from the backup of system state data. Full logging was turned on so that all the files and folders that were backed up are listed, along with their paths and attributes.

Notice that the summary at the bottom of the file lists the number of files and directories that were backed up, along with the total bytes and total elapsed time. If there had been any errors, they would be listed here.

If you want to see the results of a backup job after it has completed and you forgot to click the Reports button or you ran an unattended job from the command line, you can access the report from the Backup utility. Click Tools, Reports from the system menu. This opens the Backup Reports dialog box, shown in Figure 7.37. From this dialog box you can view or print any of the saved reports for previously run backup jobs.

```
backup04.log - Notepad
File  Edit  Format  View  Help
wmipdskq.dll          <A>          132608   3/25/2003    7:00
wmipicmp.dll          <A>           77312   3/25/2003    7:00
wmipiprt.dll          <A>           60416   3/25/2003    7:00
wmipjobj.dll          <A>           59904   3/25/2003    7:00
wmiprov.dll           <A>          133632   3/25/2003    7:00
wmiprvsd.dll          <A>          415232   3/25/2003    7:00
wmiprvse.exe          <A>          206336   3/25/2003    7:00
wmipsess.dll          <A>           39936   3/25/2003    7:00
wmisvc.dll            <A>          134144   3/25/2003    7:00
wmitimep.dll          <A>           53760   3/25/2003    7:00
wmiutils.dll          <A>           92672   3/25/2003    7:00
Folder System State\Boot Files\C:\WINDOWS\SYSTEM32\WBEM\AdStatus
trustmon.dll          <A>           28672   3/25/2003    7:00
Folder System State\Boot Files\C:\WINDOWS\SYSTEM32\WBEM\snmp
Folder System State\Boot Files\C:\WINDOWS\SYSTEM32\WBEM\xml
wmi2xml.dll           <A>           46592   3/25/2003    7:00
Folder System State\Boot Files\C:\WINDOWS\SYSTEM32\WINDOWS MEDIA\server
Folder System State\Boot Files\C:\WINDOWS\SYSTEM32\WINDOWS MEDIA\SERVER
Folder System State\Boot Files\C:\WINDOWS\SYSTEM32\WINDOWS MEDIA\SERVER
Folder System State\Boot Files\C:\WMPUB\wmiislog
Folder System State\COM+ Class Registration Database
ComRegDb.bak          <A>           22232   4/16/2003    9:29
Folder System State\Registry
default               <A>          204800   5/27/2003    6:25
SAM                   <A>           36864   5/27/2003    6:25
SECURITY              <A>           45056   5/27/2003    6:25
software              <A>        10842112   5/27/2003    6:25
system                <A>         2273280   5/27/2003    6:25
Backup completed on 5/27/2003 at 6:37 PM.
Directories: 158
Files: 2366
Bytes: 419,058,531
Time:  10 minutes and  50 seconds

----------------------
```

FIGURE 7.36◀
The backup log showing full reporting.

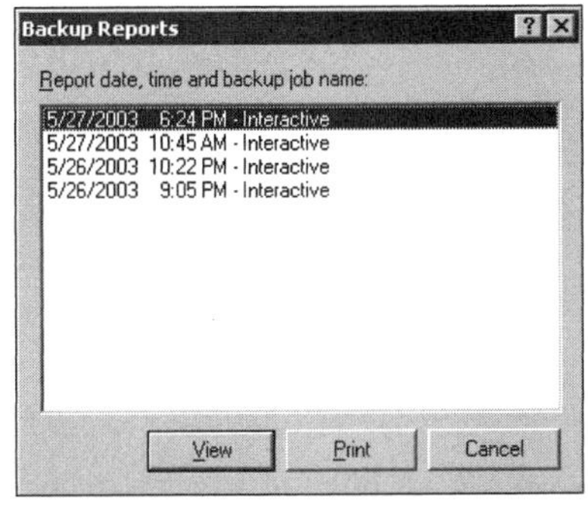

FIGURE 7.37▲
The Backup Reports dialog box allows you to select from previously saved backup logs.

Restoring Backup Data

It doesn't do you any good to back up all this data if it can't be restored. Fortunately, the Windows Server 2003 Backup program is also capable of restoring the data that you backed up. The restore procedures work very similar to the backup procedures—as a matter of fact, most use the same wizards, and it's just a matter of selecting different options. The two major differences are that there is no command-line equivalent to the GUI version of the program, and a restore can't be scheduled to run unattended.

To restore data files using the Restore Wizard, perform the procedure outlined in Step by Step 7.7.

STEP BY STEP

7.7 Restoring Data Using the Restore Wizard

1. From the Start menu, click Start, All Programs, Accessories, System Tools, Backup.

continues

continued

2. The Backup or Restore Wizard appears. From the Backup or Restore screen shown in Figure 7.38, you can select to either back up or restore files and settings. Select Restore Files and Settings and then click the Next button to continue.

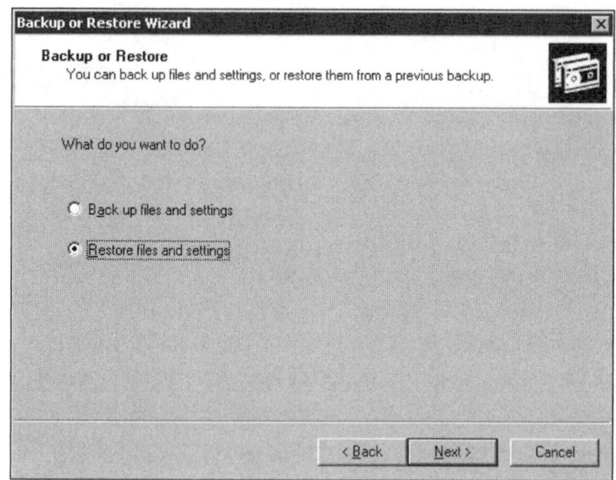

FIGURE 7.38
Select to restore files and settings.

3. From the What to Restore screen, shown in Figure 7.39, select the files and backup set to restore and then click the Next button to continue.

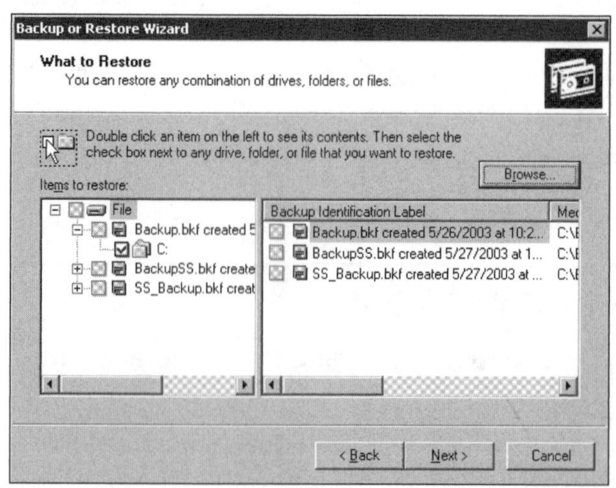

FIGURE 7.39
The What to Restore screen allows you to select the files, folders, and backup set to use to restore your data. You can click the Browse button to catalog the backup media.

4. From the Completing the Backup or Restore Wizard screen, shown in Figure 7.40, examine the selected restore settings. If any settings are not correct, click the Back button to reconfigure them. If everything is correct, click the Finish button.

FIGURE 7.40
The Completing the Backup or Restore Wizard summary screen. If you want to specify additional restore options, click the Advanced button.

5. If you click the Advanced button, the Where to Restore screen, shown in Figure 7.41, opens. This screen allows you to select from the following options: Original Location, Alternate Location, and Single Folder. Select the location for the restore and then click the Next button to continue.

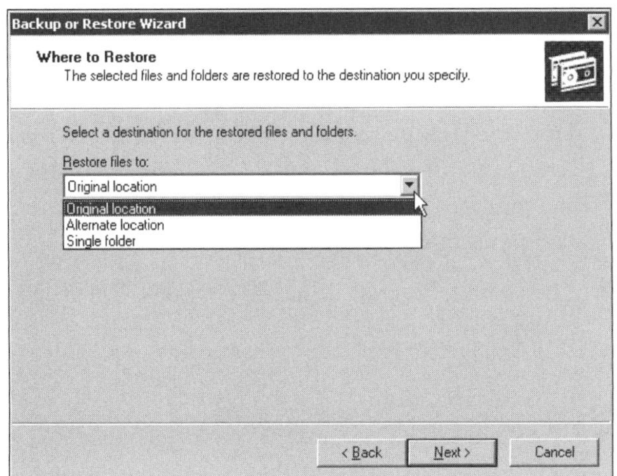

FIGURE 7.41
The Where to Restore screen. These options allow you to restore the files to an alternate location so that the original files will not be overwritten. You can also select to restore all selected files to a single folder.

continues

continued

6. From the How to Restore screen, shown in Figure 7.42, you can select how the restore process handles existing files. The default is not to overwrite them. Select the desired option and then click the Next button to continue.

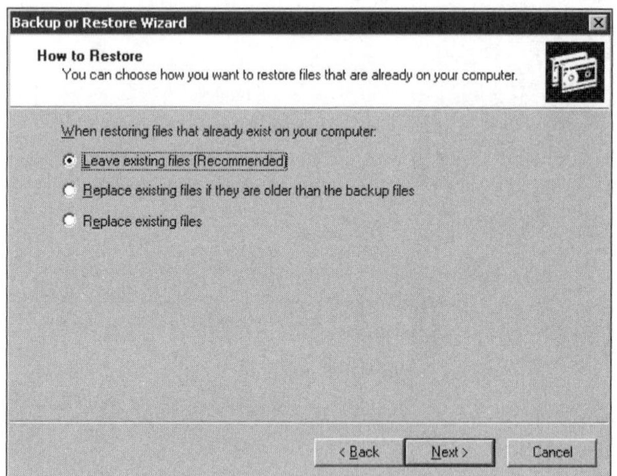

FIGURE 7.42
The How to Restore screen. The options here allow you to leave the existing files, replace them, or only replace them if they are older than the files on the backup media.

7. From the Advanced Restore Options screen, shown in Figure 7.43, you can select other restore options. You can restore the files using the security settings they were saved with (this is only for NTFS volumes). You can also select to restore junction points, which are logical pointers to files and folders on other drives, or you can select whether to preserve the volume mount points. Select the desired options and then click the Next button to continue.

8. From the Completing the Backup or Restore Wizard screen, examine the selected restore settings. If any settings are not correct, click the Back button to reconfigure them. If everything is correct, click the Finish button.

9. The Restore Progress dialog box appears, displaying the progress of the restore.

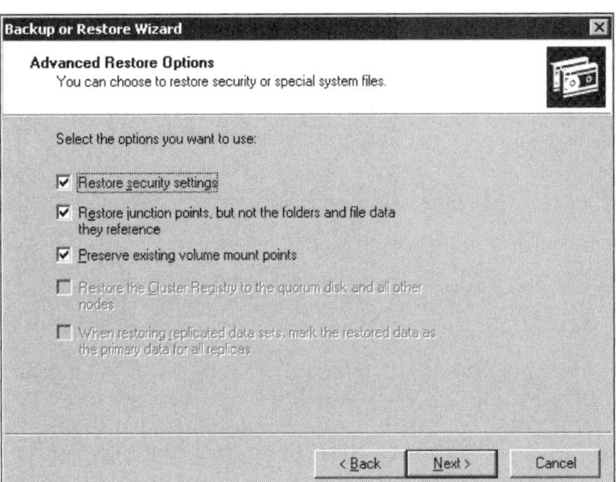

FIGURE 7.43
The Advanced Restore Options screen. These are the miscellaneous options that don't fit anywhere else.

Restoring System State Data

As discussed earlier, the Backup program in Windows Server 2003 only allows you to restore the system state data on a local computer. You are not allowed to back up and restore the system state on a remote computer. Although you can't selectively back up components of the system state, you can restore the following system state components to an alternate location:

- Registry
- SYSVOL folder
- System boot files
- Cluster configuration (if installed)

The Active Directory, IIS Metabase, COM+ Class Registration, Certificate services databases, and the Windows File Protection folder cannot be restored to an alternate location.

To restore the system state data on a Windows Server 2003 server (not a domain controller), perform the procedure outlined in Step by Step 7.8.

STEP BY STEP

7.8 Restoring System State Data Using the Restore Wizard

1. From the Start menu, click Start, All Programs, Accessories, System Tools, Backup.
2. The Backup or Restore Wizard appears. From the Backup or Restore screen, you can select to either back up or restore files and settings. Select Restore Files and Settings and then click the Next button to continue.
3. From the What to Restore screen, shown in Figure 7.44, select System State from the backup set to restore. Then click the Next button to continue.

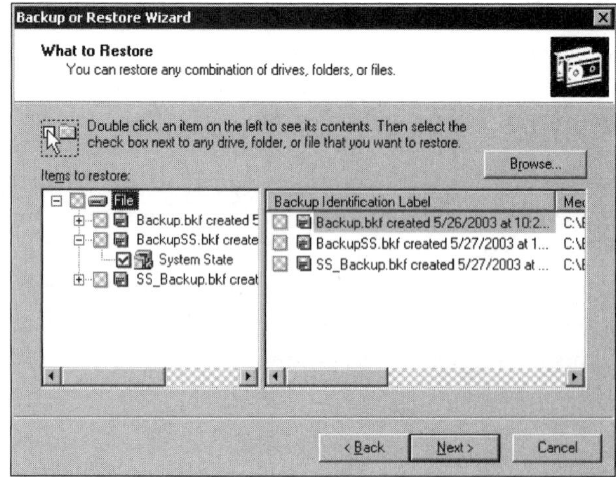

FIGURE 7.44
Selecting System State from a backup set.

4. From the Completing the Backup or Restore Wizard screen, examine the selected restore settings. If any settings are not correct, click the Back button to reconfigure them. If everything is correct, click the Finish button.
5. If you click the Advanced button, the Where to Restore screen opens. This screen allows you to select from the following options: Original Location, Alternate Location, and Single Folder. Select the location for the restore and then click the Next button to continue.

6. If you've selected to restore to the original location, you receive the warning shown in Figure 7.45.

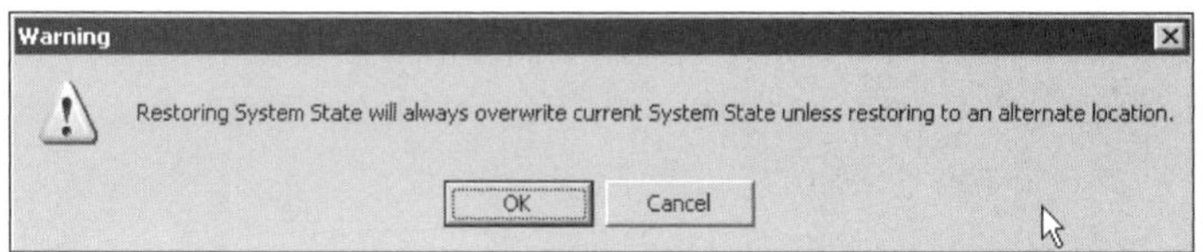

FIGURE 7.45
System state data will be overwritten.

7. From the How to Restore screen, you can select how the restore process handles existing files. The default is not to overwrite them. Note that these options do not apply to the system state restore; they are shown by default. Click the Next button to continue.
8. From the Advanced Restore Options screen, you can select other restore options. You can restore the files using the security settings they were saved with (this is only for NTFS volumes). You can also select to restore junction points, which are logical pointers to files and folders on other drives, or you can select whether to preserve the volume mount points. Note that these options only apply if you are restoring other files with your system state data. Ignore them. Then click the Next button to continue.
9. From the Completing the Backup or Restore Wizard screen, examine the selected restore settings. If any settings are not correct, click the Back button to reconfigure them. If everything is correct, click the Finish button.
10. The Restore Progress dialog box appears, displaying the progress of the restore.
11. After the restore completes, restart the server.

NOTE

For More Information For information on how to restore system state data on a domain controller, see the section titled "Using Directory Services Restore Mode to Recover System State Data," later in this chapter.

GUIDED PRACTICE EXERCISE 7.1

It is very important to always have a current backup of system state data, especially for domain controllers. The Windows Server 2003 Backup utility includes a built-in scheduler that allows you to schedule the backup to occur on a recurring basis.

For this exercise, your job is to automate the backup of system state data on your server. The data should be backed up every weekday evening at 11:00 p.m.

What is the best way to accomplish this in Windows Server 2003? On your own, try to develop a solution that involves the least amount of downtime.

If you would like to see a possible solution, follow these steps:

Estimated Time: 20 minutes

1. From the Start menu, click Start, All Programs, Accessories, System Tools, Backup.
2. The Backup or Restore Wizard appears.
3. From the Backup or Restore screen, select Backup Files and Settings and then click the Next button to continue.
4. From the What to Back Up screen, select the option to choose what to back up. Then click the Next button to continue.
5. From the Items to Back Up screen, click the My Computer entry to expand the tree. Select the System State entry and then click the Next button to continue.
6. From the Backup Type, Destination, and Name screen, you can select to back up to a tape or file, specify where to save the backup, and provide a name for the backup. Select the desired options and then click the Next button to continue.
7. From the Completing the Backup or Restore Wizard screen, examine the selected backup settings. If any settings are not correct, click the Back button to reconfigure them. If everything is correct, click the Advanced button.
8. From the Type of Backup screen, click the Next button to continue.

9. From the How to Back Up screen, click the Next button to continue.
10. From the Backup Options screen, click the Next button to continue.
11. From the When to Back Up screen, click the Set Schedule button.
12. The Schedule Job dialog box appears. Select the option to run the task daily at 11:00 p.m. Select the desired days to run the backup. When you're finished, click OK to save.
13. Back on the Schedule Job dialog box, click the OK button.
14. The Set Account Information dialog box appears. Enter the user account and password that you want the backup job to run as. Then click the OK button.
15. Back at the When to Back Up screen, click Next to continue.
16. From the Completing the Backup or Restore Wizard screen, examine the selected backup settings. If any settings are not correct, click the Back button to reconfigure them. If everything is correct, click the Finish button.

USING OTHER RECOVERY TOOLS

Although a good backup can allow the system administrator to recover from a variety of problems, a full server restore can be time consuming. Sometimes a server might have a problem that can be repaired by changing its configuration or replacing a small number of files. Windows Server 2003 includes a number of utilities that allow the system administrator (and even a user, in the case of Volume Shadow Copy) to recover from various problems. In this section we examine these utilities and show how and when they are used.

Restoring Data from Shadow Copy Volumes

Although hardware errors can sometime result in data loss, industry studies have shown that at least one third of all data loss is caused by human error, usually accidental file deletion or modification. Although these types of errors can be rectified by restoring the affected file or folder from a current backup, this requires the intervention of a system administrator or other overworked IT professional.

The other problem with restoring from a backup is that backups are usually performed outside of normal business hours, usually at night. If a user accidentally overwrites a file that he has been working on all day at 4:00 p.m., the version on the backup tape does not reflect any changes made that day, so all the changes will be lost.

This situation can be averted using the Volume Shadow Copy service in Windows Server 2003. The Volume Shadow Copy service allows users to view the contents of shared folders as they existed at specific points in time and to restore a previous copy of a file. This reduces the calls to administrators to restore accidentally deleted or overwritten files.

The Volume Shadow Copy feature in Windows Server 2003 works by setting aside a configurable amount of space, either on the same or a different volume. This space is used to save any changes to the files accessed via a share on the volume that Volume Shadow Copy is enabled on. These changes are added by making a block-level copy of any changes that have occurred to files since the last shadow copy. Only the changes are copied, not the entire file. As new shadow copies are added, the oldest one is purged either when you run out of allocated space or when the number of shadow copies reaches 64.

Shadow copies are turned on for an entire volume, not just for specific files and folders. When the Volume Shadow Copy service runs, it takes a snapshot of the files and folders on the volume. When a file is changed and saved to a shared folder, Volume Shadow Copy writes the previous version of the file to the allocated space. If the file is saved again before Volume Shadow Copy has run again, a second copy is not saved to the shadow copy storage area. A second copy cannot be saved to the storage area until the service has run again. The Volume Shadow Copy service can be configured to run at any time; the default schedule is for it to run weekdays at 7:00 a.m. and 12:00 p.m.

Shadow copies are configured on a Windows Server 2003 server. Before they are configured, you should plan how they should be configured. The following guidelines apply:

- Volume Shadow Copy is enabled for all shared folders on a volume; you can't just select a few.
- The minimum storage space you can allocate for shadow copies is 100MB.
- The storage space can be allocated on the same or on another volume.
- The default storage size allocated is 10% of the volume; however, you can increase the size at any time.
- When estimating the size to allocate, you must consider both the number and size of the files in the shared folders as well as how often they will be updated.
- Remember that when the storage limit is reached, the oldest shadow copies will be deleted.
- If you decide to store your shadow copies on another volume, the existing shadow copies will be deleted.
- The default configuration values for shadow copies are 100MB of space, with a scheduled update at 7:00 a.m. and 12:00 p.m. on weekdays.
- Using a separate volume to store shadow copies is highly recommended for heavily used file servers.
- Performing a shadow copy more than once an hour is not recommended.
- Shadow copies do not work properly on dual-boot systems.

To configure Volume Shadow Copy on a volume, perform the procedure outlined in Step by Step 7.9:

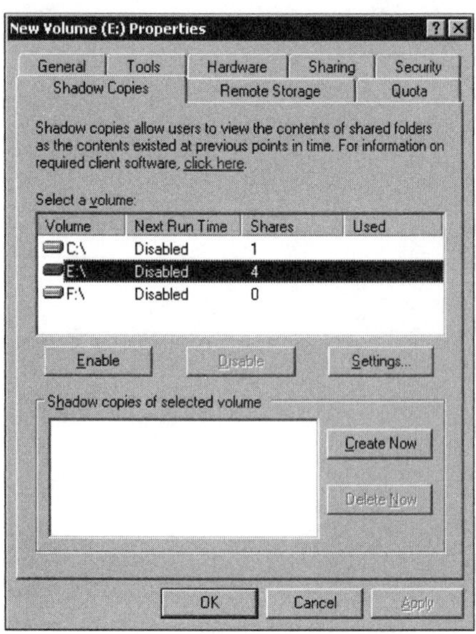

FIGURE 7.46▲
The New Volume Properties dialog box's Shadow Copies tab.

FIGURE 7.47▶
The shadow copies confirmation box. Make sure you understand the conditions and then click Yes.

STEP BY STEP

7.9 Turning on Shadow Copy

1. From Windows Explorer or My Computer, right-click the root of the volume on which you want to enable Volume Shadow Copy.
2. The New Volume Properties dialog box appears. From this Properties dialog box, click the Shadow Copies tab. This displays the view shown in Figure 7.46.
3. From the Shadow Copies tab, highlight the volume on which you want to enable shadow copies and then click the Enable button. The Enable Shadow Copies confirmation box shown in Figure 7.47 is displayed. Read the text, and then click the Yes button to continue.

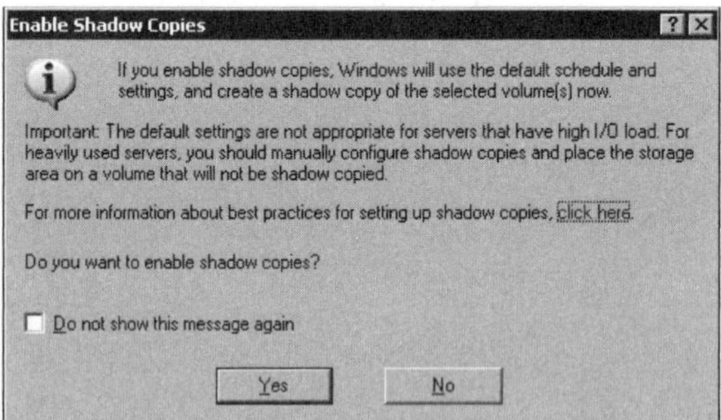

4. After the volume is processed, the information on the Shadow Copies tab is updated, as shown in Figure 7.48. From this tab you can force an update of the shadow copies by clicking the Create Now button.

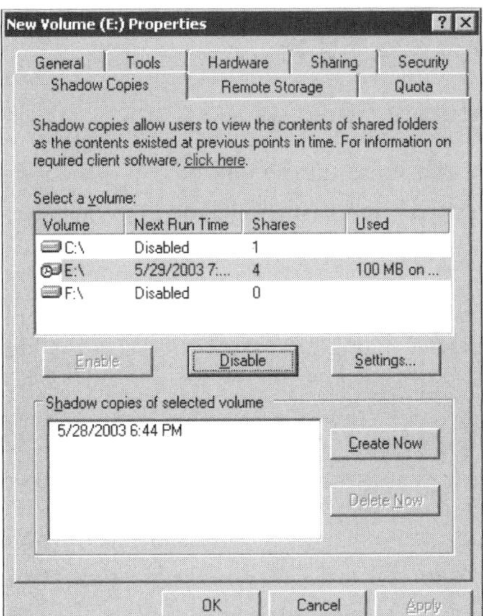

FIGURE 7.48

The updated Shadow Copies tab. As you can see, the default space and schedule items were configured.

After Volume Shadow Copy is enabled on the server, a client must be installed on the workstation so that the previous versions of the files are visible. Microsoft supplies a Shadow Copy client for Windows XP, Windows 2000 Professional, and Windows 98 users. The client is located in the `%systemroot%\system32\clients\twclient` folder on Windows Server 2003. The client software is referred to as *Previous Versions*. Windows Server 2003 and later operating systems have the Previous Versions client built in. The installation file, `twcli32.msi`, is a Microsoft installer file; you can copy it to a share that is accessible by your users.

To view files using the Previous Versions client, perform the procedure outlined in Step by Step 7.10.

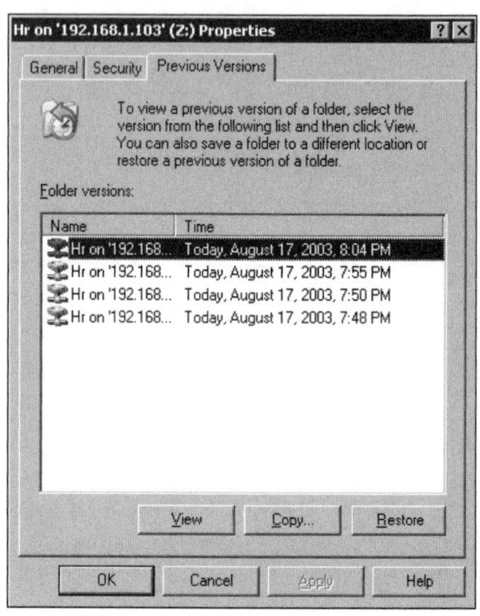

FIGURE 7.49
The Previous Versions tab, showing the versions available. You can view or copy the various versions of files in the shared folder to another location, or you can restore them to the shared folder.

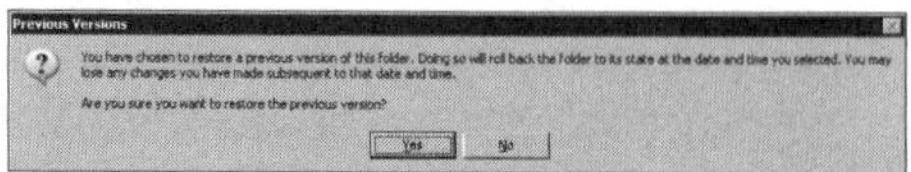

FIGURE 7.50
The Previous Versions confirmation prompt. Make sure you understand the ramifications before you click Yes.

STEP BY STEP

7.10 Restoring Previous Versions

1. Map to a share on the volume for which you enabled Volume Shared Copies. Right-click the share and select Properties.
2. The Folder Properties dialog box appears. From this Properties dialog box, click the Previous Versions tab, as shown in Figure 7.49.
3. From the Folder Properties dialog box, select the version to restore and then click the Restore button to continue.
4. The Previous Versions confirmation prompt appears, as shown in Figure 7.50. Remember that restoring a folder overwrites every file in that folder. Click Yes to continue.

The following buttons are available from the Previous Versions tab:

- **View**—This button allows you to view the contents of the selected version of the shared folder. You can only view the files; you cannot edit them.
- **Copy**—This button allows you to copy some or all of the files to a different location.
- **Restore**—This button restores the files in the shared folder to their state at the time the selected version was made. This overwrites all the existing files in the shared folder with the previous versions. Use this option with care.

Shadow copies are good for the following scenarios:

- **Recovering files that were accidentally deleted**—If someone accidentally deletes a file, he or she can recover a previous version using the Previous Versions client.
- **Recovering files that were overwritten**—If someone normally creates new files using the Save As method, sometimes he or she might click Save instead and overwrite the original file. The user can recover a previous version of the file using the Previous Versions client.

- **Checking the changes made between file versions**—The user can look at the previous versions of the file to see what changes have been made.

Shadow copies work with compressed or encrypted files and retain whatever permissions were set on these files when the shadow copies were taken.

NOTE

Keep Your Backup Plan Using shadow copies is `not` a valid replacement for a well-planned backup procedure.

Advanced Options Menu

The Advanced Options menu allows you to select from a variety of options that can be used to troubleshoot and repair server startup and driver problems. The following options are available on the Windows Server 2003 Advanced Options menu, as shown in Figure 7.51:

- **Safe Mode**—This option starts Windows Server 2003 with the basic drivers for the mouse, video, monitor, mass storage, and keyboard. This option is recommended when you suspect that a recently installed application is causing problems. You can boot into this mode and uninstall the application.
- **Safe Mode with Networking**—This option starts Windows Server 2003 with the basic drivers, plus the network drivers. This option is handy for testing basic network connectivity.
- **Safe Mode with Command Prompt**—This option starts Windows Server 2003 with the basic drivers and opens a command prompt window instead of the desktop. This option is useful when the first two Safe Mode options are unable to start the server.
- **Enable Boot Logging**—This option starts Windows Server 2003 normally but logs a list of all device drivers, services, and their status that the system attempts to load to `%systemroot%\ntblog.txt`. This is a good option to select to diagnose system startup problems.
- **Enable VGA Mode**—This option starts Windows Server 2003 normally but forces it to load the basic VGA driver. This option is useful for recovering from the installation of a bad video driver.

EXAM TIP

Volume Shadow Copy Clients Volume Shadow Copy clients are not available for Windows 95, Me, or any version of NT.

- **Last Known Good Configuration**—This option starts Windows Server 2003 with the contents of the Registry from the last time the user logged on to the system. This is helpful when recovering from a configuration error. For example, if you install a new driver and then the system crashes or fails to start, you can remove these changes by selecting Last Known Good Configuration when rebooting. When this option is selected, any configuration changes made after the last logon are lost. It is important to note that as soon as you log on to the server, the current drivers and Registry information become the last known good configuration. Therefore, if you suspect a driver problem, don't reboot and log on because you cannot roll back the changes using this option.
- **Directory Services Restore Mode**—This option is used to restore the Active Directory database and SYSVOL on a domain controller. It is listed only on a domain controller.
- **Debugging Mode**—This options starts Windows Server 2003 normally but sends debugging information over a serial cable to another computer. This option is for software developers.
- **Start Windows Normally**—This option bypasses the menu options and starts Windows Server 2003 without any modifications.
- **Reboot**—This option reboots the computer.
- **Return to OS Choices Menu**—If multiple operating systems are installed, selecting this option returns you to the boot menu.

FIGURE 7.51
The Windows Server 2003 Advanced Options Menu screen showing the Safe Mode option selected.

```
Windows Advanced Options Menu
Please select an option:

    Safe Mode
    Safe Mode with Networking
    Safe Mode with Command Prompt

    Enable Boot Logging
    Enable VGA Mode
    Last Known Good Configuration (your most recent settings that worked)
    Directory Services Restore Mode (Windows domain controllers only)
    Debugging Mode

    Start Windows Normally
    Reboot
    Return to OS Choices Menu

Use the up and down arrow keys to move the highlight to your choice.
```

Although Microsoft recommends using Last Known Good Configuration as the first step in diagnosing a problem, you can also start and log on to the server using one of the Safe Mode options. Unlike a normal logon, the Safe Mode options do not update the Last Known Good Configuration information, so it's still an option if you try Safe Mode first.

If your startup problem does not appear when you start the system in Safe Mode, you can eliminate the default settings and minimum device drivers as problems. Using Safe Mode, you can diagnose the problem and remove the faulty driver, or you can restore the proper configuration.

NOTE

Other Recovery Options If your server does not start properly using Safe Mode or Last Known Good Configuration, you might have to boot to the Recovery Console or restore your system files using the Automated System Recovery (ASR) feature.

Last Known Good Configuration

The Last Known Good Configuration option allows you to restore the system to the state it was in at the time of the last logon. Whenever a user logs on to the console of a server, the hardware configuration and settings are stored in the Registry key `HKLM\System\CurrentControlSet`. This configuration is then backed up to another key, usually `ControlSet001`. If you install a driver or make a configuration change after you log on, this new information is saved to the `CurrentControlSet` key. If your changes result in a blue screen or other problems, you can restart your server and then go into the Advanced Options Menu and select Last Known Good Configuration. This allows you to select and boot with the configuration information backed up from the `CurrentControlSet` key at the last logon. This should allow you to boot properly, although the new drivers will no longer be present.

You must remember that the previous configuration information is overwritten with the current configuration every time you complete a logon to a server. Therefore, if you reboot and log on to the server, the good configuration entry will have been overwritten by the bad configuration entry. Make sure you understand the sequence of system events so that you don't lose this recovery option.

To reboot a server using the Last Known Good Configuration option, perform the procedure outlined in Step by Step 7.11.

STEP BY STEP

7.11 Using the Last Known Good Configuration

1. Restart the server. If Windows Server 2003 is the only operating system installed, you have to press F8 early in the boot process, just after the POST screen disappears. Otherwise, when you see the prompt Please Select the Operating System to Start, press the F8 key at the first OS screen, as shown in Figure 7.52.

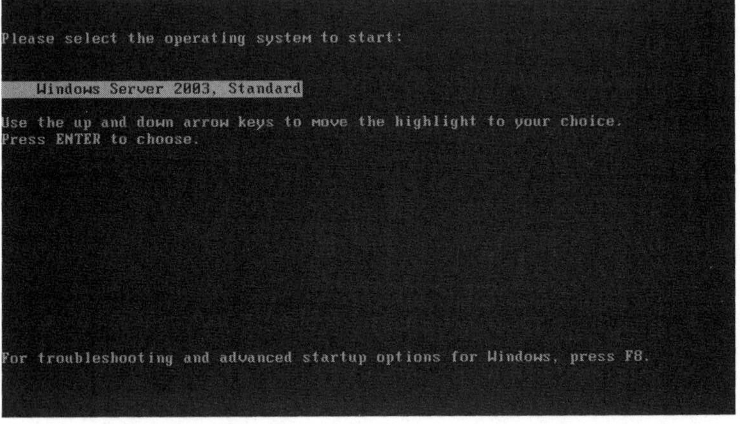
Please select the operating system to start:
Windows Server 2003, Standard
Use the up and down arrow keys to move the highlight to your choice.
Press ENTER to choose.
For troubleshooting and advanced startup options for Windows, press F8.

FIGURE 7.52
The boot menu screen.

2. The Advanced Options Menu screen appears, as shown in Figure 7.53. On the Advanced Options Menu screen, use the arrow keys to select the Last Known Good Configuration option.

FIGURE 7.53
The Advanced Options Menu screen showing the various options available. You can select one of the Safe Mode options or other assorted options.

```
Windows Advanced Options Menu
Please select an option:

    Safe Mode
    Safe Mode with Networking
    Safe Mode with Command Prompt

    Enable Boot Logging
    Enable VGA Mode
    Last Known Good Configuration (your most recent settings that worked)
    Directory Services Restore Mode (Windows domain controllers only)
    Debugging Mode

    Start Windows Normally
    Reboot
    Return to OS Choices Menu

Use the up and down arrow keys to move the highlight to your choice.
```

3. You're now back at the operating system screen, as shown in Figure 7.54. Select the operating system you want to start and then press the Enter key.

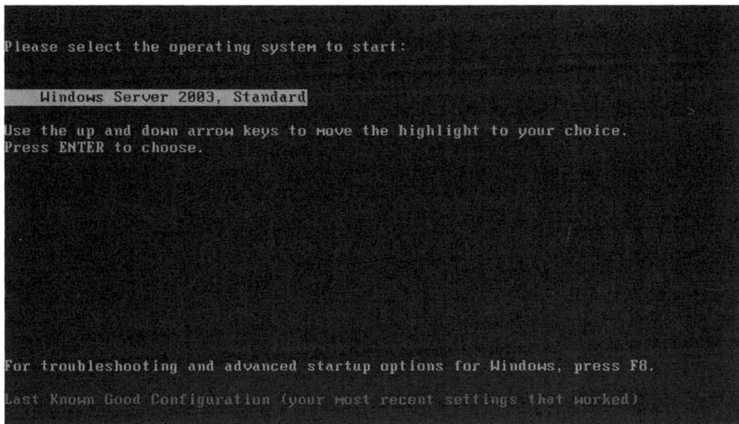
Please select the operating system to start:
Windows Server 2003, Standard
Use the up and down arrow keys to move the highlight to your choice.
Press ENTER to choose.
For troubleshooting and advanced startup options for Windows, press F8.
Last Known Good Configuration (your most recent settings that worked)

FIGURE 7.54
The boot menu screen again. Note that it informs you that you're in Last Known Good Configuration mode.

After the server boots, it should run normally. However, any configuration or driver changes made since the last logon are gone.

Safe Mode

The Windows Server 2003 Safe Mode option is a recovery tool carried over from the Windows 9x product line. This tool allows you to start your system with a minimal set of device drivers and services loaded.

Safe Mode is useful for those situations in which you load a new driver or software program or make a configuration change that results in an inability to start your system. You can use Safe Mode to start your system and remove the driver or software that is causing the problem.

To get into Safe Mode, perform the procedure outlined in Step by Step 7.12.

STEP BY STEP

7.12 Starting in Safe Mode

1. Restart the server. If Windows Server 2003 is the only operating system installed, you have to press F8 early in the boot process, just after the POST screen disappears. Otherwise, when you see the prompt Please Select the Operating System to Start, press the F8 key at the first OS screen.

2. The Advanced Options Menu screen appears, as shown in Figure 7.55. On the Advanced Options Menu screen, use the arrow keys to select one of the Safe Mode startup options and then press Enter.

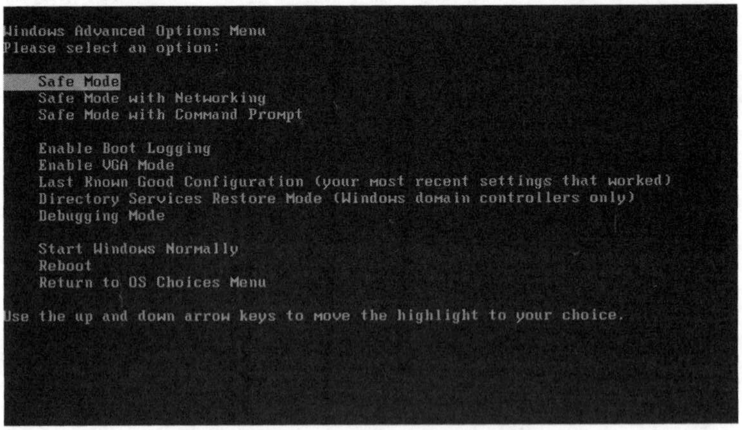

```
Windows Advanced Options Menu
Please select an option:

    Safe Mode
    Safe Mode with Networking
    Safe Mode with Command Prompt

    Enable Boot Logging
    Enable VGA Mode
    Last Known Good Configuration (your most recent settings that worked)
    Directory Services Restore Mode (Windows domain controllers only)
    Debugging Mode

    Start Windows Normally
    Reboot
    Return to OS Choices Menu

Use the up and down arrow keys to move the highlight to your choice.
```

FIGURE 7.55
The Advanced Options Menu screen showing the selection of Safe Mode.

3. You're now back at the operating system screen, as shown in Figure 7.56. Select the operating system you want to start and then press the Enter key. The server boots.

4. When you come to the logon screen shown in Figure 7.57, log on to the server.

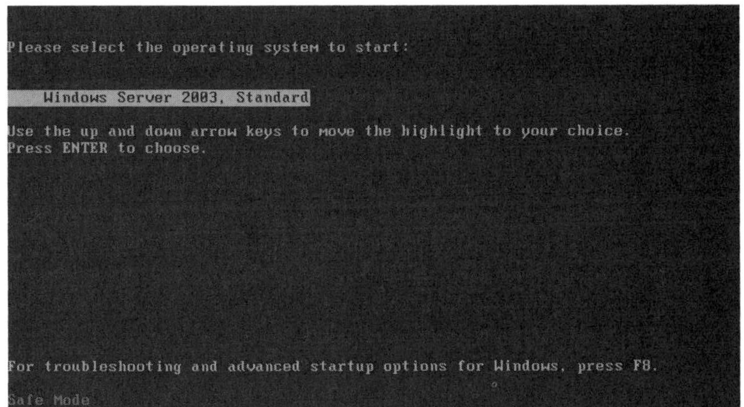

FIGURE 7.56
The boot menu screen again. Note that it informs you that you're in Safe Mode.

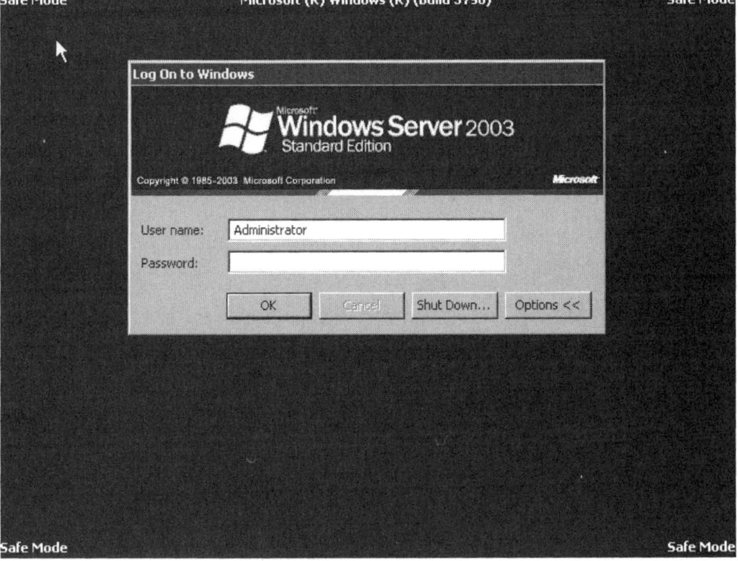

FIGURE 7.57
The Windows Server 2003 logon screen in Safe Mode. Notice that you're in VGA mode.

Remember that the capabilities vary depending on which Safe Mode option you select. For instance, the Safe Mode with Command Prompt option presents you with a command prompt window, and the Windows GUI will not be started, as shown in Figure 7.58.

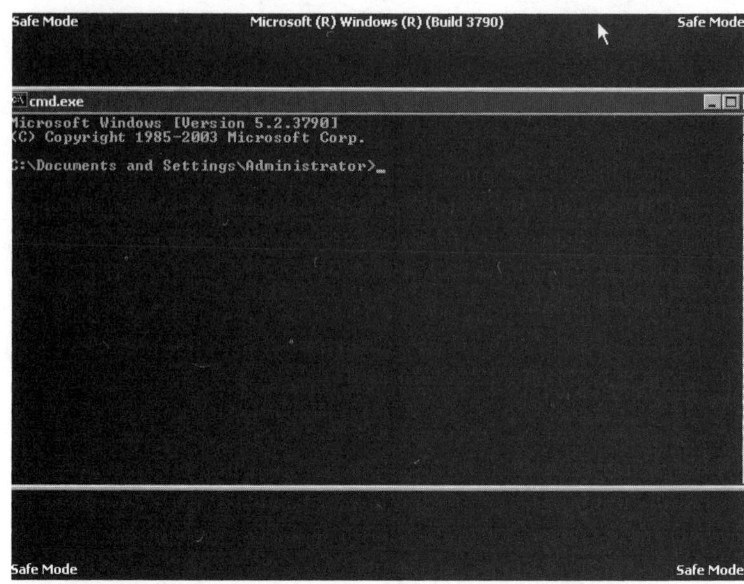

FIGURE 7.58
Windows Server 2003 server in Safe Mode with Command Prompt mode. Notice that you're in VGA mode and are limited to a command prompt window.

Recovery Console

For those situations in which the tools and methods available via Safe Mode are not enough to recover from a server failure, or if Safe Mode will not boot the server, Microsoft has provided an additional tool called the *Recovery Console*. The Recovery Console is a DOS-like command-line interface in which you can perform a limited set of commands and disable system services. Unlike booting from a DOS disk, the Recovery Console allows you limited access to files on an NTFS-formatted volume.

The Recovery Console is not installed by default; you must install it manually after you have installed Windows Server 2003 or run it from the product CD. To install the Recovery Console, perform the procedure outlined in Step by Step 7.13.

STEP BY STEP

7.13 Installing the Windows Server 2003 Recovery Console

1. Load the Windows Server 2003 CD-ROM.

2. Open a command prompt, access the Windows Server 2003 CD-ROM, and enter the `\i386\winnt32 /cmdcons` command.

3. Click the Yes button when the Windows Setup window, shown in Figure 7.59, appears.

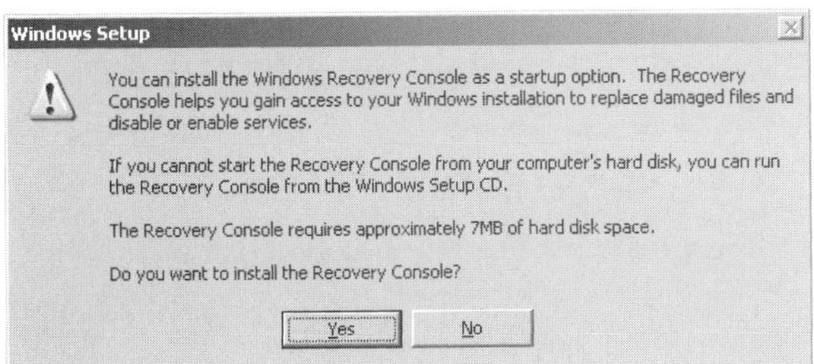

FIGURE 7.59
The Recovery Console confirmation prompt. Click Yes to install.

4. When the setup procedure completes, restart the server.

The Recovery Console option is added to the Windows Server 2003 boot menu, as shown in Figure 7.60.

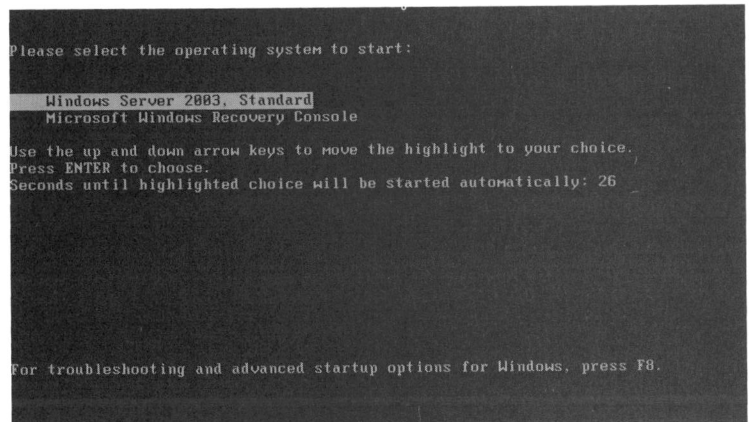

FIGURE 7.60
The Windows Server 2003 boot menu showing the addition of the Recovery Console.

If your system fails and you don't have the Recovery Console installed, or if you are having startup problems, you can run Recovery Console from the Windows Server 2003 CD-ROM.

To run the Recovery Console from a CD-ROM or a floppy, perform the procedure outlined in Step by Step 7.14.

NOTE

No More Boot Floppies Windows Server 2003 does not come with startup floppies, or with any method of creating them.

STEP BY STEP

7.14 Running the Recovery Console from a CD-ROM

1. Insert the desired media type and start the server.
2. In the Windows Server 2003 Setup procedure, select the option to repair the operating system.
3. Select Recovery Console as your repair method.
4. The system boots to the Recovery Console screen shown in Figure 7.61.

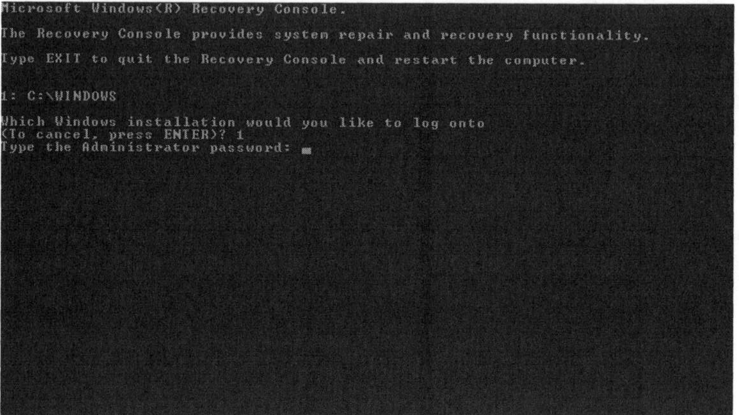

Microsoft Windows(R) Recovery Console.
The Recovery Console provides system repair and recovery functionality.
Type EXIT to quit the Recovery Console and restart the computer.
1: C:\WINDOWS
Which Windows installation would you like to log onto
(To cancel, press ENTER)? 1
Type the Administrator password:

FIGURE 7.61
The Windows Server 2003 Recovery Console showing the logon screen.

After you start the Recovery Console, either from a CD or from the hard disk, you will be prompted for the operating system number to log on to and the Administrator password, as shown in Figure 7.61. On a member server, this is the local Administrator password. However, on a domain controller this is not the domain or local Administrator password; instead, it's the Directory Services Restore Mode password, which you were prompted to create during the `dcpromo` procedure you used to install Active Directory.

After you log on, the commands listed in Table 7.2 are available.

TABLE 7.2

RECOVERY CONSOLE COMMANDS

Command	*Description*
`Attrib`	Changes the attributes of files and folders.
`Batch`	Used to execute commands from a text file.
`Bootcfg`	Used to query, configure, or change the `boot.ini` file.
`CD`	Used to change the directory.
`Chdir`	Used to change the directory.
`Chkdsk`	Repairs disk errors.
`Cls`	Clears the screen.
`Copy`	Copies a file.
`Del`	Deletes files.
`Delete`	Deletes files.
`Dir`	Used to display a list of files and directories.
`Disable`	Used to disable a service or driver.
`Diskpart`	Used to manage partitions and volumes.
`Enable`	Used to enable a service or driver.
`Exit`	Closes the console and reboots the server.
`Expand`	Extracts a file from the Windows CAB files.
`Fixboot`	Writes a new boot sector.
`Fixmbr`	Used to repair the master boot record.
`Format`	Used to format a drive.
`Help`	Lists the available commands.
`Listsvc`	Lists the installed services and drivers.
`Logon`	Used to log on to another Windows installation.
`Map`	Displays a list of mapped drives.
`MD`	Used to create a directory.
`Mkdir`	Used to create a directory.
`More`	Used to display a text file. Same as `Type`.
`RD`	Used to delete a directory.
`Ren`	Used to rename a file.

continues

TABLE 7.2 *continued*

RECOVERY CONSOLE COMMANDS

Command	*Description*
`Rename`	Used to rename a file.
`Rmdir`	Used to delete a directory.
`Set`	Used to display and set environment variables.
`Systemroot`	Sets the current directory to the systemroot.
`Type`	Used to display a text file. Same as `More`.

As you can see, the Recovery Console allows you to perform a variety of tasks, such as formatting a drive; copying, deleting, or renaming files; and starting and stopping services. However, there are some limitations:

- You only have access to `%systemroot%` and its subfolders, the root partitions of `%systemdrive%`, any other partitions, floppy drives, and CD-ROMs.
- You cannot copy a file from the hard disk to a floppy, but you can copy a file from a floppy, a CD-ROM, or another hard disk to your hard disk.

Using Directory Services Restore Mode to Recover System State Data

On a domain controller, the Active Directory files are restored as part of the system state. The system state on a domain controller consists of the following items:

- Active Directory (NTDS)
- The boot files
- The COM+ Class Registration database
- The Registry
- The system volume (SYSVOL)
- Files in the Windows File Protection folder

The individual components cannot be backed up or restored separately; they can only be handled as a unit, as we discussed in the previous section "System State Backups."

When a single domain controller fails, and the other domain controllers are still operational, it can be repaired and the data restored using a current backup tape. After Active Directory is restored, the domain controller coordinates with the other domain controllers to synchronize any changes that were made to the Active Directory on the other domain controllers since the backup tape was created. This process is called a *nonauthoritative restore.* This is the type of system state restore we performed earlier in this chapter.

Windows Server 2003 assigns an Update Sequence Number (USN) to each object created in Active Directory. This allows Active Directory to track updates and prevents it from replicating objects that have not changed. When you perform a normal file restore of the Active Directory, all the data that is restored is considered old data and will not be replicated to the other domain controllers. This data is considered to be nonauthoritative (old and out of date) because the objects have lower USNs. All the objects contained in the other copies of Active Directory on the other domain controllers that have higher USNs than the objects in the restored data will be replicated to the restored domain controller so that all copies of Active Directory are consistent. A nonauthoritative restore is the default restore mode for Active Directory and is used most often.

However, in specific circumstances, such as the accidental deletion of a group or an OU, it may be necessary to perform an authoritative restore. When you perform an authoritative restore, the USNs on the objects in the copy of the Active Directory database that is restored to the domain controller are reset to a number higher than the current USNs so that all the data that is restored is no longer considered old data. This allows the objects in the restore job to overwrite newer objects on the other domain controllers.

> NOTE
>
> **Authoritative Restore** An authoritative restore cannot be performed while a domain controller is online—the domain controller must be restarted into Directory Services Restore Mode, which is an option available from the Advanced Options Menu.

To perform an authoritative restore, perform the procedure outlined in Step by Step 7.15.

STEP BY STEP

7.15 Performing an Authoritative Restore

1. Restart the server. If Windows Server 2003 is the only operating system installed, you have to press F8 early in the boot process, just after the POST screen disappears. Otherwise, when you see the prompt Please Select the Operating System to Start, press the F8 key at the first OS screen.

2. The Advanced Options Menu screen appears, as shown in Figure 7.62. On the Advanced Options screen, use the arrow keys to select Directory Services Restore Mode.

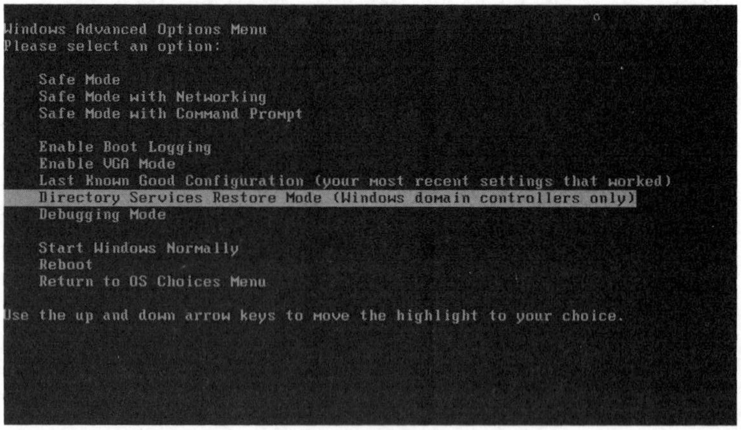

FIGURE 7.62
The Advanced Options Menu screen showing the selection of Directory Services Restore Mode.

3. You're now back at the operating system screen. Select the operating system you want to start and then press the Enter key. The server boots.

4. The server boots into Directory Services Restore Mode. From the Windows Server 2003 logon screen, log on using the Directory Services Restore Mode password. This is not the normal Administrator password. This is the password that was entered during the `dcpromo` procedure.

5. Start the Windows Server 2003 Backup program by selecting Start, All Programs, Accessories, System Tools, Backup.

6. The Backup or Restore Wizard appears. Click the highlighted Advanced Mode link to open the Backup utility.

7. From the Backup utility's Advanced Mode window, select the Restore and Manage Media tab.

8. From the Restore and Manage Media tab, double-click the backup set that contains the backup of the system state data that you want to restore.

9. In the right pane of the Restore and Manage Media tab, shown in Figure 7.63, select System State and then click the Start Restore button to continue.

10. A confirmation prompt warns you that your current system state data will be overwritten. Click OK to continue.

11. When the Confirm Restore dialog box appears, click the Advanced button.

12. From the Advanced Restore Options dialog box, shown in Figure 7.64, select the When Restoring Replicated Data Sets, Mark the Restored Data As the Primary Data for All Replicas check box, and then click the OK button.

13. Click the OK button in the Confirm Restore dialog box.

14. On the Windows Server 2003 boot menu, select the operating system to start and press Enter.

15. The server boots into Directory Services Restore Mode. From the Windows Server 2003 logon screen, log on using the Directory Services Restore Mode password. This is not the normal Administrator password. This is the password that was entered during the `dcpromo` procedure.

16. Open a command prompt window and type `ntdsutil`. Then press Enter.

17. At the command prompt, type `Authoritative Restore` and then press Enter.

18. Type `Restore Database` and then press Enter. When prompted, click OK and then click Yes.

19. After the command has completed, enter `quit` twice and reboot the domain controller. The domain controller now replicates the restored Active Directory object to the other domain controllers.

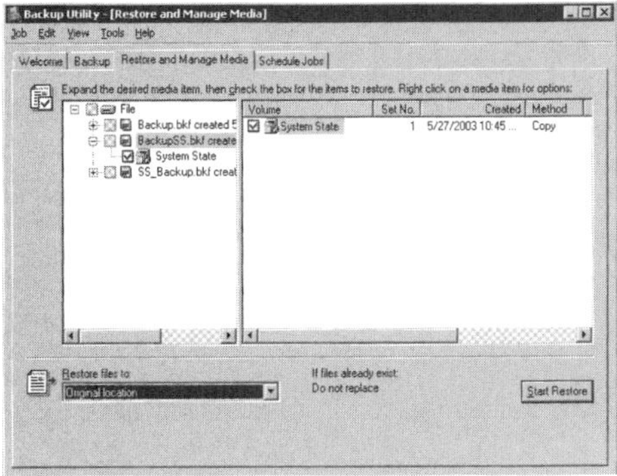

FIGURE 7.63
The Restore and Manage Media tab. Select the desired backup set and then select System State.

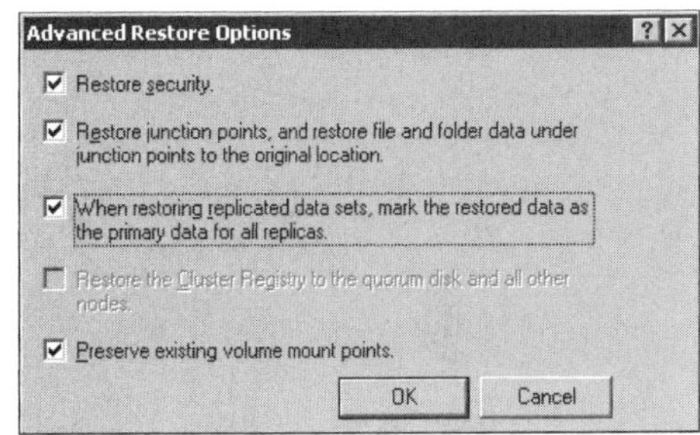

FIGURE 7.64
The Advanced Restore Options dialog box showing the authoritative restore selection.

WARNING

Partial Authoritative Restores
When you're performing a partial authoritative restore, it is very important that you only restore the specific item that needs to be restored. If the entire Active Directory is restored, you could inadvertently write over newer objects. For example, the naming context of Active Directory contains the passwords for all the computer accounts and trust relationships. These passwords are automatically changed approximately every 30 days. If the existing values are overwritten by the restore, and the passwords have been renegotiated since that backup was created, the computer accounts will be locked out of the domain and the trust relationships will be dropped. For more information, see Microsoft Knowledge Base Article Q216243, "Impact of Authoritative Restore on Trusts and Computer Accounts."

NOTE

Containers, Not OUs The default Active Directory folders shown in the root of the Active Directory Users and Computers MMC are actually containers and not Organizational Units:

- Users
- Builtin
- Computers

When referencing these containers, you have to use the `CN=` attribute and *not* the `OU=` attribute.

An authoritative restore is used most often in situations where an Active Directory object such as a user, group, or Organizational Unit (OU) has been accidentally deleted and needs to be restored.

If only a single Active Directory object is accidentally deleted, it is possible to restore only that object from a backup tape by performing a *partial* authoritative restore. This is accomplished by restoring from the last backup before the object was deleted. The procedure to perform this type of restore is very similar to the full Active Directory authoritative restore shown in the previous section.

To restore an object, you must know its common name (CN), the Organization Unit (OU), and the domain (DC) in which the object was located. For example, to restore the ABC St. Louis User OU in the `abc.com` domain after entering `Authoritative Restore` in step 17 of the previous procedure, you would enter the following command:

```
Restore Subtree "OU=ABC St. Louis User,DC=abc,DC=com"
```

This command restores all the objects that have been deleted in the ABC St. Louis User OU since the backup tape was created.

To restore a user, you would use the following command:

```
Restore Subtree "CN=JDoe,OU=ABC St. Louis User,DC=ABC,DC=com"
```

To restore a printer, you would use this command:

```
Restore Subtree "CN=DeskJet 3rdfloor,OU=ABC St. Louis User,DC=abc,DC=com"
```

After the command has completed, enter `quit` twice and reboot the domain controller. The domain controller now replicates the restored Active Directory object to the other domain controllers.

IN THE FIELD

MORE ABOUT AUTHORITATIVE RESTORES

In some situations, restoring user and/or group objects will not restore the corresponding group backlinks. For more information on how to work around this issue, see Microsoft Knowledge Base Article Q280079, "Authoritative Restore of Groups Can Result in Inconsistent Membership Information Across Domain Controllers."

GUIDED PRACTICE EXERCISE 7.2

You are the administrator of a network that includes multiple Windows Server 2003 servers used for file and print services for a small chemical company. You have a small but well-trained staff of senior administrators, with a couple junior administrators you are training.

One of the junior administrators is processing a request from Human Resources to delete the user account of an employee who has left the company. This user was named John Betty, and he worked in Executive Services. Unfortunately, there is a lady named Betty John who also works in Executive Services, and the junior administrator accidentally deleted her user account instead of John Betty's. What's even worse, Betty John is one of the senior vice presidents.

What is the best way to restore the deleted user account in Windows Server 2003? On your own, try to develop a solution that would involve the least amount of downtime.

If you would like to see a possible solution, follow these steps:

Estimated Time: 40 minutes

1. Restart one of the domain controllers. If Windows Server 2003 is the only operating system installed, you have to press F8 early in the boot process, just after the POST screen disappears. Otherwise, when you see the prompt Please Select the Operating System to Start, press the F8 key at the first OS screen.
2. The Advanced Options Menu screen appears. On the Advanced Options screen, use the arrow keys to select Directory Services Restore Mode.
3. You're now back at the operating system screen. Select the operating system you want to start and then press the Enter key. The server boots.

continues

continued

4. The server boots into Directory Services Restore Mode. From the Windows Server 2003 logon screen, log on using the Directory Services Restore Mode password. This is not the normal Administrator password. This is the password that was entered during the `dcpromo` procedure.
5. Start the Windows Server 2003 Backup program by selecting Start, All Programs, Accessories, System Tools, Backup.
6. The Backup or Restore Wizard appears. Click the highlighted Advanced Mode link to open the Backup utility.
7. From the Backup utility's Advanced Mode window, select the Restore and Manage Media tab.
8. From the Restore and Manage Media tab, double-click the backup set that contains the backup of the system state data that you want to restore.
9. In the right pane of the Restore and Manage Media tab, select System State and then click the Start Restore button to continue.
10. A confirmation prompt warns you that your current system state data will be overwritten. Click OK to continue.
11. When the Confirm Restore dialog box appears, click the Advanced button.
12. From the Advanced Restore Options dialog box, select the When Restoring Replicated Data Sets, Mark the Restored Data As the Primary Data for All Replicas check box, and then click the OK button.
13. Click the OK button in the Confirm Restore dialog box.
14. On the Windows Server 2003 boot menu, select the operating system to start and press Enter.
15. The server boots into Directory Services Restore Mode. From the Windows Server 2003 logon screen, log on using the Directory Services Restore Mode password. This is not the normal Administrator password. This is the password that was entered during the `dcpromo` procedure.
16. Open a command prompt window and type `ntdsutil`. Then press Enter.

17. At the command prompt, type `Authoritative Restore` and then press Enter.

18. Type `Restore Subtree "CN=Betty John,OU=Executive Services,DC=yourcompany,DC=com"`, and then press Enter. When prompted, click OK and then click Yes.

19. After the command has completed, enter `quit` twice and reboot the domain controller. The domain controller now replicates the restored Active Directory object to the other domain controllers.

Implementing Automated System Recovery (ASR)

Most of the recovery procedures we have looked at so far are not much use if more than a handful of the boot partition files are missing or damaged. Although in certain modes you have the ability to copy files from the operating system CD-ROM, this can become a nightmare if your boot partition has sustained major damage.

Although previous versions of Windows used the Emergency Repair Disk (ERD) to assist in this type of situation, beginning in Windows 2000, it became unwieldy to save enough files to a floppy to restore the Registry and other files necessary to rebuild a boot partition. To rectify this situation, Windows Server 2003 includes a new feature called *Automated System Recovery (ASR).*

ASR works by making a backup of the system and boot partitions (if different) to tape or other media. It then saves the catalog and other operating system information, such as system state, and disk partition information to a floppy disk.

> NOTE
>
> **System and Boot Partitions**
> Remember from Chapter 1, "Managing Server Storage Devices," that the boot partition contains the operating system files, whereas the system partition contains the startup files, such as `Ntldr` and `Ntdetect.com`. In most situations, the system and boot partitions are on the same volume.

When a problem occurs that cannot be fixed by using any of the other repair and recovery methods, or if you have replaced a failed boot drive, you need to restore the boot partition. Using ASR, this is as simple as booting your server from the Windows Server 2003 CD-ROM, and then inserting the floppy disk and the backup media created by the ASR process. The boot partition is automatically restored for you.

ASR installs a generic installation of Windows Server 2003 and then uses this generic installation to mount and restore your boot partition from the backup media created by ASR. This process not only restores the information on your boot drive, it also restores the disk signatures and re-creates the boot partition or volume, if necessary. It does not recover or delete any data volumes.

The advantage of using ASR is that it automates the restoration of your server. For example, in previous versions of Windows NT and Windows 2000, after a disk failure, you would be required to do the following:

1. Repartition and format the new hard drive.
2. Load a generic installation of Windows, including any specialized drivers.
3. Restore the system and boot partitions from a backup tape.

With ASR, after booting from the Windows Server 2003 CD-ROM, you insert the ASR floppy and the backup tape, and all of these steps are performed for you.

ASR should be run on a regular basis so that the backup media contains the most current configuration to be used for server recovery. ASR is implemented using the Windows Server 2003 Backup utility's Automated System Recovery Wizard.

The ASR Wizard can be used to create an ASR backup set using the procedure outlined in Step by Step 7.16.

STEP BY STEP

7.16 Creating an ASR Backup

1. From the Start menu, click Start, All Programs, Accessories, System Tools, Backup.
2. The Backup or Restore Wizard appears. Click the highlighted Advanced Mode link to open the Backup utility.

3. From the Backup utility's Advanced Mode window, shown in Figure 7.65, select the Automated System Recovery Wizard button.
4. The ASR Wizard opening screen appears. Click Next to continue.
5. The Backup Destination screen appears, as shown in Figure 7.66. Select the desired options and then click Next to continue.

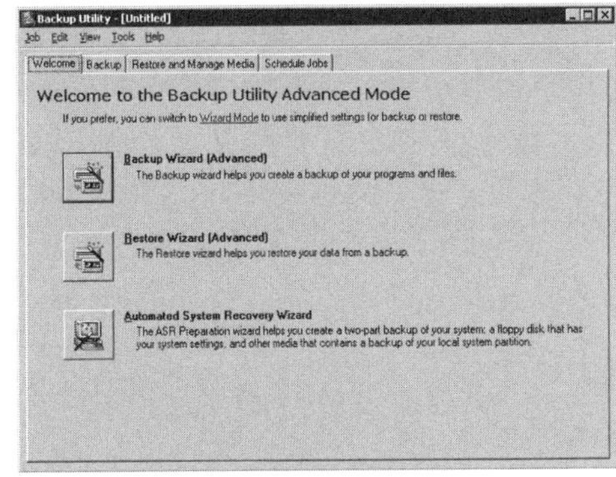

FIGURE 7.65▲
The Backup utility's Advanced Mode screen displaying the ASR Wizard button.

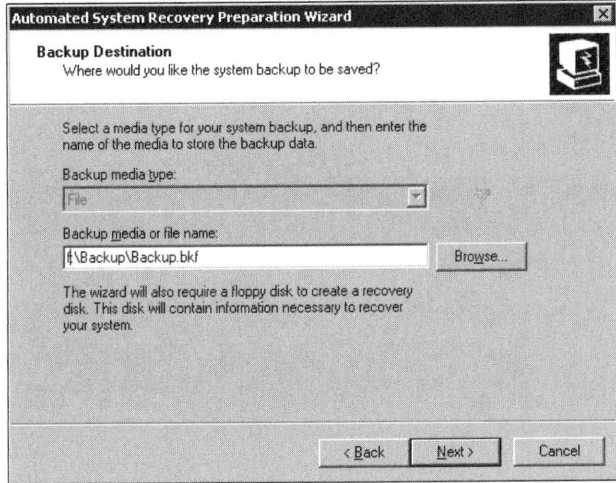

FIGURE 7.66◄
Select the backup media. This can be a tape, file, CD-RW, or ZIP drive.

6. The Completing the Wizard screen appears. Click Finish to continue.
7. The Backup program backs up the boot partition to your selected media. When prompted, insert a blank, formatted floppy disk.

To repair your system using ASR, you must start from the Windows Server 2003 CD. During the setup process, select F2, when prompted, and then insert the floppy disk and the backup media.

When needed, ASR can be used to restore a server using the procedure outlined in Step by Step 7.17.

STEP BY STEP

7.17 Restoring an ASR Backup

1. Load the Windows Server 2003 CD-ROM in your CD-ROM drive.

2. Restart the server. When you see the prompt shown in Figure 7.67, press the F2 key.

FIGURE 7.67
Press the F2 key to start ASR.

3. When the prompt shown in Figure 7.68 appears, insert the floppy disk and press the Enter key.

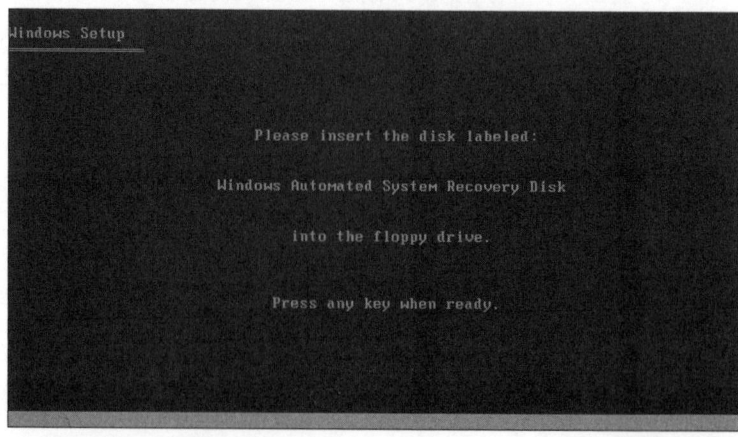

FIGURE 7.68
Insert the ASR floppy disk when prompted

ASR uses the setup configuration files stored on the floppy disk to restore the boot partition to its state at the time the ASR media set was built.

EXAM TIP

Know the Recovery Methods You should be familiar with the various recovery methods for Windows Server 2003, as well as when and how to use each one.

IN THE FIELD

SLIPSTREAMING OPERATING SYSTEM CD-ROMS

Several of the procedures in this section refer to using the original installation CD-ROM to copy files from or as part of the recovery procedure. However, after a server has been operational for awhile, you have probably installed a service pack or two (or three), and the files on the original CD-ROM no longer match the ones on your server. Because some of the recovery procedures require you to overwrite operating system files on the server with files from the operating system CD-ROM, it's best to use a slipstream CD-ROM that contains a service pack–updated version of the operating system instead of the original CD-ROM. Instructions on how to create a slipstreamed operating system CD-ROM can usually be found in the `Readme` file included with the service packs.

PLANNING FOR DISASTER RECOVERY

In this chapter we have covered a variety of tools and procedures that can be implemented in Windows Server 2003 to protect your servers and data in case of a disaster. However, disaster planning and recovery involves more than learning a few procedures; it has to be part of an overall strategy. Just firing up Windows Backup and filling up media with data does not make a good disaster-recovery plan. You have to have a plan in place for what to do with your backups when you need them.

A good disaster-recovery plan starts with the basics:

- What kind of disasters are you planning for?
- What are you going to do when a disaster occurs?

When making your disaster-recovery plan, you should prepare for not only common daily occurrences, such as users or administrators accidentally deleting files, but also more serious problems, such as tornadoes, hurricanes, and extended power outages.

Your disaster-recovery plan should be documented. If the chief technology officer walks into your office and starts asking what-if questions, you should be able to reach into your desk and pull out a binder than contains a detailed layout of what disasters you have planned for, what the contingencies are, who to contact, and where the materials you need (such as spare parts, offsite media, passwords, and so on) are stored and how to obtain them.

Copies of this disaster-recovery "cookbook" should be distributed to the personnel who have a part in recovery. In addition, this cookbook should be updated frequently as new hardware and software are added to your network or as additional personnel are added or removed. This should be a "living" document.

To keep this document effective, you should schedule frequent test runs to verify that the procedures work and that necessary personnel are comfortable with them. Feel free to make liberal use of screenshots in the documentation. Just like the old adage says, "a picture is worth a thousand words," especially when you're in the middle of a disaster and trying to recover.

Implementing and Using Good Backup Procedures

As part of your disaster-recovery plan, you should have solid backup and restore procedures. Here are some of the recommended best practices for backups:

- **Test your backups**—This can help to identify not only bad tapes but also bad procedures.
- **Train additional personnel**—In the case of a disaster, you might need to replace administrators who are busy elsewhere.
- **Preinstall the Recovery Console on all servers**—This allows you to recover quicker because you won't need to hunt down the Windows Server 2003 CD-ROM.
- **Back up both the system state and the data together**—This allows you to protect yourself from a hard disk failure and makes it easier for you to locate backup sets because everything should be on a single set.

- **Use the Automated System Recovery feature**—This not only protects you from the failure of a boot disk, but because the restore is fully automated, it allows you to work on other things while the process completes.
- **Always create and review the backup logs**—This lets you know whether a backup procedure has failed. There is nothing worse that starting the restore on a critical server and finding out that the backup media is blank because the backup failed.
- **Don't disable the Volume Shadow Copy backup feature**—The Volume Shadow Copy backup feature allows you to back up open files. If this option is turned off, some files will not be backed up.
- **Rotate your backup media**—Rotating backup media helps to insulate you from media failures.

Managing and Rotating Backup Storage Media

After spending a lot of time and effort backing up your servers, it can all be negated by a bad tape or a tape that was overwritten when it shouldn't have been. There are several standard-industry practices for managing and rotating backup storage media. For proper disaster-recovery protection, they should be followed.

For example, if you use the same tape or tapes every day, they soon become worn out. There is nothing worse than being in the middle of restoring critical files when you discover that a backup tape cannot be read because of an error. Best practices for working with backup tapes recommend that you cycle tapes so that they are not used too frequently, and that you track their in-service date. You should have a plan in place for the tapes to be replaced either when they are showing errors in the backup log or sometime before their "end of life," as recommended by the manufacturer of the tape.

Let's look at a typical weekly backup schedule and the differences in the media required for a full restore (see Tables 7.3 and 7.4).

TABLE 7.3

WEEKLY BACKUP SCHEDULE USING NORMAL AND INCREMENTAL BACKUPS

Day	*Backup Type*	*Media Required for Full Restore*
Monday	Normal	Monday
Tuesday	Incremental	Monday and Tuesday
Wednesday	Incremental	Monday, Tuesday, and Wednesday
Thursday	Incremental	Monday, Tuesday, Wednesday, and Thursday
Friday	Incremental	Monday, Tuesday, Wednesday, Thursday, and Friday

TABLE 7.4

WEEKLY BACKUP SCHEDULE USING NORMAL AND DIFFERENTIAL BACKUPS

Day	*Backup Type*	*Media Required for Full Restore*
Monday	Normal	Monday
Tuesday	Differential	Monday and Tuesday
Wednesday	Differential	Monday and Wednesday
Thursday	Differential	Monday and Thursday
Friday	Differential	Monday and Friday

In both cases, you should use five media sets (one or more tapes) each week. These tapes should be stored in a fireproof media safe during the week, and the previous week's backup should be stored offsite in a secure, climate-controlled location. A common practice is to have three or four sets of backup media so that there is a longer period before older data is overwritten. This protects the system administrator from a user who deletes a file just before he leaves for a two-week vacation and then wants his file back when he returns to work. These backups can be supplemented by a monthly, quarterly, or even yearly normal backup that can be kept for a longer period of time.

CASE STUDY: SOUTHERN WINDS

ESSENCE OF THE CASE

Here are the essential elements in this case:

- ▶ Back up all the critical data.
- ▶ Provide a good disaster-recovery strategy.
- ▶ Prepare for catastrophic events.
- ▶ Provide for recoverability with the least amount of hands-on time.

SCENARIO

Frank runs a small Application Service Provider (ASP) that caters to several local small businesses that can't afford to have their own server farm and IT staff. Frank's business consists of five Web servers, two database servers, and three servers hosting Windows Server 2003 Terminal Services sessions. All his clients access his server farm either through a VPN or via one of the Web servers.

Because he is in effect running the business for a number of small companies, Frank realizes that the ability to recover quickly from hardware and software failures, as well as from user-created problems, is essential. In addition, because Frank is located in a part of Florida that is known for the frequency and ferocity of its hurricanes, he has to have a good backup plan in place. This is in addition to the fact that this ASP is a business that Frank runs on the side, apart from his full-time job.

ANALYSIS

After a close examination of the needs for Frank's business, it should be possible to address these needs using the built-in Windows Server 2003 backup and recovery tools.

To ensure the recoverability of his servers and the data they contain, Frank should set up a backup schedule. He should perform a full backup once a week, with differential backups (because the restore is quicker) the other days of the week. In addition, he should use a rotating schedule for the backup tapes and make sure that the previous week's tapes are stored offsite in a hurricane-resistant location, such as a bank vault.

continues

Case Study: Southern Winds

continued

Frank should set up Automated System Recovery (ASR) on all his servers. This feature will allow him to restore his servers to operation quickly in case of a catastrophic system failure. In addition, he should install the Recovery Console on all his servers, which will allow him to repair a variety of boot and system file–related problems easily and quickly.

An item that should reduce the time Frank has to devote to customer support would be to enable the Volume Shadow Copy Service (VSS) on selected volumes. This feature enables the end users to restore previously saved copies of their files due to accidental deletion or file corruption, without requiring intervention from Frank. The following table provides an overview of the requirements and solutions in this case study.

OVERVIEW OF THE REQUIREMENTS AND SOLUTIONS IN THIS CASE STUDY

Requirement	Solution Provided By
Back up all the critical data.	Configuring Windows Server 2003 Backup to save all critical files
Provide a good disaster-recovery strategy.	Incorporating the Recovery Console, Automated System Recovery, and a good backup schedule
Prepare for catastrophic events.	Setting up a rotating backup schedule and storing tapes offsite
Provide for recoverability with the least amount of users hands-on time.	Enabling the Volume Shadow Copy Service (so that can recover some of their own files) and configuring the backups to run automatically

CHAPTER SUMMARY

This chapter, "Managing and Implementing Disaster Recovery," covered the main features in Windows Server 2003 used for protecting and restoring server configurations and data in case of disasters of various types. To summarize, this chapter contained the following main points:

- **Planning for disaster recovery**—This includes planning for and working with the procedures involved in creating a disaster-recovery plan.
- **Using Windows Backup**—This includes saving and recovering both system state data and user data.
- **Using recovery tools**—This includes using the disaster-recovery tools built in to Windows Server 2003, such as Automated System Recovery, Last Known Good Configuration, the Recovery Console, and Safe Mode.

KEY TERMS

- Incremental backup
- Differential backup
- Backup selection file
- Recovery Console
- Safe Mode
- System state
- Last Known Good Configuration
- Emergency Repair Disk (ERD)
- Automated System Recovery (ASR)

APPLY YOUR KNOWLEDGE

Exercises

7.1 Using Last Known Good Configuration

A very common problem in Windows is the installation and recovery from the effects of bad device drivers. The effects of a faulty device driver can range from poor performance to a blue screen. As a system administrator, you need to be able to recover from this type of incident.

What is the best way to accomplish this in Windows Server 2003? On your own, try to develop a solution that involves the least amount of downtime.

If you would like to see a possible solution, follow these steps:

Estimated Time: 20 minutes

1. Open Regedit. Delete the Registry key `HKLM\SYSTEM\CurrentControlSet\Control\SystemBootDevice`.
2. Restart the server. You should get a blue screen, possibly with the message "Inaccessible Boot Device."
3. Restart the server. If Windows Server 2003 is the only operating system installed, you have to press F8 early in the boot process, just after the POST screen disappears. Otherwise, when you see the prompt Please Select the Operating System to Start, press the F8 key at the first OS screen.
4. The Advanced Options Menu screen appears. On this screen, use the arrow keys to select the Last Known Good Configuration option.
5. You're now back at the operating system screen. Select the operating system you want to start and then press the Enter key. The server boots normally.

7.2 Using the Recovery Console

Another common problem in Windows is the corruption of system files. This prevents a server from booting properly, or it can result in a system STOP error. It is important to understand the capabilities and limitations of the tools used to correct these types of situations.

For this exercise, one of the Windows Server 2003 system files is corrupt. The server will no longer boot. Even Safe Mode is not available. Your job is to fix the server while incurring the least amount of downtime.

What is the best way to accomplish this in Windows Server 2003? On your own, try to develop a solution that involves the least amount of downtime.

If you would like to see a possible solution, follow these steps:

Estimated Time: 20 minutes

1. Open either My Computer or Windows Explorer. Select Tools, Folder Options and then click the View tab. Unhide the hidden files.
2. In the root folder on the boot drive, remove the read-only attribute from the `boot.ini` file.
3. Make a copy of `boot.ini` and name it `boot.sav`.
4. Open `boot.ini` with a text editor and delete all the lines under `[operating systems]`.
5. Save the file.
6. Reboot the server. You should get a boot error, most likely "Cannot find NTLDR."
7. Insert the Windows Server 2003 CD-ROM and start the server.
8. In the Windows Server 2003 Setup procedure, select the option to repair the operating system.

APPLY YOUR KNOWLEDGE

9. Select Recovery Console as your repair method.
10. The system boots to the Recovery Console screen.
11. Select the operating system to load. This will probably be number 1.
12. Enter the Administrator password.
13. From the command prompt, type `del boot.ini`.
14. From the command prompt, type `ren boot.sav boot.ini`.
15. Type Exit to restart the server. It should boot normally.

Review Questions

1. What are the different types of backups available in Windows Server 2003?
2. What is the main difference between Safe Mode and the Recovery Console?
3. Which backup type(s) does not change the archive bit?
4. What groups automatically have Backup and Restore rights?
5. What three things are required to restore a server using Automated System Recovery?
6. What can you do if you need to run the Recovery Console but haven't installed it on your servers?

Exam Questions

1. Bob is the system administrator for Good Times Inc., a manufacturer of various leisure-time accessories. The Good Times network consists of 12 Windows Server 2003 servers, 10 Windows 2000 servers, and 700 Windows XP Professional clients.

   Bob's boss wants to have all the servers backed up from a single location. Because the company has a limited budget due to the current economic slowdown, Bob can afford to buy a new tape changer, but his software budget is limited.

   Required Result:

   All servers should be backed up to a designated backup server.

   Optional Desired Results:

   Back up system state data on all servers.

   Back up the Registry on all servers.

   Proposed Solution:

   Buy a tape changer and install it on one of the Windows Server 2003 servers. This server is the backup server. The Windows Server 2003 version of Windows backup will be used.

   Evaluation of Proposed Solution:

   Which result(s) does the proposed solution produce?

   A. The proposed solution produces the required result but neither of the optional results.

   B. The proposed solution produces the required result and one of the optional results.

APPLY YOUR KNOWLEDGE

C. The proposed solution produces the required result and both the optional results.

D. The proposed solution does not produce the required result.

2. Mary scheduled Windows Backup to run unattended during the night to back up her server. When she came in the next day, she examined the backup logs, and the backup not only took a lot longer to complete than she thought it would, but there were also messages in the log about skipped open files. What is Mary's problem?

   A. She left too many files open.

   B. She ran the command-line version of Backup instead of the GUI version.

   C. Volume Shadow Copy was disabled.

   D. She forgot to dump her SQL database before starting the backup.

3. Volume Shadow Copy is enabled on a volume that hosts the user data files. On Friday, a user tries to use the Previous Versions client to access a copy of a file that she has been working on every day that week. However, she only has versions from Wednesday forward. What is the most likely problem?

   A. The Volume Shadow Copy Service wasn't enabled until Wednesday.

   B. The user doesn't have the proper rights to see all the files.

   C. The area designated for Volume Shadow Copy is too small.

   D. She hasn't saved a copy of the file since Wednesday.

4. First Star Bank is a small bank and holding company based in the Midwest. It has a small IT staff, so it tries to automate as many tasks as possible. First Star Bank is currently in the process of upgrading its servers from Windows NT 4.0 to Windows Server 2003. The company has been using `NTBACKUP.EXE` and `AT.EXE` from Windows NT 4.0 to back up and restore its environment using a series of batch files and scripts.

   Required Result:

   All servers should be backed up using the command-line version of `NTBACKUP.EXE` in a script.

   Optional Desired Results:

   Restore selected folders via automated scripts.

   Schedule backups using `AT.EXE`.

   Proposed Solution:

   First Star Bank intends to continue using the Windows Server 2003 version of `NTBACKUP.EXE` for its backups and restores by modifying the existing scripts to handle the differences in command-line syntax between versions.

   Evaluation of Proposed Solution:

   Which result(s) does the proposed solution produce?

   A. The proposed solution produces the required result but neither of the optional results.

   B. The proposed solution produces the required result and one of the optional results.

   C. The proposed solution produces the required result and both the optional results.

   D. The proposed solution does not produce the required result.

APPLY YOUR KNOWLEDGE

5. John, a junior system administrator, just loaded new video drivers on a Windows Server 2003 server. After the install, he rebooted the server and immediately received a blue screen. What's the quickest way for John to recover from this problem?

   A. Rebuild the server using Automated System Recovery (ASR).

   B. Go into Safe Mode, delete the driver, and reboot.

   C. Boot into the Recovery Console, delete the driver, and reboot.

   D. Boot the server and select Last Known Good Configuration.

6. Jane is one of the network administrators for Big Company, Inc. Jane is responsible for managing and maintaining all the database servers in the organization. As part of her duties, Jane maintains current backups of all the servers she is responsible for, along with various boot disks and other items necessary for recovery purposes.

   One day, Jane comes to work and one of her servers has blue screened. It seems that one of the junior administrators was upgrading device drivers and, after he rebooted, got a blue screen. Jane proceeds to try Last Known Good Configuration, then Safe Mode, and then the Recovery Console, but those methods don't seem to repair the problem. What is her next step?

   A. Rebuild the server using Automated System Recovery (ASR).

   B. Go into Safe Mode, restore the system state data, and reboot.

   C. Boot into the Recovery Console, restore the system state data, and reboot.

   D. Repair the server using the Emergency Repair Disk (ERD).

7. John has been newly hired as the system administrator for a small legal firm. The chief information officer has explained to him that the firm's legal documents are stored on the servers, and they must be recoverable in case of a hardware failure or natural disaster. John has decided to back up his servers every day.

   Required Result:

   All servers should be backed up overnight.

   Optional Desired Results:

   Servers must be backed up in the shortest period of time.

   Servers must be recoverable in the shortest period of time.

   Proposed Solution:

   John uses Windows Server 2003 Backup to schedule a normal backup for Friday night, with incremental backups scheduled for the other days.

   Evaluation of Proposed Solution:

   Which result(s) does the proposed solution produce?

   A. The proposed solution produces the required result but neither of the optional results.

   B. The proposed solution produces the required result and one of the optional results.

APPLY YOUR KNOWLEDGE

C. The proposed solution produces the required result and both the optional results.

D. The proposed solution does not produce the required result.

8. John has been newly hired as the system administrator for a small legal firm. The chief information officer has explained to him that the firm's legal documents are stored on the servers and they must be recoverable in case of a hardware failure or natural disaster. John has decided to back up his servers every day.

Required Result:

All servers should be backed up overnight.

Optional Desired Results:

Servers must be backed up in the shortest period of time.

Servers must be recoverable in the shortest period of time.

Proposed Solution:

John uses Windows Server 2003 Backup to schedule a normal backup for Friday night, with differential backups scheduled for the other days.

Evaluation of Proposed Solution:

Which result(s) does the proposed solution produce?

A. The proposed solution produces the required result but neither of the optional results.

B. The proposed solution produces the required result and one of the optional results.

C. The proposed solution produces the required result and both the optional results.

D. The proposed solution does not produce the required result.

9. As part of his disaster-recovery plan, Don plans to back up both of his domain controllers on a regular basis. Because his domain controllers don't have other roles, such as being the file or print server, Don decides to only back them up once a week. Don's company has two locations connected by T1 lines.

Required Result:

All domain controllers should be recoverable.

Optional Desired Results:

Domain controllers must be recoverable in the shortest period of time.

Domain controllers must be recoverable with no loss of data.

Proposed Solution:

John uses Windows Server 2003's Automated Server Recovery feature to back up each domain controller once a week.

Evaluation of Proposed Solution:

Which result(s) does the proposed solution produce?

A. The proposed solution produces the required result but neither of the optional results.

B. The proposed solution produces the required result and one of the optional results.

C. The proposed solution produces the required result and both the optional results.

D. The proposed solution does not produce the required result.

APPLY YOUR KNOWLEDGE

10. As part of his disaster-recovery plan, Don plans to back up both of his domain controllers on a regular basis. Because his domain controllers don't have other roles, such as being the file or print server, Don decides to only back them up once a week. Don's company has two locations connected by T1 lines.

    Required Result:

    All domain controllers should be recoverable.

    Optional Desired Results:

    Domain controllers must be recoverable in the shortest period of time.

    Domain controllers must be recoverable with no loss of data.

    Proposed Solution:

    John uses Windows Server 2003's Automated Server Recovery feature to back up each domain controller once a week. John designates one of his locations as a hot site, and he places a domain controller there that will be backed up every day.

    Evaluation of Proposed Solution:

    Which result(s) does the proposed solution produce?

    A. The proposed solution produces the required result but neither of the optional results.

    B. The proposed solution produces the required result and one of the optional results.

    C. The proposed solution produces the required result and both the optional results.

    D. The proposed solution does not produce the required result.

11. Fred reboots one of his Windows Server 2003 domain controllers and receives the message that `NTOSKRNL.EXE` cannot be found. What is the quickest way to repair this problem?

    A. Boot his server from a DOS disk and copy the `NTOSKRNL.EXE` file from the Windows Server 2003 CD-ROM.

    B. Boot his server from the Recovery Console and copy the `NTOSKRNL.EXE` file from the Windows Server 2003 CD-ROM.

    C. Boot his server from Safe Mode and copy the `NTOSKRNL.EXE` file from the Windows Server 2003 CD-ROM.

    D. Boot his server from the Windows Server 2003 CD-ROM and select the Repair option. Then copy the `NTOSKRNL.EXE` file from the Windows Server 2003 CD-ROM.

12. Your Windows Server 2003 uses a SCSI adapter that is not included on the Hardware Compatibility List (HCL). You install an updated driver for the SCSI adapter. When you start the computer, you receive the following STOP error:

    `"INACCESSIBLE_BOOT_DEVICE."`

    Which of the following procedures can you use to resolve the problem?

    A. Start the computer in Safe Mode. Reinstall the old driver for the SCSI adapter.

    B. Start the computer by using a Windows Server 2003 bootable floppy disk. Reinstall the old driver for the SCSI adapter.

    C. Start the computer by using the Windows Server 2003 CD-ROM. Load the Recovery Console and replace the SCSI driver.

    D. Recover the system and boot partitions using ASR.

APPLY YOUR KNOWLEDGE

13. You are trying out a TCP/IP Registry hack that you saw in a magazine. After carefully making the change using Regedit, you reboot your server. However, it hangs on the logon screen. What is the best way to correct this problem?

    A. Restart the server in Safe Mode. Undo the Registry change.

    B. Restart the computer and boot to the Recovery Console. Undo the Registry change.

    C. Restart the server and select Last Known Good Configuration from the Advanced Options Menu screen.

    D. Restart the server in Safe Mode with Networking. Undo the Registry change.

14. You are the administrator of a Windows Server 2003 Active Directory domain with multiple sites. As part of your job, you perform daily system state backups on your domain controllers. Unfortunately, one of your junior administrators opened a file that contains a virus on one of your domain controllers. This virus seems to have deleted several users and groups in your Active Directory database on one of your domain controllers. What action should you take?

    A. Quickly unplug the domain controller from the network, format the hard drive, and recover from backup.

    B. On one of the other domain controllers, use Windows Backup to restore the system state data. Run Ntdsutil.

    C. On one of the other domain controllers, boot into Directory Service Restore mode. Use Windows Backup to restore the system state data. Run Ntdsutil.

    D. On one of the other domain controllers, boot into Safe Mode. Use Windows Backup to restore the system state data. Run Ntdsutil.

15. You are the administrator of a Windows Server 2003 Active Directory domain with multiple sites. As part of your job, you perform daily system state backups on your domain controllers. Unfortunately, one of your junior administrators opened a file that contains a virus on one of your domain controllers. This virus seems to have deleted several users and groups in your Active Directory database on several domain controllers. What action should you take?

    A. Unplug the domain controller from the network, format the hard drive, and recover from backup.

    B. On one of the other domain controllers, use Windows Backup to restore the system state data. Run Ntdsutil.

    C. On one of the other domain controllers, boot into Directory Service Restore mode. Use Windows Backup to restore the system state data. Perform an authoritative restore.

    D. On one of the other domain controllers, boot into Safe Mode. Use Windows Backup to restore the system state data. Run Ntdsutil.

APPLY YOUR KNOWLEDGE

Answers to Review Questions

1. Windows Server 2003 supports five types of backups: Normal, Copy, Differential, Incremental, and Daily.
2. Whereas Safe Mode boots the server with a set of default drivers, the Recovery Console uses its own mini-version of Windows Server 2003 to boot. The Recovery Console only supports a limited number of command-line utilities.
3. Copy, Differential, and Daily backups do not change the archive bit.
4. The Administrators and Backup Operators groups are automatically assigned Backup and Restore rights.
5. The Automated System Recovery restore procedure requires the Windows Server 2003 CD-ROM and the floppy disk and backup media created by the ASR backup.
6. You can run the Recovery Console from the Windows Server 2003 CD-ROM.

Answers to Exam Questions

1. **A.** The solution satisfies the required result, but it does not satisfy either of the optional results. Although Windows Backup can be used to back up remote servers, it cannot back up the Registry or the system state data on remote computers.
2. **C.** When Volume Shadow Copy is enabled, whenever the backup encounters an open file, a snapshot is copied to another area on disk, and that copy of the file is backed up. Volume Shadow Copy is enabled by default for backups, but it can be deselected if desired.
3. **C.** The most likely cause is that the Volume Shadow Copy area is too small. Volume Shadow Copy can store only 64 copies, and it starts deleting the oldest versions when it reaches that number or when it runs out of disk space.
4. **B.** The proposed solution meets the required result and only one of the optional results. Even though the GUI version of Windows Backup has a built-in scheduler, you can still use the command-line version of `NTBACKUP.EXE` in a script that's scheduled using `AT.EXE`. However, the Windows Server 2003 command-line version of `NTBACKUP.EXE` can only back up files, it cannot restore them.
5. **D.** Although any of the other answers would work, the quickest way to recover from a bad driver install is to boot the server using Last Known Good Configuration.
6. **A.** The next recovery step to attempt after Jane has tried Last Known Good Configuration, Safe Mode, and the Recovery Console is Automated System Recovery. ASR deletes and reformats the boot partition and then reloads it from backup. Restoring the system state data usually will fix a driver problem because it restores the Registry, but that had already been tried. The ERD doesn't exist in Windows Server 2003 (it has been replaced by ASR).

APPLY YOUR KNOWLEDGE

7. **B.** Performing a normal backup once a week and an incremental backup on the other days provides the required result and one of the optional results. An incremental backup only backs up the files that have changed since the last backup, so it typically results in the shortest backup time over the scheduled period. However, the restore time can potentially be longer depending on the day of the failure. For example, if the failure is on a Wednesday, John will need to restore the full backup from Friday, plus restore from the tape for every day since then.

8. **B.** Performing a normal backup once a week and a differential backup on the other days provides the required result and one of the optional results. A differential backup backs up the files that have changed since the last normal backup, so it typically results in a longer backup time each day because there are more files to be backed up. This results in a longer backup time over the scheduled period. However, the restore time is less because you never have to restore more than two tapes. For example, if the failure is on a Wednesday, John will need to restore the full backup from Friday, plus the tape from Tuesday.

9. **B.** The proposed solution meets the required result and one of the optional results. Automated System Recovery can be used to back up and recover the operating system–related files on a server. This includes all the files on a server that is only being used as a domain controller. Because ASR is automated, it can be used to recover a server in a shorter period of time. However, performing a backup only once a week could cause a potential loss of data if all the domain controllers are lost and the Active Directory changes since the last backup cannot be replicated to the recovered domain controller from another domain controller.

10. **C.** The proposed solution meets the required result and both the optional results. Automated System Recovery can be used to back up and recover the operating system–related files on a server. This includes all the files on a server that is only being used as a domain controller. Because ASR is automated, it can be used to recover a server in a shorter period of time. By backing up a domain controller in a hot site once a day, even if all domain controllers are lost, the hot site domain controller can be recovered and used to replicate the current Active Directory changes to the other domain controllers.

11. **B.** A DOS disk won't be able to read an NTFS disk, which is what's installed by default on a domain controller. Safe Mode won't be available if the `NTOSKRNL.EXE` file is corrupted or missing. The Repair option from the install procedure requires the ASR recovery media. Because the Recovery Console uses its own mini-version of Windows Server 2003 to boot the server, it can be used to copy and repair system files.

12. **C, D.** Safe Mode does not work because the boot partition is inaccessible due to the driver problem. There is no boot floppy for Windows Server 2003. The Recovery Console has its own copy of Windows Server 2003 so that you can still boot to it. ASR will also work.

APPLY YOUR KNOWLEDGE

13. **C.** Restarting a server and selecting Last Known Good Configuration is the quickest and easiest way to correct most bad Registry edits.

14. **A.** Because the virus has only affected a single domain controller, you should take it off the network before it replicates changes to the other domain controllers. Then you should rebuild the domain controller from backup.

15. **C.** Because the problem has started replicating to other domain controllers, your only choice is to perform an authoritative restore, which overwrites the bad copy of the AD database with a good copy from your backups.

Suggested Readings and Resources

1. Microsoft Official Curriculum Course 2275: Maintaining a Microsoft Windows Server 2003 Environment
   - Module 7: Managing Disaster Recovery
2. Microsoft Official Curriculum Course 2270: Updating Support Skills from Microsoft Windows 4.0 to the Windows Server 2003 Family
   - Module 16: Implementing Disaster Protection
3. Disaster Recovery Whitepaper: `http://www.microsoft.com/technet/treeview/default.asp?url=/technet/prodtechnol/windowsserver2003/proddocs/deployguide/sdcbc_sto_gqda.asp`
4. Shadow Copy Whitepaper: `http://www.microsoft.com/windowsserver2003/docs/SCR.doc`
5. Non-Microsoft Resources:
   - Boswell, William. *Inside Windows Server 2003*. New Riders, 2003. ISBN 0735711585.
   - Matthews, Marty. *Windows Server 2003: A Beginners Guide*. McGraw-Hill, 2003. ISBN 0072193093.
   - Minasi, Mark, et al. *Mark Minasi's Windows XP and Server 2003 Resource Kit*. Sybex, 2003. ISBN 0782140807.
   - Minasi, Mark, et al. *Mastering Windows Server 2003 Server*. Sybex, 2003. ISBN 0782141307.
   - Shapiro, Jeffrey, et al. *Windows Server 2003 Bible*. John Wiley & Sons, 2003. ISBN 0764549375.

PART 

Final Review

Fast Facts

Practice Exam

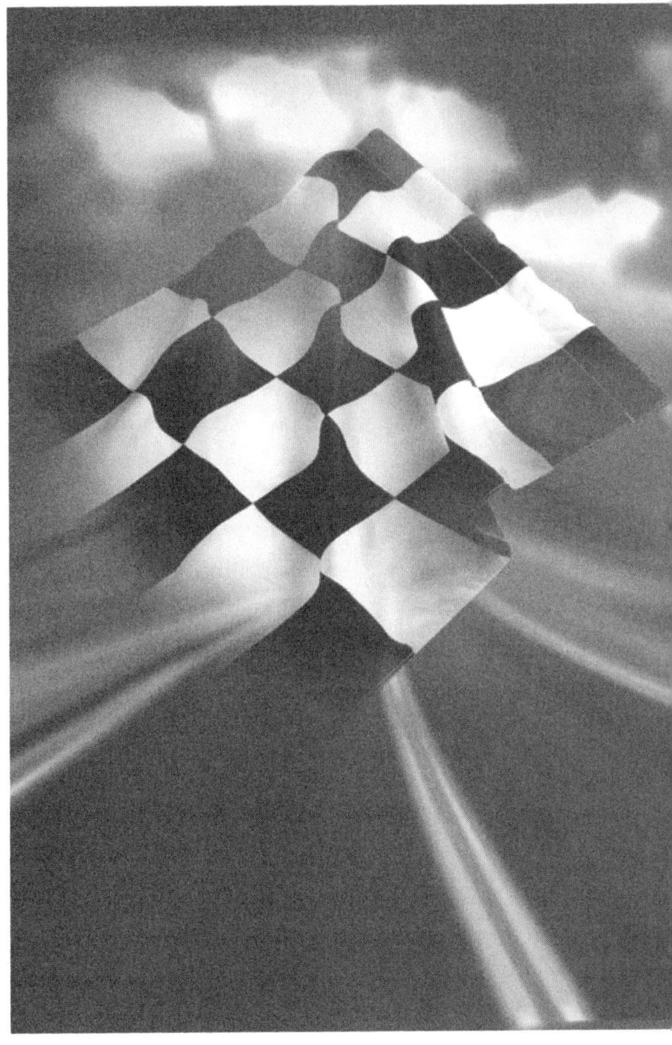

Fast Facts

70-290

The preceding chapters in this book covered the objectives for exam 70-290: Managing and Maintaining a Windows Server 2003 Environment. Hopefully, you took the time not only to read through the study material but also to work through the exercises. After working through this material a few times, you should be ready to tackle the exam.

This final chapter is intended to provide the material that you look through just before you go into the testing center. Organized by chapter topic, this review covers the most important points you will need to be familiar with for the exam.

MANAGING SERVER STORAGE DEVICES

The first chapter of this book covered the disk subsystem and working with the file systems that are supported in Windows Server 2003.

Managing Basic Disks and Dynamic Disks

Windows Server 2003 supports two types of physical disk configurations: basic and dynamic. A single physical disk must be one type or the other; however, you can intermingle the physical disk types in a multiple-disk server.

Basic Disks

When a new disk is installed in Windows Server 2003, it is installed as a basic disk. The basic disk type has been used in all versions of Microsoft Windows since version 1.0, OS/2, and MS-DOS. This allows a basic disk created in Windows Server 2003 to be recognized by these earlier operating systems. A basic disk splits a physical disk into units called *partitions.* Partitions allow you to subdivide your physical disk into separate units of storage. There are two types of partitions: primary and extended. On a single physical hard disk you can have up to four primary partitions, or three primary partitions and an extended partition. The basic disk is the only type supported in versions of Windows prior to Windows 2000.

Dynamic Disks

Dynamic disks were first introduced in Windows 2000 and are the preferred disk type for Windows Server 2003. Unlike a basic disk, a dynamic disk is divided into volumes instead of partitions. Although a clean installation of Windows Server 2003 will create a basic disk by default, any additional disks can be added as basic or dynamic disks. In addition, after the initial installation, the basic disk can be converted to a dynamic disk.

Unlike basic disks, which use the original MS-DOS–style master boot record (MBR) partition tables to store primary and logical disk-partitioning information, dynamic disks use a private region of the disk to maintain a *Logical Disk Manager (LDM)* database, which contains the volume types, offsets, memberships, and drive letters of the volumes on that physical disk.

The following are the five types of volumes available using dynamic storage disks:

- **Simple volumes**—Simple volumes are similar to a basic storage partition.
- **Spanned volumes**—Spanned volumes can take various amounts of disk space, from 2 to 32 physical disks, to create one large volume. Spanned volumes provide no fault tolerance. Actually, they can be more prone to failure than other types of volumes because if any disk should fail, the entire set is lost. The advantage of using spanned volumes is that you can quickly add more storage space without adding additional drive letters.
- **Striped volumes**—Striped volumes write data to physical disks (from 2 to 32) in 64KB sequential stripes. The first stripe is written to the first disk, the second stripe is written to the second disk, and so forth. Striped volumes, also known as *RAID-0,* provide no fault tolerance. The advantage provided by striped volumes lies in the overall disk I/O performance increase of the computer as the total disk I/O is split among all the disks in the volume.
- **RAID-1 volumes (mirrored volumes)**—RAID-1 volumes, also known as *mirrored volumes,* provide fault-tolerant data storage using two physical disks. Data is written simultaneously to each physical disk so that they all contain identical information. If one of the drives in a mirrored volume fails, the system will continue to run using the other volume(s). The total volume capacity will be equal to that provided by one of the physical disks.
- **RAID-5 volumes**—RAID-5 volumes are similar to striped volumes in that they use multiple disks—in this case, from 3 to 32 physical disks—of the same size. The total volume capacity will be equal to that provided by the number of physical disks minus one. Data is written sequentially across each physical disk and contains both data and parity information. For example, if you create a volume using four 1GB disks, your usable storage would be 3GB because 1GB is devoted to storing the parity information.

The parity information from the set is used to rebuild the set should one disk fail, thus providing fault tolerance. RAID-5 volumes in Windows Server 2003 cannot sustain the loss of more than one disk in the set while still providing fault tolerance.

Unlike Windows NT 4.0, Windows Server 2003 does not support the creation or use of any of these configurations on a basic disk. If any of these volumes are present on a basic disk in a server that is upgraded to Windows Server 2003, or are added after Windows Server 2003 is installed, they will no longer be accessible.

File Systems

Two main file systems are recognized by Windows Server 2003:

- **File Allocation Table (FAT)**—Windows Server 2003 is able to read partitions formatted in two versions of FAT: the 16-bit version (FAT16), supported by early versions of MS-DOS, and the 32-bit version (FAT32), first introduced with Windows 95 OEM Service Release 2 (OSR2). For FAT16 partitions, the maximum size is 4GB. In theory, FAT32 partitions support a maximum size of 2,047GB. However, there is a 32GB limitation on creating FAT32 partitions in Windows Server 2003.
- **The NT File System (NTFS)**—NTFS is designed to provide a high-performance, secure file system for Windows Server 2003. It also supports selective file, folder, and volume compression or encryption and auditing. In addition, NTFS supports security assigned at the file, folder, or volume level.

NTFS Compression

Native file and folder compression is one of the many benefits of using NTFS. NTFS compression and EFS encryption are mutually exclusive. That is, you cannot both compress and encrypt a file or folder at the same time. Because NTFS compression is a property of a file, folder, or volume, you can have uncompressed files on a compressed volume or a compressed file in an uncompressed folder.

In addition, several rules apply when you move or copy compressed files and folders. The possible outcomes of moving or copying NTFS-compressed files or folders are as follows:

- Moving an uncompressed file or folder to another folder on the same NTFS volume results in the file or folder remaining uncompressed, regardless of the compression state of the target folder.
- Moving a compressed file or folder to another folder results in the file or folder remaining compressed after the move, regardless of the compression state of the target folder.
- Copying a file to a folder causes the file to take on the compression state of the target folder.
- Overwriting a file of the same name causes the copied file to take on the compression state of the target file, regardless of the compression state of the target folder.
- Copying a file from a FAT folder to an NTFS folder results in the file taking on the compression state of the target folder.
- Copying a file from an NTFS folder to a FAT folder results in all NTFS-specific properties being lost.

Managing and Troubleshooting Hardware Devices

A *device driver* is a program that passes requests between the operating system and the device.

Windows File Protection

Device drivers and other system files are automatically protected against improper replacement by the Windows File Protection facility. This facility runs in the background (invisible to the user and the administrator) and is alerted whenever a file in a protected folder is changed. It determines whether the new version of the file is signed. If it isn't, Windows File Protection automatically rolls back the file to the version kept in the `%systemsroot%\system32\dllcache` folder. If the desired version of the file is not in the `dllcache` folder, Windows File Protection asks for the Windows Server 2003 CD-ROM to be mounted and then copies the file from there.

An administrator can run the System File Checker (`SFC.EXE`) to explicitly schedule a scan of the system files either immediately, at the next reboot, or at every reboot. Also, if the `dllcache` folder is corrupted or needs to be repopulated for some other reason, the administrator can run the System File Checker with the `/purgecache` switch to cause the folder to be emptied and reloaded.

Resource Settings

Resource settings are mechanisms by which a device can communicate with other hardware or the operating system. The following list details the four types of resources:

- **Direct memory access (DMA)**—Allows a device to read from the computer's memory, or to write to it, without using the computer's processor (CPU). Each device using DMA must have a DMA channel dedicated for its use.
- **Interrupt request line (IRQ)**—A hardware channel line over which a device can interrupt the CPU for service. Some devices can share an IRQ line; others must have a dedicated IRQ.
- **Input/output (I/O) port**—Another channel through which data is transferred between a device and the CPU. It acts like an area of memory that can be read from, and written to, by the device and the CPU. I/O ports cannot be shared.
- **Memory address**—An area of memory allocated to the device driver for communication between the device and the operating system.

If two devices attempt to use the same resources, and the particular resource is not sharable, one or both of the devices may be unusable.

Some older devices, such as most Industry Standard Architecture (ISA) bus expansion cards, cannot share resources, however. And many of them, even with a Plug and Play driver, cannot have their resource settings configured by the operating system.

Driver Signing

Microsoft has provisions in Windows Server 2003 for confirming that device drivers have passed a certain level of testing and that they have not been changed since the testing was accomplished. This is done by including a digital signature in the device driver that combines Microsoft's software-signing certificate and a digest of the code that implements the driver. Signed driver files are distributed through the following methods and can be found on the Windows Server 2003 CD-ROM:

- Windows service packs
- Hotfix distributions
- Operating system upgrades
- Windows Update

For the greatest device driver security, many administrators want to ensure that only signed device drivers are loaded. To achieve this, Windows Server 2003 can be configured to refuse to load unsigned drivers.

MANAGING USERS, COMPUTERS, AND GROUPS

Here are some points to remember about user accounts:

- Every user account is assigned a unique Security Identifier (SID).
- SIDs are never reused.
- An account can be renamed without losing any of the permissions assigned to it because the SID doesn't change.
- User, computer, and group accounts are created and managed using the Active Directory Users and Computers MMC.
- Local users and groups are created using the Local Users and Groups snap-in.
- `csvde` and `ldifde` can be used to import and export users and groups.

Password Complexity

Password complexity is determined by the domain account policies. If enabled, this policy requires that passwords meet the following minimum requirements:

- They must not contain all or part of the user's account name.
- They must be at least six characters in length.
- They must contain characters from three of the following four categories:
    - English uppercase characters (*A* through *Z*)
    - English lowercase characters (*a* through *z*)
    - Base-10 digits (0 through 9)
    - Nonalphabetic characters (such as !, $, #, %)

Managing Local, Roaming, and Mandatory User Profiles

The settings for a user's work environment are stored in a file known as the *user profile.* This file is automatically created the first time a user logs on to a computer running any version of Windows, and any changes to the environment (Favorites, Start menu items, icons, colors, My Documents, Local Settings, and so on) are saved when the user logs off. The profile is reloaded when the user logs on again. Summary Table 1 lists the components of a user profile (from Windows Server 2003 Help and Support):

SUMMARY TABLE 1

USER PROFILE FOLDERS AND THEIR CONTENTS

User Profile Folder	*Contents*
Application Data	Program-specific data (for example, a custom dictionary). Program vendors decide what data to store in this user profile folder.
Cookies	User information and preferences.
Desktop	Desktop items, including files, shortcuts, and folders.
Favorites	Shortcuts to favorite locations on the Internet.
Local Settings	Application data, history, and temporary files. Application data roams with the user by way of roaming user profiles.
My Documents	User documents and subfolders.
My Recent Documents	Shortcuts to the most recently used documents and accessed folders.
NetHood	Shortcuts to My Network Places items.
PrintHood	Shortcuts to printer folder items.
SendTo	Shortcuts to document-handling utilities.
Start Menu	Shortcuts to program items.
Templates	User template items.

The user profiles facility allows several people to use the same computer running Windows and each to see his or her own desktop. There are three types of user profiles:

- **Local profile**—This profile exists only on the computer where it was created.
- **Roaming profile**—This profile is stored on a file share so that the user will see the same desktop no matter where he or she is logged on.
- **Mandatory profile**—This profile is typically created for a group of users. After the profile is configured as desired, it is renamed `NTUser.dat`. All users will have the same desktop, and the profile cannot be changed.

The Four Domain Functionality Levels

The default domain functionality level of a domain installed on a new Windows Server 2003 machine is Windows 2000 mixed (which was called "mixed mode" in Windows 2000). At this level, a domain can contain domain controllers on computers running Windows NT, Windows 2000, or Windows Server 2003.

Once you have removed all Windows NT domain controllers from the domain, you can increase the domain functionality level to Windows 2000 native or to Windows Server 2003. At the Windows 2000 native level, you get the improved group capabilities of Active Directory as delivered in Windows 2000, such as the ability to "nest" groups and the availability of groups of Universal scope.

The most advanced level of domain functionality is the Windows Server 2003 level. Only domains where there are no Windows 2000 or Windows NT domain controllers can be raised to this level of domain functionality.

A fourth level of domain functionality is known as *Windows Server 2003 interim.* Both Windows NT and Windows Server 2003 domain controllers can exist in a domain at this level. As with the Windows 2000 mixed level, enhanced group functionality cannot be used!

Group Types

The two types of groups are as follows:

- **Distribution**—Used for email distribution lists only. Cannot be used to assign permissions for resource access.
- **Security**—Used for the assignment of permissions for resource access and for email distribution.

Group Scope

A way of classifying a group is by defining its *scope.* This means determining what locations the members can come from and where the resources can be located that the group can be granted access permissions to. In Summary Table 2, the first column lists the scope of the group object (Domain Local, Global, or Universal), the second column lists the object types that can be members of this kind of group, and the third column lists the locations of the resources that a group can be given access to.

Note that in several cases, the characteristics of the group object differ depending on the functionality of the domain.

SUMMARY TABLE 2

GROUP SCOPES AND APPLICABLE MEMBERS AND RIGHTS

Scope	*Can Include*	*Can Be Granted Access to Resources In...*
Domain Local	Accounts, Global groups, and Universal groups from any domain and, in Windows 2000 native or Windows Server 2003 functionality level domains, other Domain Local groups from the same domain as the group object.	The local domain
Global	In domains at the Windows 2000 mixed level or at the Windows Server 2003 interim level, only accounts from the same domain as the group object. In Windows 2000 native or Windows Server 2003 functional level domains, accounts and other global groups from the same domain as the group object.	Any domain in the forest and any domain in any other forest that trusts the local domain
Universal	(Not available in domains at the Windows 2000 mixed level or the Windows Server 2003 interim level.) Accounts, Global groups, and Universal groups from any domain.	Any domain in the forest and any domainin any other forestthat trusts the local domain

In larger networks, the recommended usage of groups is this:

- Make accounts members of Global groups.
- Make Global groups members of Domain Local groups.
- Assign resource access permissions to the Domain Local groups.

MANAGING AND MAINTAINING ACCESS TO RESOURCES

The process of working with share and NTFS permissions has always been a major focus on Microsoft exams. Make sure you have a complete understanding of how the different permissions are applied when you access a folder over the network versus accessing it from the server console.

Managing File System Permissions

Permissions define the type of access that is granted to a user or group for an object such as a file, folder, or share. Permissions can be assigned to local users or groups, or if the server is a member of a domain, permissions can be assigned to any user or group that is trusted by that domain.

If you are sitting at the server or workstation console, only the NTFS file and folder access permissions apply. However, if you are trying to access the files across the network via a shared folder, both the file and the share permissions will apply.

NTFS Permissions

NTFS permissions can be granted to either users or groups. By default, the Administrators group can assign permissions to all files and folders on a server.

The following permissions apply to a file:

- **Read**—This permission allows you to read the contents of a file and its attributes, including file ownership and assigned permissions.
- **Read & Execute**—This permission includes all the Read permissions in addition to the ability to run applications.
- **Write**—This permission includes all the Read permissions in addition to the ability to overwrite the file and change its attributes.
- **Modify**—This permission includes all the Read & Execute and the Write permissions in addition to the ability to modify and delete the file.
- **Full Control**—This permission includes all the Modify permissions in addition to allowing you to take ownership of a file and configure the permissions to it.

The following permissions apply to a folder and to the files and subfolders contained in that folder:

- **Read**—This permission allows you to read the contents of a folder and its attributes, including ownership and assigned permissions.
- **Read & Execute**—This permission includes all the Read permissions in addition to the ability to run applications.
- **Write**—This permission includes all the Read permissions in addition to the ability to create new files and subfolders and change the folder's attributes.
- **Modify**—This permission includes all the Read & Execute and the Write permissions in addition to the ability to modify and delete the folder.
- **Full Control**—This permission includes all the Modify permissions in addition to allowing you to take ownership of a folder and configure the permissions to it.

The creator or owner of a file or folder will automatically have the Full Control permission for that object. In addition to the basic permissions, NTFS also allows you to assign more granular special permissions. Special permissions are generally a subset of the basic NTFS permissions. This allows you to limit access to a file or folder to specific tasks. Special permissions apply to both files and folders. The owner of a file or folder will always have the right to modify permissions.

By default, when you assign file and folder permissions, these permissions are automatically applied to the files and folders underneath them in the hierarchy. This means that any permissions applied at the root of an NTFS drive will flow down to files and folders at the lowest level, unless the inheritance has been removed. In addition, if you create a file or folder in an existing folder, the permissions in effect for that folder will apply to the new objects.

Here are a few key points to remember about inherited permissions:

- Inherited Deny permissions will be overridden by an explicit Allow permission.
- Explicit permissions will always take precedence over inherited permissions.

NTFS file and folder permissions are *cumulative.* This means that the effective permissions will be a combination of the permissions granted to the user and those permissions granted to any group the user is a member of. The exception to this is Deny Access, which overrules everything else.

Several rules apply when you move or copy NTFS files and folders. The possible outcomes of moving or copying NTFS files or folders are as follows:

- Moving a file or folder to another folder on the same NTFS volume results in the file or folder retaining its permissions, regardless of the permissions configured on the target folder.
- Moving a file or folder to a different NTFS volume results in the file or folder assuming the permissions of the target folder.
- Moving a file or folder from a FAT volume to an NTFS volume results in the file or folder assuming the permissions of the target folder.
- Moving a file or folder from an NTFS volume to a FAT volume results in all NTFS-specific properties being lost.
- Copying a file to another folder on the same NTFS volume results in the file assuming the permissions of the target folder.
- Copying a file or folder to a different NTFS volume results in the file or folder assuming the permissions of the target folder.
- Copying a file or folder from a FAT volume to an NTFS volume results in the file assuming the permissions of the target folder.
- Copying a file or folder from an NTFS volume to a FAT volume results in all NTFS-specific properties being lost.

Share Permissions

Share permissions apply only when a file or folder is accessed over the network through a shared folder. When a folder is shared, by default the Everyone group is granted Read access. Only members of the Administrators, Server Operators, and Power Users group are permitted to share folders. Only three permissions are allowed for a shared folder:

- Read
- Change
- Full Control

When you're accessing the contents of a shared folder on an NTFS volume, the effective permission for the object is a combination of the share and NTFS permissions applied to the object. The effective permission will always be the most restrictive.

Encrypting File System (EFS)

Encrypting File System (EFS) is similar to NTFS compression in that it allows the user to selectively encrypt files and folders as desired. After a file is encrypted, all file operations continue transparently for the user who performed the encryption. However, unauthorized users cannot access the files. NTFS compression and EFS encryption are mutually exclusive. That is, you cannot both compress and encrypt a file or folder at the same time. Here are some additional points to keep in mind:

- Only files and folders on NTFS volumes can be encrypted.
- If a folder is encrypted, all files and folders contained in that folder will be automatically encrypted.
- Encrypted files will be unencrypted when they are moved or copied to a non-NTFS volume.
- Moving or copying encrypted files to an unencrypted folder on an NTFS volume will not decrypt them.
- A recovery agent is an authorized individual who is able to decrypt data in the event that the original certificate is unavailable, such as when an employee leaves the company.
- A recovery agent can be any user assigned that role.

Terminal Services Fundamentals

Windows Terminal Services is designed to distribute the Windows 32-bit desktop to clients that are usually not able to run it. Although at the client it appears that the application is running locally, all processing is actually occurring on the server. The only processing that occurs at the client involves displaying the user interface and accepting input from the keyboard and mouse. Terminal Services consists of three major components:

- **Multiuser server core**—This is a modified version of the Windows Server 2003 kernel that allows the operating system to support multiple concurrent users and share resources.
- **Client software**—The Remote Desktop Connection (RDC) client software provides the user interface. It can be installed on a PC, Windows terminal, or handheld device. It provides the look and feel of the standard Windows interface.
- **Remote Desktop Protocol (RDP)**—This is the protocol that provides communication between the server and the client software. It runs only on TCP/IP.

Terminal Services is available in two modes: Remote Desktop for Administration (formerly called *Remote Administration mode*) and Application Server mode. Remote Desktop for Administration mode is used to provide remote server management. Unlike in Windows 2000, where the Remote Administration mode was an option, the Remote Desktop for Administration mode is automatically installed in Windows Server 2003. However, incoming connections are disabled by default. With Windows Server 2003 Terminal Services in Remote Desktop for Administration mode, you are allowed two concurrent sessions, plus a console session to the Windows server.

Application Server mode requires that each remote connection have a Windows Server 2003 Terminal Services user or device Client Access License (TS CAL). These licenses are separate from the normal Windows Client Access Licenses (CALs) and must be installed and managed using a Terminal Services licensing server. If a license is not installed within 90 days, the client will no longer be able to access the server.

Two types of Terminal Services licensing servers are built in to Windows Server 2003:

- **Enterprise License server**—An Enterprise License server should be used when you have Windows Server 2003 Terminal Services servers located in several domains. This is the default.
- **Domain License server**—A Domain License server is used if you want to segregate licensing by domain, or if you're supporting a Windows NT 4.0 domain or a workgroup.

To install applications on a Terminal Services server in Application Server mode, you must be in Install mode. This can be accomplished by installing programs via the Add/Remove Programs applet in the Control Panel or via the Change User command. When you're connecting via the RDC client, the following resources can be mapped between the server and the client session:

- Client drives
- Client printers
- Clipboard
- Printers
- Serial ports
- Sound

MANAGING AND TROUBLESHOOTING SERVERS

In this section, the tools used to manage a Windows Server 2003 server are covered, with an emphasis on remote tools. In addition, IIS 6.0 and the Software Update Services are summarized.

Remote Assistance

In a Remote Assistance session, you can grant a remote user the ability to observe your desktop as you are working. You can exchange messages via a chat session, or you can talk to each other if you both have the required sound cards and microphones. You can even grant a remote user the ability to take over your desktop to make changes and run programs. After enabling Remote Assistance, you must issue an invitation before anyone can connect to your machine. This invitation can be sent to the other user via one of the following methods:

- Windows Messenger (the preferred method)
- Email
- Disk

If you are accessing a Remote Assistance computer that is behind a firewall, port 3389 must be open.

Internet Information Services (IIS)

IIS is no longer installed as a default component. In addition, even after it is installed, it will present only static pages. If your Web site requires the use of ASP or other dynamic content, you must manually enable the support for each feature.

In addition, during an upgrade from a previous version of Windows, IIS will be installed; however, the service will be disabled, and you must start it manually.

IIS 6.0 allows you to run your Web applications in either of two different modes:

- IIS 5.0 Isolation Mode
- Worker Process Isolation Mode

IIS 5.0 Isolation Mode is used to run older IIS 5.0–compatible applications that will not run natively in IIS 6.0. By default, a Web server that is upgraded from a previous version of IIS will be enabled in IIS 5.0 Isolation Mode.

In Worker Process Isolation Mode, applications and processes can be separated into *application pools*, which are sets of one or more applications assigned to a set of one or more worker processes. An application pool can contain Web sites, applications, and virtual directories. Each application pool is isolated from the others. Because of this, a failure or memory leak will affect only the processes running in that application pool and will have no effect on any of the other functions in other application pools.

In Windows Server 2003, you can either run in IIS 5.0 Isolation Mode or Worker Process Isolation Mode, but not both simultaneously on the same server. IIS 6.0 can be managed via the following four methods:

- The IIS Manager MMC
- Administration scripting
- Manually editing the configuration file
- The Remote Administration Web site

IIS Metabase

The IIS Metabase is used to store most configuration information for IIS. The Metabase can be backed up using the IIS Manager MMC. The backup is stored in the `%systemroot%\system32\inetsrv\` folder. By default, IIS will keep the last 10 Metabase backups; these previous backups are stored in the `%systemroot%\system32\inetsrv\history` folder. To restore the IIS Metabase, select Backup, Restore Configuration from the IIS Manager MMC. The backups will be displayed by filename as well as by the date and time they were backed up.

Virtual Servers

When you're hosting multiple Web sites on a single server, each Web site must have a unique identity. This is accomplished by using the following identifiers:

- **Unique IP address**—Commonly used for Web sites accessed over the Internet. Required when Secure Sockets Layer (SSL) is being used.
- **Host header name**—Commonly used over both the Internet and intranets.
- **TCP port number**—Rarely used on production Web servers.

When using multiple IP addresses to identify the Web sites on your server, you can either install multiple network interface cards (NICs), each with a unique IP address, or just assign multiple IP addresses to a single NIC.

Authentication Mechanisms

Authenticated access is used to integrate the Web server with Windows security. The user is required to present a user ID and password to access Web site resources. These user IDs and passwords are stored either as local accounts on the Web server or in the Active Directory domain database. When anonymous access is disabled, all users who attempt to access the Web site will be prompted for a user ID and password. Authentication is also required when the Web site resources are protected via NTFS permissions.

Four types of authenticated access are available:

- **Integrated Windows authentication**—If the Web server and the client are members of trusted domains, the browser will pass the user ID and password to the Web server automatically and the user will not be prompted for a password. This method does not work through some firewalls but is fine for intranets. The password is transmitted as a hash value.
- **Digest authentication**—This method is supported only if the client is using Internet Explorer 5 or later, in an Active Directory domain, and the password must be stored in clear text. However, this method will work through most firewalls. The password is transmitted as an MD5 hash value.
- **Basic authentication**—This is the least-secure method because it transmits the password as clear text. However, it is supported by just about any browser available. Basic authentication is usually used in combination with SSL so that the passwords are encrypted.

- **.NET Passport authentication**—This is a new feature in Windows Server 2003. This method uses the Passport authentication system that Microsoft is marketing to e-commerce Web sites. It allows a user to create a single sign-on that is honored across various Passport-enabled sites. Authentication is performed by a central Passport authentication server. When Passport authentication is selected, a default domain must be specified.

Software Update Services

Microsoft Software Update Services (SUS) can be installed on an internal Windows 2000 or Windows Server 2003 server that can download all critical updates as they are posted to Windows Update. Administrators can also receive email notification when new critical updates have been posted.

The client computers and servers can be configured through Group Policy or the Registry to contact the internal SUS server for updates, instead of going out over the Internet to the Microsoft servers. The SUS clients can be configured to point to a specific SUS server. This way, in a WAN environment, they will always receive updates from the server that is closest to them. The client is configured to often check its local SUS server for updates. Older versions of the Automatic Update client do not support SUS. The correct version is included with the following:

- Windows XP Service Pack 1 or later
- Windows 2000 Service Pack 3 or later
- All versions of Windows Server 2003

Monitoring and Optimizing Server Performance

This section summarizes the tools and procedures used to monitor and optimize the performance of a Windows Server 2003 server. Items covered include Task Manager, Performance Monitor, Event Viewer, and System Monitor.

Event Viewer

The Event Viewer is used to view event log files that are updated by the operating system and various services and applications running on your server. Typically, events will be written to the logs for any significant occurrence that a user or administrator should be aware of. All Windows Server 2003 systems have at the very least these three logs:

- **The System log file**—Records events related to system operation, most often associated with device drivers and services such as DHCP or WINS. Most of the information you will find here is related to the stopping and starting of services or the failure of a system component.
- **The Application log file**—Records events related to applications, programs, and utilities, usually not native Windows Server 2003 components. Examples are database programs, email servers, and print messages. The information that is recorded here is determined by the application developer, and it will usually consist of informational messages, errors, or warnings. This log is also used to store the alerts that are generated by the Performance Logs and Alerts tool.

- **The Security log file**—Records events related to security and auditing. Typical events include valid and invalid logon attempts and the accessing of resources, such as opening, reading, or deleting a file or folder. The types of events recorded in this log can be configured via the audit policy. In previous versions of Windows, the Security log would not record any information until an audit policy was enabled. In Windows Server 2003, security logging is enabled by default.

If the DNS service is installed on your server, the DNS log will be available. The DNS log file records events related to the operation of the DNS service. If you're having name-resolution problems on your network, this is the first place to look.

In addition, Active Directory domain controllers will have the following logs:

- **The Directory Service log file**—Records events related to the operation of the Active Directory service. Typical events you will see in this log are related to communication between domain controllers and Global Catalog servers.
- **The File Replication Service log file**—Records events related to the replication of the SYSVOL folder and the DFS tree.

Auditing

Auditing is the process of recording user and system activities on the network. These events are recorded in the Windows Server 2003 Security log, which is one of the logs contained in the Event log. When you configure auditing, you decide which events you wish to track and against what object. Typical activities that can be tracked are valid and invalid logon attempts, creating and opening files, and changes in user rights. A typical entry in the Security log will show the following:

- The time and date the event occurred
- The event performed
- The user account that performed the event
- The success or failure of the event

An audit policy is used to define the events that will be recorded in the Windows Server 2003 Security logs. Audit policies are created and applied similar to the other types of policies using the Group Policy snap-in. Auditing is turned on by default in Windows Server 2003.

Task Manager

The Task Manager can be used to monitor and manage the state of active applications, including a real-time view of the system resources assigned to each application. Task Manager also allows you to observe applications that have stopped responding, to increase or decrease their priority, and to terminate them.

Windows Server 2003 subdivides processing time to applications using different classes of priority levels. Priority levels are assigned numbers from 0 to 31. Applications and noncritical operating system functions are assigned levels of 0 to 15, whereas real-time functions such as the operating system kernel are assigned levels of 16 to 31. The normal base priority is 8.

Task Manager does not allow you to set a process to a specific number; it only allows you to set priority classes. The priority classes are as follows:

- **Realtime**—Priority 24
- **High**—Priority 13
- **AboveNormal**—Priority 9
- **Normal**—Priority 8
- **BelowNormal**—Priority 7
- **Low**—Priority 4

Performance Monitor

The Performance Monitor tool is actually made up of two separate Microsoft Management Console (MMC) snap-ins: System Monitor and Performance Logs and Alerts.

System Monitor

Each subsystem within Windows Server 2003 has more than one object that exists in System Monitor. Each object has several monitoring functions called *counters*. Each counter offers insight into a different aspect or function of the object. The System Monitor snap-in allows you to view real-time performance data contained in the counters from your system. In addition, System Monitor allows you to review performance data that is stored in a log file created with the Performance Logs and Alerts snap-in. Here's a list of the objects you need to monitor closely for performance issues:

- Memory
- Processor
- Physical disk
- Network

Performance Logs and Alerts

The Performance Logs and Alerts MMC snap-in allows you to log performance data over a period of time and save it to a log file for later viewing. Two logging options are available: Counter Logs and Trace Logs. Counter logs allow you to record data about hardware usage and the activity of system services from local or remote computers. You can configure logging to occur manually or automatically based on a defined schedule. Trace logs record data as a certain activity, such as disk I/O or a page fault, occurs. When the event occurs, the provider sends the data to the log service. The log data can be saved in the following file formats:

- **Text file (CSV)**—Comma-delimited format, for import into spreadsheet or database programs.
- **Text file (TSV)**—Tab-delimited format, for import into spreadsheet or database programs.
- **Binary file**—This is the default for use with the System Monitor snap-in. Data is logged into this file until it reaches the maximum limit. The default maximum file size is 1MB, but this can be changed when you configure settings for the file from the Log Files tab of the Log Properties dialog box by clicking the Configure button.
- **Binary circular file**—Data is logged into this file until it reaches the maximum limit. Then the file is overwritten, starting at the beginning of the file. The default maximum file size is 1MB, but this can be changed when you configure settings for the file from the Log Files tab of the Log Properties dialog box by clicking the Configure button.
- **SQL**—Data is logged directly into an existing SQL database.

The Alerts container is used to define threshold alerts. These can be used with real-time measurements or with historical log files. An alert is issued when a specific counter crosses a defined threshold value. When this occurs, a trigger event is initiated. You can select several actions to be performed when an alert threshold is reached:

- **Log an entry in the application event log**—If a threshold is reached, Windows Server 2003 will create an entry in this log and you can view it in the Application event log found in the Event Viewer.
- **Send a network message to**—This allows you to send a message to a user or computer via the Messenger service.

- **Start performance data log**—This starts logging to a predefined counter log. This is useful if you are trying to see what happens to system performance when a specific event occurs.
- **Run this program**—This can be any program that can be run from a command line. For example, it might be a program that performs some type of system maintenance, such as compressing files.

Monitoring Memory Performance

Here are some counters to watch to monitor memory performance:

- **Memory: Cache Faults/sec**—This condition usually indicates an insufficient amount of RAM on your system. However, it can also be caused by running a combination of apps, such as running a read-intensive application at the same time as an application that is using an excessive amount of memory.
- **Memory: Page Faults/sec**—If this counter averages above 200 for low-end systems or above 600 for high-end systems, excess paging is occurring.
- **Memory: Available Bytes**—Less than 4MB indicates insufficient RAM on the system, thus causing the system to perform excessive paging.
- **Paging File: % Usage Peak**—If this number nears 100% during normal operations, the maximum size of your paging file is too small, and you probably need more RAM.

Monitoring Disk Performance

Unlike in previous versions of Windows, Windows Server 2003 enables the disk counters by default. Here are some key performance counters for the disk subsystem:

- **PhysicalDisk: Avg. Disk Queue Length**—The number of queued requests should not exceed the number of spindles in use, plus 2.
- **PhysicalDisk: % Disk Time**—It is not uncommon for this counter to regularly hit 100% on active servers. Sustained percentages of 90% or better, however, might indicate that a storage device is too slow. This usually is true when its Avg. Disk Queue Length counter is constantly above 2.
- **PhysicalDisk: Avg. Disk sec/Transfer**—Indicates the average time, in seconds, for a disk transfer.

Monitoring Processor Performance

To identify problems with the processor, you should monitor the following counters:

- **Processor: % Processor Time**—If this counter remains above 80% for an extended period, you should suspect a CPU bottleneck. (There will be an instance of this counter for each processor in a multiprocessor system.)
- **Processor: % Total Processor Time**—If this value remains consistently higher than 80%, at least one of your CPUs is a bottleneck.
- **System: Processor Queue Length**—A sustained value of 2 or higher for this counter indicates processor congestion.

Monitoring Network Performance

To identify performance problems with the network interface, you should monitor the following counters:

- **Network Interface: Bytes Total/sec**—If the highest observed average is less than 75% of the expected value, communication errors or slowdowns might be occurring that limit the NIC's rated speed.

- **Network Interface: Output Queue Length**—If this averages above 2, you are experiencing delays.
- **Network Interface: Packets/sec**—Sharp declines that occur while the queue length remains non-zero can indicate protocol-related or NIC-related problems.

Implementing and Monitoring Disk Quotas

Disk quotas provide a method of controlling the amount of space a user has access to on a file server. You can also use the disk quota feature to monitor the space in use by your users. Disk quotas are disabled by default. All events related to disk quotas are sent to the event logs. Here are some of the key points to remember about disk quotas:

- Disk quotas do not apply to members of the local Administrators account.
- The files contained on a volume converted from FAT to NTFS will not count against user quotas because they will initially be owned by the local administrator and will count against the administrator's quota. Files created or moved to the volume after the conversion has been completed are owned by the user.
- Disk quotas cannot be applied on a per-folder basis. They can only be applied on a per-volume basis.
- If a physical disk has multiple volumes, a quota must be applied separately to each volume.
- Disk usage is based on all files that the user creates, copies, or takes ownership of.
- File compression cannot be used to prevent a user from exceeding his or her quota. Disk quotas are based on the actual file size, not the compressed file size.
- Disk quotas affect the free size that an installed application will see during the installation process.
- Disk quotas can be enabled on local or network volumes and on removable drives formatted with NTFS.
- Disk quotas are not available on any volume or partition formatted using a version of Windows prior to Windows 2000. Disk quotas are available only on NTFS volumes or partitions formatted by Windows 2000 or later.

Managing and Monitoring Print Queues

Here are some key terms to remember print queues:

- **Print job**—The sequence of data and print device commands sent to the print device
- **Spooler**—The service that manages the documents that are waiting to be printed
- **Spool file**—The file that stores the print data while it's waiting to be printed
- **Print queue**—The list of print jobs currently in the spooler
- **Print server**—A computer, usually a Windows Server 2003 machine, that you install and share the print drivers on
- **Printer driver**—The software that enables the operating system to communicate to the printing device
- **Print device**—The physical printer
- **Local printer**—Any print device that is directly attached and controlled by the print server
- **Network printer**—Any print device that is directly attached to the network

Printer pooling is a form of load balancing in that two or more print devices are represented by a single virtual printer. The users send their print jobs to what looks like a single printer. The print server then queues the print jobs in the order that they were submitted. For printer pooling to work successfully, the following conditions must be met:

- **The printers must use the same print driver**—They don't all have to be the same exact model, just as long as they will give the same results using a common printer driver.
- **They must all be connected to the same print server**—This is because they have to share the same driver and print queue.
- **They should be located in close proximity to each other**—Because the user will have no way of knowing which printer the print job ends up on, it's best to have them all in the same room.

You can set up several logical printers connected to a single physical printer. Each logical printer can have slightly different configurations (but use the same print driver) and can be assigned to different people. For example, different users could be assigned different logical printers with different priorities. The priority sets the default importance of the print jobs in the queue. Priorities can be set from 1 to 99. The job assigned the highest number will be printed first. Summary Table 3 shows the given predefined roles:

SUMMARY TABLE 3

GROUP-SPECIFIC ROLES

Group	*Print*	*Manage Documents*	*Manage Printer*
Administrators	X	X	X
Creator Owner		X	
Everyone	X		
Power Users	X	X	X
Print Operators	X	X	X
Server Operators	X	X	X

MANAGING AND IMPLEMENTING DISASTER RECOVERY

This objective covers the tools and procedures necessary to back up and recover your server in the event of a disaster, either large or small.

Windows Backup

Windows Backup allows you to back up files and folders on FAT16, FAT32, and NTFS volumes. However, if you have backed-up data on an NTFS volume, restoring to either type of FAT volume will result in a loss of configured file and folder permissions, in addition to the loss of encryption and compression attributes.

To back up and restore a Windows Server 2003 server, you must be a member of the local Administrators or the Backup Operators group. If you are a member of the local Administrators or the Backup Operators group on a domain controller, you can back up and restore a file on any computer that is a member of the domain or has a two-way trust relationship with the domain. If you are not a member of either of these groups, you will only be able to back up the files you are the owner of or those you have at least Read permissions for.

Windows Server 2003 has five backup options, as detailed in the following list. Each type varies as to what is backed up and whether or not the archive bit is set. The *archive bit* is a file attribute that is turned on when a file is created or modified, and it is cleared whenever a file is successfully backed up. It is used to let the backup software know which files need to be backed up based on whether they have just been created or whether modifications to previously backed-up files have happened since the last backup.

Here's the list of backup options in Windows Server 2003:

- **Normal**—A normal backup (sometimes referred to as a *full backup*) is used to back up all the files and folders you select, regardless of the setting of the archive bit. It then changes the archive bit of the files to show that they were backed up.
- **Copy**—A copy backup is used to back up the desired files and folders. It does not read or change the archive bit.
- **Daily**—A daily backup is used to back up only the files and folders that have been created or modified on that day. It does not read or change the archive bit.
- **Differential**—A differential backup is used to back up only the files and folders that have been created or modified since the last normal or incremental backup. It does not change the archive bit. However, it reads the archive bit to determine which files need to be backed up.
- **Incremental**—An incremental backup is used to back up only the files and folders that have been created or modified since the last normal or incremental backup. It reads the archive bit to determine which files need to be backed up as well as clears the archive bit of the files that were backed up.

System State Backups

System State data is a collection of data that contains the operating system configuration of the server. For all Windows Server 2003 operating systems, the System State data includes the following:

- Registry
- COM+ Class Registration database
- System boot files
- The system files included in the Windows File Protection area

The System State data also includes the Certificate Services database (if the server is operating as a certificate server). If the server is a domain controller, the System State data also includes the Active Directory Services database and the SYSVOL directory. The System State will include the IIS Metabase or the Cluster Service configuration if these features are installed on the server. Due to their interdependencies, these components cannot be backed up or restored separately.

Restoring System State Data

Although you can't selectively back up components of the System State, you can restore the following System State components to an alternate location:

- Registry
- SYSVOL folder
- System boot files
- Cluster configuration (if installed)

The Active Directory, IIS Metabase, COM+ Class Registration and Certificate Services databases, and the Windows File Protection folder cannot be restored to an alternate location.

Volume Shadow Copy

By using Volume Shadow Copy with Windows Backup, you can back up most open files. When Volume Shadow Copy is used during a backup and an open file is encountered, a snapshot is taken of the file. This is an exact copy of the file, and it is saved to another area on the disk. This copy is then saved via the Backup utility.

Volume Shadow Copy offers the following advantages:

- Users cannot be locked out by the Backup program.
- Open files are not skipped.
- The backup procedure completes faster.
- Applications can write data to a file during a backup.
- Volume Shadow Copy eliminates the need for additional third-party software in most cases.
- Backups can be performed during business hours.

The Volume Shadow Copy Service (VSS) allows users to view the contents of shared folders, as they existed at specific points in time, and to restore a previous copy of a file. The Volume Shadow Copy feature works by setting aside a configurable amount of space, either on the same or a different volume. This space is used to save any changes to the files on the volume that Volume Shadow Copy is enabled on. These changes are added by making a block-level copy of any changes that have occurred to files since the last shadow copy. Only the changes are copied, not the entire file. As new shadow copies are added, the oldest one will be purged when you either run out of allocated space or the number of shadow copies reaches 64. The following guidelines apply:

- Volume Shadow Copy is enabled at the volume level.
- The minimum storage space you can allocate for shadow copies is 100MB.
- The storage space can be allocated on the same volume that Volume Shadow Copy is enabled on, or on another volume.
- The default storage size allocated will be 10% of the volume; however, you can increase the size at any time.
- When estimating the size to allocate, you must consider both the number and size of the files on the volume as well as how often they will be updated.
- Remember that when the storage limit is reached, the oldest shadow copies will be deleted.
- If you decide to store your shadow copies on another volume, the existing shadow copies will be deleted.
- The default configuration for shadow copies is for a scheduled update at 7:00 a.m. and 12:00 p.m. on weekdays.
- Using a separate volume to store shadow copies is highly recommended for heavily used file servers.
- Shadow copies will not work properly on dual-boot systems.

A Volume Shadow Copy client is required for Windows XP, Windows 2000 Professional, and Windows 98 users. The client is located in the `%systemroot%\system32\clients\twclient` folder on Windows Server 2003 systems.

Advanced Options Menu

The Advanced Options menu allows you to select from a variety of options that can be used to troubleshoot and repair server startup and driver problems. The following options are available on the Windows Server 2003 Advanced Options menu:

- **Safe Mode**—This option starts Windows Server 2003 with the basic drivers for the mouse, video, monitor, mass storage, and keyboard.
- **Safe Mode with Networking**—This option starts Windows Server 2003 with the basic drivers, plus the network drivers.
- **Safe Mode with Command Prompt**—This option starts Windows Server 2003 with the basic drivers and opens a command window instead of the desktop.
- **Enable Boot Logging**—This option starts Windows Server 2003 normally but logs a list of all the device drivers and services, along with their status, that the system attempts to load. This information is logged to `%systemroot%\ntblog.txt`.
- **Enable VGA Mode**—This option starts Windows Server 2003 normally but forces it to load the basic VGA driver.
- **Last Known Good Configuration**—This option starts Windows Server 2003 with the contents of the Registry from the last time the user logged on to the system.
- **Directory Services Restore Mode**—This option is used to restore the Active Directory database and SYSVOL folder on a domain controller. It will be listed only on a domain controller.
- **Debugging Mode**—This options starts Windows Server 2003 normally but sends debugging information over a serial cable to another computer.
- **Boot Normally**—This option bypasses the menu options and starts Windows Server 2003 without any modifications.

Unlike a normal logon, the Safe Mode options do not update the Last Known Good Configuration information. Therefore, it will still be an option if you try Safe Mode first.

Recovery Console

The Recovery Console is a DOS-like command-line interface in which you can perform a limited set of commands and start and stop system services. Unlike booting from a DOS disk, the Recovery Console allows you access to files on an NTFS-formatted volume.

The Recovery Console is not installed by default; you must install it manually after you have installed Windows Server 2003. It can also be run from the Windows Server 2003 CD-ROM. After you log on, the commands in Summary Table 4 are available:

SUMMARY TABLE 4

RECOVERY CONSOLE COMMANDS

Command	*Description*
`Attrib`	Changes the attributes of files and folders
`Batch`	Executes commands from a text file
`CD`	Changes the directory
`Chdir`	Changes the directory
`Chkdsk`	Repairs disk errors
`Cls`	Clears the screen
`Copy`	Copies files
`Del`	Deletes files
`Delete`	Deletes files
`Dir`	Displays a list of files and directories
`Disable`	Used to disable a service or driver
`Diskpart`	Used to manage partitions and volumes
`Enable`	Used to enable a service or driver
`Exit`	Closes the console and reboots the server
`Expand`	Extracts a file from the Windows CAB files or expands compressed files from the Windows Server 2003 CD-ROM

continues

SUMMARY TABLE 4 *continued*

RECOVERY CONSOLE COMMANDS

Command	*Description*
`Fixboot`	Writes a new boot sector
`Fixmbr`	Used to repair the master boot record
`Format`	Used to format a drive
`Help`	Lists the available commands
`Listsvc`	Lists the installed services and drivers
`Logon`	Logs on to the server
`Map`	Displays a list of local drive partitions and their mappings
`MD`	Creates a directory
`Mkdir`	Creates a directory
`More`	Displays the contents of a text file and pauses when the screen is full
`RD`	Used to delete a directory
`Ren`	Used to rename a file
`Rename`	Used to rename a file
`Rmdir`	Used to delete a directory
`Systemroot`	Sets the current directory to the systemroot
`Type`	Displays the contents of a text file and pauses when the screen is full

There are some limitations, however:

- You have access only to `%systemroot%` and its subfolders, the root partitions of `%systemdrive%`, any other partitions, floppy drives, and CD-ROMs.
- You cannot copy a file from the hard disk to a floppy, but you can copy a file from a floppy, a CD-ROM, or another hard disk to your hard disk.

Recovering System State Data by Using Directory Services Restore Mode

On a domain controller, the Active Directory files are restored as part of the System State. The System State on a domain controller consists of the following:

- Active Directory (NTDS)
- The boot files
- The COM+ Class Registration database
- The Registry
- The system volume (SYSVOL)
- Files in the Windows File Protection folder

The individual components cannot be backed up or restored separately; they can only be handled as a unit.

When Active Directory is in a corrupted state on all the domain controllers, it will be necessary to restore AD from tape and force the replication of the restored data to all the other domain controllers. This type of operation is called an *authoritative restore.* An authoritative restore will cause the data that is restored from tape to overwrite the corrupted data that is stored on all the domain controllers.

If only a single Active Directory object is accidentally deleted, it is possible to restore only that object from a backup tape by performing a partial authoritative restore.

To restore an object, you will need to know its common name (CN), the Organizational Unit (OU), and the domain (DC) the object was located in. First, boot into Directory Restore mode and start the `NTDSUtil` utility. For example, to restore the ABC St. Louis User OU, in the `abc.com` domain, you would enter the following command:

```
Restore Subtree "OU=ABC St. Louis User,DC=abc,DC=com"
```

Implementing Automated System Recovery (ASR)

Automated System Recovery (ASR) works by making a backup of the boot partition onto tape or other media. It then saves the catalog and other operating system information, such as System State and disk partition information, to a floppy disk.

When a problem occurs that cannot be fixed by using any of the other repair and recovery methods, or if you have replaced a failed boot drive, you will need to boot your server from the Windows Server 2003 CD-ROM and then insert the floppy disk and the backup media that was created by the ASR process.

ASR installs a generic version of Windows Server 2003 that is used to mount and restore your boot partition from the backup media created by ASR. This process not only restores the information on your boot drive, it also restores the disk signatures and re-creates the boot partition or volume, if necessary. It will not recover or delete any data volumes, however.

Practice Exam

This exam consists of 60 questions that reflect the material covered in the chapters and are representative of the types of questions you should expect to see on the actual exam.

The answers to these questions appear in their own section following the exam. It is strongly suggested that when you take this exam, you treat it just as you would an actual exam at the test center. Time yourself, read carefully, and answer all the questions to the best of your ability.

Most of the questions do not simply require you to recall facts but require deduction on your part to determine the best answer. Most questions require you to identify the best course of action to take in a given situation. Many of the questions are verbose, requiring you to read them carefully and thoroughly before you attempt to answer them. Run through the exam, and for questions you miss, review any material associated with them.

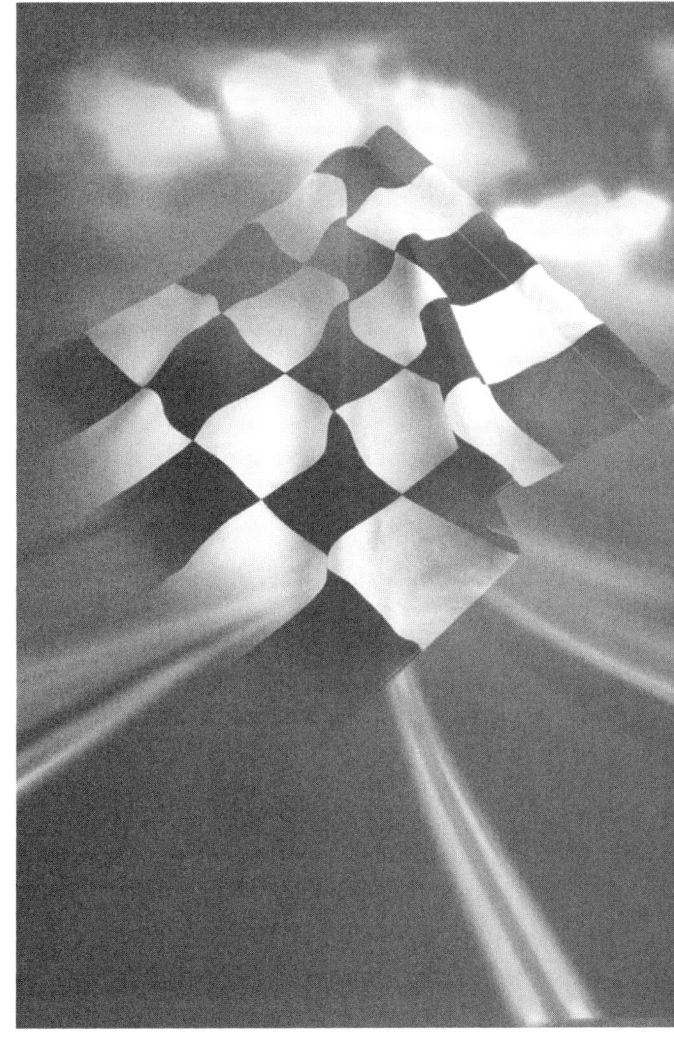

1. You are building a Windows Server 2003 server that is to be used as a database server for your company. Deciding that hardware RAID is the way to go, you purchase a new controller card that supports RAID-5. After you install the new card and start your server, the controller card does not appear in Device Manager. What do you need to do to get the hardware working correctly?

   A. Shut down the server, reinstall the device, and restart the server.

   B. Use the Add/Remove Programs applet in Control Panel to install the drivers for the controller card.

   C. Use the Add Hardware applet in Control Panel to install the controller card.

   D. Use the Device Manager utility to install the controller card.

2. You are the administrator of a network that has several Windows Server 2003 servers. When starting your mail server, you receive a blue screen. The Recovery Console was not preloaded. How will you boot to it?

   A. By using a PXE-capable NIC.

   B. From the Windows Server 2003 CD-ROM.

   C. From the Windows Server 2003 boot disks.

   D. It's not possible to boot to the Recovery Console if it's not preinstalled.

3. Mary has installed four disks on her Windows Server 2003 server that she wants to configure as a RAID-5 array. However, it doesn't seem to be working. What is the most likely cause of Mary's problem?

   A. The server hard disks are configured as dynamic disks.

   B. The server hard disks are configured as basic disks.

   C. The controller does not support a RAID-5 configuration.

   D. Mary was not made a member of the Enterprise Admins group.

4. You are the network administrator for a small manufacturing firm. Due to a downturn in the economy, you are unable to upgrade your servers, so you must make due with the hardware you currently own. You're running out of disk space on your file server. What steps can you take to keep the file server from becoming full?

   A. Enable disk quotas.

   B. Use the Disk Defragmenter to consolidate free space.

   C. Enable disk quotas and set warning limits.

   D. Enable disk quotas and enable limits.

5. Joe is the network administrator for a mid-sized network that consists of 20 Windows Server 2003 servers and 700 Windows XP workstations. As all good administrators should, he subscribes to several security newsletters. One day he receives a newsletter that tells him that Microsoft has just released an Internet Explorer security patch with a rating of critical. How can Joe get this patch applied to all of his servers and workstations in the least amount of time?

   A. Download the patch from Microsoft and apply it to all of his computers.

   B. Use Windows Update Services to apply the patch to his computers.

   C. Use the Software Update Service (SUS) to apply the patch to all his computers.

   D. Write code to apply the patch via a logon script.

6. You are a user at a small legal firm. While working with a small database, you attempt to save a file and are denied access because you are out of disk space. You check the NTFS disk quotas and see that you have 50MB of free space remaining, but your database file is only 40MB. What is the problem?

   A. You need to reconfigure the NTFS permissions.

   B. You need to reconfigure the disk quotas to give you more space.

   C. The disk is compressed.

   D. You have a virus.

7. You are the administrator of a small network. You have a Windows Server 2003 server that you suspect is going to need a memory upgrade. Which of the following tools allows you to see how much memory is being used by your applications? (Choose all correct answers.)

   A. System Monitor

   B. Performance Logs and Alerts

   C. Task Manager

   D. Performance Monitor

8. You have a Windows Server 2003 server that seems to be sluggish. Which of the following devices should you monitor closely? (Choose all correct answers.)

   A. Memory

   B. Video

   C. Application load time

   D. Processor

   E. Network interface card

9. You are the network administrator for a small advertising firm. Most of the data on your file servers consists of zipped graphics files. You're running out of disk space on your file server. What steps can you take to keep the file server from becoming full?

   A. Enable drive compression.

   B. Use the Disk Defragmenter to consolidate free space.

   C. Enable drive compression and set it to Maximum.

   D. Enable disk quotas and enable limits.

10. You are the only system administrator for your company. You have decided to take a long-overdue and well-deserved vacation. Before you go, you want to give one of your users the ability to run backups. To which groups should you add her user account to give her the proper permissions? (Choose all correct answers.)

    A. Server Operators

    B. Power Users

    C. Account Operators

    D. Administrators

    E. Backup Operators

11. You have just finished building a new Windows Server 2003 server. As part of your build checklist, you need to create an Emergency Repair Disk. What Windows Server 2003 utility should you use to create an Emergency Repair Disk?

    A. Rdisk

    B. MakeERD

    C. Windows Server 2003 Backup

    D. ERDclone

    E. None of the above

12. You are the administrator for Widgets, Inc. The Director of Information Security is extremely security conscious. She wants you to install all Microsoft security patches within 48 hours of their release to the Windows Update site. On which of the following clients can this be accomplished using SUS? (Choose all correct answers.)

    A. Windows Server 2003 servers

    B. Computers with Windows XP Service Pack 1

    C. Computers with Windows 2000 Service Pack 1

    D. Computers with Windows NT 4.0 Service Pack 6

13. Your Windows Server 2003 network consists of various client computers, including many Windows 95 and Windows 98 clients. You have a new application that runs only on Windows Server 2003 or Windows XP, to which all your users need access. What can you do to give all your users access to this new application quickly and relatively cheaply?

    A. Upgrade all your client machines to Windows XP and install the new software.

    B. Install a new server with Windows Server 2003 configured in Remote Administration mode, and install the application on the server.

    C. Install a new server with Windows Server 2003 configured in Application mode, and install the application on the server.

    D. None of the above.

14. You are the new junior administrator for a Windows Server 2003 server running IIS 6.0. The CIO is extremely security conscious. She wants you to view the audit logs daily. What utility do you use to view audit information?

    A. Audit Log Viewer

    B. Log Viewer

    C. Event Viewer

    D. Audit Viewer

    E. Event Audit Viewer

15. Mary is the lead administrator for a small manufacturing firm located in the Southeast. A user in one of the branch offices calls Mary and requests her help on a Windows XP problem. Mary attempts to assist the user over the telephone, but the user is having trouble describing what he is seeing on his screen. Which technologies in Windows Server 2003 or Windows XP can Mary use to fix this problem? (Choose all correct answers.)

    A. Remote Desktop for Administration

    B. Terminal Services

    C. Remote Assistance

    D. Remote Administrator

16. You have purchased new hardware and are moving a group of shared folders to a new Windows Server 2003 server. After moving the folders and their contents using Copy, you make the server available again to the users. Soon, your telephone rings with users complaining that they can't see the file shares. What steps must you perform to fix the problem?

    A. You need to reconfigure the NTFS permissions.

    B. You need to reconfigure the share permissions.

    C. You need to restart the Server service on the new server.

    D. You need to reshare the shares.

    E. You need to give the shares unique names.

17. You are installing a new network application that requires a configuration script to be run when a user logs on to the network. What is the best way to configure this for a Windows Server 2003–based network?

    A. Configure a startup script on the user's computer.

    B. Add a logon script entry to the user account configuration in Active Directory Users and Groups.

    C. Use Group Policy.

    D. Add a drive mapping to the user profile.

18. You are configuring a Windows NT workstation that you are going to use to manage your Windows Server 2003–based network. Which one of the following tools should you install on your workstation?

    A. The administration tools for Windows Server 2003

    B. The Active Directory Users and Groups MMC

    C. The Terminal Services client

    D. User Manager for Domains

19. You are the administrator for an engineering firm. The Director of Research is extremely security conscious. She wants you to set up a file share so that common users will not have access to it or be able to browse it. However, specified users in the Research department should be able to access it easily. In addition, various contractors will need to access the file share for limited periods of time.

    Required Result:

    Set up a secure file share for the Research department.

    Optional Desired Results:

    Common users should not have access to it.

    As contractors come and go, access to the share should be easily granted and denied.

    Proposed Solution:

    Create the engineering file share. Assign the specified user accounts the appropriate permissions. Delete any default permissions for any other user or group.

    Evaluation of Proposed Solution:

    Which result(s) does the proposed solution produce?

    A. The proposed solution produces the required result but neither of the optional results.

    B. The proposed solution produces the required result and one of the optional results.

    C. The proposed solution produces the required result and both the optional results.

    D. The proposed solution does not produce the required result.

20. You are the administrator for an engineering firm. The Director of Research is extremely security conscious. She wants you to set up a file share so that common users will not have access to it or be able to browse it. However, specified users in the Research department should be able to access it easily. In addition, various contractors will need to access the file share for limited periods of time.

    Required Result:

    Set up a secure file share for the Research department.

Optional Desired Results:

Common users should not have access to it.

As contractors come and go, access to the share should be easily granted and denied.

Proposed Solution:

Create the engineering file share. Create a group called SecureEng and assign it the appropriate permissions. Add the users to this group. Delete any default permissions for any other user or group.

Evaluation of Proposed Solution:

Which result(s) does the proposed solution produce?

A. The proposed solution produces the required result but neither of the optional results.

B. The proposed solution produces the required result and one of the optional results.

C. The proposed solution produces the required result and both the optional results.

D. The proposed solution does not produce the required result.

21. You have attached an external IrDA device on serial port 1 of your Windows Server 2003 server to communicate with a printer. What step should you take to install the device?

A. Install the drivers using Device Manager.

B. Use the Add Hardware Wizard to install the device.

C. Use the Add Printers applet.

D. Restart the server and let Plug and Play detect the device.

22. You are the administrator for a customer service department. This department is a heavy fax user, so you replace the existing fax card in the department's Windows Server 2003 server with one that has better features. While reading the installation instructions, you notice that they clearly state that no other fax devices or fax drivers can be present in the server.

Required Result:

Install a new fax card in the Customer Service Windows Server 2003 server.

Optional Desired Results:

There can be no other fax devices present in the server.

There can be no other fax drivers installed in the server.

Proposed Solution:

Shut down the server, remove the old fax card, and replace it with the new one. Restart the server and allow Plug and Play to recognize the new fax card and install the drivers.

Evaluation of Proposed Solution:

Which result(s) does the proposed solution produce?

A. The proposed solution produces the required result but neither of the optional results.

B. The proposed solution produces the required result and one of the optional results.

C. The proposed solution produces the required result and both the optional results.

D. The proposed solution does not produce the required result.

23. You are the administrator for a customer service department. This department is a heavy fax user, so you replace the existing fax card in the department's Windows Server 2003 server with one that has better features. While reading the installation instructions, you notice that they clearly state that no other fax devices or fax drivers can be present in the server.

    Required Result:

    Install a new fax card in the Customer Service Windows Server 2003 server.

    Optional Desired Results:

    There can be no other fax devices present in the server.

    There can be no other fax drivers installed in the server.

    Proposed Solution:

    Open Device Manager and remove the entries for the old fax card. Shut down the server, remove the old fax card, and replace it with the new one. Restart the server and allow Plug and Play to recognize the new fax card and install the drivers. Open Device Manager and check to make sure that there are no entries for the old card and that there are no unknown devices with the yellow question mark icon.

    Evaluation of Proposed Solution:

    Which result(s) does the proposed solution produce?

    A. The proposed solution produces the required result but neither of the optional results.

    B. The proposed solution produces the required result and one of the optional results.

    C. The proposed solution produces the required result and both the optional results.

    D. The proposed solution does not produce the required result.

24. You are the administrator for Merger, Inc. The specialty of your company is purchasing other companies and adding their resources to your company. You currently have 3,000 users distributed over 20 locations. Your company has purchased another company and wants the users in the new company to have user accounts on your Windows Server 2003 network. The new company is using a Windows 2000–based network.

    Required Result:

    Add the users from the new company to your Windows Server 2003 domain.

    Optional Desired Results:

    Modify the distinguished name field to reflect the fact that they are now part of Merger, Inc.

    Add the new users to the NewCompany group.

    Proposed Solution:

    Using the csvde utility, export the user accounts from the new company's Active Directory, make the necessary changes, import them into the Merger, Inc. directory, and then add them to the NewCompany group.

    Evaluation of Proposed Solution:

    Which result(s) does the proposed solution produce?

    A. The proposed solution produces the required result but neither of the optional results.

    B. The proposed solution produces the required result and one of the optional results.

C. The proposed solution produces the required result and both the optional results.

D. The proposed solution does not produce the required result.

25. You are the administrator for Merger, Inc. The specialty of your company is purchasing other companies and adding their resources to your company. You currently have 3,000 users distributed over 20 locations. Your company has purchased another company and wants the users in the new company to have user accounts on your Windows Server 2003 network. The new company is using a Windows 2000–based network.

Required Result:

Add the users from the new company to your Windows Server 2003 domain.

Optional Desired Results:

Modify the distinguished name field to reflect the fact that they are now part of Merger, Inc.

Add the new users to the NewCompany group.

Proposed Solution:

Using the ldifde utility, export the user accounts from the new company's Active Directory, make the necessary changes, import them into the Merger, Inc. directory, and then add them to the NewCompany group.

Evaluation of Proposed Solution:

Which result(s) does the proposed solution produce?

A. The proposed solution produces the required result but neither of the optional results.

B. The proposed solution produces the required result and one of the optional results.

C. The proposed solution produces the required result and both the optional results.

D. The proposed solution does not produce the required result.

26. You are the backup operator for NETPower, Inc. The specialty of your company is installing and maintaining UPS systems for mid-sized to large companies. You just upgraded to Windows Server 2003 from Windows NT 4.0, and you want to ensure that the proper files are backed up on your servers.

Required Result:

Back up all the files on your servers.

Optional Desired Results:

Back up the system state data.

Back up open files.

Proposed Solution:

Set up a backup procedure where Automated System Recovery is run every night.

Evaluation of Proposed Solution:

Which result(s) does the proposed solution produce?

A. The proposed solution produces the required result but neither of the optional results.

B. The proposed solution produces the required result and one of the optional results.

C. The proposed solution produces the required result and both the optional results.

D. The proposed solution does not produce the required result.

27. You are the backup operator for NETPower, Inc. The specialty of your company is installing and maintaining UPS systems for mid-sized to large companies. You just upgraded to Windows Server 2003 from Windows NT 4.0, and you want to ensure that the proper files are backed up on your servers.

    Required Result:

    Back up all the files on your servers.

    Optional Desired Results:

    Back up the system state data.

    Back up open files.

    Proposed Solution:

    Set up a backup procedure where a normal backup is run every night. Select the option to back up the system state data.

    Evaluation of Proposed Solution:

    Which result(s) does the proposed solution produce?

    A. The proposed solution produces the required result but neither of the optional results.

    B. The proposed solution produces the required result and one of the optional results.

    C. The proposed solution produces the required result and both the optional results.

    D. The proposed solution does not produce the required result.

28. After scheduling a normal backup to run on Sunday night, you want to only back up the files and folders that have changed the rest of the week. What type of backup should you perform on the other days of the week?

    A. Normal

    B. Daily

    C. Incremental

    D. Partial

29. You are working with your Windows Server 2003 server when you receive a blue screen. When you reboot your server you see the following message:

```
Windows cannot access the following registry key:

HKEY_LOCAL_MACHINE\System
```

    What can you do to recover from this error?

    A. Rebuild the server using Automated System Recovery (ASR).

    B. Go into Safe Mode, delete the SCSI driver, and reboot.

    C. Boot into the Recovery Console, delete the video driver, and reboot.

    D. Boot the server and select Last Known Good Configuration.

30. You are the administrator of a Windows Server 2003 Web farm for Widgets, Inc. The Director of Information Services is extremely price conscious. She has contracted with a local consulting firm to write various Web applications. However, although reasonably priced, this consulting company does not have a good reputation. Other customers have complained that the consulting company's apps keep crashing their Web servers. Unfortunately, she wants you to run the consulting company's applications on the same Web servers where you are currently running mission-critical Web applications.

    Required Result:

    Protect the mission-critical applications from other apps.

Optional Desired Results:

Implement the solution quickly.

Implement the solution without purchasing additional hardware.

Proposed Solution:

Move all the mission-critical applications to a specific group of servers. Segregate the new applications on their own servers.

Evaluation of Proposed Solution:

Which result(s) does the proposed solution produce?

A. The proposed solution produces the required result but neither of the optional results.

B. The proposed solution produces the required result and one of the optional results.

C. The proposed solution produces the required result and both the optional results.

D. The proposed solution does not produce the required result.

31. You are the administrator of a Windows Server 2003 Web farm for Widgets, Inc. The Director of Information Services is extremely price conscious. She has contracted with a local consulting firm to write various Web applications. However, although reasonably priced, this consulting company does not have a good reputation. Other customers have complained that the consulting company's apps keep crashing their Web servers. Unfortunately, she wants you to run the consulting company's applications on the same Web servers where you are currently running mission-critical Web applications.

Required Result:

Protect the mission-critical applications from other apps.

Optional Desired Results:

Implement the solution quickly.

Implement the solution without purchasing additional hardware.

Proposed Solution:

Segregate the new applications into their own application pool on each server.

Evaluation of Proposed Solution:

Which result(s) does the proposed solution produce?

A. The proposed solution produces the required result but neither of the optional results.

B. The proposed solution produces the required result and one of the optional results.

C. The proposed solution produces the required result and both the optional results.

D. The proposed solution does not produce the required result.

32. You are the proud owner of a Windows Server 2003 server. After you have installed your applications, you have decided to create a baseline of system performance. What is the best tool to use to accomplish this?

A. Performance Monitor

B. Performance Logs and Alerts

C. Task Manager

D. System Monitor

33. Your Windows Server 2003 server seems sluggish. You want to figure out what's wrong, so you run Performance Logs and Alerts and see the following averages:

Processor: % ProcessorTime: 50

System: Processor Queue Length: 1

Memory: Pages/sec: 10

PhysicalDisk: Avg. Disk Queue Length: 4

Paging File: % Usage: 25

What should you do to improve performance?

A. Add memory.

B. Add a faster processor.

C. Add a faster hard disk.

D. Replace the hard disk with a faster one.

34. Your Windows Server 2003 server seems sluggish. You want to figure out what's wrong, so you run Performance Logs and Alerts and see the following averages:

Processor: % ProcessorTime: 95

System: Processor Queue Length: 6

Memory: Pages/sec: 10

PhysicalDisk: Avg. Disk Queue Length: 2

Paging File: % Usage: 25

What should you do to improve performance?

A. Add memory.

B. Add a faster processor.

C. Add a faster hard disk.

D. Replace the hard disk with a faster one.

35. You are the administrator of a Windows Server 2003 Terminal Services load-balanced application farm. You have identical applications installed on all your servers. Everything is running fine, except your database administrators complain that if they start a Terminal Services session where they are doing a database rebuild in the office and then try to reconnect to that session from their home computer, they get a new session. What can you do to fix this issue?

A. Install and configure Session Directory.

B. Increase the disconnect timeout.

C. Increase the idle timeout.

D. Give the database admin administrative rights for the network.

36. After reading about all the new features in Windows Server 2003 Terminal Services, Joe decides to install a new test server to see whether everything he has heard is true. Joe installs and configures the new server, loads a few sample applications, and then requests a few users to try it out. However, it seems that only two people can log on to Terminal Services at a time. What is the most likely cause of this problem?

A. Joe didn't install the Session Directory.

B. Joe didn't install and activate the Terminal Services licensing server.

C. The server is in Remote Desktop for Administration mode.

D. The users are still using the older Terminal Services client.

37. After reading about all the new features in Windows Server 2003 Terminal Services, Joe decides to upgrade all the servers in his Terminal Services farm to Windows Server 2003. After the upgrades are completed, he installs a new application that features audio prompts. When trying to use the application, the end users don't hear anything. What is the most likely cause of this problem?

A. Joe didn't install the Session Directory.

B. Joe didn't enable audio support.

C. Audio support is only available with the Citrix add-on.

D. The users are still using the older Terminal Services client.

38. After Joe gets his Windows Server 2003 Terminal Services servers up and running, he has to work out the licensing issues. If Joe has the following users, what Client Access Licenses (CALs) should he purchase?

    - 30 computers
    - 10 handheld devices
    - 20 users who use both handhelds and computers

    A. 60 Terminal Services CALs

    B. 60 Terminal Services device CALs

    C. 60 Terminal Services user CALs

    D. 20 Terminal Services user CALs and 40 Terminal Services device CALs

39. You are creating a Windows Server 2003 server cluster when you discover that your dynamic disks are not supported. What method can you use to convert your dynamic disks back to basic disks?

    A. You cannot convert a dynamic disk back to a basic disk.

    B. Use `Format /basic`.

    C. Use `Convert /basic`.

    D. In the Disk Management snap-in, right-click the disk and select Revert to Basic Disk.

40. You are building a new Windows Server 2003 server to host a SQL database. This server must provide good performance in addition to fault tolerance. How should you configure the disk subsystem?

    A. RAID-5

    B. RAID-0

    C. RAID-1

    D. RAID-3

41. You are trying out the driver-signing feature of Windows Server 2003 in your test lab. You configure Group Policy to block the installation of unsigned drivers by end users. However, when you log in to test the policy, you are able to install an unsigned driver without any problems. What is the most likely cause of this problem?

    A. You logged on as administrator.

    B. You forgot to save the policy.

    C. You forgot to refresh Group Policy after applying the configuration. The changes should take effect after you use the `secedit` command.

    D. You forgot to refresh Group Policy after applying the configuration. The changes should take effect after you use the `gpupdate` command.

42. Your Windows Server 2003 server seems sluggish. You suspect that the disk subsystem is the bottleneck. Using the Performance Logs and Alerts utility, which counters should you be monitoring? (Choose all correct answers.)

    A. % Disk Time

    B. % Disk Queue

    C. Disk Seeks/Sec

    D. Disk Queue Length

43. George is building a new server for a database application. The user of the server wants the server to be fault tolerant, so George decides to use Windows Server 2003's mirroring capabilities to create a mirrored set for the boot/system partition. If George has the following drives available, what will be the effective capacity of his boot/system partition?

    - Drive 1: 18GB
    - Drive 2: 9GB

A. 9GB

B. 18GB

C. 27GB

D. 13.5GB

44. George decides to add a RAID-5 array to the new server he is building for the database application. If George has the following drives available, what will be the effective capacity of his RAID-5 array?

- Drive 1: 18GB
- Drive 2: 18GB
- Drive 3: 36GB
- Drive 4: 36GB

A. 108GB

B. 72GB

C. 54GB

D. 60GB

45. Your Windows Server 2003 server seems sluggish. You suspect that the CPU might be the bottleneck. Using the Performance Logs and Alerts utility, which counters should you be monitoring? (Choose all correct answers.)

A. % Processor Time

B. % Processor Page Faults

C. Processor Interrupts/Sec

D. Processor Queue Length

46. It's late Friday afternoon and you want to finish a database query so that you can go home. Using Task Manager, what priority can you set the database process to so that it will finish quicker?

A. Normal

B. High

C. AboveNormal

D. Priority 15

47. You are the administrator for Good Times, Inc. The Director of IT is extremely security conscious. She doesn't want any user being able to use a blank password. Which of the following password policies should you use to accomplish this? (Choose all correct answers.)

A. Password Length

B. Passwords Must Meet Complexity Requirements

C. Minimum Password Length

D. Require Non-Blank Password

48. In addition to the non-blank passwords requirement, your extremely security-conscious Director of IT wants you to increase the level of audit logging performed for user logons. If there are going to be more items audited, what other step should you take?

A. Increase the log-retention length.

B. Increase the size of the Event log.

C. Increase the size of the Security log.

D. Increase the size of the Audit log.

49. You're the system administrator for a fairly large corporation. Your corporation has a mix of network clients and platforms. You want to use Windows Server 2003 Terminal Services so that all clients see the same desktop. Which of the following platforms are *not* supported by the Windows Server 2003 version of Terminal Services? (Choose all correct answers.)

A. Handheld devices (iPAQ, HP, and so on)

B. Apple Macintosh

C. Red Hat Linux

D. Windows for Workgroups

50. The Director of Human Resources is extremely security conscious. She wants you to set up a folder for her department on a Windows Server 2003 server so that common users will not have access to it. However, specified users in the HR department should be able to access it easily over the network.

Required Result:

Set up a secure folder for Human Resources so that HR users will be able to access it over the network.

Optional Desired Results:

Common users should not have access to the contents of the folder.

Administrators should not be able to casually view the files.

Proposed Solution:

Create a folder named HRSecure and share it. Set the share permissions for the HRSecure folder to grant the specified HR users Full Control permission. Delete any share permissions that are specified for any other user or group.

Evaluation of Proposed Solution:

Which result(s) does the proposed solution produce?

A. The proposed solution produces the required result but neither of the optional results.

B. The proposed solution produces the required result and one of the optional results.

C. The proposed solution produces the required result and both the optional results.

D. The proposed solution does not produce the required result.

51. The Director of Human Resources is extremely security conscious. She wants you to set up a folder for her department on a Windows Server 2003 server so that common users will not have access to it. However, specified users in the HR department should be able to access it easily over the network.

Required Result:

Set up a secure folder for Human Resources so that HR users will be able to access it over the network.

Optional Desired Results:

Common users should not have access to the contents of the folder.

Administrators should not be able to casually view the files.

Proposed Solution:

Create a folder named HRSecure and share it. Set the NTFS and share permissions for the HRSecure folder to grant the specified HR users Full Control permission. Delete any NTFS or share permissions that are specified for any other user or group.

Evaluation of Proposed Solution:

Which result(s) does the proposed solution produce?

A. The proposed solution produces the required result but neither of the optional results.

B. The proposed solution produces the required result and one of the optional results.

C. The proposed solution produces the required result and both the optional results.

D. The proposed solution does not produce the required result.

52. You are one of the system administrators for a bank with multiple locations. Due to employee shortages, your tellers have to rotate between banks, as needed. The tellers need to always have the same files and desktop available. Which Windows Server 2003 technology should you implement to make this happen?

    A. Shared Profiles

    B. Roaming profiles

    C. Mandatory profiles

    D. Distributed File System (DFS)

53. You are one of the system administrators for a bank with multiple locations. Due to employee shortages, your tellers have to rotate between banks, as needed. All banks are connected to the logon and file servers in the headquarters location by 128K lines. The tellers need to always have the same files and desktop available. Which Windows Server 2003 technology should you implement to make this happen?

    A. Terminal Services

    B. Roaming profiles

    C. Mandatory profiles

    D. Distributed File System (DFS)

54. You've just installed new SCSI drivers and your server has blue screened. Which Windows Server 2003 server startup option will recover from this problem?

    A. Safe Mode

    B. Safe Mode with Networking

    C. Automated System Recovery

    D. Last Known Good Configuration

55. Which of the following methods cannot be used to start the Recovery Console in Windows Server 2003? (Choose all correct answers.)

    A. Operating system menu

    B. Windows Server 2003 boot disks

    C. Windows Server 2003 CD-ROM

    D. Network share

56. Mary has been tasked by her boss with saving money. She decides that instead of purchasing new servers, she will set up user quotas and file compression in order to make the existing servers last longer. Unfortunately, Mary has servers of various vintages. Which operating system cannot use user quotas?

    A. Windows NT 4.0

    B. Windows Server 2003

    C. Windows 2000 Server

    D. Windows XP Professional

57. The CIO of your financial services company resigns without warning. Her personal folders contain several files that the Securities and Exchange Commission (SEC) needs access to. The folders have the following permission:

    CIO: Full Control

    All the user folders, including one for the SEC, are located on a server formatted with NTFS. What's the quickest way to give the SEC access to these files?

    A. Reset the password on the CIO's account and then give the SEC the user ID and the new password.

    B. Assign ownership of the files to the SEC.

C. Take ownership of the files and give the SEC Full Control permission.

D. Move the files to the SEC's folders.

58. In an effort to conserve space on your file servers, you enable disk quotas on every user volume. However, the user data still seems to be increasing in size. What is the most likely problem?

A. You're using FAT32 volumes.

B. You assigned the quotas to the wrong groups.

C. Quota limits are not enabled by default.

D. The default quota limits are set too high.

59. Stan is a system administrator who works with a mixture of Windows 2000 and Windows Server 2003 servers. The shipping department has asked him to install a new application that will require a couple different folders that users will need Read/Write access to. He installs the application, creates a couple shared folders on a couple different servers, tests the application, and then hands it over to the shipping department. Soon, his phone begins to ring. It seems that users cannot access all the folders. What is the most likely cause of this problem?

A. Stan is using FAT32 volumes.

B. Stan assigned the wrong permissions to the wrong groups.

C. One folder is on Windows 2000; the other is on Windows Server 2003.

D. Stan set quota limits too low.

60. You are the administrator for a utility company. Your company is part of a utility cooperative that shares infrastructure and information to keep costs down. You have published coal and natural gas futures prices on your Web site. However, due to the sensitive nature of this data, this information must be secure. What steps should you perform to allow other companies access to this data while making it secure from unauthorized users? (Choose all correct answers.)

A. Turn anonymous access off.

B. Configure the Web site to support Integrated Authentication.

C. Install and configure a certificate and SSL.

D. Configure the Web site to support Basic Authentication.

E. Encrypt the data in the shared folders.

ANSWERS AND EXPLANATIONS

1. **C.** Non–Plug and Play hardware, or hardware that is not automatically recognized, must be added via the Add Hardware applet in the Control Panel. Reinstalling the hardware will not cause it to be recognized; therefore, answer A is incorrect. Installing drivers will not accomplish anything if the hardware is not recognized; therefore, answer B is incorrect. The Device Manager does not assist in installing new hardware directly; therefore, answer D is incorrect.

2. **B.** The server can be booted to the Recovery Console using the Windows Server 2003 CD-ROM. Booting from a PXE-capable NIC is used only for the Remote Installation Service (RIS); therefore, answer A is incorrect. Unlike previous versions of Windows, Windows Server 2003 does not come with boot disks; therefore, answer C is incorrect. Answer D is incorrect because you can boot into the Recovery Console using the Windows Server 2003 CD-ROM.

3. **B.** The most likely reason for Mary not being able to create a RAID-5 array in this situation is that the disks are basic disks, not dynamic disks. Dynamic disks are required to create RAID-5 arrays; therefore, answer A is incorrect. Because Windows Server 2003 supports software RAID, a hardware RAID controller is not required; therefore, answer C is incorrect. Being a member of the Enterprise Admins group is not a requirement to create a RAID-5 array; therefore, answer D is incorrect.

4. **D.** To enforce a quota, you must set limits. Just enabling disk quotas tracks usage, but nothing else; therefore, answer A is incorrect. Consolidating free space won't result in any extra space; therefore, answer B is incorrect. Enabling warning limits allows the administrator to see who is running out of configured space; therefore, answer C is incorrect.

5. **C.** Although all the listed solutions would work, the quickest and easiest solution is to use Software Update Services (SUS) to automatically download the patch from Microsoft and apply it to all the computers; therefore, answers A, B, and D are incorrect.

6. **C.** In addition to disk quotas, a Windows Server 2003 server's NTFS drives support file and folder compression. Disk quotas are based on uncompressed file size; therefore, your database file may take up more than the displayed size-on-disk figure. An NTFS permissions problem or a virus would not give you an out-of-space message; therefore, answers A and D are incorrect. Users do not have the authority to configure quotas; therefore, answer B is incorrect.

7. **A, C.** Both System Monitor and Task Manager allow you to see the current performance of your applications. The Performance Logs and Alerts snap-in allows you to log data and create alerts only, and the Performance Monitor utility was used in previous versions of Windows; therefore, answers B and D are incorrect.

8. **A, D, E.** Although video performance might be important on a workstation, on a server the big four are memory, processor, physical disk, and network card; therefore, answer B is incorrect. Answer C is incorrect because application load time is not a device.

9. **D.** To enforce a quota, you must set limits. Zip files are already compressed, so disk compression has little, if any, effect; therefore, answers A and C are incorrect. Consolidating free space won't result in any extra space; therefore, answer B is incorrect.

10. **D, E.** You need to add her user account to the Administrators and Backup Operators groups to provide the proper permissions to perform backups. The Server Operators, Power Users, and Account Operators groups do not have the proper file-level permissions to back up files; therefore, answers A, B, and C are incorrect.

11. **E.** Windows Server 2003 does not use an Emergency Repair Disk; therefore, answers A, B, C, and D are all incorrect.

12. **A, B.** To support SUS, client computers must be running the updated Automatic Updates client and Windows 2000 (Service Pack 2), Windows XP, or Window Server 2003; therefore, answers C and D are incorrect.

13. **C.** The quickest and probably cheapest way to distribute the application is to set up a Windows Server 2003 server with Terminal Services running in Application Server mode. In Application Server mode, Terminal Services can support multiple concurrent users, whereas Remote Desktop for Administration mode limits you to two concurrent connections. If your desktops are still running Windows 95 and Windows for Workgroups, it's unlikely they could be upgraded to Windows XP quickly or cheaply; therefore, answers A, B, and D are incorrect.

14. **C.** The audit information is recorded in the Security Log under Event Viewer; therefore, answers A, B, D, and E are all incorrect.

15. **A, B, C.** Although either Remote Desktop for Administration or Terminal Services allows Mary to work on the Windows XP client, the Remote Assistance feature allows both Mary and the user to see and control the desktop on the client. The Remote Administrator feature does not exist; therefore, answer D is incorrect.

16. **A, B, D.** When a shared folder is moved, it is no longer shared. When it is moved to a different server, it assumes the NTFS permissions of the target folder, which probably won't be the same as the original folder. Restarting the Server service or giving the shares new names will not cause nonshared folders to appear as shares; therefore, answers C and E are incorrect.

17. **C.** Although you can still assign a logon script via the user profile, the recommended method in Windows Server 2003 is to assign logon scripts via Group Policy; therefore, answers A, B, and D are incorrect.

18. **C.** You should install the Terminal Services client so that you can access your servers remotely. The Windows Server 2003 administration tools can only be installed on Windows XP and Windows Server 2003 computers; therefore, answer A is incorrect. The Active Directory Users and Groups MMC, whether it is the Windows 2000 or Windows 2003 version, will not run on Windows NT; therefore, answer B is incorrect. Although User Manager for Domains works in a mixed-mode Windows Server 2003 domain, it doesn't provide much functionality; therefore, answer D is incorrect.

19. **B.** The solution satisfies the required result and one of the optional results. Although the solution allows only the designated users to access the file share, it's going to be a lot of work to reassign permissions to each one as contractors come and go.

20. **C.** The solution satisfies the required result and both the optional results. The solution allows only the designated users to access the file share, and there is less work involved long term because you must only add or remove the contractors accounts from the SecureEng group.

21. **B.** External devices attached to serial ports must be installed using the Add Hardware Wizard. Only internal devices, or devices attached to certain parallel ports, can be installed using Plug and Play or via Device Manager; therefore, answers A and D are incorrect. The Add Printers applet can only be used to install printers, not communication devices; therefore, answer C is incorrect.

22. **A.** The solution satisfies the required result but neither of the optional results. Although the solution should install the new card correctly, the old drivers are still present.

23. **C.** The solution satisfies the required result and both the optional results. To completely remove all traces of an old device from a server, you must use Device Manager to remove the drivers before physically removing the device.

24. **B.** The solution satisfies the required result and one of the optional results. Although the csvde utility can be used to import and export user accounts, it does not have the ability to modify them or add them to groups. However, you can modify the file manually after it is exported from the old directory. Then it can be imported to the new directory.

25. **C.** The solution satisfies the required result and both the optional results. The ldifde utility can be used to import, export, modify, or delete records. In addition, it can be used to add users to a group by modifying the group with the LDIF file.

26. **D.** The solution does not produce the required result. Although Automated System Recovery backs up and restores the boot partition and disk signatures, it does not back up or restore any data volumes.

27. **C.** The solution satisfies the required result and both the optional results. A normal backup backs up all files on the server, including the system state data. The Volume Shadow Copy feature is enabled by default, which backs up open files.

28. **C.** An incremental backup is used to back up only the files and folders that have been created or modified since the last normal or incremental backup. It reads the archive bit to determine which files need to be backed up. It then changes the archive bit of the files that were backed up so that the next time the backup program is run, the file is not backed up again unless it was changed. A normal backup backs up all the files, whereas a daily backup backs up only the files created or modified that day; therefore, answers A and B are incorrect. A partial backup does not exist; therefore, answer D is incorrect.

29. **D.** Restarting a server and selecting Last Known Good Configuration is the quickest and easiest way to correct most problems with the `SYSTEM` Registry key; therefore, answers A, B, and C are incorrect.

30. **B.** The solution satisfies the required result and one of the optional results. Although moving the applications works, in a Web farm of any size, this could take a while.

31. **C.** The solution satisfies the required result and both the optional results. The native mode of IIS 6.0 is Worker Process Isolation mode. In this mode, applications and processes can be separated into application pools. An *application pool* is a set of one or more applications assigned to a set of one or more worker processes. An application pool can contain Web sites, applications, and virtual directories. Each application pool is isolated from the others. Because of this, a failure or memory leak affects only the processes running in that application pool and has no effect on any of the other functions in other application pools.

32. **B.** The Performance Logs and Alerts tool can be used to capture baseline data that can be viewed in the System Monitor. Performance Monitor was the tool used in Windows NT 4.0; therefore, answer A is incorrect. Task Manager is not suited for baselining; therefore, answer C is incorrect. Although System Monitor is used to display performance data, it can't log it to create a baseline; therefore, answer D is incorrect.

33. **D.** Typically, a Disk Queue Length of more than 2 is a problem. To fix this, you should replace the disk with a faster one. Although adding a faster disk might help a little, the existing disk will still be a bottleneck; therefore, answer C is incorrect. All the other settings are within an acceptable range; therefore, answers A and B are incorrect.

34. **B.** Typically, a Processor Queue Length of more than 2 is a problem, especially if ProcessorTime is over 80%. All the other settings are within an acceptable range; therefore, answers A, C, and D are incorrect.

35. **A.** Because NLB uses the IP address of the client when routing, it can reconnect to a disconnected session. However, in those situations where the user has moved to another computer or received a different IP address via DHCP, the user receives a new session chosen at random from the group of servers. The Session Directory is a database that indexes the sessions using the username instead of the IP address. Session Directory allows disconnected sessions to be reconnected by using the username to look up the location of a disconnected session. Simply prolonging the session by increasing the disconnect and the idle timeout, or granting administrative rights, will have no effect on session routing; therefore, answers B, C and D are incorrect.

36. **C.** Terminal Services in Remote Desktop for Administration mode supports only two concurrent connections, plus a console session. A new server has a 120-day grace period for client licenses; therefore, answer B is incorrect. Answer A is incorrect because the Session Directory is useful only for session routing among multiple Terminal Services servers. Any Terminal Services client can be used to connect to a Windows Server 2003 Terminal Services server, albeit with less functionality; therefore, answer D is incorrect.

37. **D.** A common problem with Terminal Services involves connecting to the server with the older Terminal Services RDP 4.0 client instead of the RDC 5.0 client (included with Windows 2000) or the RDC 5.1 client (included with Windows XP or Windows Server 2003). The clients look and function in a similar manner; however, the advanced functionality that is enabled in RDC 5.0 and 5.1, such as audio support and keyboard mapping, is not available with the older Terminal Services 4.0 RDP clients. Session Directory allows disconnected sessions to be reconnected by using the username to look up the location of a disconnected session. It has no effect on audio; therefore, answer A is incorrect. Audio support is enabled, by default, and doesn't require the Citrix add-on; therefore, answers B and C are incorrect.

38. **D.** New with Windows Server 2003 is the concept of user Client Access Licenses and device Client Access Licenses. These allow organizations additional license options. For example, if a Terminal Services user connects via multiple devices, such as an office PC, a home PC, and a handheld device, he would purchase a user license instead of a device license. PCs or other devices that support multiple users would require a device license. The standard TS CAL is only for Windows 2000 Terminal Services servers.

39. **A.** After a basic disk is converted to a dynamic disk, it can't be converted back to a basic disk. The only way to revert to using a basic disk is to back up the data, reinitialize the disk, repartition it, and restore the data; therefore, answers B, C, and D are incorrect.

40. **A.** RAID-5 provides the best compromise between performance and fault tolerance; therefore, answers B and C are incorrect. RAID-3 is not supported by Windows Server 2003; therefore, answer D is incorrect.

41. **D.** Except for security changes, Group Policies are not immediately applied. Windows Server 2003 uses the `gpupdate` command to apply policies immediately. Administrative privilege is not at issue because you logged in as a regular user to test the policy; therefore, answer A is incorrect. Policies are saved automatically as they are configured; therefore, answer B is incorrect. Previous versions of Windows used the `secedit` command; therefore, answer C is incorrect.

42. **A, D.** If the Disk Queue Length is above 2, or the % Disk Time is a sustained 80% or better, the disk unit is the most likely bottleneck. Disk Seeks/Sec is not a good indicator of a bottleneck because you would need to correlate the results with the disk access time, and % Disk Queue is not a valid option; therefore, answers B and C are incorrect.

43. **A.** The space available is 9GB. When a mirrored set is created, it is sized to be equivalent to the smallest volume; therefore, answers B, C, and D are incorrect.

44. **C.** The space available is 54GB. When a RAID-5 array is created, it uses no more than the size of the smallest configured area on each volume. In addition, the equivalent of one volume is dedicated to storing parity information; therefore, answers A, B, and D are incorrect.

45. **A, D.** If the Processor Queue Length is above 2, or the % Processor Time is a sustained 80% or better, the processor is the most likely bottleneck. % Processor Page Faults doesn't exist; therefore, answer B is incorrect. A high value for Processor Interrupts/Sec usually indicates a bad card or system device; therefore, answer C is incorrect.

46. **B.** Although setting the process to AboveNormal, which is a priority 9 is better than Normal, which is an 8, High is a priority 13; therefore, answers A and C are incorrect. Priorities are not assigned via number; therefore, answer D is incorrect.

47. **B, C.** The password complexity rules are rather involved, but require that the minimum length be six characters. Alternatively, you can set the Minimum Password Length policy to 1. This prevents users from attempting to use blank passwords. The options Password Length and Require Non-Blank Password do not exist; therefore, answers A and D are incorrect.

48. **C.** The Security log is the place where the audit events are stored. Increasing the log-retention time might make things worse if the log is not set to overwrite old data; therefore, answer A is incorrect. There are no logs specifically named Audit or Event; therefore, answers B and D are incorrect.

49. **C, D.** Windows for Workgroups and Linux clients are only available from third parties. Pocket PC devices and Apple Macintosh are supported, although you might have to download the client from Microsoft; therefore, answers A and B are incorrect.

50. **B.** The solution satisfies the required result and one of the optional results. Securing the shared folder and granting permissions only to the HR group prevents common users from accessing the folder over the network. However, because the permissions are assigned at the share level, anyone sitting at the console can browse the files without any problem.

51. **C.** The solution satisfies the required result and both the optional results. Securing the shared folder and granting permissions only to the HR group prevents common users from accessing the folder over the network. Additionally, setting the NTFS permissions prevents anyone sitting at the console from casually browsing the files. However, an administrator can still take ownership of the files.

52. **B.** Roaming profiles allow the users' desktop and the contents of their folders, such as My Documents, to follow them from computer to computer. Shared Profiles is not a valid option; therefore, answer A is incorrect. Although mandatory profiles always present users with the same desktop, their files are not available unless some sort of drive mapping is implemented; therefore, answer C is incorrect. DFS would not enable the required functionality; therefore, answer D is incorrect.

53. **A.** Windows Server 2003 Terminal Services is the only viable option here. It allows the user desktop and files to remain at the headquarters location, and only screen updates and keystrokes are transmitted over the WAN. Although roaming profiles are a nice feature, they tend to get rather large. With such a low-bandwidth link, a typical profile downloading over the WAN would saturate the link; therefore, answer B is incorrect. Although mandatory profiles always present users with the same desktop, their files are not available unless some sort of drive mapping is implemented; therefore, answer C is incorrect. DFS would allow the user files to be stored in multiple locations, but that doesn't affect the desktop, and the file replication between multiple locations could potentially saturate the WAN link; therefore, answer D is incorrect.

54. **D.** The Last Known Good Configuration option starts the server using the `Hardware` key that was in use the last time the server was successfully booted. It overwrites the new, and potentially bad, SCSI drivers that you just installed. The options in answers A and B will not be effective because they will still be using the defective drivers to boot the server. Automated System Recovery would potentially fix the problem, but only if you had already created a backup set previous to installing the faulty drivers; therefore, answer C is incorrect.

55. **B, D.** The Windows Server 2003 Recovery Console cannot be started from a network share, and Windows Server 2003 no longer includes boot disks. Using the operating system menu and the Windows Server 2003 CD-ROM are both viable options for starting the Recovery Console; therefore, answers A and C are incorrect.

56. **A.** Windows NT 4.0 is the only listed operating system that does not support disk quotas. This is because it uses NTFS version 4.0, whereas all the other listed operating systems use NTFS 5.0, which has quota, compression, and encryption support built in; therefore, answers B, C, and D are incorrect.

57. **B.** Unlike previous versions of Windows, in Windows Server 2003, the administrator can assign the ownership of files and folders. Moving the files would not work because files moved to a different folder on an NTFS partition retain their existing permissions; therefore, answer D is incorrect. The other options would work, but they take more steps; therefore, answers A and C are incorrect.

58. **C.** When quotas are enabled, they track only the space used by each user. Quota limits are not enabled by default; they must be manually configured. Quotas are not supported on FAT32 volumes; therefore, answer A is incorrect. Quotas cannot be assigned by group, and there are no default quota limits; therefore, answers B and D are incorrect.

59. **C.** One major difference between Windows 2000 and Windows Server 2003 is the default permissions for file shares. In Windows 2000, the default is Everyone - Full Control. In Windows Server 2003, the default is Everyone - Read. Using Shared folders on a FAT32 volume wouldn't make a difference in access through a share, as long as the permissions were configured correctly. Also, if the permissions were assigned to the wrong groups, that wouldn't explain why the users can access some folders and not others; therefore, answers A and B are incorrect. Quotas were not mentioned; therefore, answer D is incorrect.

60. **A, C, D.** You need to follow these steps to use Secure Sockets Layer (SSL) to require authentication and encrypt all data passing between the user computer and the Web site; therefore, answers B and E are incorrect.

PART 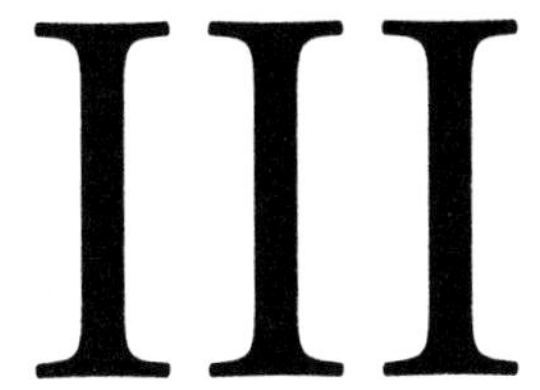

APPENDIXES

APPENDIX A

Key Resources Online

To prepare you to handle the new challenges of Windows Server 2003, Microsoft and others have developed numerous sources of information and support. Resources are available to help you get up to speed on the new platform and to support it after you have implemented it.

The Internet has always been known for its sense of community, so it should come as no surprise that a wealth of Windows Server 2003 information is available—most of it for free.

Microsoft Resources

A good source of information about Microsoft Certification Exams comes from Microsoft itself. Because its products and technologies—and the exams that go with them—change frequently, the best place to go for exam-related information is on the Microsoft Training and Certification Web site.

If you haven't already visited the Microsoft Certification site, do so right now. The Microsoft Training and Certification home page resides at `www.microsoft.com/traincert/default.asp`.

The Microsoft Training and Certification home page is a portal to information about current and soon-to-be-released exams, events, and resources to assist you in preparing for your exam.

> **NOTE** The Microsoft Training and Certification home page might be replaced by something new and different by the time you read this appendix because things change regularly on the Microsoft site. Should this happen, be sure to read the section at the end of this appendix titled "Coping with Change on the Web."

The following are some key locations on the Microsoft Web site pertaining to Windows Server 2003:

- **The home page for Windows Server 2003**—`http://www.microsoft.com/windowsserver2003/default.mspx`
- **Preparation Guide for Exam 70-290**—`http://www.microsoft.com/traincert/exams/70-290.asp`
- **Microsoft Training and Certification newsgroups**—You can exchange information with others who are studying for or have passed the 70-290 exam and other Microsoft exams: `http://communities.microsoft.com/newsgroups/default.asp?icp=certification&slcid=us`
- **NNTP server**—Microsoft hosts a large number of newsgroups to support its various products. Most questions will be answered by your peers, but Microsoft support personnel occasionally join in: `http://msnews.microsoft.com`
- **Microsoft Windows Server 2003 Deployment Kit**—`http://www.microsoft.com/windowsserver2003/techinfo/reskit/deploykit.mspx`

- **Microsoft Windows Server 2003 Resource Kit**—Contains useful tools and tips and is occasionally the source of a few extra points on the exam: `http://www.microsoft.com/windowsserver2003/techinfo/reskit/resourcekit.mspx`
- **Windows Server 2003 technical overviews**—`http://www.microsoft.com/windowsserver2003/techinfo/overview/default.mspx`
- **Product documentation for Windows Server 2003 Standard Edition**—`http://www.microsoft.com/technet/treeview/default.asp?url=/technet/prodtechnol/windowsserver2003/proddocs/server/default.asp`
- **Product documentation for Windows Server 2003 Enterprise Edition**—`http://www.microsoft.com/technet/treeview/default.asp?url=/technet/prodtechnol/windowsserver2003/proddocs/entserver/default.asp`
- **Product documentation for IIS 6.0**—`http://www.microsoft.com/technet/treeview/default.asp?url=/technet/prodtechnol/windowsserver2003/proddocs/server/iiswelcome.asp`
- **Storage Management How-to Guide**—`http://support.microsoft.com/common/canned.aspx?R=d&H=Windows%20Server%202003%20Storage%20Management%20How-to%20Guide&LL=kbwinnetsearch%20or%20kbwinserv2003search&Sz=kbstoragedev&sd=gn`
- **Windows Server 2003 Terminal Services How-to Guide**—`http://support.microsoft.com/common/canned.aspx?R=d&H=Windows%20Server%202003%20Terminal%20Services%20How-to%20Guide&LL=kbwinnetsearch%20or%20kbwinserv2003search&Sz=kbtermserv&sd=gn`
- **Windows Server 2003 Active Directory How-to Guide**—`http://support.microsoft.com/common/canned.aspx?R=d&H=Windows%20Server%202003%20Active%20Directory%20How-to%20Guide&LL=kbwinnetsearch%20or%20kbwinserv2003search&Sz=kbactivedirectory&sd=gn`
- **Windows Server 2003 Networking and Communications How-to Guide**—`http://support.microsoft.com/common/canned.aspx?R=d&H=Windows%20Server%202003%20Networking%20and%20Communications%20How-to%20Guide&LL=kbwinnetsearch%20or%20kbwinserv2003search&Sz=kbnetwork&sd=gn`
- **Windows Server 2003 Management Services How-to Guide**—`http://support.microsoft.com/common/canned.aspx?R=d&H=Windows%20Server%202003%20Management%20Services%20How-to%20Guide&LL=kbwinnetsearch%20or%20kbwinserv2003search&Sz=kbmgmtsvc&sd=gn`
- **Microsoft Knowledge Base**—An online database of known problems and solutions for Microsoft products: `http://support.microsoft.com/default.aspx?scid=fh;[ln];kbhowto`
- **Microsoft Security & Privacy**—An up-to-date source of security information pertaining to Microsoft products: `http://www.microsoft.com/security/`
- **Microsoft Security reporting email**—To report a security exposure to Microsoft, send an email to `secure@microsoft.com`
- **Microsoft TechNet**—Features technical articles on most Microsoft business products and operating systems: `http://www.microsoft.com/technet/`
- **Microsoft's service pack and hotfix FTP site**—Houses all the latest Microsoft fixes and service packs: `ftp://ftp.microsoft.com/bussys`

Third-party Internet Resources

The information resources available online for Windows Server 2003 are not limited to Microsoft. Various companies, organizations, and even individuals offer information about Windows Server 2003 on the Web:

- **Ask a Question of the Experts**—AllExperts is the oldest and largest free Q&A service on the Internet. It features a roster of volunteers who will attempt to answer your computer-related questions: `http://www.allexperts.com/getExpert.asp?Category=2073`
- **@stakeL0pht Heavy Industries**—A security-oriented Web site, @stake offers the latest news on vulnerabilities in Windows Server 2003 and other operating systems: `http://www.atstake.com/`
- **Brainbuzz**—A comprehensive site with forums, discussion groups, white papers, and a job database: `http://www.brainbuzz.com`
- **CramSession**—A great Windows site with forums and a job database: `http://www.cramsession.com`
- **C|Net's Download.COM**—`http://www.download.com/`
- **C|Net's Shareware.COM**—Although the C|Net sites are light on technical content, they are a great source for finding the latest freeware and shareware: `http://www.shareware.com/`
- **Computerwire**—A subscription-based, custom news and market research service that allows you to preselect your daily technical news: `http://www.computerwire.info`
- ***ComputerWorld***—The online site of one of the industry's oldest news and technical subscription newspapers. Features industry profiles, technical articles, and product reviews for various platforms: `http://www.computerworld.com/`
- **Enterprise IT Planet**—A comprehensive Windows site that includes freeware, shareware, job listings, technical forums, white papers, and more: `http://products.enterpriseitplanet.com/`
- ***eWeek***—A weekly technical newspaper featuring industry news, product reviews, and technical articles (available online or via subscription): `http://www.zdnet.com/eweek/`
- **Google Groups**—Google newsgroups features a search engine that allows you to search for discussion threads in previous postings in newsgroups. The content is available for a four-year period: `http://groups.google.com/`
- ***Enterprise Computing***—A biweekly magazine available in both print and online versions that features product reviews and technical articles. A subscription newsletter is also available: `http://www.entmag.com/`
- **InfoWorld**—A weekly technical newspaper featuring industry news, product reviews, and technical articles (available online or via subscription): `http://www.infoworld.com/`
- ***Microsoft Certified Professional Magazine***—A good site that features articles, forums, and online chats pertaining to certification topics. A private area is available to MCSEs: `http://www.mcpmag.com/`
- **Net Admin Tools**—A compendium of tips, tricks, white papers, and freeware for network administrators: `http://www.netadmintools.com/`

- **Netmation's Index of Windows Resources**—An index of links to Windows Web sites: `http://www.netmation.com/listnt.htm`
- **NTWare.com**—A download site that features Windows software: `http://www.ntware.com/`
- **Paperbits' Support Center for Windows NT**—This site has hints, technical tips, and drivers for the various versions of Windows: `http://www.paperbits.com/`
- **Paul Thurrott's SuperSite for Windows**—This site features breaking news on Windows, product reviews, and a detailed Windows FAQ: `http://www.winsupersite.com/`
- **TechRepublic**—A site with lots of articles relating to Windows and networking in general: `http://www.techrepublic.com`
- **The Association of Windows NT System Professionals (NT*Pro)**—NT*Pro is a professional association that provides a technical, educational, and support forum for computer professionals with an interest in Windows Server, BackOffice technologies, and related server and development issues. Membership is free: `http://www.ntpro.org`
- **Symantec Security Response**—A listing of the latest virus threats and security vulnerabilities: `http://www.sarc.com/avcenter/`
- **SearchWin2000.com**—A Windows-specific portal run by TechTarget. Its home page features current Windows news summaries with links to the original articles. There are also links to Windows XP articles, and there is a selection of Windows XP–related white papers. The portal also sponsors a chat session with IT industry insiders, usually about once a week. It also features a subscription newsletter. TechTarget runs a line of similar portals for Solaris, HP IBM AS/400, S/390, and other platforms: `http://searchwin2000.com`
- **Somarsoft**—Free utilities for the reporting of security, directory, Registry, and event information under Windows NT/2000/XP/2003: `http://www.somarsoft.com/`
- **Sysinternals**—The Sysinternals Web site features advanced utilities, technical information, and source code related to Windows NT/2000/2003 internals: `http://www.sysinternals.com`
- **Sunbelt Software**—Sunbelt has a large selection of tools and utilities for Windows Server 2003: `http://www.sunbelt-software.com/`
- **TechWeb**—High-tech industry news: `http://www.techweb.com/`
- **Tek-Tips**—Online forums for Windows and other platforms: `http://www.tek-tips.com/`
- **The Thin Net's Windows Links**—`http://thethin.net/winnt.cfm`
- **TUCOWS**—Arguably the best download site on the Web. TUCOWS has mirror sites just about everywhere: `http://www.tucows.com/`
- ***Windows & .NET Magazine***—A monthly hard-copy magazine that adds articles online for subscribers: `http://www.win2000mag.com/`
- **Windows Server 2003 Tips, Registry Hacks, and More**—`http://www.jsiinc.com/reghack.htm`
- **Windows Tips**—`http://www.chami.com/tips/windows/`
- **WinPlanet**—Windows tips, news, and technical articles: `http://www.winplanet.com/`
- **WinSite**—Windows freeware and shareware of all kinds: `http://www.winsite.com/`
- **World of Windows Networking**—Lots of Windows Server 2003 tips, downloads, and technical articles: `http://www.wown.com/j_helmig/winxppro.htm`

- **WUGNET**—The WindowsUsers Group Web site features news, tips, and articles about Windows Server 2003: `http://www.wugnet.com/`
- **X-Force's Computer Threats and Vulnerabilities**—Security news, including a searchable database: `http://www.iss.net/`
- **ZDNet**—The online home of *PC Magazine* and other Ziff-Davis publications: `http://www.zdnet.com/`

Listservers

Listservers are a very valuable resource for someone who is studying for an exam. They give you access to others who are also studying for an exam or who are working with Windows Server 2003. Most of these lists are open to anyone who is interested. This interaction can be very valuable, and it is free. Here are some Listservers to check out:

CAUTION

Some of the mailing lists can get pretty busy in terms of message volume per day; therefore, you might want to consider subscribing in digest mode. Alternately, you could set up a folder for each group and use an email rule to sort incoming messages.

- **Internet Security Systems (ISS) mailing lists**—ISS sponsors several mailing lists that feature "hot off the press" security exposures for Windows products. To sign up, go to `http://www.iss.net/security_center/maillists/`
- **Saluki**—This site features Listservers covering a variety of technical issues, including Windows Server 2003: `http://www.saluki.com`
- **NT-Tools**—Sunbelt Software hosts this site. In addition to the Windows Server 2003 Listserver, there are other Listservers for other subjects, including Exchange, Windows System Administration, and a list where you can post your resume: `http://www.sunbelt-software.com/community.cfm`
- **NTBugtraq**—This is a mailing list for the discussion of security exploits and security bugs in Windows and related applications: `http://www.ntbugtraq.com/`
- **A list of security-related mailing Listservers for Windows Server 2003 and other Microsoft products**—`http://oliver.efri.hr/~crv/security/mlist/mlist. html`

Email Newsletters

A variety of newsletters are available that cover Windows Server 2003 and associated technologies. Most are delivered to your inbox weekly, in either text or HTML format.

- **Internet Security Systems (ISS)**—Sponsors the *Connections* newsletter, which features new security threats and information-protection tips. To sign up, go to `http://www.iss.net/security_center/maillists/`.
- ***Microsoft Certified Professional Magazine***—Sponsors a weekly newsletter that includes links to articles on its Web site, breaking news in the certification world, and a schedule of its certification online chats. You can subscribe at `http://mcpmag.com`.
- **TechRepublic**—Sponsors several weekly and biweekly newsletters relating to Windows and networking in general. You can subscribe at `http://www.techrepublic.com`.

- **Tech Target**—Sponsors a multitude of newsletters featuring just about any Information Technology–related topic. To get a list of the available newsletters, go to `http://www.techtarget.com`.
- ***Windows & .NET Magazine***—Sponsors various newsletters relating to the Windows environment. To subscribe, go to `http://email.winnetmag.com/winnetmag/winnetmag_prefctr.asp`.
- **WinInfo**—This is a newsletter run by Paul Thurrott. It's also known as SuperSite for Windows. To subscribe, go to `http://www.winsupersite.com/`.
- **Woody's Office Watch**—Publishes several free weekly newsletters that cover all the Office products and Windows versions. Sign up at `http://www.woodyswatch.com/index.asp`.

Training

These companies offer Windows Server 2003 information, online training, computer-based training, or live training that will help to prepare you for working with Microsoft Windows Server 2003:

- **Global Knowledge**—One of the largest training providers, with worldwide locations. Global Knowledge offers online and classroom training covering a variety of technologies and can be reached at `http://www.globalknowledge.com`.
- **Learn 2 Store**—The Learn 2 Store is an online training site. Learn 2 Store can be reached at `http://www.tutorials.com/`.
- **Pinnacle Training**—Offers both online and classroom training in a variety of technologies. Pinnacle can be reached at `http://www.pinnacletraining.com/`.
- **Wave Technologies**—Offers both online and classroom training at various locations. Wave Technologies also has an intensive boot camp for those seeking certification training and can be reached at `http://wave.netg.com/`.

Coping with Change on the Web

Sooner or later, all the information I've shared with you about the Microsoft Training and Certification Web site and the other Web-based resources mentioned in this appendix and throughout this book will go stale or be replaced by newer information. In some cases, the URLs you find here may lead you to their replacements; in other cases, the URLs will go nowhere, leaving you with the dreaded "404 File not found" error message. When that happens, don't give up.

There's always a way to find what you want on the Web if you're willing to invest some time and energy. Most large or complex Web sites (such as the Microsoft site) offer a search engine. On all of Microsoft's Web pages, a Search button appears along the top edge of the page. As long as you can get to the Microsoft site (it should stay at `www.microsoft.com` for a long time), use this tool to help you find what you need.

The more focused you can make a search request, the more likely the results will include information you can use. For example, you can search for the string

```
"training and certification"
```

to produce a lot of data about the subject in general, but if you're looking for the preparation guide for Exam 70-290, "Managing and Maintaining a Windows Server 2003 Environment," you'll be more likely to get there quickly if you use a search string similar to the following:

```
"Exam 70-290" AND "preparation guide"
```

Likewise, if you want to find the Training and Certification downloads, try a search string such as this:

```
"training and certification" AND "download page"
```

Finally, feel free to use general search tools—such as `www.google.com`, `www.search.com`, `www.altavista.com`, and `www.excite.com`—to look for related information. Although Microsoft offers great information about its certification exams online, there are plenty of third-party sources of information and assistance that need not follow Microsoft's party line. Therefore, if you can't find something immediately, intensify your search.

APPENDIX B

General Networking Resources and Bibliography

As you observed in the previous appendix, there are a great number of Windows Server 2003 information resources on the Internet. However, as you will soon find out, there are nearly as many in print. In this appendix, we provide a selection of resources that we recommend—a collection of the best of the best. These resources are available to help you get up to speed on the new platform and to help you support it after you have implemented it.

Publications

This is a list of recommended publications. Most of them are specifically for Windows Server 2003, whereas others are included because they provide general networking knowledge:

- *Connected Home Magazine.* A magazine that focuses on using Windows and related technologies in the home environment. `http://www.connectedhomemag.com/`.
- *Microsoft Certified Professional Magazine.* A magazine that focuses on Microsoft-related certification topics but also includes good technical information. You can get subscription information from `http://mcpmag.com/`.
- *Windows and .NET Magazine.* A monthly magazine that focuses on the latest technology in the Windows platform. To subscribe, go to `http://www.winnetmag.com/`.
- Aleksey, Tchekmarev, et al. *Windows .NET Server 2003 Domains and Active Directory.* A-List Publishing, 2002. ISBN 1931769001.
- Balladelli, Micky and Jan De Clercq. *Mission-Critical Active Directory: Architecting a Secure and Scalable Infrastructure.* Digital Press, 2001. ISBN 1555582400.
- Borge, Stein. *Managing Enterprise Systems with the Windows Script Host.* APress, 2001. ISBN 1893115674.
- Boswell, William. *Inside Windows Server 2003.* New Riders, 2003. ISBN 0735711585.
- Carl-Mitchell, Smoot and John S. Quarterman. *Practical Internetworking with TCP/IP and UNIX.* Addison-Wesley, 1993. ISBN 0201586290.
- Charles, Kackie. *Windows 2000 Routing and Remote Access Services.* New Riders, 2000. ISBN 0735709513.
- Cheswick, William and Steven M. Bellovin. *Firewalls and Internet Security: Repelling the Wily Hacker.* Addison-Wesley, 2001. ISBN 0201633574.

- Comer, Douglas E. *Internetworking with TCP/IP: Principles, Protocols, and Architecture, Vols. I–III.* Prentice Hall, 1995, 1996, 1997. ISBNs 0132169878, 0139738436, and 0138487146.
- Craddock, John P., et al. *Active Directory Forestry: Investigating and Managing Objects and Attributes for Windows 2000 and Windows Server 2003.* Kimberry Associates, 2003. ISBN 0954421809.
- Davies, Joseph. *Microsoft Windows Server 2003 TCP/IP Protocols and Services Technical Reference.* Microsoft Press, 2003. ISBN 0735612919.
- Eck, Thomas. *Windows NT/2000 ADSI Scripting for System Administration.* New Riders, 2000. ISBN 1578702194.
- Fortenberry, Thaddeus. *Windows 2000 Virtual Private Networking.* Que, 2000. ISBN 1578702461.
- Graham, Jeffrey, et al. *Windows 2000 DNS.* New Riders, 2000. ISBN 0735709734.
- Habraken, Joe. *Sams Teach Yourself Microsoft Windows Server 2003 in 24 Hours.* Sams, 2003. ISBN 0672324946.
- Henrickson, Hethe, et al. *IIS 6: The Complete Reference.* McGraw-Hill, 2003. ISBN 0072224959.
- Hipson, Peter D. *Mastering Windows XP Registry.* Sybex, 2002. ISBN 0782129870.
- Honeycutt, Jerry. *Introducing Microsoft Windows Server 2003.* Microsoft Press, 2003. ISBN 0735615705.
- Internet Security Systems, Inc. *Microsoft Windows 2000 Security Technical Reference.* Microsoft Press, 2000. ISBN 073560858X.
- Jones, Don. *Windows Server 2003 Weekend Crash Course.* John Wiley & Sons, 2003. ISBN 0764549251.
- Jones, Don, et al. *Microsoft Windows Server 2003 Delta Guide.* Sams, 2003. ISBN 0789728494.
- King, Robert. *Mastering Active Directory for Windows Server 2003.* Sybex, 2003. ISBN 0782140793.
- Knittel, Brian. *Windows XP Under the Hood: Hardcore Windows Scripting and Command Line Power.* Que, 2002. ISBN 0789727331.
- Kokoreva, Olga. *Windows XP Registry: A Complete Guide to Customizing and Optimizing Windows XP.* A-List Publishing, 2002. ISBN 193176901X.
- Kouti, Sakari, et al. *Inside Active Directory: A System Administrator's Guide.* Addison Wesley, 2001. ISBN 0201616211.
- Lissoir, Alain. *Leveraging WMI Scripting.* Digital Press, 2003. ISBN 1555582990.
- Lissoir, Alain. *Understanding WMI Scripting.* Digital Press, 2003. ISBN 1555582664.
- Liu, Cricket, et al. *DNS and Bind, 4th Edition.* O'Reilly & Associates, 2001. ISBN 0596001584.
- Matthews, Marty. *Windows Server 2003: A Beginner's Guide.* McGraw-Hill, 2003. ISBN 0072193093.
- McClure, Stuart. *Hacking Exposed: Network Security Secrets and Solutions.* McGraw-Hill Osborne, 2001. ISBN 0072193816.
- Microsoft Corp. *Microsoft Internet Information Services (IIS) 6.0 Resource Kit.* Microsoft Press, 2003. ISBN 0735614202.
- Microsoft Corp. *Microsoft Windows Server 2003 Deployment Kit.* Microsoft Press, 2003. ISBN 0735614865.
- Microsoft Corp. *Microsoft Windows Server 2003 Resource Kit.* Microsoft Press, 2003. ISBN 0735614717.

- Microsoft Corp. *Microsoft Windows XP Professional Administrators Pocket Consultant.* Microsoft Press, 2001. ISBN 0735613818.
- Microsoft Corp. *Microsoft Windows XP Professional Resource Kit.* Microsoft Press, 2001. ISBN 0735614857.
- Minasi, Mark, et al. *Mark Minasi's Windows XP and Server 2003 Resource Kit.* Sybex, 2003. ISBN 0782140807.
- Minasi, Mark, et al. *Mastering Windows Server 2003.* Sybex, 2003. ISBN 0782141307.
- Minasi, Mark, et al. *Mastering Windows XP Professional.* Sybex, 2001. ISBN 0782129811.
- Morimoto, Rand, et al. *Microsoft Windows Server 2003 Unleashed.* Sams, 2003. ISBN 0672321548.
- Moskowitz, Jeremy, et al. *Windows 2000: Group Policy, Profiles, and IntelliMirror.* Sybex, 2001. ISBN 0782128815.
- Mulcare, Mike, et al. *Active Directory Services for Microsoft Windows .NET Server Technical Reference.* Microsoft Press, 2002. ISBN 0735615772.
- Nowshadi, Farshad and Norman Buskell. *Managing Windows NT/NetWare Integration.* Addison-Wesley, 1998. ISBN 0201177846.
- Olsen, Gary L. and Ty Loren Carlson. *Windows 2000 Active Directory Design and Deployment.* Que, 2000. ISBN 1578702429.
- Peikari, Cyrus. *Windows .NET Server Security Handbook.* Prentice Hall, 2002. ISBN 0130477265.
- Perlmutter, Bruce. *Virtual Private Networking: A View from the Trenches.* Prentice Hall, 2000. ISBN 0130203351.
- Pogue, David. *Windows XP Home Edition: The Missing Manual.* O'Reilly and Associates, 2002. ISBN 0596002602.
- Que. *MCSE Windows Server 2003 Core Exam Cram 2 Pack.* Que, 2003. ISBN 0789729768.
- Que. *MCSE Windows Server 2003 Core Training Guide.* Que, 2003. ISBN 0789729776.
- Rampling, Blair. *Windows Server 2003 Security Bible.* John Wiley & Sons, 2003. ISBN 076454912X.
- Rhoton, John. *The Wireless Internet Explained.* Digital Press, 2001. ISBN 1555582575.
- Rhoton, John. *Wireless Security Explained.* Digital Press, 2002. ISBN 1555582842.
- Ruest, Nelson, and Danielle Ruest. *Windows Server 2003: Best Practices for Enterprise Deployments.* McGraw-Hill Osborne, 2003. ISBN 007222343X.
- Russel, Charlie, et al. *Microsoft Windows Server 2003 Administrator's Companion.* Microsoft Press, 2003. ISBN 0735613672.
- Ruth, Andy and Bob Collier. *Windows 2000 Dynamic DNS: Concise Guide.* Que, 2000. ISBN 0789723352.
- Scheil, Dennis. *MCSE Designing a Microsoft Windows Server 2003 Active Directory and Network Infrastructure Exam Cram 2.* Que, 2003. ISBN 0789730154.
- Shapiro, Jeffrey, et al. *Windows Server 2003 Bible.* John Wiley & Sons, 2003. ISBN 0764549375.
- Shema, Mike, et al. *Anti-Hacker Tool Kit.* McGraw-Hill Osborne, 2002. ISBN 0072222824.

- Shimonski, Robert. *Windows 2000 and Windows Server 2003 Clustering and Load Balancing.* McGraw-Hill Osborne, 2003. ISBN 0072226226.
- Shinder, Debra L. *Scene of The Cybercrime: Computer Forensics Handbook.* Syngress Media, Inc., 2002. ISBN 1931836655.
- Shinder, Thomas W., et al. *Configuring Windows 2000 Server Security.* Syngress Media, Inc., 2000. ISBN 1928994024.
- Simmons, Curt. *Windows XP Headaches: How to Fix Common (and Not So Common) Problems in a Hurry.* McGraw-Hill Osborne, 2002. ISBN 0072224614.
- Simmons, Curt. *Windows XP Secrets.* John Wiley & Sons, 2001. ISBN 0764548522.
- Sivakumar, Srinivasa, et al. *IIS 6 Programming Handbook.* Wrox Press, 2003. ISBN 1861008392.
- Sjouwerman, Stu, et al. *Microsoft Windows XP Power Pack.* Que, 2003. ISBN 0789728583.
- Stanek, William. *Essential Windows XP Command Reference.* Self-Published, 2002. ISBN 1575450461.
- Stanek, William. *Microsoft IIS 6.0 Administrator's Pocket Consultant.* Microsoft Press, 2003. ISBN 0735615608.
- Stanek, William. *Microsoft Windows Server 2003 Administrator's Pocket Consultant.* Microsoft Press, 2003. ISBN 0735613540.
- Stevens, W. Richard. *TCP/IP Illustrated, Vols. I, II, and III.* Addison-Wesley, 1994. ISBNs 0201633469, 020163354X, and 0201634953.
- Tittel, Ed, et al. *Windows Server 2003 for Dummies.* John Wiley & Sons, 2003. ISBN 0764516337.
- Tulloch, Mitch. *IIS 6 Administration.* McGraw-Hill, 2003. ISBN 0072194855.
- Tyler, Denise. *Windows XP Home and Professional Editions Instant Reference.* Sybex, 2001. ISBN 0782129862.
- Wilensky, Marshall and Candace Leiden. *TCP/IP for Dummies, Second Edition.* John Wiley & Sons, 1997. ISBN 0764500635.
- Williams, Robert, et al. *The Ultimate Windows Server 2003 System Administrator's Guide.* Addison Wesley, 2003. ISBN 0201791064.
- Wong, William. *Windows 2000 DNS Server.* McGraw-Hill Osborne, 2000. ISBN 0072124326.

APPENDIX C

Glossary of Technical Terms

In this appendix, we provide definitions for the list of key terms that appeared at the end of each chapter. In addition, we have included some other definitions that might be helpful.

A

Account Lockout A security feature that is used to disable an account when certain procedures are violated, such as the number of times a user attempts to log on unsuccessfully.

Active Directory A centralized resource and security management, administration, and control mechanism in Windows Server 2003 that is used to support and maintain a Windows Server 2003 domain. The Active Directory is hosted by domain controllers.

Active Directory Users and Computers The MMC used to manage users, groups, computer accounts, and resources, as well as OUs and Group Policies.

Advanced Configuration and Power Interface (ACPI) ACPI is the current standard for communication with a motherboard's Basic Input/Output System (BIOS). With ACPI, all devices that have power-management capabilities (such as sleep mode or hibernation) can be controlled by the operating system. This allows the operating system to selectively shut down devices not currently in use, to give maximum battery life to portable computing devices. ACPI is also needed for the OnNow Device Power Management initiative, which allows a user to start his or her computer by simply touching any key on the computer's keyboard. ACPI is installed only if all components detected during setup support power management.

application pool A set of one or more applications assigned to a set of one or more IIS worker processes. An application pool can contain Web sites, applications, and virtual directories. Each application pool is isolated from the others. Because of this, a failure or memory leak will only affect the processes running in that application pool and will have no effect on any of the other functions in other application pools.

Application Server mode The Application Server mode of Terminal Services allows the system administrator to load common applications that can be shared by multiple users. Although an unlimited number of connections is supported, each connection requires a license, called a *Terminal Server Client Access License (TSCAL).*

auditing The recording of the occurrence of a defined event or action.

Audit Policy A policy used to track access to resources. Typical events include valid or invalid logon attempts and the accessing of resources such as the opening, reading, or deletion of a file or folder.

Automated System Recovery (ASR) ASR works by making a backup of the boot partition and System State to tape or other media and then saving the catalog and other operating system information, such as disk partition information, to a floppy disk. When a problem occurs that cannot be fixed by using any of the other repair and recovery methods, or when you have replaced a failed boot drive, you can restore the boot partition by booting your server from the Windows Server 2003 CD and then inserting the diskette and the backup media created by the ASR process.

B

backup selection file This selection file contains the names of the files and folders that you want to be backed up. The selection file must be created using the GUI version of Windows Backup.

basic disk When a new disk is installed in Windows Server 2003, it is installed as a basic disk. The basic disk type has been used in all versions of Microsoft Windows dating back to 1.0, OS/2, and MS-DOS. This allows a basic disk created in Windows Server 2003 to be recognized by these earlier operating systems. A basic disk splits a physical disk into units called *partitions*. Partitions allow you to subdivide your physical disk into separate units of storage.

Basic Input/Output System (BIOS) The interface that allows an operating system to communicate with the hardware devices on the computer.

boot partition The partition that contains the operating system files.

`BOOT.INI` The `BOOT.INI` file contains the physical path to the location of the folder that contains the operating system files. The `BOOT.INI` file can contain paths to multiple operating systems. At boot time, you will be presented with a menu so that you can choose which operating system to start.

C

certificate A digital signature issued by a third party (called a *Certificate Authority*, or *CA*) that claims to have verified the identity of a server or an individual.

Check Disk A utility that checks the file and folder structure of your hard disk. You can also have Check Disk check the physical structure of your hard disk. Check Disk can perform repairs as required.

client A computer on a network that requests resources or services from some other computer.

compression The process of compacting data to save disk space.

computer account The computer account is a security principal, and it can be authenticated and granted permissions to access resources. A computer account is automatically created for each computer running Windows NT (or later operating systems) when the computer joins the domain.

counters Each object has several monitoring functions called *counters*. Each counter offers insight into a different aspect or function of the object. For example, the memory object has counters called % Committed Bytes in Use, Available Bytes, Page Faults/sec, and more. System Monitor takes the readings from these counters and presents the information to you in a human-readable format.

CSV (Comma Separated Variable) A file format that is used by various utilities in Windows Server 2003 for import and export.

D

defragmention The process of reorganizing files so that they are stored contiguously on the hard drive.

device driver A device-specific software component used by an operating system to communicate with a device. The device driver is responsible for passing requests between the operating system and the device.

device driver rollback The ability to easily restore a device driver to the previous version. This can be accomplished either manually via the Device Manager applet or automatically via Windows File Protection.

Device Manager A Windows Server 2003 administrative tool used to install, configure, and manage hardware devices.

differential backup A differential backup is used to back up only the files and folders that have been created or modified since the last normal or incremental backup. It does not change the archive bit.

digital signature A digital signature is used to ensure that the identity of the provider of the signature is who they say they are.

direct memory access (DMA) DMA allows a device to read or write to the computer's memory, without using the computer's processor (CPU). Each device using DMA must have a DMA channel dedicated for its use.

disabled account An inactive account that cannot be used for accessing resources.

Disk Cleanup A tool used to regain access to hard drive space through deleting temporary, orphaned, or downloaded files, emptying the Recycle Bin, compressing little-used files, and condensing index catalog files.

Disk Defragmenter The application built in to Windows Server 2003 for defragmenting hard disks.

Disk Management console The MMC snap-in that is used to manage the physical and logical disks in a Windows Server 2003 server.

disk quota A disk quota provides a way of controlling or monitoring how much space a user is allowed to use on a volume.

domain controller A computer that authenticates the domain logons and maintains a Windows Server 2003 domain's Active Directory, which stores all information and relationships about users, groups, policies, computers, and resources.

domain functionality level Windows Server 2003 domains can be in four different functional levels, and those levels impact what type of groups are possible, the type of replication supported, and other features.

Domain Name Service (DNS) A naming system used to translate hostnames to IP addresses and to locate resources on a TCP/IP-based network.

driver signing All drivers from Microsoft and approved vendors are signed. A signed driver is one whose integrity is verified by Microsoft and digitally approved for installation. Windows Server 2003 can be configured to refuse to install any unsigned drivers.

dynamic disk A dynamic disk is divided into volumes instead of partitions. A clean install of Windows Server 2003 will create a basic disk, and any additional disks can be added as basic or dynamic disks. After the initial installation, the basic disk can be converted to a dynamic disk. Dynamic disks cannot be accessed by DOS.

E

Emergency Repair Disk (ERD) A disk that can be used to repair a failed system; it is no longer available in Windows Server 2003.

Encrypting File System (EFS) A file system supported by Windows Server 2003 that provides the encryption of data stored on NTFS volumes.

event ID Event ID is a field in every Event Log entry that can be used to identify the event type. This ID number can be used to aid in the troubleshooting of server problems.

Event Viewer A utility built in to Windows Server 2003 that is used to view and manage the various logs of Windows Server 2003.

extended partition An extended partition can only be created on a basic disk, and you can create a theoretically unlimited number of logical drives inside that partition.

F

FAT A file system originally developed for use with DOS. FAT does not include support for security or enhanced partition features such as compression.

FAT32 First introduced with Windows 95 OEM Service Release 2 (OSR2), FAT32 includes support for larger partitions, up to 32GB in Windows Server 2003.

fault tolerant Describes a system that's able to keep operating, even when a component has failed.

file share A folder that is visible to other computers over the network. Access to the share is controlled by share permissions.

File Signature Verification File Signature Verification inspects the files in a location you specify and tells you whether they are unsigned.

G–H

Group Policies Group Policies can be assigned at the domain, OU, or site level and are used to manage computers, users, and resources.

Hardware Compatibility List (HCL) A list of hardware devices supported by Windows. A version of the HCL is found on the Windows Server 2003 distribution CD, but a Web site version is updated regularly at `www.microsoft.com/hwdq/hcl/`.

Hardware Troubleshooter An online aid used to help diagnose problems with device drivers and hardware.

I–K

incremental backup An incremental backup is used to back up only the files and folders that have been created or modified since the last normal or incremental backup. It reads the archive bit to determine which files need to be backed up. It then changes the archive bit of these backed-up files so that the next time the backup program is run, these files will not be backed up again unless they are changed.

input/output (I/O) port A I/O port is a channel through which data is transferred between a device and the CPU. It acts like an area of memory that can be read from, and written to, by the device and the CPU.

instance The terminology used to refer to multiple occurrences of the same type of object, such as in a multiprocessor server, in System Monitor. A separate instance exists for each processor.

Internet Information Services (IIS) A full-featured Web-hosting platform for building Web pages through true distributed, dynamic Web sites.

interrupt request (IRQ) An IRQ line is a hardware channel line over which a device can interrupt the CPU for service. Some devices can share an IRQ line; others must have a dedicated IRQ.

L

Last Known Good Configuration A startup option that allows you to restore the system to the state it was in at the time of the last logon.

LDAP LDAP stands for *Lightweight Directory Access Protocol* and is an industry-standard protocol for accessing directories and the primary access control protocol for Active Directory.

LDAP Data Interchange Format (LDIF) LDIF is a definition of how data can be exchanged between LDAP-based directories.

ldifde ldifde is short for *LDIF Directory Exchange.* The ldifde utility can be used to import, export, modify, and delete records in an LDAP-based directory.

Licensing A Windows Server 2003 utility used to configure and manage the license of Windows Server 2003 and installed applications.

Local Users and Groups The MMC snap-in used to create and manage local users and groups on workstations and member servers.

M–N

managed computer A computer that is managed by the administrator through restrictive profiles and Group Policies.

Master Boot Record (MBR) The MBR contains a pointer to the location of the active partition on the hard drive, as well as the code needed to begin the startup process.

MMC The Microsoft Management Console (MMC) is the de facto tool for administering anything and everything in Windows Server 2003. The MMC itself does none of the administration; it is simply a shell into which administration tools called *snap-ins* can be added, modified, and removed.

mirrored volume A fault-tolerant disk configuration in which data is written to two hard disks, rather than one, so that if one disk fails, the data remains accessible.

nested group When a group is a member of another group. Nested groups are allowed only at certain domain functionality levels.

NT File System (NTFS) The preferred file system of Windows 2003, NTFS supports file-level security, encryption, compression, auditing, and more.

O

OnNow Device Power Management The intent of the OnNow Device Power Management initiative is to allow a user to start his or her computer by simply touching any key on the computer's keyboard.

Organizational Unit (OU) A container in Active Directory that can be used to hold users, groups, and resources. Group Policy is assigned via OUs.

P–Q

partition Partitions allow you to subdivide your physical disk into separate logical units of storage.

performance The measurement of how efficiently a system runs.

permissions Permissions are used to control access, and the type of access granted, to a resource.

Plug and Play A technology that allows an operating system to recognize a device, install the correct driver, and enable the device automatically.

policy A component that automatically configures user settings.

primary partition A primary partition can be used to store a boot record so that you can boot your server from that partition. A hard disk can be configured with one or more (up to four) primary partitions. Primary partitions are only used on basic disks.

print device The piece of hardware that most people refer to as a *printer.*

print driver The software that enables the operating system to communicate with the printing device. The role of the print driver is to accept commands from the operating system and translate them into commands that the print device will understand.

print queue The contents of the spool file. Users have the ability to view the print queue by using the Print Manager applet.

print server The print server manages the printer driver settings for all printers connected to it.

print spooler Also known as the *spool file*, the print spooler is a service on the print server that manages the data to be printed. This service also contains the print data and the print device–specific commands needed to format the printed output.

R

RAID-0 RAID-0 volumes write data to anywhere from 2 to 32 physical disks in 64KB sequential stripes. The first stripe is written to the first disk, the second stripe is written to the second disk, and so forth. RAID-0 provides no fault tolerance. The advantage provided by RAID-0 lies in the overall disk I/O performance increase of the computer as the total disk I/O is split among all of the disks in the volume.

RAID-1 RAID-1, also known as a *mirrored volume,* provides fault-tolerant data storage using two physical disks. Data is written simultaneously to each physical disk so that both contain identical information. If one of the drives in a mirrored volume fails, the system will continue to run using the other volume. The total volume capacity will be equal to that provided by one of the physical disks.

RAID-5 RAID-5 volumes are similar to striped volumes in that they use multiple disks, in this case from 3 to 32 physical disks of the same size. The total volume capacity will be equal to that provided by the number of physical disks minus one. Both data and parity information are written sequentially across each physical disk. For example, if you create a volume using four 1GB disks, your usable storage would be 3GB because 1GB is devoted to storing the parity information. The parity information from the set is used to rebuild the set should one disk fail, thus providing fault tolerance. RAID-5 volumes in Windows Server 2003 cannot sustain the loss of more than one disk in the set while still providing fault tolerance.

Recovery Console A command-line control system used in system recovery in the event of a failure of a core system component or driver. Through the Recovery Console, you can use simple commands to restore the operating system to a functional state.

Remote Assistance You can use Remote Assistance to grant a remote user the ability to observe your desktop as you are working. You can exchange messages via a chat session, or you can talk to each other if you both have the required sound cards and microphones. You can even grant a remote user the ability to take over your desktop to make changes and run programs.

remote control The process of taking control of a user session or console on a remote computer.

Remote Desktop for Administration With Windows Server 2003 Terminal Services in Remote Desktop for Administration mode, you are allowed two concurrent sessions, plus a console session to the Windows server. These sessions can be used to remotely access any programs or data on the server.

Remote Desktop Protocol (RDP) This protocol provides communication between the server running Terminal Services and the RDP client software. RDP runs only on TCP/IP.

Remote Installation Services (RIS) RIS can be used to automate the installation of Windows 2000 or later operating systems.

resource settings The mechanism by which a device can communicate with other hardware or the operating system.

S

Safe Mode A startup option that starts Windows Server 2003 with the basic drivers for the mouse, video, monitor, mass storage, and keyboard.

Secure Sockets Layer (SSL) SSL is used with HTTP to encrypt all traffic between the browser and the Web server.

security descriptor The access-control information that is assigned to every object.

Security log The log in Event Viewer that contains events relating to security and auditing.

Session Directory A service that creates a database on a server that contains a record of the current sessions being hosted by a load-balanced cluster of Windows Server 2003 Terminal Servers. This database indexes the sessions by user name instead of IP address. The user name is used to look up the location of a disconnected session when the user is trying to log on to the Terminal Services server again. After it is determined which server is hosting the session that the user was disconnected from, his or her logon is routed to that server.

simple volume A simple volume is the equivalent of a partition on a basic disk.

Software Update Services (SUS) SUS is a service installed on an internal Windows 2000 or Windows Server 2003 server that can download all critical updates as they are posted to Windows Update. The client computers and servers can be configured through Group Policy or the Registry to contact the internal SUS server for updates, instead of going out over the Internet to the Microsoft servers. SUS is basically an internal version of the Windows Update service, with the exception that the network administrator has the option to control which updates get downloaded from Microsoft and which ones get installed on the computers in the environment.

spanned volume A spanned volume takes various amounts of disk space from 2 to 32 physical disks to create one large volume. Spanned volumes provide no fault tolerance; actually, they can be more prone to failure than other types of volumes because if any one disk should fail, the entire set is lost. The advantage of a spanned volume is that you can quickly add more storage space.

striped volume A striped volume writes data to 2 to 32 physical disks in 64KB sequential stripes. The first stripe is written to the first disk, the second stripe is written to the second disk, and so forth. Striped volumes, also known as *RAID-0*, provide no fault tolerance. The advantage provided by using a striped volume lies in the overall disk I/O performance increase of the computer because the total disk I/O is split among all the disks in the volume.

System File Checker The System File Checker (`SFC.EXE`) is used to verify that the protected system files have not been overwritten.

System Monitor System Monitor is used to track the performance of your Windows Server 2003 server.

system partition On an Intel-based system, the system partition contains the `BOOT.INI`, `NTDETECT.COM`, and `NTLDR` files. These files tell the server how to start the operating system. The system partition is also known as the *active partition*.

system state A collection of data that contains the operating system configuration of the server.

T

Terminal Services Windows Server 2003 includes Terminal Services, which allows thin clients to be employed as network clients. Terminal Services grants remote access to applications and offers limitation controls over application access.

Transmission Control Protocol/Internet Protocol (TCP/IP) The most popular protocol suite in use today, TCP/IP was originally based on the network protocols developed by the Department of Defense. TCP/IP is the protocol used on the Internet.

U

uninterruptible power supply (UPS) A device used to protect computers and other electronic equipment from power loss, surges, spikes, and brownouts. A UPS uses batteries to ensure that a device can continue operating briefly during a power loss.

user profile The file where the settings for a user's work environment are. This file is automatically created the first time a user logs on to a computer running any version of Windows, and any changes to the environment (favorites, Start menu items, icons, colors, My Documents, local settings) are saved when the user logs off. The profile is reloaded when the user logs on again.

user rights The actions that the user of a particular account is permitted to perform on a system.

user template A preconfigured account that is saved with various characteristics. This account is copied whenever another user account with the same characteristics needs to be created.

V–Z

virtual private network (VPN) An extension of a network that can be accessed securely through a public network such as the Internet.

Web Service Extensions The EXE and DLL files required for the specific function that is enabled. For example, for Active Server Pages to be used, the `asp.dll` file must be enabled. To get a list of the files required for each Web Service Extension, in the IIS Manager MMC, highlight the desired extension and click the Properties button.

Windows File Protection (WFP) WFP runs in the background and is alerted whenever a file in a protected folder is changed. It determines whether the new version of the file is signed. If it isn't, Windows File Protection automatically rolls back the file to the version kept in the `%systemroot%\system32\dllcache` folder.

Windows Internet Naming Service (WINS) A service that dynamically maps IP addresses to NetBIOS computer names used by Microsoft operating systems other than Windows Server 2003.

Windows Server 2003 Readiness Analyzer A utility that can be run on a server to check the software and hardware components for compatibility with Windows Server 2003.

Windows Update A Microsoft Web site (`http://windowsupdate.microsoft.com/`) that provides an automated source of operating system fixes, security patches, and updated drivers.

APPENDIX **D**

What's on the CD-ROM

This appendix provides a brief summary of what you'll find on the CD-ROM that accompanies this book. For a more detailed description of the PrepLogic Practice Exams, Preview Edition exam-simulation software, see Appendix E, "Using the PrepLogic Practice Exams, Preview Edition Software." In addition to the PrepLogic Practice Exams, Preview Edition software, the CD-ROM includes an electronic version of the book, in Portable Document Format (PDF), and the source code used in the book.

The PrepLogic Practice Exams, Preview Edition Software

PrepLogic is a leading provider of certification training tools. Trusted by certification students worldwide, PrepLogic is the best practice exam software available. In addition to providing a means of evaluating your knowledge of this book's material, PrepLogic Practice Exams, Preview Edition features several innovations that help you improve your mastery of the subject matter.

For example, the practice tests allow you to check your score by exam area or domain, to determine which topics you need to study further. Another feature allows you to obtain immediate feedback on your responses, in the form of explanations for the correct and incorrect answers.

PrepLogic Practice Tests, Preview Edition exhibits all the full-test simulation functionality of the Premium Edition but offers only a fraction of the total questions. To get the complete set of practice questions, visit `www.preplogic.com` and order the Premium Edition for this and other challenging exam training guides.

For a more detailed description of the features of the PrepLogic Practice Exams, Preview Edition software, see Appendix E.

An Exclusive Electronic Version of the Text

As mentioned previously, the CD-ROM that accompanies this book also contains an electronic PDF version of this book. This electronic version comes complete with all figures as they appear in the book. You can use Acrobat's handy search capability for study and review purposes.

APPENDIX E

Using the PrepLogic Practice Exams, Preview Edition Software

This book includes a special version of the PrepLogic Practice Exams software, a revolutionary test engine designed to give you the best in certification exam preparation. PrepLogic offers sample and practice exams for many of today's most in-demand and challenging technical certifications. A special Preview Edition of the PrepLogic Practice Exams software is included with this book as a tool to use in assessing your knowledge of the training guide material while also providing you with the experience of taking an electronic exam.

This appendix describes in detail what PrepLogic Practice Exams, Preview Edition is, how it works, and what it can do to help you prepare for the exam. Note that although the Preview Edition includes all the test simulation functions of the complete retail version, it contains only a single practice test. The Premium Edition, available at `www.preplogic.com`, contains a complete set of challenging practice exams designed to optimize your learning experience.

The Exam Simulation

One of the main functions of PrepLogic Practice Exams, Preview Edition is exam simulation. To prepare you to take the actual vendor certification exam, PrepLogic is designed to offer the most effective exam-simulation available.

Question Quality

The questions provided in PrepLogic Practice Exams, Preview Edition are written to the highest standards of technical accuracy. The questions tap the content of this book's chapters and help you review and assess your knowledge before you take the actual exam.

The Interface Design

The PrepLogic Practice Exams, Preview Edition exam-simulation interface provides you with the experience of taking an electronic exam. This enables you to effectively prepare to take the actual exam by making the test experience familiar. Using this test simulation can help eliminate the sense of surprise or anxiety you might experience in the testing center because you will already be acquainted with computerized testing.

The Effective Learning Environment

The PrepLogic Practice Exams, Preview Edition interface provides a learning environment that not only tests you through the computer but also teaches the material you need to know to pass the certification exam. Each question includes a detailed explanation of the correct answer, and most of these explanations provide reasons as to why the other answers are incorrect. This information helps to reinforce the knowledge you already have and also provides practical information you can use on the job.

Software Requirements

PrepLogic Practice Exams requires a computer with the following:

- Microsoft Windows 98, Windows Me, Windows NT 4.0, Windows 2000, or Windows XP
- A 166MHz or faster processor
- A minimum of 32MB of RAM
- 10MB of hard drive space

> **NOTE**
> **Performance** As with any Windows application, the more memory, the better the performance.

Installing PrepLogic Practice Exams, Preview Edition

You install PrepLogic Practice Exams, Preview Edition by following these steps:

1. Insert the CD-ROM that accompanies this book into your CD-ROM drive. The Autorun feature of Windows should launch the software. If you have Autorun disabled, select Start, Run. Go to the root directory of the CD-ROM and select `setup.exe`. Click Open and then click OK.
2. The Installation Wizard copies the PrepLogic Practice Exams, Preview Edition files to your hard drive. It then adds PrepLogic Practice Exams, Preview Edition to your Desktop and the Program menu. Finally, it installs test engine components to the appropriate system folders.

Removing PrepLogic Practice Exams, Preview Edition from Your Computer

If you elect to remove PrepLogic Practice Exams, Preview Edition, you can use the included uninstallation process to ensure that it is removed from your system safely and completely. Follow these instructions to remove PrepLogic Practice Exams, Preview Edition from your computer:

1. Select Start, Settings, Control Panel.
2. Double-click the Add/Remove Programs icon. You are presented with a list of software installed on your computer.

3. Select the PrepLogic Practice Exams, Preview Edition title you want to remove. Click the Add/Remove button. The software is removed from your computer.

HOW TO USE THE SOFTWARE

PrepLogic is designed to be user friendly and intuitive. Because the software has a smooth learning curve, your time is maximized because you start practicing with it almost immediately. PrepLogic Practice Exams, Preview Edition has two major modes of study: Practice Exam and Flash Review.

Using Practice Exam mode, you can develop your test-taking abilities as well as your knowledge through the use of the Show Answer option. While you are taking the test, you can expose the answers along with detailed explanations of why answers are right or wrong. This helps you better understand the material presented.

Flash Review mode is designed to reinforce exam topics rather than quiz you. In this mode, you are shown a series of questions but no answer choices. You can click a button that reveals the correct answer to each question and a full explanation for that answer.

Starting a Practice Exam Mode Session

Practice Exam mode enables you to control the exam experience in ways that actual certification exams do not allow. To begin studying in Practice Exam mode, you click the Practice Exam radio button from the main exam-customization screen. This enables the following options:

- **The Enable Show Answer button**—Clicking this button activates the Show Answer button, which allows you to view the correct answer(s) and full explanation(s) for each question during the exam. When this option is not enabled, you must wait until after your exam has been graded to view the correct answer(s) and explanation(s) for each question.
- **The Enable Item Review button**—Clicking this button activates the Item Review button, which allows you to view your answer choices. This option also facilitates navigation between questions.
- **The Randomize Choices option**—You can randomize answer choices from one exam session to the next. This makes memorizing question choices more difficult, thereby keeping questions fresh and challenging longer.

On the left side of the main exam-customization screen, you are presented with the option of selecting the preconfigured practice test or creating your own custom test. The preconfigured test has a fixed time limit and number of questions. Custom tests allow you to configure the time limit and the number of questions in your exam.

The Preview Edition on this book's CD-ROM includes a single preconfigured practice test. You can get the complete set of challenging PrepLogic Practice Exams at `www.preplogic.com` to make certain you're ready for the big exam.

You click the Begin Exam button to begin your exam.

Starting a Flash Review Mode Session

Flash Review mode provides an easy way to reinforce topics covered in the practice questions. To begin studying in Flash Review mode, you click the Flash Review radio button from the main exam-customization screen. Then you either select the preconfigured practice test or create your own custom test.

You click the Begin Exam button to begin a Flash Review mode session.

Standard PrepLogic Practice Exams, Preview Edition Options

The following list describes the function of each of the buttons you see across the bottom of the screen:

> NOTE
>
> **Button Status** Depending on the options, some of the buttons will be grayed out and inaccessible—or they might be missing completely. Buttons that are appropriate are active.

- **Exhibit**—This button is visible if an exhibit is provided to support the question. An *exhibit* is an image that provides supplemental information that is necessary to answer a question.
- **Item Review**—This button leaves the question window and opens the Item Review screen, from which you can see all questions, your answers, and your marked items. You can also see correct answers listed here, when appropriate.
- **Show Answer**—This option displays the correct answer, with an explanation about why it is correct. If you select this option, the current question is not scored.
- **Mark Item**—You can check this box to flag a question that you need to review further. You can view and navigate your marked items by clicking the Item Review button (if it is enabled). When your exam is being graded, you are notified if you have any marked items remaining.
- **Previous Item**—You can use this option to view the previous question.
- **Next Item**—You can use this option to view the next question.
- **Grade Exam**—When you have completed your exam, you can click Grade Exam to end your exam and view your detailed score report. If you have unanswered or marked items remaining, you are asked if you would like to continue taking your exam or view the exam report.

Seeing the Time Remaining

If your practice test is timed, the time remaining is displayed in the upper-right corner of the application screen. It counts down the minutes and seconds remaining to complete the test. If you run out of time, you are asked if you want to continue taking the test or if you want to end your exam.

Getting Your Examination Score Report

The Examination Score Report screen appears when the Practice Exam mode ends—as a result of time expiration, completion of all questions, or your decision to terminate early.

This screen provides a graphical display of your test score, with a breakdown of scores by topic domain. The graphical display at the top of the screen compares your overall score with the PrepLogic Exam Competency Score. The PrepLogic Exam Competency Score reflects the level of subject competency required to pass the particular vendor's exam. Although this score does not directly translate to a passing score, consistently matching or exceeding this score does suggest that you possess the knowledge needed to pass the actual vendor exam.

Reviewing Your Exam

From the Your Score Report screen, you can review the exam that you just completed by clicking the View Items button. You can navigate through the items, viewing the questions, your answers, the correct answers, and the explanations for those questions. You can return to your score report by clicking the View Items button.

CONTACTING PREPLOGIC

If you would like to contact PrepLogic for any reason, including to get information about its extensive line of certification practice tests, you can do so online at `www.preplogic.com`.

Customer Service

If you have a damaged product and need to contact customer service, please call the following number:

800-858-7674

Product Suggestions and Comments

PrepLogic values your input! Please email your suggestions and comments to `feedback@preplogic.com`.

LICENSE AGREEMENT

YOU MUST AGREE TO THE TERMS AND CONDITIONS OUTLINED IN THE END USER LICENSE AGREEMENT ("EULA") PRESENTED TO YOU DURING THE INSTALLATION PROCESS. IF YOU DO NOT AGREE TO THESE TERMS, DO NOT INSTALL THE SOFTWARE.

Index

SYMBOLS

A

B

C

D

E

F

G

H

I-J

K-L

M

N

O

P

Q

R

S

T

U

V

W

X-Z